A PANORAMA OF CHRISTIAN HYMNODY

A PANORAMA
OF
CHRISTIAN HYMNODY

Erik Routley

G.I.A. PUBLICATIONS, INC.

7404 So. Mason Ave. Chicago, Illinois 60638

IN MEMORIAM

NATHANIEL MICKLEM, D.D.

preacher, teacher, scholar, wit

who guided my feet into this path

ACKNOWLEDGMENTS

Grateful acknowledgment is made to the following holders of copyright for permission to reprint material under their control. Hymns so covered are identified by the number they appear under in this volume.

3	From THE MARTIN LUTHER CHRISTMAS BOOK, translated and arranged by Roland H. Bainton. Copyright © MCMXLVIII, by W. L. Jenkins. Published by Muhlenberg Press. Used by permission
5	From THE MENNONITE HYMNAL, copyright © 1969 by Herald Press, Scottdale, PA, and Faith and Life Press, Newton, KS
6	Dr. Ernest A. Payne, C.H., Oxford, England
91, 583	Nathaniel Micklem, Abingdon, Berks., England
144, 145, 150, 151, 188, 265, 266, 267, 268	From the *English Hymnal*, by permission of Oxford University Press, 37 Dover Street, London, W.I. England
155	J. M. Dent & Sons, 26 Albermarle Street, London, W.I. England
161	Search Press Ltd., 2-10 Jerdan Place, London, England
189	From *The Lutheran Hymnal* © 1941 by Concordia Publishing House, 3558 So. Jefferson Ave., St. Louis, MO 63118
191, 193B, 194A, 200, 257, 258, 259, 260, 261, 262	From the *Yattendon Hymnal* by permission of Oxford University Press, 37 Dover Street, London, W.I. England
195A, 549, 550, 551, 552	Church Pension Corporation, 800 Second Avenue, New York 10017
256	A. P. Watt, Ltd., London
263, 264	Schott & Co., Ltd., 48 Marlborough Street, London, England
269, 459, 497, 498, 499, 500, 505, 506, 507, 508, 571, 573, 574	Used by permission of Oxford University Press, 37 Dover Street, London, England
320B	From the *Revised Church Hymnary 1927* by permission of Oxford University Press, 37 Dover Street, London, W.I. England
323, 324	The Editor's Literary Estate and Chatto and Windus Ltd., 40 William IV Street, London, England
407, 408	Broadman Press, 127 Ninth Avenue No., Nashville, TN 37203
450, 451, 477	United Reformed Church, 86 Tavistock Place, London, England
452	A. D. Peters & Co. Ltd., 10 Buckingham Street, London, England
453	Community of the Resurrection, Mirfield, Yorks., England
454, 456, 458, 460, 461, 462, 463, 465, 466, 486	From *Enlarged Songs of Praise* by permission of Oxford University Press, 37 Dover Street, London, England
455	Industrial Christian Fellowship, St. Katharine Cree Church, Leadenhall Street, London, ECl England
467, 468, 509	Hymns Ancient and Modern, 7 Chichester Court, Pevensey Garden, Worthing, Sussex, England
469, 470, 471	Rev. A. F. Bayly, Chelmsford, Essex, England
472, 473	The Rev. T. C. Hunter-Clare, Leics., England
474	From the *BBC Hymn Book* by permission of Oxford University Press, 37 Dover Street, London, W.I. England
475, 476	Invicta Productions, The Old Sun, Alresford, Hampshire, England
478, 479	The Rev. Dr. George Caird, Oxford, England
481	H. C. Piggott, Brighton, England
483, 484	The Society for Promoting Christian Knowledge, Marylebone Road, London, England
488, 489, 490, 491, 493, 494, 495, 496, 503, 504, 521, 522, 523, 524, 528, 529, 530, 531, 532, 533	Galaxy Music Inc., 2121 Broadway, New York 10023
491, 492	The Rev. John B. Geyer, Chelmsford, Essex, England
501, 502	The Venerable Timothy Dudley-Smith, Norwich, England
510, 511, 514, 515, 526, 527	Geoffrey Chapman Ltd. 35 Red Lion Square, London, WCl England
512, 513	Faber Music Ltd. 3 Queen Square, London, England
516	The Rev. Archibald M. Hunter, D.D., Ayr., Scotland
517	The Rev. Dr. Ian Pitt-Watson, Aberdeen, Scotland

519, 520, 535, 576	The Rev. T. C. Micklem, J.P., Oxford, England
525	British Weekly, London, England
543	Abingdon Press, 201 Eighth Avenue South, Nashville, TN 37202
544, 553, 564	The Hymn Society of America, Wittenberg University, Springfield, OH 45501
545	Dr. Elinor Downs, Bronxville, N.Y.
554	Lutheran Council in the USA, 360 Park Avenue So., New York 10010
557	From *The Hymnal of the United Church of Christ.* Copyright © 1974 United Church Press, Philadelphia, PA
561	Board of Regents of Victoria University, Toronto, Canada
562	The Venerable T. H. O'Driscoll, Vancouver, B.C., Canada
563	The Rev. John E. Speers, Barrie, Ont., Canada
578	From WESTMINSTER PRAISE edited by Erik Routley, copyright © 1976 by Hinshaw Music Inc., Chapel Hill, NC 27514
584	Mrs. Frank W. Price, Lexington, VA 24450
591	The Rev. John Hoad, Princeton, NJ 08540
592	Lutterworth Press, Lake House, Farnham Road, Guildford, Surrey, England

Every effort has been made to trace owners of copyright material, but if any have been overlooked or gone unacknowledged here because replies to applications were not received, we shall be happy to correct these omissions in a future edition if they are reported to us.

TABLE OF CONTENTS

INTRODUCTION

This book has a threefold purpose; and it is right to say that two, at least, of these purposes were aroused in my mind by the privilege I have recently been granted, of teaching the study of hymns in two institutions in America.

The first purpose of the book is to provide pleasure, a pleasure which I discover to be now wholly hidden from those friends in America whom I admire and love so much as to wish to share it with them. That is the godly and sensible pleasure of *reading* hymns. I do not mean reading them communally in church, which strikes me as a miserable substitute for that cheerful song which is now the delight of all Christian communions. I mean reading them in solitude, reading them as lyric poetry. When one does this, their crudities and roughness, which any literary critic must observe, which the best lover of hymns must admit, and which some Christians (among them my revered C. S. Lewis) have openly despised, become softened by the associations of communal song which these texts must inevitably carry. There will be a tune in the reader's mind; if there is not, a glance at the Appendix will provide one. (He is likely, especially in America, to have a music copy about the house). But when I remember how in my own youth, say thirty years back, men and women in so many branches of the church in England, my home country, would read their hymnals as eagerly and regularly as they read their Bibles, and would, if whipped off to hospital, reach for the hymn book as well as the Bible, I simply grieve to think that this particular pleasure and religious nourishment is withheld from so many or ignored by so many in these later days.

The reason for that in my own country is simple laziness. In America it is less blameworthy, at least in the innocent reader. It is now the custom in America to print all hymnals with the texts interlined between the music staves. The advantages of this are the certain one of saving paper—it is indeed more economical—and the dubious one of making hymns easier to sing; in respect of which I am bound to say that in the ordinary congregation I have not detected any greater readiness in America than in my own country to sing unfamiliar tunes, which is what makes me think that second advantage doubtful. Being, however, resigned to the inevitable continuance of a practice which makes it impossible to read the text as it should be read, I thought it right here to provide an anthology of hymn texts set out, for the most part, in the manner in which their authors wrote them. Then, I thought, my reader can have the best of both worlds: a full music edition for worship, or for musical pleasure at home, and this book for his more intimate meditation.

Now I am aware, and what I said above implies, that a hymn without its tune is incomplete. And just as it is unwise to use literature above a certain level of greatness as the libretto of an opera (as Sir Donald Tovey once pointed out), so there is a level beyond which literature cannot rise if it is to be good hymnody. The most obvious restraint on poetic inspiration and technique is the need, in a hymn, to use regular stresses, which gives its text, in the reading, a sing-song monotony which no master of poetry would tolerate in his verse for a moment. Indeed, it is a very clear necessity in the writing of large-scale poetry that the rhythm should be injected with surprise and vitality precisely by the conflict between the regular metre which is the framework and the more natural flow of the words which are disciplined but, in a true poet's hands, never constricted by that framework. Similarly, in great poetry the sense of a sentence will not end with the end of a line; it is, indeed, important that it should not always do so. In a hymn, it must. A 'run-on' from line to line, especially where there is an important natural break in the music, provides discomfort in singing. (On this matter see further the note on #45 in article 4).

Probably it is less necessary to warn the reader against being too impatient with the 'in-group' language, mythology and thought-forms of evangelical hymnody. It is perfectly true that during one period—that between Watts and Bridges—a certain vocabulary was understood to have significance for author and reader who were connected by the language of the Bible. The pervasive 'blood', the Wesleyan 'interest', the whole complex of Atonement theology which could be conveyed to pious singers by the use of certain cue-words is part of a system towards which a modern reader must exercise imaginative forbearance, especially when he has not a tune to carry him through these rough places. But it is worth persevering.

Another pleasure the reader may perhaps receive with gratitude (that is my hope) is that of being able now and then to let an author talk himself out. Our usual conventions make it necessary to limit the length of hymns to something between twelve and, at the most, forty lines. Modern hymn writers know this and write accordingly. Not so always the classical writers, whose ecstasy and energy might carry them much farther. It is interesting to notice that Isaac Watts very rarely goes beyond the demands of reasonable prudence, though in one hymn, which we have included here, he does run to 72 lines; and, given the right amount of goodwill, would any reader really wish it shorter, however legitimate the demand of a singer would be? Is there not some satisfaction in being able to see the whole delectable autobiographical length of Addison's 'Gratitude' (47), or in being able to relax into the expansive joy of Nicolai's 'Wie schon leuchtet' (188)? To follow Charles Wesley through the 84 agonized, yet in the end triumphant, lines of 'Wrestling Jacob' (62), even though a perfectly good 24-line hymn in congregational use can be made out of it, is something of a privilege, especially if one has one's Bible open at Genesis 32. In a few cases the restoration of an original text bespeaks a powerful, even indignant, conviction in your editor; for I do regard it as something of a crime to omit, as hymnals so often do, the fourth stanza of 'When I survey the wondrous cross'; and I equally think it no bad thing for any who are familiar with 'Our God, our help in ages past' (44) in the significantly emasculated version beginning 'O God . . .' to read the whole of that section of Watts' Psalm 90, and feel again the overpowering solemnity of that sometimes over-used piece; or, in another mood, to enjoy the picturesque stanzas of 'Jesus shall reign' (43) that are now never sung (even if my American friends think Watts somewhat insular in confining his picture of western civilization to Europe).

My second purpose in furnishing this book has also something to do with America. In this blessed land, the subject of hymnology is taught. (It is not, in the length and breadth of Britain, unless perhaps it appears on the occasional Scottish curriculum). My gratitude to the U.S.A. owes much to its having permitted me to teach the subject here. Now this is very difficult if the only textbook you have is the hymnal of the denomination favoured by the teaching institution. It's not likely that the seminary chapel will have more than one, or at most two, books. It will surely be handy for an instructor and his or her pupils to have, within the covers of a single volume, a conspectus of the literature of hymnody. Reference can always be made to the standard hymnals, and of course, such references will have to be made in respect of tunes. And (copyright materials excepted) there is always the friendly Xerox machine to provide copies of any non-copyright material you need that I have omitted.

But it is with that in mind that I have arranged the material in the form you will find. When the book is used for other purposes, its indexes will help the reader to handle it as he wishes; but for teaching purposes, one needs to survey the story of hymnody from the viewpoint on which twentieth-century Americans or Britishers inevitably stand. Hymnody of our kind begins with Luther, is submerged under metrical psalmody, and emerges again with Watts. The peculiar glories of seventeenth-century poetry were very largely unknown to English-speaking hymn singers before Robert Bridges and Percy Dearmer brought them to our notice at the beginning of the twentieth century. So George Herbert comes later than he would appear in an ordinary poetry-anthology. Similarly, hymns from the Latin and from the German flooded into the English books in the later nineteenth century, ancient though many of them are; and therefore (excepting Luther, who must clearly have his place right at the beginning) that is where you find them here. In my own teaching, anyhow, that is the line I take. Anybody can take a different one and use this book equally well.

The third person I have my eye on is the hymnal editor. I have observed a tendency lately among editors to receive into any newly projected hymnal a text and tune as what we may call a package deal; or, to use a more elegant metaphor, to regard marriages between texts and tunes as made in heaven and indissoluble. Whether I am acting on the principle that hymnody moves in a permissive society, or whether on the higher principle that there is no marrying or giving in marriage in heaven, I leave it to a psychoanalyst to determine; but I know for sure that some marriages between texts and tunes, though of long standing, are calamitous (the most scandalous of all being that commonly honored in America in respect of 'When I survey the wondrous cross'). I think editors may well be assisted, if they do not care to examine books of English provenance that use a different printing format, by having a collection of texts to study; this assistance may come through their being able simply to judge the words without having to disentangle them from a music-stave, or through their being the more readily able to find better tunes for those ineptly paired at present, or by having a more complete text to select from than the standard hymnals provide.

I do have to say, however, that this book should not be regarded as a pedantically faithful presentation of original spellings and punctuations. Most of the time there is no advantage in being anything else; but for one thing, I wish my devotional reader to have a text that he or she can easily read, and therefore I have, with one or two exceptions, modernised the spelling; for another, the use of capitals in such authors as Watts is, to a modern eye, distracting, and I have usually followed modern customs there (but not in the reprinting of his very first hymn, which I thought we might see exactly as he wrote it); for a third, I happen to think that the old custom of beginning every line of poetry with a capital is, for these purposes, over-ponderous, and that it has the special disadvantage of making it difficult to see when, as occasionally happens, the syntax runs through the end of a stanza, as it does at sts. 4-5 of 'Jesus shall reign' [43]. For ease of reading, I have followed a uniform system except in those few places where for a special reason I reproduced an older style.

In respect of the two greatest sources, any editor or interested reader will find punctilious exactitude wholly satisfied in Dr. Selma Bishop's great work on Isaac Watts: *Hymns and Spiritual Songs*, and in F. W. Baker's no less important study, *Representative Verse of Charles Wesley*. But in any case an editor will go as near as he can to the original before deciding what emendations will be prudent. In two cases I have refused to reproduce the original; that is where the word 'bowels' is so often written by the classicals for 'mercies' and where 'worms' represents 'creatures of no importance.' Nobody now is going to feel underprivileged in being deprived of a few words which have become grotesque in ways which their original users could not have foreseen. Any editor who wishes to restore these is welcome, but not with help from me.

One final word. This, of course, is not a hymnal. It is a 'panorama of hymnody.' No reader will be so ill-advised as to think that I include here all the hymns I love best, or that I approve, for public worship, of everything I have put in. That is far from being the case. A panorama will include some disagreeable sights, the world being what it is. No reader will find here everything he hoped for, any more than I do. I could easily have included forty great pieces of Watts, and as many of Wesley, and it is gratifying to have to admit that I could have found many more pieces from the period 1965-75 than I have found room for. However, I do claim that a tolerable degree of justice has been achieved for all legitimate forms of hymnody—at least for all that can be transcribed without music and still make sense.

Having thus assigned my book to the categories of *uti* and *frui*—of usefulness and enjoyment—I leave it in the hope that it may appear on some bedside tables, and on some academic desks, and perhaps do something towards recovering for the hymn writer that long-lost claim to be, in a humble form, a man of letters.

E. R.
Princeton, N. J.

A PANORAMA OF CHRISTIAN HYMNODY

ARTICLE 1: LUTHER AND NICOLAI (1-6)

Hymnody as it is now understood throughout Christendom began with Martin Luther–or so it is convenient to say. That statement must at once be qualified by an historical maxim which is irrefutable in whatever field one chooses to apply it. This is that whenever popular belief ascribes the inception of some great movement to any given person, that person will always be found to be not the first, not often even the second, to express the ideas, affect the style, or long for the achievement which is attributed to the famous 'Founder.' The Reformation itself we regard as owed to Luther; but how many persons, groups, and movements looked in that direction, without succeeding in making it a continent-wide operation, for two hundred years before Luther, as tradition has it, nailed up his Theses? English hymnody, we shall later observe, regards its founder as Isaac Watts. Thirty years before his time, the Baptist Benjamin Keach was writing freely-composed hymns, though nobody now sings them. The Oxford Movement we say was founded by John Keble, and we judge its greatest mind to have been J. H. Newman. But a look at the content of Keble's hymns, all written before the Movement started, and at the developing thought in a few small groups before it became a Movement, even a look at the thought of John Wesley in his earliest days of ministry, will indicate not only that this movement had roots in a remoter past, but that many of the suppositions we entertain about it need to be modified if we take into account the earlier utterances of its own leading figures, especially the hymns of Keble. The renaissance of English church music, especially of hymnody, we properly attribute to Percy Dearmer and Vaughan Williams in the *English Hymnal* of 1906; but the things they there said with such emphasis and success had already been said by G. R. Woodward in his early carol collections from 1894 onwards and by Robert Bridges in his *Yattendon Hymnal* of 1899. What it is necessary to say of any 'founder' is that he, influenced by certain obscurer and more local figures and movements, or responding to needs already made known at that lower level, made an achievement of what before his time was a dream, or an eccentricity, or a hope. It was so with Luther and hymnody.

What we mean when we ascribe this historical role to Luther is that it was he who successfully propagated the idea that the communal singing of Christian songs could be an integral part of public worship. People had plenty of religious songs before his time; but not at the Mass, not at the centre of worship, and not songs known all over Europe. The story of the carols, the *Laudi Spirituali*, and the songs of pre-Reformation dissenting groups is a story of what happened outside the church, or far from the church's liturgical centre, and mostly also of what happened locally. It is quite different from the story that begins with Luther.

It will be familiar to any reader that there was a medieval hymnody, a great store of Latin texts (to which at a later stage we shall attend), many of which in translation are familiar to the English-speaking world. But these were for the monastic choirs to sing, not for the congregation; and the style of music to which they were set (plainsong) was kept very carefully clear of secular associations and influences.

Not but what Luther's hymnody was influenced by these medieval songs; often he rewrote a plainsong tune in a style which he reckoned ordinary people could easily sing, and, as we see with our #1, more than once he recast a medieval text to transform it into material suitable for a congregation to use as a song of its faith.

The best source for the study of Luther's own hymns is Volume 53 of the Augsburg edition of Luther's Works, where all 37 of them, texts and music, are set out (the texts in the translation of George Macdonald). The very first hymn there given, *Ein Neues Lied*, provides a great surprise and establishes a great principle. The surprise is in its content, for it is a pugnacious song celebrating the deaths of two early Reformation martyrs and trouncing their detractors. It is a polemical ballad of the most red-blooded kind, very little like the dogmatic style which we usually associate with Luther. The principle established is in his using for the tune a melody based on the form of the troubadour and Minnesinger songs, the court music, or, you might almost say, 'classical music' of his time. The idea that Luther used 'popular tunes,' in so far as it is put about to give credibility to the modern use of vulgar music, should at once be disposed of. The sources of the Luther tunes are either the monastic plainsong or the kind of music the aristocracy enjoyed.

It is difficult to resist the theory–though it has never been officially sanctioned by scholars–that Luther's hymn-writing began with a quite overt imitation of these aristocratic ballads, and that, as it were, finding he had a gift for this kind of thing, he then turned to what one is obliged to call more serious writing; at least, to matters of more enduring importance. Our ## 1-4 give a reasonable conspectus of his various styles: the adapted and developed medieval sequence at # 1; the metricized and Christianized Psalm at # 2 (which reminds us that psalmody was the almost invariable Christian praise at the Mass during the Middle Ages); the domestic Christmas carol at # 3; and the famous battle-song at # 4. These show Luther's versatility in providing people with Christian songs. Dogma and drama are unusually combined in his forceful texts. Notice how in # 1 the drama in the old Sequence (the conversation with Mary) is replaced by the spiritual drama of the Eucharist, and how, on the other hand, the pivotal and arresting phrase *Mors et vita duello conflixere mirando* is gratefully retained. Note also how New Testament Scriptures are used to illuminate Psalm 130 in # 2 in a manner almost foreshadowing Isaac Watts. Contrast these immensities with the homeliness of # 3, written for his own family with a child playing the part of the angel, the other children joining in the heavenly chorus, and everybody singing the final doxology. In any company, of course, # 4 is unique. Taking its opening lines from Psalm 46, it summons the Reformed world to arms against the oppressions of those Establishment figures who were mustering all their forces to stop what had by this date (about 1528) become a menace they could no longer ignore. Everybody now sings this song as a hymn of spiritual confidence, including modern Catholics; but its original meaning is quite unquestionable. Still, it has inspired so many fine translators that it has now gone quite beyond Luther's control.

A great hymn writer tends to stifle the next generation. Charles Wesley did so almost completely, and there is hardly a Methodist hymn of any importance to be found before 1900. (Watts, that other pioneer, did not have this effect; others at once, and successfully, imitated and developed his style. We cannot here stop to ask why this was, but it is an interesting and important point of difference between him and the Wesleys.) By the same token, there is not much text-writing in the Lutheran church for a generation after Luther's death. We shall not come back to the Lutherans until we reach # 188.

But that other stream of the Reformation, the radical Anabaptists, produced a style of hymnody with which only Luther's very first hymn has much in common. Anabaptist hymnody mostly has not turned out to be exportable; those most faithful to this tradition today are the conservative branches of the Mennonites in the U. S. A., among whom the *Ausbund*, last revised in 1622, is still in use. This is a collection of hymns in German, many of which are historical songs recounting the heroic witness of vintage Anabaptists under persecution, and it is nothing out of the way for one of these to run as far as twenty stanzas. One or two exceed thirty. Anabaptism, in the 16th century, was a faith which Luther neither understood nor wanted to understand; his special facility in making converts from the upper reaches of society was the opposite of their homespun, common-man approach. And their ballads were just such songs as would appeal to groups of people who proudly claimed, as did Paul writing to Corinth, that their ranks number 'not many wise men after the flesh, not many mighty, not many noble' which was really a claim that Luther could never have made. Our # 5 is a short selection made for the American Mennonite Hymnal (1969) from a 27-stanza original and has the characteristic 'vintage' Anabaptist emphasis on personal suffering and sacrifice. The first official *Ausbund* appeared in 1583, and this was # 11 in that book. Our # 6, which is translated complete and is unusually brief, is # 131 in that book, being part of a supplement added in 1622. Its translator is the eminent English Baptist historian Dr. Ernest Payne, and this is the only Anabaptist hymn known to Britishers. Some idea of the expansive manner of most Anabaptist hymns will be gathered from the fact that the present edition of the *Ausbund*, including the 1622 additions, uses 812 pages to print 140 pieces (texts only).

It will be the end of the 16th century, and our Article 13, before we can again take up the tale of mainstream German hymnody.

MARTIN LUTHER
1483-1546

1

A   **HG 111**

Christ lag in Todesbanden,	Christ Jesus lay in death's strong bands
für unsre Sünd gegeben,	for our offences given;
der ist wieder erstanden	but now at God's right hand he stands.
und hat uns bracht das Leben.	and brings us light from heaven.
Des wir sollen fröhlich sein,	Wherefore let us joyful be
Gott loben und dankbar sein	and sing to God right thankfully
und singen Halleluja,	loud songs of Hallelujah!
Halleluja.	Hallelujah!

★   ★   ★

Es war ein wunderlich Krieg,	It was a strange and dreadful strife
da Tod und Leben rungen;	when life and death contended;
Das Leben behielt den Sieg,	the victory remained with life,
es hat den Tod verschlungen.	the reign of death was ended;
Die Schrift hat verkündet das,	stript of power, no more he reigns,
wie ein Tod den andern frass,	an empty form alone remains;
ein Spott aus dem Tod ist worden.	his sting is lost for ever.
Halleluja.	Hallelujah!

★   ★   ★

So feiern wir das hoh Fest	So let us keep the festival
mit Herzensfreud und Wonne,	whereto the Lord invites us;
das uns der Herr scheinen lässt.	Christ is himself the joy of all,

Er ist selber die Sonne,	the sun that warms and lights us;
der durch seiner Gnaden Glanz	by his grace he doth impart
erleucht' unsre Herzen ganz;	eternal sunshine to the heart;
der Sünden Nacht ist vergangen.	the night of sin is ended.
Halleluja.	Hallelujah!

Wir essen und leben wohl	Then let us feast this Easter day
zum süssen Brot geladen,	on the true Bread of heaven.
der alte Sauerteig nicht soll	The word of grace hath purged away
sein bei dem Wort der Gnaden.	the old and wicked leaven. (1 Cor. 5:6-8)
Christus will die Kost uns sein	Christ alone our souls will feed,
und speisen die Seel allein;	he is our meat and drink indeed,
der Glaub will keins andern leben.	faith lives upon no other.
Halleluja.	Hallelujah!

Enchiridion, 1524

tr. **Richard Massie**, 1800-87,
Spiritual Songs . . ., 1854

B

Victimae paschali
laudes immolent Christiani.
Agnus redemit oves;
Christus innocens Patri
reconciliavit peccatores.

Mors et vita duello
conflixere mirando;
dux vitae mortuus
regnat vivus.

Dic nobis, Maria,
quid vidisti in via?

'Sepulchrum Christi viventis,
et gloriam vidi resurgentis;
angelicos testes,
sudarium et vestes.
Surrexit Christus spes mea,
praecedet suos in Galilea.'

Credendum est magis soli Mariae veraci
quam Judaeorum turbae fallaci,
scimus Christum resurrexisse
ex mortuis vere.
Tu nobis, victor rex, miserere.

Easter Sequence, ascr. to Wipo, chaplain to Emperors Conrad II and Henry III, d. 1050.

Christians, to the Paschal Victim
offer your thankful praises!
A Lamb the sheep redeemeth:
Christ, who only is sinless,
reconcileth sinners to the Father.

Death and Life have contended
in that combat stupendous:
the Prince of Life, who died, reigns immortal.

Speak, Mary, declaring
what thou sawest wayfaring:

'The tomb of Christ, who is living,
the glory of Jesus' Resurrection;
bright angels attesting,

the shroud and napkin resting.
Yea, Christ my hope is arisen:
to Galilee he goes before you.'

Happy they who bear the witness
Mary's word believing
above the tales of Jewry deceiving.
Christ indeed from death is risen,
our new life obtaining;
have mercy, Victor King, ever reigning!

Tr. in the *English Hymnal*, 1906, based
on *Antiphoner and Grail*, 1880

2
PSALM 130   HG 838

Aus tiefer Not schrei ich zu dir,	From depths of woe I raise to thee
Herr Gott, erhör mein Rufen.	the voice of lamentation;
Dein gnädig Ohren kehr zu mir	Lord, turn a gracious ear to me
und meine Bitt sie öffen;	and hear my supplication.
denn so du willst das sehen an,	If thou shouldst be extreme to mark
was Sünd und Unrecht ist getan,	each secret sin and misdeed dark,
wer kann, Herr, vor dir bleiben?	O who could stand before thee?
Bei dir gilt nichts denn Gnad und Gunst,	To wash away the crimson stain,
die Sünde zu vergeben,	grace, grace alone availeth;
est ist doch unser Tun umsonst	our works, alas! are all in vain;
auch in dem besten Leben.	in much the best life faileth:
vor dir niemand sich rühmen kann,	no man can glory in thy sight,
des muss dich fürchten jedermann	all must alike confess thy might
und deiner Gnade leben.	and live alone by mercy.
Darum auf Gott will hoffen ich,	Therefore my trust is in the Lord,
auf mein Verdienst nicht bauen;	and not in mine own merit;
auf ihn mein Herz soll lassen sich	on him my soul shall rest: his word
und seiner Güte trauen,	upholds my fainting spirit:
die mir zusagt sein wertes Wort;	his promised mercy is my fort,
das ist mein Trost und treuer Hort,	my confort and my sweet support;
des will ich allzeit harren.	I wait for it with patience.
Und ob es währt bis in die Nacht	What though I wait the livelong night,
un wieder an den Morgen,	and till the dawn appeareth,
doch soll mein Herz an Gottes Macht	my heart still trusteth in his might;
verzweifeln nicht noch sorgen.	it doubteth not nor feareth:
So tu Israel rechter Art,	so let the Israelite in heart,
der aus dem Geist erzeuget ward	born of the Spirit, do his part
	(John 1:47)
und seines Gotts erharre.	and wait till God kappeareth.
Ob bei uns ist der Sünden viel,	Although our sin is great indeed,
bei Gott ist viel mehr Gnade;	God's mercies far exceed it;
sein Hand zu helfen hat kein Ziel,	his hand can give the help we need,
wie gross auch sei der Schade.	however much we need it:
Er ist allein der gute Hirt,	he is the Shepherd of the sheep
der Israel erlosen wird	who Israel doth guard and keep,
	(Ps. 80:1)
aus seinen Sünden allen.	and shall from sin redeem him.

Etlich Christliche Lieder, 1524   **RICHARD MASSIE**, 1854

3
THE ANGEL'S SONG   HG 884

(Angel)	(Angel)
Vom himmel hoch da komm ich her,	From heaven high I come to earth.
ich bring euch gute neue Mär,	I bring you tidings of great mirth.
der guten Mär bring ich so viel,	This mirth is such a wondrous thing
davon ich singn und sagen will.	that I must tell you all and sing.
Euch ist ein Kindlein heut geborn	A little child for you this morn
von einer Jungfrau auserkorn,	has from a chosen Maid been born;
ein Kindelein so zart und fein,	a little child, so tender, sweet
das soll eur Freud und Wonne sein.	that you must skip upon your feet.
Es ist der Herr Christ, unser Gott,	He is the Christ, our God indeed,
der will euch führn aus aller Not,	who saves you all in every need.
er will eur Heiland selber sein,	He will himself your Savior be,
von allen Sünden machen rein.	from all wrongdoing make you free.
Er bringt euch alle Seligkeit,	He brings you every one to bliss, -
die Gott der Vater hat bereit',	the Heavenly Father sees to this -
das ihr mit uns im Himmelreich	You shall be here with us on high,
sollt leben nun und ewiglich.	here shall you live and never die.
So merket nun das Zeichen recht,	Look now, you children, at the sign,
die Krippe, Windelein so schlect;	a manger cradle, far from fine,
da findet ihr das Kind gelegt,	a tiny baby you wil see;
das alle Welt erhalt und trägt.	upholder of the world is he.
(Children)	(Children)
Des lasst uns alle fröhlich sein	How glad we'll be if this is so!
und mit den Hirten gehn hinein,	With all the angels let us go
zu sehn, was Gott uns hat beschert,	to see what God for us has done
mit seinem lieben Sohn verehrt.	in sending us his own dear Son.
Merk auf, mein Herz, und sieh dorthin:	Look, look, my heart, and let me peek.
was liegt doch in dem Krippelein?	Whom in the manger do you seek?
Wes ist das schone Kindelein?	Who is that lovely little one?
Es ist das liebe Jesulein.	The baby Jesus, God's own Son.
Sei mir willkommen, edler Gast!	Be welcome, Lord, be now our guest.
Den Sünder nicht verschmahet hast	By you poor sinners have been blessed.
und kommst ins Elend her zu mir;	In nakedness and cold you lie.
wie soll ich immer danken dir?	How can I thank you, how can I?
Ach Herr, du Schöpfer aller Ding,	O Lord, who made and molded all,
wie bist du worden so gering,	how did you come to be so small
dass du da liegst auf dürrem Gras,	that you could lie upon dry grass,
davon ein Kind und Esel ass!	the fodder of the ox and ass?
Und wär die Welt vielmal so weit,	And if the world were twice as wide
von Edelstein und Gold bereit',	with gold and precious stones inside,
so war sie doch dir viel zu klein,	still such a cradle would not do
zu sein ein enges Wiegelein.	to hold a babe as great as you.
Der Sammet und die Seiden dein,	The velvet and the silken ruff,
das ist grob Heu und Windelein,	for these the hay is good enough,
darauf du König gross und reich	Here lies a prince and Lord of all,
herprangst, als wärs dein Himmelreich.	a king within an ass's stall.

Das hat also gefallen dir,
die Wahrheit anzuzeigen mir,
wie aller Welt Macht, Ehr und Gut
vor dir nichts gilt, nichts hilft noch
tut.

Ach mein herzliebes Jesulein,
mach dir ein rein sanft Bettelein,
zu ruhen in meins Herzens
Schrein,
dass ich nimmer vergesse dein.

Davon ich allzeit fröhlich sei,
zu springen, singen immer frei
das rechte Susaninne schon
mit Herzenslust den süssen Ton.

(ALL)
Lob, Ehr sei Gott im höchsten
Thron,
der uns schenkt seinen eingen
Sohn;
des freuen sich der Engel Schar'
und singen uns solch neues Jahr.

You wanted so to make me know
that you had let all great things go.
You had a palace in the sky:
you left it there for such as I.

O dear Lord Jesus, for your head
now will I make the softest bed.
The chamber where this bed shall
be
is in my heart, inside of me.

Now I can play the whole day long.
I'll dance, and sing for you a song,
a soft and soothing lullaby,
so sweet that you will never cry.

(ALL)
To God who sent his only Son

be glory, laud and honor done.

Let all the choir of heaven rejoice,
the new ring in with heart and
voice.

Klug's *Gesangbuch*, 1535

tr. **Roland Bainton**,* 1948

4
GOD IS OUR REFUGE AND STRENGTH
(Ps. 46:1)   HG 847

Ein' feste Burg ist unser Gott,
ein' gute Wehr und Waffen.
Er hilft uns frei aus aller Not
die uns jetzt hat betroffen.
Der alte böse Feind
Mit Ernst er es jetzt meint;
Gross' Macht und viele List
Sei' grausam' Rustung ist;
auf Erd'n ist nicht sein's Gleichen.

Mit uns'rer Macht ist nichts getan,
wir sind gar bald verloren;
Es streit't für uns der rechte Mann,
den Gott hat selbst erkoren.
Und fragst du Wer der ist?
Er heisset Jesus Christ,
Der Herre Zebaoth;
und ist kein and'rer Gott;
Das Feld muss er behalten.

Und wenn die Welt voll Teufel wär'
und wollt' uns gar verschlingen,
so fürchten wir uns nicht zu sehr,
es soll uns doch gelingen.
Der Fürst von dieser Welt
wie sauer er sich stellt,
so tut er uns doch nicht;
das Macht, er ist gericht't,
Ein Wörtlein kann ihn fällen.

Das Wort sie sollen lassen stah'n
und kein'n Dank dazu haben;
er ist bei uns wohl suf dem Plan
mit seinem Geist und Gaben.
Nehmen sie uns den Leib,
Gut, Ehre, Kind und Weib;
Lass fehren nur dahin,
sie haben's kein'n Gewinn;

das Reich muss uns doch bleiben.

Klug's *Gesangbuch*, 1529

A mighty fortress is our God,
a bulwark never failing;
our helper he amid the flood
of mortal ills prevailing.
For still our ancient foe
doth seek to work us woe;
his craft and power are great,
and armed with cruel hate
on earth is not his equal.

Did we in our own strength confide
our striving would be losing,
were not the right Man on our side,
the Man of God's own choosing.
Dost ask who that may be?
Christ Jesus, it is he;
Lord Sabaoth his name,
from age to age the same,
and he must win the battle.

And though this world, with devils filled,
should threaten to undo us,
we will not fear, for God hath willed
his truth to triumph through us.
The prince of darkness grim,
we tremble not for him;
his rage we can endure,
for lo, his doom is sure;
one little word shall fell him.

That word above all earthly powers,
no thanks to them, abideth;
the Spirit and the gifts are ours
through him who with us bideth.
Let goods and kindred go,
this mortal life also;
the body they may kill;
God's truth abideth still,
his kingdom is for ever.

(See also 330)

FREDERICK H. HEDGE, *Hymns for the Church of Christ*, 1853

5
BLESSED ARE YOU WHEN YOU ARE PERSECUTED

He who would follow Christ in life
must scorn the world's insult and strife
and bear his cross each day.
For this alone leads to the throne;
Christ is the only way.

Christ's servants follow him to death, (1 Pet. 1:7)
and give their body, life and breath
on cross and rack and pyre.
As gold is tried and purified
they stand the test of fire.

Renouncing all, they choose the cross,
and, claiming it, count all as loss,
Ev'n home and child and wife.
Forsaking gain, forgetting pain,
they enter into life.

JORG WAGNER, 1527*, tr. **David Augsburger**, 1962*

6
THE LORD'S PRAYER

Our Father God, thy name we praise,
  to thee our hymns addressing,
and joyfully our voices raise,
  thy faithfulness confessing:
assembled by thy grace, O Lord,
we seek fresh guidance from thy Word:
  now grant anew thy blessing.

Touch, Lord, the lips that speak for thee,
  set words of truth before us,
that we may grow in constancy,
  the light of wisdom o'er us.
Give us this day our daily bread;
may hungry souls again be fed;
  may heavenly food restore us.

Lord, make thy pilgrim people wise,
  the gospel message knowing,
that we may walk with lightened eyes
  in grace and goodness growing.
The righteous must thy precepts heed;
thy Word alone supplies their need,
  from heaven their succor flowing.

As with our brethren here we meet,
  thy grace alone can feed us,
as here we gather at thy feet
  we pray that thou wilt feed us.
The power is thine, O Lord divine,
the kingdom and the rule are thine.
  May Jesus Christ still lead us!

LEONAERDT CLOCK, c. 1590,* tr.
Ernest A. Payne, 1962,* from *Ausbund*,
Ed. of 1622

ARTICLE 2:
METRICAL PSALMODY AND HYMNODY, 1549-1700 (7-31)

The only way in which Lutheran hymnody (so far as texts go) impinged on English culture in the 16th century was through the translations of the English Coverdale and the Scottish Wedderburn brothers. Coverdale's version of *Christ is erstanden* can occasionally be found in carol books (*University Carol Book* 183, for example) and his version of a fragment of our # 3 also appears here and there. The Wedderburns are chiefly famous now for having introduced a Scottish version of *In dulci jubilo* on which modern English versions are based. But this translated material did not turn out to be the foundation of English hymnody.

It was the influence of Calvin, not that of Luther, that was decisive in the shaping of both the English and the Scottish reformed churches. In our field the effect of that influence was to restrict congregational song quite firmly to psalmody. And although there was much interaction in the musical field (for that which you can hear, you cannot shut out as you can that which you can see; we were not born with ear-flaps), there was an impassable frontier between the psalm-style and the hymn-style. For metrical psalmody in its English form is not hymnody based on the psalms; it is the very words of the English version of the psalter rearranged, so far as is possible, into metrical form for singing. Calvin himself, having encountered

Clément Marot, the French court-poet who was amusing the French court in the 1530s with metrical psalmody for purely secular and recreational purposes, decided that this style was what would be appropriate to the reformed Church as he envisaged it; and in Marot, and even more in his friend Beza, who carried on the work, he was as fortunate as he was in the incomparable musician Bourgeois, who set these new metrical psalms to music. The French metrical psalms, then, are a passable sort of literature. The French Psalter, when completed in 1562, had 125 meters (and 110 tunes) for its 150 psalms, many of the meters wayward, expansive and beautiful.

As luck would have it, an English psalm-style was developing at the same time through the work of Thomas Sternhold (d. 1549), who, as Groom of the Royal Wardrobe, sought to entertain and educate the young King Edward VI (who was ten when he became king in 1547) by arranging the psalter in the style of the English and Scottish ballads, using their meter. Sternhold at his death left 37 of these done into meter; and perhaps nothing would have come of this had it not been for the flight of so many English Protestant divines to Geneva in 1553 when King Edward's successor, Queen Mary, came to the throne and at once reacted violently towards the old Catholic faith.

Anyone entering the great church at Geneva in 1553 would have found a psalter of 83 psalms (the 1551 edition) in use, and could hardly fail to be impressed with the sonorous simplicity of the French psalms and their music. From the first it was clear to the exiles from Scotland and England that metrical psalmody could be a most appropriate vehicle for public praise. But there were difficulties. It was found, naturally enough, that hardly any Genevan tune would fit an English psalm unless the psalm were retranslated in the Genevan meter. Ingenious devices for adapting the Genevan style of tune to the English meters took a while to work out; the first attempts were less successful than some historians claim. But the conflict remained between a literary desire to write poetry, which the fine Genevan meters looked like encouraging, and the pious desire to keep as close as possible to the language of the newly translated Book of Psalms.

By 1562 the whole English Psalter had been done into ballad meter. It contained a handful of concessions to the Genevan style, of which the best known are the Old Hundredth and the Old 124th (thus called because they are versions of psalms in this 1562 collection which fairly soon became known as the *Old Version*). These indeed were the only psalms not in ballad meter that became popular at once–although there are a dozen others in Genevan meters which though constantly reprinted we may guess remained largely unused.

The style of 1562 is illustrated in ## 9 and 10. 'Sternhold and Hopkins' (which is another name for this Old Version, taken from its two chief authors) is now scarcely sung at all; only Psalm 18 (10) has been taken seriously by modern editors. It's a fine, long psalm of 50 verses and contains a number of couplets which, carefully selected, make a good hymn. But the theologically-minded reader may well pause to reflect on how those Calvinists who so rigorously confined public praise to psalmody assimilated the spiritual complacency of old King David in the Third Part as here quoted.

One other thing must be noted about this historic and now embalmed 1562 collection. That is its title, which is worth quoting.

The Whole Booke/of Psalmes, collected into Eng/lish metre by T. Starnhold I. Hopkins/ & others: conferred with the Ebrue,/

with apt notes to synge the withal, Faithfully perused and alow/ed according to thordre appo/inted in the Queenes Maiesties Iniunctions./§ Very mete to be vsed of all sortes of people priuately for / their solace & comfort: laying apart all / vngodly/ Songes and Ballades, which tende only to the / norishing of vyce, and corrupting of youth. . . .

The 'Iniunctions' of 1559 had indeed very cautiously provided for the singing of 'a Hymn' (a term which by common consent was interpreted as a 'metrical psalm or canticle') at public worship in the Church of England; but the promoters of this collection especially commend it for private use in the home. And indeed it was such private use which provided the largest market for copies of this psalter and which encouraged the making of truly English music for it.

Now, so far as official edict went, this remained the official book of praise throughout the Church of England for 134 years, without any authorized competitors. Scotland produced its own psalter, a parallel but quite independent version, sharing only a few of the 'Geneva-type' versions, including Psalms 100 and 124 (8). This appeared first in 1564 (an example of its contents is at # 11), and it lasted 96 years. Its final revision came in 1650 and produced the Scottish Psalter which is known in the Church of Scotland and all presbyterian communions affiliated with it to this day. This, whose contents are too well known to need much quotation (see ## 12-14), was made by a committee of the Westminster Assembly, which reviewed all the most reasonable private efforts that had been made in intervening years to improve the original, including some that were made for Dissenting congregations. And it will be noted especially here how the primary need to keep as close as possible to the words of the King James Bible overcame any impulse to write what flows naturally as poetry; with the result, so familiar, of syntactical inversions like 'He makes me down to lie,' and 'God keep for ever will.' In the final Scottish version every psalm appears in Common Meter, but some have alternative versions (like, again, 100 and 124); and one or two English compositions are slipped in among these.

But it is only quite recently that the Scottish Psalter has made any impact at all on hymn singing outside the Scottish-centered Presbyterian churches. 'The Lord's my Shepherd' (9e) would now be regarded as a universally popular hymn; but this development is almost entirely the work of the 20th century. The English Methodists have used it since 1876; the Congregationalists took it in 1916; the Baptists waited until 1933, and as for the Church of England, the first widely-used hymnal to take it was the Anglican Hymn Book of 1965, if we do not count the ecumenical BBC Hymn Book (1951) and a much more obscure book, Church Hymnal for the Christian Year (1917). There is little doubt that the sudden rise to popularity of the tune CRIMOND, used at the wedding of Princess Elizabeth (now Queen Elizabeth II) in November 1947 did much to make widely known a psalm which, though venerable, had till then served a minority constituency.

The English metrical psalter was officially revised in 1696 by Nahum Tate, the Poet Laureate, and Nicholas Brady, being known thereafter as 'Tate and Brady' or the 'New Version.' This version was a good deal smoother than the former, and two fragments from it, Psalms 34 and 42, have been received into the general repertory (## 15, 16). This did not replace the Old Version; that version was still being printed in the mid-19th century having run through well over 300 editions. The New Version actually had more success in the U.S.A., where in the 18th century it was very widely used, particularly by Episcopals.

Very little was permitted to public praise beyond the Psalter,

but in the Old Version there was an appendix containing some additional matter. This consisted of: the metrical Veni Creator (found also in the Book of Common Prayer, 1549); the Gospel Canticles (Benedictus, Magnificat, Nunc Dimittis); the Lord's Prayer; the Ten Commandments, followed by a 'prayer' (Long Meter, no doubt to carry the Genevan 'Commandments' tune thus adapted); the Athanasian Creed; the Lamentation of a Sinner (# 17); a second Lamentation in Long Meter; a hymn, 'Preserve us, Lord, by thy dear word,' founded on an older hymn by Luther and using his tune; and three Glorias. The first (C.M.) 'Lamentation' was retained until quite recently in the general repertory, judicious selections and revisions usually overtaking it; so it stands as the oldest original English hymn in continuous and authorized use.

The Scottish Psalter of 1564 and 1650 had no such appendix; the large appendix of 'Paraphrases' came later, in 1781, and is dealt with in its proper place (## 96-102). But the New Version did indeed have a Supplement. To be exact, it had two: one textual, and one musical, the musical one of 1708 being an important musical source (it contains the tune now well known to 'Our God our help in ages past' as well as several other important first appearances). The textual supplement was somewhat expanded, containing, besides the material above (sometimes conservatively revised), the Te Deum; a second (L.M.) Veni Creator (not that at # 160 which was in the 1662 Prayer Book alongside the 1549 version); the Apostles' Creed; a second (L.M.) Lord's Prayer; 'The Song of the Angels' (22); two Easter hymns; two hymns from the Book of Revelation; a post-Communion Thanksgiving Hymn; the Benedicite; and 'A Hymn on the divine Use of Musick' (21) of which more in a moment. The Athanasian Creed and 'Preserve us, Lord,' were dropped.

As has been hinted, private psalters were not uncommon in the 17th century; some of them were designed simply for domestic use, others for use by those congregations which braved the hazards of dissenting from the Church of England. (This was illegal and punishable in the England of those days.) Several psalters, including especially those of Francis Rous and Zachary Boyd, were consulted in the revision of the Scottish Psalter; but none seem to have been used by Tate and Brady, who made a fresh start in their revision. Ainsworth's Psalter of 1612 was in the hands of the Pilgrim Fathers when they arrived in America in 1620, though it cannot be regarded as literature of any merit, and the attempt to bring back the long and complicated Genevan tunes, quite unsuccessful in England, was impeded even among the sturdy pioneers by the awkward diction of Ainsworth's Psalter. The most distinguished author of a complete metrical psalter was King James VI of Scotland, who by then had become King James I of England (the book was not printed until 1631 when he had been dead six years); but his metrical schemes made it impossible for it to be substituted in either country for what was in use, an example (which is as literary work very favourably comparable with other versions) is at # 328. George Sandys' Psalms of 1637, not a complete version, are of interest chiefly in having generated some tunes by the leading English composer of the day (Henry Lawes: see # 28). The versions of Phineas Fletcher and of Sir Philip Sidney and his sister Mary, Countess of Pembroke (who probably wrote our example # 26), were, of course, far better literature and not intended in any sense for ecclesiastical use. Notice how Fletcher (27) brings the New Testament in at the end, almost in the style of the later Isaac Watts.

Ex hypothesi, there was no hymn writing, at least officially, beyond the Psalter supplements we mentioned. George

Wither, however, did produce in 1623 *Hymns and Songs of the Church*, and fell foul of the law for doing so without the necessary licence (which he could never have obtained anyhow), spending a while in prison for his pains. This has some splendidly crusty lyric in it (see # 23); and an added distinction was the appendix of tunes by Orlando Gibbons (1583-1625), the last of England's great madrigalists. Wither later put together *The Hallelujah* (1641) in which were several psalm-versions.

One of the most interesting of all the later psalters is that of John Playford, second edition 1677; for this contains certain hymns not before found in psalters. One of these was the Cosin 'Veni Creator' (160 B), another was # 21, 'On the divine Use of Musick' (which had been in the 1671 edition); two others (18 and 19) are from a Roman Catholic source. Roman Catholicism was officially taboo in England since 1558 and was subject to the same interdicts and penalties as nonconformity; but the known sympathy of Charles II (1660-85) with the Catholics caused some easement of their difficulties during his reign, and in 1668 a book of hymns appeared edited by John Austin, who drew much on the work of the very great mystical poet Crashaw. The two above-mentioned found their way into Playford, one being a translation from a Latin office-hymn (see also # 140). A hymn by Austin from that source, not in Playford, is also given as # 20.

Thomas Ken's very famous trio (the third is not now in use) at # 29 were written for a school, Winchester College, which was in some respects outside the jurisdiction of the hierarchy; and the visionary John Mason, in his *Songs of Praise*, 1694, produced some astonishing literature (30, 31) which, however, was hardly sung at all before the 20th-century editors discovered him.

If then one excepts the versifications of Prayer Book Canticles and spriptural passages especially associated with the Liturgy, and of the Creeds, there is, stretching it as far as we can, a repertory of hardly a dozen hymns available to 17th-century churchgoers. The Catholic hymnody, such as it was, soon returned 'underground,' and apart from the Baptist Benjamin Keach, none of whose work survives now although he wrote a good deal between about 1673 and 1691, even the nonconformists have nothing to say. The understanding of this makes a proper preparation for the explosion of evangelical hymnody in the following century.

See:

Millar Patrick, *Four Centuries of Scottish Psalmody*, Oxford University Press, London, 1949
The Scottish Psalter of 1635, Edited by N. Livingston, McClure and Macdonald, Glasgow, 1864
J. W. McMeeken, *A History of the Scottish Metrical Psalms*, McCullough & Co., Glasgow, 1872

7
PSALM 100   HG 20

Vous qui la terre habitez,
chantez tout haut a Dieu, chantez:
servez à Dieu joyeusement,
venez devant lui gaiement.

Sachez qu'il est le Souverain,
qui sans nous, nous fit de la main,
nous, dis-je son vrai peuple acquis,
et le troupeau de son pasquis.

Entrez és portes d'icelui,
louez-le et célébrez chez lui,

par tout son honneur avancez:
et son tres-saint Nom benissez.

Car il est Dieu plein de bonté,
et dure sa benignité
a jamais: voire du Tres-haut
la vérité jamais ne faut.

Theodore Beza, * in *Genevan Psalter*, 1551

All people that on earth do dwell,
    sing to the Lord with chereful voyce:
him serve with feare, his praise forthe tell:
    come ye before him and reioyce.

The Lord, ye knowe, is God in dede:
    without our aide, he did us make:
We are his folke: he doth us fede,
    and for his shepe he doeth us take.

Oh, entre then his gates with praise:
    approche with ioye his courtes unto.
Praise, laude and blesse his name alwayes
    for it is semely so to do.

For why: the Lord our God is good:
    his mercie is for euer sure:
his trueth at all times firmely stoode
    and shall from age to age indure.

William Kethe, d. 1594, in *Four Score and Seven Psalmes of David*, 1561

8
PSALM 124   A

Or peut bien dire Israël maintenant,
    Si le Seigneur pour nous n'eust point esté,
    si le Seigneur nôtre droit n'eust porté,
quand tout le monde à grand fureur venant
    pour nous meurtri dessus nous s'est jeté,

déjà fuissons vifs devorez par eux,
    veu la fureur ardente des pervers:
    déjà fuissons sous les eaux a l'envois;
et tout ainsi qu'un flot impetueux
    nous eussent tous abusmez et couverts.

Par dessus nous leurs gros et forts torrens
    eussent déjà passé et repassé.
    Loué soit Dieu, lequel n'a point laissé
le peuple sien tomber entre leurs dents
    pour le manger, comme ils avoient pensé.

Comme l'oiseau du filé de defait
    de l'oiseleur, nous sommes échapez,
    rompant le laqs qui nous eust attrapez:
voilà comment le grand Dieu qui a fait
    et terre et ciel, nous a dévelopez.

Theodore Beza, * in the *Genevan Psalter*, 1551

B

Now Israel	may say, and that truly,
if that the Lord	had not our cause maintain'd,
if that the Lord	had not our right sustain'd,
when all the world	against us furiously

made their uproars   and said we should all die;

then long ago
   and swallowed quick   they had devour'd us all
Such was their rage   for aught that we could deem.
And as the floods   as we might well esteem.
so had they now   with mighty force do fall,
    our lives ev'n brought to thrall.

The raging streams
   had long ago   most proud in roaring noise,
   Praised be God   o'erwhelmed us in the deep:
from bloody teeth,   which doth us safely keep
   which as a prey   and their most cruel voice,
    to eat us would rejoice.

Even as a bird
   escapes away   from fowlers gin or pen
   broke are the nets   right so it fared with us;
God that made heaven   and we escaped thus.
   his name hath sav'd   and earth, is our help then,
    us from these wicked men.

WILLIAM WHITTINGHAM, in *The Whole Book of Psalmes* (Sternhold & Hopkins, 1562)

Note: Here and at ## 9 B, 9 C, 10 and 11 we preserve the printing convention used in all early singing editions of the *Old Version*, in which long lines were divided at the natural *caesura*, where the unskilled singer would take breath.

C

Now Israel may say, and that truly,
   if that the Lord had not our cause maintain'd;
   if that the Lord had not our right maintain'd,
     when cruel men against us furiously
     rose up in wrath to make of us their prey;

then certainly they had devour'd us all,
   and swallow'd quick, for ought that we could deem;
   such was their rage, as we might well esteem.
     and, as fierce floods before them all things drown,
     so had they brought our soul to death quite down.

The raging streams, with their proud swelling waves,
   had then our soul o'erwhelmed in the deep.
   But bless'd be God, who doth us safely keep,
     and hath not giv'n us for a living prey
     unto their teeth and bloody cruelty.

Ev'n as a bird out of the fowler's snare
   escapes away, so is our soul set free:
   broke are their nets, and thus escaped we.
     Therefore our help is in the Lord's great name,
     who heav'n and earth by his great power did frame.

Revised in the *Scottish Psalter*, 1650
(as still used in the Church of Scotland)

9

PSALM 23

A

Mon Dieu me paist sous sa puissance haute,
c'est mon berger, de rien je n'aurai faute.
   En toict bien seur, joignat les beaux herbages,
   coucher me fait, me mene aux clairs rivages,
traitte ma vie en douceur tres humaine,
et pour son Nom par droits sentiers me mene.
Si seurement, que quand au val viendroye
d'ombre de mort rien de mal ne craindroye:
   acr avec moi tu es a chacune heure,
   pius ta houlette et conduite m'asseure.

Tu enrichis de vivres necessaires
ma table aux yeux de tous mes adversaires.

Tu oincts mon chef d'huiles et senteurs bonnes,
et jusqu'aux bords pleine tasse me donnes:
   voire et ferras que cette faveur tuenne
   tant que vivrai compagnie me tienne:
si que toujours de faire ai esperance
en la maison du Seigneur demeurance.

CLEMENT MAROT,* in *Strasbourg Psalter*, 1545

B

My Shepherd is the living Lord,
in pastures fair, near pleasant
               streams   nothing therefore I need:
    he setteth me to feed.
He shall convert and glad my soul   and bring my mind in frame:
to walk in paths of righteousness,   for his most holy Name.

Yea, tho' I walk in vale of death,   yet will I fear no ill:
thy rod and staff doth comfort me,   and thou art with me still.
And in the presence of my foes   my table thou shalt spread:
thou wilt fill full my cup, and thou   anointed hast my head.

Thro' all my life thy favour is   so frankly shewed to me,
that in thy house for evermore   my dwelling place shall be.

THOMAS STERNHOLD,* d. 1549, in *The Whole Booke of Psalmes*, 1562

★   ★   ★   ★   ★

C

The Lord is only my support   and he that doth me feed:
how can I then lack anything   whereof I stand in need?
In pastures green he leadeth me   where I do safely lie:
and after leads me to the streams   which run most pleasantly.

And when I find myself near lost   then doth he me home take
conducting me in his right paths   even for his own name's sake.
And tho' I were even at death's
               door   yet would I fear no ill:
for both thy rod and shepherd's
              crook   afford me comfort still.

Thou hast my table richly spread   in presence of my foe:
thou hast my head with balm
            refresh'd,   my cup doth overflow.
And finally while breath doth last   thy grace shall me defend
and in the house of God will I   my life for ever spend.

WILLIAM WHITTINGHAM, in *The Whole Booke of Psalmes*, 1562

D

The Lord is only my support,
   and he that doth me feed:
how can I then lack anything
   whereof I stand in need?
He doth me fold in coats most safe,
   the tender grass fast by:
and after driv'th me to the streams
   which run most pleasantly.

And when I feel myself near lost,
   then doth he me home take:
conducting me in his right paths
   even for his own Name's sake.

And though I were even at death's door,
   yet would I fear none ill:
for by thy rod, and shepherd's crook
   I am comforted still.

Thou hast my table richly deckt
   in despite of my foe:
thou hast my head with balm refresh'd,
   my cup doth over-flow.
And finally, while breath doth last,
   thy grace shall me defend:
and in the house of God will I
   my life for ever spend.

Revised from above: in Scottish Psalter, 1564

E   HG 705

The Lord's my shepherd: I'll not want,
   he makes me down to lie
in pastures green: he leadeth me
   the quiet waters by.
My soul he doth restore again:
   and me to walk doth make
within the paths of righteousness
   ev'n for his own Name's sake.

Yea, though I walk in death's dark vale,
   yet will I fear none ill:
for thou art with me; and thy rod
   and staff me comfort still.
My table thou hast furnished
   in presence of my foes;
my head thou dost with oil anoint,
   and my cup overflows.

Goodness and mercy all my life
   shall surely follow me:
and in God's house for evermore
   my dwelling-place shall be.

Scottish Psalter, 1650

F   HG 693

The God of love my shepherd is,
   and he that doth me feed;
while he is mine and I am his,
   what can I want or need?

He leads me to the tender grasse
   where I both feed and rest;
then to the streams that gently passe:
   in both I have the best.

Or if I stray, he doth convert
   and bring my minde in frame:
and all this not for my desert,
   but for his holy name.

Yea, in death's shadie black abode
   well may I walk, not fear:
for Thou art with me; and thy rod
   to guide, thy staff to bear.

Nay, thou dost make me sit and dine,
   ev'n in my enemies sight:
my head with oyl, my cup with wine
   runnes over day and night.

Surely thy sweet and wondrous love
   shall measure all my dayes;
and as it never shall remove,
   so neither shall my praise.

GEORGE HERBERT (1593-1632), *The Temple*, 1633

10
from PSALM 18

(original spelling and lining: read across the page)

The First Part

O God, my strength and fortitude,   of force I must love thee:
Thou art my castle and defence   in my necessity.
My God, my rock, in whom I trust,   the worker of my wealth:
My refuge, buckler, and my shield,   the horn of all my health.

When I sing laud unto the Lord,   most worthy to be serv'd,
Then from my foes I am right sure   that I shall be preserv'd.
The pangs of death did compass
                              me,   and bound me ev'rywhere
The flowing waves of wickedness   did put me in great fear.

The sly and subtil snares of hell,   were round about me set:
And for my life there was prepar'd   a deadly trapping net.
I was beset with pain and grief,   did pray to God for grace:
And he forthwith heard my
                       complaint   out of his holy place.

Such is his pow'r that in his wrath   he made the earth to quake:
Yea, the foundation of the mount   of Basan for to shake.
And from his nostrils went a
                         smoke,   when kindled was his ire:
And from his mouth went burning
                          coals   of hot consuming fire.

The Lord descended from above,   and bow'd the heav'ns most high;
And underneath his feet he cast   the darkness of the sky.
On cherubs and on cherubims   full royally he rode:
And on the wings of mighty winds   came flying all abroad.

★   ★   ★

The Third Part

But evermore I have respect   to his law and decree:
His statutes and Commandments I   cast not away from me.
But pure, and clean, and un-
                       corrupt   appear'd before his face:
and did refrain from wickedness,   and sin in ev'ry case.

The Lord therefore will me reward,   as I have done aright:
And to the cleanness of my hands   appearing in his sight,
For, Lord, with him that holy is   wilt thou be holy too:
And with the good and vertuous
                           men,   thou wilt uprightly do.

And for the loving and elect   thy favour wilt reserve:
And thou wilt use the wicked men   as wicked men deserve.
For thou dost save the simple folk   in trouble when they lie:
And dost bring down the counte-
                         nance   of them that look full high.

The Lord will light my candle so,   that it shall shine full bright:
The Lord my God will make also   my darkness to be light.
For by thy help an host of men   discomfit, Lord, I shall:
By thee I scale and over-leap   the strength of any wall.

Unspotted are the ways of God,   his word is purely try'd:
He is a sure defence to such   as in his faith abide.

For who is God except the Lord?   for other there is none:
Or else who is omnipotent,   saving our God alone.

THOMAS STERNHOLD,* d. 1549
(1562) - vv 1-10, 21-30

STERNHOLD AND HOPKINS,
The Old Version, 1561

11
MAGNIFICAT

My soul doth magnifie the Lord,   my spirit evermore
rejoiceth in the Lord my God,   who is my Saviour.
And that because he did regard   and had respect unto
the low estate of his hand-maid   and let the mighty go.

For now behold all nations and   the generations all,
from this time forth for evermore   shall me right blessed call.
Because he hath me magnified,   who is the Lord of might:
whose name be ever sanctifi'd,   and praised day and night.

For with his mercy and his grace   all men he doth inflame:
thro'out the generations all   that fear his holy Name.
He shew'd strength with his
            mighty arm   and made the proud to start:
with all imaginations that   were in their wicked heart.

He hath put down the mighty ones   from their supernal seat:
he did exalt the meek in heart,   even from their low estate.
The hungry he replenished   with all things that were good
and thro' his pow'r he made the
               rich   oft times to want their food.

And calling to remembrance his   great mercy very well,
hath holpen up most graciously   his servant Israel.
According to his promise made   to Abraham before:
and to his seed successively   to stand for evermore.

[original punctuation]

The Scottish Psalters: 1564,
1650

12
PSALM 145, vv. 1-6

O Lord, thou art my God and King,
  undoubtedly, I will thee praise:
I will extol and blessings sing
  unto thine holy name always.

From day to day I will thee bless
  and laud thy name world without end.
For great is God, most worthy praise,
  whose greatness none may comprehend.

Race shall thy works praise unto race:
  and so declare thy power, O Lord.
The glorious beauty of thy grace,
  and wondrous works, will I record.

And all men shall the power (O God,)
  of all thy fearful Acts declare:
and I to publish all abroad
  thy greatness at no time will spare.

JOHN CRAIG, Minister of Holyrood,
in *Scottish Psalter,* 1564

13
PSALM 24   HG 828

The earth belongs unto the Lord,
  and all that it contains;
the world that is inhabited,
  and all that there remains.
For the foundations thereof
  he on the seas did lay,
and he hath it established
  upon the floods to stay.

Who is the man that shall ascend
  into the hill of God?
or who within his holy place
  shall have a firm abode?
Whose hands are clean, whose heart is pure,
  and unto vanity
who hath not lifted up his soul,
  nor sworn deceitfully.

He from th'Eternal shall receive
  the blessing him upon,
and righteousness, ev'n from the God
  of his salvation.
This is the generation
  that after him enquire,
O Jacob, who do seek thy face
  with their whole heart's desire.

Ye gates, lift up your heads on high;
  ye doors, that last for aye
be lifted up, that so the King
  of glory enter may.
But who of glory is the King?
  The mighty Lord is this;
ev'n that same Lord, that great in migh'
  and strong in battle is.

Ye gates, lift up your heads; ye doors,
  doors that do last for aye
be lifted up, that so the King
  of glory enter may.
But who is he that is the King
  of glory? Who is this?
The Lord of hosts, and none but he
  the King of glory is.

Scottish Psalter, 1650

14
PSALM 116

I love the Lord, because my voice
  and prayers he did hear.
I, while I live, will call on him,
  who bow'd to me his ear.
Of death the cords and sorrows did
  about me compass round;
the pains of hell took hold on me,
  I grief and trouble found.

Upon the name of God the Lord
  then did I call, and say,
'Deliver thou my soul, O Lord,
  I do thee humbly pray.'
God merciful and righteous is,
  yea, gracious is our Lord.
God saves the meek: I was brought low,
  he did me help afford.

I'll of salvation take the cup,
  on God's name will I call:
I'll pay my vows now to the Lord
  before his people all.
Dear in God's sight is his saints' death,
  thy servant, Lord, am I;
thy servant sure, thine handmaid's son:
  by bands thou didst untie.

Thank-offerings I to thee will give,
  and on God's name will call.
I'll pay my vows now to the Lord
  before his people all;
within the courts of God's own house,
  within the midst of thee,
O city of Jerusalem,
  praise to the Lord give ye.

vv. 1-6, 13-19, *Scottish Psalter,* 1650

15
PSALM 42   HG 53

As pants the hart for cooling
              streams
  when heated in the chase;
so longs my soul, O God, for thee
  and thy refreshing grace.

For thee, my God, the living God,
  my thirsty soul doth pine;
O when shall I behold thy face,
  thou Majesty divine?

Tears are my constant food, while
              thus
  insulting foes upbraid,
'Deluded wretch, where's now
            thy God,
  and where thy promis'd aid?'

I sigh whene'er my musing
            thoughts
  those happy days present,
when I with troops of pious
            friends
  thy temple did frequent;

when I advanc'd with songs of
            praise
  my solemn vows to pay;
and led the joyful sacred throng
  that kept the festal day.

Why restless, why cast down, my
            soul?
  Trust God, and he'll employ
his aid for thee, and change these
            sighs
  to thankful hymns of joy.

My soul's cast down, O God, and
            thinks
  on thee and Sion still;
from Jordan's banks, from Her-
         mon's heights,
  and Missar's humbler hill.

One trouble calls another on
  and, bursting o'er my head,
fall spouting down, till round my
            soul
  a roaring sea is spread.

But when thy presence, Lord of
            life,
  has once dispelled this storm,
to thee I'll midnight anthems sing,
  and all my vows perform

God of my strength, how long
            shall I,
  like one forgotten, mourn?
forlorn, forsaken, and expos'd
  to my oppressors' scorn.

My heart is pierced as with a sword,
  whilst thus my foes upbraid,
'Vain boaster, where is now thy God?
  and where his promised aid?'

Why restless, why cast down, my soul?
  hope still; and thou shalt sing
the praise of him who is thy God,
  thy health's eternal spring.

TATE AND BRADY, *New Version,* 1696

16
From PSALM 34   HG 747

Through all the changing scenes of life,
  in trouble and in joy,
the praises of my God shall still
  my heart and tongue employ.

Of his deliverance I will boast,
  till all that are distress'd
from my example comfort take
  and soothe their griefs to rest.

O magnify the Lord with me;
  with me exalt his name:
when in distress to him I called,
  he to my rescue came.

The hosts of God encamp around
  the dwellings of the just;
deliv'rance he affords to all
  who in his succour trust.

O! make but trial of his love,
  experience will decide
how blest are they, and only they,
  who in his truth confide.

Fear him, ye saints, and ye will then
  have nothing else to fear;
make you his service your delight,
  he'll make your wants his care.

A hymn fashioned out of Ps. 34, verses
1-4, 7-9 in **TATE & BRADY,** *New Version,* 1696

JOHN MARCKANT, fl. 1561

17
THE LAMENTATION OF A SINNER   HG 543

O Lord, turn not thy face away
  from him that lies prostrate,
lamenting sore his sinful life
  before thy mercy gate,
which thou dost open wide to those
  that do lament their sin;
O shut it not against me, Lord,
  but let me enter in.

Call me not to a strict account
  how I have livèd here:
for then I know right well, O Lord,
  most vile I shall appear.
I need not to confess my life,
  for surely thou canst tell
what I have been, and what I am
  thou knowest very well.

★   ★   ★

So come I to the throne of grace,
  where mercy doth abound:
desiring mercy for my sin,
  to heal my deadly wound.
O Lord, I need not to repeat
  what I do beg or crave:
for thou dost know before I ask
  the thing that I would have.

Mercy, good Lord, mercy I ask,
  this is the total sum:
for mercy, Lord, is all my suit,
  O let thy mercy come.

> In Day's edition (1561) of **STERNHOLD
> & HOPKINS**, *Psalms*, sts. 3-4 omitted.

JOHN AUSTIN*
1613-69

18
A HYMN FOR SUNDAY

Behold, we come, dear Lord, to thee,
  and bow before thy throne:
we come to offer on our knee
  our vows to thee alone.

Whate'er we have, whate'er we are
  thy bounty freely gave:
thou dost us here in mercy spare,
  and wilt hereafter save.

But O! can all our store afford
  no better gifts for thee!
Thus we confess thy riches, Lord,
  and thus our poverty.

'Tis not our tongue or knee can pay
  the mighty debt we owe:
far more we should than we can say,
  far lower than we bow.

Come then, my soul, bring all thy pow'rs,
  and grieve thou hast no more:
bring every day thy choicest hours,
  and thy great God adore.

But above all, prepare thy heart
  on this his own blest day,
in its sweet task to bear thy part
  and sing, and love, and pray.

> *Devotions in the Antient Way of Of-
> fices,* 1668

19
IAM LUCIS ORTO SIDERE
A Morning Hymn

Now that the Daystar doth arise,
beg we of God with humble cries
all hurtful things to keep away,
while we devoutly spend the day;

our tongues to guide, so that no strife
may breed disquiet in all our life:
to shut and close the wandering eye,
lest it doth let in vanity;

to keep the heart most pure and free
from fond and troubled fantasie;
to tame proud flesh, while we deny 't
a too full cup and wanton diet;

that when the day-light shall go out,
time bringing on the night about,
we may, by leaving worldly ways,
neglect no time our God to praise.

> Medieval Latin text (cf. # 139), tr. **R.
> Cranshaw*** and **John Austin**, 1668

20

Hark, my soul, how everything
strives to serve our bounteous King;
each a double tribute pays,
sings its part, and then obeys.

Nature's chief and sweetest choir
him with cheerful notes admire;
chanting every day their lauds,
while the grove their song applauds.

Though their voices lower be,
streams have too their melody;
night and day they warbling run,
never pause, but still sing on.

All the flowers that gild the spring
hither their still music bring;
if heaven bless them, thankful, they
smell more sweet, and look more gay.

Only we can scarce afford
this short office to our Lord:
we, on whom this bounty flows,
all things gives, and nothing owes.

Wake! for shame, my sluggish heart,
Wake! and gladly sing thy part;
learn of birds, and springs, and flowers
how to use thy nobler powers.

Call whole nature to thine aid;
since 'twas he whole nature made;
join in one eternal song,
who to one God all belong.

Live for ever, glorious Lord!
live by all thy works adored,
One in Three, and Three in One,
thrice we bow to thee alone.

> 'For Monday at Lauds,' *Devotions,*
> 1668

Anonymous

21
ON THE DIVINE USE OF MUSICK

We sing to thee, whose wisdom formed
  the curious organ of the ear;
and thou, who gav'st us voices, Lord,
  our grateful songs in kindness hear.

We'll joy in God, who is the spring
  of lawful joy and harmless mirth:
whose boundless love is fitly called
  the harmony of heaven and earth.

Those praises, dearest Lord, aloud
  our humblest sonnets shall rehearse;
which rightly tun'd, are rightly styl'd
  the MUSICK of the Universe.

And whilst we sing we'll consecrate
  that too too much prophaned Art,
by off'ring up with ev'ry tongue
  in ev'ry song a flaming heart.

We'll hallow pleasure, and redeem
   from vulgar use our precious voice:
those lips which wantonly have sung
   shall serve our turn for nobler joys.

Thus we will imitate on earth,
   poor mortals still, the heavenly quires:
and with high notes, above the clouds
   we'll send with words more rais'd desires.

And that Above we may be sure,
   when we come there our part to know:
whilst we live here, at Home and Church
   we'll practice singing oft below.

Glory and praise be given most
   to Father, Son and Holy Ghost:
Hallelujah, Hallelujah,
Hallelujah, Hallelujah.

In **JOHN PLAYFORD**, *The Whole
Book of Psalms*, 1677

NAHUM TATE
1652-1715

22
SONG OF THE ANGELS: The Nativity of our
Blessed Saviour. Luke 2:8-15   HG 816

While Shepherds watched their flocks by night,
   all seated on the ground,
the Angel of the Lord came down
   and glory shone around.

'Fear not,' said he, (for mighty dread
   had seized their troubled mind),
'glad tidings of great joy I bring
   to you and all mankind.'

'To you, in *David's* Town this day
   is born, of *David's* line
the Saviour, who is Christ the Lord,
   and this shall be the sign:

'The heavenly Babe you there shall find
   to humane View display'd,
all meanly wrapped in swathing bands,
   and in a manger laid.'

Thus spake the Seraph, and forthwith
   appear'd a shing throng
of Angels, praising God, and thus
   address'd their joyful song:

'All glory be to God on high,
   and to the earth be peace;
good will henceforth, from Heaven to men
   begin, and never cease.'

In *A Supplement to the New Version*,
1708

GEORGE WITHER, * 1588-1667

23
ASCENSION DAY

To God with heart and cheerful voice
   a triumph song we sing;
and with true thankful hearts rejoice
   in our almighty King;

yea, to his glory we record
   (who were but dust and clay)
what honour he did us afford
   on his ascending day.

The human nature, which is late   (Ps. 8)
   beneath the angels was
now raisèd from that meaner state
   above them hath a place.
And at man's feet all creatures bow
   which through the whole world be,
for at God's right hand thronèd now
   in glory sitteth he.

Each door and everlasting gate   (Ps. 24:7)
   to him hath lifted been;
and in a glorious wise thereat
   our King is entered in.
Whom if to follow we regard,
   with ease we safely may,
for he hath all the means prepared,
   and made an open way.   (Heb. 10:20)

Then follow, follow on apace,
   and let us not forego
our Captain, till we win the place
   that he hath scaled unto;
and for his honour, let our voice
   a shout so hearty make,
the heavens may at our mirth rejoice,
   and earth and hell may shake.

Song 57 (st. 3 omitted) in *Hymns and
Songs of the Church*, 1623

24
PSALM 148

The Lord of heaven confess,
   on high his glory raise.
Him let all angels bless,
   him all his armies praise.
     Him glorify
       sun, moon and stars;
       ye higher spheres
     and cloudy sky.

From God your beings are,
   him therefore famous make;
you all created were,
   when he the word but spake.
     And from that place,
       where fixed you be
       by his decree
     you cannot pass.

Praise God from earth below,
   ye dragons and all deeps:
fire, hail, clouds, wind and snow,
   whom in command he keeps.
     Praise ye his name,
       hills great and small,
       trees low and tall;
     beasts wild and tame;

all thing that creep or fly.
   Ye kings, ye vulgar throng,
all princes mean or high;
   both men and virgins young,

ev'n young and old
exalt his name;
for much his fame
should be extolled.

O let God's name be praised
above both earth and sky;
for he his saints hath raised
and set their horn on high;
ev'n those that be
of Israel's race,
near to his grace,
the Lord praise ye.

Psalms of David, 1632; *Scottish Psalter*,
1650

25
A GENERAL INVITATION TO PRAISE GOD

Come, oh come in pious lays
sound we God Almighty's praise;
hither bring in one consent
heart, and voice, and instrument.
Music add of every kind;
sound the trump, the cornet
                              wind;
strike the viol, touch the lute;
let no tongue or string be mute;
    nor a creature dumb be found
    that hath either voice or sound.

Let those things which do not live
in still music praises give;
lowly pipe, ye worms that creep,
on the earth, or in the deep:
loud aloft your voices strain,
beasts and monsters of the main:
birds, your warbling treble sing;
clouds, your peals of thunder ring:
    sun and moon, exalted higher,
    and bright stars, augment this
                              choir.

Come, ye sons of human race,
in this chorus take a place;
and amid the mortal throng,
be you masters of the song.
Angels, and supernal powers,
be the noblest tenor yours;
let, in praise of God, the sound
run a never-ending round;
    that our song of praise may be
    everlasting, as is He.

From earth's vast and hollow
                              womb,
music's deepest bass may come;
seas and floods, from shore to
                              shore,
shall their counter-tenors roar.
To this consort, when we sing,
whistling winds your descant
                              bring;
that our song may over-climb
all the bounds of space and time,
    and ascend from sphere to
                              sphere
    to the great Almighty's ear.

So from heaven, on earth he shall
let his gracious blessings fall;
and this huge wide orb we see
shall one choir, one temple be;
where, in such a praise, full tone
we shall sing what he hath done,
that the cursed fiends below
shall thereat impatient grow.
    Then, oh come, in pious lays,
    sound we God Almighty's praise.

Hymn 1 in *The Hallelujah*, 1641

MARY SIDNEY,* Countess of
Pembroke (Lady Mary Her-
bert) 1561-1621

26
from PSALM 139

O Lord, in me there lieth nought
but to thy search revealèd lies;

for when I sit
thou markest it:
no less thou notest when I rise:
yea, closest closet of my thought
hath open windows to thine eyes.

Thou walkest with me when I walk;
when to my bed for rest I go
I find thee there
and everywhere;
not youngest thought in me doth grow,
no, not one word I cast to talk
but, yet unuttered, thou dost know.

If forth I march, thou goest before;
if back I turn, thou comest behind;
so forth nor back
thy guard I lack
nay, on me too thy hand I find.
Well I thy wisdom may adore,
but never reach with earthy mind.

To shun thy notice, leave thine eye,
O! whither might I take my way?
To starry sphere?
Thy throne is there.
To dead men's undelightsome stay?
There is thy walk, and there to lie
unknown in vain I should assay.

O sun, whom light nor flight can match,
suppose thy lightful flightful wings
thou lend to me,
and I could flee
so far as thee the evening brings,
even led to west he would me catch,
nor should I lurk with western things.

Do thou thy best, O secret night
in sable veil to cover me,
thy sable veil
shall vainly fail;
with day unmasked my night shall be;
for night is day, and darkness light,
O Father of all lights, to thee.

*The Psalms of David . . . begun by the
noble and learned gent, Sir Philip Sidney, Knt., and finished by the Right
Honourable the Countess of Pembroke, his Sister . . . (no date: between
1603 and 1621)*

PHINEAS FLETCHER*
1582-1650

27
PSALM 130

From the deeps of grief and fear
O Lord to thee my soul repairs:
from thy heaven bow down thine ear;
let thy mercy meet my prayers.
O if thou mark'st
what's done amiss,
What soul so pure
can see thy bliss?

But with thee sweet mercy stands,
sealing pardons, working fear:
wait, my soul, wait on his hands;
wait mine eye, oh wait mine ear:

If he his eye
   or tongue affords,
watch all his looks,
   catch all his words.

As a watchman waits for day,
   and looks for light, and looks again;
when the night grows old and grey,
   to be relieved he calls amain:
      so look, so wait,
         so long mine eyes,
      to see my Lord,
         my Sun, arise,

Wait, ye saints, wait on your Lord;
   for from his tongue sweet mercy flows:
wait on his cross, wait on his word;
   upon that Tree Redemption grows.
      He will redeem
         his Israel
      from sin and wrath,
         from death and hell.

The Purple Island, 1633

GEORGE SANDYS*
1577-1644

28
PSALM 8

Lord, how illustrious is thy Name,
whose power both heaven and earth proclaim!
Thy glory thou hast set on high
above the marble-arched sky,

The wonders of thy power thou hast
in mouths of babes and sucklings placed,
that so thou might'st thy foes confound,
and who in malice most abound.

When I pure heaven, thy fabric, see,
the moon and stars disposed by thee;
O what is man, or his frail race,
that thou should'st such a shadow grace!

Next to thy angels most renowned,
with majesty and glory crowned,
the king of all thy creatures made,
that all beneath his feet hast laid;

all that on dales or mountains feed,
that shady woods or deserts breed;
what in the airy regions glide,
or through the rolling ocean slide.

Lord, how illustrious is thy name,
whose power both heaven and earth proclaim!

*A Paraphrase Vpon the Divine Poems
. . . , 1638*

THOMAS KEN, 1637-1711

29
MORNING, EVENING AND MIDNIGHT HYMNS
HG 63

Morning
Awake, my soul, and with the sun
thy daily stage of duty run,
shake off dull sloth, and joyful rise
to pay thy morning sacrifice.

Thy precious time misspent, re-
         deem,
each present day thy last esteem,
Improve thy talent with due care,
for the Great Day thyself prepare.

By influence of the Light divine
let thy own light to others shine.
Reflect all heaven's propitious
         ways
in ardent love, and cheerful
         praise.

Wake, and lift up thyself, my heart,
and with the angels bear thy part,
who all night long unwearied sing
high praise to the eternal King.

All praise to thee who safe hast
         kept
and hast refreshed me while I
         slept.
Grant, Lord, when I from death
         shall wake
I may of endless light partake.

★ ★ ★ ★

Evening
All praise to thee, my God, this
         night
for all the blessings of the light.
Keep me, O keep me, King of
         kings
beneath thine own almighty
         wings.

Forgive me, Lord, for thy dear Son
the ill that I this day have done;
that with the world, my self and
         thee
I, ere I sleep, at peace may be.

Teach me to live, that I may
         dread
the grave as little as my bed;
teach me to die, that so I may
rise glorious at the awful day.

★ ★ ★ ★

Midnight
My God, now I from sleep awake,
the sole possession of me take.
From midnight terrors me secure,
and guard my heart from thoughts
         impure.

Bless'd Angels! while we silent lie,
you hallelujahs sing on high,
you joyful hymn the ever-Bless'd
before the Throne, and never rest.

I with your choir caelestial join
in offering up a hymn divine;
with you in heaven I hope to
         dwell,
and bid the night and world fare-
         well.

Heav'n is, dear Lord, where e'er
         thou art,
O never then from me depart;
for to my soul 'tis hell to be
but for one moment void of thee.

Lord, I my vows to thee renew,
disperse my sins like morning
         dew.
Guard my first springs of thought
         and will
and with thyself my Spirit fill.

Direct, control, suggest this day
all I design, or do, or say,
that all my powers with all their
         might
in thy sole glory may unite.

★ ★ ★ ★

O! may my soul on thee repose
and with sweet sleep mine eye-
         lids close,
sleep that may me more vig'rous
         make
to serve my God when I awake.

When in the night I sleepless lie,
my soul with heavenly thoughts
         supply;
let no ill dreams disturb my rest,
no powers of darkness me molest.

O may my Guardian while I sleep
close to my bed his vigil keep,
his love angelical instill,

★ ★ ★ ★

O may I always ready stand
with my lamp burning in my
         hand;
may I in sight of heaven rejoice
when e'er I hear the Bridegroom's
         voice.

(Doxology after all parts)
*Praise God, from whom all bless-
         ings flow,
praise him, all creatures here be-
         low;
praise him above, he heavenly
         host
praise Father, Son and Holy Ghost.*

A Manual of Prayers, 1695; text of 1709
5 stanzas omitted from pt. 1, 5 from pt.
2, 7 from pt. 3.

JOHN MASON, 1645-94
from
Songs of Praise, 1694

30
A GENERAL SONG OF PRAISE TO ALMIGHTY GOD

HG 300

How shall I sing that Majesty
  which angels do admire!
Let dust in dust and ashes lie,
  sing, sing, ye heavenly choir.
Thousands of thousands stand around
  thy throne, O God most high;
ten thousand times ten thousand sound
  thy praise; but who am I?

Thy brightness unto them appears
  whilst I thy footsteps trace;
a sound of God comes to my ears,
  but they behold thy face.
They sing, because thou art their Sun;
  Lord, send a beam on me;
for where heaven is but once begun,
  there hallelujahs be,

Enlighten with faith's light my heart,
  enflame it with love's fire,
then shall I sing and bear a part
  with that celestial choir.
I shall, I fear, be dark and cold,
  with all my fire and light;
yet when thou dost accept their gold,
  Lord, treasure up my mite.

                        Lk. 21:1

How great a being, Lord, is thine,
  which doth all beings keep.
Thy Knowledge is the only line
  to sound so vast a deep.
Thou art a sea without a shore,
  a sun without a sphere;
thy time is now and evermore,
  thy place is everywhere.

                (st. 1-4 of 12)

31
A SONG OF PRAISE FOR THE LORD'S DAY

My Lord, my Love, was crucified,
  he all the pains did bear;
but in the sweetness of his rest
  he makes his servants share.
How sweetly rest thy saints above,
  which in thy bosom lie!
The church below doth rest in hope
  of that felicity.

Thou, Lord, who daily feedst thy sheep,
  mak'st them a weekly Feast:
thy flocks meet in their several folds

  upon this Day of Rest.
Welcome and dear unto my soul
  are these sweet feasts of love;
but what a sabbath shall I keep
  when I shall rest above!

I bless thy wise and wondrous love
  which binds us to be free;
which makes us leave our earthly snares
  that we may come to thee.
I come, I wait, I hear, I pray:
  thy footsteps, Lord, I trace:
I sing to think this is the way
  unto my Saviour's face.

These are my preparation days:
  and when my soul is drest,
these sabbaths shall deliver me
  to mine eternal rest.

ARTICLE 3: ISAAC WATTS (32-44)

Isaac Watts needs little introduction here, though he repays the closest study that anyone can afford to give him. The son of an elder of an Independent (Congregational) church in Southampton, born in 1674, precociously literate and learned, finally becoming a minister of a church of that communion in London, Watts is the liberator of hymnody in English. He cannot, as we have seen, be called positively its inventor; but, according to the principle mentioned in Article I, he was its first successful practitioner. There are four sources for his work: *Horae Lyricae*, 1705 (which contains not only hymns but some poetry in other forms), *Hymns and Spiritual Songs*, 1707, *Divine and Moral Songs*, 1715 (a very small collection divided into 'Divine Songs' and 'Moral Songs,' both for children), and *The Psalms of David Imitated in the Language of the New Testament*, 1719. Pieces from all four collections are still in common use, but it is the second and fourth which contain his best known hymns. Only one now in common use comes from any other source: this is 'Am I a soldier of the Cross?' for which see the *Hymnal Guide*.

Watts' hymns were the consequence of his dissatisfaction with the metrical psalters. He had reason to be discontented with their literature, but far more he was unhappy that Christians were not allowed to sing, apart from the meagre allowance provided in the psalter supplements, about Christian doctrine. The accepted story is that in about 1690, at the age of 16, he mentioned to his father that the hymnody in church was dull and profitless, and on his father's replying, 'Then write something better,' he promptly did, and our # 32 was the result.

This text should be studied with care. In it is the germ of all the 700-odd pieces he subsequently wrote. One notices that it is in the psalm meter; and all his hymns were written in psalm meters, so that known psalm tunes could carry them. It is, secondly, founded on a lyric passage in Revelation, a passage to which he often later returned, and is indeed so close a paraphrase of that passage that it was admitted in 1781 to the *Scottish Paraphrases* (see Article 8 below). But thirdly, the final stanza gives the hymn an existential quality which is really the principle of the hymn's liberation. In that stanza the congregation is no longer reciting the Biblical words but making its own prayer, and this is what finally unlocks the secret of hymnody.

Watts' style is close to that of the metrical psalters, but of course, being no longer bound by the necessity of packing in the words of the Authorized Version of the Bible, he does not need to strain his sentence structure and can write more freely. He still uses rhyme and rhyme is, here and in the psalters, a most necessary aid to memory when hymns are being 'lined out,' that is, sung by dictation and not from a book. Like so many other practical necessities in hymns (a musical parallel is the 'gathering note' in the old psalm-tunes), what here begins as a conventional necessity becomes an integral part of the poetry in skilled hands, so that it remained with us until very recently as, in all but a few unusual meters, a hymnic necessity.

It has to be admitted, as soon as you read Watts in any quantity, that he could descend to bathos. It is out of place to include his more risible examples in the quoted texts, but one of his finest pieces, 'Begin, my tongue, some heavenly theme,' contains a stanza which can hardly be printed now:

> He said, *Let the wide Heav'n be spread,*
> And Heaven was stretched abroad;
> 'Abrah'm, *I'll be thy God,'* He said,
> and he was *Abrah'm's* God.

But the incongruity of that is the consequence not of a failure on his part to write properly but on a shifting of taste and custom in the use of words and phrases. The effect of 'worms' and 'bowels' (see introduction, p. iv) is nowadays always absurd, but it was not so to him nor to his people.

It is the quality of free and uninhibited writing which produces so often that epigrammatic style that is always the mark of the great hymn writer. The memorable phrase, packing immense amounts into a few simple words, is what makes a hymn live. The last stanza of 'When I survey,' or the third of 'Nature with open volume,' two of his supreme moments, are examples to any hymn writer. The zest of mind which produces such fine religious conceits as the third stanza of # 40 is what we first find in Watts, and what after him we look for in any writer worth considering.

His *Hymns*, 1707, are in three books: the first, hymns closely paraphrasing scripture; the second (more fertile in material acceptable to modern editors), 'spiritual songs' of freer range; and the third, communion hymns. All this, as well as the material in the 1705 book, was completed before he was 33 years old. In reading him, one wants to suspend a facile modern resistance to the diction and rhythm of the 18th century and to enjoy the positive gifts of this extraordinary writer.

This section contains nothing from *Divine and Moral Songs*; one hymn from there is at # 296 (see Article 16). But the *Psalms* produce two of his very best known pieces (## 43 and 44).

The *Psalms* are, in a way, a more dramatic gesture even than the *Hymns*, for, as he expressed it himself in a famous preface which well repays the trouble of finding and reading it, Watts here endeavours 'to make David speak like a Christian.' References to strictly Old Testament places, people and events are often replaced with Christian references, so that, in the famous example (43), 'Jesus shall reign' translates 'His Kingdom shall endure from sea to sea,' the Hebrew priest-king being replaced by Christ himself. 'Israel' often becomes 'the Church,' or, in other contexts, 'Britain' (a reference that now always has to be altered). Watts' psalter is not quite complete; it omits a few psalms, though to compensate this Watts frequently translates a psalm in two or even three versions, throwing the emphasis in different directions or employing different meters. Example 44 shows the original text of his second version, part 1, of Psalm 90.

Watts is represented always by a few hymns in modern hymnals. The most generous selection in a current hymnal is that in *Congregational Praise* (1951) which gives 45 of his hymns. American hymnals rarely come near that figure; the *Worshipbook* (1972), for example, presents ten of his texts, in only one case avoiding abridgment, expansion or alteration. This is quite normal nowadays.

Bibliography:

Selma Bishop: *Isaac Watts, Hymns and Spiritual Songs*: a textual study London, Faith Press, 1962

Selma Bishop: *Isaac Watts' Hymns and Spiritual Songs*, A Publishing History and Bibliography, Ann Arbor, Mich., Pierian Press, 1974

A. P. Davis: *Isaac Watts, His Life and Works*, London, Independent Press, 1943

H. Escott: *Isaac Watts, Hymnographer*, London, Independent Press, 1962

D. Fountain: *Isaac Watts Remembered*, Worthing (England), H. E. Walter, 1974

ISAAC WATTS, 1674-1748
HG 10

32

(original spelling, punctuation and capitalization)

Behold the Glories of the Lamb
 Amidst his Father's Throne:
Prepare new Honours for his Name,
 And Songs before unknown.

Let Elders worship at his Feet,
 The Church adore around,
With Vials full of Odours sweet,
 And Harps of sweeter sound.

Those are the Prayers of the Saints,
 And these the Hymns they raise:
Jesus is kind to our Complaints,
 He loves to hear our Praise.

Eternal Father, who shall look
 Into thy Secret Will?
Who but the Son should take that Book,
 And open every Seal?   (Rev. 5:2)

He shall fulfil thy great Decrees,
 The Son deserves it well;
Lo, in his Hand the Sov'reign Keys
 Of Heav'n, and Death, and Hell.

Now to the Lamb that once was slain,
 Be endless Blessings paid;
Salvation, Glory, Joy remain
 Forever on thy Head.

Thou hast redeem'd our Souls with Blood,
 Hast set the Pris'ners free,
Hast made us Kings and Priests to God,
 And we shall reign with Thee.

The World of Nature and of Grace
 Are put beneath thy Pow'r;
Then shorten these delaying Days
 And bring the promis'd Hour.

ISAAC WATTS' first hymn. *Hymns* I 1: 'A new Song to the Lamb that was slain'; Rev. 5:6, 8, 9, 10, 12

33
GOD EXALTED ABOVE ALL PRAISE

Eternal Pow'r! whose high abode
becomes the grandeur of a GOD;
Infinite length! beyond the bounds
where stars revolve their little rounds.

The lowest step about thy seat
rises too high for Gabriel's feet:
in vain the tall archangel tries
to reach thy height with wond'ring eyes.

Thy dazzling beauties while he sings,
he hides his face behind his wings;
and ranks of shining thrones around
fall worshipping, and spread the ground.

Lord, what shall earth and ashes do?
We would adore our Maker too;
from sin and dust to thee we cry,
'The GREAT, the Holy, and the HIGH!'

Earth from afar has heard thy fame,
and babes have learnt to lisp thy name:
but oh! the glories of thy mind
leave all our soaring thoughts behind.

God is in heaven, and men below;
be short our tunes; our words be few;
a sacred rev'rence checks our songs,
and praise sits silent on our tongues.

Horae Lyricae, 1705, Book I

34
THE OFFICES OF CHRIST: from Several Scriptures
HG 375

Join all the glorious names
of wisdom, love and power,
that ever mortals knew,
that angels ever bore:
All are too mean to speak his worth,
too mean to set my *Saviour* forth. (John 4:47)

But O what gentle terms,
what condescending ways
doth our *Redeemer* use
to teach his heav'nly grace!
Mine eyes with joy and wonder see
what forms of love he bears for me.

Array'd in mortal flesh
he like an *Angel* stands, (Dan. 6:22)
and holds the promises
and pardons in his hands,
commission'd from his Father's throne
to make his grace to mortals known.

Great *Prophet* of my God, (Acts 3:22)
my tongue would bless thy name;
by thee the joyful news
of our salvation came;
the joyful news of sins forgiv'n,
of hell subdu'd, and peace with heav'n.

Be thou my *Counsellor*, (Is. 9:6)
my *Pattern*, and my *Guide*; (John 13-15; Is. 55:4)
and thro' this desert land
still keep me by thy side.

O let my feet ne'er run astray,
nor rove, nor seek the crooked way.

I love my *Shepherd*'s voice, (Ps. 23)
his watchful eyes shall keep
my wandering soul among (John 10:1-10)
the thousands of his sheep: (Matt. 18)
he feeds his flock, he calls their names,
his bosom bears the tender lambs.

To this dear *Surety*'s hand (Gen. 43:9)
will I commit my cause;
he answers and fulfils
his Father's broken laws.
Behold my soul at freedom set!
My Surety paid the dreadful debt.

Jesus, my great *High-Priest* (Heb. 5:10)
offer'd his blood and dy'd;
my guilty conscience seeks
no Sacrifice beside.
His powerful blood did once atone;
and now it pleads before the Throne.

My *Advocate* appears (1 John 2:1)
for my defence on high,
The Father bows his ear,
and lays his thunder by.
Not all that hell or sin can say
shall turn his heart, his love away.

My dear Almighty *Lord*, (1 Tim. 6:15)
my *Conqueror* and my *King*, (Rev. 6:2; Acts 17:7)
Thy scepter, and thy *Sword*,
thy reigning grace, I sing.
Thine is the power; behold I sit
in willing bonds before thy feet.

Now let my soul arise,
and tread the Tempter down;
my *Captain* leads me forth (Heb. 2:10)
to conquest and a crown.
A feeble saint shall win the day,
Tho' death and hell obstruct the way.

Should all the hosts of death
and powers of hell unknown
put their most dreadful forms
of rage and mischief on;
I shall be safe, for *Christ* displays (Rev. 11:15)
superior power and guardian-grace.

Hymns, I 150

35
A PROSPECT OF HEAVEN MAKES DEATH EASY
HG 726

There is a land of pure delight,
where saints immortal reign;
infinite day excludes the night,
and pleasures banish pain.

There everlasting spring abides,
and never withering flowers;
death like a narrow sea divides
this heav'nly land from ours.

Sweet fields beyond the swelling floor
   stand drest in living green;
so to the *Jews* old *Canaan* stood,
   while *Jordan* rolled between.

But timorous mortals start and shrink
   to cross this narrow sea,
and linger shivering on the brink,
   and fear to launch away.

O could we make our doubts remove,
   these gloomy doubts that rise,
and see the *Canaan* that we love
   with unbeclouded eyes; -

could we but climb where *Moses* stood,
   and view the landscape o'er,
not Jordan's stream, nor death's cold flood
   should fright us from the shore.

Hymns, II 66

36
THE CHRISTIAN RACE
Is. 40:28-31

Awake, our souls, (away our fears,
   let every trembling thought be gone)
awake, and run the heavenly race,
   and put a cheerful courage on.

True, 'tis a strait and thorny road,
   and mortal spirits tire and faint,
but they forget the mighty God
   that feeds the strength of every saint:

thee, mighty God, whose matchless power
   is ever new and ever young,
and firm endures while endless years
   their everlasting circles run.

From thee the overflowing spring
   our souls shall drink a fresh supply,
while such as trust their native strength
   shall melt away and droop and die.

Swift as an eagle cuts the air
   we'll mount aloft to thine abode,
on wings of love our souls shall fly,
   nor tire amidst the heavenly road.

Hymns, I 48

37
THE EXAMPLES OF CHRIST AND THE SAINTS
HG 218

Give me the wings of faith, to rise
   within the veil, and see
the saints above, how great their joys,
   how bright their glories be.

Once they were mourning here below
   and wet their couch with tears;   (Ps. 6:6)
they wrestled hard, as we do now,
   with sins, and doubts, and fears.

I ask them whence their victory came,
   they, with united breath,

ascribe their conquest to the Lamb,
   their triumph to his death.

They marked the footsteps that he trod,
   (his zeal inspired their breast:)
and following the incarnate God
   possess the promised rest.

Our glorious Leader claims our praise
   for his own pattern given,
while the long cloud of witnesses
   shows the same path to heaven.

Hymns, II 140.

38
CRUCIFIXION TO THE WORLD BY THE CROSS
OF CHRIST Gal. 6:14   HG 804

When I survey the wond'rous Cross
   where the young Prince of Glory dy'd,†
my richest gain I count but loss,
   and pour contempt on all my pride.

Forbid it, Lord, that I should boast
   save in the death of Christ my God;
all the vain things that charm me most,
   I sacrifice them to his blood.

See from his head, his hands, his feet
   sorrow and love flow mingled down;
did e'er such love and sorrow meet,
   or thorns compose so rich a crown?

His dying crimson, like a robe
   spreads o'er his body on the Tree;
then am I dead to all the globe,
   and all the globe is dead to me.

Were the whole realm of nature mine,
   that were a present far too small;
love so amazing, so divine
   demands my soul, my life, my all.

Hymns, III 7

†Watts himself altered this line in all editions after the first to the form
now familiar.

39
CHRIST CRUCIFY'D: THE WISDOM AND POWER
OF GOD

Nature with open volume stands
   to spread her Maker's Praise abroad
and every labour of his hands
   shows something worthy of a God.

But in the Grace that rescu'd Man
   his brightest form of Glory shines;
here on the Cross 'tis fairest drawn
   in precious Blood and crimson Lines.

Here his whole Name appears complete,
   nor Wit can guess, nor Reason prove
which of the Letters best is writ,
   the Power, the Wisdom, or the Love.

Here I behold his inmost Heart,
   where Grace and Vengeance strangely join,

piercing his Son with sharpest Smart
   to make the purchas'd Pleasures mine.

O the sweet Wonders of that Cross,
   where God the Saviour loved and dy'd!
Her noblest Life my Spirit draws
   from his dear Wounds, and bleeding Side.

I would for ever speak his Name
   in sounds to mortal Ears unknown,
with Angels join to praise the Lamb,
   and worship at his Father's throne.

Hymns, III 10

40
INCOMPARABLE FOOD: OR, THE FLESH AND BLOOD OF CHRIST

The banquet that we eat
   is made of heavenly things.
Earth hath no dainties half so sweet
   as our Redeemer brings.

In vain had *Adam* sought
   and search'd his garden round,
for there was no such blessed fruit
   in all that happy ground.

Th' angelic host above
   can never taste this food,
they feast upon their Maker's love,
   but not a Saviour's blood.

On us th' Almighty Lord
   bestows this matchless grace,
and meets us smiling at his Board,
   with pleasure in his face.

Come, all ye drooping saints
   and banquet with the King,
the Wine will drown your sad complaints,
   and tune your voice to sing.

Salvation to the name
   of our adorèd *Christ*:
thro' the wide Earth his grace proclaim,
   and glory in the high'st.

Hymns, III 17, st. 3-8

41
GLORY IN THE CROSS: OR, NOT ASHAM'D OF CHRIST CRUCIFY'D

At thy command, our dearest Lord,
   here we attend thy dying feast;
thy blood like wine adorns thy board,
   and thine own flesh feeds every guest.

Our faith adores thy bleeding love,
   and trusts for life in one that dy'd;
we hope for heav'nly crowns above
   from a Redeemer crucify'd.

Let the vain world pronounce it shame,
   and fling their scandals on the cause;
we come to boast our Saviour's name,
   and make our triumphs in his cross.

With joy we tell the scoffing age
   he that was dead has left his tomb,
he lives above their utmost rage
   and we are waiting till he come.

Hymns, III 19

42
PSALM 23
HG 472

My Shepherd will supply my need,
   Jehovah is his name;
in pastures green he makes me feed
   beside the living stream.

He brings my wandering spirit back
   when I forsake his ways;
and leads me, for his mercy's sake,
   in paths of truth and grace.

When I walk thro' the shades of death,
   thy presence is my stay;
a word of thy supporting breath
   drives all my fears away.

Thy hand, in sight of all my foes,
   doth still my table spread;
my cup with blessings overflows,
   thine oil anoints my head.

The sure provisions of my God
   attend me all my days;
O may thy house be mine abode,
   and all my work be praise!

There would I find a settled rest,
   (while others go and come)
no more a stranger or a guest,
   but like a child at home.

Psalms of David Imitated, 1719

43
PSALM 72, Second Part
Christ's Kingdom among the Gentiles
HG 367

Jesus shall reign where'er the sun
   does his successive journeys run;
his kingdom stretch from shore to shore,
   till moons shall wax and wane no more.

Behold the Islands with their Kings,
   and *Europe* her best tribute brings;
from *North* to *South* the Princes meet
   to pay their homage at his feet.

There *Persia* glorious to behold,
   there *India* stands in *Eastern* Gold;
and barbarous nations at his word
   submit and bow and own their Lord.

For him shall endless pray'r be made,
   and praises throng to crown his head;
his name like sweet perfume shall rise
   with every morning sacrifice;†

†The semicolon at the end of this line, indicating that this and the following stanza are one continuous sentence, is not in any of the editions of Watts' hymns but is a wholly acceptable conjecture first offered by the English classical scholar Robert L. Arrowsmith and incorporated in the text in *Hymns for Church and School* (1964), #123.

people and realms of every tongue
dwell on his love with sweetest song;
and infant-voices shall proclaim
their early blessings on his name.

Blessings abound where'er he reigns,
the prisoner leaps to lose his chains,
the weary find eternal rest,
and all the sons of want are blest.

Where he displays his healing power
death and the curse are known no more;
in him the tribes of *Adam* boast
more blessings than their father lost.

Let every creature rise and bring
peculiar honours to our king;
angels descend with songs again,
and earth repeat the long *Amen*.

Psalms of David Imitated, 1719

44
PSALM 90:1-5
Man Frail and God Eternal   HG 592

Our God, our help in ages past,
  our hope for years to come,
our shelter from the stormy blast,
  and our eternal home.

Under the shadow of thy throne
  thy saints have dwelt secure;
sufficient is thine arm alone,
  and our defence is sure.

Before the hills in order stood,
  or earth received her frame,
from everlasting thou art God,
  to endless years the same.

Thy Word commands our flesh to dust,
  Return, ye sons of men;
all nations rose from Earth at first,
  and turn to earth again.

A thousand ages in thy sight
  are like an evening gone;
short as the watch that ends the night
  before the rising sun.

The busy tribes of flesh and blood,
  with all their lives and cares,
are carried downwards by the flood
  and lost in following years.

Time, like an ever-rolling stream
  bears all its sons away;
they fly, forgotten as a dream
  dies at the opening day.

Like flow'ry fields the nations stand
  pleas'd with the morning light;
the flowers beneath the Mower's hand
ly withering e'er 'tis night.

Our God, our help in ages past,
  our hope for years to come,

be thou our guard while troubles last,
  and our eternal home.

Psalms of David Imitated, 1719

ARTICLE 4:
AFTER WATTS AND BEFORE THE WESLEYS (45-52)

'After' and 'Before' are not so much chronological as stylistic terms here. The group of hymns that follows includes some that were written before Watts had finished and some written after Charles Wesley had begun; but the importance of this interim period between the two great hymnic explosions can hardly be overstated.

In it the current is flowing two ways. In ## 44-9 we see the source of a new style, in 50-52, three pieces by Philip Doddridge, we have the work of a devoted disciple of Watts.

The two fragments of Pope's *Messiah* (44) should be studied closely. The whole poem of 108 lines should, if possible, be consulted. (It is No. 227 in the *Oxford Book of Christian Verse*.) It first appeared in *The Spectator*, whose founding editor was Joseph Addison, on 12 May 1712. Pope was by that time the leading poet of British life, and he was about to bring to its highest perfection a style of writing which is always primarily associated with his name: the didactic and philosophical poem in heroic couplets (rhymed decasyllables). In the *Essay on Man*, his masterpiece, Pope showed how this meter could express in poetic terms a long argument and drive it home with that quality for which it proved to be particularly suited– wit. Pope at his best evokes a quite different kind of smile from that which the lyric poets of the 17th century produce. He builds on Dryden rather than on Milton, whose blank verse, using the same metrical line, has a totally different effect.

What I think has not been hitherto pointed out is the effect, to Pope as unexpected as it was unintended, that this had on hymnody. While the heroic couplet is not in any sense a natural meter for hymnody (the few hymns that exist in rhymed tens do not sound at all like Pope's couplets) there is one thing that they do have in common with the hymn style, and that is that, quite unlike the blank verse of Milton and Shakespeare, they depend for their effect on the coincidence of the sentence with the end of a couplet. The 'run-on' is essential to the rhythm of blank verse; it is rare in heroic couplets. In our short extract there is only one place, line 102, where the sense runs over the end of a couplet, and that is in fact the only place in the whole poem where it does so. Similarly, and for obvious practical reasons, the 'run-on' is always regarded as exceptional in hymn writing.

Now, it cannot escape the most casual eye that in section (a) of # 44 there are several phrases that are familiar to hymn singers. The whole poem is a catena of paraphrases from the Old Testament prophets; but what is more remarkable is the very clear announcement that lines 29, 37, 39-40 are the source of stanzas 1 and 4 of Doddridge's 'Hark the glad sound' (52), and that lines 38 and 43-4 are the source of stanza 5 of Wesley's 'O for a thousand tongues' (60). (A much later American hymn (372) quotes line 37.)

When we add the much better-known fact that the first line of 'Love divine' (66) is imitated from Dryden, and that the last is taken verbatim from the fourth line of Addison's *Gratitude* (47), we know what Charles Wesley read in his youth, and what kind of literature inspired his forms of expression. In the less-known Wesley hymns there is much use of classical allusion, and, in his poetry, plenty of picturesque admixture of classical proper names of the kind familiar in Milton and in Pope (and seen in line 100 of our second extract at # 44).

This piece, we repeat, appeared in Addison's *Spectator* in May 1712. In several Saturday issues in July, August, and September of the same year, Addison included hymns of his own (see the *Hymnal Guide* for details, at 621) which were written in imitation and in admiration of Isaac Watts, whose *Hymns* had appeared five years earlier. Of the five that Addison wrote, three (46-8) are in very wide use still, and all are to be found in current hymnals. (The *English Hymnal* contains all five, at nos. 92, 297, 491, 511, 524, only 511 being abridged.) Three are in Watts' Common Meter; the other two use six and eight line stanzas of eight syllables, and both these (46, 48) are psalm paraphrases. His hymns are, however, as characteristically an Anglican layman's work of the period as Watts' are the work of a dissenting Calvinist minister. They sacrifice (if that is the word you want to use) Watts' fervour for a smoothness and urbanity of diction that Watts never rose to and never particularly aimed at. They are more palatable than much of Watts to people who value good literature, less so to those who value the in-group intensity of religious diction. Men of letters have often expressed special admiration of # 48, and the compilers of the Scottish Paraphrases of 1781, severe enough in all conscience in their dogmatic standards, included our 47 (in full) and 48, with 'When rising from the bed of death' as three of the five hymns they permitted to be appended to their scriptural paraphrases; the other two are by Watts.

'Christians, awake' (49) is worth reading in its entirety alongside the Pope fragments. Pope's poem was not 'discovered' as hymn material until the first American Episcopal *Hymnal* of 1826 included a cento that uses lines 85-6, 97-8, 87-94 and 105-8, the only alteration being the reduction of the final line by two syllables. Byrom's poem, his Christmas present to his daughter in 1749, was sung, as tradition has it, the very next year by the choir of the church that he attended in Manchester, and it was made into a regular hymn by Cotterill in 1819. Here again we see the attractions of the 'heroic couplet' as a vehicle of hymnody. We would give much to know just what selection of lines was sung on that Christmas in 1750 when the magnificent tune was first heard.

Philip Doddridge (50-52) was an industrious hymn writer, almost all of whose work first saw the light of publication after his death. He wrote his hymns at different times to illustrate his preaching, being a minister of the same communion as Watts. His work is, on the whole, cavalierly treated by modern hymnals and the best known hymn attributed to him, 'O God of Bethel' (96) contains very little of his original work. In this, at least for the first four stanzas, and in # 101, the Scottish revisers on the whole improved him; but they were interested in that part of his work which stayed closest to the letter of Scripture. This he frequently did, as in # 52, which in its full version is a very uneven piece of work, and makes a far better hymn if every other stanza is left out. But when he is writing more freely he is often very eloquent, and though they are far from well known, ## 50 and 51 may well be his finest pieces: 50 showing an unusually compressed and poised style that certainly owes a good deal to the Augustans (whose leader was this same Pope); and 51, besides being positively the first hymn on the social applications of the Gospel ever to be written (if we discount Watts' not infrequent effusions on the Popish Plot), is also a beautiful example of disciplined rhetorical power. Other work of his in the current hymnals is always worth looking at, though it does not often rise quite to this standard.

The one other well-known hymn of the 'interim' period, which again owes much to Watts but shows something of the new literary freedom, is Simon Browne's 'Come, gracious Spirit' (*HG* 124); as now sung, however, this text is much altered from the original and is an improvement on it.

ALEXANDER POPE, 1688-1744

45   HG 621

(a)   Hark! a glad sound the lonely desert cheers;
Prepare the way! a God, a God appears: (30)
A God, a God! the vocal hills reply,
The rocks proclaim th' approaching Deity.
Lo, earth receives him from the bending skies!
Sink down, ye mountains, and ye valleys, rise,
With heads declin'd, ye cedars homage pay; (35)
Be smooth, ye rocks, ye rapid floods, give way!
The Saviour comes! by ancient bards foretold:
Hear him, ye deaf, and all ye blind, behold!
He from thick films shall purge the visual ray,
and on the sightless eyeball pour the day: (40)
'Tis he th' obstructed paths of sound shall clear,
and bid new music charm th' unfolding ear:
the dumb shall sing, the lame his crutch forego,
and leap exulting like the bounding roe.
No sigh, no murmur the wide world shall hear, (45)
from every face he wipes off every tear.

(lines 29-46)

★   ★   ★

(b)   Rise, crown'd with light, imperial Salem, rise! (85)
Exalt thy tow'ry head, and lift thy eyes!
See, a long race thy spacious courts adorn;
See future sons, and daughters yet unborn,
In crowding ranks on ev'ry side arise,
Demanding life, impatient for the skies! (90)
See barb'rous nations at thy gates attend,
walk in thy light, and in thy temple bend;
See thy bright altars throng'd with prostrate kings,
And heap'd with products of Sabaean springs!
For thee Idumé's spicy forests blow, (95)
And seeds of gold in Ophir's mountains glow.
See heav'n its sparkling portals wide display,
And break upon thee in a flood of day!
No more the rising Sun shall gild the morn,
Nor ev'ning Cynthia fill her silver horn; (100)
But lost, dissolv'd in thy superior rays
One tide of glory, one unclouded blaze
O'erflow thy courts: the light himself shall shine
Reveal'd, and God's eternal day be thine!
The seas shall waste, the skies in smoke decay, (105)
Rocks fall to dust, and mountains melt away;
But fix'd his word, his saving pow'r remains; -
Thy realm for ever lasts, thy own Messiah reigns!

(lines 85-108)

The Messiah, 1712 (see article 4)

JOSEPH ADDISON
1672-1719

46
PSALM 23:1-4   HG 704

The Lord my pasture shall prepare,
and feed me with a shepherd's care;
his presence shall my wants supply,
and guard me with a watchful eye;

my noonday walks he shall attend,
and all my midnight hours defend.

When in the sultry glebe I faint,
or on the thirsty mountain pant,
to fertile vales and dewy meads
my weary wandering steps he leads,
where peaceful rivers, soft and slow,
amid the verdant landscape flow.

Though in the paths of death I tread,
with gloomy horrors overspread,
my steadfast heart shall fear no ill,
for thou, O Lord, art with me still;
thy friendly crook shall give me aid,
and guide me through the dreadful shade.

Though in a bare and rugged way
through devious lonely wilds I stray,
thy bounty shall my pains beguile;
the barren wilderness shall smile,
with sudden greens and herbage crowned,
and streams shall murmur all around.

The Spectator, 26 July, 1712

47
GRATITUDE HG 800

When all thy mercies, O my God!
my rising soul surveys,
transported with the view, I'm lost
in wonder, love and praise.

O how shall words, with equal warmth,
the gratitude declare
that glows within my ravish'd heart!
but thou canst read it there.

Thy providence my life sustain'd,
and all my wants redrest,
when in the silent womb I lay
and hung upon the breast.

To all my weak complaints and cries
thy mercy lent an ear,
ere yet my feeble thoughts had learn'd
to form themselves in pray'r.

Unnumber'd comforts to my soul
thy tender care bestowed,
before my infant heart conceived
from whom those comforts flow'd.

When in the slippery paths of youth
with heedless steps I ran;
thine arm, unseen, convey'd me safe,
and led me up to man.

Through hidden dangers, toils and deaths,
it gently clear'd my way;
and through the pleasing snares of vice,
more to be fear'd than they.

When worn with sickness, oft hast thou
with health renew'd my face;
and, when in sins and sorrows sunk,
reviv'd my soul with grace.

Thy bounteous hand with worldly bliss
hath made my cup run o'er;
and in a kind and faithful friend,
hath doubled all my store.

Ten thousant thousand precious gifts
my daily thanks employ;
nor is the least a cheerful heart,
that tastes these gifts with joy.

Through ev'ry period of my life
thy goodness I'll proclaim;
and after death, in distant worlds,
resume the glorious theme.

When nature fails, and day and night
divide thy works no more,
my ever grateful heart, O Lord,
thy mercy shall adore.

Through all eternity to thee
a joyful song I'll raise;
for oh! eternity's too short
to utter all thy praise.

The Spectator, 9 August, 1712

48
PSALM 19:1-6 HG 716

The spacious firmament on high,
with all the blue ethereal sky,
and spangled heavens, a shining frame,
their great Original proclaim.
Th' unwearied sun from day to day
does his Creator's pow'r display;
and publishes to every land
the work of an Almighty hand.

Soon as the ev'ning shades prevail,
the moon takes up the wondrous tale,
and, nightly to the listening earth
repeats the story of her birth;
while all the stars that round her burn,
and all the planets in their turn
confirm the tidings as they roll
and spread the truth from pole to pole.

What though in solemn silence all
move round the dark terrestrial ball?
what though no real voice, no sound,
amidst their radiant orbs be found?
In reason's ear they all rejoice,
and utter forth a glorious voice;
for ever singing, as they shine,
'The hand that made us is divine.'

The Spectator, 23 August, 1712

JOHN BYROM
1692-1763

49
CHRISTIANS, AWAKE HG 119

This now famous Christian hymn was first written as a continuous Ode. But the tradition is that the Christmas following that for which it was written, the choir of the nearby parish church came and sang it under its author's windows, with the tune composed by its music director John Wainwright. One must suppose therefore that for that purpose it was divided into stanzas, though we do not know how. It came into use as a hymn in 1819. It is printed below so that the reader can distinguish the lines that form the modern versions (they vary from book to book); it should be noted that the couplet beginning 'Tread in his steps . . . ,' excellently though it matches the spirit of the original, is not in the poem as Byrom wrote it.

Christians, awake, salute the happy Morn
Whereon the Saviour of the World was born.
Rise to adore the Mystery of Love
Which hosts of Angels chanted from above;
With them the joyful Tidings first begun
Of God incarnate and the Virgin's Son.
Then to the watchfull Shepherds it was told,
Who heard th' Angelic Herald's Voice—behold!
I bring good tidings of a Saviour's Birth
To you and all the Nations upon Earth.
This Day hath God fulfill'd his promised Word,
This day is born a Saviour, Christ the Lord.
  In David city, shepherds, ye shall find
  The long foretold redeemer of Mankind
  Wrapt up in swadling Claoths, be this the Sign,
  A Cratch contains the holy Babe divine.
He spake, & straightway the celestial Quire
In Hymns of joy unknown before conspire
The Praises of redeeming Love they sung
and Heav'n's whole Orb with Hallelujahs rung.
God's highest Glory was their Anthem still,
Peace upon Earth, & mutual Good Will.
To Bethlehem straight th' enlightened Shepherds ran*
To see the Wonder God had wrought for Man.
They saw their Saviour as the Angel said,
The swaddled Infant in the Manger laid.
  Joseph and Mary a distressed pair
  Guard the sole Object of th' Almighty's Care;
  To human eyes none present but they two
  Where Heaven was pointing its concentred View.
Amaz'd the wondrous Story they proclaim,
The first Apostles of his Infant Fame.
  But Mary kept and pondered in her Heart
  The heav'nly Vision which the Swains impart.
  They to their flocks & praising God return
  With hearts no doubt that did within them burn.

  Let us like these good Shepherds then employ
  Our grateful voices to proclaim the Joy.
Like Mary let us ponder in our mind
God's wondrous Love in saving lost Mankind,
  Artless and watchful as these favour'd Swains,
  While virgin Meekness in the Heart remains.
Trace we the Babe who has retrieved our loss
From his poor manger to his bitter Cross.
  Follow we him who has our Cause maintain'd†
  And Man's first heav'nly State shall be regained.
Then may we hope, th'Angelic Thrones among,
To sing, redeem'd, a glad Triumphal Song.
He that was born upon this joyful Day
Around us all his Glory shall display;
Sav'd by his Love, incessant we shall sing
of Angels and of Angel-men the King.

(1749)

_____

*The four lines beginning with this are altered and conflated to two in modern use.
†'Tread in his steps' is from this line and the next.

PHILIP DODDRIDGE
1702-51

Hymns (ed. J. Orton)
1755

50
EBENEZER, or God's Helping Hand Review'd and Acknowledg'd. 1 Sam. 7:12

My helper God! I bless his name;
the same his power, his grace the same.
The tokens of his friendly care
open, and crown, and close the year.

I 'midst ten thousand dangers stand
supported by his guardian hand;
and see, when I survey my ways,
ten thousand monuments of praise.

Thus far his arm has led me on;
thus far I make his mercy known;
and, while I tread this desert land,
new mercies shall new songs demand.

My grateful soul, on *Jordan*'s shore
shall raise one sacred pillar more:
then bear, in his bright courts above
inscriptions of immortal love.

No. 23

51
Relieving Christ in his poor Saints
Matt. 25:40   HG 361

Jesus, my Lord, how rich thy grace!
  thy bounties how complete!
How shall I count the matchless sum?
  or pay the mighty debt?

High on a throne of radiant light
  dost thou exalted shine;
what can my poverty bestow
  when all the worlds are thine?

But thou hast brethren here below,
  the partners of thy grace,
and wilt confess their humble names
  before thy Father's face.

In them thou may'st be clothed, and fed,
  and visited, and cheered,
and in their accents of distress
  my Saviour's voice is heard.

Thy face with rev'rence and with love
  I in thy poor would see;
O let me rather beg my bread
  than hold it back from thee.

No. 188

52
CHRIST'S MESSAGE
Luke 4:18, 19   HG 267

Hark, the glad sound! the Saviour comes,
  the Saviour promised long!

let every heart prepare a throne,
and every voice a song.

On him the Spirit largely pour'd
exerts its sacred fire:
wisdom and might, and zeal and love
his holy breast inspire.

He comes the prisoners to release
in *Satan's* bondage held;
the gates of brass before him burst,
the iron fetters yield.

He comes from thickest films of vice
to purge the mental ray,
and on the eyeballs of the blind
to pour celestial day.

He comes the broken heart to bind,
the bleeding soul to cure,
and with the treasures of his grace
to enrich the humble poor.

The silver trumpets publish loud
the Jub'lee of the Lord;   (Lev. 25)
our debts are all remitted now,
our heritage restored.

Our glad hosannas, Prince of peace,
thy welcome shall proclaim,
and heaven's eternal arches ring
with thy beloved name!

See also ## 96 and 101.

ARTICLE 5:
CHARLES WESLEY AND HIS FAMILY (53-72)

This part of our story must begin with John, Charles Wesley's even more celebrated elder brother. John was a hymnologist and a translator but not, it is usually thought, a hymn writer. (We must admit that the ascription of all translations to John and all original hymns to Charles is nowhere supported in anything they themselves said or wrote; but it is an educated guess which there is no serious reason for disturbing.) One of the many distinctions enjoyed by Charles is the preparation of the first hymnal published in America–the Charlestown hymnal of 1737 which he compiled in the course of his unfortunate and ill-starred mission to Georgia. This event took place before what he refers to as his 'conversion' (May 24, 1738); but the hymnal is not without interest. It contains, for the first time, a hymn by his father (53) and one by his elder brother (54) which show something of the style of Isaac Watts; and this collection also has for the first time 'Before Jehovah's awful throne,' rewritten in its first stanza by John Wesley from Watts' Psalm 100. Naturally there is nothing here by Charles Wesley, who seems not to have begun hymn writing until after his own 'conversion,' three days before John's, so Isaac Watts is inevitably the chief contributor. But there are several others by Charles' father and brother, and six hymns made out of poems by George Herbert (for whom see Article 20).

John's contact with the German pietists, especially the Moravians as newly gathered under their great leader Zinzendorf, inspired him to learn German, and to make a number of translations not always in the meters of the originals, but showing a command of language which introduces a quite new note into hymnody and which he shared with his more prolific brother (see 55, 56, 195B, 202B).

But once Charles got under way in his 1739 collection, he began a hymnic output which is unmatched anywhere in the literature for volume, variety, and distinction of style. The truth about the volume cannot be more precisely stated than as it is put by F. Baker (see bibliography) who finds that he wrote 8,989 religious poems. Not all qualify as hymns, but it is usually said that something over 6,000 do. Charles lived fifty years from the year of his conversion, so this total works out at 3.4 poems per week, assuming him to have died in the act of writing. If a skeptic says that it would be difficult to avoid writing badly in such an output, and if a kinder critic murmurs that it must have been impossible to avoid repetition, the only honest answer is that it is still remarkable how many indispensable hymns everybody now admits him to have written, and what a high standard of doctrine, eloquence, and lyricism he reaches in so many of them. Not that he is an unhonoured prophet. The English Methodist Hymn Book of 1904 contained 980 hymns, of which 440 are his; its 1933 successor, almost exactly the same length, could not cut him down below 243. Many hymnals of all denominations contain twenty.

Watts was an Independent. Wesley was a priest of the Church of England. In any of those hymnals which have a theological rather than liturgical arrangement you tend to find Watts near the beginning, Wesley coming into his own in the seasons of the Church's year and, of course, in hymns of Christian experience. Watts was the hymn writer primarily of the glory of God as a good Calvinist heart apprehended it. Wesley was the celebrator of Christ and of the Holy Spirit. In *Congregational Praise* (which I choose because of its theological arrangement) Watts has fourteen entries before Wesley's first, and twenty-one before Wesley's third, while in the second half of the book Wesley has 26 to Watts' ten.

Charles Wesley's two overriding passions were the celebration of the Church's year, stemming from his faithfulness to his prayer-book, and (that to which he gave even freer rein) hymns exalting the glory of Christ and the bliss of conversion. He is the first and, surely for all time, the greatest evangelical hymn writer. Not infrequently he is didactic, but he is hardly ever anything but ecstatic. Such a pressure of devotion needed the discipline of doctrine, and this we find in him to a degree that is the measure of his outstanding pre-eminence among evangelicals. The simplest and most 'popular' of his hymns (like 'Hark the herald,' or its original, for which see #59) abound in scriptural echoes and allusions; the profoundest abound equally (see # 58). His treatment of Scripture is the poet's as much as the preacher's; for most of the time he uses Scripture to illuminate itself, often providing a mosiac of quotations which produce a new and magnificent pattern, as in 'Love divine,' # 66. The direct paraphrasing of Scripture he hardly attempts before 1762, in which year he produced a small collection of hymns, mostly short and all exquisite, which are largely paraphrases of Matthew Henry's Commentary (1700) - see ## 69-71. The majestic 'Come, O thou Traveller' (62) is not really so to be thought of; it is rather a meditation on a mystery. In its full length it is moving, though hardly singable; and yet in the 4-stanza selection still to be found in hymnals that have not wholly lost their consciences it becomes an utterance of perfect clarity and trenchant communicativeness.

Wesley used over eighty meters compared with Watts' handful. Some are most entertaining and light-hearted (like that of # 68), others grave and measured, like the six-eights of which he was especially fond. The gate that Watts had opened Wesley joyously entered; and the field that Watts sowed he reaped, literally, a hundredfold. If one considers these two as two mountain ranges, then perhaps Watts can boast the highest peak. Wesley, it may be fair to say, never quite reached the height of 'When I survey' and 'Nature with open volume'; but the average level of Wesley is probably higher, considered as literature. Watts could occasionally come down to a thump of bathos; Wesley sometimes flounders. But between them they ensured, the one in his quiet London congregation, the other anywhere from the tin-mines of Cornwall to the coalpits of Newcastle, that the Christian Faith should never be without songs for its full expression.

It is just possible, however, that Watts scores over Wesley in one respect. Perhaps, over two centuries after their hymns were written, Watts uses less 'in-group' language; perhaps at his best he is more public, easier to offer to Christians whose faith is not learned or intense. Wesley is much more for those who have travelled far. You come to 'When I survey' long before you come to 'Eternal beam of light divine' (57) which is perhaps the hymn of Wesley's that can be most fairly compared with Watts' masterpieces. Yes, you find Wesley near the end of the road, and yet, as the reader will see, I have, as a disciple of Watts' own communion, had to close my anthology not with a Wesley but with a Watts—whose last two lines say what Wesley never quite said and perhaps never really was likely to say.

See:

F. Baker and G. W. Williams, *John Wesley's First Hymn Book* (Charleston: Dalcho Historical Society and London, Wesley Historical Society, 1964)

J. L. Nuelsen, *John Wesley and the German Hymn* (Rev. A. S. Holbrook, Calverley, Pudsey, Yorkshire, 1972)

F. Baker, *Representative Verse of Charles Wesley* (Epworth Press, 1962)

E. Rattenbury, *The Evangelical Doctrines of Charles Wesley's Hymns* (Epworth, 1941)

E. Rattenbury, *The Eucharistic Hymns of John and Charles Wesley* (Epworth, 1948)

H. Bett, *The Hymns of Methodism* (Epworth, 1913, 1945)

H. Bett, *The Hymns of Charles Wesley: a Study of their Structure* (Epworth, 1953)

B. L. Manning, *The Hymns of Wesley and Watts* (Epworth, 1942)

J. A. Kay, *Wesley's Prayers and Praises* (Epworth, 1958)

H. A. Hodges and A. M. Allchin, *A Rapture of Praise* (Hodder & Stoughton, 1966)

J. Lawson, *The Christian Year with Charles Wesley* (Epworth, 1966)

SAMUEL WESLEY, SENIOR
1662-1735

53
ON THE CRUCIFIXION

Behold the Saviour of mankind
  nail'd to the shameful Tree!
How vast the love that him inclin'd
  to bleed and die for thee!

Hark how he groans! while Nature shakes,
  and earth's strong pillars bend!
The temple's veil in sunder breaks,
  the solid marbles yield.

'Tis done! the precious ransom's paid;
  'Receive my soul,' he cries:
see where he bows his sacred head!
  He bows his head and dies.

But soon he'll break death's envious chain
  and in full glory shine;
O Lamb of God, was ever pain,
  was ever love like thine!

> as printed in *A Collection of Psalms and Hymns*, Charlestown, N. Carolina, by its editor, John Wesley, who omits 2 stanzas of the original

SAMUEL WESLEY, JUNIOR*
1691-1739

54
HYMN TO GOD THE FATHER

Hail, Father, whose creating call
  unnumbered worlds attend,
Jehovah, comprehending all,
  whom none can comprehend!

In light unsearchable inthron'd
  which angels dimly see;
the Fountain of the God-head own'd
  and foremost of the Three.

From thee thro' an eternal Now
  The Son, thine Offering, flow'd;
an everlasting Father thou,
  as everlasting God.

Nor quite display'd to worlds above,
  nor quite on earth conceal'd:
by wondrous, unexhausted love
  to mortal men reveal'd:

supreme and all-sufficient God,
  when Nature shall expire
and worlds created by thy nod
  shall perish by thy fire.

Thy name *Jehovah* be ador'd
  by creatures without end,
whom none but thy essential Word
  and Spirit comprehend.

> SAMUEL WESLEY, JR., 1691-1739 in *Poems on Several Occasions*, 1736 and in the Charlestown *Collection*, 1737

JOHN WESLEY
1703-91
(translations)

55
THOU HIDDEN LOVE OF GOD   HG 741

Thou hidden love of God, whose height,
  whose depth unfathomed, no man knows;
I see from far thy beauteous light,
  inly I sigh for thy repose:
my heart is pained, nor can it be
at rest, till it finds rest in thee.

Thy secret voice invites me still
  the sweetness of thy yoke to prove;
and fain I would: but though my will
  be fixt, yet wide my passions rove;
yet hindrances strew all the way;
I aim at thee, yet from thee stray.

'Tis mercy all, that thou hast brought
   my mind to seek her peace in thee!
Yet while I seek, but find thee not,
   no peace my wandering soul shall see:
O when shall all my wanderings end,
and all my steps to thee-ward tend?

Is there a thing beneath the sun,
   that strives with thee my heart to share?
Ah, tear it thence, that thou alone
   may'st reign, unrivalled Monarch there;
from earthly loves I must be free
ere I can find repose in thee.

O hide this self from me, that I
   no more, but Christ in me may live.   (Gal. 2:20)
My vile affections crucify,
   nor let one darling lust survive:
In all things nothing may I see,
nothing desire or seek, but thee.

O Love, thy sov'reign aid impart,
   to save me from low-thoughted care!
Chase this self-will through all my heart,
   through all its latent mazes there,
make me thy duteous child that I
ceaseless may 'Abba, Father' cry.   (Rom. 8:15-16)

Ah no! ne'er will I backward turn:
   thine wholly, thine alone I am!
Thrice happy he who views with scorn
   earth's toys, for thee his constant flame!
O help, that I may never move
from the blest footsteps of thy love!

Each moment draw from earth away
   my heart that lowly waits thy call;
speak to my inmost soul, and say,
   'I am thy love, thy God, thy All!'
To feel thy power, to hear thy voice,
to taste thy love, is all my choice.

Psalms and Hymns, 1738 (text of 1780), translated from 'Verborgne Gottes-liebe du' of Gerhard Tersteegen, 1697-1769 (1729)

56
THE BELIEVER'S TRIUMPH   HG 371

Jesus, thy blood and righteousness
my beauty are, my glorious dress: (Is. 61:10)
'midst flaming worlds, in these arrayed,
with joy shall I lift up my head.

Bold shall I stand in that great day;
for who ought to my charge shall lay?   (Rom. 8:33)
Fully absolved through these I am,
from sin and fear, from guilt and shame.

The holy, meek, unspotted Lamb
who from the Father's bosom came,
who died for me, even me to atone,
now for my Lord and God I own.   (Jn. 20:28)

Lord, I believe thy precious blood,   (Lev. 16:2)
which at the mercy seat of God   (Heb. 9:4, 13-14)
for ever doth for sinners plead,
for me, even for my soul was shed.

Lord, I believe, were sinners more
than sands upon the ocean-shore,
thou hast for all a ransom paid,
for all a full atonement made.

When from the dust of earth I rise
to claim my mansion in the skies,   (Jn. 14:2)
even then shall this be all my plea,
'Jesus hath lived, hath died, for me.'

Thus Abraham, the friend of God,   (Rom. 4:3)
thus all heaven's armies bought with blood,
Saviour of sinners thee proclaim;
sinners, of whom the chief I am.   (1 Tim. 1:15)

Jesu, be endless praise to thee,
whose boundless mercy hath for me,
for me, and all thy hands have made,
an everlasting ransom paid.

Ah, give to all, Almighty Lord,
with power to speak thy gracious word,
that all who to thy wounds will flee
may find eternal life in thee.

Thou God of power, thou God of love,
let the whole world thy mercy prove!
Now let thy word o'er all prevail!
Now take the spoils of death and hell.

O let the dead hear now thy voice!
Now bid thy banished ones rejoice!
Their beauty this, their glorious dress,
Jesus, thy blood and righteousness.

Hymns and Sacred Poems, 1740, translated from 'Christi Blut und Gerechtigheit' of N. L. von Zinzendorf, 1700-60 (1739).

See also ## 195B, 202B

CHARLES WESLEY
1707-88
HG 1

57
IN AFFLICTION

Eternal beam of light divine,
   Fountain of unexhausted love,
in whom the Father's glories shine   (Heb. 1:3)
   through earth beneath and heav'n above! -

Jesu, the weary wanderer's rest,
   give me thine easy yoke to bear,   (Matt. 11:30)
with stedfast patience arm my breast,   (1 Tim. 6:11)
   with spotless love and holy fear.

Thankful I take the cup from thee,
   prepared and mingled by thy skill:
though bitter to the taste it be,
   powerful the wounded soul to heal.   (Matt. 20:23)

Be thou, O Rock of ages, nigh:
   so shall each murmuring thought be gone,
and grief and fear and care shall fly
   as clouds before the mid-day sun.

Speak to my warring passions, 'Peace';
   say to my trembling heart, 'Be still:'   (Mk. 4:39)

Thy power my strength and fortress is,
    for all things serve thy sovereign will.

O death, where is thy sting? where now
    thy boasted victory, O grave?   (1 Cor. 15:55)
Who shall contend with God? or who
    can hurt whom God delights to save?

Hymns and Sacred Poems, 1739

58
FREE GRACE   HG 39

And can it be, that I should gain
    an interest in the Saviour's Blood!
Died he for me?—who caused his pain!
    for me?—who him to death pursu'd.
Amazing Love! how can it be
that thou, my God, shouldst die for me?

'Tis mystery all! The immortal dies!
    who can explore his strange design?
In vain the first born Seraph tries
    to sound the depths of love divine.   (1 Pet. 1:12)
'Tis mercy all! Let earth adore,
let angel-minds enquire no more.

He left his Father's throne above,
    (so free, so infinite his grace!)
emptied himself of all but love,   (Phil. 2:8)
    and bled for *Adam*'s helpless race:
'Tis mercy all, immense and free,
for, O my GOD! it found out me!

Long my imprison'd Spirit lay
    fast bound in sin and nature's night:
thine eye diffused a quick'ning ray:
    I woke; the dungeon flam'd with light;   (Acts 16:25-6)
my chains fell off, my heart was free,
I rose, went forth, and followed thee.

Still the small inward voice I hear,
    that whispers all my sins forgiv'n;
still the atoning Blood is near,
    that quench'd the wrath of hostile heav'n.   (Eph. 2:13-14)
I feel the life his wounds impart;
I feel my Saviour in my heart.

No condemnation now I dread,   (Rom. 8:1)
    Jesus, and all in him, is mine;
alive in him, my living Head,
    and clothed in righteousness divine,
bold I approach the eternal throne   (Heb. 4:16)
and claim the crown, through Christ my own!

Hymns & Sacred Poems, 1739

59
HYMN FOR CHRISTMAS-DAY   HG 268

Hark, how all the welkin rings   (Luke 8:15)
'Glory to the King of kings!
'Peace on earth and mercy mild,
'God and sinners reconcil'd!'

Joyful all ye nations rise,
join the triumph of the skies,
universal nature say,
'Christ the Lord is born to-day!'

Christ, by highest heaven adored,
Christ, the everlasting Lord,
late in time behold him come,   (Gal. 4:4)
offspring of a Virgin's womb.

Veil'd in flesh, the Godhead see,
hail th' incarnate Deity!
Pleas'd as man with men to appear
Jesus, our Immanuel here!

Hail the heaven-born Prince of peace!   (Is. 9:7)
Hail the Sun of righteousness!   (Mal. 4:2)
Light and life to all he brings,
ris'n with healing in his wings.

Mild, he lays his glory by,   (Phil. 2:8)
born,—that man no more may die,
born to raise the sons of earth,
born—to give them second birth.   (John 3:5)

Come, Desire of nations, come,   (Hag. 2:7)
fix in us thy humble home,
rise, the Woman's conquering seed,
bruise in us the serpent's head.   (Gen. 3:15)

Now display thy saving pow'r,
ruined nature now restore,
now in mystic union join
thine to ours, and ours to thine.

Adam's likeness, Lord, efface,   (Rom. 6:6)
stamp thy image in its place,   (Heb. 1:3)
second Adam from above,   (1 Cor. 15:45)
reinstate us in thy love.

Let us thee, tho' lost, regain,
thee, the Life, the inner Man: (Eph. 3:16)
O! to all thyself impart,
form'd in each believing heart.

Hymns & Sacred Poems, 1739
The familiar opening 'Hark the herald
angels sing' first appeared in G. Whitefield's Collection, 1753; and the 10-
line stanza in the 1791 edition of *Tate &
Brady*, among the additional hymns.

60
FOR THE ANNIVERSARY DAY OF ONE'S CONVERSION

(The stanzas set to the left-hand margin are those selected by John Wesley in his
1780 Hymn Book, to which he gave the title, 'Exhorting, and Beseeching to return
to God.')

Glory to God, and praise and love
    be ever, ever given;
by saints below, and saints above,
    the Church in earth and heaven.

On this glad day the glorious Sun
    of Righteousness arose,   (Mal. 4:2)
on my benighted soul he shone,
    and filled it with repose.

Sudden expired the legal strife,
    'twas then I ceased to grieve,
My second, real, living life
    I then began to live.

Then with my *heart* I first believ'd,
    believ'd with faith divine,

power with the Holy Ghost received   (Acts 10:38)
to call the Saviour *mine.*

I felt my Lord's atoning Blood
close to *my* soul applied;
me, me, he lov'd—the Son of God!
for *me,* for *me* he died!

I found, and own'd his promise true,
ascertain'd of *my* part,
my pardon pass'd in heaven I *knew*
when written on my heart.

O for a thousand tongues to sing
my dear Redeemer's praise!
The glories of my God and King,
the triumphs of his grace.

My gracious Master, and my God,
assist me to proclaim,
to spread through all the earth abroad
the honours of thy name.

Jesus, the name that charms our fears,
that bids our sorrows cease;
'tis musick in the sinner's ears,
'tis life and health and peace!

He breaks the power of cancell'd sin;
he sets the prisoner free;
his blood can make the foulest clean;
his blood availed for me.

He speaks, and listening to his voice
new life the dead receive,
the mornful, broken hearts rejoice,
the humble poor *believe.*

Hear him, ye deaf, his praise, ye dumb,
your loosen'd tongues employ,
ye blind, behold your Saviour come,
and leap, ye lame, for joy.

Look unto him, ye nations, own
your God, ye fallen race!
Look, and be saved through faith alone,
be justified by grace!

See all your sins on Jesus laid;
the Lamb of God was slain,
his soul was once an offering made
for *every soul* of man.

Harlots, and publicans, and thieves,
in holy triumph join!
Sav'd is the sinner that believes
from crimes as great as mine.

Murtherers, and all ye hellish crew,
ye sons of lust and pride,
believe the Saviour died for you;
for me the Saviour died.

Awake from guilty nature's sleep.   (Eph. 5:15)
and Christ shall give you light,
cast all your sins into the deep,
and wash the *Ethiop* white.   (Jer. 13:23)

With me, your Chief, you then shall *know,*   (1 Tim. 1:15)
shall feel your sins forgiven;

anticipate your heaven below
and own, that love is heaven.

Hymns and Sacred Poems, 1740

61
A MORNING HYMN   HG 116

Christ, whose glory fills the skies,
Christ, the true, the only Light,
Sun of Righteousness, arise,   (Mal. 4:2)
triumph o'er the shades of night:
Day-spring from on high, be near: (Lk. 1:78)
Day-star, in my heart appear.

Dark and cheerless is the morn
unaccompanied by thee.
Joyless is the day's return,
till thy mercy's beams I see;
till they inward light impart,
glad my eyes, and warm my heart.

Visit then this soul of mine,
pierce the gloom of sin, and grief,
fill me, radiancy divine,
scatter all my unbelief,
more and more thyself display,
shining to the perfect day.   (Prov. 4:18)

Hymns and Sacred Poems, 1740

62
WRESTLING JACOB   HG 138

*   Come, O thou Traveller unknown,   (Gen. 32:24-31)
whom still I hold, but cannot see;
my company before is gone,
and I am left alone with thee;
with thee all night I mean to stay
and wrestle till the break of day.

*   I need not tell thee who I am,
my misery, or sin declare;
thyself hast called me by my name,
look on thy hands, and read it there;   (Is. 49:16)
But who, I ask thee, who art thou?
Tell me thy name, and tell me now.

In vain thou strugglest to get free;
I never will unloose my hold;
art thou the Man that died for me?
the secret of thy love unfold;
wrestling I will not let thee go
till I thy name, thy nature know.

Wilt thou not yet to me reveal
thy new, unutterable name?
Tell me, I still beseech thee, tell,
to know it now resolved I am;
wrestling I will not let thee go
till I thy name, thy nature know.

'Tis all in vain to hold thy tongue,
or touch the hollow of my thigh;   (Gen. 32:25)
though every sinew be unstrung,
out of my arms thou shalt not fly;
wrestling I will not let thee go
till I thy name, thy nature know.

What though my shrinking flesh complain,
  and murmur to contend so long?
I rise superior to my pain;
  when I am weak, then I am strong.   (2 Cor. 12:10)
And when my all of strength shall fail
I shall with the God-Man prevail.

My strength is gone, my nature dies,
  I sink beneath thy mighty hand,
faint to revive, and fall to rise;
  I fall, and yet by faith I stand;
I stand, and will not let thee go
till I thy name, thy nature know.

* Yield to me now, for I am weak;
  but confident in self-despair:
speak to my heart, in blessings speak,
  be conquered by my instant prayer.
Speak or thou never hence shalt move,
and tell me if thy name is Love.

* 'Tis Love! Tis Love! thou diedst for me,
  I hear thy whisper in my heart;
the morning breaks, the shadows flee,
  pure universal love thou art.
To me, to all, thy mercies move,
thy nature, and thy name is Love.

My prayer hath power with God; the Grace
  unspeakable I now receive;
through faith I see thee face to face,
  I see thee face to face, and live:
in vain I have not wept and strove;
thy nature, and thy name is Love.

I know thee, Saviour, who thou art,
  Jesus, the feeble sinner's friend;
nor wilt thou with the night depart,
  but stay, and love me to the end;
thy mercies never shall remove;
thy nature, and thy name is Love.

The Sun of Righteousness in me
  hath rose with healing in his wings,   (Mal. 4:2)
withered my nature's strength; from thee
  my soul its life and succour brings;
my help is all laid up above,   (Col. 1:5)
thy nature, and thy name is Love.

Contented now upon my thigh
  I halt, till life's short journey end;
all helplessness, all weakness, I
  on thee alone for strength depend,
nor have I power, from thee to move;
thy nature, and thy name is Love.

Lame as I am, I take the prey,
  hell, earth and sin with ease o'ercome;
I leap for joy, pursue my way,
  and as a bounding hart fly home
thro' all eternity to prove
thy nature, and thy name is Love.

Hymns and Sacred Poems, 1742
* normal hymn selection

63
GOD WITH US

Let earth and heaven combine,
  angels and men agree
to praise in songs divine
  th'incarnate Deity,
our God contracted to a span,
incomprehensibly made man.

He laid his glory by,   (Phil. 2:5)
  he wrapp'd him in our clay,
unmark'd by human eye
  the latent Godhead lay:
infant of days he here became,
and bore the lov'd Immanuel's name.

See in that Infant's face
  the depths of Deity,
and labour, while ye gaze
  to sound the mystery;
in vain: ye angels gaze no more,   (1 Pet. 1:12)
but fall, and silently adore.

Unsearchable the love
  that hath the Saviour brought,
the grace is far above
  or men or angels' thought;
suffice for us that God, we know,
our God, is manifest below.

He deigns in flesh to appear,
  widest extremes to join,
to bring our vileness near,
  and make us all-divine;
and we the life of God shall know,
for God is manifest below.

Made perfect first in love,   (1 Jn. 4:17)
  and sanctified by grace,
we shall from earth remove
  and see his glorious face;
his love shall then be fully showed,
and man shall [then] be lost in God.

Nativity Hymns, 1745

64
VICTIM DIVINE   HG 768

Victim Divine, thy grace we claim
  while thus thy precious death we shew,
once offer'd up a spotless Lamb
  in thy great Temple here below,
thou didst for all mankind atone,
and standest now before the throne.   (Heb. 10:22)

Thou standest in the holiest place,
  as now for guilty sinners slain,
thy Blood of Sprinkling speaks, and prays   (Heb. 12:24)
  all-prevalent for helpless man;
thy blood is still our ransom found,
and spreads salvation all around.

The Smoke of thine Atonement here   (Matt. 27:51;
  darken'd the sun and rent the veil,   Heb. 10:20)
made the new Way to Heaven appear,
  and showed the great Invisible:
well pleased in thee our God looked down,   (Mk. 1:11)
and called his rebels to a crown.

He still respects thy sacrifice,
    its savour sweet dot!. always please,
the Offering smokes through earth and skies,
    diffusing life and joy and peace;
to these thy lower courts it comes
and fills them with divine perfumes.

We need not now go up to heaven   (Rom. 10:6)
    to bring the long-sought Saviour down;
thou art to all already given;
    thou dost ev'n now thy banquet crown.
To every faithful soul appear
and show thy Real Presence here.

Hymns on the Lord's Supper, 1745

65
DESIRING TO LOVE   HG 544

O Love divine, how sweet thou art!
When shall I find my longing heart
    all taken up by thee?
I thirst, I faint, and die, to prove
the greatness of redeeming love,
    the love of Christ to me.

Stronger his love than death or hell;   (Cant. 8:6)
its riches are unsearchable,   (Rom. 11:33)
    the first-born sons of light
desire in vain its depth to see;
they cannot reach the Mystery,
    the length, the breadth, and height.   (Eph. 3:18-19)

God only knows the love of God.
O that it now were shed abroad
    in this poor stony heart!   (Ezek. 36:26)
For love I sigh, for love I pine:
this only portion, Lord, be mine,
    be mine this better part.   (Lk. 10:41)

O that I could for ever sit
with *Mary*, at the Master's feet!
    Be this my happy choice!
My only care, delight and bliss,
my joy, my heav'n on earth, be this,
    to hear the bridegroom's voice.   (Mk. 2:19)

O that with humbled *Peter* I
could weep, believe, and thrice reply,   (Jn. 21:15)
    my faithfulness to prove!
Thou know'st, for all to thee is known,
thou know'st, O Lord, and thou alone,
    thou know'st, that thee I love.

O that I could, with favour'd *John*,
recline my weary head upon   (Jn. 13:23)
    the dear Redeemer's breast!
from care, and sin, and sorrow free,
give me, O Lord, to find in thee
    my everlasting rest.

Thy only Love do I require,
nothing on earth beneath desire,
    nothing in heaven above;   (Ps. 73:25)
let earth, and heaven, and all things go,
give me thine only love to know,
    give me thine only love.

Festival Hymns, 1746

66
LOVE DIVINE   HG 442

Love divine, all loves excelling,
    Joy of heaven, to earth come down,
fix in us thy humble dwelling,
    all thy faithful mercies crown;
Jesu, thou art all compassion,
    pure unbounded love thou art,
visit us with thy salvation,   (Ps. 106:4)
    enter every trembling heart.

Come, Almighty to deliver,
    let us all thy life receive,
suddenly return, and never,   (Mal. 3:1)
    never more thy temples leave.
Thee we would be always blessing,
    serve thee as thy hosts above,
pray, and praise thee without ceasing,
    glory in thy perfect love.

Finish then thy new creation,   (2 Cor. 5:17)
    pure and spotless let us be,   (Eph. 5:27)
let us see thy great salvation
    perfectly restored in thee;
chang'd from glory into glory,   (2 Cor. 3:18)
    till in heaven we see thy face,   (1 Cor. 13:12)
till we cast our crowns before thee,   (Rev. 4:10)
    lost in wonder, love and praise.

Redemption Hymns, 1747; stanza 2 omitted as in John Wesley's first Collection, 1780

67
BEFORE WORK   HG 208

Forth in thy name, O Lord, I go,
    my daily labour to pursue,
thee, only thee, resolved to know
    in all I think, or speak, or do.

The task thy wisdom hath assigned
    O let me cheerfully fulfil;
in all my works thy presence find,
    and prove thine acceptable will.   (Rom. 12:2)

Preserve me from my calling's snare,
    and hide my simple heart above,   (Col. 3:2)
above the thorns of choking care,   (Matt. 13:22)
    the gilded baits of worldly love.   (1 Jn. 2:16)

Thee may I set at my right hand
    whose eyes my inmost substance see,   (Ps. 139:2)
and labour on at thy command,
    and offer all my works to thee.

Give me to bear thy easy yoke,   (Matt. 11:30)
    and every moment watch and pray,   (Matt. 26:41)
and still to things eternal look,
    and hasten to thy glorious day;   (Phil. 1:6)

for thee delightfully employ
    whate'er thy bounteous grace hath given,
and run my course with even joy,
    and closely walk with thee to heaven.   (Gen. 5:22)

Hymns and Sacred Poems, 1749

68
FOR NEW YEAR'S DAY
HG 130

Come, let us anew
our journey pursue,
roll round with the year,
and never stand still till the Master appear;
his adorable will
let us gladly fulfil,
and our talents improve
by the patience of hope and the labour of love.

Our life is a dream,
our time as a stream
glides swiftly away,
and the fugitive moment refuses to stay,
the arrow is flown,
the moment is gone,
the millennial year
rushes on to our view, and Eternity's here!

O that each in the day
of His coming may say,
'I have fought my way through;   (2 Tim. 4:7)
I have finished the work thou didst give me to do.'
O that each from his Lord
may receive the glad word,
'Well and faithfully done!   (Matt. 25:21)
Enter into my joy, and sit down on my throne!'

Hymns for New Year's Day, 1750

SCRIPTURE HYMNS (1962) (based on the Commentary of Matthew Henry on each passage)
69
Exodus 13:21

Captain of Israel's host, and guide
of all who seek that land above,
beneath thy shadow we abide,
the cloud of thy protecting love,
our strength thy grace, our rule thy word,
our end, the glory of the Lord.

By thine unerring spirit led
we shall not in the desert stray,
the light of man's direction need,
or miss our providential way;
as far from danger as from fear
while Love, almighty Love, is near.

70
2 Chronicles 29:5

('The filling of our hands with the service of God intimates that we must serve him only, serve him liberally, and serve him in the strength of grace derived from him' - M.H.)

Lord, in the strength of grace
with a glad heart and free
myself, my residue of days
I consecrate to thee;
thy ransom'd servant, I
restore to thee thine own,
and from this moment live, or die
to serve my God alone.

71
Leviticus 8:35
HG 1

('We have every one of us a charge to keep, an eternal God to glorify, an immortal soul to provide for, needful duty to be done, our generation to serve; and it must be our daily care to keep this charge, for it is the charge of the Lord our Master, who will shortly call us to account about it, and it is at our utmost peril if we neglect it. Keep it, *that ye die not.*' - M.H.)

A charge to keep I have,
a God to glorify,
a never-dying soul to save
and fit it for the sky;
to serve the present age,
my calling to fulfil:
O may it all my powers engage
to do my Master's will.

Arm me with jealous care
as in thy sight to live,
and O! thy servant, Lord, prepare
a strict account to give.
Help me to watch and pray,
and on thyself rely,
assured, if I my trust betray,
I shall for ever die.

(In modern use the last couplet usually reads:
and let me ne'er my trust betray,
but press to realms on high.

The alteration dates from 1904.)

72
FOR THE LORD'S DAY
HG 134

Come, let us with our Lord arise,   (Col. 1:3)
our Lord, who made both earth and skies,
who died to save the world he made,
and rose triumphant from the dead;
he rose, the Prince of life and peace,
and stamped the day for ever his.

This is the day the Lord hath made,   (Ps. 118:24)
that all may see his power displayed,
may feel his resurrection's power,   (Phil. 3:10)
and rise again, to fall no more,
in perfect righteousness renewed,
and filled with all the life of God.

Then let us render him his own,
with solemn prayer approach the throne,
with meekness hear the gospel word,
with thanks his dying love record,
our joyful hearts and voices raise
and fill his courts with songs of praise.

Honour and praise to Jesus pay
throughout his consecrated day,
be in all Jesu's praise employed,
nor leave a single moment void,
with utmost care the time improve,
and only breathe his praise and love.

CHARLES WESLEY, *Hymns for Children,* 1763

See also # 297.

ARTICLE 6:
THE EARLY EVANGELICALS, 1740-1780 (73-84)

It was natural enough that the hymnody of the Wesleys should generate, during their long lifetime, much imitation. They had completed the liberation; others entered into their labours without much delay.

Charles Wesley had published two books containing many of his best-known and finest hymns when John Cennick, one of John's first lay preachers (but an unstable character who soon left him) began to publish. Cennick's gifts were those of a miniaturist, as ## 74 and 75 show. 74 has the best kind of modest economy of expression; 75, and its companion, 'Ere I sleep,' have a special charm because of their meter, which later Charles Wesley used but which Cennick seems to have discovered first. 'Children of the heavenly King,' in many books still, is another piece which with judicious editorial pruning has had deserved success. Beyond these there is not much in Cennick that we need to recover today.

The massive *Yigdal*, # 73, is a different story. Here is Thomas Olivers, the London cobbler, drinking deep of the Wesleyan love of Scripture (all the Scriptural allusions here included are his) and transforming the old Jewish hymn of praise (*Yigdal* is from a root meaning 'greatness') into an ecstatic and apocalyptic Christian song; some of its lines are now too rough for normal use, but its generous length leaves at least five stanzas which remain indispensable.

To the same period belongs what is so surprisingly the only Welsh hymn which in translation has found a place in popular affection, # 76. It is not easy to say why Offa's Dyke has proved so impassable. The English have a liking for Welsh tunes, though their taste is not always what would please a true Welsh connoisseur, but the hymnody of the Welsh evangelicals who were aroused by the missions of Whitefield and his followers has remained in Wales, and one has to read a Welsh hymnal to see their texts. This one, translated jointly by the Welsh author and his brother, has all the grandeur that a true affection for Scripture could give it.

The Baptists in Britain have been surprisingly backward in the production of hymns acceptable outside their immediate circle. They were not without their writers, and they could rise to excellence, as ## 77 and 83 indicate. 77 has again the modesty and naturalness we find in Cennick at his best; 83, which is worth looking at in both its original and its later versions, is on the grand scale, and it has been a wise instinct that has moved modern editors to make it more manageable by removing the refrain and altering a few rough phrases. The same author's 'Come, thou Fount of every blessing' is perhaps more famous but in its original form less singable, and in edited forms is usually too far from the original to appear here; its most practicable and at the same time authentic form is probably that in *Congregational Praise* (442).

The appearance of Toplady's two texts here sufficiently demonstrates the way in which hymnody ignores the frontiers set up by religious dispute, for Toplady's fanatical hatred of John Wesley is one of the best-known facts in church history. Toplady, the Vicar of Broadhembury in East Devon, is best known as the author of a hymn (80) which is now less sung than formerly but which in its day has had countless admirers. It is certainly the only hymn of his which was ever in wide use without abridgment; but #79 is not only a practicable fragment of a longer and uneven original, but is indeed, thus pruned, a hymn in the very best Calvinist tradition. 'Inspirer and hearer of prayer,' cut down usually to two stanzas as 'A Sovereign

Protector I have,' provides another very fine devotional piece. 'Object of my first desire,' after an unpromising start, contains many excellent lines. Toplady's brief life of 38 years falls wholly within not merely the lives but the writing lives of the Wesleys. He is the most famous example of the kind of tortured spirit which contributed so much to the praise and devotion of 18th-century Evangelicals and Calvinists. Joseph Hart ('Come, Holy Spirit, come') is such another, and of course Robert Robinson (83) was of this kind in his youth.

Three anonymous hymns, ## 78, 81-2, represent perhaps a more sober and less ambitious strain in hymnody, though they all come from the Evangelical tradition. The Easter Hymn (78) settled down to its present form in one of the many music books of this tradition which bridged the gap between the decorous psalm-singing tradition and that of the new hymnody by providing for the metrical psalms a new kind of flexible and expressive tune, and adding a modest number of doctrinal hymns, somewhat in the style of the 1708 *Supplement to the New Version*, (article 2). It is originally based on a Latin text, *Surrexit Christus Hodie*, but in this form, now well known, departs some distance from it. The other two, 81-2, are the two best-known examples (and in their brevity and sobriety of diction they are very good indeed) of the hymnody generated by the great charity-houses founded in the mid-century by Evangelicals inspired by the social passion of the Wesleys. The Foundling Hospital, an orphanage in London, was not only the most famous of these, but it amounted, in its propagation of children's choral singing, almost to a nonconformist cathedral foundation. Many fine tunes first appeared in the hymnals of this institution and of the Magdalen Hospital, a comparable house for 'fallen women,' and it is always worth noting that the original association of # 82 was undoubtedly with Haydn's tune AUSTRIA, and it is at least a respectable opinion that the two should never have been separated in later hymnals. (It is surprising that in Britain only the *Methodist Hymn Book* and *Hymns Ancient and Modern*, among standard hymnals, preserve this association.)

The section closes with the great hymn 'All hail the power,' whose celebration of the visions of the Book of Revelation can be described only as heraldic in its boldness. This text, first appearing in its full form in 1780, has often suffered alteration, most of which is quite needless. It generated two great tunes, MILES LANE in England and CORONATION in America, within a very short time of its composition, each of which is its composer's only known composition, and each of which in its own way admirably reflects the soaring spirit of the text.

See:

Erik Routley, *I'll Praise My Maker* (Independent Press, 1951)

THOMAS OLIVERS
1725-99

73
A HYMN TO THE GOD OF ABRAHAM

HG 692

In Three Parts, adapted to a celebrated Air sung by the Priest, Signior Leoni, &c, at the Jews' Synagogue, in London

PART THE FIRST

The God of Abrah'm praise	(Ex. 3:6)
who reigns enthron'd above;	
ancient of everlasting days,	(Dan. 7:22)
and God of Love;	(2 Cor. 13:11)

JEHOVAH, GREAT I AM   (Ex. 6:3, 3:14)
by earth and heav'n confest;   (Rev. 4:8-11)
I bow and bless the sacred Name
   for ever bless'd.   (Rom. 1:25)

The God of Abrah'm praise,
  at whose supreme command   (Gen. 12:1)
from earth I rise - and seek the joys
   at his right hand:
I all on earth forsake,   (Gen. 12:4)
  its wisdom, fame and power;
and him my only portion make,   (Gen. 15:1)
   my Shield and Tower.   (Ps. 18:2)

The God of Abrah'm praise,
  whose all-sufficient grace   (Gen. 17:1)
shall guide me all my happy days   (Gen. 28:15)
   in all my ways:
he calls a worm his friend!   (James 2:23)
he calls himself my God!   (Ex. 3:6)
and he shall save me to the end   (1 Pet. 1:5)
   thro' Jesu's blood.

He by himself hath sworn,   (Gen. 22:16-17)
  I on his oath depend,   (Rom. 4:20-1)
I shall on eagle's wings up-borne   (Ex. 19:4)
   to heaven ascend;
I shall behold his face,   (John 17:24)
I shall his power adore,   (Ex. 15:2)
and sing the wonders of his grace   (Ps. 145:1; 146:2)
   for evermore.

PART THE SECOND

Tho' nature's strength decay   (Gen. 15:4, 6; Rom. 4:19)
  and earth and hell withstand,   (Ex. 5:2)
to Canaan's bounds I urge my way,   (Ex. 14:15)
   at his command:
the wat'ry deep I pass,   (Ex. 14:22)
  with Jesus in my view;   (Ex. 13:21)
and through the howling wilderness   (Ex. 13:18)
   my way pursue.

The goodly land I see,   (Ex. 3:8)
  with peace and plenty bless'd;   (Deut. 8:7-9)
a land of sacred liberty,   (Lev. 25:42)
   and endless rest.   (Ex. 33:14)
There milk and honey flow,   (Ex. 3:8)
  and oil and wine abound   (Deut. 32:13-14)
and trees of life for ever grow,   (Is. 61:3)
   with mercy crown'd.

There dwells the Lord our King,   (Gen. 14:18; Heb. 7:1-2)
THE LORD OUR RIGHTEOUSNESS   (Jer. 33:16)
(Triumphant o'er the world and sin)   (Eph. 4:8; Phil. 2:9-11)
  the Prince of Peace: (Is. 9:6)
On Sion's sacred height,   (Ps. 50:2)
  his kingdom still maintains;
and glorious with his saints in light   (Is. 24:23)
   for ever reigns.

He keeps his own secure,   (Ps. 12:7)
  He guards them by his side,
arrays in garments, white and pure   (Rev. 4:4; 19:7-8)
  his spotless bride;   (Eph. 5:27)
with streams of sacred bliss   (Rev. 7:17; 22:1)
with groves of living joys -
with all the fruits of Paradise   (Rev. 2:7; 22:2)
   he still supplies.

PART THE THIRD

Before the great THREE-ONE   (Rev. 7:9-10)
  they all exulting stand;
and tell the wonders he hath done
   thro' all their land:
the list'ning spheres attend,   (Rev. 7:11-12)
  and swell the growing fame;
and sing, in songs which never end
   the wondrous NAME.

The God who reigns on high,   (Rev. 4:8)
  the great arch-angels sing,
and* 'Holy, Holy, Holy,' cry,
  'ALMIGHTY KING!
Who was, and is, the same;
  and evermore shall be;
JEHOVAH - FATHER - GREAT I AM!
  WE WORSHIP THEE.'

*'Sing the following parts of this verse *slow* and *solemn*' (T.O.)

Before the Saviour's face   (Rev. 5:8-10; 15:24)
  the ransom'd nations bow;
o'erwhelmed at his almighty grace,
   for ever new:
he shews his prints of love -   [Jn. 20:27]
  they kindle - to a flame!
and sound thro' all the worlds above
   the slaughter'd LAMB.

The whole triumphant host,   (Rev. 5:13; 19:1-7)
  give thanks to God on high;
'Hail, FATHER, SON and HOLY GHOST,'
  they ever cry:
Hail, Abraham's God - and *mine*!   (Ps. 89:26; Jn. 20:17, 28)
(I join the heavenly lays)   (Ps. 103:1-5)
All might and majesty are thine   (Rev. 4:11; 5:12; 7:10, 12)
  and endless praise.

Probably written in London between 1763 and 1770. Included in John Wesley's
Pocket Hymn Book, 1785.
The Scripture-references are included by the author.

JOHN CENNICK
1718-55
HG 69

74
DIVINE PROTECTION

Be with me, Lord, where'er I go;
teach me what thou wouldst have me do;
suggest whate'er I think or say;
direct me in the narrow way.

Prevent me, lest I harbour pride,
lest I in my own strength confide;
show me my weakness, let me see
I have my power, my all, from thee.

Assist and teach me how to pray;
incline my nature to obey;
what thou abhorrest let me flee,
and only love what pleases thee.

*Sacred Hymns for the Children of God
in their Pilgrimage*, 1741

75
MORNING HYMN

Rise, my soul, adore thy Maker!
  Angels praise,
    join thy lays;
  with them be partaker.

Father, Lord of every spirit,
  in thy light
    lead me right,
  through my Saviour's merit.

Never cast me from thy Presence
  till my soul
    shall be full
  of thy blessed Essence.

O my Jesus, God almighty,
  pray for me
    till I see
  thee in Salem's city.

Holy Ghost, in Jesus given,
  be my guide,
    lest my pride
  shut me out of heaven.

Thou by night wast my protector:
  with me stay
    all the way
  ever my Director.

Holy, Holy, Holy Giver
  of all good,
    life and food,
  reign, adored for ever!

Sacred Hymns . . . , 1741

76
GUIDE ME, O THOU GREAT JEHOVAH

HG 258

Arglwydd, arwain trwy'r anialwch
  fi bererin gwael ei wedd,

nad oes ynof nerth na bywyd,
  fel yn gorwedd yn y bedd;

  Hollaluog   (Ex. 16:4)
  Ydyw'r un a'm cwyd i'r lan.

Agor y ffynnonau melus
            (Ex. 17:6)
  sydd yn tarddu o'r Graig i maes;

'rhyd yr anial mawr canlyned
            (Ex. 40:38)
  afon iachawdwriaeth gras

  Rho imi hyny;
dim i mi ond dy fwynhau.
            (Gen. 15:1)

Ynddiriedaf yn dy allu,
            (Jos. 4:16)
  mawr yw'r gwaith a wnest
            erioed;
ti gest angau, ti gest uffern,

  ti gest Satan dan dy droed,
    Pen Calfaria,
nac ed hwnw byth o'm cof.

William Williams, *Alleluia*, 1745

Guide me, O thou great Jehovah,
  pilgrim through this barren
                    land;
I am weak, but thou art mighty;
  hold me with thy powerful
                    hand;
  Bread of heaven,
  feed me till I want no more.

Open now the crystal fountain

  whence the healing stream
                doth flow;
let the fiery cloudy pillar

  guide me all my journey
                through.
  Strong deliverer,
  be thou still my strength and
                shield.

When I tread the verge of Jordan

  bid my anxious fears subside,

Death of death, and hell's de-
                struction,
  land me safe on Canaan's side;
    songs of praises
I will ever give to thee.

Peter Williams, *Hymns on Various Sub-jects*, 1771, and others.

BENJAMIN BEDDOME*
1717-95

77
JOINING THE CHURCH

Witness, ye men and angels, now,
  before the Lord we speak;
to him we make our solemn vow,
  a vow we dare not break:

that long as life itself shall last
  ourselves to Christ we yield;
nor from his cause will we depart,
  or ever quit the field.

We trust not in our native strength,
  but on his grace rely,
that, with returning wants, the Lord
  will all our need supply.

O guide our doubtful feet aright,
  and keep us in thy ways:
and while we turn our vows to prayers,
  turn thou our prayers to praise.

*Hymns Adapted to Public Worship or
Family Devotion*, 1817 (posth.)

Anonymous

78
EASTER HYMN

HG 347

Jesus Christ is risen to-day
            Alleluia!
our triumphant holy day,
            Alleluia!
who did once upon the cross,
            Alleluia!
suffer to redeem our loss,
            Alleluia!

Hymns of praise then let us sing,
            Alleluia!
unto Christ our heavenly King
            Alleluia!
who endured the cross and grace
            Alleluia!
sinners to redeem and save
            Alleluia!

But the pains that he endured
            Alleluia!
our salvation have procured
            Alleluia!
Now above the sky he's King;
            Alleluia!
where the angels ever sing
            Alleluia!

ARNOLD'S *Compleat Psalmodist*,
1749; lines 1-3 from *Divine Songs*,
1708; line 5 from Supplement to *Tate
and Brady*, 1816.

AUGUSTUS MONTAGUE
TOPLADY, 1740-78
HG 3

79
FOR I AM PERSUADED

When we in darkness walk,
nor feel the heavenly flame,
then is the time to trust our God,
and rest upon his name.

Soon shall our doubts and fears
subside at his control!
His loving-kindness shall break through
the midnight of the soul.

Wait till the shadows flee,
wait thine appointed hour;
wait till the bridegroom of thy soul
reveals his love with pow'r.

His grace will to the end
stronger and brighter shine;
nor present things, nor things to come   (Rom. 8:37)
shall quench the spark divine.

Blest is the man, O God,
that stays himself on thee!
who wait for thy salvation, Lord,
shall thy salvation see.

Gospel Magazine (1772); sts. 7, 8, 13,
3, 16.

80
A LIVING AND DYING PRAYER FOR THE HOLIEST
BELIEVER IN THE WORLD   HG 623

Rock of Ages, cleft for me   (Is. 26:4; Zech. 14:4)
let me hide myself in thee!
Let the water and the blood
from thy riven side which flowed   (Jn. 19:34; 1 Jn. 5:6)
be of sin the double cure;
cleanse me from its guilt and power.

Not the labours of my hands
can fulfil thy law's commands;
could my soul no respite know,
could my tears for ever flow,
all for sin could not atone:
thou must save, and thou alone.

Nothing in my hand I bring;
simply to thy cross I cling;
naked, come to thee for dress;
helpless, look to thee for grace;
foul, I to the fountain fly;
wash me, Saviour, or I die.   (Ps. 51:7)

Whilst I draw this fleeting breath, -
* when my eyes shall close in death, -
when I soar through tracts unknown -
see thee on thy Judgment-throne -
Rock of ages, cleft for me,
let me hide myself in thee!

The *Gospel Magazine*, 1776;
* altered

Anonymous, from the
Foundling Hospital Collection

81
SPIRIT OF MERCY, TRUTH AND LOVE   HG 658

Spirit of mercy, truth and love,
send thy blest influence from above,
and still from age to age convey
the wonders of this sacred day.

In every clime, in every tongue
be God's eternal praises sung;
through all the listening earth be taught
the acts our great Redeemer wrought.

Unfailing comfort, heavenly guide,
over thy favoured church preside;
still may mankind thy blessings prove,
Spirit of mercy, truth and love.

(1774)

82
PSALM 148   HG 601

Praise the Lord! ye heavens, adore him;
praise him, angels in the height;
sun and moon, rejoice before him,
praise him, all ye stars and light:
praise the Lord, for he hath spoken,
worlds his mighty voice obeyed;
laws, which never shall be broken
for their guidance hath he made.

Praise the Lord! for he is glorious;
never shall his promise fail;
God hath made his saints victorious,
sin and death shall not prevail.
Praise the God of our salvation;
hosts on high, his power proclaim;
heaven and earth, and all creation
laud and magnify his name!

(1796)

ROBERT ROBINSON
1735-90
HG 141

83
PRAISE TO THE REDEEMER
for Christmas
A   HG 453

Mighty God! while angels bless thee,
may an infant lisp thy name?
Lord of men, as well as angels,
thou art every creature's theme.
Hallelujah
Hallelujah, Amen.

Lord of every land and nation,
Ancient of eternal days!
sounded through the wide creation
be thy just and lawful praise:

For the grandeur of thy nature,
grand beyond a seraph's thought;
for created works of power,
works with skill and kindness wrought:

For thy providence, that governs
　　through thine empire's wide domain;
wings an angel, guides a sparrow,
　　blessed be thy gentle reign.

But thy rich, thy free redemption,
　　dark through brightness all along:
thought is poor, and poor expression,
　　who dare sing that awful song?

Brightness of the Father's glory,
　　shall thy praise unuttered lie?
Fly, my tongue, such guilty silence!
　　sing the Lord who came to die.

Did archangels sing thy coming?
　　Did the shepherds learn their lays?
Shame would cover me ungrateful
　　should my tongue refuse to praise.

From the highest throne of glory
　　to the cross of deepest woe;
all to ransom guilty captives:
　　flow, my praise, for ever flow.

Go, return, immortal Saviour!
　　Leave thy footstool, claim thy throne;
thence return, and reign for ever,
　　be the kingdom all thine own.

　　　　　　　1774; in Middleton's *Hymns*, 1793

B

The same, in modern use. (The rearrangement of stanzas, with omission of st. 7, is due to Dr. R. W. Dale, 1879: the text here given, as in *Congregational Praise*, 1951, restores a few words amended by Dale)

Mighty God, while angels bless thee,
　　may a mortal sing thy name?
Lord of men as well as angels,
　　thou art every creature's theme;
Lord of every land and nation,
　　Ancient of eternal days,
sounded through the wide creation
　　be thy just and endless praise.

For the grandeur of thy nature -
　　grand beyond a seraph's thought -
for the wonders of creation,
　　works with skill and kindness wrought,
for thy providence that governs
　　through thine empire's wide domain,
wings an angel, guides a sparrow,
　　blessed be thy gentle reign.

But thy rich, thy free redemption,
　　dark through brightness all along -
thought is poor, and poor expression -
　　who dare sing that wondrous song?
Brightness of the Father's glory,
　　shall thy praise unuttered lie?
Break, my tongue, such guilty silence,
　　sing the Lord who came to die.

From the highest throne of glory
　　to the cross of deepest woe,
all to ransom guilty captives!
　　Flow my praise, for ever flow!
Go, return, immortal Saviour,
　　leave thy footstool, claim thy throne;
thence return and reign for ever;
　　be the kingdom all thine own!

EDWARD PERRONET
1721-92

84
ON THE RESURRECTION: THE LORD IS KING

HG 17

All hail! the pow'r of Jesu's name;
　　let angels prostrate fall;
bring forth the royal diadem
　　to crown him Lord of all.

Let high-born seraphs tune the lyre,
　　and, as they tune it, fall
before his face who tunes their choir,
　　and crown him Lord of all.

Crown him, ye morning stars of light　(Job 38:7)
　　who fixed this floating ball;
now hail the strength of Israel's might,
　　and crown him Lord of all.

Crown him, ye martyrs of our God,
　　who from his altar call;　　　　　　(Rev. 6:9)
extol the stem of Jesse's rod　　　　　(Is. 11:1)
　　and crown him Lord of all.

Ye seed of Israel's chosen race,
　　ye ransomed of the fall,
hail him who saves you by his grace,
　　and crown him Lord of all.

Hail him, ye heirs of David's line,
　　whom David Lord did call;　　　　　(Ps. 110:1)
the God incarnate, Man divine,
　　and crown him Lord of all.

Sinners! whose love can ne'er forget
　　the wormwood and the gall,　　　　(Lam. 3:19)
go, spread your trophies at his feet,
　　and crown him Lord of all.

Let every tribe and every tongue
　　that bound creation's call,
now shout in universal song
　　the crownéd Lord of all.

　　　　　　　The Gospel Magazine, April, 1780

ARTICLE 7:
THE OLNEY HYMN BOOK, 1779 (85-95)

Evangelicalism, it must be understood, was not the same as nonconformity; it never has been, and the Wesleys and Toplady, among those we have already encountered, were Anglican priests. But even the Wesleys could not hope to touch the whole of so widespread an institution as the Anglican church, and there were plenty of places where hymnody was quite unknown, so far as it was not contained within the metrical psalters. Such a place was Olney, the Buckinghamshire village (now part of the late 20th-century new city of Milton Keynes) where John Newton was perpetual curate, and William Cowper a prominent layman. The book of *Olney Hymns* was put together in a very short time by these two men as a means of widening and deepening the religious life of those rustics, and no single book, not even the collections of Watts and the Wesleys, has been, as a collection, more influential on the course of hymnody.

The story of Newton and Cowper has been told often enough

not to need repetition here. The briefest biography of Newton must contain the information that he ran away to sea, joined the merchant navy, deserted and was brought back and punished, and that he rose to the command of a ship engaged in the infamous slave trade. His conversion was the result partly of the faithfulness of his fiancée, Mary Catlett, and partly of reading St Thomas à Kempis. But he found great difficulty in getting any bishop to ordain him when he sought orders, and until he was 57 found nothing more distinguished than this perpetual curacy (a now defunct order in the Church of England which in effect meant the burden of parish work without the usual sources of clerical emolument) in the heart of the British countryside. Only in 1782 did he receive a rectory, and this was in the City of London and a position of some distinction (St Mary Woolnoth, near the Bank of England and almost next door to the Mansion House).

Cowper (he is pronounced Cooper), the first man of letters to become a major hymn writer and one of the very small handful who ever did, was of course the only man in the parish on Newton's intellectual level. He was naturally Newton's closest friend, but for other reasons his most difficult and demanding parishioner, for Cowper was a pathological depressive, haunted by a sense of guilt and failure, whose mind became gradually more and more clouded until in his last decade he was to all intents and purposes insane. Newton made use of him, as much for his friend's good as for anyone else's, about the parish, and the most effective way in which he did so was to enlist his help in compiling a hymn book. In the end Cowper's contribution was 68 hymns, and Newton's 280. Even if it ever was Newton's intention to let Cowper write the whole book, they probably laboured on it together, and certainly Newton's lyric gift, so different from Cowper's, is one which the church would have been the poorer for missing.

Newton wears his heart on his sleeve: he is direct, candid, and uncomplicated. As literature perhaps his work cannot be expected to match Cowper's, but the five in our selection show him at his best. 'How sweet the name,' # 85, still one of the best known of all hymns, is as tender as any medieval mystic's devotion and as open and durable as Watts; perhaps stanza 4 is rightly omitted in modern books, but who would wish to spare, or to alter, any more of it? No. 86, here given in the most satisfactory of contemporary versions (st. 3, with an abundance of weak rhymes, is unhappily still used in America at the expense of the dogmatic and triumphant stanzas 4-5), is as scripturally ingenious as anything in Wesley. In # 87 we have the honest teacher instructing his flock, and in the monumental 88, the old sailor recalling the hazards of his early career; the picturesque crudity of its language here is all scriptural, and worth wrestling with. The song is still a great experience if it is sung to the old psalm tune, OLD 104TH. For sheer simplicity based on a profound New Testament text, # 89 is as good as anything he wrote; for the rest, consult your hymnal, and if it is an educated one, it will have more good texts to add to these.

It was an inspired providence that brought together in one book the energy and zest of Newton and the gentle, withdrawn talent of Cowper. 'O for a closer walk' is one of Cowper's best known (90), and at once we detect the hesitating and wistful spirit that produced it. The terse and simple lines of 'Hark, my soul,' # 92, interweaving scriptural thoughts very much in Newton's style, combine with a typically tender interpretation of the text 'lovest thou me?' to make a hymn worthy of a finer tune than the one which is so often set to it that the

text is in danger of being suffocated out of the repertory. No. 93 is, in the Newton style again, didactic and thoughtful, the work of a compassionate teacher who has patience with the believer's difficulties. Nos. 94 and 95 express Christian faith and hope in contrasting styles, the one dark, the other (almost uniquely in Cowper), bright and buoyant.

These all speak for themselves. It is # 91 that needs special treatment. It is the most difficult case in all hymnodic criticism. In its original version, with the opening, 'There is a fountain filled with blood drawn from Emmanuel's veins,' it has secured the affection of many devoted disciples and earned the execration of as many people who find it crudely revolting. Often in this collection we preserve a crude text (as we do in # 88) because it is worth inviting a reader to suspend his frown or his instinct to reject it in order that a true message may come through which if it were altered would be smothered. It is not so here. The passage behind this opening stanza is this, in the King James Version of Zechariah 13:1:

> In that day there shall be a fountain opened to the house of David and the inhabitants of Jerusalem for sin and for uncleanness.

Cowper's intention is to identify this, through an accepted course of typology, with the blood of Christ shed on the Cross. Were it not that a later English poet whose gifts I should not place much below Cowper's has produced an amendment that reflects the original Scripture more faithfully (in the words 'for sin') and that introduces the majesty and pathos of the Atonement with no less sureness and without the graceless literalism into which the usually sensitive Cowper was betrayed, I could not pursue this argument, though I should still have included the hymn.

But my reasons go beyond this. For one thing, this amendment is at present wholly unknown to editors, and therefore nowadays the hymn appears only in those collections which do not make much allowance for the antipathetic reaction I have mentioned; for another, when the hymn is printed it often ends at stanza 5, or, much worse, is further abridged and presented with a spurious chorus (and, to crown it all, a shockingly complacent and jaunty tune), so that contemporary associations with it are further corrupted. Among current books in England and America, only the *English Hymnal* prints the full text now, and this, of course, in its original form. It is inexcusable also, by omitting the last eight lines, to make the hymn more depressing than Cowper meant it to be, or, by treating it as some hymnals do, to make it more casual and commonplace than Cowper could ever have conceived it to be. As we have it here it is something which no serious reader can lightly dismiss.

See:

David Cecil: *The Stricken Deer*
B. Martin: *The Life of John Newton*

JOHN NEWTON, 1725-1807
The *Olney Hymns*, 1779
HG 37

85
THE NAME OF JESUS
HG 301

How sweet the name of Jesus sounds   (Cant. 1:3)
  in a believer's ear!
It soothes his sorrows, heals his wounds,
  and drives away his fear.

It makes the wounded spirit whole,
    and calms the troubled breast;
'tis manna to the hyngry soul,
    and to the weary rest.

Dear name! the rock on which I build,
    my shield and hiding-place;
my never-failing treasury, filled
    with boundless stores of grace.

By thee my pray'rs acceptance gain,
    although with sin defiled;
Satan accuses me in vain,
    and I am own'd a child.

Jesus! my Shepherd, Husband, Friend,
    my Prophet, Priest and King,
my Lord, my life, my way, my end,
    accept the praise I bring.

Weak is the effort of my heart,
    and cold my warmest thought;
but when I see thee as thou art,
    I'll praise thee as I ought.

Till then I would thy love proclaim
    with every fleeting breath;
and may the music of thy name
    refresh my soul in death.

I 57

86
THE CITY OF GOD
Isaiah 33:20-1

HG 220

Glorious things of thee are spoken,
    Zion, city of our God!   (Ps. 87:3)
He, whose word cannot be broken
    form'd thee for his own abode:
on the Rock of Ages founded   (Is. 26:4)
    what can shake thy sure repose?
With salvation's walls surrounded,   (Is. 60:18)
    thou may'st smile at all thy foes.

See! the streams of living waters,   (Ezek. 47:1)
    springing from eternal love,
well supply thy sons and daughters   (Ps. 46:4)
    and all fear of want remove:
who can faint while such a river   (Rev. 22:1)
    ever flows their thirst to assuage?
Grace, which like the Lord, the giver
    never fails from age to age.

★   ★   ★

Bless'd inhabitants of Zion,
    wash'd in the Redeemer's blood!
Jesus, whom their hopes rely on,
    makes them kings and priests to God. (Rev. 1:5-6)
'Tis his love his people raises
    over self to reign as king,
and, as priests, his solemn praises
    each for a thank-offering brings.

Saviour, if of Zion's city
    I through grace a member am,   (Ps. 87:6)
let the world deride or pity,
    I will glory in thy name:

fading is the worldling's pleasure -
    all his boasted pomp and show;
solid joys and lasting treasure
    none but Zion's children know.

I 60 (St. 3 omitted)

87
THE CREATURES IN THE LORD'S HANDS

The water stood like walls of brass
to let the sons of Israel pass,   (Ex. 14:21)
and from the rock in rivers burst   (Ex. 17:6)
at Moses' pray'r, to quench their thirst.

The fire, restrain'd by God's commands,
could only burn his people's bands;   (Dan. 3:27)
too faint, when he was with them there
to singe their garments or their hair.

At Daniel's feet the lions lay   (Dan. 6:22)
like harmless lambs, nor touched their prey:
and ravens, which on carrion fed
procured Elijah flesh and bread.   (3 Kgs. 17:6)

Thus creatures only can fulfil
their great Creator's holy will;
and when his servants need their aid,
his purposes must be obey'd.

So, if his blessing he refuse,
their pow'r to help they quickly lose;
sure as on creatures we depend,
our hopes in disappointment end.

Then let us trust the Lord alone,
and creature-confidence disown;
nor if they threaten need we fear,
they cannot hurt if he be near.

If instruments of pain they prove,
still they are guided by his love;
as lancets by the surgeon's skill
which wound to cure, and not to kill.

II 97

88
I WILL TRUST AND NOT BE AFRAID   HG 74

Begone, unbelief,
    my Saviour is near,
and for my relief
    will surely appear:
by pray'r let me wrestle
        (Gen. 32:24)
    and he will perform;
        (Phil. 1:6)
with Christ in the vessel
        (Mk. 4:38)
    I smile at the storm.

Though dark be my way,
    since he is my guide
'tis mine to obey,   (Deut. 29:29)
    'tis his to provide. (Matt. 6:31)
Though cisterns be broken
        (Jer. 2:13)
    and creatures all fail,
the word he hath spoken
    will surely prevail.

His love in time past
    forbids me to think
he'll leave me at last
    in trouble to sink. (Matt. 14:31)
Each sweet Ebenezer
        (1 Sam. 7:12)
    I had in review
confirms his good pleasure
    to help me quite through.

Determined to save,
    he watched o'er my path
when, Satan's blind slave,
    I sported with death;
and can he have taught me
    to trust in his name,
and thus far have brought me
    to put me to shame?

Why should I complain
of want or distress?
Temptation or pain?
he told me no less:
the heirs of salvation,
I know from his word,
through much tribulation
must follow their Lord.

(Mk. 8:34)

How bitter that cup
no heart can conceive,
which he drank quite up
that sinners might live.

(Mk. 14:36)

His way was much rougher
and darker than mine;
did Jesus thus suffer,
and shall I repine?

Since all that I meet
shall work for my good, (Rom. 8:18)
the bitter is sweet,
the med'cine is food;
though painful at present,
'twill cease before long,
and then, O! how pleasant
the conqueror's song!

III 37

What peaceful hours I once enjoy'd!
how sweet their mem'ry still!
But they have left an aching void
the world can never fill.

Return, O holy Dove, return,
sweet messenger of rest;   (Gen. 8:11)
I hate the sins that made thee mourn   (Eph. 4:30)
and drove thee from my breast.

The dearest idol I have known,
whate'er that idol be,
help me to tear it from thy throne,
and worship only thee.

So shall my walk be close with God,
calm and serene my frame;
so purer light shall mark the road
that leads me to the Lamb.

I 3

89
PERSEVERANCE

Rejoice, believer, in the Lord,
who makes your cause his own;
the hope that's built upon his word
can ne'er be overthrown.

Though many foes beset your road,
and feeble is your arm,
your life is hid with Christ in God   (Col. 3:3)
beyond the reach of harm.

Weak as you are, you shall not faint,
or fainting, shall not die;
Jesus, the strength of every saint
will aid you from on high.

Though sometimes unperceived by sense,
faith sees him always near,
a guide, a glory, a defence;
then what have you to fear?

As surely as he overcame
and triumph'd once for you;
so surely you that love his name
shall in him triumph too.   (Rom. 8:39)

III 84

WILLIAM COWPER
1731-1800
Olney Hymns, 1779
HG 235

90
WALKING WITH GOD
Gen. 5:24

HG 507

O for a closer walk with God,
a calm and heavenly frame,
a light to shine upon the road
that leads me to the Lamb!

Where is the blessedness I knew
when first I saw the Lord?
Where is the soul-refreshing view
of Jesus and his word?

91
PRAISE FOR THE FOUNTAIN OPENED   HG 724

There springs a fountain, where for sin   (Zach. 13:1)
Immanuel was slain;
and sinners who are washed therein
are cleansed from every stain. *

The dying thief rejoiced to see   (Lk. 23:43)
that fountain in his day;
and there have I, as vile as he,
washed all my sins away.

Thy resurrection and thy blood
shall never lose their power
till all the ransomed Church of God
be saved, to sin no more.

E'er since by faith I saw the stream
thy flowing wounds supply,
redeeming love has been my theme
and shall be, till I die.

Then in a nobler, sweeter song
I'll sing thy power to save, -
when this poor lisping, stammering tongue
lies silent in the grave.

Lord, I believe thou hast prepared
(unworthy though I be,)
for me a blood-bought free reward,
a golden harp for me!

'Tis strung, and tuned for endless years,
and formed by power divine
to sound in God the Father's ears
no other name but thine.

_____

*see preceding article

179;
st. 1 and 3 amended by Nathaniel
Micklem

92
LOVEST THOU ME?
John 21:16
HG 266

Hark, my soul, it is the Lord;
'tis thy Saviour, hear his word;
Jesus speaks, and speaks to thee:
'Say, poor sinner, lov'st thou me?'

'I delivered thee when bound,
and, when bleeding, heal'd thy wound, -
sought thee wandering, set thee right   (Matt. 18:12)
turned thy darkness into light.   (Eph. 5:14)

'Can a woman's tender care
cease toward the child she bare?
Yes, she may forgetful be,   (Is. 49:15)
yet will I remember thee.

'Mine is an unchanging love,
higher than the heights above,
deeper than the depths beneath,
free and faithful, strong as death.   (Cant. 8:6)

'Thou shalt see my glory soon,   (Lk 23:43)
when the work of grace is done, -
partner of my throne shalt be;
say, poor sinner, lov'st thou me?'

Lord, it is my chief complaint
that my love is weak and faint;
yet I love thee and adore,
oh for grace to love thee more!

I 118

93
EXHORTATION TO PRAYER

What various hindrances we meet
in coming to the mercy-seat!
Yet who that knows the worth of pray'r
but wishes to be often there?

Pray'r makes the darken'd cloud withdraw, (Ex. 19:18, 20)
pray'r climbs the ladder Jacob saw,   (Gen. 28:12)
gives exercise to faith and love,
brings every blessing from above.

Restraining pray'r, we cease to fight:
pray'r makes the Christian's armour bright: (Eph. 6:18)
and Satan trembles when he sees
the weakest saint upon his knees.

While Moses stood with arms spread wide (Ex. 17:8-12)
success was found on Israel's side;
but when through weariness they failed,
that moment *Amalek* prevail'd.

Have you no words? Ah, think again:
words flow apace when you complain,
and fill your fellow-creature's ear
with the sad tale of all your care.

Were half the breath thus vainly spent
to heaven in supplication sent,
your cheerful song would oftener be,
'Hear what the Lord has done for me.'   (Ps. 66:16)

II 60

94
LIGHT SHINING OUT OF DARKNESS
John 13:7
HG 235

God moves in a mysterious way
his wonders to perform;
he plants his footsteps in the sea,   (Ps. 77:19)
and rides upon the storm.

Deep in unfathomable mines   (Rom. 11:30)
of never-failing skill
he treasures up his bright designs
and works his sovereign will.

Ye fearful saints, fresh courage take, -
the clouds ye so much dread
are big with mercy, and shall break
in blessings on your head.

Judge not the Lord by feeble sense,
but trust him for his grace:
behind a frowning providence
he hides a smiling face.

His purposes will ripen fast,
unfolding every hour;
the bud may have a bitter taste,
but sweet will be the flower.

Blind unbelief is sure to err,
and scan his work in vain;
God is his own interpreter
and he will make it plain.

III 15

95
JOY AND PEACE IN BELIEVING
HG 649

Sometimes a light surprises
that Christian while he sings;
it is the Lord, who rises
with healing in his wings.   (Mal. 4:2)
When comforts are declining,
he grants the soul again
a season of clear shining   (2 Sam. 23:4)
to cheer it after rain.

In holy contemplation
we sweetly then pursue
the theme of God's salvation,
and find it ever new: (Lam. 3:26)
set free from present sorrow,
we cheerfully can say,
'E'vn let the unknown morrow
bring with it what it may.'   (Matt. 6:34)

It can bring with it nothing
but he will bear us through;
who gives the lilies clothing   (Matt. 6:28)
will clothe his people too;
beneath the spreading heavens
no creature but is fed;
and he who feeds the ravens
will give his children bread.

Though vine nor fig-tree neither (Hab. 3:17-8)
　　their wonted fruit should bear,
though all the field should wither,
　　nor flocks nor herd be there:
yet God the same abiding,
　　his praise shall tune my voice;
for, while in him confiding,
　　I cannot but rejoice.

III 48

ARTICLE 8:
THE SCOTTISH PARAPHRASES (96-102)

Scotland has its own way of performing Christian praise, and it is hardly too much to say that even the legitimizing of hymnody in Scotland in the mid-19th century hardly disturbed this settled habit between the publication of the first Psalter in 1564 and that of the Third Edition of the Church Hymnary in 1973.

For a Scot, the metrical psalms in the 1650 version are the centre of all praise. In this he is like a medieval Catholic, for whom hymnody was always secondary to psalmody. And until the year 1781 nothing but psalmody was permitted in any part of the Church of Scotland. (Certain of the most conservative Scottish communions still preserve this rule.) But it was perhaps inevitable that a Watts-like protest against the singer's being confined to the Old Testament for his praise should be heard sooner or later. It was heard in the General Assembly of 1741. By resolution of that Assembly certain men were deputed to draw up a short collection of paraphrases of Scripture passages in psalm-meter which should then be submitted, as are all resolutions of that Assembly, to the Presbyteries for their judgment. A collection of 45 pieces was presented to Assembly in 1745 and duly copied and distributed to the Presbyteries. It appears (from Maclagan's account) that it proved impossible to bring the Assembly to a decision, because, for one reason and another, many Presbyteries withheld their replies, the excuse being that the times were disturbed (they were indeed; 1745 was not the best of all years in which to initiate a project of this sort in Scotland). By 1751, though some work of revision had been done on the recommendation of the Assembly, the project was officially laid aside.

The matter was reactivated some 25 years later, and this time came to a successful conclusion. Working on the 1745 and 1751 drafts, and adding more from other sources, the committee brought in, and the Assembly accepted, a collection of 67 pieces. Of these, 32 were taken from the Old Testament and 35 from the New. Every piece was scrutinized by the new committee, and the result of their work is a homogeneous collection which looks as if it were all written by one hand. In fact a number of the paraphrases come from the works of the few writers in the Calvinist tradition available to be drawn on. Clearly nothing in the Wesleyan style would do, but 23 pieces are altered from Isaac Watts; two or three more are based on his work but depart very widely from it; five are based on hymns by Philip Doddridge; nine are untraceable; the rest are by ministers who contributed to the earlier or the later collection, or by members of the editorial committee, of whom the best known are Logan and Cameron.

Virtually nothing passed unaltered through the editorial committee's hands; Paraphrase 64 is the only one, according to Maclagan, that suffered no alteration through the editions of 1754, 1751, and 1781 (and it is not a particularly meritable piece). The very famous Doddridge paraphrase (96) was greatly improved, as to its first four stanzas, by the paraphrasers, though their fifth introduced a legalistic note which while not contradicted in the Scripture at that point comes uneasily to Christians. Even Tate's 'While shepherds' (our 22) was altered in a few details.

The ruthlessness of this revision produced one awkward controversy which has never been satisfactorily cleared up. We are content to attribute our ## 97 and 101 to Michael Bruce, the young poet who died at 21; but Logan claimed them as his, and indeed he certainly worked on them before they were finally published. As to Paraphrase 18 (97) it has to be said that a version like it was in the 1745 book (before Bruce was born), and Bruce can only have revised it; but Paraphrase 58 (100) may indeed be Bruce's work, even if again it was gone over by Logan. It is the only Paraphrase in anything but Common Meter, and is an alternative to Paraphrase 57 on the same passage. Those who wish to go into the matter will need to chase it through many pages of contemporary and later dispute.

This collection, anyhow, was the hymn book of the Church of Scotland for nearly a century after its publication, and many pieces from it have found their way into later and non-Scottish collections. This must be credited to the revisers, who certainly did their work very faithfully. Among Scots the collection is second only to the Psalms. I may say that so great is the gap between the psalms and paraphrases on one hand and the hymns on the other even to this day, that I heard an elder of a famous church in Edinburgh say, of a certain paraphrase which appeared also in the hymn book, that he disapproved of its being announced by the minister as Hymn 365 and preferred, with weighty emphasis, that it be always known as Paraphrase Eighteen. The separate psalter, with paraphrases, was discarded officially only in 1973 when a new hymnal appeared which included selected psalms and paraphrases among the hymns. My elder is not on record as having commented on the fact that Psalm 23 is now Hymn 387.

See:

Douglas J. Maclagan, *The Scottish Paraphrases*, Edinburgh, 1889

THE SCOTTISH PARA-
PHRASES, 1781
HG 76

96
PARAPHRASE TWO: Gen. 28:20-22　　HG 512

O God of Bethel, by whose hand
　　thy people still are fed;
who through this weary pilgrimage
　　hast all our fathers led;
our vows, our prayers, we now present
　　before thy throne of grace:
God of our fathers, be the God
　　of their succeeding race.

Through each perplexing path of life
　　our wandering footsteps guide;
give us each day our daily bread
　　and raiment fit provide.
O spread thy covering wings around
　　till all our wanderings cease,
and at our Father's loved abode
　　our souls arrive in peace.

Such blessings from thy gracious hand
　　our humble prayers implore;

and thou shalt be our chosen God
and portion evermore.

Based on **P. Doddridge** (1755)

97
PARAPHRASE EIGHTEEN: Is. 2:2-6   HG 79

Behold! the mountain of the Lord
in latter days shall rise
on mountain tops above the hills,
and draw the wondering eyes.
To this the joyful nations round,
all tribes and tongues shall flow;
'Up to the hill of God', they'll say,
'and to his house we'll go.'

The beam that shines from Sion hill
shall lighten every land;
the King who reigns in Salem's towers
shall all the world command.
Among the nations he shall judge;
his judgments truth shall guide;
his sceptre shall protect the just,
and quell the sinner's pride.

No strife shall rage, nor hostile feuds
disturb those peaceful years;
to ploughshares men shall beat their swords,
to pruning-hooks their spears.
No longer hosts encountering hosts
shall crowds of slain deplore:
they hang the trumpet in the hall
and study war no more.

Come then, O house of Jacob! come
to worship at his shrine;
and, walking in the light of God,
with holy beauties shine.

Probably by **Michael Bruce**, 1746-67,
revising an older text (1751)

98
PARAPHRASE NINETEEN: Is: 9:2-7   HG 709

The race that long in darkness pined
have seen a glorious light;
the people dwell in day, who dwelt
in death's surrounding night.
To hail thy rise, thou better Sun!
the gathering nations come,
joyous, as when the reapers bear
the harvest treasures home.

For thou our burden hast removed,
and quelled th' oppressor's sway,
quick as the slaughtered squadrons fell
in Midian's evil day.
To us a Child of hope is born,
to us a Son is giv'n;
him shall the tribes of earth obey,
him all the hosts of heav'n.

His name shall be the Prince of Peace,
for evermore adored,
the Wonderful, the Counsellor,
the great and mighty Lord.

His power increasing still shall spread,
his reign no end shall know;
justice shall guard his throne above,
and peace abound below.

JOHN MORISON, 1749-98

99
PARAPHRASE THIRTY: Hosea 6:1-4   HG 133

Come, let us to the Lord our God
with contrite hearts return;
our God is gracious, nor will leave
the desolate to mourn.
His voice commands the tempest forth,
and stills the stormy wave;
and though his arm be strong to smite,
'tis also strong to save.

Long hath the night of sorrow reigned,
the dawn shall bring us light:
God shall appear, and we shall rise
with gladness in his sight.
Our hearts, if God we seek to know,
shall know him, and rejoice;
his coming like the morn shall be,
like morning songs his voice.

As dew upon the tender herb
diffusing fragrance round;
as showers that usher in the spring
and cheer the thirsty ground:
so shall his presence bless our souls,
and shed a joyful light;
that hallowed morn shall chase away
the sorrows of the night.

JOHN MORISON, 1749-98

100
PARAPHRASE FIFTY-EIGHT: Heb. 4:14-16   HG 814

Where high the heavenly temple stands,
the house of God not made with hands,
a great High Priest our nature wears,
the guardian of mankind appears.
He who for men their surety stood,
and poured on earth his precious blood,
pursues in heaven his mighty plan,
the Saviour and the friend of man.

Though now ascended up on high,
he bends on earth a brother's eye;
partaker of the human name,
he knows the frailty of our frame.
Our fellow-sufferer yet retains
a fellow-feeling of our pains;
and still remembers in the skies
his tears, his agonies and cries.

In every pang that rends the heart
the Man of Sorrows has a part;
he sympathises with our grief,
and to the sufferer brings relief.
With boldness therefore at the throne,
let us make all our sorrows known;
and ask the aid of heavenly power
to help us in the evil hour.

MICHAEL BRUCE, 1746-67

101
PARAPHRASE SIXTY: Heb. 13:20-1   HG 186

Original by Philip Doddridge, 1755

Father of peace, and God of love,
   we own thy Pow'r to save;
that Pow'r by which our Shepherd
                   rose
   victorious o'er the grave,

We triumph in that Shepherd's
                  Name,
   still watchful for our Good;
who brought th' eternal Cove-
               nant down,
   and seal'd it with his Blood

So may thy Spirit seal my Soul,
   and mould it to thy Will;
that my fond Heart no more may
                stray,
   but keep thy Cov'nant still.

Still may we gain superior
              Strength,
   and press with Vigour on,
till full Perfection crown our
              Hopes,
and fix us near thy Throne.

Version by ? John Logan, 1781

Father of peace, and God of love!
   we own thy power to save,
that power by which our Shep-
                 herd rose
   victorious o'er the grave.
Him from the dead thou
             brought'st again
   when, by his sacred blood,
confirmed and sealed for ever-
               more
   th' eternal Covenant stood.

O may thy Spirit seal our souls,
   and mould them to thy will,
that our weak hearts no more may
                stray,
   but keep thy precepts still!

that to perfection's sacred height
   we nearer still may rise,
and all we think, and all we do
   be pleasing in thine eyes.

102
PARAPHRASE SIXTY-THREE: 1 John 3:1-4   HG 76

Behold, th' amazing gift of love
   the Father hath bestowed
on us, the sinful sons of men,
   to call us sons of God!
Concealed as yet this honour lies,
   by this dark world unknown,
a world that knew not when he came
   ev'n God's eternal Son.

High is the rank we now possess;
   but higher we shall rise;
though what we shall hereafter be
   is hid from mortal eyes:
our souls, we know, when he appears,
   shall bear his image bright;
for all his glory, full disclosed,
   shall open to our sight.

A hope so great, and so divine,
   may trials well endure;
and purge the soul from sense and sin,
   as Christ himself is pure.

? **John Logan**, 1748-88, revised from Isaac Watts (1707)

ARTICLE 9:
FROM EVANGELICAL TO ROMANTIC (103-129)

'The Romantic' has as many colours as the rainbow, but for our purposes it may broadly be described as including emphases on the personal rather than the public, the distant rather than the easily tractable, the adventurous rather than the cautious, the imaginative rather than the rational. If we speak so (and William Blake would, aside from his hatred of anything so clear cut, mostly have approved), then it is clear that the romantic has affinities with the Evangelical, and is always suspected by the Calvinistic culture.

There is much about the Wesleyan enterprise that is romantic: the sheer adventure of it; all that travelling; the exposure of evangelists to danger; the pursuit of a far-off but always visible goal; and the free rein given to personal expressions of religion. Wesley does not suspect Nature quite as deeply as a faithful Calvinist must.

Therefore the romantic strain in hymnody issues very naturally from the Evangelical, even when it is best seen in the work of people who hardly described themselves technically as Evangelicals. In the section 103-129, we see exactly how this works out.

Numbers 103-105 are Evangelical. Thomas Haweis's moving little poem on the words of the penitent thief is intensely personal in a manner worthy of Wesley himself. The two magnificent dogmatic utterances of Thomas Kelly are Evangelical, in the sense of urging a total commitment to the mystery of the Cross, and Calvinistic, in their resurrection-background. (Kelly, an Irish judge and a Protestant, wrote an enormous number of hymns; we can forgive him all the doggerel in the vast majority of his hymns for these two perfect pieces).

But with # 106 comes a change. No. 106 is the work of a vicar who was more or less a contemporary of Jane Austen and therefore of the alarming clerics that appear in her novels: an absentee incumbent who lived in Torquay while leaving his midlands parish in the hands of a curate. But it is, first and last, a missionary hymn, and so are the much greater examples of James Montgomery that immediately follow (107-109).

Now, the missionary explosion of 1792-1810 is romanticism coming to life in English religion. It is, of course, Evangelism, but it is also remote, adventurous, and perilous. Missionaries really were eaten by cannibals. It was a sharing of experience, not an extension of a system. The very existence of the London Missionary Society, founded in 1795, and its famous peroration in its constitution, which averred that its purpose was not the imposition of any church system (it was at first a wholly non-denominational mission) but to spread 'the glorious Gospel of the Blessed God,' is romanticism at its best.

Should it have been said before this that romanticism is not in any known sense a pejorative word? It is so used by people who have certain theories about organs, and it is used with a special tone of contempt by certain theologians, but I do not so use it here. All the captivating enthusiasms, all the endearing weaknesses, of the Protestant missionary enterprise of this time was romantic, and perhaps the fact that some other missions promoted from elsewhere have in our own time come to stickier ends has something to do with an inhibition which suffocated true romance in the hearts and minds of their promoters. That is material for somebody else's Ph.D.

At any rate, James Montgomery, the greatest of English lay hymn writers, focuses this argument in the shape of his life and the cast of his missionary hymns. Here was a young-middle-aged radical, a journalist working for a radical editor who was sent to prison for his political opinions, taking over the paper when the editor disappeared and promoting every philanthropic and humanitarian cause he could reach—a romantic political writer to his finger tips. Our # 107 was evoked by news of a special victory in the South Seas. Was there ever a more romantic (still in the best sense) interpretation of Psalm 72 than # 108? Compare it with # 43! The sense of distance, of the trajectory of preaching, is nowhere more vividly expressed than in # 109. The specially personal and devotional note so sanely and unaffectedly sounded in ## 110-113 is equally of the romantic tradition. Romance is not irrational, though it is impatient of pedantry; what better shows that than these beautifully wrought devotional pieces? Montgomery wrote probably 300 hymns, often dashing them off for special occasions (# 109 was written for a local missionary celebration in Leeds) and revising them later at leisure. Many others, of which one can say just what we have said of these, are scattered over the hymnals.

'Romantic' is also a proper description of # 114, if one recalls its author's background. This author is a diplomat, business-man, and *traveller*; the sight of the charred iron cross that was all that remained of the burnt-out cathedral on the island of Macao inspired the hymn. And it is very proper that we are able to include in # 115 some lines of Sir Walter Scott, the father of all romantic novelists in English literature. This is, by design, a Christian's prayer for the conversion of the Jews and is not now seen in hymnals. (1927 was the date of the last to include it.)

I have insisted that romanticism is not to be regarded as contemptible; but it is fair to point out that it can be perverted. When it is corrupt it becomes loathsome enough. The most obvious perversions of it are the habit of being preoccupied with what is distant at the expense of what is immediately present; Charles Dickens sufficiently disposed of the corrupt 'missionary' mentality in his devastating character sketches of Mrs. Jellyby and Mrs. Pardiggle in *Bleak House*, women who, in their pursuit of benefit for people far away, neglected and abused their own families. The romantic can be irrational, anarchic, egotistical and impossible to communicate with. It can escape from present duties in contemplation of imaginary ones. And, of course, it can always dispense itself from the duty of being corrected by new evidence. That happened to many missionary hymns of the less meritable kind and to much devotional poetry as well.

But we have to say that there was more than a touch of the romantic about the Oxford Movement itself. The historical judgments of some of those who wished to bring the Middle Ages back were as shaky as Sir Walter Scott's; the zeal with which they sought to reconstruct the system of office-hymns could blind them to the occasional anachronism and even bathos produced by the less inspired of the texts they trans-lated.

That their hymn writers (in articles 11 and 14) were not worse than they were was undoubtedly to the credit of the writers featured in ## 116-129. Bishop Heber (not a bishop when he wrote his hymns) showed a warmth and grace which at this moment were badly needed. 'Holy, Holy, Holy' (116) is more impressionistic than theological; it proved, once Dykes had given it a tune, too easy to sing and has suffered badly from the batterings of incompetent hymn-choosers. But it was Tenny-son's favourite hymn, and one can see why. No. 117 is equally impressionistic, but (almost fatally) attractive. No. 118 is a Communion hymn, but hardly a Eucharistic one. No. 119 is a tender, naturalistic meditation. This is very different from what the Calvinists prescribed. Nothing became Heber so much as his inclusion in his collection of one hymn that was not his, # 120, which is surely the finest lyric written in the whole of the 19th century.

And Keble, one of the Oxford Movement's architects, is, as a hymn writer, a pure romantic. He collected his hymns in *The Christian Year* when he was 35, and the collection became a best-seller which paid for the reconstruction of his country

parish church. Many of the 'hymns' are really extended poetic meditations, and the fragments now in common use are much better understood when read in the context of their sur-rounding verses. No. 123 happens to be a hymn well known in a grossly distorted version which uses two of its verses and two platitudinous rhymes by another writer. In its original form it has an immense sense of distance, the more effective because of its restricted meter. And as for # 124, this is romantic in its interest in created nature and its contented contempla-tion of it as it is.

'O worship the King,' in its full text a splendid piece of writ-ing, is as romantic an interpretation of Psalm 104, which lends itself especially to such treatment, as # 108 was of Psalm 72. And the much-loved H. F. Lyte, though scriptural and evan-gelical in his emphases, always writes good literature and is rarely deserted by an exquisite lyric gift. Perhaps the centrally 'romantic' hymn of all hymns is the intensely personal yet, as it has proved, wholly universal hymn, 'Abide with me' (128), which again can be read most profitably in its full version.

As a tailpiece we include # 129, one of the handful of hymns left by the young priest Joseph Anstice. His others are actually more overtly romantic than this one, but what he might have become had he lived longer, as a hymn writer with a touch of Watts about him illuminated by the lyric gifts of the romantics, is a question which # 129 poses forcefully.

This small section, covering a short but important age, indi-cates how a group of writers demonstrated, just in time, that 'the system' need not suffocate literature. Had they not done so, the Oxford Movement might have been a good deal more stuffy than it was.

THOMAS HAWEIS
1734-1820

103
REMEMBER ME
Luke 23:39   HG 564

O Thou, from whom all goodness flows,
    I lift my heart to thee;
in all my sorrows, conflicts, woes,
    Dear Lord, 'Remember me!'

While on my poor distressèd heart
    my sins lie heavily,
my pardon speak, new peace impart,
    in love 'Remember me!'

Temptations sore obstruct my way,
    to shake my faith in thee;
O give me strength, Lord, as my day;
    for good 'Remember me!'

Distrest with pain, disease and grief,
    this feeble body see;
grant patience, rest, and kind relief,
    Hear! and 'Remember me!'

When in desertion's dismal night
    thy face I cannot see;
then, Lord, arise with glorious light,
    and still 'Remember me!'

If on my face for thy dear name
    shame and reproaches be,
all hail, reproach, and welcome, shame,
    if thou 'Remember me!'

The hour is near, consign'd to death
  I wait thy just decree;
Saviour, with my last parting breath,
  I'll cry, 'Remember me!'

Carmina Christo, 1792

The cross he bore is life and health,
  though shame and death to him;
his people's hope, his people's wealth,
  their everlasting theme.

Hymns . . . , 1820

THOMAS KELLY
1769-1855
HG 406

104
GOD FORBID THAT I SHOULD GLORY
Gal. 6:14   HG 787

We sing the praise of him who died,
  of him who died upon the cross;
the sinner's hope let men deride,
  for this we count the world but loss.   (Gal. 6:14)

Inscribed upon the cross we see
  in shining letters, 'God is love';   (Mk. 15:26)
he bears our sins upon the tree;   (1 Pet. 2:24)
  he brings us mercy from above.

The cross! it takes our guilt away;
  it holds the fainting spirit up;
it cheers with hope the gloomy day,
  and sweetens every bitter cup.

It makes the coward spirit brave,
  and nerves the feeble arm for fight;
it takes its terror from the grave,
  and gilds the bed of death with light;

the balm of life, the cure of woe,
  the measure and the pledge of love,
the sinners' refuge here below,
  the angels' theme in heaven above.

Hymns (Dublin), 1815   Based on a hymn by Samuel Medley,
                          1738-99)

105
CHRIST PERFECT THROUGH SUFFERINGS
Heb. 2:10   HG 695

The head that once was crowned with thorns
  is crowned with glory now:
a royal diadem adorns
  the mighty Victor's brow.

The highest place that heaven affords
  is his, is his by right,
the King of kings and Lord of lords,   (Rev. 19:16)
  and heaven's eternal light;

the joy of all who dwell above,
  the joy of all below,
to whom he manifests his love,
  and grants his name to know.

To them the cross, with all its shame,
  with all its grace, is given:
their name an everlasting name,
  their joy the joy of heaven.   (Lk. 10:20)

They suffer with their Lord below,   (2 Tim. 2:12)
  they reign with him above,
their profit and their joy to know
  the mystery of his love.

JOHN MARRIOTT
1780-1825

106
LET THERE BE LIGHT   HG 744

Thou, whose almighty word
chaos and darkness heard,
  and took their flight;
hear us, we humbly pray;
and, where the gospel's day
sheds not its glorious ray,
  let there be light!   (Gen. 1:3)

Thou, who didst come to bring
on thy redeeming wing
  healing and sight,
health to the sick in mind,
sight to the inly blind,
oh, now to all mankind
  let there be light!

Spirit of truth and love,
life-giving, holy Dove,
  speed forth thy flight!
Move on the waters' face,
bearing the lamp of grace,
and in earth's darkest place
  let there be light!

Holy and blessed Three,
Glorious Trinity,
  Wisdom, Love, Might!
Boundless as ocean's tide,
rolling in fullest pride,
through the earth, far and wide
  let there be light!

1813; in *Evangelical Magazine,* 1825:
text of 1861

JAMES MONTGOMERY
1771-1854
HG 6

107
THE LORD GOD OMNIPOTENT REIGNETH
HG 269

Hark! the song of jubilee,
  loud as mighty thunders' roar,
or the fulness of the sea
  when it breaks upon the shore:
Alleluia! for the Lord
  God omnipotent shall reign;
Alleluia! let the word
  echo round the earth and main.

Alleluia! hark the sound,
  from the depths unto the skies,
wakes above, beneath, around,
  all creation's harmonies;
see Jehovah's banner furled,
  sheathed his sword; he speaks - 'tis done,

and the kingdoms of this world   (Rev. 11:15)
  are the kingdoms of his Son.

He shall reign from pole to pole
  with illimitable sway;
he shall reign when like a scroll   (Rev. 6:14)
  yonder heavens are passed away;
then the end; beneath his rod   (1 Cor. 15:24)
  man's last enemy shall fall;
Alleluia! Christ in God,
  God in Christ, is all in all.   (Col. 3:11)

Evangelical Magazine, April, 1818;
author's revision, 1853

108
THE REIGN OF CHRIST
Psalm 72   HG 261

Hail to the Lord's Anointed!
  Great David's greater Son;
Hail, in the time appointed,
  his reign on earth begun!
He comes to break oppression,
  to set the captive free,
to take away transgression,
  and rule in equity.

He comes in succour speedy
  to those who suffer wrong;
to help the poor and needy,
  and bid the weak be strong;
to give them songs for sighing,
  their darkness turn to light,
whose wouls, condemned and dying
  were precious in his sight.

By such shall he be fearéd
  while sun and moon endure;
beloved, obeyed, reveréd;
  for he shall judge the poor
through changing generations,
  with justice, mercy, truth,
while stars maintain their stations,
  or moons renew their youth.

He shall come down like showers
  upon the fruitful earth,
and love, joy, hope, like flowers
  spring in his path to birth:
before him on the mountains,
  shall Peace, the herald, go;
and righteousness, in fountains
  from hill to valley flow.

Arabia's desert ranger
  to him shall bow the knee,
the Ethiopian stranger
  his glory come to see:
with offerings of devotion,
  ships from the isles shall meet,
to pour the wealth of ocean
  in tribute at his feet.

Kings shall bow down before him,
  and gold and silver bring;
all nations shall adore him,
  his praise all people sing:

for he shall have dominion
  o'er river, sea and shore,
far as the eagle's pinion
  or dove's light wing can soar.

For him shall prayer unceasing
  and daily vows ascend;
his kingdom still increasing,
  a kingdom without end:
the mountain dews shall nourish
  a seed in weakness sown,
whose fruit shall spread and flourish,
  and shake like Lebanon.

O'er every foe victorious,
  he on his throne shall rest,
from age to age more glorious,
  all-blessing and all-blest;
the tide of time shall never
  his covenant remove;
his name shall stand for ever;
  that name to us is Love.

Evangelical Magazine, May 1822;
author's revision, 1853

109
THE SPIRIT ACCOMPANYING THE WORD OF GOD
HG 563

O Spirit of the living God,
  in all thy plenitude of grace,
where'er the foot of man hath trod,
  descend on our apostate race.

Give tongues of fire and hearts of love
  to preach the reconciling word;
give power and unction from above
  whene'er the joyful sound is heard.

Be darkness at thy coming, light:
  confusion, order in thy path;
souls without strength inspire with might;
  bid mercy triumph over wrath.

O Spirit of the Lord, prepare
  all the round earth her God to meet;
breathe thou abroad like morning air
  till hearts of stone begin to beat.

Baptize the nations; far and nigh
  the triumphs of the cross record:
the name of Jesus glorify,
  till every kingdom call him Lord.

God from eternity hath willed
  all flesh shall his salvation see:
so be the Father's love fulfilled,
  the Saviour's sufferings crowned through thee.

The Christian Psalmist, 1825; revised
from text of 1823

110
LORD, TEACH US TO PRAY   HG 435

Lord, teach us how to pray   (Luke 11:1)
  with reverence and with fear;
though dust and ashes in thy sight
  we may, we must draw near.

We perish if we cease from prayer;
  O grant us power to pray;
and when to meet thee we prepare,
  Lord, meet us by the way.

God of all grace, we come to thee
  with broken, contrite hearts;   (Ps. 51:17)
give, what thine eye delights to see,
  truth in the inward parts.   (Ps. 51:6)

Give deep humility, the sense
  of godly sorrow give;
a strong desiring confidence
  to hear thy voice and live;

faith in the only sacrifice
  that can for sin atone;
to cast our hopes, to fix our eyes,
  on Christ, on Christ alone;

patience to watch, and wait, and weep
  though mercy long delay;
courage, our fainting souls to keep
  and trust thee, though thou slay.   (Job 13:15)

Give these, - and then thy will be done;
  thus strengthened with all might,
we by thy Spirit and thy Son
  shall pray, and pray aright.

              COTTERILL'S *Selection*, 1819; author's
              revision, 1825.

111
THE SKILL OF PRAYER   HG 608

Prayer is the soul's sincere desire,
  uttered or unexpressed;
the motion of a hidden fire
  that trembles in the breast.

Prayer is the burden of a sigh,
  the falling of a tear,
the upward glancing of an eye
  when none but God is near.

Prayer is the simplest form of speech
  that infant lips can try;
prayer the sublimest strains that reach
  the Majesty on high.

Prayer is the contrite sinner's voice,
  returning from his ways,
while angels in their songs rejoice
  and cry, 'Behold, he prays!'

Prayer is the Christian's vital breath,
  the Christian's native air,
his watchword at the gates of death:
  he enters heaven with prayer.

The saints in prayer appear as one
  in word and deed and mind,
while with the Father and the Son
  sweet fellowship they find.

Nor prayer is made by man alone;
  the Holy Spirit pleads,
And Jesus on the eternal throne
  for sinners intercedes.

O thou, by whom we come to God,
  the Life, the Truth, the Way,   (Jn. 14:6)
the path of prayer thyself hast trod:
  Lord, teach us how to pray.   (Lk. 11:1)

              COTTERILL'S *Selection*, 1819; author's
              revision of 1853

112
PSALM 63   HG 518

O God, thou art my God alone,
  early to thee my soul shall cry,
a pilgrim in a land unknown,
  a thirsty land whose springs are dry.

O that it were as it hath been
  when, praying in the holy place,
thy power and glory I have seen,
  and marked the footsteps of thy grace!

Yea, through this rough and thorny maze
  I follow hard on thee, my God;
thine hand unseen upholds my ways;
  I safely tread where thou hast trod.

Thee, in the watches of the night,
  when I remember on my bed,
thy presence makes the darkness light;
  thy guardian wings are round my head.

Better than life itself thy love,
  dearer than all beside to me;
for whom have I in heaven above,
  or what on earth, compared with Thee?   (Ps. 73:24)

Praise with my heart, my mind, my voice,
  for all thy mercy I will give;
my soul shall still in God rejoice;
  my tongue shall bless thee while I live.

              Songs of Zion, 1822

113
THE FAMILY TABLE   HG 68

Be known to us in breaking bread,   (Lk. 24:35)
  but do not then depart;
Saviour, abide with us, and spread
  thy table in our heart.

There sup with us in love divine,
  thy body and thy blood,
that living bread, that heavenly wine
  be our immortal food.

              The Christian Psalmist, 1825

SIR JOHN BOWRING
1792-1872
HG 230

114
GLORYING IN THE CROSS
Gal. 6:14   HG 336

In the Cross of Christ I glory,
  towering o'er the wrecks of time;
all the light of sacred story
  gathers round its head sublime.

When the woes of life o'ertake me,
hopes deceive and fears annoy,
never shall the Cross forsake me,
Lo! it glows with peace and joy.

When the sun of bliss is beaming
light and love upon my way,
from the Cross the radiance streaming
adds more lustre to the day.

Bane and blessing, pain and pleasure
by the Cross are sanctified;
peace is there which knows no measure
joys that through all time abide.

In the Cross of Christ I glory,
towering o'er the wrecks of time;
all the light of sacred story
gathers round its head sublime.

Hymns. . . ., 1825

SIR WALTER SCOTT
1771-1832
HG 846

115
EXODUS

When Israel, of the Lord belov'd
out of the land of bondage came,
her fathers' God before her moved,
an awful Guide, in smoke and flame.   (Ex. 40:38)

By day, along the astonished lands
the cloudy pillar glided slow;
by night, Arabia's crimsoned sands
returned the fiery column's glow.

There rose the choral hymn of praise,
and trump and timbrel answered keen   (Ex. 15:1)
and Zion's daughters poured their lays
with priest's and warrior's voice between.

No portents now their foes amaze;
forsaken Israel wanders lone;
their fathers would not know thy ways,
and thou hast left them to their own.

But, present still, though now unseen,
when brightly shines the prosperous day,
be thoughts of thee a cloudy screen
to temper the deceitful ray.

And O, when stoops on Judah's path
in shade and storm, the frequent night,
be thou, long-suffering, slow to wrath,
a burning and a shining light!

The Song of Rebecca, in *Ivanhoe*, ch.
35, 1819; first used as a hymn, 1833

REGINALD HEBER, Bishop
1783-1826
Hymns (Posth.) 1827
HG 93

116
HOLY! HOLY! HOLY!   HG 289

Holy, Holy, Holy! Lord God Almighty!
Early in the morning our song shall rise to thee;
Holy, Holy, Holy! merciful and mighty,
God in three Persons, blessed Trinity!

Holy, Holy, Holy! all the saints adore thee,
casting down their golden crowns around the glassy sea,
Cherubim and seraphim falling down before thee,
who wert and art, and evermore shalt be.

Holy, Holy, Holy! though the darkness hide thee,
though the eye of sinful man thy glory may not see,
only thou art holy, there is none beside thee
perfect in power, in love and purity.

Holy, Holy, Holy! Lord God Almighty!
All thy works shall praise thy name in earth and sky and sea;
Holy, Holy, Holy! merciful and mighty!
God in three Persons, blessed Trinity.

117
BRIGHTEST AND BEST   HG 96

Brightest and best of the sons of the morning,
dawn on our darkness, and lend us thine aid,
star of the east, the horizon adorning,
guide where our infant Redeemer is laid!

Cold on his cradle the dewdrops are shining,
low lies his head with the beasts of the stall;
angels adore him, in slumber reclining,
Maker, and Monarch, and Saviour of all.

Say, shall we yield him, in costly devotion,
odours of Edom and offerings divine;
gems of the mountain, and pearls of the ocean,
myrrh from the forest, or gold from the mine?

Vainly we offer each ample oblation,
vainly with gifts would his favour secure;
richer by far is the heart's adoration,
dearer to God are the prayers of the poor.

118
BREAD OF THE WORLD   HG 93

Bread of the world, in mercy broken,
wine of the soul, in mercy shed,
by whom the words of life were spoken,
and in whose death our sins are dead:
look on the heart by sorrow broken,
look on the tears by sinners shed,
and be thy feast to us the token
that by thy grace our souls are fed.

119
ETERNITY

I praised the earth, in beauty seen
with garlands gay of various green;
I praised the sea, whose ample field
shone glorious as a silver shield;
and earth and ocean seemed to say,
'Our beauties are but for a day!'

I praised the sun, whose chariot roll'd
on wheels of amber and of gold;
I praise the moon, whose softer eye
gleam'd sweetly through the summer sky!
And moon and sun in answer said,
'Our days of light are numbered'.

O God! O good beyond compare!
If thus thy meaner works are fair!
If thus thy bounties gild the span
of ruin'd earth and sinful man,
how glorious must the mansion be
where thy redeem'd shall dwell with thee!

HENRY HART MILMAN
1791-1868
HG 524

120
PALM SUNDAY
HG 619

Ride on! ride on in majesty!
Hark, all the tribes 'Hosanna!' cry;
thine humble beast pursues his road
with palms and scattered garments strowed.

Ride on! ride on in majesty!
In lowly pomp ride on to die;
O Christ, thy triumphs now begin
o'er captive death and conquered sin.

Ride on! ride on in majesty!
the wingéd squadrons of the sky
look down with sad and wondering eyes
to see the approaching sacrifice.

Ride on! ride on in majesty!
Thy last and fiercest strife is nigh;
the Father on his sapphire throne
expects his own anointed Son.

Ride on! ride on in majesty!
In lowly pomp ride on to die;
bow thy meek head to mortal pain,
then take, O God, thy power, and reign.

Heber's *Hymns*, 1827

JOHN KEBLE, 1792-1866
from *The Christian Year*, 1827
HG 83

121
MORNING
HG 480

Oh! timely happy, timely wise,
hearts that with rising morn arise!
Eyes that the beam celestial view
which evermore makes all things new!   (Rev. 21:5)

New every morning is the love   (Lam. 3:26)
our wakening and uprising prove;
through sleep and darkness safely brought,
restored to life, and power, and thought.

New mercies, each returning day,
hover around us while we pray;
new perils past, new sins forgiven,
new thoughts of God, new hopes of heaven.

If on our daily course our mind
be set to hallow all we find,
New treasures still, of countless price
God will provide for sacrifice.   (Gen. 22:8)

Old friends, old scenes, will lovelier be
as more of heaven in each we see:
some softening gleam of love and prayer
shall dawn on every cross and care.

★   ★   ★

We need not bid, for cloistered cell,
our neighbour and our work farewell,
nor strive to wind ourselves too high
for sinful man beneath the sky:

the trivial round, the common task
would furnish all we ought to ask;
room to deny ourselves; a road
to bring us, daily, nearer God.

Seek we no more; content with these,
let present rapture, comfort, ease,
as heaven shall bid them, come and go -
the secret, this, of rest below.

Only, O Lord, in thy dear love
fit us for perfect rest above;
and help us, this and every day,
to live more nearly as we pray.

Sts. 1-4, 10-12 omitted

122
EVENING
Luke 24:29
HG 668

'Tis gone, that bright and orbéd blaze,
fast fading from our wistful gaze;
yon mantling cloud has hid from sight
the last faint pulse of quivering light

★   ★   ★

Sun of my soul, thou Saviour dear,
it is not night if thou be near:
oh, may no earth-born cloud arise
to hide thee from thy servant's eyes.

When round thy wondrous works below
my searching rapturous glance I throw,
tracing out wisdom, power and love,   (cf. # 39)
in earth or sky, in stream or grove; -

or by the light thy words disclose
watch Time's full river as it flows,
scanning thy gracious Providence,
where not too deep for mortal sense; -

when with dear friends sweet talk I hold,
and all the flowers of life unfold; -   (Lk. 24:32)
let not my heart within me burn
except in all I thee discern.

★   ★   ★

Abide with me from morn till eve,
for without thee I cannot live:
abide with me when night is nigh,
for without thee I dare not die.

★   ★   ★

If some poor wandering child of thine
have spurned, to-day, the voice divine,
now, Lord, the gracious work begin;
let him no more lie down in sin.

Watch by the sick; enrich the poor
with blessings from thy boundless store:
be every mourner's sleep tonight,
like infant's slumbers, pure and light.

Come near and bless us when we wake,
ere through the world our way we take:
till in the ocean of thy love
we lose ourselves in heaven above.

sts. 2, 7, 9-11 omitted

123
BLESSED ARE THE PURE IN HEART
Matt. 5:8

HG 83

Bless'd are the pure in heart,
for they shall see our God,
the secret of the Lord is theirs,
their soul is Christ's abode.

Might mortal thought presume
to guess an angel's lay,
such are the notes that echo through
the courts of heaven to-day.

Such the triumphal hymns
on Sion's Prince that wait,
in high procession passing on
towards his temple-gate.

Give ear, ye kings - bow down,
ye rulers of the earth -
This, this is He; your Priest by grace,
your God and King by birth.

No pomp of earthly guards
attends with sword and spear,
and, all-defying, dauntless look
their monarch's way to clear:

yet there are more with him
than all that are with you -
the armies of the highest Heaven,
all righteous, good and true.

★　★　★

His throne, thy bosom blest,
O Mother undefiled -
that throne, if aught beneath the skies
beseems the sinless Child.

Lost in high thoughts, 'whose son
the wondrous Babe might prove,'
her guileless husband walks beside,
bearing the hallow'd dove.   (Lk. 2:24)

★　★　★

But who is he, by years
bow'd, but erect in heart,
whose prayers are struggling with his tears?
'Lord, let me now depart.   (Lk. 2:29)

'Now hath thy servant seen
thy saving health, O Lord:
'Tis time that I depart in peace,
according to thy word.'

Yet swells the pomp; one more   (Lk. 2:36)
comes forth to bless her God:
full fourscore years, meek widow, she
her heavenward way hath trod.

She who to earthly joys
so long had given farewell,
now sees, unlook'd for, Heaven on earth,
Christ in his Israel.

Wide open from that hour
the temple gates are set,
and still the saints rejoicing there
the holy Child have met.

★　★　★

Still to the lowly soul
he doth himself impart,
and for his dwelling and his throne
chooseth the pure in heart.

(sts. 7, 10, 16 omitted)

124
For SEPTUAGESIMA
Romans 1:20

HG 723

There is a book, who runs may read,   (Hab. 2:2)
which heavenly truth imparts,
and all the lore its scholars heed,
pure eyes and Christian hearts.

The works of God above, below,
within us and around,
are pages in that book, to show
how God himself is found.

The glorious sky embracing all
is like the Maker's love,
wherewith encompass'd, great and small
in peace and order move.

The Moon above, the Church below,
a wondrous race they run,
but all their radiance, all their glow
each borrows of its Sun.

★　★　★

One Name above all glorious names
with its ten thousand tongues
the everlasting Sea proclaims
echoing angelic songs.

The raging fire, the roaring Wind,   (Heb. 12:29)
thy boundless power display;
but in the gentler breeze we find   (Jn. 3:8)
thy Spirit's viewless way.

Two worlds are ours: 'Tis only sin
forbids us to descry
the mystic heaven and earth within,
plain as the sea and sky.

Thou, who hast given me eyes to see
and love this sight so fair,
Give me a heart to find out thee,
and read thee everywhere.

Sts. 5-8 omitted

SIR ROBERT GRANT
1779-1838

125
PSALM 104

HG 575

O worship the King,
  all glorious above,
O gratefully sing
  his power and his love;
our Shield and Defender,
  the Ancient of Days,
pavilioned in splendour
  and girded with praise.

O tell of his might,
  o sing of his grace,
whose robe is the light,
  whose canopy, space.

His chariots of wrath
  the deep thunder clouds form,
and dark is his path
  on the wings of the storm.

This earth, with its store
  of wonders untold,
Almighty, thy power
  hath founded of old;
hath stablished it fast
  by a changeless decree,
and round it hath cast
  like a mantle, the sea.

Thy bountiful care
   what tongue can recite?
It breathes in the air,
   it shines in the light;
it streams from the hills,
   it descends to the plain
and sweetly distils
   in the dew and the rain.

Frail children of dust,
   and feeble as frail,
in thee do we trust,
   nor find thee to fail;

thy mercies, how tender,
   how firm to the end,
our Maker, Defender,
   Redeemer and Friend.

O measureless might,
   Ineffable love,
while angels delight
   to hymn thee above,
thy humbler creation,
   though feeble their lays,
with true adoration
   shall lisp to thy praise.

Christian Psalmody (**E. Bickersteth**),
1833

HENRY FRANCIS LYTE
1793-1847
HG 5

126
PRAISE, MY SOUL!
Psalm 103

HG 597

Praise, my soul, the King of heaven;
   to his feet thy tribute bring!
Ransomed, healed, restored, forgiven,
   who like me his praise should sing?
     Praise Him! Praise Him!
Praise the everlasting King!

Praise Him for his grace and favour
   to our fathers in distress!
Praise him, still the same for ever,
   slow to chide, and swift to bless!
     Praise Him! Praise Him!
Glorious in his faithfulness!

Father-like, he tends and spares us;
   well our feeble frame he knows.
In his hands he gently bears us,
   rescues us from all our foes.
     Praise Him! Praise Him!
widely as his mercy flows.

Frail as summer's flower we flourish:
   blows the wind, and it is gone.
But, while mortals rise and perish,
   God endures unchanging on.
     Praise Him! Praise Him!
Praise the high eternal One!

Angels, help us to adore him;
   ye behold him face to face:
sun and moon, bow down before him;
   dwellers all in time and space.
     Praise Him! Praise Him!
Praise with us the God of grace!

The Spirit of the Psalms, 1834

127
MY BELOVED IS MINE, AND I AM HIS
HG 405

[The author adds to his title 'Imitated from Quarles,' referring to a poem by
Francis Quarles, 1592-1644, beginning 'Ev'n like two little bank-dividing brooks.'
The imitation consists in the use of the phrase which ends each stanza]

Long did I toil, and knew no earthly rest;
   far did I rove, and found no certain home:
at last I sought them in his sheltering breast,
   who opes his arms, and bids the weary come. (Matt. 11:28)
With him I found a home, a rest divine;
and I since then am his, and he is mine.

Yes, he is mine! and nought of earthly things,
   not all the charms of pleasure, wealth, or power,
the fame of heroes, or the pomp of kings,
   could tempt me to forego his love an hour.
Go, worthless world, I cry, with all that's thine!
Go! I my Saviour's am, and he is mine.

The good I have is from his stores supplied:
   the ill is only what he deems the best.
He for my Friend, I'm rich with nought beside;
   and poor without him, though of all possessed.
Changes may come - I take, or I resign,
content, while I am his, and he is mine.

Whate'er may change, in him no change is seen,
   a glorious Sun, that wanes not, nor declines:
above the clouds and storms he walks serene,
   and on his people's inward darkness shines.
All may depart - I fret not, nor repine,
while I my Saviour's am, and he is mine.

He stays me falling; lifts me up when down;
   reclaims me wandering; guards from every foe;
plants on my worthless brow the victor's crown,
   which in return before his feet I throw,
grieved that I cannot better grace his shrine,
who deigns to own me his, as he is mine.

While here, alas! I knew but half his love,
   but half discern him, and but half adore;
but when I meet him in the realms above,
   I hope to love him better, praise him more,
and feel, and tell, amid the choir divine,
how fully I am his, and he is mine.

Poems, chiefly religious, 1833

128
ABIDE WITH US, FOR IT IS TOWARD EVENING
Luke 24:29

HG 5

Abide with me! Fast falls the eventide;
The darkness thickens. Lord, with me abide.
When other helpers fail, and comforts flee,
Help of the helpless, O abide with me!

Swift to its close ebbs out life's little day;
earth's joys grow dim, its glories pass away;
change and decay in all around I see.
O Thou who changest not, abide with me!

Not a brief glance I beg, a passing word;
but as thou dwell'st with thy disciples, Lord,
familiar, condescending, patient, free, -
come, not to sojourn, but abide with me.

Come not in terrors, as the King of kings;
but kind and good, with healing in thy wings,
tears for all woes, a heart for every plea,
come, Friend of sinners, and abide with me.

Thou on my head in early youth didst smile;
and though rebellious and perverse meanwhile,
thou hast not left me, oft as I left thee.
On to the close, O Lord, abide with me!

I need thy presence every passing hour.
What but thy grace can foil the Tempter's power?
Who like thyself my guide and stay can be?
Through cloud and sunshine, O, abide with me.

I fear no foe with thee at hand to bless:
ills have no weight, and tears no bitterness.
Where is death's sting? Where, grave, thy victory? (1 Cor. 15:55)
I triumph still, if thou abide with me.

Hold thou thy cross before my closing eyes,
speak through the gloom, and point me to the skies;
Heaven's morning breaks, and earth's vain shadows flee!
In life, in death, O Lord, abide with me!

Manuscript of 1847; Remains, 1850

JOSEPH ANSTICE
1808-36
HG 536

129
THE HEEDLESS WORLD

When came in flesh the incarnate Word,
  the heedless world slept on,
and only simple shepherds heard
  that God had sent his Son.

When comes the Saviour at the last,
  from east to west shall shine
the awful pomp, and earth aghast
  shall tremble at the sign.

Then shall the pure of heart be blest;
  as mild he comes to them,
as when upon the Virgin's breast
  he lay at Bethlehem:

as mild to meek-eyed love and faith,
  only more strong to save;
strengthened by having bowed to death,
  by having burst the grave.

Lord, who could dare see thee descend
  in state, unless he knew
thou art the sorrowing sinner's friend,
  the gracious and the true?

Dwell in our hearts, O Saviour blest;
  so shall thine advent's dawn
'twixt us and thee, our bosom-guest,
  be but the veil withdrawn.

Hymns (posth.), 1836

ARTICLE 10:
EARLY 19TH CENTURY DISSENT (130-136)

The first third of the 19th century produces very little hymnody from the dissenting denominations who had shot their bolt in the previous age. Methodists saw no need to add to what John Wesley had collected for them in 1780: a book of about 500 hymns, most of which were his or his brother's. Baptists were similarly content with the work of their 18th-century writers, who mostly seemed to write what lasted a generation or two and then began to get tired. Samuel Medley and John Ryland were their best writers, but for the most part they were happy with Watts. Presbyterians of the non-Scottish kind had been troubled by dissensions which produced the Unitarian connection, reducing orthodox Presbyterianism to a small though elite body which, in pursuit of orthodoxy, was content with the metrical psalter.

It might have been so with the Congregationalists, who were in the direct line of succession from Isaac Watts, had it not been for an historical accident. During the 18th century, Congregational churches were self-governing bodies which, although their one constitutional document, the *Savoy Declaration*, 1658, explicitly warned them against it, tended to be isolationist. Evangelical pressures caused them, from about 1787 onwards, to group themselves in local 'Unions' by counties, and the same pressures eventually resulted in their forming themselves into a national 'Union' in 1831. (As a total group they were called 'The Congregational Union' from then until 1966, and 'The Congregational Church' from 1966 until they became in 1972 part of the United Reformed Church in England and Wales.) The formation of this national body, whose Assembly met first in 1832, was the occasion for the commissioning of a national hymnal, which appeared as the *Congregational Hymn Book* in 1836. As it happened, this released a small but important stream of new hymnody. Its general editor, Josiah Conder, happened to be a very gifted hymn writer.

Conder's work appears in ## 133-6, and it is very interesting in the way it reacts to the romantic hymnody of the Anglicans whom we have just been discussing. It is clearly founded on the style of Watts; ## 133 and, even more, 136 have the festive and theologically ecstatic touch of Watts, and Watts would have been proud of either. Perhaps in the tiny but perfect # 134 there is a touch of Wesley. But # 135 is a versification (one of several Conder made) of a Prayer Book Collect. All this, and a study of other hymns he wrote, places Conder as a dogmatic Calvinist with a cultural 'finish' which the earlier Calvinists did not aspire to. He is not naturalistic, not personal, not experimental; he adds the only kind of hymnody that a Calvinist body could find acceptable at that time. It is interesting that the Baptists formed themselves into a Union in 1813, but their first general hymnal did not appear until 1858, *Psalms and Hymns*, and in it they did not produce a figure comparable to Conder. The first Congregational hymnal was, of course, mostly Watts, and the later edition of 1855 contained nearly 300 hymns by him; but the fact that hymn-writing was never quite extinguished in Watts' own communion must be credited largely to the special genius of Conder.

Two other hymns by Congregationalists appear in this section. Andrew Reed's 'Spirit divine' (131) was written for a united Evangelical Good Friday service. (That small point indicates the objectivity with which people of that kind placed theology above the customs of the Church's Year; there is every possible theological reason for invoking the Holy Spirit on Good Friday when one remembers what is written in John 14:16.) But Thomas Binney's superb 'Eternal Light' (130), as a purely romantic hymn of the best sort, the Dissenting answer to 'Abide with me,' did not find a place in official Congregational hymnals until 1859, and perhaps this was because by that time

Binney had become so famous a leader in that church. Here indeed is the romantic 'distance,' the spiritual adventure, the mystical speculation, and the work of a man who was an artist through and through. (Binney's single-handed efforts to introduce poetry and order and beauty into Congregational worship were responsible for whatever resistance to philistinism that communion managed to raise in the 19th century; see our reference to him when we come to T. T. Lynch in article 14.)

The Society of Friends, as might be expected, produces few hymns, because the English form of that culture does not sing at worship. Most Quaker hymns come from 19th-century America or 20th-century Britain. Bernard Barton's very neat and orthodox meditation on Psalm 119:89 (132) deserves a place in any book and is probably the earliest Quaker hymn to remain in the repertory, although, naturally, it was not used by Quakers in his time.

THOMAS BINNEY
1798-1874

130
THE ETERNAL LIGHT   HG 171

Eternal Light! Eternal Light!
  how pure the soul must be,
when, placed within thy searching sight,
it shrinks not, but with calm delight
  can life, and look on thee.

The spirits that surround thy throne
  may bear the burning bliss;
but that is surely theirs alone,
since they have never, never known
  a fallen world like this.

O how shall I, whose native sphere
  is dark, whose mind is dim,
before th' Ineffable appear,
and on my naked spirit bear
  the uncreated beam?

There is a way for man to rise
  to that sublime abode;
an offering and a sacrifice,
a Holy Spirit's energies,
  an Advocate with God.

There, these prepare us for the sight
  of holiness above
the sons of ignorance and night
may dwell in the eternal light
  through the eternal love!

1826; in *Psalms and Hymns*, 1858

ANDREW REED
1787-1862

131
COME, GREAT SPIRIT!   HG 656

Spirit divine, attend our prayers,
  and make this house thy home;
descend with all thy gracious powers,
  O come, great Spirit, come!

Come as the light - to us reveal
  our emptiness and woe;
and lead us in the paths of life
  where all the righteous go.

Come as the fire - and purge our hearts
  like sacrificial flame;
let our whole soul an offering be
  to our Redeemer's name.

Come as the dew, and sweetly bless
  this consecrated hour;
may barrenness rejoice to own
  thy fertilizing power.

Come as the dove - and spread thy wings,
  the wings of peaceful love;
and let thy church on earth become
  blest as the church above.

Come as the wind - with rushing sound
  and pentecostal grace;
that all of woman born may see
  the glory of thy face.

Spirit divine, attend our prayers,
  make a lost world thy home;
descend with all thy gracious powers,
  O come, great Spirit, come!

Evangelical Magazine, June, 1829

BERNARD BARTON
1784-1849

132
LAMP OF OUR FEET
Ps. 119:105   HG 383

Lamp of our feet, whereby we trace
  our path when wont to stray;
stream from the fount of heavenly grace;
  brook by the traveller's way;

bread of our souls, whereon we feed,
  true manna from on high;
our guide and chart, wherein we read
  of realms beyond the sky;

pillar of fire through watches dark,
  or radiant cloud by day;
when waves would whelm our tossing bark,
  our anchor and our stay;

Word of the ever-living God,
  will of his glorious Son,
without thee how could earth be trod,
  or heaven itself be won?

Lord, grant that we aright may learn
  the wisdom it imparts,
and to its heavenly teaching turn
  with simple, childlike hearts.

The Reliquary, 1836; text modified, 1855

JOSIAH CONDER
1789-1855
HG 92

133
THE LORD IS KING
HG 701

The Lord is King; lift up thy voice,   (Ps. 99:1)
O earth, and all ye heavens rejoice.
From world to world the joy shall ring:
the Lord omnipotent is King.

The Lord is King; who then shall dare
resist his will, distrust his care,
or murmur at his wise decrees,
or doubt his royal promises?

The Lord is King; child of the dust,
the Judge of all the earth is just: (Gen. 18:25)
holy and true are all his ways;
let every creature speak his praise.

He reigns! ye saints, exalt your strains:
your God is King, your Father reigns;
and He is at the Father's side,
the Man of Love, the Crucified.   (Heb. 1:3)

Come, make your wants, your burdens known   (Heb. 4:16)
he will present them at the throne;
and angel bands are waiting there
his messages of love to bear.   (John 1:51)

O! when his wisdom can mistake,
his might decay, his love forsake,
then may his children cease to sing,
'The Lord omnipotent is King.'

Alike pervaded by his eye
all parts of his dominion lie;
this world of ours, and worlds unseen,
and thin the boundary between.

One Lord, one empire, all secures,
he reigns - and life and death are yours.   (1 Cor. 3:16)
Through earth and heaven one song shall ring:
'The Lord omnipotent is King.'

The Star in the East, 1824

134
BREAD OF HEAVEN
HG 92

Bread of heaven! on thee I feed,
for thy flesh is meat indeed.   (John 6:35)
Ever may my soul be fed
with this true and living bread:
day by day with strength supplied
through the life of him who died.

Vine of heaven! thy blood supplies
this blest cup of sacrifice.
'Tis thy wounds my healing give:
to thy cross I look, and live.
Thou my life! O let me be
rooted, grafted, built on Thee.   (Eph. 3:17)

The Star in the East, 1824

135
HEAD OF THE CHURCH

Head of the Church, our risen Lord!
who by thy Spirit dost preside
o'er the whole body; by whose word
they all are ruled and sanctified:

our prayers and intercessions hear
for all thy family at large,
that each, in his appointed sphere,
his proper service may discharge,

So, through the grace derived from thee,
in whom all fulness dwells above,
may thy whole church united be
and edify itself in love.

Congregational Hymn Book, 1836

136
THE EVERLASTING WORD

Thou art the everlasting Word,
    the Father's only Son;
God manifestly seen and heard,
    and heaven's beloved One:
Worthy, O Lamb of God, art thou
that every knee to thee should bow.

In thee, most perfectly expressed
    the Father's glories shine;
of the full deity possessed,
    eternally divine: . . .

True image of the infinite,   (Heb. 1:2)
    whose essence is concealed;
brightness of uncreated light;
    the heart of God revealed: . . .

But the high mysteries of thy name
    an angel's grasp transcend:
the Father only - glorious claim -
    the Son can comprehend: . . .   (Luke 10:22)

Yet loving thee, on whom his love
    ineffable doth rest,
thy glorious worshippers above
    as one with thee, are blest: . . .

Throughout the universe of bliss,
    the centre thou, and Sun,
the eternal theme of praise is this
    to heaven's beloved One:
Worthy, O Lamb of God, art thou
that every knee to thee should bow.

Congregational Hymn Book, 1836

ARTICLE 11:
HYMNS FROM LATIN SOURCES (137-176)

Latin hymnody has had so great an influence on English-speaking hymnody that it must be approached here from both ends. It appears so late in the course of this work because it did not make any notable impact on English hymn singing until the mid-nineteenth century. But although Martin Luther gave hymnody a 'new start,' there is a sense in which Latin hymnody is the source of all the rest.

(a) THE LATIN TEXTS

Latin hymnody begins with St Ambrose, Bishop of Milan (340-397). The Christian Church had received from the Emperor Constantine in 313 a legitimacy which it had never before had, and therefore it began only then to develop its public ministry. But already in the fourth century the Church was divided linguistically into the Greek-speaking half (in the East) and the Latin-speaking half (in the West); the metropolis of the Greek-speaking half was Byzantium (Constantinople), and that of the Latin-speaking half, Rome. The two halves of the church preserved always an uneasy détente until they finally separated in 1054 into what are still known as the Eastern Orthodox and the Roman Catholic communions. It seems as if the earliest hymnody of the Christian Church was certainly in Greek (see # 177), but the earliest public hymnody (so to call it) was in Latin. The pre-eminence of the Latin-speaking Church in the matter of discipline and organization is obviously connected with the fact that both halves of the church began their lives within the Roman empire.

Ambrose's hymnody is referred to more than once by his devoted friend and disciple, St Augustine of Hippo. Exactly what its purpose was is not as easy to determine as one might expect. There is, on the one hand, the *Te Deum Laudamus*, a prose composition which was at one time attributed to him but is now thought to have been composed a little later. On the other hand there is quite certainly our # 137, *Deus creator omnium*, which Augustine knew and quoted more than once.

Now, looking at that text, what does its purpose appear to have been? Why, it has two very clear subjects. The first is the personal discipline of the Christian community, and the second is the praise of God the Trinity in the final stanza (which is the oldest Latin doxology). Further, it is clearly a hymn to be sung at the close of the day. One theory of its origin is that it, and others like it, were composed by Ambrose for the comfort of Christians who were upholding the Faith during the Arian controversy (A.D. 325-381). That controversy produced situations close to civil war in many places; the nearest thing to it in modern times is the situation in Ireland from 1916 onwards. And the point of dispute was the relation between the first two Persons of the Trinity; the end-products included the so-called 'Nicene' Creed, and the patristic formulations of the Nature of Christ. Possibly hymns of this kind, with their affirmations of trinitarian belief in their doxologies, were another such product; and if, as some say, the Arians, finally judged unorthodox, invented the custom of setting their beliefs to music and singing them in defiance of the Christians from whom they separated themselves, it is plausible to believe that a gifted Christian writer like Ambrose would be moved to provide something for his own people to sing. If, further, the custom was to sing after the day's disputes and fightings had died down, this would explain the evening references.

But whether or not that is true, it is more important, and historically safer, to notice the other aspect of this text. This suggests a company of Christians living together under discipline. Such companies were indeed forming themselves just at this time. The great question whether Christianity was only for spiritual athletes, or whether the athletes were to be regarded as having a special role among a much larger company of 'ordinary' Christians, is as old as the days of St Paul. But for all sorts of reasons a movement began in the fourth century which ran an uninterrupted course, disputed by nobody, until at least the thirteenth century, based on the principle that while all souls in Christendom were regarded as the Church's charge, in every community it was necessary for there to be a company of specially committed souls who engaged in contemplation, prayer, and liturgy, and who, to all intents, did the ordinary people's praying for them.

These communities developed into those medieval monasteries which gathered to themselves not only a special Christian ministry but a monopoly of learning and culture. The only people who could read and write were members of these communities; they preserved the literature of Christianity and indeed became, through their monopoly, the censors of literature. What they did not write down did not get preserved, for from one age to another very different ideas of what it was proper for a Christian lay brother to transcribe and edit prevailed.

Inevitably then, the worship of God was controlled and fashioned in these communities. Mass was celebrated regularly, and on high days the laity would attend, though normally they would not in any modern sense participate. Ancillary services were gradually devised to punctuate the round of work and contemplation in which the monks were primarily engaged.

These services were known as 'offices' (duties), and they were performed solely by the members of the religious community. It was for these that the whole system of 'Office hymns' in the early middle ages was set up. And broadly speaking the period during which 'Office hymns' were written divides itself into the Early, running perhaps 200 years after Ambrose's time, and the Middle, running from about 600 to about 1100. The Later period is that in which other forms of hymnody principally flourished.

By about 1200 at the latest, all these communities had their Office-books and breviaries in which hymns of this sort were written. When one remembers that the church served by this hymnody reached from Sicily to Northumbria, it is not surprising that variations are found from one place to another; scholarly analyses of all this are readily available, and we need not pause here to go into them. The English-speaking versions of Latin hymnody are mostly based on the selections used at Sarum (Salisbury), with occasional additions from York.

Clearly, however, it did not all happen at once. Our # 138 is a good example of a very early hymn in the style of Ambrose, though not his own, and ## 139-144 can be taken closely with it. These five form the series of hymns composed probably in the Early period to go with the domestic Offices of the monasteries; ## 139-43 refer respectively to services held at 6 and 9 a.m. and at 6, and (about) 9 p.m.: # 144 is for 'Matins,' a service held in the small hours before dawn. (*Nocte surgentes*, 'Getting up in the middle of the night,' expresses this exactly; Dearmer's very good English version, for fairly obvious reasons, suppresses that particular point and turns it into a hymn to be sung after daybreak.)

The subject matter of all these hymns, apart from their doxologies, is still domestic and personal. (It may be noted that doxologies soon became adjustable units, so that one used different forms at different seasons; that would explain why Neale does not reflect the changed doxology in the text of # 143.) The morning suggests challenge, the evening, death. There are all manner of devices of the devil peculiar to the successive times of day against which the Christian prays to be defended. Indeed, the whole business looks to a modern Protestant Christian somewhat gloomy, and introverted. But two things have to be remembered: One is that the separateness and sanctity of the monastic life was a tough assignment and was believed to deliver substantial spiritual rewards, but at a high price; the other is that the objective praise of God was provided by the psalter, and hymns were still regarded as very much an appendix to the Psalms, which contained for these people the strong meat of Christian praise. The two things the Psalms do not mention are the monastic life and the doctrine of the Trinity. These the hymns provided, and they were not expected to provide more.

But as time went on it was natural for hymnody to develop a more didactic and imaginative style. Touches of typology and scriptural adventure appear in the series for the days of the week (EH 51-62), and in ## 145-50 in our series there is a handful of distinguished seasonal hymns that make the most of their opportunities. Note the scriptural richness of # 145, with its references to four very diverse examples of the efficacy of prayer and fasting before our Lord's ministry. No. 146 is especially rich at the beginning with its references to the Exodus, the white robes of baptismal candidates on Easter Eve, the altar as symbol of the Cross, and Christ's final triumph as a fulfilment of Scripture. Here at last we have real New Testament hymnody, real competition with the Psalter. No. 148 tells the Easter story in simpler and more strictly narrative terms. No. 149, by Ambrose, was found useful as soon as celebrations of seasonal and festive offices became the rule; # 150 expresses the heraldry of Michaelmas; and # 147, a very early hymn on the Trinity, is a good deal more than a formal doxology.

It will be noticed that two meters only are used for these hymns. One is the octosyllabic meter, which generated the English Long Meter and which was exclusively used by St Ambrose and his direct imitators. Rhyme is not used in the earlier examples of this meter; it is fitfully and inconsistently used a little later. The other meter is Sapphic, as in ## 144, 147, and 150; this, unlike octosyllables, was a classical Latin meter. If Pope Gregory I is the author of # 144, he probably introduced it to hymnody. Rhyme never appears in this meter, and it is one of the few traditional hymn meters which when used in English can with perfect naturalness dispense with rhyme.

(b) SEQUENCES

Nos. 151-3, with which # 1B can be taken, are examples of 'Sequence,' which is a quite different form of medieval hymnody. It originates with the setting of words to the musical flourishes that had grown up as glosses on the music of the 'Alleluia,' which is a liturgical unit in the Mass. The earliest we know of is # 151, which is in prose and is not seasonal. The Easter Sequence (1B) is not much later and is also in prose, though it is a little more regular and rhythmical. Nos. 152 and 153, a good deal later, are in verse and show how the Sequence, as it were, dropped off the Alleluia altogether and became a separate unit with its own tune. These, together with ## 10, 22, 172 and 253 in the English Hymnal, show also how Sequences came to be associated with especially festive occasions. The genesis of Sequences, indeed, exposes the tension so much felt in the medieval church at all stages between the impulse to extend music, especially on festivals, beyond what the texts required, and the more austere principle that suspected any music that was not adequately supported by words. Sequences developed for all the major festivals, and their later manifestations show a very high level of lyric artistry, as in the way every third line throughout # 152 follows the same rhyme independently of the other rhyming couplets (beautifully reflected in Neale's translation), and as in the tender diction and profound thought of the Dies Irae (153). Later medieval liturgies always found a place for these fine compositions.

(c) LATIN LYRIC

But many familiar hymns from the Latin are translated from poems which fall altogether outside the liturgical system, even though much later they found a place in it. Our # 164, a difficult case, cannot quite be so described; but the rest in the series 154-167 are the work of poets who, even when they wrote in hymn-like meters, did not necessarily expect their material to be sung in church.

Christian Latin lyric begins in the 4th century, and Prudentius (154, 155) was one of a circle of poets who had a special ministry to perform. There is always a danger that Christianity will part company with high culture. In that troubled time the danger was very great, and it was very much increased by the influence of Julian the Apostate, emperor 361-3, who, in the course of a reign of only 600 days, managed to have more influence on the society of his time than anybody except Constantine had had for the previous 200 years. That influence was wholly anti-Christian and pro-cultural; he made much of the legend, often before put about by Christianity's opponents, that the faith was fundamentally philistine, and could not hope to compete with true learning, philosophy, and poetry. As had happened before, and as until recently one could count on happening since, the effect on the Christians was to stimulate their best philosophical and poetic minds, Prudentius was one of these. No. 154 is part of a longer poem in the Ambrosian style, no doubt written in imitation of Ambrose, but # 155 introduced for the first time a new meter, and is a selection of verses from a long poem in defence of the faith designed to show that being a Christian did not prevent one's being either a poet or a reasoner. Most of it is less lyrical than the part which has now become so famous.

It should at once be noted that although many of these pieces now have tunes that are thought of as inseparable from them, the tunes were always set to them later than the time of their composition; the tune to # 155, for example, appears first in the 12th century.

Venantius Fortunatus (156), a younger contemporary of Justinian, living long after the fall of the Roman Empire, is perhaps the greatest of all the early lyricists. Pange Lingua, a panorama of the credal facts of Christ's life with its great peroration on the Cross, is very nearly untranslatable, and we have called in a team of translators to make our composite version. The other piece, its companion in octosyllables, Vexilla Regis, has defeated every known translator so far, which is the only reason we omit it here.* We are here in a very different literary world from that of the Office hymns.

The earliest known British hymn, # 157, has much in common with the Middle period Office hymns for festal occasions; and the excellent and mystical Urbs Beata (158) builds on the foundation of Fortunatus. (The note given with the hymn is important for its understanding.)

'All glory, laud and honour' (159) is a popular rendering of a piece in the most famous of the classical lyric meters—Elegiacs. Fortunatus had used this meter for his Salve Festa Dies (see EH 624, 628 etc.). It was brought to its height in secular poetry by Ovid. This and # 160 are the two Latin lyrics, apart from Office hymns, that seem to have survived from the depths of the so-called Dark Ages.

Veni Creator (160) is another hymn that looks like an Office

*See EH 94 for Neale's orthodox translation and the Canadian Hymn Book (1971) 445 for a very good, though incomplete, rendering by J. W. Grant. (Here and elsewhere EH signifies the English Hymnal, 1906 and 1933.)

hymn, but is not; it is a devotional prayer to the Holy Spirit which has by long tradition been especially associated with ordinations. More about this when we deal with the translations.

Peter Abélard (161, 551) was, as is well known, the most acute philosopher of his time, but he was also a supreme poet. He wrote these and several other hymns for the House of the Paraclete, of which Heloise became Abbess. Here is another new meter, unexampled in Christian Latin literature, complete with a fully worked-out rhyme scheme.

The incredible *Hora Novissima* (162) was originally a satirical poem of 2,966 lines mostly devoted to the corruptions and social evils of church and state in medieval Europe. The part that Neale translated is that which contrasts the delights of heaven with these unpleasantnesses. Here again we have a unique Latin meter, all-dactylic hexameters, which only a poet of quite unusual dexterity could have attempted. This, of course, was never intended to be sung and never was used as a hymn until Neale translated it.

No more was the equally celebrated # 163 (implausibly attributed to the Abbot who became prosecuting counsel when Abélard was indicted for heresy) designed for singing; it was a 42-stanza meditation on the love of Christ in the Ambrosian style, with an intermittent rhyme-scheme that is not carried through the whole poem.

That brings us to ## 164 and 165. No. 164 was composed by St Thomas Aquinas at the invitation of the reigning Pope, about 1263, for the new Office of Corpus Christi and looks like one of the first hymns written in this fashion 'to order'; two others accompanied it, the *Verbum Supernum* (EH 330) and *Lauda Sion*, (EH 317), the second of which is roughly in the form of a metrical Sequence. No. 165 is still attributed to St Thomas by hymnal editors, but it has been shown by the British scholar F. J. E. Raby not to have been his. The three authentic hymns all begin with a first line already familiar in medieval worship. No. 164 shares its first line with # 156; it rehearses the actual story of the Last Supper in language that makes an extended interpretative note necessary at the hymn. No. 165 is simpler and, unlike the three by St Thomas, highly personal. The reference to the 'Pelican' in st. 6 recalls the ancient belief that the pelican feeds her young with her own blood.

Another medieval devotion of great poetic beauty is *Stabat Mater*, 166, of which some stanzas are well known in English. It will be seen how rhyme is now firmly established. (St Thomas uses it; Fortunatus, in the hymn whose first line he echoes, did not.)

Almost at the end of the Middle Ages, St Thomas à Kempis wrote a good deal of poetry which was fairly soon found to make good hymnody, and # 167 is the best known and finest example of that.

(d) LATER LYRICS

Hymnody in the Roman Catholic Church did not stop with the Middle Ages. For a while it died down. The Council of Trent incepted the counter-Reformation with a thorough overhaul of liturgical procedures and a revision of hymn texts which eventually produced the *Roman Breviary*, in which the various usages that had become current in different places during the late Middle Ages were organized into a single system. While this went on, and for a time afterwards, no new hymnody was called for. Our # 168, which comes from the very turn of the Middle Ages, is a narrative carol that had no liturgical place then or later, agreeable though it has proved to be for modern singers.

But there was a great deal of tune-writing, especially in Germany, where a considerable stream of hymnals appeared in the last century. One of these produced the now universally loved tune LASST UNS ERFREUEN, 'All creatures of our God and King.' No. 169 is a text that was slipped into one of these hymnals.

France, in the next generation or two, was the scene of a considerable liturgical revival in the course of which many new Latin texts were written, especially by de Santeuil (170-1) and Coffin (173-4). Indeed a glance over this handful of hymns, ## 169-176, indicates that there was a certain amount of activity all over Europe. No. 176 comes from Portugal. But it was in France that the greatest activity seems to have taken place, and this included the adaptation and composition of a whole series of new metric tunes to provide music for people for whom the obligatory plainsong of the counter-Reformation was proving too demanding. The subject matter of these new hymns varied considerably, taking in all the mannerisms of the old medieval hymnody without usually adding much to them. The old domestic 'in group' Office hymn is reflected in # 174, the seasonal Office hymn in ## 170-1, the devotional lyric in # 176.

Nos. 172 and 175, now among the twenty most-used hymns in all Christendom, are especially popular products of this revival. *Veni Immanuel* is a versification of part of the late medieval devotion called the 'Great O's of Advent' or 'the O antiphons' (for an English text see *EH* 734), never quite complete and a popular rather than liturgical piece in that it clearly intends all the stanzas to be sung consecutively, whereas the 'Great O's' were designed to be said one sentence at a time on each of the eight days before Christmas. *Adeste Fideles*, its original text being sts. 1-2, 7-8 of the version we have here, is, almost certainly, the composition of an English music copyist who spent most of his life at Douay in France, right in the heart of the liturgical revival. It is, as it is now given, one of the few hymns written by three identifiable hands.

(e) THE TRANSLATORS

The impulse to translate Latin hymns came from the Oxford Movement, one of whose aims was the revival of medieval liturgies and values. That Movement is dated from 1833 and it is clear at once that the translators lost no time in beginning their work. One of the first shots to be fired must have been Isaac Williams' eloquent translation at # 170, which was in the British Magazine in 1836 before being included in his large collection of *Hymns Translated from the Paris Breviary*, 1839. The other translators of this first generation represented in our collection were John Chandler, 1806-76 (*Hymns of the Primitive Church*, 1837), Edward Caswall, 1814-87 (*Lyra Catholica*, 1849), and John Mason Neale, 1818-66. John Henry Newman (## 440-442), one of the Movement's leaders, produced a number of translations of which we do not here have an example; another leader, Keble, wrote all his hymns before the Movement began (see 121-4).

The chief problem before a translator, as we shall see again when we come to the German hymns, is in the tension between the demands of faithful transcription and those of his own poetic imagination. It will be noticed that Williams, Caswall, and Chandler have no scruples about altering the meter of the original. Williams, in our example (170), uses an old English meter; so does Chandler in # 139, and so does Caswall in ## 154 and 163A. Their object then was to make the old Latin look like an English hymn; Williams certainly allows his expansive meter to give him scope for plenty of vivid writing. The problem is made much more difficult when a translator tries so to translate that the original tune—if there is one ascertainable—can be sung to the English version, that is, to keep the original meter. Now it has often been said of Neale, and of those who amended or imitated him, that their translations read stiffly and creakily in places, and we have to admit that Neale is the father of the pedantic 'translator's English' that has brought the Office hymns and saints-day hymns into disrepute among many. It has to be remembered, of course, that Neale must have worked incredibly fast. To produce the contents of the *Hymnal Noted*, 1852, (our chief source for his versions from Latin), together with nearly everything else he translated from Latin, well before his fortieth year, he must have worked at high pressure. There were also original hymns and carols in his collection by then; only the Greek originals seem to have occupied him later. But the truth is, as anyone can see, that it is when he can choose his meter that his poetic instinct is allowed the needful freedom. We find this especially in *Hora Novissima* (162), which has verse after verse of ecstatic and resounding beauty. In two other well-known cases in our book he abandons the original meter: in # 159, 'All glory, laud and honour,' though here he did indeed make another translation in elegiacs so that the plainsong tune could be used (it is a poorish piece compared with the justly popular version we know); and in 'O quanta qualia,' # 161, which had no 'proper tune' and where he felt free to give up the ferocious challenge of reproducing Abélard's continuous rhyming dactyls. (His translation is everywhere accessible, 'O what their joy and their glory must be'; we have substituted Ronald Knox's because it is rather closer to the original meter.)

But Neale must be honoured as an industrious worker who not infrequently produced a fine version and who set an example upon which others improved (whose later versions we often substitute for his), but which, without the initial challenge of his imperfections, they might never have used as an occasion for developing their gifts.

One other translator whose neglect of original meters paid dividends in good writing was J. R. Woodford. It is very unusual to see an original in L. M. reduced in meter so drastically as he reduces that of # 173; but his six-syllable lines achieve a quite remarkable spaciousness. His translation of part of # 165 we thought too well known to need a place here, since it is incomplete; but it makes a very good English hymn, and with a little cheating actually goes to the tune associated with the original. (See *EH* 331.)

Only one American translator of Latin texts finds a place in this section—that very fine writer, Ray Palmer (163B, 169B). He keeps the meter of 163, but abandons that of 169; in both cases he produces very good literature indeed.

For the rest, we refer the reader to the *Hymnal Guide* for information about the more modern translators we have pressed into service, noting only that at # 174 we have an unusual piece in a translation by a 20th-century English Presbyterian of the 17th-century text by Charles Coffin. Leslie Bunn has not only translated it, but translated it with surpassing grace, and since this is his only extant contribution to hymnody (he was one of the most learned hymnologists of his age), we are glad to pay tribute to him here.

Office Hymns

137
DEUS CREATOR OMNIUM

[The original of this hymn by St Ambrose is quoted twice by St Augustine; once, in *De Musica* (c. 389) as an example of meter, and again in his Confessions (c. 410) where he tells how it comforted him on the evening of the day of his mother's funeral. It can be regarded as the text which inspired the creation of the later system of Office hymns, and therefore, in the translation provided by the *English Hymnal*, stands first in this section]

Creator of the earth and sky,
ruling the firmament on high,
clothing the day with robes of light,
blessing with gracious sleep the night,

that rest may comfort weary men
and brace to useful toil again,
and soothe awhile the harrassed mind,
and sorrow's heavy load unbind,

day sinks; we thank thee for thy gift;
night comes; and once again we lift
our prayer and vows and hymns, that we
against all ills may shielded be.

Thee let the secret heart acclaim,
thee let our tuneful voices name,
round thee our chaste affections cling,
thee sober reason own as King;

that when black darkness closes day,
and shadows thicken round our way,
faith may no darkness know, and night
from faith's clear beam may borrow light.

Rest not, my heaven-born mind and will:
rest, all ye thoughts and deeds of ill;
may faith its watch unwearied keep,
and cool the dreaming warmth of sleep.

From cheats of sense, Lord, keep me free,
and let my heart's depth dream of thee;
let not my envious foe draw near,
to break my rest with any fear.

Pray we the Father and the Son,
and Holy Ghost: O Three in One,
Blest Trinity, whom all obey,
guard thou thy sheep by night and day.

ST AMBROSE, 339-397. Tr. **Charles Bigg**, 1906

138
CHRISTE QUI LUX ES ET DIES

[This, written in imitation of St Ambrose's style, and certainly earlier than 532, when it is first referred to, became one of the most widely used of all 'Office hymns' when the system was brought into use in the Middle period. It is also the text of several motets by well-known Tudor composers]

Christe qui lux es et dies,
noctis tenebras detegis,
lucisque lumen crederis
lumen beatum praedicans;

precamur, sancte Domine,
defende nos in hac nocte;
sit nobis in te requies,
quietam noctem tribue.

O Christ, who art the Light and Day,
thou drivest darksome night away!
We know thee as the Light of light,
illuminating mortal sight.

All-holy Lord, we pray to thee,
keep us tonight from danger free;
grant us, dear Lord, in thee to rest,
so be our sleep in quiet blest.

oculi somnum capiant,

cor ad te semper vigilet,
dextera tua protegat
famulos qui te diligunt.

defensor noster aspice,
insidiantes reprime,
guberna tuos famulos,

quos sanguine mercatus es.

memento nostri, Domine,
in gravi isto corpore,
qui es defensor animae,

adesto nobis, Domine.

Deo Patri sit gloria,

eiusque soli Filio,
cum Spiritu Paraclito,

et nunc et in perpetuum.

And while the eyes soft slumber
take,
still be the heart to thee awake;
be thy right hand upheld above
thy servants resting in thy love.

Yea, our Defender, be thou nigh
to bid the powers of darkness fly:
keep us from sin, and guide for
good
thy servants purchased by thy
Blood.

Remember us, dear Lord, we pray,
while in this mortal flesh we stay:
'Tis thou who dost the soul
defend -
be present with us to the end.

Blest Three in One and One in
Three,
Almighty God, we pray to thee
that thou wouldst now vouchsafe
to bless
our fast with fruits of righteousness.

Early period

Hymns of the
Little Hours

W. J. COPELAND (HG 499), 1848

139   HG 854

[PRIME]
Iam lucis orto sidere
Deum precemur supplices
ut in diurnis actibus
nos servet a nocentibus.

linguam refraenans temperet

ne litis horror insonet;

visum fovendo contegat

ne vanitates hauriat.

sint pura cordis intima,

absistat et vecordia,
carnis terat superbiam

potus cibique parcitas.

ut cum dies abscesserit
noctemque sors reduxerit
mundi per abstinentiam

ipsi canamus gloriam.

Deo Patri sit gloria
eiusque soli Filio
sancto simul cum Spiritu
nunc et per omne saeculum.

Now that the daylight fills the sky
we lift our hearts to God on high,
that he, in all we do or say,
would keep us free from harm
to-day,

would guard our hearts and
tongues from strife,
from anger's din would hide our
life:
from all ill sights would turn our
eyes:
would close our ears from vanities:

would keep our inmost conscience pure;
our souls from folly would secure:
would bid us check the pride of
sense
with due and holy abstinence.

So we, when this new day is gone,
and night in turn is drawing on,
with conscience by the world
unstained
shall praise his name for victory
gained.

All laud to God the Father be;
all laud, eternal Son, to thee;
all laud, as is for ever meet
to God the Holy Paraclete.

140

[TERCE]
Nunc sancte nobis Spiritus,

unum Patri cum Filio,
dignare promptus ingeri

nostro refusus pectori.

Os, lingua, mens, sensus, vigor

confessionem personent;

flammescat igne caritas,

accendat ardor proximos.

praesta, Pater piissime,
Patrique compar unice,

cum Spiritu Paraclito,
et nunc et in perpetuum.

Come, Holy Ghost, with God the
Son,
and God the Father, ever one:
shed forth thy grace within our
breast,
and dwell with us, a ready guest.

By every power, by heart and
tongue,
by act and deed, thy praise be
sung:
inflame with perfect love each
sense,
that others' souls may kindle
thence.

O Father, that we ask be done,
through Jesus Christ, thine only
Son,
who with the Holy Ghost and thee
shall live and reign eternally.

141

[SEXT]
Rector potens, verax Deus,
qui temperas rerum vices,

splendore mane illuminas
et ignibus meridiem.

Extingue flammas litium,
aufer calorem noxium,
confer salutem corporum

verumque pacem cordium.

praesta, Pater piissime,
Patrique compar unice,

cum Spiritu Paraclito,
et nunc et in perpetuum.

O God of Truth, O Lord of might,
who orderest time and change
aright,
and send'st the early morning ray,
and light'st the glow of perfect
day;

extinguish thou each sinful fire,
and banish every ill desire:
and while thou keep'st the body
whole,
shed forth thy peace upon the
soul.

O Father, that we ask be done
through Jesus Christ, thine only
Son,
who with the Holy Ghost and thee
shall live and reign eternally.

142

[NONE]
Rerum Deus tenax vigor,
immotus in te permanens,

lucis diurnae tempora

successibus determinans,

largire lumen vespere,

quo vita nusquam decidat,

sed praemium mortis sacrae
perennis instet gloria.

O God, creation's secret force,
thyself unmoved, all motion's
source,
who from the morn till evening's
ray
through all its changes guid'st the
day,

grant us, when this short life is
past,
the glorious evening that shall
last:
that by a holy death attained
eternal glory may be gained.

praesta, Pater piissime,
Patrique compar unice,

cum Spiritu Paraclito,
et nunc et in perpetuum.

O Father, that we ask be done
through Jesus Christ, thine only
Son,
who with the Holy Ghost and thee
shall live and reign eternally.

143   HG 878

[COMPLINE]
Te lucis ante terminum,
rerum creator, poscimus,
ut pro tua clementia
sis praesul et custodia.

Before the ending of the day,
Creator of the world, we pray
that with thy wonted favour, thou
wouldst be our guard and keeper
now.

procul recedant somnia

et noctium phantasmata,
hostemque nostrum comprime
ne polluantur corpora.

From all ill dreams defend our
eyes,
from nightly fears and fantasies;
tread under foot our ghostly foe
that no pollution we may know.

praesta, Pater omnipotens,
per Jesum Christum Dominum,

qui tecum in perpetuum

regnat cum sancto Spiritu.

* O Father, that we ask be done
through Jesus Christ thine only
Son,
who with the Holy Ghost and
thee
shall live and reign eternally.

Early period

J. M. NEALE (HG 2), 1852
* see preceding article

144   HG 862

[MATINS]
Nocte surgentes vigilemus omnes,
semper in psalmis meditemur, atque
    viribus totis Domino canamus
        dulciter hymnos.

ut pio regi pariter canentes
cum suis sanctis mereamur aulam
    ingredi coeli, simul et beatam
        ducere vitam.

praestet hoc nobis Deitas beata
Patris et Nati pariterque sancti
    Spiritus, cuius reboatur omni
        gloria mundo.

? ST GREGORY, 540-604

- - - - - - - -

Father, we praise thee, now the night is over,
active and watchful, stand we all before thee;
    singing, we offer prayer and meditation:
        thus we adore thee.

Monarch of all things, fit us for thy mansions;
banish our weakness, health and wholeness sending;
    bring us to heaven, where thy saints united
        joy without ending.

All holy Father, Son and equal Spirit,
Trinity blessed, send us thy salvation;
    thine is the glory, gleaming and resounding
        through all creation.

PERCY DEARMER (HG 88), 1906

145

Clarum decus ieiunii
monstratur orbi caelitus.
quod Christus auctor omnium

cibis dicavit abstinens.

The glory of these forty days
we celebrate with songs of praise;
for Christ, by whom all things
were made
himself has fasted and has prayed.

hob Moyses carus Deo (Ex. 19:
14, 19)
legisque lator factus est;
hos Heliam per aera (3 Kgs. 19:
5-6)
curru levavit igneo. (4 Kgs. 2:11)

Alone and fasting Moses saw

the loving God who gave the Law;
and to Elijah, fasting, came

the steeds and chariots of flame

hinc Daniel mysteria (Dan. 6:
16-28)
victor leonum viderat;
per hoc amicus intimus (Jn. 3:
29)
sponsi Iohannes claruit.

So Daniel trained his mystic sight,

delivered from the lion's might;
and John, the Bridegroom's
friend, became
the herald of Messiah's name.

haec nos sequi dona, Deus,

exempla parsimoniae;

tu robur auge mentium

dans spiritale gaudium

Then grant us, Lord, like them to
be
full oft in fast and prayer with
thee;
our spirits strengthen with thy
grace,
and give us joy to see thy face.

praesta, Pater, per Filium,
praesta per almum Spiritum,
cum his per aevum triplici
unus Deus cognomine.

Father and Son and Spirit blest,
to thee be every prayer addrest.
who art in threefold Name adored
from age to age, the only Lord.

Middle period
(possibly of English origin)

MAURICE F. BELL (HG 838), 1906

146
EASTER   HG 833

Ad coenam Agni providi,

et stolis albis candidi,

post transitum Maris Rubri

Christo canamus Principi;

The Lamb's high banquet we
await,
in snow-white robes of royal
state:
and now, the Red Sea's channel
past,
to Christ our Prince we sing at last.

cuius corpus sanctissimum
in ara Crucis torridum:
cruore eius roseo
gustando, vivimus Deo.

Upon the Altar of the Cross
his body hath redeemed our loss:
and tasting of his roseate blood,
our life is hid with him in God.

Protecti Paschae vespero

a devastante Angelo,
erepti de durissimo

Pharaonis imperio.

That Paschal Eve God's arm was
bared,
the devastating Angel spared:
by strength of hand our hosts
went free
from Pharaoh's ruthless tyranny.

Iam Pascha nostrum Christus est,

qui immolatus Agnus est:

sinceritatis azyma
caro eius oblata est.

Now Christ our Paschal Lamb is
slain,
the Lamb of God that knows no
stain,
the true Oblation offered here,
our own unleavened Bread sincere.

O vere dignis Hostia,

per quam fracta sunt Tartara,
redempta plebs captivata
reddita vitae praemia.

consurgit Christus tumulo,
Victor redit de barathro,

tyrannum trudens vinculo

et reserans Paradisum.

Gloria tibi Domine,

qui surrexisti a mortuis,
cum Patre et sancto Spiritu
in sempiterna saecula.

Middle period

O Thou, from whom hell's monarch flies,
O great, O very Sacrifice,
thy captive people are set free,
and endless life restored in thee.

For Christ, arising from the dead,
from conquered hell victorious
sped:
and thrust the tyrant down to
chains,
and Paradise for man regains.

To thee who, dead, again dost
live,
all glory, Lord, thy people give;
all glory, as is ever meet,
to Father and to Paraclete.

J. M. NEALE (HG 2), 1852

147
TO THE TRINITY
HG 866

O Pater sancte mitis atque pie,
o Jesu Christe Fili venerande
paracliteque Spiritus o alme,
    Deus aeterne,

trinitas sancta unitasque firma,
deitas vera, bonitas immensa,
lus angelorum, salus orphanorum,
    spesque cunctorum,

serviunt tibi cuncta quae creasti;
te tuae cunctae laudant creaturae;
nos quoque tibi psallimus devoti;
    tu nos exaudi.

gloria tibi, omnipotens Deus,
trinus et unus, magnus et excelsus;
te decet hymnus, honor laus et decus   (Ps. 65:1)
    nunc et in aevum.

- - - - - - - - -

Father most holy, merciful and loving,
Jesu, Redeemer, ever to be worshipped,
life-giving Spirit, Comforter most gracious,
    God everlasting;

three in a wondrous Unity unbroken,
one perfect Godhead, love that never faileth,
light of the angels, succour of the needy,
    hope of all living;

all thy creation serveth its creator,
thee every creature praiseth without ceasing;
we too would sing thee psalms of true devotion:
    hear, we beseech thee.

Lord God almighty, unto thee be glory,
one in three Persons, over all exalted.
Thine, as is meet, be honour, praise and blessing
    now and for ever.

A. E. ALSTON, 1904

148
EASTER SONG
HG 837

Aurora lucis rutilat,

caelum laudibus intonat,

mundus exultans iubilat,

gemens infernus ululat,

cum rex ille fortissimus

mortis confractis viribus,

pede conculcans tartara,

solvit catena miseros.

ille, qui clausus lapide

custoditur cum milite,

triumphans pompa nobili
victor surgit de funere.

solutis iam gemitibus

et inferni doloribus,
quia 'surrexit Dominus'

resplendens clamat angelus.

. . . . .

tristes erant apostoli

de nece sui Domini
quem poena mortis crudeli

saevi damnarunt impii.

. . . . .

sermone blando angelus
praedixit mulieribus:
'in Galilaea Dominus

videndus est quantocius.'

illae dum pergunt concite

apostolis hoc dicere,
videntes eum vivere

osculantur pedes Dei.

quo agnito, discipuli

in Galilaeam propere
pergunt, videre faciem

desideratam Domini.

. . . . .

claro paschali gaudio
sol mundo nitet radio
cum Christum iam apostoli

visu cernunt corporeo.

Light's glittering morn bedecks
the sky,
heaven thunders forth its victor-
cry;
the glad earth shouts its triumph
high,
and groaning hell makes wild
reply,

while he the King of glorious
might
treads down Death's strength in
Death's despite,
and trampling Hell by victor's
right,
brings forth his sleeping saints to
light.

Fast barred beneath the stone of
late
in watch and ward where soldiers
wait,
now shining in triumphant state,
he rises victor from death's gate.

Hell's pains are loosed, and tears
are fled;
captivity is captive led;
the angel, crowned with light,
hath said,
'The Lord is risen from the dead.'

. . . . .

The Apostles' hearts were full of
pain,
for their dear Lord so lately slain,
that Lord his servants' wicked
train
with bitter scorn had dared ar-
raign.

. . . . .

With gentle voice the angel gave
the women tidings at the grave;
'Forthwith your Master shall ye
see:
he goes before to Galilee.'

And while with fear and joy they
pressed
to tell these tidings to the rest,
their Lord, their living Lord, they
meet,
and see his form, and kiss his feet.

The Eleven, when they hear, with
speed
to Galilee forthwith proceed;
that there they may behold once
more
their Lord's dear face, as oft before.

. . . . .

In this our bright and paschal day
the sun shines out with purer ray:
when Christ, to earthly sight made
plain,
the glad Apostles see again.

ostensa sibi vulnera	The wounds, the riven wounds he shows
in Christi carne fulgida	in that his flesh with light that glows,
resurrexisse Dominum	with public voice both far and nigh
voce fatentur publica.	the Lord's arising testify.
rex Christe clementissime,	O Christ, the King who lov'st to bless,
tu corda nostra posside,	do thou our hearts and souls possess;
ut tibi laudes debitas	to thee our praise that we may pay
reddamus omni tempore.	to whom our laud is due, for ay.
+ + + + +	+ + + + +
quaesumus, auctor omnium,	We pray thee, King with glory decked,
in hoc paschali gaudio	in this our Paschal joy, protect
ab omni mortis impetu	from all that death would fain affect
tuum defende populum.	thy ransomed flock, thine own elect.
gloria tibi, Domine	To thee who, dead, again dost live,
qui surrexisti a mortuis,	all glory, Lord, thy people give:
cum patre et sancto spiritu	all glory, as is ever meet,
in sempiterna saecula.	to Father and to Paraclete.

Early period   **J. M. NEALE** (HG 2), 1852

(Note: In early liturgies the hymn was divided either in two parts, the first ending at st. 5, or in three, the first ending at st. 4, the second at st. 8; in either case the two doxology verses were sung after any separated part. The hymn 'That Easter day with joy was bright,' very well known in the USA, is the revision of the last 5 stanzas of this hymn made in *Hymns Ancient and Modern*, 1861. Neale's original, although less smooth than the revision, is here given to show how, in sts. 1-6, he preserves a four-line rhyme, which the Latin author abandoned after st. 1.)

149
FOR APOSTLES   HG 690

Aeterna Christi munera	Th' eternal gifts of Christ the King,
apostolorum gloriam	th' Apostles' glorious deeds, we sing:
palmas et hymnos debitos	and while due hymns of praise we pay,
laetis canamus mentibus;	our thankful hearts cast grief away.
ecclesiarum principes,	The church in these her princes boasts,
belli triumphales duces,	these victor chiefs of warrior hosts:
caelestis aulae milites,	the soldiers of the heavenly hall,
et vera mundi lumina.	the lights that rose on earth for all.
devota sanctorum fides,	'Twas thus the yearning faith of Saints,
invicta spes credentium,	th' unconquered hope that never faints,
perfecta Christi caritas	the love of Christ that knows not shame,
mundi tyrannum conterit.	the Prince of this world overcame.
in his Paterna gloria,	In these the Father's glory shone;
in his voluntas Spiritus,	in these the will of God the Son;
in his triumphat Filius,	in these exults the Holy Ghost;
coelum repletur gaudio.	through these rejoice the heavenly host.

Patri, simulque Filio,	Redeemer, hear us of thy love,
tibique sancte Spiritus,	that, with the glorious band above,
sicut fuit, sit iugiter	hereafter, of thine endless grace
saeclum per omne gloria.	thy servants also may have place.

ST AMBROSE (HG 865), 339-397
Roman Breviary Text

J. M. NEALE (HG 2), 1852

150
SAINT MICHAEL AND ALL ANGELS   HG 112

Christe, sanctorum decus angelorum,
gentis humanae sator et Redemptor,
caelitum nobis tribuas beatas
    scandere sedes.

Angelus pacis Michael in sedes
caelitus nostras veniat, serenae
auctor ut pacis lacrimosa in orcum
    bella releget.

Angelus fortis Gabriel, ut hostes
pellat antiquos at amica caelo,
quae triumphator statuit per orbem,
    templa revisat.

Angelus nostrae medicus salutis
adsit e caelo Raphael, ut omnes
sanet aegrotos dubiosque vitae
    dirigat actus.

Virgo dux pacis genetrixque lucis
et sacer nobis chorus angelorum
semper assistat, simul et micantis
    regia coeli.

? **RABANUS MAURUS**, 10th cent.

- - - - - - - - - - -

Christ, the fair glory of the holy angels,
thou who hast made us, thou who o'er us rulest,
grant of thy mercy unto us thy servants
    steps up to heaven.

Send thy Archangel, Michael, to our succour;
peacemaker blessed, may he banish from us
striving and hatred, so that for the peaceful
    all things may prosper.

Send thy Archangel, Gabriel the mighty;
herald of heaven, may he from us mortals
spurn the old serpent, watching o'er the temples
    where thou art worshipped.

Send thy Archangel, Raphael the restorer
of the misguided ways of men who wander,
who at thy bidding strengthens soul and body
    with thine anointing.

May the blest Mother of our God and Saviour,
may the assembly of the saints in glory,
may the celestial companies of angels
    ever assist us.

ATHELSTAN RILEY, 1906

Sequences

151
THE ALLELUIATIC SEQUENCE

Cantemus cuncti melodum nunc 'Alleluia'

The strain upraise of joy and praise, 'Alleluia!'

in laudibus aeterni regis
haec plebs resultet, Alleluia!

to the glory of our King
let the ransomed people sing, 'Alleluia!'

hoc denique caelestes chori
cantant in altum, Alleluia!

And the choirs that dwell on high
shall re-echo through the sky, 'Alleluia!'

hoc beatorum per prata
paradisiaca
psallat concentus Alleluia!

they through the fields of Paradise
that roam,
the blessed ones, repeat through
that bright home, 'Alleluia!'

quin et astrorum micantia
luminaria
iubilent altum Alleluia!

the planets glittering on their
heavenly way,
the shining constellations join and
say, 'Alleluia!'

nubium cursus, ventorum volatus,
fulgurum coruscatio
et tonitruum sonitus

Ye clouds that onward sweep,
ye winds on pinions light,
ye thunders, echoing loud and
deep,

dulce consonent simul Alleluia!

ye lightnings wildly bright
in sweet consent unite your
Alleluia!

fluctus et undae,
imber et procellae,
tempestas et serenitas,
cauma, gelu, nix, pruinae,
saltus, nemora, pangant Alleluia!

Ye floods and ocean billows!
Ye storms and winter snow!
Ye days of cloudless beauty,
Hoar frost and summer glow!
Ye groves that wave in spring
and glorious forests, sing, 'Alle-
luia!'

hinc variae volucres creatorem

First let the birds, with painted
plumage gay,

laudibus concinite cum Alleluia!

exalt their great Creator's praise,
and say 'Alleluia!'

ast illinc respondeant voces altae

Then let the beasts of earth, with
varying strain

diversarum bestiarum, Alleluia!

join in Creation's hymn, and cry
again, 'Alleluia!'

Istinc montium celsi vertices
sonent Alleluia!

Here let the mountains thunder
forth sonorous, 'Alleluia!'

illinc vallium profunditates

there, let the valleys sing in gentler

saltent Alleluia!

chorus, 'Alleluia!'

tu quoque maris iubilans abysse,
dic Alleluia!

Thou jubilant abyss of ocean cry
'Alleluia!'

nec non terrarum molis

ye tracts of earth and continents
reply,

immensitates, Alleluia!

'Alleluia!'

nunc omne genus humanum
laudans
exultet Alleluia!

To God who all creation made

et creatori grates frequentans
consonet Alleluia!

the frequent hymn be duly paid
'Alleluia!'

hoc denique nomen audire igitur
delectatur Alleluia!

This is the strain, the eternal strain,
the Lord of all things loves:
'Alleluia!'

hoc etiam carmen caeleste
comprobat
ipse Christus Alleluia!

This is the song, the heavenly
song, that
Christ himself approves:
'Alleluia!'

nunc vos o socii cantate laetantes

Alleluia!

Wherefore we sing, both heart
and voice
awaking, 'Alleluia!'

et vos pueruli respondete semper

Alleluia!

and children's voices echo,
answer
making, 'Alleluia!'

nunc omnes canite simul Alleluia
Domino
Alleluia Christo,
Pneumatique Alleluia

Now from all men be outpoured
Alleluia to the Lord;
with Alleluia evermore
the Son and Spirit we adore.

laus Trinitati aeternae,

Alleluia! Alleluia!
Alleluia! Alleluia! Alleluia!
Alleluia!

Praise be done to the Three in
One,

Alleluia! Alleluia!
Alleluia! Alleluia!

NOTKER BALBULUS, 10th cent.

J. M. NEALE(HG 2), 1852
[for the Easter Sequence *Victimae
Paschali* see 1 B]

152
THE GOLDEN SEQUENCE   HG 881

Veni sancte Spiritus
et emitte caelitus
  lucis tuae radium;
veni pater pauperum;
veni, dator munerum;
  veni, lumen cordium.

Come, thou holy Paraclete,
and from thy celestial seat
  send thy light and brilliancy:
Father of the poor, draw near,
giver of all gifts, be here:
  come, the soul's true radiancy.

consolator optime,
dulcis hospes animae,
  dulce refrigerium,
in labore requies,
in aestu temperies,
  in fletu solacium.

Come, of comforters the best,
of the soul the sweetest guest -
  come in toil refreshingly:
thou in labour rest most sweet,
thou art shadow from the heat,
  comfort in adversity.

o lux beatissima,
reple cordis intima
  tuorum fidelium:
sine tuo numine

O thou Light, most pure and blest,
shine within the inmost breast
  of thy faithful company.
Where thou art not, man hath
nought;

nihil est in homine,
  nihil est innoxium.

every holy deed and thought
comes from thy divinity.

lava quod est sordidum,
riga quod est aridum,
  sana quod est saucium.
flecte quod est rigidum,
fove quod est languidum,
  rege quod est devium,

What is soiléd, make thou pure;
what is wounded, work its cure;
  straighten what goes erringly.
what is frozen, warmly tend,
what is rigid, gently bend,
  what is parchéd, fructify;

da tuis fidelibus	Fill thy faithful, who confide
in te confidentibus	in thy power to guard and guide,
sacrum septenarium;	with thy sevenfold mystery:
da virtutis meritum;	here thy grace and virtue send:
da salutis exitum,	grant salvation to the end,
da perenne gaudium.	and in heaven felicity.

? STEPHEN LANGTON, d. 1228

J. M. NEALE (HG 2), 1852

153
DIES IRAE   HG 846

Dies irae, dies illa,	Day of wrath and doom impending,
solvet saeclum in favilla,	David's word with Sibyl's blending!
teste David cum Sibylla.	heaven and earth in ashes ending!
quantus tremor est futurus,	O what fear man's bosom rendeth,
quando iudex est venturus,	when from heaven the Judge descendeth,
cuncta stricte discussurus!	on whose sentence all dependeth!
tuba mirum spargens sonum	Wondrous sound the trumpet flingeth,
per sepulcra regionum	through earth's sepulchres it ringeth;
coget omnes ante thronum.	all before the throne it bringeth.
mors stupebit et natura,	Death is struck, and nature quaking
cum resurget creatura	all creation is awaking,
iudicanti responsura.	to its Judge an answer making.
liber scriptus proferetur,	Lo, the book exactly worded,
in quo totum continetur,	wherein all hath been recorded;
unde mundus iudicetur.	thence shall judgment be awarded.
iudex ergo cum sedebit,	When the Judge his seat attaineth,
quidquid latet, apparebit;	and each hidden deed arraigneth,
nil inultum remanebit.	nothing unavenged remaineth.
quid sum miser tunc dicturus,	What shall I, frail man, be pleading?
quem patronum rogaturus,	who for me be interceding,
cum vix iustus sit securus?	when the just are mercy needing?
rex tremamdae maiestatis,	King of majesty tremendous,
qui salvandos salvas gratis,	who dost free salvation send us,
salva me, fons pietatis;	Fount of pity then befriend us!
recordare, Jesu pie,	Think, kind Jesu! - my salvation
quod sum causa tuae viae;	caused thy wondrous incarnation;
ne me perdas illa die.	leave me not to reprobation.
quaerens me sedisti lassus	Faint and weary thou hast sought me,
redemisti crucem passus,	on the cross of suffering bought me;
tantus labor non sit cassus.	shall such grace be vainly brought me?
iuste iudex ultionis,	Righteous Judge, for sin's pollution,
donum fac remissionis	ere that day of retribution
ante diem rationis.	grant thy gift of absolution.

ingemisco tanquam reus,	Guilty now I pour my moaning,
culpa rubet vultus meus;	all my shame with anguish owning;
supplicanti parce, Deus.	spare O God thy suppliant groaning!
qui Mariam absolvisti	Through the sinful woman shriven,
et latronem exaudisti,	through the dying thief forgiven,
mihi quoque spem dedisti.	thou to me a hope hast given.
preces meae non sunt dignae;	Worthless are my prayers and sighing,
sed tu bonus fac benigne	yet, good Lord, in grace complying,
ne perenne cremer igne.	rescue me from fires undying.
inter oves locum praesta,	With thy sheep a place provide me,
et ab haedis me sequestra,	from the goats afar divide me,
statuens in parte dextra.	to thy right hand do thou guide me.
confutatis maledictis,	When the wicked are confounded,
flammis acribus addictis,	doomed to shame and woe unbounded,
voca me cum benedictis.	call me with thy saints surrounded.
oro supplex et acclinis;	Low I kneel, with heart submission;
cor contritum quasi cinis;	see like ashes my contrition!
gere curam mei finis.	help me in my last condition.
(lacrymosa dies illa,	Ah! that day of tears and mourning!
quae resurget ex favilla	from the dust of earth returning
iudicandum homo reus,	man for judgment must prepare him;
huis ergo parce deus.	spare. O God, in mercy spare him!
Pie Jesu Domine,	Lord all-pitying, Jesu blest,
dona eis requiem.)	grant them thine eternal rest.

THOMAS OF CELANO, fl. 1215

W. J. IRONS, 1848, text of St. 1 as *English Hymnal*, 1906

(Note on DIES IRAE)

The Latin poem, by Thomas of Celano, friend and biographer of St Francis of Assisi, consisted of the 17 three-line stanzas ending 'gere curam mei finis,' and was designed as a personal meditation on death and the Judgment. When it came into liturgical use, the six lines at the end, which break the rhyme-scheme, were added. The poem now takes its place in the history of hymnody partly because of the sonorous and dramatic beauty of some, though perhaps not all, of its Latin lines, and partly because it has inspired so many poets and musicians of later times. Its liturgical use was in its being the one Christian hymn sung at the Requiem Mass; therefore in musical settings of the Mass it took a central place. Moreover, its plainsong melody opens with a phrase that several composers, notably Berlioz and Rachmaninoff, have woven into secular compositions.

It has to be admitted that the only English translation in the original meter (that given above) cannot be rated higher than a brave attempt to translate the original; it makes it possible to sing the original plainsong in English, but it misses too many of the overtones of the Latin to be called a classic version. Recognizing this, we add here a prose translation, the first five sections of which (each corresponding to six lines of the original) are taken from *Hymns for Church and School*, 1964, and the rest of which is added here to complete the poem.

1. That Day, the Day of Wrath, will dissolve the world into ashes, as David and the Sibyl testify. What a trembling will there be, when the Judge will come, who will sternly examine all things!
2. The trumpet will scatter a wonderful sound through the tombs of all parts of the world; it will compel all men before the throne. Death and nature will be astonished into silence when creation arises to answer him who judges.
3. The written book will be produced in which is contained the whole record

from which the world will be judged. Therefore when the judge makes his review, whatever is hidden will come to light; nothing will remain unavenged.

4. What am I then to say, in my wretchedness? Whom shall I call on as my defending counsel, seeing that the righteous man is scarcely safe? King of aweful majesty, who dost freely save those who are to be saved, save me, thou fount of pity!

5. Remember, kind Jesus, that I am the cause of thy journey: do not destroy me on that day. Thou didst sit in weariness when searching for me; thou didst redeem me by enduring the Cross. Let not all that labour be in vain.

6. Righteous judge to whom vengeance belongs, give thy pardon before the day of reckoning comes. My guilt makes me cry out; my blame makes me blush. Hear my prayer, O God, and spare me.

7. Thou didst pardon Mary; thou didst hear the thief's prayer, and in this thou hast given me hope. My prayers are not fit to be heard; but thou wilt be kind, and not let me burn in eternal fire.

8. Give me a place with the sheep: separate me from the goats; put me at thy right hand. When the wicked are doomed in shame to the fires of bitterness, call my name with those who are blessed.

9. Humbly, prostrate, I pray: my heart is ground to ashes by penitence; look upon my fate with mercy.

10. Oh, what a day of tears and lamentation, when man, waiting for judgment, rises from earth's ashes: spare him in that day! Kind Lord Jesus, give them rest!

Medieval Latin Lyrics

154
THE CITY OF BETHLEHEM   HG 870

O sola magnarum urbium
major Bethlem, cui contigit

ducem salutis caelitus
incorporatum gignere:

quem stella, quae solis rotam
vincit decore ac lumine,
venisse terris nuntiat

cum carne terrestri Deum.

videre postquam illum magi,
eoa promunt munera,
stratique votis offerunt
tus, myrrham, et aurum regium.

regem Deumque adnuntiant
thesaurus et fragrans odor
turis Sabaei, ac myrrheus
pulvis sepulcrum praeducet

gloria tibi Domini,
qui apparuisti hodie,
cum Patre et sancto Spiritu
in sempiterna saecula.

PRUDENTIUS (HG 843), 4th century

Bethlehem, of noblest cities
    none can once with thee compare;
thou alone the Lord from heaven
    didst for us incarnate bear.

Fairer than the sun at morning
    was the star that told his birth;
to the lands their God announcing,
    his beneath a form of earth.

By its lambent beauty guided
    see the eastern Kings appear;
see them bend, their gifts to offer,
    gifts of incense, gold and myrrh.

Solemn things of mystic meaning
    incense doth the God disclose,
gold, a royal child proclaimeth,
    myrrh a future tomb foreshows.

Holy Jesu, in thy brightness
    to the gentile world displayed,
with the Father and the Spirit
    endless praise to thee be paid.

EDWARD CASWALL (HG 21), 1849

155
CORDE NATUS   HG 843

Corde natus ex parentis
    ante mundi exordium
A et O cognominatus,
    ipse fons et clausula
omnium quae sunt, fuerunt,
    quaeque post futura sunt
        saeculorum saeculis

ipse iussit, et creata,
    dixit ipse, et facta sunt,

terra, coelum, fossa, ponti,

Of the Father's heart begotten,
    ere the world from chaos rose,
he is Alpha: from that Fountain
    all that is and hath been flows;
he is Omega, of all things
    yet to come the mystic close,
        evermore and evermore.

By his word was all created;
    he commanded and 'twas done
        (Ps. 33:9)
earth and sky and boundless
                        ocean,

trina rerum machina,
quaque in his vigent sub alto

solis et lunae globo. . . .

corporis formam caduci,
    membra morti obnoxia
induit, ne gens periret
    primoplasti ex germine,
merserat quam lex profundo

    noxialis tartaro. . . .

O beatus ortus ille,

    virgo cum puerpera

edidit nostram salutem

    foeta sancto Spiritus,
et puer Redemptor orbis

    os sacratum protulit. . . .

ecce, quem vates vetustis
    concinebant saeculis
quem prophetarum fideles
    paginae spoponderant,
emicat promissus olim

    cuncta collaudent eum. . . .

psallat altitudo coeli,

    psallant omnes angeli,
quidquid est virtutis usquam
    psallat in laudam Dei,
nulla linguarum silescat,
    vox et omnis consonet. . . .

Macte Iudex mortuorum,

    macte Rex viventium,
dexter in parentis arce

    qui cluis virtutibus,

omnium venturus inde
    iustus ultor criminum. . . .

te senes et te iuventus,
    parvulorum te chorus,
turba matrum virginumque,
    simplices puellulae
voce concordes pudicis
    perstrepant concentibus. . . .

Tibi, Christe, sit cum Patre,

    Hagioque Pneumate,
hymnus, melos, laus perennis,

    gratiarum actio,

universe of three in one,
    all that sees the moon's soft radiance,
    all that breathes beneath the
                        sun. . . .

He assumed this mortal body,
    frail and feeble, doomed to die,
that the race from dust created
    might not perish utterly,
which the dreadful law had sentenced
    in the depths of hell to lie, . . .

O how blest that wondrous birthday,
    when the Maid the curse retrieved,
brought to birth mankind's salvation;
    by the Holy Ghost conceived;
and the Babe, the world's Redeemer
    in her loving arms received. . . .

This is he, whom seer and sybil
    sang in ages long gone by;
this is he of old revealéd
    in the page of prophecy;
lo! he comes, the promised Saviour;
    let the world his praises cry! . . .

Sing, ye heights of heaven, his
                        praises;
    angels and archangels, sing!
Wheresoe'er ye be, ye faithful,
    let your joyous anthems ring,
every tongue his name confessing,
    countless voices answering. . . .

Hail! thou Judge of souls departed;
    hail! of all the living King!
On the Father's right hand
                        throned,
    through his courts thy praises
                        ring,
toll at last for all offences
    righteous judgment thou shalt
                        bring. . . .

Now let old and young uniting
    chant to thee harmonious lays,
maid and matron hymn thy glory,
    infant lips their anthem raise,
boys and girls together singing
    with pure heart their song of
                        praise. . . .

Christ, to thee with God the Father
    and O Holy Ghost, to thee,
hymn and chant and high thanksgiving
    and unwearied praises be,

honor, virtus, victoria
regnum aeternaliter,
saeculorum saeculis.

PRUDENTIUS, 4th century (cento)

honour, glory and dominion
and eternal victory
evermore and evermore.

sts. 1-8 by **R. F. DAVIS**, 1905, based on
J. M. NEALE, 1852; st. 9: text of 1861.

156
VENERATION OF THE CROSS HG 868

Pange, lingua, gloriosi

praelium certaminis,
et super crucis tropaeum
dic triumphum nobilem,
qualiter redemptor oribis
immolatus vicerit.

de parentis protoplasti
fraude factor condolens,
quando pomi noxialis
morte morsu conruit,
ipse lignum tunc notavit,
dama ligni ut solveret.

hoc opus nostrae salutis
ordo depoposcerat,
multiformis perditoris
arte ut artem falleret,
et medelam ferret inde
hostis unde laeserat.

quando venit ergo sacri

plenitudo temporis,
missus est ab arce Patris
Natus, orbis conditor,
atque ventre virginali
carne factus prodiit.

vagit infans inter arta
conditus praesepia,
membra pannis involuta
virgo mater adligat,

et pedes manusque, crura
stricta pingit fascia.

lustra sex qui iam peracta
tempus implens corporis,
se volente, natus ad hoc,

passione deditus,
Agnus in crucis levatur
immolandus stipite.

hic acetum, fel, harundo,

sputa, clavi, lancea;
mite corpus perforatur;
sanguis, unda profluit;
terra, pontus, astra, mundus

quo lavantur flumine.

crux fidelis, inter omnes
arbor una nobilis,

Sing, my tongue, how glorious battle

glorious victory became;
and above the Cross, His trophy,
tell the triumph and the fame:
tell how he, the earth's Redeemer,
by his death for man o'ercame. *

God in pity saw men fallen,
shamed and sunk in misery
when he fell on death by tasting
fruit of the forbidden tree;
then another tree was chosen
which the world from death
should free. †

Thus the scheme of our salvation
was of old in order laid,
that the manifold deceiver's
art by art might be outweighed,
and the lure the foe put forward
into means of healing made. †

Therefore when the appointed fulness
of the holy time was come,
he was sent, who maketh all things
forth from God's eternal home;
thus he came to earth, incarnate,
offspring of a maiden's womb †

Laid within a narrow manager,
uttering but an infant sound,
while the Virgin-Mother fastens
swaddling clothes his limbs around,
in the tightly girded linen
God's own hands and feet are bound. §

Thirty years fulfilled among us,
perfect life in low estate -
born for this, and self surrendered,
to his passion dedicate,
on the Cross the Lamb is lifted
for his people immolate. †

His the nails, the spear, the spitting,
reed and vinegar and gall;
from his patient body pierced
blood and water streaming fall:
earth and sky and stars and mankind
by that stream are cleansed all. †

Faithful Cross, above all other,
one and only noble Tree!

nulla talem silva profert
flore, fronde, germine,
dulce lignum dulce clavo
dulce pondus sustinens.

flecte ramos, arbor alta;
tensa laxa viscera,
et rigor lentescat ille,
quem dedit nativitas,

ut superni membra regis
mite tendas stipite.

sola digna tu fuisti
ferre pretium saeculi,
atque portum praeparare
nauta mundo naufrago,
quem sacer cruor perunxit
fusus Agni corpore.

gloria et honor Deo
usquequo altissimo,
una Patri, Filioque,
inclito Paraclito,
cuius honor et potestas
in aeterna saecula.

VENANTIUS FORTUNATUS
530-609

None in foliage, none in blossom,
none in fruit thy peers may be:
sweetest wood and sweetest iron,
sweetest weight is hung on thee.

Bend thy boughs, O Tree of glory!
thy relaxing sinews bend;
for a while the ancient rigour
that thy birth bestowed, suspend;
and the King of heavenly beauty
on thy bosom gently tend.

Thou alone wast counted worthy
this world's ransom to uphold;
for a shipwrecked race preparing
harbour, like the Ark of old;
with the sacred Blood anointed
from the smitten Lamb that rolled.

To the Trinity be glory,
everlasting, as is meet:
equal to the Father, equal
to the Son, and Paraclete:
Trinal Unity, whose praises
all created things repeat.

Translation composite.
* William Mair and A. W. Wotherspoon in *Scottish Mission Hymnal*, 1912
† Percy Dearmer, 1867-1936, in *English Hymnal*, 1906
§ Compilers of *Hymns Ancient and Modern*, 1904.
The last 4 stanzas, J. M. Neale in *Medieval Hymns*, 1851, upon whose translation all the others are based.

157
ASCENSION HG 852

Hymnum canamus gloriae,

hymni novi nunc personent;

Christus novo cum tramite

ad Patris ascendit thronum.

Apostoli tunc mystico

in monte stantes Chrismatis
cum Matre clara Virgine
Jesu videbant gloriam.

Quos alloquentes angeli,

'quid astra stantes cernitis?

Salvator hic est,' inquiunt,
'Jesus triumpho nobili.'

Sicque venturum asserunt
quemadmodum hunc viderunt
summa polorum culmina
scandere Jesus splendida.

da nobis illuc sedula
devotione tendere
quo te sedere cum Patre

in arce regni credimus.

Sing we triumphant hymns of praise,

new hymns to heaven exulting raise;

Christ, by a road before untrod (Heb. 10:20)

ascendeth to the throne of God.

The holy apostolic band (Acts 1:1-11)
upon the Mount of Olives stand,
and with the Virgin-Mother see
Jesus' resplendent majesty.

To whom the angels, drawing nigh,
'Why stand and gaze upon the sky?
This is the Saviour,' thus they say,
'This is his noble triumph day.'

Again shall ye behold him, - so
as ye to-day have seen him go,
in glorious pomp ascending high
up to the portals of the sky.

O grant us thitherward to tend,
and with unwearied hearts ascend
toward thy kingdom's throne, where thou,
as is our faith, art seated now.

tu esto nostrum gaudium

qui es futurus praemium,

sit nostra in te gloria
per cuncta semper saecula.

gloria tibi, Domine,
qui scandis supra sidera,
cum Patre et Sancto Spiritu
in sempiterna saecula.

THE VENERABLE BEDE, 673-735

Be thou our joy and thou our
                                          guard,
who art to be our great Reward:
                                    (Gen. 12:1)
our glory and our boast in thee
for ever and for ever be!

All glory, Lord, to thee we pay,
ascending o'er the stars to-day:
all glory, as is ever meet,
to Father and to Paraclete.

BENJAMIN WEBB (HG 545), 1852

158
THE HEAVENLY CITY AS A FIGURE
OF THE EARTHLY CHURCH   HG 879

Urbs beata Jerusalem,
   dicta pacis visio,
quae construitur in caelis
   vivis ex lapidibus   (1 Pet. 2:5)
et angelis coornata
   ut sponsata comite,
                          (Rev. 21:1ff)

nova veniens e caelo,
   nuptali thalamo
praeparata, ut sponsata

   copuletur Domino;
plateae et muri eius
   ex auro purissimo.

portae nitent margaritis,

   adytis patentibus,
et virtute meritorum
   illuc introducitur
omnis qui pro Christi nomine

   hic in mundo premitur.

tunsionibus, pressuris
   expoliti lapides,

suisque aptantur locis
   per manum artificis;
disponuntur permansuri

   sacris aedificiis.

. . . . .

Angularis fundamentum

   lapis Christus missus est
                          (1 Pet. 2:6)
qui compage parietis

   in utroque nectitur,
quem Sion sancta suscepit,
   in quo credens permanet.

omnis illa Deo sacra
   et dilecta civitas,
plena modulis in laude
   et canore iubilo,
trinum Deum unicumque
   cum favore praedicat.

Blessed city, heavenly Salem,
   vision dear of peace and love,
who, of living stones upbuilded
   art the joy of heaven above,
and with angel cohorts circled
   as a Bride to earth dost move: -

from celestial realms descending,
   ready for the nuptial bed,
to his presence, decked with
                                    jewels,
   by her Lord shall she be led:
all her streets, and all her bulwarks
   of pure gold are fashioned.

Bright with pearls her portal
                                    glitters;
   it is open evermore;
and by virtue of his merits,
   thither faithful souls may soar,
who for Christ's dear name in this
                                      world
   pain and tribulation bore.

Many a blow and biting sculpture
   polished well those stones
                                    elect,
in their places now compacted
   by the heavenly Architect,
who therewith hath willed for
                                      ever
   that his Palace should be
                                    decked.

. . . . .

Christ is made the sure founda-
                                      tion
   and the precious corner-stone,
who, the twofold walls sur-
                                    mounting
   binds them closely into one:
holy Sion's help for ever
   and her confidence alone.

All that dedicated city
   dearly loved by God on high,
in exultant jubilation
   pours perpetual melody;
God the One and God the Trinal
   singing everlastingly.

Hos in templo, summe Deus,

   exoratus adveni,
et clementi bonitate
   precum vota suscipe;
largam benedictionem
   hic infunde iugiter.

his promereantur omnes
   petita acquirere,
et adepta possidere
   cum sanctis perenniter,

paradisum introire
   translati in requiem.

glori et honor Deo
   usquequo altissimo,
una Patri Filioque
   inclito Paraclito,
cui laus est et potestas
   per aterna saecula.

Middle period

To this temple, where we call
                                    thee,
   come, O Lord of hosts, to-day!
With thy wonted lovingkindness
   hear thy people as they pray;
and thy fullest benediction
   shed within its walls for ay.

Here vouchsafe to all thy servants
   that they supplicate to gain:
here to have and hold for ever
   those good things their prayers
                                    obtain;
and hereafter in thy glory
   with thy blessed ones to reign.

Laud and honour to the Father,
   laud and honour to the Son;
laud and honour to the Spirit;
   ever three and ever one:
consubstantial, co-eternal,
   while unending ages run.

J. M. NEALE (HG 2), 1852

(Note: the division of this hymn at st. 4 goes back to medieval liturgical custom.
Those who cheerfully sing part II of the English translation, with or without the
opening verse, hardly know from what deep waters of mythological metaphor
they have been delivered. Three basic ideas run in uneasy counterpoint in part I:
(a) the 'marriage' of the heavenly Jerusalem and the victorious Christ, from Rev.
21; (b) the physical process of building and planning a city, and (c) the notion
of Christ as the corner-stone and his members as 'living stones,' from 1 Peter 2.
Usually, as soon as one metaphor looks like becoming unmanageable, the poet
shifts to another; but in st. 4 the blows of hammers and nicks of chisels are meta-
phorical: they represent the refining tribulations through which the Divine
Architect causes his saints (his 'living stones') to pass on the way to perfection.
All this prefaces the prayer of the church militant, which comes in the second
Part and which is more familiar.)

159
PALM SUNDAY   HG 15

Gloria laus et honor
   tibi sint, rex Christe redemptor,
cui puerile decus
   prompsit Hosanna pium.

Israel es tu rex Davidis
   et inclyta proles,
nomine qui in Domini
   rex benedicte venis.

coetus in excelsis te laudat
   caelicus omnis
et mortalis homo,
   et cuncta creata simul.

plebs Hebraea tibi
   cum palmis obvia venit:
cum prece, voto hymnis

   adsumus ecce tibi.

hi tibi passuro
   solvebant munia laudis;

nos tibi regnanti
   pangimus ecce melos.

hi placuere tibi;
   placeat devotio nostra,
rex pie, rex clemens
   cui bona cuncta placent.

All glory, laud and honour
   to thee, Redeemer, King,
to whom the lips of children
   made sweet hosannas ring.

Thou art the King of Israel,
   thou David's royal Son,
who in the Lord's name comest,
   thou King and blessed One.

The company of angels
   are praising thee on high:
and mortal men, and all things
   created make reply.

The people of the Hebrews
   with palms before thee went;
our praise and prayer and
                                    anthems
   before thee we present.

In hast'ning to thy Passion,
   they raised their hymns of
                                    praise;
in reigning 'midst thy glory,
   our melody we raise.

Thou didst accept their praises:
   accept the prayers we bring,
who in all good delightest,
   thou good and gracious King!

gloria laus et honor
  tibi sit, rex Christe redemptor,
cui puerile decus
  prompsit Hosanna pium.

THEODULPH OF ORLEANS, c. 821

All glory, laud and honour
  to thee, Redeemer, King,
to whom the lips of children
  made sweet hosannas ring.

J. M. NEALE (HG 2), 1852, (St. 1, text of 1861)

Teach us to know the Father, Son,
and thee, of both, to be but One;
that through the ages all along
this may be our endless song:

Praise to thy eternal merit,
Father, Son and Holy Spirit.

JOHN COSIN, 1627

160
VENI CREATOR SPIRITUS HG 880
A

Veni, Creator Spiritus,
mentes tuorum visita,

imple superna gratia
quae tu creasti pectora;

qui Paraclitus diceris,
donum Dei, altissimi,
fons vivus, ignis, caritas,
et spiritalis unctio.

tu septiformis munere,

dextrae Dei tu digitus,
tu rite promisso Patris
sermone ditans guttura.

accende lumen sensibus,
infunde amorem cordibus,

infirma nostri corporis
virtute firmans perpeti.

hostem repellas longius,
pacemque dones protinus;

ductore sit te praevio
vitemus omne noxium.

per te sciamus da Patrem,
noscamus atque Filium,

te utriusque Spiritum
credamus omni tempore.

? RABANUS MAURUS, 10th cent.

Come, O Creator Spirit, come,
and make within our hearts thy
                              home;
to us thy grace celestial give,
who of thy breathing move and
                              live.

O Comforter, that name is thine,
of God most high the gift divine;
the well of life, the fire of love,
our souls' anointing from above.

Thou dost appear in sevenfold
                              dower
the sign of God's almighty power;
the Father's promise, making rich
with saving truth our earthly
                              speech.

Our senses with thy light inflame,
our hearts to heavenly love re-
                              claim;
our bodies' poor infirmity
with strength celestial fortify.

Our mortal foe afar repel,
grant us henceforth in peace to
                              dwell;
and so to us, with thee for guide,
no ill shall come, no harm betide.

May we by thee the Father learn,
and know the Son, and thee dis-
                              cern,
who art of both; and thus adore
in perfect faith for evermore.

ROBERT BRIDGES (HG 9), 1899

(C)

Creator Spirit, by whose aid
the world's foundations first were laid,
come, visit every pious mind;
come, pour thy joys on human kind;
from sin and sorrow set us free,
and make thy temples worthy thee.

O Source of uncreated light,
the Father's promised Paraclete!
Thrice-holy fount, thrice-holy fire,
our hearts with heavenly love inspire;
come, and thy sacred unction bring
to sanctify us while we sing.

Plenteous of grace, descend from high
rich in thy sevenfold energy;
thou strength of his almighty hand
whose power does heaven and earth command;
proceeding Spirit, our defence, *
who dost thy gift of tongues dispense,
and crown'st thy gift with eloquence!

Refine and purge our earthly parts;
but oh, inflame and fire our hearts!
Make us eternal truths receive,
and practise all that we believe;
give us thyself, that we may see
the Father and the Son by thee.

Immortal honour, endless fame,
attend the almighty Father's name;
the Saviour Son be glorified,
who for lost man's redemption died;
and equal adoration be,
eternal Paraclete, to thee.

JOHN DRYDEN, 1631-1700

* when this appears in hymnals, this line, or the whole stanza, is normally dropped.

This, probably the most celebrated of Latin hymns in English-speaking use, is translated above by one poet Laureate; below we give the more familiar translation (less accurate) by a Bishop of Durham, and the highly-wrought version by another Laureate.

(B)

Come, Holy Ghost, our souls inspire
and lighten with celestial fire;
thou the anointing Spirit art,
who dost thy sevenfold gifts impart:

thy blessed unction from above
is comfort, life, and fire of love;
enable with perpetual light
the dulness of our blinded sight:

anoint and cheer our soiléd face
with the abundance of thy grace:
keep far our foes, give peace at home;
where thou art guide no ill can come.

161
O QUANTA QUALIA HG 571

O quanta qualia sunt illa sabbata
quae semper celebrat superna curia;
quae fessis requies, quae merces fortibus,
cum erit omnia Deus in omnibus.

Quis Rex, quae curia, quale palatium,
quae pax, quae requies, quod illud gaudium?
huius participes exponant gloriae
si quantum sentiunt possint exprimere.

vere Jerusalem est illa civitas,
cuius pax iugis est summa iucunditas,
ubi non praevenit rem desiderium,
nec desiderio minus est praemium.

Ibi molestiis finita omnibus
securi cantiza Sion santabiums,
et iuges gratiae de donis gratiae
beata referet plebs tibi, Domine.

Illic nec sabbato succedit sabbatum,
perpes laetitia sabbatizantium,
nec ineffabiles cessabunt iubili
quos decantabiums et nos et angeli.

nostrum est interim mentes erigere,
et totis patriam votis appetere,
et ad Jerusalem a Babylonia
post longa regredi tandem exilia.

perenni Domino perpes sit gloria,
ex quo sunt, per quem sunt, in quo sunt omnia;
ex quo sunt, Pater est, per quem sunt, Filius,
in quo sunt, Patris et Filii Spiritus.

PETER ABELARD (HG 34), 1079-1142.
See also 551.

O what high holiday, past our declaring,
safe in his palace God's courtiers are sharing,
rest after pilgrimage, spoil after fighting!
God, all in all, is their crown and requiting.

Truly Jerusalem's townsmen we call them -
peace everlasting doth fold and enthral them;
never they crave, but the boon hath been granted,
never that boon leaves their hope disenchanted.

Wondrous that King, and his lieges who reign there,
wondrous the peace and the joy they attain there;
could they but tell of that rapture, who feel it!
Had we but ears, or they words to reveal it!

Yet in the meanwhile our eyes thither turn we;
home of our hearts, for thy loveliness yearn we:
long though this Babylon's exile detaineth,
yonder we press, where a city remaineth.

Free from all cares that on earth can annoy us,
Sion's sweet anthems shall wholly employ us,
grateful at last for those infinite graces
time nor eternity ever effaces.

Holidays still one another o'ertaking
give them fresh joy of their holiday-making;
still of that chorus the echoes are ringing.
Angels and men join together in singing.

Praise to the Godhead unceasingly give we,
of whom, in whom and by whom ever live we,
God all-creating and God all-sustaining,
God in three Persons eternally reigning.

RONALD A KNOX, 1940

162
HORA NOVISSIMA   HG 851

Latin	English

Hora novissima
tempora pessima
  sunt, vigilemus.
Ecce minaciter
imminet arbiter,
  ille supremus, -
	The world is very evil,
	  the times are waxing late;
	be sober and keep vigil,
	  the Judge is at the gate;

imminet, imminet
  ut mala terminet,
  aequa coronet,
recta remuneret,
anxia liberet,
  aethera donet.
	the Judge who comes in mercy,
	  the Judge who comes with
	                    might
	to terminate the evil,
	  to diadem the right.

curre vir optime;
lubrica reprime,
  praefer honesta,
fletibus angere,
flendo merebere,
  caelica festa.
luce replebere
iam sine vespere,
  iam sine luna;
lux nova lux ea,
lux erit aurea,
  lux erit una.
	Arise, arise, good Christian,
	  let right to wrong succeed;
	let penitential sorrow
	  to heavenly gladness lead,
	to light that has no evening,
	  that knows no moon or sun,
	the light so new and golden,
	  the light that is but one.

Hic breve vivitur,
hic breve plangitur,
  hic breve fletur;
non breve vivere,
non breve plaudere,
  retribuentur.
O retributio!
stat brevis actio,
  vita perennis;
o retributio!
caelica mansio
  stat luce plenis.
	Brief life is here our portion,
	  brief sorrow, short-lived care;
	the life that knows no ending,
	  the tearless life, is there.
	O happy retribution:
	  short toil, eternal rest;
	for mortals and for sinners
	  a mansion with the blest.

sunt modo praelia,
postmodo praemia, -
  qualia? plena:
plena refectio,
nullaque passio,
  nullaque poena.
spe modo vivitur,
et Sion angitur
  a Babylone;
nunc tribulatio,
tunc recreatio,
  sceptra, coronae.
	And now we fight the battle,
	  but then shall wear the crown
	of full and everlasting
	  and passionless renown.
	And now we watch and struggle,
	  and now we live in hope,
	and Sion in her anguish
	  with Babylon must cope.

qui modo creditur,
ipse videbitur,
  atque scietur,
ipse videntibus
  attribuetur.
mane videbitur,
umbra fugabitur,
  ordo patebit;
mane nitens erit,
et bona qui gerit
  ille nitebit.
	But he whom now we trust in
	  shall then be seen and known,
	and they who know and see him
	  shall have him for their own.
	The morning shall awaken,
	  the shadows shall decay,
	and each true-hearted servant
	  shall shine as doth the day.

pars mea, rex meus,
in proprio Deus
  ipse decore
visus amabitur,
  auctor in ore.
tunc Jacob Israel
 	
et Lia tunc Rahel
  efficietur;
	There God our King and Portion,
	  the fulness of his grace,
	shall we behold for ever
	  and worship face to face.
	Then Jacob into Israel
	  from earthlier self
	                    estranged,
	and Leah into Rachel
	  for ever shall be changed.

tunc Syon atria
pulchraque patria
    perficietur.

Urbs Sion aurea,
patria lactea,
    vice decora,
omne cor obruis,
omnibus obstruis
    et cor et ora.
nescio, nescio
quae iubilatio,
    lux tibi qualis,
quam socialia
guadia, gloria,
    quam specialis.

Sunt Sion atria
conjubilantia,
    martyra plena,
cive micantia,
principe stantia,
    luce serena.
sunt ibi pascua
mentibus afflua
    praestita sanctis;
regis ibi thronus,
agminis et sonus
    est epulantis.
gens duce splendida,
contio candida
    vestibus albis,
sunt sine fletibus
in Sion aedibus,
    sedibus almis.

Tu locus unicus
illeque caelicus
    es paradisus.
non tibi lacrima
sed placidissima
    gaudia, risus.
lux tua mors crucis
atque caro ducis
    est crucifixi;
laus, benedictio,
conjubilatio
    personat ipsi.

O bona patria,
num tua gaudia
    teque videbo?
o bona patria,
num tua praemia
    plena videbo?
plaude cinis meus,
est tua pars Deus:
    eius es, et sis.

BERNARD OF CLUNY, fl. 1140-1150

Then all the halls of Sion
    for ay shall be complete,
and in the land of beauty
    all things of beauty meet.

Jerusalem the golden,
    with milk and honey blest,
beneath thy contemplation
    sink heart and voice opprest.
I know not, oh, I know not
    what social joys are there,
what radiancy of glory,
    what bliss beyond compare.

They stand, those halls of Sion,
    conjubilant with song,
and bright with many an angel,
    and many a martyr throng;
the Prince is ever with them,
    the daylight is serene;
the pastures of the blessed
    are decked in glorious sheen.

There is the throne of David,
    and there, from sin released,
the song of them that triumph,
    the shout of them that feast;
and they who with the Leader
    have conquered in the fight,
for ever and for ever
    are clad in robes of white.

O one, O only mansion!
    O paradise of joy!
where tears are ever banished,
    and smiles have no alloy.
The Cross is all thy splendour,
    the Crucified thy praise;
his laud and benediction
    thy ransomed people raise.

O sweet and blessed country,
    shall I ever see thy face?
O sweet and blessed country,
    shall I ever win thy grace?
Exult, O dust and ashes,
    the Lord shall be thy part:
his only his for ever
    thou shalt be, and thou art.

J. M. NEALE (HG 2), 1858

163
DULCIS JESU MEMORIA   HG 857
A

Dulcis Jesu memoria,
dans vera cordis gaudia:
sed super mel et omnia
dulcis eius praesentia.

Jesu, the very thought of thee
    with sweetness fills the breast;
but sweeter far thy face to see,
    and in thy presence rest.

nil canitur suavius,

auditur nil iucundius,
nil cogitatur dulcius,
quam Jesus Dei filius.

Jesu spes paenitentibus,
quam pius es petentibus,
quam bonus te quaerentibus!

sed quid invenientibus?

nec lingua potest dicere,

nec littera exprimere;
experto potes credere
quid sit Jesum diligere.

tu esto nostrum gaudium,
qui es futurus praemium;
sit nostra in te gloria
per cuncta semper saecula.

Jesu, rex admirabilis
et triumphator nobilis,
dulcedo ineffabilis,
totus desiderabilis.

quando cor nostrum visitas,
tunc lucet ei veritas,
mundi vilescit vanitas,
et intus fervet caritas.

te nostra, Jesu, vox sonet,
nostri te mores exprimet,
te corda nostra diligant
et nunc et in perpetuum.

mane nobiscum, Domine,
et nos illustra lumine;
pulsa mentis caligine,
mundum reple dulcedine.

Jesu, flos matris virginis,
favus mirae dulcedinis,
laus, honor tibi numinis,
regnum beatitudinis.

Uncertainly attributed to **ST BERNARD OF CLAIRVAUX**, 1090-1153; but may be by an anonymous English author.

No voice can sing, no heart can
                              frame
nor can the memory find
a sweeter sound than Jesus' name,
    the Saviour of mankind.

O hope of every contrite heart,
    O joy of all the meek,
to those who ask, how kind thou
                              art,
    how good to those who seek?

But what to those who find! ah
                              this
    nor tongue nor pen can show;
the love of Jesus, what it is,
    none but his loved ones know.

Jesus, our only joy be thou,
    as thou our prize wilt be;
in thee be all our glory now
    and through eternity.

O Jesu, King most wonderful,
    thou Conqueror renowned,
thou sweetness most ineffable
    in whom all joys are found!

When once thou visitest the heart,
    then truth begins to shine,
then earthly vanities depart,
    then kindles love divine.

Thee, Jesu, may our voices bless,
    thee may we love alone,
and ever in our lives express
    the image of thine own.

Abide with us, and let thy light
    shine, Lord, on every heart;
dispel the darkness of our night,
    and joy to all impart.

Jesus, our love and joy, to thee,
    the Virgin's holy Son,
all might and praise and glory be
    while endless ages run.

EDWARD CASWALL (HG 21), 1849

B
JESU DULCEDO CORDIUM

[The following translation, using another selection from the 42 stanzas of the original poem, comes from America; although American hymnody is dealt with at a later stage, it seems reasonable to include it here. It is one of the best known and finest of American hymns.]

Jesu, dulcedo cordium.
fons vitae, lumen mentium,

excedis omne gaudium

et omne desiderium.

Jesu, spes paenitentibus,

quam pius es petentibus,

Jesu! thou joy of loving hearts!
    Thou fount of life, thou light of
                              men!
from the best bliss that earth
                              imparts
    we turn unfilled to thee again.

Thy truth unchanged hath ever
                              stood,
    thou savest those that on thee
                              call;

quam bonus te quaerentibus!	to them that seek thee, thou art good:
sed quid invenientibus?	to them that find thee, all in all.
qui te gustant, esuriunt;	We taste thee, O thou living Bread,
qui bibunt, adhuc sitiunt;	and long to feast upon thee still;
desiderare nesciunt	we drink of thee, the fountain-head,
nisi Jesum quem cupiunt.	and thirst our souls from thee to fill.
quocunque loco fuero	Our restless spirits yearn for thee,
mecum Jesum desidero,	where'er our changeful lot is cast,
quam laetus cum invenero,	glad when thy gracious smile we see,
quam felix cum tenuero!	blest when our faith can hold thee fast.
mane nobiscum, Domine,	O Jesus, ever with us stay,
nos tuo replens lumine:	make all our moments calm and bright;
pulsa noctis caligine,	chase the dark nights of sin away,
mundum reple dulcedine.	shed o'er the world thy holy light.

as above   RAY PALMER (HG 370), 1858

164
ST THOMAS' HYMN OF THE EUCHARIST
HG 867

Pange lingua gloriosi	Of the glorious Body telling,
corporis mysterium	O my tongue, the mysteries sing;
sanguinisque pretiosi	and the blood, all price excelling,
quem in mundi pretium	which for this world's ran-soming,
fructus ventris generosi	in a noble womb once dwelling,
rex effudit gentium.	he shed forth, the Gentiles' King.
nobis datus, nobis natus	Given for us, for us descending
ex intacta virgine,	of a Virgin to proceed,
et in mundo conversatus,	Man with man in converse blending
sparso verbi semine,	scattered he his Gospel seed:
sui moras incolatus	till his sojourn drew to ending,
miro clausit ordine.	which he closed in wondrous deed.
in supremae nocte cenae	At the last great Supper seated,
recumbens cum fratribus,	circled by his brethren's band,
observata lege plene	all the law required, completed
cibis in legalibus	in the feast its statutes planned,
cibum turbae duodenae	to the Twelve himself he meted
se dat suis manibus.	for their food with his own hand.
Verbum caro panem verum	Word made flesh, by word he maketh
verbo carnem efficit,	very bread his flesh to be;
fitque sanguis Christi merum,	man in wine Christ's blood par-taketh,
etsi sensus deficit;	and if senses fail to see,
ad firmandum cor sincerum	faith alone the true heart waketh
sola fides sufficit.	to behold the mystery.

tantum ergo sacramentum	Therefore we, before it bending,
veneremur cernui,	this great Sacrament adore:
et antiquum documentum	types and shadows have their ending
novo cedat ritui:	in the new Rite evermore:
praestet fides supplementum	faith, our outward sense amend-ing,
sensuum defectui.	maketh good defects before.
Genitori Genitoque	Honour, laud and praise address-ing
laus et iubilatio,	to the Father and the Son,
salus, honor, virtus quoque	might ascribe we, virtue, bless-ing,
sit et benedictio;	and eternal benison:
procedenti ab utroque	Holy Ghost, from Both progress-ing,
compar sit laudatio.	equal laud to thee be done!

ST THOMAS AQUINAS, c. 1263   **J. M. NEALE** (HG 2), 1852

Note on PANGE LINGUA.

This is probably the densest and most difficult hymn ever written, a characteristic product of the most massive intellect of the Middle Ages. St Thomas was invited to write this and two other hymns for the Feast of Corpus Christi by Pope Urban IV. In PANGE LINGUA, poetry embraces not only history, but also theology and liturgical belief. While St Thomas, in faultless Latin, conveys with precision every overtone of his thought, we can forgive poor Neale for being defeated. He makes St Thomas just about singable in English, but he has to bend his vocabulary and submit to obscurity to an extent which he usually avoids.

St. 1:   The Incarnation and the Atonement are at once brought together in lines 5-6;

St. 2:   similarly the earthly ministry (lines 3-4) is joined on to the Last Supper (lines 5-6) which is seen as its climax;

St. 3:   here the Last Supper is the center of attention; the reference to 'the law' recalls the fact that (as St Thomas believed and as most agree) the Last Supper was a Passover meal, prescribed by Jewish custom, here trans-formed. St Thomas is, of course, not quite faithful to Scripture in implying that all twelve Disciples were present;

St. 4:   in line 1, Christ is The Word, and the second 'word' in the line is that 'word of institution' (as liturgists call it) which gave the new significance to the Bread and the Wine. Transubstantiation, which St Thomas himself clarified as a doctrine, is here affirmed to be a process which faith alone can comprehend;

St. 5:   it is the Sacrament, in Catholic liturgy, which is revered; hence Neale's 'it' where the hymnals often write 'him.' Hebrews 8 lies behind the 'types and shadows' passage.

165
ADORO TE DEVOTE   **HG 867**

Adoro te devote, latens Deitas
quae sub his figuris vere latitas:
tibi se cor meum totum subicit,
quia te contemplans totum deficit.

visus, tactus, gustus in te fallitur,
sed auditu solo tuto creditur;
credo quidquie dixit Dei Filius,
nil hoc verbo Veritatis verius.

In cruce latebat sola Deitas,
at hic latet simul et humanitas;
ambo tamen credens atque confitens
peto quod petivit latro poenitens.

plagas sicut Thomas non intueor,
Deum tamen meum te confiteor;
fac me tibi semper magis credere,
in te spem habere, te diligere.

O memoriale mortis Domini,
panis vivus, vitam praestans homini:
praesta meae menti de te vivere,
et te illi semper dulci sapere.

Pie pellicane, Jesu Domine,
me immundum munda tuo sanguine;
cuius una stilla salvum facere
totum mundum quit ab omni scelere.

Jesu, quem velatum nunc aspicio,
oro fiat ilud, quod tam sitio,
ut te revelata cernens facie,
visu sim beatus tuae gloriae.

Anonymous, first in a manuscript of
1323.

The translation of this (incomplete) most used in church, 'Thee we adore,' is
by J. R. Woodford, 1852, and it forms a satisfactory vehicle of public devotion,
even if–possibly because–it steers carefully round the more inaccessible subtleties of the original. Since it has inspired two of England's greatest poets who
would otherwise not appear in this collection, we give below the translation
first of Crashaw, and then, in the original meter, of Gerard Manley Hopkins.

(A)

With all the powers my poor soul hath
of humble love and loyal faith,
thus low, my God, I bow to thee,
whom too much love bowed lower for me.

Down, down, proud sense, discourses die,
and all adore faith's mystery!
Faith is my skill, faith can believe
as fast as love new laws can give.

Faith is my force, faith strength affords
to keep pace with those powerful words:
and words more sure, more sweet than they
Love could not think, truth could not say.

O dear memorial of that death,
which still survives, and gives us breath,
live ever, bread of life, and be
my food, my joy, my all to me.

O soft-self-wounding Pelican!
whose breast weeps balm for wounded man,
that blood, whose least drops sovereign be
to wash my worlds of sin from me.

* Come, glorious Lord, my hopes increase,
and fill my portion in thy peace:
come, hidden life, and that long day
for which I languish, come away,

* when this dry soul those eyes shall see,
and drink the unsealed source of thee;
when glory's sun faith's shade shall chase,
then for thy veil give me thy face.

* These 2 sts. translate st. 7 in the
original.

Adapted by **JOHN AUSTIN***, 1668,
from the translation of **Richard Cra-
shaw***, 1613-50.

(B)

Godhead here in hiding, whom I do adore
masked by these bare shadows, shape and nothing more,
see, Lord, at thy service low lies here a heart
lost, all lost in wonder at the God thou art.

Seeing, touching, tasting are in thee deceived;
how says trusty hearing? That shall be believed;
what God's Son hath told me, take for truth I do;
truth himself speaks truly, or there's nothing true.

On the Cross thy Godhead made no sign to men;
here thy very manhood steals from human ken;
both are my confession, both are my belief,
and I pray the prayer of the dying thief.

I am not like Thomas, wounds I cannot see,
but can plainly call thee Lord and God as he;
this faith each day deeper be my holding of,
daily make me harder hope and dearer love.

O thou our reminder of Christ crucified,
living Bread, the life of us for whom he died,
lend this life to me then; feed and feast my mind,
there be thou, the sweetness man was meant to find.

Bring the tender tale true of the Pelican;
bathe me, Jesus Lord, in what thy bosom ran -
blood that but one drop of has the power to win
all the world forgiveness of its world of sin.

Jesus whom I look at shrouded here below,
I beseech thee send me what I thirst for so,
some day to gaze on thee face to face in light
and be blest for ever with thy glory's light.

GERARD MANLEY HOPKINS, 1844-89
(first published 1918)

166
STABAT MATER   HG 876

[The Latin hymn is a prayer to the Virgin; in Anglican use it was so translated as
to keep clear of that worship of the Virgin which some felt unable to accept. The
following translation is that used in the *English Hymnal*, which contains elements
from the earlier work of one Anglican and one Roman Catholic translator.]

Stabat Mater dolorosa	At the cross her station keeping
iuxta crucem lacrimosa	stood the mournful Mother weeping
dum pendebat Filius;	close to Jesus at the last,
cuius animam gementem,	through her soul, of joy bereavéd,
contristantem et dolentem	bowed with anguish, deeply grievéd,
pertransivit gladius.	now at length the sword hath passed. (Lk. 2:35)
O quam tristis et afflicta	O that blessed one, grief-laden,
fuit illa benedicta	blessed Mother, blessed Maiden,
Mater unigeniti!	Mother of the holy One;
Quae maerebat et dolebat	O that silent, ceaseless mourning,
pia Mater dum videbat	O those dim eyes, never turning
nati poenas inclyti!	from that wondrous, suffering Son.
Quis est homo qui non fleret	Who on Christ's dear Mother gazing,
Matrem Christi si videret	in her trouble so amazing,
in tanto supplicio?	born of woman, would not weep?
quis non posset contristari,	Who on Christ's dear Mother thinking,
Christi matrem contemplari	such a cup of sorrow drinking,
dolentem cum Filio?	would not share her sorrow deep?
pro peccatis suae gentis	For his people's sins, in anguish,
vidit Jesum in tormentis	there she saw the Victim languish,
et flagellis subditum.	bleed in torments, bleed and die:
vidit suum dulcem Natum	saw the Lord's anointed taken;

moriendo desolatum
  dum emisit spiritum.

Eia Mater, fons amoris,
me sentire vim doloris
  fac, ut tecum lugeam.
Fac, ut ardeat cor meum
in amando Christum Deum
  ut sibi complaceam.

Sancta Mater, istud agas
crucifixi fige plagas
  cordi meo valide.
Tui Nati vulnerati,
tam dignati pro me pati
  poenas mecum divide.

Fac me tecum pie flere,
crucifixo condolere
  donec ego vixero;
juxta crucem tecum stare
et me tibi sociare
  in planctu desidero.

Virgo virginum praeclara
mihi iam non sis amara,
  fac me tecum plangere.
Fac ut portem Christi mortem,
passionis fac consortem
  et plagas recolere.

Fac me plagis vulnerari,

fac me cruce inebriari
  et cruore Filii.
Flammis ne urar successus,

per te, Virgo, sim defensus

  in die iudicii.

Christe, cum sit hinc exire,
da per Matrem me venire
  ad palmam victoriae.

Quando corpus morietur,
fac ut animae donetur
  paradisi gloria.

JACOPONE DA TODI, 1230-1306

saw her Child in death forsaken;
  heard her last expiring cry.

(In the Passion of my Maker
be my sinful soul partaker,
  may I with her bear my part;
of his passion bear the token,
in a spirit bowed and broken
  bear his death within my heart.)

May his wounds both wound and
              heal me,
he enkindle, cleanse, anneal me,
  be his cross my hope and stay.
May he, when the mountains
              quiver,
from that flame which burns for
              ever
  shield me on the judgment day.

Jesu, may thy cross defend me,
and thy saving death befriend me,
  cherished by thy deathless
              grace;
when to dust my soul returneth
grant a soul that to thee yearneth
  in thy Paradise a place.

Tr. **R. Mant**, 1837, **Aubrey de Vere**, 1884
and compilers of the *English Hymnal*,
1906

(Note: a translation was made by **E. Caswall** in 1849, in meter 77.7.77.7)

167
THE LENGTH, THE BREADTH, THE HEIGHT

HG 545

O amor quam ecstaticus!

quam effluens, quam nimius!
qui Deum Dei Filium

unum fecit mortalium!

Non invisit nos Angelo,
seu supremo seu infimo,
carnis assumens pallium
venit ad nos per se ipsum.

O Love, how deep, how broad,
             how high,
it fills the heart with ecstasy,
that God, the Son of God, should
             take
our mortal form for mortals' sake.

He sent no angel to our race
of higher or of lower place,
but wore the robe of human frame
himself, and to this lost world
             came.

nobis baptisma suscipit,
nobis jejunans esurit,
nobis et Satan hunc tentat,
nobis tentantem superat.

nobis orat et praedicat,
pro nobis cuncta factitat,
verbis, signis et actibus

nos quaerens, non se, penitus.

pro nobis comprehenditur,
flagellatur, conspuitur,

crucis perfert patibulum,

pro nobis tradit spiritum.

nobis surgit a mortuis,
nobis se transfert superis,
nobis suum dat Spiritum,
in robur, in solatium.

Deo Patri sit gloria,

per infinita saecula,
cuius amore nimio
salvu sumus in Filio.

ST THOMAS A KEMPIS (HG 402),
1379-1471

For us he was baptized, and bore
his holy fast, and hungered sore;
for us temptation sharp he knew,
for us the tempter overthrew.

For us he prayed, for us he taught,
for us his daily works he wrought,
by words and signs and actions
             thus
still seeking not himself, but us.

For us to wicked men betrayed,
scourged, mocked, in purple robe
            arrayed,
he bore the shameful cross and
           death,
for us at length gave up his breath.

For us he rose from death again;
for us he went on high to reign:
for us he sent his Spirit here
to guide, to comfort and to cheer.

To him whose boundless love has
            won
salvation for us through his Son,
to God the Father, glory be
both now and through eternity.

BENJAMIN WEBB, 1852

Later Latin Lyrics

168
YE SONS AND DAUGHTERS

HG 562

O Filii et filiae,
rex caelestis, rex gloriae,

morte revixit hodie. *Alleluia!*

et Maria Magdalenae (Mark 16:1)
at Jacobi et Salome
venerunt corpus unguere. . . .

in albis sedens angelus
          (Mark 16:7)
praedixit mulieribus,
'In Galilaea est Dominus'. . . .

discipulis adstantibus (John 20:19)
in medio stetit Christus,

dicens 'pax vobis omnibus' . . . .

postquam audivit Didymus (John
          20:24)
quia surrexerat Jesus,
remansit fide dubis. . . .

'Vide, Thoma, vide latus, (John 20:
          27)
vide pedes, vide manus;
noli esse incredulus'. . . .

Alleluia! Alleluia! Alleluia!
O sons and daughters, let us sing!
the King of heaven, the glorious
            King
o'er death to-day rose triumph-
           ing;
           Alleluia!

That Easter morn, at break of day
the faithful women went their way
to seek the tomb where Jesus
           lay. . . .

An angel clad in white they see,

who sat, and spake unto the three,
'Your Lord is gone to Galilee'. . . .

That night the apostles met in fear;
amidst them came their Lord most
           dear,
and said, 'my peace be on all
           here' . . . .

When Thomas first the tidings
           heard,
how they had seen the risen Lord,
he doubted the disciples' word. . . .

'My piercéd side, O Thomas, see;

my hands, my feet, I show to thee;
not faithless, but believing be.' . . .

quando Thomas vidit Christum,
pedes, latus, suum, manus,

dixit 'tu es Deus meus.' . . .

No longer Thomas then denied;
he saw the feet, the hands, the
side;

'Thou art my Lord and God,' he
cried. . . .

beati qui non viderunt   (John
20:29)

et firmiter crediderunt;

vitam aeterman habebunt. . . .

How blest are they who have not
seen,
and yet whose faith hath constant
been!
for they eternal life shall win. . . .

in hoc festo sanctissimo
sit laus et iubilatio;

benedicamus Domino. Alleluia!

On this most holy day of days,
to God your hearts and voices
raise
in laud and jubilee and praise.
Alleluia!

J. TISSERAND, d. 1494

Tr. based on **J. M. Neale**, 1851 (1861)

169
FOOD FOR TRAVELLERS   HG 864
A

O esca viatorum,
o panis angelorum,
  o manna caelitum,
esurientes ciba,
dulcedine non priva
  cor te quaerentium.

O food of men wayfaring,
the Bread of Angels sharing,
  O manna from on high!
we hunger; Lord, supply us,
nor thy delights deny us,
  whose hearts to thee draw nigh.

o lympha, fons amoris,
qui puro salvatoris
  e corde profluis,
te sitientes pota;
haec sola nostra vota;
  his una sufficis.

O stream of love past telling,
O purest fountain, welling
  from out the Saviour's side!
We faint with thirst, revive us,
of thine abundance give us,
  and all we need provide.

o Jesu, tuum vultum
quem colimus occultum
  sub panis specie,
fac ut remoto velo
aperta nos in caelo
  cernamus acie.

O Jesu, by thee bidden,
we here adore thee, hidden
  'neath forms of bread and wine.
Grant, when the veil is riven,
we may behold, in heaven
  thy countenance divine.

Anon. c. 1661

Tr. **Athelstan Riley** (HG 112), 1906

B

O bread to pilgrims given,
  O food that angels eat,
O manna sent from heaven
  for heaven-born natures meet:
give us, for thee long pining,
  to eat till richly filled;
till, earth's delights resigning,
  our every wish is stilled.

O Fountain, purely flowing
  forth from that sacred heart,
our Saviour's grace bestowing,
  true wine of life thou art.
O let us, freely tasting
  our spirit's thirst assuage;
thy goodness, never wasting,
  avails from age to age.

Jesus, this feast receiving,
  we thee unseen adore;
thy faithful word believing,
  we take, and doubt no more:
give us, thou true and loving,
  on earth to live in thee;
then, death the veil removing,
  thy glorious face to see.

Tr. **Ray Palmer** (HG 370), 1858, st. 2
altered as in *Hymns for Celebration*,
1974

170
THE POWER OF THE WORD   HG 164

Supreme quales, arbiter
tibi ministros eligis,
tuas opes qui vilibus

vasis amas committere!   (2 Cor.
4:7)

Christum sonant: versae ruunt
arces superbae daemonum;
circum tubis clangentibus (Jos.
6:20

sic versa quondam moenis.

haec nempe plena lumine
tu vasa frangi praecipis;
lux inde magna rumpitur,
ceu nube scissa fulgura.

fac, Christe, caelestes tubae
somno graves nos excitent:
accensa de te lumina
pellant tenebras mentium.

totum per orbem nuntii
nubes velut citi colant:
verbo graves, Verbo Deo,
tonant, coruscant, perpluunt.

uni sit et trino Deo
suprema laus, summum decus,
de nocte qui nos ad suae
lumen vocavit gloriae. (1 Pet. 2:9)

J. B. DE SANTEUIL (HG 101), 1686

Disposer supreme, and Judge of the earth
  who choosest for thine the meek and the poor;
to frail earthen vessels, and things of no worth
  entrusting thy riches which ay shall endure;

those vessels soon fail, though full of thy light,
  and at thy decree are broken and gone;
thence brightly appeareth thy truth in its might
  as though the clouds riven the lightnings have shone.

Like clouds are they borne to do thy great will,
  and swift as the winds about the world go;
the Word with his wisdom their spirits doth fill;
  they thunder, they lighten, their waters o'erflow.

Their sound goeth forth, 'Christ Jesus the Lord!'
  then Satan doth fear, his citadels fall;
as when the dread trumpets went forth at thy word,
  and one long blast shattered the Canaanite's wall.

O loud be their trump, and stirring their sound,
  to rouse us, O Lord, from slumber of sin!
The lights thou hast kindled in darkness around,
  O may they awaken our spirits within!

All honour and praise, dominion and might,
  to God, Three in One, eternally be,
who round us hath shed his own marvellous light
  and called us from darkness his glory to see.

ISAAC WILLIAMS (HG 71), 1836

171
VEILED IN FLESH   HG 334

Divine crescebas puer;

crescendo discebas mori:
haec destinata tunc erant

mortis tuae praeludia.

satus Deo, volens tegi,
elegit obscurum patrem;
qui fecit aeternas domos

domo latet sub paupere.

caelum manus quae sustinent

fabrile contrectant opus;
supremus astrorum parens
fit ipse vilis artifex.

tremenda cuius praepetes
mandata portant spiritus,
cui pronus orbis subditur,

se sponte fabro subicut.

qui natus es de virgine,
Jesu, tibi sit gloria
cum Patre cumque Spiritu
in sempiterna saecula.

J. B. DE SANTEUIL (HG 101), 1689

In stature grows the heavenly
child,
with death before his eyes;
a Lamb unblemished, meek and
mild,
prepared for sacrifice.

The Son of God his glory hides
with parents mean and poor;
and he who made the heaven
abides
in dwelling-place obscure.

Those mighty hands that stay the
sky
no earthly toil refuse;
and he who set the stars on high
an humble trade pursues.

He before whom the angels stand,
at whose behest they fly,
now yields himself to man's
command,
and lays his glory by.

Jesu, the Virgin's holy Son,
we praise thee and adore,
who art with God the Father One
and Spirit evermore.

J. CHANDLER (HG 52), 1837

172
VENI IMMANUEL   HG 502

Veni veni Emmanuel;

captivum solve Israel,
qui gemit in exilio,
privatus Dei Filio.
   gaude, gaude, Emmanuel
nascetur pro te, Israel.

veni, o Jesse virgula;

ex hostis tuos ungula
de specu tuos tartari

educ et antro barathri.

   gaude, gaude, Emmanuel
nascetur pro te, Israel.

veni, veni, o Oriens;

solare nos adveniens;
noctis depelle nebulas

dirasque noctis tenebras.

   gaude, gaude, Emmanuel
nascetur pro te, Israel.

veni, Clavis Davidica;

regna reclude caelica;

O come, O come, Immanuel
(Is. 7:14)
and ransom captive Israel
that mourns in lonely exile here
until the Son of God appear.
   Rejoice! Rejoice! Immanuel
shall come to thee, O Israel.

O come, thou Rod of Jesse, free
(Is. 11:1)
thine own from Satan's tyranny;
from depths of hell thy people
save
and give them victory o'er the
grave.
   Rejoice! Rejoice! Immanuel
shall come to thee, O Israel.

O come, thou Dayspring come
and cheer   (Lk. 1:78)
our spirits by thine advent here;
disperse the gloomy clouds of
night
and death's dark shadows put to
flight.
   Rejoice! Rejoice! Immanuel
shall come to thee, O Israel.

O come, thou Key of David,
come,   (Is. 22:22)
and open wide our heavenly
home;   (Rev. 3:7)

fac iter tutum superum,

at claude vias inferum.
   gaude, gaude, Emmanuel
nascetur pro te, Israel.

veni, veni, Adonaï,

quo populo in Sinaï
legem dedisti vertice
in maiestate gloriae.
   gaude, gaude, Emmanuel
nascetur pro te, Israel.

Anon. 1710

make safe the way that leads on
high,
and close the path to misery.
   Rejoice! Rejoice! Immanuel
shall come to thee, O Israel.

O come, O come, thou Lord of
might (Ex. 20)
who to thy tribes on Sinai's height
in ancient times didst give the law
in cloud and majesty and awe.
   Rejoice! Rejoice! Immanuel
shall come to thee, O Israel.

J. M. NEALE (HG 2), 1852; text altered,
1868

173
GOD FROM ON HIGH HATH HEARD   HG 853

Iam desinant suspiria;
audivit ex alto Deus:
caeli patescunt; en adest
promissa pax mortalibus.

profunda noctis otia
caelestis abrumpit chorus,
natumque festo carmine
annuntiat terris Deum.

specum sacratum pervigil
dum turba pastorum subit,
eamus et castis pia
cunis feramus oscula.

at qualis nobis panditur
instantibus spectaculum
praesepe, faenum, fasciae,
parens inops, infans puer.

tunc ille, Christe, Filius
et splendor aeterni Patris?
illumne cerno, qui levi
orbem pugillo sustinet?

sic est: verenda, queis lates,
fides penetrat nubila:
agnosco quem proni vident
tremunt, adorant angeli.

agis magistrum vel tacens:
ex hac cathedra nos doces
vitare quod carni placet,
caro quod horret perpeti.

castos amores nutriens,
sanans tumentes spiritus,
divine nostris o puer
praecordiis innascere.

C. COFFIN (HG 52), 1736

God from on high hath heard!
let sighs and sorrows cease;
the skies unfold, and lo!
descends the gift of peace!

Hark on the midnight air
celestial voices swell:
the hosts of heaven proclaim
'God comes on earth to dwell.'

Haste with the shepherds; see
the mystery of grace;
a manger-bed, a child
is all the eye can trace.

Is this the eternal Son
who on the starry throne
before the world began
was with the Father one?

Yes, Faith can pierce the cloud
which shrouds his glory now;
and hail him Lord and God
to whom all creatures bow.

Faith sees the sapphire throne
where angels evermore
adoring, tremble still,
and trembling still, adore.

O Child! thy silence speaks
and bids us not refuse
to bear what flesh would shun,
to spurn what flesh would
choose.

Fill us with holy love,
heal thou our earthly pride;
be born within our hearts,
and ever there abide.

J. R. WOODFORD (HG 834), 1852

174
A CHRISTIAN COMMUNITY   HG 263

O quam iuvat fratres, Deus,

unum quibus Christus caput

Christ is our Head, our strength,
our life,
our only and sufficient good;

vitale robur sufficit
uno moveri spiritu.

then, Lord, let unity inspire
   and aid our common brother-
                          hood.

quam dulce laudes dicere
una tibi cunctos domo,

Melodious let our mingled praise
   from this fair house to thee
                         ascend;

precumque ceu facta manu,
inferre vim gratam tibi.

and our petitions, strong as deeds,
   in thine approving Presence
                          blend.

hanc quisque diligat domum;
hanc pace concors recreet:
vae dira qui spargit malus
dissensionum semina.

Let here tranquility abound,
   as all in loving concord strive;
no bitter seed of enmity
   unto a baleful harvest thrive.

sed damna cedunt in lucrum

te, Christe, diligentibus:

augent coronas praelia;
prosuntque, dum nocent, mali.

Yet unto those who love thee,
                          Lord,
   all things together work for
                          good:
from injuries we gain a spur,
   a crown by agony and blood.

vox blanda saevit tristius,
dum pectus incautum subit,

lapusque caeco dulcibus
laudum venenis inficit.

More grievous is the cruel tongue
   that flatters with envenomed
                          art -
with honeyed insincerity
   corrupts the blind and heedless
                          heart.

praesta, beata Trinitas,
ut caritate mutua

prosimus alter alteri,
regnemus at polo simul.

Here then, O Trinity most blest,
   the humble grace to each be
                          given
to love his neighbour as himself,
   till thou enthrone us all in
                          heaven.

C. COFFIN (HG 52), 1736

L. H. BUNN, 1954

175
O COME, ALL YE FAITHFUL   HG 500

Adeste fideles,
laeti triumphantes,
venite, venite in Bethlehem;

O come, all ye faithful,
joyful and triumphant,
O come ye, O come ye to
                       Bethlehem;

natum videte
regem angelorum,
venite, adoremus Dominum.

come and behold him
born the King of angels:
*O come, let us adore him,
                    Christ the Lord.*

Deum de Deo,
lumen de lumine,
gestant puellae viscera:

God of God,
Light of light,
Lo! he abhors not the virgin's
                          womb;

Deum verum,
genitum, non factum. . . .

Very God
begotten, not created. . . .

* En grege relicto
humiles ad cunas
vocati pastores adproperant;

* See how the shepherds,
summoned to his cradle,
leaving their flocks, draw nigh
                    with lowly fear;

et nos ovanti
gradu festinemus. . . .

we too will thither
bend our joyful footsteps. . . .

† Stella duce Magi
Christum adorantes
aurum thus et myrrham dant
                          munera:

* Lo! star-led chieftains,
Magi, Christ adoring,
offer him incense, gold and
                          myrrh;

Jesu infanti
corda praebeamus. . . .

we to the Christ-Child
bring our hearts' oblations: . . .

* Aeterni parentis
splendorem aeternum
velatum sub carne videbimus;

† The splendour eternal
of eternal Godhead
veiled with infirmities of flesh
                       we see:

Deum infantem
pannis involutum. . . .

hiding his glory,
swaddling clothes he
                      weareth: . . .

* pro nobis egenum
et foeno cubantem,
piis foveamus amplexibus:

* Child, for us sinners,
poor and in the manger,
fain we embrace thee with awe
                      and love;

sic nos amantem
quis non redamaret? . . .

who would not love thee,
loving us so dearly? . . .

Cantet nunc Io!
chorus angelorum,
cantet nunc aula coelestium,

Sing, choirs of angels,
sing in exultation,
sing, all ye citizens of heaven
                          above;

Gloria
in excelsis Deo. . . .

Glory to God
in the highest! . . .

Ergo qui natus
die hodierna
Jesu tibi sit gloria:
Patris aeterni
verbum caro factum! . . .

Yea, Lord, we greet thee,
born this happy morning,
Jesu, to thee be glory given;
Word of the Father
now in flesh appearing. . .

from a ms. of **J. F. WADE**, 1751
(*) Abbé E. J. F. Borderies, 1822,
(†) *Paroissien Romain*, Paris, c. 1868

Later form of tr. by **F. Oakeley**, 1845
(*) Percy Dearmer (HG 88) in *English
Hymnal*, 1906
(†) Ronald A. Knox (HG 866), in *West-
minster Hymnal*, 1940

176
THE HEART OF JESUS   HG 757

Summi parentis Filio,
patri futuri saeculi,
pacis beatae principi,
promamus ore canticum.

To Christ, the Prince of Peace,
and Son of God most high,
the Father of the world to come,
we lift our joyful cry.

qui vulneratus pectore
amoris ictum pertulit,
amoris urens ignibus
ipsum qui amantem diligunt.

Deep in his heart for us
the wound of love he bore,
that love which he enkindles still
in hearts that him adore.

Jesu, doloris victima,
quis te innocentem compulit
dura ut apertum lancea
latus pateret vulneri?

O Jesu, victim blest,
what else but love divine
could thee constrain to open thus
that sacred heart of thine?

o fons amoris inclyte,
o vena aquarum limpida,
a flamma adurens crimina,
o cordis ardens caritas!

O wondrous fount of love,
O well of waters free,
O heavenly flame, refining fire,
O burning charity!

in corde, Jesu, iugiter
reconde nos, et uberi
dono fruamur gratiae

Hide us in thy dear heart,
Jesu, our Saviour blest,
so shall we find thy plenteous
                          grace

caelique tandem praemiis.

and heaven's eternal rest!

Roman Breviary, Lisbon, 1786

E. CASWALL (HG 21), 1849; altd., 1861

ARTICLE 12:
HYMNS FROM GREEK SOURCES (177-187)

The hymnody of the Greek-speaking church has contributed less to Western hymnody than that of the Latin church for reasons which, after reading Article 11, will be obvious.

Greek hymnody took forms quite different from the Latin and was used for quite different purposes. The short selection we here give shows how diverse those forms and purposes were.

The 'Lamplighting hymn' (177) was already well known in about 365 A.D., when St Basil mentions it as a familiar hymn. It certainly goes back into the days when Christians worshipped 'underground' (literally so when they were in the catacombs), and when 'light' had a special significance for people whose only safe place of worship was in the dark. It is also just about the first Greek hymn to find an English translation. John Keble (see article 9) made a version of it in what approximates to the original meter. His translation is slightly obscure here and there, and we add a second which is more literal and was made for a modern recension of the original Greek melody. Robert Bridges also translated it metrically, to go with the Genevan tune for the *Nunc Dimittis*, in his Yattendon Hymnal; this, 'O gladsome Light,' appears in many current hymnals.

We may suppose that there were plenty of hymns before this one. The New English Bible translation of Ephesians 5:13-14 makes it quite clear that the quotation 'Awake thou that sleepest' is presumed by those translators to be from a hymn. Many other passages in the Epistles and Revelation are thought similarly to be fragments of hymns.

But nothing that one can call organized hymnody appeared until the 7th century at earliest. The period 700-900 saw the writing and singing of massive festal songs known as Canons and Contakions consisting of long odes with florid music, mostly referring to the Resurrection, and especially associated with Easter. Our ## 178 and 179 come from two of these. The originals are in wayward meters which cannot be reproduced for English singing, so J. M. Neale took his own line about meter, and, as always when he allowed himself to do that, produced translations which run beautifully and catch the festive spirit of the originals.

Other English hymns have been made out of Greek prayers: liturgical, like ## 180-2, or private, like ## 183-5. We owe most of these to 'Oxford Movement' translators who valued the originals for their liturgical and devotional messages, and certainly in ## 180-2 we have a trio of magnificent liturgical hymns. The translations by the Scottish minister John Brownlie are also very valuable, ## 184-5 being particularly good, and also 'O King, enthroned on high' (*EH* 454). The original of # 184 is a poem by one of the outstanding Christian Greek poets; that of # 185 is now unascertainable.

Neale's delicious carol 'A great and mighty wonder' (186) was written in this meter because he tended to use it when he was free to choose; the arrangement with a refrain made out of stanza 3, for the SPOTLESS ROSE tune, was a happy inspiration of the editors of the *English Hymnal*.

Of # 187, and one or two others including 'Art thou weary,' Neale wrote that since they bore no closer relation to a Greek original than having been suggested by a single phrase, they ought to be regarded as hymns mostly of his own invention. This, in his favourite meter again, is a particularly pleasant one.

For detailed information about Greek hymnody see E. Wellesz, *Byzantine Music and Hymnography*, 1947.

177
AT THE LIGHTING OF THE LAMPS
Phōs Hilaron

(A) The earliest English Translation, following the line-scheme of the Greek:

> Hail, gladdening light, of his pure glory poured
> who is the immortal Father, heavenly, blest;
> Holiest of holies, Jesus Christ our Lord!
>
> Now we are come to the sun's hour of rest,
> the lights of evening round us shine,
> we hymn the Father, Son and Holy Spirit divine.
>
> Worthiest art thou at all times to be sung
>   with undefiled tongue,
> Son of our God, giver of life, alone:
> therefore in all the world thy glories, Lord, they own.

JOHN KEBLE (HG 83), 1834

(B) A new translation, following the meter of the Greek as set to the original tune.

> Christ, gladdening light of holy glory,
> glory of God, heavenly Father immortal,
> the holy blessed one, our Lord Jesus Christ:
>
> we come now to the peaceful hour of sunset;
> we see the star of evening shine;
> we sing to the Father, the Son and the Holy Spirit, one God.
>
> You are worthy at all times to be praised
> and honoured with pure and pious songs,
> God's only Son, our only life-giver:
> wherefore all the world gives glory to you, its Master.

E. R., 1972

(C) A lyric translation set to a Genevan hymn tune

> O gladsome light, O grace
> of God the Father's face,
> the eternal splendour wearing:
> celestial, holy, blest,
> our Saviour, Jesus Christ,
> joyful in thine appearing;
>
> now e'er day fadeth quite
> we see the evening light,
> our wonted hymn outpouring;
> Father of might unknown,
> thee, his incarnate Son
> and Holy Spirit adoring.
>
> To thee of right belongs
> all praise of holy songs,
> O Son of God, lifegiver;
> thee therefore, O most high,
> the world doth glorify
> and shall exalt for ever.

ROBERT BRIDGES (HG 9), 1899

178
EASTER HYMN   HG 148

[No attempt is ever made in English translations to preserve Greek meters. We provide a literal translation of the Greek originals, where it is appropriate, to compare with the versification that follows.]

All peoples: let us sing praise to him who has delivered Israel from Pharaoh's bitter bondage, and who has led him through the depths of the sea dry-shod, by a way of victory, to his glory.

Today is the spring of souls, for Christ, like the sun shining after a dark winter, has shone out again after three days, driving away the winter of our sin; we sing praise to him, to his glory.

On this royal light-bringing day of days, the gift-bearing Queen of seasons brings joy to the chosen people of the church, ceaselessly praising the risen Christ.

Neither the gates of death, nor the seals on the tomb, nor the keys of its doors, held you back, O Christ; but risen, Master, you gave your Peace to your friends, a gift which exceeds all understanding.

Come, ye faithful, raise the strain
  of triumphant gladness!
God has brought us, Israel,
  into joy from sadness:
loosed from Pharaoh's bitter yoke
  Jacob's sons and daughters,
led them with unmoistened foot
  through the Red Sea waters.

'Tis the spring of souls to-day:
  Christ hath burst his prison;
and from three days' sleep in death
  as a sun hath risen.
All the winter of our sins,
  long and dark, is flying
from his light, to whom we give
  laud and praise undying.

Now the Queen of seasons bright
  with the day of splendour,
with the royal feast of feasts,
  comes its joy to render:
comes to glad Jerusalem,
  who with true affection
welcomes, in unwearied strains
  Jesus' Resurrection.

Neither might the gates of death,
  nor the tomb's dark portal
nor the watchers, nor the seal
  hold these as a mortal;
but to-day amidst thy friends*
  thou didst stand, bestowing
that thy peace, which evermore
  passeth human knowing.

J. M. NEALE (HG 2), 1862,
*(one line altd.)

179
THE DAY OF RESURRECTION   HG 687

A day of resurrection! People, proudly tell of it. A Passover, a Passover of the Lord! For Christ, who is God, has brought us over from death to life, from earth to heaven, and we are singing songs of victory.

Let us purify our affections, as we prepare to see the risen Christ flashing in the unapproachable light of his resurrection, and as we prepare to hear him clearly saying 'Greeting to you!'; so we sing songs of victory.

Let the heavens be duly joyful; let the earth exult; let the universe, visible and invisible, keep festival; for Christ our eternal joy is risen.

The day of Resurrection!
  Earth! tell it out abroad!
The Passover of gladness!
  the Passover of God!
From death to life eternal, -
  from this world to the sky,
our Christ hath brought us over
  with hymns of victory.

Our hearts be pure from evil,
  that we may see aright
the Lord in rays eternal
  of Resurrection-light:
and, listening to his accents,
  may hear so calm and plain
his own 'All hail!' and hearing
  may raise the victor strain!

Now let the heavens be joyful!
  let earth her song begin!
Let the round earth keep triumph,
  and all that is therein:
Invisible and visible,
  their notes let all things blend -
for Christ the Lord hath risen -
  our Joy that hath no end.

ST JOHN OF DAMASCUS, tr. **J. M. Neale** (HG 2), 1862 (later version of first line)

180
LET ALL THE EARTH KEEP SILENCE BEFORE HIM
Hab. 2:20   HG 388

[From the Prayer at the opening of the Eucharist in the Liturgy of St James, found in both Greek and Syriac in the mid-4th century.]

Let all mortal flesh keep silence, and with fear and trembling stand;
ponder nothing earthly-minded, for with blessing in his hand
Christ our God to earth descendeth our full homage to demand.

King of kings, yet born of Mary, as of old on earth he stood,
Lord of lords, in human venture—in the Body and the Blood—
he will give to all the faithful his own self for heavenly Food.

Rank on rank the host of heaven spreads its vanguard on the way,
as the Light of light descendeth from the realms of endless day,
that the powers of hell may vanish as the darkness clears away.

At his feet the six-winged Seraph: Cherubim with sleepless eye,
veil their faces to the Presence, as with ceaseless voice they cry,
'Alleluia! Alleluia! Alleluia! Lord most high.'

tr. **Gerard Moultrie**, 1864

181
AFTER COMMUNION   HG 665

[Originally in Syriac, from a closing prayer at the Eucharist in the Liturgy of Malabar, observed in the 5th century in the Nestorian Church of South India.]

Strengthen for service, Lord, the hands
  that holy things have taken;
let ears that now have heard thy songs
  to clamour never waken.

Lord, may the tongues which 'Holy' sang
  keep free from all deceiving;
the eyes which saw thy love be bright
  thy blessed hope perceiving.

The feet that tread thy holy courts
  from light do thou not banish;
the bodies by thy Body fed
  with thy new life replenish.

PERCY DEARMER (HG 88), 1906, altered from a hymn by C. W. Humphreys.

182
FROM GLORY TO GLORY   HG 212

[From the closing prayer at the Eucharist in the Liturgy of St James, 4th century.]

Making the journey from glory to glory, we sing praise to you, the Saviour of our souls. Glory to the Father, and to the Son, and to the Holy Spirit, now and always to ages of ages. We praise you, Saviour of our souls.

Making the journey from strength to strength, completing all our service in your temple, we now pray you, Lord our God, to count us worthy of your utter love for mankind; make straight our journey; plant us firmly in the fear of you, and deem us worthy of the heavenly Kingdom, in Christ Jesus our Lord, with whom you are to be praised, and with the all-holy, righteous and life-giving Spirit, now and always, to ages of ages.

From glory to glory advancing, we praise thee, O Lord;
thy name with the Father and Spirit be ever adored.

From strength unto strength we go forward on Sion's highway,
to appear before God in the City of infinite day.

Thanksgiving and glory and worship, and blessing and love
one heart and one song have the saints upon earth and above.

Evermore O Lord, to thy servants thy presence be nigh;
ever fit us by service on earth for thy service on high.

C. W. HUMPHREYS, 1906

183
THE PRAYER OF BISHOP SYNESIUS   HG 426

Christ, Son of the most high God, remember your servant, a man of
sinful heart, who writes this; send deliverance from sorrows and griefs
to my soul, born in sin; Jesus, Saviour, grant me to see your divine
radiance, so that having seen, I may sing a song, praises in my soul,
praises in my body, to the Father with the great Holy Spirit.

Lord Jesus, think on me,
and purge away my sin;
from earthborn passions set me free,
and make me pure within.

Lord Jesus, think on me,
with care and woe opprest;
let me thy loving servant be,
and taste thy promised rest.

Lord Jesus, think on me,
amid the battle's strife;
in all my pain and misery
be thou my health and life.

Lord Jesus, think on me,
nor let me go astray;
through darkness and perplexity
point thou my heavenly way.

Lord Jesus, think on me
when flows the tempest high;
when on doth rush the enemy,
O Saviour be thou nigh.

Lord Jesus, think on me,
that, when the flood is past,
I may the eternal brightness see,
and share thy joy at last.

SYNESIUS OF CYRENE, c. 375-430; tr.
A. W. Chatfield, 1876.

184
PRAYER FOR PURITY   HG 533

O Light that knew no dawn,
that shines to endless day,
all things in earth and heaven
are lustred by thy ray;
no eye can to thy throne ascend,
nor mind thy brightness comprehend.

Thy grace, O Father, give,
that I may serve with fear,
above all boon, I pray,
grant me thy voice to hear;
from sin thy child in mercy free
and let me dwell in light with thee;

that, cleansed from stain of sin,
I may meet homage give,
and, pure in heart, behold   (Matt. 5:3)
thy beauty while I live;

clean hands in holy worship raise   (Ps. 26:6)
and thee, O Christ my Saviour, praise.

In supplication meek
to thee I bend the knee;
O Christ, when thou shalt come   (Lk. 23:42)
in love remember me,
and in thy kingdom, by thy grace
grant me a humble servant's place.

Thy grace, O Father, give,
I humbly thee implore,
and let thy mercy bless
thy servant more and more.
All grace and glory be to thee
from age to age eternally.

ST GREGORY OF NAZIANZUS, c. 325-
395, tr. J. Brownlie (HG 531), 1900

185
THE KING IN HIS BEAUTY   HG 699

The King shall come when morning dawns
and light triumphant breaks,
when beauty gilds the eastern hills
and life to joy awakes.

Not as of old a little child
to bear and fight and die,
but crowned with glory, like the sun
that lights the morning sky.

O brighter than the rising morn
when he, victorious, rose,
and left the lonesome place of death
despite the rage of foes.

O brighter than that glorious morn
shall this fair morning be
when Christ our King in beauty comes,
and we his face shall see!   (Is. 33:20)

The King shall come when morning dawns,
and light and beauty brings;
Hail, Christ the Lord! thy people say,
come quickly, King of kings.

Anonymous Greek hymn: tr. J.
Brownlie (HG 531), 1907

186
THE DIVINE PARADOX   HG 2

Today is achieved a great and unimaginable wonder: a Virgin gives
birth, her maidenhood intact; the Word is made flesh, and yet is not
separated from the Father. Angels sing praises with the shepherds, and
we shout with them: 'Glory to God in the highest, and peace upon
earth.'

All the angels are dancing in heaven, and keep festival to-day; the
whole creation rejoices, since our Saviour, the Lord, is born in Bethlehem; the age of the idols comes to an end, and Christ reigns for ever.

A great and mighty wonder!
a full and holy cure!
the Virgin bears the infant
with Virgin-honour pure!

The Word becomes incarnate,
   and yet remains on high:
and Cherubim sing anthems
   to shepherds from the sky.

And we with them triumphant
   repeat the hymn again:
'To God on high be glory,
   and peace on earth to men!'

While thus they sing your Monarch,
   those bright angelic bands,
rejoice, ye vales and mountains!
   ye oceans, clap your hands!

Since all he comes to ransom,
   by all be he adored,
the Infant born in Bethlehem,
   the Saviour and the Lord!

And idol forms shall perish,
   and error shall decay'
and Christ shall wield his sceptre,
   our Lord and God for aye.

ST GERMANOS, 634-734; tr. **J. M. Neale**, 1862

187
THE WEIGHT OF GLORY   HG 520

O happy band of pilgrims,
   if onward ye will tread,
with Jesus as your Fellow,
   to Jesus as your Head!

O happy if ye labour
   as Jesus did for men;
O happy if ye hunger
   as Jesus hungered then.   (Matt. 4:1)

The Cross that Jesus carried
   he carried as your due;
the Crown that Jesus weareth,
   he weareth it for you.

The faith by which ye see him,
   the hope in which ye yearn,
the love that through all troubles
   to him alone will turn,

what are they but vaunt-couriers   (Heb. 11:1)
   to lead you to his sight?
what are they save the effluence
   of uncreated light?

The trials that beset you,
   the sorrows ye endure,
the manifold temptations
   that death alone can cure,

what are they but his jewels
   of right celestial worth?
what are they but the ladder   (Gen. 28:20)
   set up to heaven on earth?

O happy band of pilgrims,
   look upward to the skies,
where such a light affliction   (2 Cor. 4:17)
   shall win you such a prize!

J. M. NEALE (HG 2), 1862, suggested by a Greek poem.

ARTICLE 13:
HYMNS FROM GERMAN AND ITALIAN SOURCES (188-205)

Perhaps it is harder for most hymn singers to imagine a world without 'Now thank we all our God' than a world without 'All glory, laud and honour'; but the historical fact is that before the mid-nineteenth century virtually no hymns from the German language were known in England. The exceptions were John Wesley's translations (55-6, 197-8) and possibly a stray translation from Gerhardt by A. M. Toplady, 'Holy Ghost, dispel our sadness,' which is now better known in America than in England.

The reason for the mid-century interest in German hymnody is quite different from that which produced the Latin and Greek hymns in the preceding section. Neale and company made versions of the Latin and Greek hymns because they deplored the historical and religious isolationism of the English church and sought to recover the liturgical disciplines–and with them, the hymnody–of the Middle Ages. The German originals are not medieval but post-Lutheran, not Catholic but Protestant, and the protest of the translators of these, who were contemporaries of the liturgical translators, was against England's geographical isolationism. Or you can say that a general interest in foreign travel and the beginning of the process which has so recently produced political and economic efforts towards European unity aroused in the English a new desire to share the praises of that country which was the real birthplace of congregational hymnody. German scholarship, especially in theology, was becoming known in England, and very disturbing the English often found it. German literature was beginning to find a response. German music, of course, was insisting on being heard.

Catherine Winkworth (1827-78) is the translator from German who corresponds to J. M. Neale in the Latin field. Her *Lyra Germanica*, in two parts (1856, 1858), contains her first attempts to communicate German lyric to English readers. But that is exactly how to put it: the *Lyra Germanica* was not intended as a book to sing from, and it contained no music. Therefore it did not matter too much that fairly often she did not reproduce the German meters. She was usually fairly close to them but did not feel it necessary to be precise. See her translation at # 199 for an example of this. In adjusting meters to make it easier to write in familiar English styles, she followed John Wesley, who made less attempt than she did to preserve original meters.

Personal contact with the Baron Bunsen, German Ambassador to Britain, inspired this work, but contact with musicians immediately after it was published persuaded her that a hymnal consisting of her translations with music would fill a need. So she produced the *Chorale-Book for England* in 1863, containing 200 pieces. Some were new (such as ## 190 and 191, the two most famous of all her translations), but some were revised versions of pieces in the earlier books, adjusted to carry their proper German tunes. (English readers can see an example of this happening by turning to # 159 in the *Methodist Hymn Book*, which is the 1858 version, and comparing it with # 381 in *Congregational Praise*, which is the 1863 revision, of her translation of Luther's 130th Psalm, for the original of which see # 2 in this collection.) She was very fortunate in her musical collaborators: Sterndale Bennett, one of the best English composers of his time; and Otto Goldschmid (husband of Jenny Lind), one of the best musicologists. The 1863 book therefore becomes one of the most fertile sources of familiar hymnody from the German.

Before this time, the only English translator of German hymns whose work has lasted was John Wesley, who, just before his 'conversion' in 1738, translated many German pieces, especially from the work of pietist authors who were almost his contemporaries. (In the Wesley *corpus* it is usually understood that Charles Wesley wrote original hymns while John was content to translate.) The style of these translations is always lofty and eloquent–see our ## 195 and 202–but Wesley always felt free not only to use meters which would in those days carry tunes familiar to the English singers but also to paraphrase. In 1774, Toplady, author of 'Rock of Ages,' translated a Gerhardt hymn, 'Holy Ghost, dispel our sadness,' without in his own works acknowledging that it was a translation. Nowadays this is normally sung not in his (or Gerhardt's) original meter but as rearranged in 8.7.8.7 D. (See, e.g., *Worshipbook* 342, which carries two of the original seven stanzas.) These apart, it was Catherine Winkworth's contemporaries who supplemented her own great work: Emma Frances Bevan (201); the Scottish sisters, Sarah Findlater ('Jesus still lead on') and Jane Borthwick (203); and Frances E. Cox (whose 'Jesus lives!' is especially fine; and see also our # 198). Another Scot, Richard Massie, often achieves an eloquence which translators usually find it necessary to renounce (see our 1 and 2), and of course 'Ein' feste Burg' generated many excellent translations of which yet another Scot, Thomas Carlyle, wrote that which is most famous in Britain. We have included this in our Scottish section at # 330, but the American translation is at # 4, and both these come slightly before the main wave of English translations, 'Ein' feste Burg' being, as we said in article 1, something of a special case.

Apart from that, and one other (190) which we are about to mention, English translation from German was really begun in the 1850s, and historically it was a function of the new interest in Britain in foreign literature and in scholarship. But it brought into English hymnody a new strain of devotion which only the Germans of the period 1650-1750 (plus a few earlier pioneers) could provide.

We said in article 1 that Luther's personal contribution to hymnody, mainly dogmatic and creedal though with some surprising and lively excursions into other areas, discouraged other 16th-century writers from adding much. And really nothing of great importance happens in German hymnody until the great pietist movement of the mid-17th century. But although it was Paulus Gerhardt (193, 194, 195) who, in *Praxis Pietatis Melica* (first edition, 1644 [lost], subsequent editions 1647, 1653 and later), set the tone of German hymnody for nearly two centuries, there were signs before him of the new style, and the secret of this is that it was generated by intense public suffering.

It is for this reason that we have waited so long before presenting the two immortal pieces which are all that, so far as we know, Philipp Nicolai, pastor of Unna in Westphalia, wrote.

Brooding in 1597 over the tragedy which had caused so much death in his congregation, a pestilence of the kind so common in those days, he wrote the music and the words of *Wachet Auf*

and *Wie schön leuchtet* (188, 189), which we give in full here. The tunes are in Luther's style, and perhaps no single tune has generated so much inspiration in subsequent composers as that of *Wie schön leuchtet*. But the texts are something quite new: *Wachet Auf* is a visionary and intensely scriptural song of the Second Coming and the comfort which suffering mortals can take in the thought of it; *Wie schön* is a passionate hymn of personal devotion to Christ (which is now almost always sung by English-speaking congregations in a totally altered version by the 18th-century hymn-writer Johannes Schlegel). These two spacious and magnificent odes come out of deep suffering, and they stand by themselves. Yet they forecast what happened a generation later when the whole of Germany was engulfed by the Thirty Years' War (1618-48).

Perhaps no war until World War I generated such a mountain of human suffering as did this one. Hymnody reflects this in its response. What one might well expect is what one gets: hymns of intense personal devotion; hymns of passionate defiance; and hymns of rich and persevering praise. One might also expect just what one gets at the conclusion of the war: a radical reassessment of religion. Christianity had, for Protestants, been subjected to fierce and distorting pressures during the period 1618-48, not least because that war was mostly a religious war. So at the end of it people looked for a religion more personal and more practical than that which mainstream Lutheranism had bequeathed. What came of it was a culture which the English would call evangelical, but which they called pietist, from the *Collegium Pietatis*, founded by Jakob Spener in 1670. This was not a campus but an 'order,' something like Methodism (which it so richly inspired) in England, or, though not in its theology, the Iona Community movement in 20th-century Scotland: a way of life which people, clerical and lay, could choose to follow. Its chief notes were deep personal devotion, hopeful and optimistic religious behaviour, Christian good works, and a special devotion to the Crucified (rather than the risen) Christ.

A glance at our ## 190-197 will illustrate this. You can see it foreshadowed in 'Ah, holy Jesus' (191), and in the angry defiance of 'Lord of our life' (190). In respect of that second one we must say that in order to get the sense of the original, one must read Catherine Winkworth's translation; the other, better literature to be sure, was made earlier by an English statesman and scholar who applied the 'war' image to the new crusade which the Tractarians of the Church of England were pursuing against unbelief and, as he surely thought, against misconceived nonconformist religion in their own country. But Pusey captures very well the truculence of the original. All that is about 1630; and then we come to # 192, the most famous now of all German hymns (much more often sung than 'Ein' feste Burg') which was originally written as a grace at table in the darkest days of the War.

With Gerhardt, ## 193-5, we begin to emerge. The truculent note fades, the personal and hopeful note is heard more strongly. The Communion hymn, # 196, expresses all the new personal radiance; and the Passiontide hymn, # 194, itself a translation from the Latin (and which, therefore, in English uses a double translation), the devotion to the Crucified. Everyday religion under pressure is classically celebrated in # 195. Nos. 193-196 all come from Gerhardt's great collection in which, in the end, 123 of his own hymns appeared, as well as many by other authors of like mind, and many magnificent settings by Johann Cruger.

This practical, personally-oriented Christian culture was

attractive not only to Protestants but also to many Catholics who had so lately been at war for their faith. The mid-17th century was the period of Port Royal and the Jansenist controversies, and the same tendency was noticeable there: impatience with an institutional religion which had cracked under the pressures of war (so far, anyhow, as the personal faith of Christians went), and a tendency to look for small groups ('churches within the church') which would really foster true religion. This again is very close to the Methodist style of the Wesleys. The Polish-born aristocrat J. A. Scheffler (197) was received into the Jesuit order at age 29 (1652) and thereafter wrote a great deal of devotional poetry of which our # 197, in the beautiful Winkworth version, is the best known in English. Its style is indistinguishable from that of the Protestant pietists.

Joachim Neander was a young and religiously ardent schoolmaster who was dismissed from his post at the age of thirty for his religious extravagances, as the authorities saw them, and died a few months later of exposure after attempting to live in a cave. He leaves us, in ## 199 and 200, two jewels of 'religious radiance,' both with an intensely personal accent. Even # 198, another fine extrovert hymn of praise by a distinguished layman (evangelicals often produce good lay hymnodists), is really a personal prayer.

The stream flows strongly from there on. Our # 201 is an evangelical piece written by a Lutheran minister whose interesting connection with J. S. Bach is mentioned in the *Hymnal Guide*; then appear the two great aristocrats, Tersteegen and Zinzendorf, who so peculiarly impressed John Wesley. Tersteegen (55, 202) was the primary poet and benefactor of 18th-century pietism, Zinzendorf (56) the re-founder of Moravianism, an evangelical culture which traced its ancestry back to John Hus (15th century) and which now flourishes very strongly in Eastern Pennsylvania as well as less conspicuously in England. Between them they produced a volume of hymnody which, with small additions only, kept the German-speaking Protestants fully supplied until the mid-20th century found that country, reacting to World War II much as it had reacted to the Thirty Years' War: undergoing a profound and creative reassessment of its national religion. (*Cantate Domino*, 1974, which we encounter in our final article, carries many examples of the 'new deal' German hymnody, and it is perhaps worth recording that in the construction of that book the German members of the editorial board refused to countenance '*Schmücke dich*' and permitted '*Jesu meine Freude*' and '*Ein' Feste Burg*' only under protest.)

But we are able to include # 203, which is a very unusual German piece indeed, being the only hymn from the period of 'Enlightenment,' the new scientific and philosophical humanism, which has found its way into English currency.

Nobody will be surprised to find that in the 19th century German was the only European language to furnish material for translation in any quantity. Only Protestant cultures were generating vernacular hymnody, and the Lutheran churches of Scandinavia and the Reformed churches of Holland leaned so heavily on their respective parent traditions that they produced little of their own. We have one Danish hymn in our repertory here (233), and more recently American Lutherans have explored Scandinavian writers, especially Nicolas Gruntvig, for the purposes of translation, not with widespread success. Nowadays, of course, the activities of the World Council of Churches and post-war revisions of theology and liturgy have caused a good deal more traffic between these cultures and those outside so that Scandinavia, especially Sweden, is

producing much original and interesting hymnody; and the Dutch, for so long wedded to the Genevan Psalter, have been making important contributions.

But two pieces from medieval Italy have found their way into the English repertory, and this is as good a place as any to consider them. Of the famous Canticle of the Sun, by St Francis of Assisi, the celebrated version, 'All creatures of our God and King,' is so universally accessible that we have here given the first English translation made of it, by Matthew Arnold. (A musical setting for this is at *Songs of Praise* 434.) 'Come down, O love divine' is the only piece from the medieval *Laudi Spirituali*—sacred songs associated chiefly with fringe-movements in the 13th and 14th centuries who began even then to explore the idea of 'alternative churches' which we have just been mentioning in the German connection—which is generally familiar. Vaughan Williams' famous tune was and has remained the reason for the availability of this exquisitely-translated piece. As yet we have nothing from Italian Protestant traditions. The Waldensians have their hymnal, but a good deal of it is translated from non-Italian Protestant sources, and the rest has up to now been judged of historic interest only. We must finally add, in reference to the St Francis hymn, that two other English translations ought certainly to be compared with the famous one that is generally sung: that of G. R. Woodward at 406 in *Songs of Syon*; and that of Howard Chandler Robbins in the American Episcopal *Hymnal 1940*.

188
SLEEPERS, WAKE! HG 885

Wachet auff, rufft uns die Stimme,
der Wächter sehr hoch auff der Zinnen,
    Wach auff, du Statt Jerusalem!
Mitternacht heisst diese Stunde,
sie ruffen uns mit hellem Munde,
    wo seidt ihr klugen Jungfrauen?
      Wohlauff! der Bräutgam kompt,
      steht auff, die Lampen nimpt,
        Halleluia!
    Macht euch bereit zu der Hochzeit,
    ihr müsset ihm entgegen gehn.

Zion hört die Wächter singen,
das Hertz thut ihr von Frewden springen,
    sie wachet und steht eilend auff:
ihr Freund kompt vom Himmel prächtig,
von Gnaden starck, von Warheit mächtig,
    Ihr Liecht wirdt hell, ihr Stern geht auff.
      Nu komm, du werthe Kron,
      Herr Jesu, Gottes Sohn.
        Hosanna!
    Wir folgen all zum Frewden Saal,
    Und halten mit das Abendmal.

Gloria sey dir gesungen
mit Menschen und Englischen Zungen,
    mit Harpffen und mit Cymbeln schön!
Von zwölff Perlen sind die Pforten
an deiner Statt, wir sind Consorten
    der Engeln hoch umb deinen Thron.
      Kein Aug hat je gespürt,
      kein Ohr hat mehr gehört
      Solche Frewde:
    Dess sind wir froh, io, io!
Ewig *in dulci jubilo.*

P. NICOLAI, 1556-1608 (*Frewden-Spiegel*, 1599)

Wake, O wake! with tidings thrilling
the watchmen all the air are filling,
　　arise, Jerusalem, arise!
Midnight strikes! no more delaying,
'The hour has come!' we hear them saying,
　　Where are ye all, ye virgins wise?
　　　　The Bridegroom comes in sight,
　　　　Raise high your torches bright!
　　　　　　Alleluia!
　　　　The wedding song
　　　　swells loud and strong:
Go forth and join the festal throng.

Sion hears the watchmen shouting,
her heart leaps up with joy undoubting,
　　She stands and waits with eager eyes;
see her Friend from heaven descending,
adorned with truth and grace unending!
　　Her light burns clear, her star doth rise.
　　　　Now come, thou precious Crown,
　　　　Lord Jesu, God's own Son!
　　　　　　Hosanna!
　　　　Let us prepare
　　　　to follow there
where in thy supper we may share.

Every soul in thee rejoices;
from men and from angelic voices
　　be glory given to thee alone!
Now the gates of pearl receive us,
thy presence never more shall leave us,
　　we stand with angels round thy throne.
　　　　Earth cannot give below
　　　　the bliss thou dost bestow.
　　　　　　Alleluia!
　　　　Grant us to raise
　　　　to length of days
the triumph-chorus of thy praise.

　　　　　　Tr. **F. C. Burkitt**, 1864-1935, in the *Eng-
　　　　　　lish Hymnal*, 1906

189
A CHRISTIAN LOVE SONG　　　　HG 888

Wie schön leuchtet der Morgenstern,
voll Gnad und Wahrheit von dem Herrn,
　　die süsse Wurzel Jesse!
Du Sohn Davids aud Jakobs Stamm,
mein König und mein Bräutigam,
　　hast mir mein Herzbesessen;
　　　　lieblich, freundlich,
　　　　schon und herrlich,
　　　　gross und ehrlich,
　　　　reich an Gaben,
hoch und sehr prächtig erhaben.

Ei meine Perl, du werte Kron,
wahr' Gottes und Marien Sohn,
　　ein hochgeborner König!
Mein Herz heisst dich ein Himmelsblum;
dein süsses Evangelium
　　ist lauter Milch und Honig.
　　　　Ei mein Blümlein
　　　　Hosianna!
　　　　Himmlich Manna,
　　　　das wir essen,
deiner kann ich nicht vergessen.

Geuss sehr tief in das Herz hinein,
du leuchtend Kleinod, edler Stein,
　　mir deiner Liebe Flamme,
dass ich, O Herr, ein Gliedmass bleib
an deinem auserwählten Leib,
　　ein Zweig an deinem Stamme.
　　　　Nach dir wallt mir
　　　　mein Gemüte,
　　　　ewig Güte
　　　　bis es findet
dich, des Liebe mich entzündet.

Von Gott kommt mir ein Freudenschein,
wenn du mich mit den Augen dein
　　gar freundlich tust anblicken.
O Herr Jesu, mein trautes Gut,
dein Wort, dein Geist, dein Leib und Blut
　　mich innerlich erquicken.
　　　　Nimm mich freundlich
　　　　in dein Arme,
　　　　Herr, erbarme
　　　　dich in Gnaden;
auf dein Wort komm ich geladen.

Herr Gott Vater, mein starker Held,
du hast mich ewig vor der Welt
　　in deinem Sohn geliebet.
Dein Sohn hat mich ihm selbst vertraut,
er ist mein Schatz, ich seine Braut,
　　drum mich auch nichts betrübet.
　　　　Eia, eia,
　　　　himmlich Leben
　　　　wird er geben
　　　　mir dort oben;
ewig soll mein Herz ihn loben.

Zwingt die Saiten in Cythara
und lasst die süsse Musica
　　ganz freudenreich erschallen,
dass ich möge mit Jesulein,
dem wünderschönen Bräutgam mein,
　　in steter Liebe wallen.
　　　　Singet, springet,
　　　　jubilieret,
　　　　triumphieret,
　　　　dankt dem Herren;
Gross ist der König der Ehren.

Wie bin ich doch so herzlich froh,
dass mein Schatz ist das A und O,　　　(Rev. 1:8)
　　der Anfang und das Ende.
Er wird mich doch zu seinem Preis
aufnehmen in das Paradeis;
　　des klopf ich in die Hände.
　　　　Amen, Amen,
　　　　komm, du schöne
　　　　Freudenkrone,
　　　　bleib nicht lange;
deiner wart ich mit Verlangen.

　　　　　　P. NICOLAI (HG 885), 1599
(Stanzas have initials forming acrostic of initials Wilhelm Ernst Graf Und Herr Zu
Waldeck, a former pupil of Nicolai.)

　　　　How lovely shines the morning star!
　　　　The nations see and hail afar
　　　　　　the light in Judah shining.
　　　　Thou David's Son of Jacob's race,
　　　　my Bridegroom and my King of grace,
　　　　　　for thee my heart is pining.

Lowly, holy,
    Great and glorious
    thou victorious
Prince of graces,
    filling all the heavenly places.

O highest joy by mortals won,
thou Son of God and Mary's Son,
    thou high-born King of ages!
Thou art my heart's most beauteous flower,
and thy blest Gospel's saving power
    my raptured soul engages.
        Thou mine: I thine:
            Sing hosanna,
            heavenly manna
        tasting, eating,
        whilst thy love in songs repeating.

Now richly to my waiting heart,
O thou my God, deign to impart
    the grace of love undying.
In thy blest body let me be,
ev'n as the branch is in the tree,
    thy life my life supplying.
        Sighing, crying
            for the savour
            of thy favour;
        resting never
        till I rest in thee for ever.

A pledge of peace from God I see
when thy pure eyes are turned to me
    to show me thy good pleasure.
Jesus, thy Spirit and thy Word,
thy body and thy blood, afford
    my soul its dearest treasure.
        Keep me kindly
            in thy favour,
            O my Saviour!
        Thou wilt cheer me;
        thy word calls me to draw near thee.

Thou, mighty Father, in thy Son
didst love me ere thou hadst begun
    this ancient world's foundation.
Thy Son hath made a friend of me,
and when in spirit him I see,
    I joy in tribulation.
        What bliss is this!
            He that liveth
            to me giveth
        life for ever;
        nothing me from him can sever.

Lift up the voice and strike the string,
let all glad sounds of music ring
    in God's high praises blended.
Christ will be with me all the way
to-day, to-morrow, every day,
    till travelling days be ended.
        Sing out, ring out
            triumph glorious,
            O victorious
        Chosen nation;
        praise the God of your salvation.

O joy to know that thou, my Friend,
art Lord, Beginning without end,
    the First and Last, eternal!

And thou at length - O glorious grace! -
wilt take me to that holy place,
    the home of joys supernal.
        Amen, Amen!
            Come and meet me!
            Quickly greet me!
        With deep yearning,
        Lord, I look for thy returning.

Tr: composite in the *Lutheran Hymnal*
(USA), 1941

190
IN TIME OF WAR   HG 431
A

Christe, du beistand deiner
        Kreuzgemeine,
eile met hilf und Rettung uns
        erscheine.
Steure den Feinden; ihre Blut-
        gedichte
    mache zu nichte.

Streite doch selber für uns arme
        Kinder
wehre dem Teufel, seine Macht
        verhinder;
alles, was kämpfet wider deine
        Glieder,
    stürze darnieder.

Frieden bei Kirch und Schule uns
        beschere,
Frieden zugleich der Obrigkeit
        gewähre.
Frieden dem Herzen, Frieden
        dem Gewissen
    gib zu geniessen.

Also wird zeitlich deine Güt er-
        hoben,
also wird ewig und ohn Ende
        loben
dich, o du Wächter deiner armen
        Herde,
    Himmel und Erde.

M. VON LÖWENSTERN, 1630

Christ, thou the champion of that
        war-worn host
who bear thy cross, haste, help
        or we are lost;
the scheme of those who long our
        blood have sought
    bring thou to nought.

Do thou thyself for us thy children
        fight,
withstand the Devil, quell his rage
        and might,
whate'er assails thy members left
        below
    do thou o'erthrow:

and give us peace: peace in the
        church and school,
peace to the powers who o'er our
        country rule,
peace to the conscience, peace
        within the heart,
    do thou impart.

So shall thy goodness here be still
        adored,
thou guardian of thy little flock,
        dear Lord,
and heaven and earth through all
        eternity
    shall worship thee.

CATHERINE WINKWORTH (HG 14),
1855

B

The same paraphrased, 1834,
by **PHILIP PUSEY**

Lord of our life and God of our
        salvation,
Star of our night, and hope of
        every nation,
hear and receive thy church's
        supplication,
    Lord God Almighty.

See round thine Ark the hungry
        billows curling,
see how thy foes their banners are
        unfurling;
Lord, while their darts enven-
        omed they are hurling,
    thou canst preserve us.

Lord, thou canst help when earth-
        ly armour faileth,
Lord, thou canst save when deadly
        sin assaileth;
Christ, o'er thy Rock nor death
        nor hell prevaileth;
    Grant us thy peace, Lord.

Peace in our hearts, our evil
        thoughts assuaging,
peace in thy church, where broth-
        ers are engaging,
peace when the world its busy war
        is waging:
    calm thy foes' raging.

Grant us thy help till backward they are driven,
grant them thy truth, that they may be forgiven;
grant peace on earth, and after we have striven,
                    peace in thy heaven.

JOHANN HEERMANN
1585-1647

191
THE INIQUITY OF US ALL

Herzliebster Jesu, was hast du verbrochen.
das man ein solch scharf Urteil hat gesprochen?
Was ist die Schuld, in was für Missetaten
                    bist du geraten?

Du wirst gegeisselt und mit Dorn gekrönet,
ins Angesicht geschlagen und verhöhnet.
Du wirst mit Essig und mit Gall getränket,
                    ans Kreuz gehenket.

Was ich doch wohl die Ursach solcher Plagen?
Ach, meine Sünden haben dich geschlagen!
Ach mein Herr Jesu, habe dies verschuldet,
                    was du erduldet.

Wie wunderbarlich ist doch diese Strafe!
Der gute Hirte leidet für die Schafe,
die Schuld bezahlt der Herre, der Gerechte,
                    für deine Knechte.

Der Fromme stirbt, der recht und richtig wandelt,
der Böse lebt, der wider Gott misshandelt,
der Mench verwirkt den Tod und ist entgangen,
                    der Herr gefangen.

O grosse Lieb, o Lieb ohn alle Masse,
die dich gebracht auf dieser Marterstrasse!
Ich lebte mit der Welt in Lust und Freuden,
                    und du musst leiden.

Ach, grosser König, gross zu allen Zieten,
wie kann ich gnugsam solche Treu ausbreiten?
Keins Menschen Herz vermag es auszudenken,
                    was dir zu schenken?

Ich kanns mit meinen Sinnen nicht erreichen,
womit doch dein Erbarmung zu vergleichen,
Wie kann ich dir denn deine Liebestaten
                    in Werk erstatten?

Doch ist noch etwas, das dir angenehme,
wenn ich des Fleisches Lüste dämpf und zähme,
dass sie aufs neu mein Herze nicht entzünden
                    mit alten Sünden.

Weils aber nicht besteht in eignen Kräften,
fest die Begirden an das Kreuz zu heften,
so gib mir deinen Geist, der mich regiere,
                    zum Guten führe.

Alsdann so wird ich deine Huld betrachten,
aus Lieb zu dir die Welt für gar nichts achten,
bemühen werd ich mich, Herr, deinen Willen,
                    stets zu erfüllen.

Ich werde dir zu Ehren alles wagen,
kein Kreuz nicht achten, keine Schmach noch Plagen,
nichts von Verfolgung, nichts von Todeschmerzen
                    nehmen zu Herzen.

Dies alles, obs für schlecht zwar ist zu schätzen,
wirst du es doch nicht gar beiseite setzen,
in Gnaden wirst du dies von mir annehmen,
                    mich nicht beschämen.

Wenn dort, Herr Jesu, wird von deinem Throne,
auf meinem Haupte stehn die Ehrenkrone,
da will ich dir, wenn alles wird wohl klingen,
                    Lob und Dank singen.

1630

Translation of **Catherine
Winkworth**, 1827-78

A

Alas, dear Lord, what law then hast thou broken,
that such sharp sentence should on thee be spoken?
Of what great crime hast thou to make confession -
                    what dark transgression?

They crown his head with thorns, they smite, they scourge him,
with cruel mockings to the cross they urge him,
they given him gall to drink, they still decry him, -
                    they crucify him.

Whence come these sorrows, whence this mortal anguish?
It is my sins for which my Lord must languish;
yes, all the wrath, the woe he doth inherit
                    'Tis I do merit!

What strangest punishment is suffered yonder!
The Shepherd dies for sheep that loved to wander!
The Master pays the debts His servants owe Him,
                    who would not know him.

There was no spot in me by sin unstained,
sick with its venom all my heart had fainted;
my heavy guilt to hell had well-nigh brought me,
                    such woe it wrought me.

O wondrous love! whose depths no heart hath sounded,
that brought thee here by foes and thieves surrounded;
all worldly pleasures, heedless, I was trying
                    while thou wast dying!

O mighty King! no time can dim thy glory!
How shall I spread abroad thy wondrous story?
How shall I find some worthy gift to proffer?
                    What dare we offer?

For vainly doth our human wisdom ponder -
thy woes, thy mercy, still transcend our wonder.
Oh how should I do aught that could delight thee?
                    Can I requite thee?

Yet unrequited, Lord, I would not leave thee,
I can renounce whate'er doth vex or grieve thee,
and quench with thoughts of thee and prayers most lowly
                    all fires unholy.

But since my strength alone will ne'er suffice me
to crucify desires that still entice me,
to all good deeds, oh let thy Spirit win me,
                    and reign within me!

I'll think upon thy mercy hour by hour,
I'll love thee so that earth must lose her power;
to do thy will shall be my sole endeavour
                    henceforth for ever.

Whate'er of earthly good this life may grant me
I'll risk for thee - no shame, no cross shall daunt me;
I shall not fear what man can do to harm me,
    nor death alarm me.

But worthless is my sacrifice, I own it,
yet, Lord, for love's sake thou wilt not disown it;
thou wilt accept my gift in thy great meekness,
    nor shame my weakness.

And when, dear Lord, before thy throne in heaven
to me the crown of joy at last is given,
where sweetest hymns thy saints for ever raise thee,
    I too shall praise thee!

1863

Paraphrase by **Robert Bridges**, 1844-1930
HG 9

B

Ah, holy Jesus, how hast thou offended
that man to judge thee hath in hate pretended?
By foes derided, by thine own rejected,
    O most afflicted!   st. 1

Who was the guilty? who brought this upon thee?
Alas, my treason, Jesus, hath undone thee;
'twas I, Lord Jesus, I it was denied thee:
    I crucified thee.   st. 3

Lo, the good Shepherd for the sheep is offered,
the slave hath sinned, and the Son hath suffered;
for man's atonement, while he nothing heedeth,
    God intercedeth.   st. 4

For me, kind Jesus, was thine incarnation,
thy mortal sorrow and thy life's oblation;
thy death of anguish and thy bitter passion
    for my salvation.

Therefore, kind Jesus, since I cannot pay thee,
I do adore thee, and will ever pray thee,
think on thy pity and thy love unswerving,
    not my deserving.   st. 13

1899

192
NOW BLESS YE THE GOD OF ALL
Ecclus. 50:11   HG 492

Nun danket alle Gott,
mit Herzen, Mund und Händen,
der grosse Dinge tut

an uns und allen Enden;
der uns von Mutterlieb
und Kindesbeinen an
unzählig viel zugut
bis hieher hat getan.

Der ewig reiche Gott
woll' uns in diesem Leben
ein immer fröhlich Herz
und edlen Frieden geben,
und uns in seiner Gnad
erhalten fort und fort,

Now thank we all our God
with heart and hands and voices,
who wondrous things hath
    done,
in whom his world rejoices;
who from our mother's arms
hath blessed us on our way
with countless gifts of love
and still is ours to-day.

O may this bounteous God
through all our life be near us
with ever joyful hearts
and blessed peace to cheer us;
and keep us in his grace,
    and guide us when perplexed,

und uns aus aller Not
erlösen hier und dort.

Lob, Ehr' und Preis sei Gott,
dem Vater und dem Sohne
und dem, der beiden gleich,
im höchsten Himmelsthrone,
dem einig höchsten Gott
als es anfänglich war
und ist und bleiben wird
jetzund und immerdar!

and free us from all ills
in this world and the next.

All praise and thanks to God
the Father now be given,
the Son, and him who reigns
with them in highest heaven,
the one eternal God,
    whom heaven and earth adore,
for thus it was, is now
and shall be evermore.

MARTIN RINCKART, 1636, 1647   **CATHERINE WINKWORTH** (HG 14), 1863

NOTE: Refer to nos. 1-6 for earlier German hymns, to 55-6 for two more Wesley translations, and to 569-71 for modern hymns from German originals.

193
AT EVENING   HG 863
(cf Virgil *Aeneid* IV 522-8) **A**

Nun ruhen all Wälder,
Vieh, Menschen, Stadt und
    Felder,
es schläft die ganze Welt;
ihr aber, meine Sinnen,
auf, auf, ihr sollt beginnen,
was eurem Schöpfer wohlgefällt.

Wo bist du, Sonne, blieben?
Die Nacht hat dich vertrieben,

    die Nacht, des Tages Feind,
Fahr hin, ein andre Sonne,
mein Jesus, meine Wonne,
gar hell in meinem Herzen
    scheint.

Das Haupt, die Füss und Hände
sind froh, dass nun zum Ende
    die Arbeit kommen sei.
Herz, freu dich, du sollst werden
vom Elend dieser Erden
und von der Sünden Arbeit frei.

Breit aus die Flügel beide,
o Jesu, meine Freude,
    und nimm dein Küchlein ein!
Will Satan mich verschlingen,
so lass die Engel singen,
'Dies Kind soll unverletzet sein.'

Auch euch, ihr meine Lieben,
soll heute nicht betrüben
    kein Unfall noch Gefahr.
Gott lass euch selig schlafen,
stell euch die güldnen Waffen
ums Bett und seiner Engel Schar.

Now all the woods are sleeping,
and night and stillness creeping

o'er city, man and beast;
but thou, my soul, awake thee,
to prayer awhile betake thee,
and praise thy Maker ere thou rest.

O Sun, where art thou vanished?
The night thy reign hath
    banished,
thy ancient foe, the Night.
Farewell, a brighter glory
my Jesus sheddeth o'er me,
all clear within me shines his light.

Now thought and labour ceases,
for night the tired releases
    and bids sweet rest begin:
my heart, there comes a morrow
shall set thee free from sorrow
and all the dreary toil of sin.

My Jesus, stay thou by me,
and let no foe come nigh me,
    safe sheltered by thy wing;
but would the foe alarm me,
oh let him never harm me,
but still thine angels round me
    sing.

My loved ones, rest securely,
from every peril surely
our God will guard your heads;
and happy slumbers send you,
and bid his hosts attend you,
and golden-armed, watch o'er
    your heads.

PAUL GERHARDT (HG 18), 1647   **CATHERINE WINKWORTH** (HG 14), 1863
sts. 1, 2, 5, 8, 9

B

The duteous day now closeth,
each flower and tree reposeth,
shade creeps o'er wild and wood:

Let us as night is falling,
on God our Maker calling,
give thanks to him, the Giver good.

Now all the heavenly splendour
breaks forth in starlight tender
from myriad worlds unknown;
and man, the marvel seeing,
forgets his selfish being
for joy of beauty not his own.

His care he drowneth yonder,
lost in the abyss of wonder;
to heaven his soul doth steal:
this life he disesteemeth,
the day it is that dreameth,
that doth from truth his vision seal.

Awhile his mortal blindness
may miss God's lovingkindness,
and grope in faithless strife:
but when life's day is over
shall death's fair night discover
the fields of everlasting life.

ROBERT BRIDGES, suggested by the
opening of the foregoing hymn, 1899

194
O SACRED HEAD

HG 871

A

Salve caput cruentatum,
totum spinis coronatum,
conquassatum, vulneratum,
harundine verberatum,
facie sputis illita,
salve, cuius dulcis vultus
immutatus et incultus
immutavit suum florem
totus versus in pallorem,
quem caeli tremit curia.

omnis vigor atque viror
hunc recessit, non admiror,
mors apparet in aspectu,
totus pendens in defectu
attritus serga macie.
sic affectus, sic despectus,
propter me sic interfectus,
peccatori tam indigno
cum amoris in te signo
appare clara facie.

in hac tua passione
me agnosce, Pastor bone;
cuius sumpsi mel ex ore,
haustum lactis ex dulcore
prae omnibus deliciis.
non me reum asperneris,
nec indignum dedigneris,
morte tibi iam vicina
tuum caput hic inclina,
in meis pausa bracchiis.

tuae sanctae passioni
me gauderem interponi,
in hac cruce tecum mori
praesta crucis amatori,

O sacred Head, sore wounded,
defiled and put to scorn;
O kingly Head, surrounded
with mocking crown of thorn:
what sorrow mars thy grandeur?
can death thy bloom deflower?
O countenance whose splendour
the hosts of heaven adore!

Thy beauty, long-desirèd
hath vanished from our sight;
thy power is all expirèd,
and quenched the Light of light.
Ah me! for whom thou diest,
hide not so far thy grace:
show me, O Love most highest,
the brightness of thy face.

I pray thee, Jesus, own me,
me, Shepherd good, for thine;
who to thy fold hast won me,
and fed with truth divine.
Me, guilty me refuse not,
incline thy face to me,
this comfort that I lose not,
on earth to comfort thee.

In thy most bitter passion
my heart to thee doth cry,
with thee for my salvation
upon the Cross to die.

sub cruce tua moriar:
morti tuae iam amarae
grates ago, Jesu care;
qui es clemens, pie Deus
fac quod petit tuus reus,
ut absque te non finiar.

dum me mori est necesse,
noli mihi tunc deesse;
in tremenda mortis hora
veni Jesu! absque mora
tuere me et libera.
cum me iubes emigrare
Jesu! care! tunc appare,
o amator amplectande
temet ipsum tunc ostende
in cruce salutifera.

Anonymous Latin lyric,
? 11th century

Ah, keep my heart thus moved
to stand thy Cross beneath,
to mourn thee, well-beloved,
yet thank thee for thy death.

My days are few, O fail not,
with thine immortal power,
to hold me that I quail not
in death's most fearful hour:
that I may fight befriended,
and see in my last strife
to me thine arms extended
upon the Cross of life.

ROBERT BRIDGES (HG 9), 1899

B

O Haupt voll Blut und Wunden,
voll Schmerz, bedeckt mit
Hohn,
O göttlich Haupt umwunden
mit einer Dornenkron'!
O Haupt, das andrer Ehren
und Kronen würdig ist,
sei mir mit frommen Zähren,
sei tausendmal gegrüsst!

Der Purpur deiner Wangen,
der Lippen frisches Rot,
all' Schönheit ist vergangen
in bitter Todesnot.
Doch strömt aus deinen Blicken
noch himmlische Geduld,
selbst Sünder zu beglücken
mit unverdienter Huld.

Ach Herr, was du erduldet,
ist alles meine Last,
ich habe das verschuldet,
was du getragen hast.
Ich, Jesu, bin's, ich Armer,
der dies verdienet hat:
O tilge, mein Erbarmer,
doch meine Missethat!

Ich danke dir von Herzen,
O Jesu, bester Freund,
für deine Todesschmerzen;
wie gut hast du's gemeint!
Ach gib, dass ich mich halte
zu dir und deiner Treu',
dass nimmermehr erkalte
im Herzen Lieb' und Reu'.

Erscheine mir zum Schilde,
zum Trost in meinem Tod,
und lass mich sehn dein Bilde
in deiner Kreuzesnot.
Da will ich nach dir blicken,
da will ich glaubensvoll,
dich seht an mein Herz drücken.
Wer so stirbt, der stirbt wohl.

PAUL GERHARDT (HG 18), 1653
(sts. 1, 3, 4, 8, 10)

O sacred head! now wounded,
with grief and shame weighed
down;
now scornfully surrounded
with thorns, thy only crown;
O sacred Head! what glory,
what bliss till now was thine!
I read the wondrous story!
I joy to call thee mine!

O noblest brow and dearest!
in other days the world
all feared when thou appearedst;*
what shame on thee is hurled!
How art thou pale with anguish,
with sore abuse and scorn;
how does that visage languish
which once was bright as morn!

What thou, my Lord, hast suffered
was all for sinners' gain;
mine, mine was the transgression,
but thine the deadly pain.
Lo! here I fall, my Saviour!
'Tis I deserve thy place;
look on me with thy favour,
vouchsafe to me thy grace.

What language shall I borrow
to thank thee, dearest Friend,
for this, thy dying sorrow,
thy pity without end?
O make me thine for ever!
and should I fainting be,
Lord, let me never, never
outlive my love to thee!

Be near when I am dying,
O show thy cross to me!
and for my succour flying,
come, Lord, to set me free.
These eyes, new faith receiving,
from Jesus shall not move,
for he who dies believing
dies safely through thy love.

J. W. ALEXANDER, 1830, 1849
* these three lines are from lines 9-10
of the Latin

195
COMMIT THY GRIEFS TO HIM   HG 840

A

Befiehl du deine Wege
  und was dein Herze kränkt
der allertreusten Pflege
  des, der den Himmel lenkt.
Der Wollen, Luft und Winden
  gibt Wege, Lauf und Bahn,
der wird auch Wege finden,
  da dein Fuss geben kann.

Dem Herren musst du trauen,
  wenn dirs soll wohlergehn;
auf sein Werk musst du schauen,
  wenn dein Werk soll bestehn.
Mit Sorgen und mit Grämen
  und mit selbsteigner Pein
lässt Gott sich gar nichts nehmen,
  es muss erbeten sein.

Dein ew'ge Treu und Gnade,
  o Vater, weiss und sieht,
was gut sei oder schade
  dem sterblichen Gëblut;
und was du dann erlesen,
  das treibst du, starker Held,
und bringst zum Stand und
                    Wesen,
  was deinem Rat gefällt.

Hoff, o du arme Seele,
  hoff und sei unverzagt!
Gott wird dich aus der Höhle,
  da dich der Kummer plagt,
mit grossen Gnaden rücken;
  erwarte nur die Zeit,
so wirst du schon erblicken
  die Sonn der schönsten Freud.

PAUL GERHARDT (HG 18), 1653
(st. 1, 2, 3, 6 of 12)

Commit thou all that grieves thee
  and fills thy heart with care
to him whose faithful mercy
  the skies above declare,
who gives the winds their courses,
  who points the clouds their way;
'tis he will guide thy footsteps
  and be thy staff and stay.

O trust the Lord then wholly,
  if thou wouldst be secure;
his work must thou consider
  for thy work to endure.
What profit doth it bring thee
  to pine in grief and care?
God only sends his blessing
  in answer to thy prayer.

Thy lasting truth and mercy,
  O Father, see aright
the needs of all thy children,
  their anguish or delight:
what loving wisdom chooseth,
  redeeming might will do,
and bring to sure fulfilment

  thy counsel good and true.

Hope on, then, broken spirit;
  hope on, be not afraid:
fear not the griefs that plague thee
  and keep thy heart dismayed:
thy God, in his great mercy,
  will save thee, hold thee fast,
and in his own time grant thee
  the sun of joy at last.

A. W. FARLANDER and WINFRED
DOUGLAS (HG 659), 1939

B

John Wesley's translation of
these stanzas

Commit thou all thy griefs
  and ways into his hands,
to his sure truth and tender care
  who heaven and earth commands.

Who points the clouds their course,
  whom winds and seas obey,
he shall direct thy wandering feet,
  he shall prepare thy way.

Thou on the Lord rely,
  so safe shalt thou go on:
fix on his work thy stedfast eye,
  so shall thy work be done.

No profit canst thou gain
  from self-consuming care;
to him commend thy cause; his ear
  attends thy softest prayer.

Thy everlasting truth,
  Father, thy ceaseless love,

sees all thy children's wants, and knows
  what best for each shall prove.

Thou everywhere hast sway,
  and all things serve thy might;
thy every act pure blessing is,
  thy path unsullied light.

★   ★   ★

Give to the winds thy fears,
  hope, and be undismayed;
God hears thy sighs, and counts thy tears,
  God shall lift up thy head.

Through waves and clouds and storms,
  he gently clears thy way;
wait thou his time, so shall this night
  soon end in joyous day.

1739

196
THE KING'S BANQUET   HG 162

Schmücke dich, O liebe Seele,	Deck thyself, my soul, with gladness,
lass die dunkle Sündenhöhle,	leave the gloomy haunts of sadness,
komm ans helle Licht gegangen,	come into the daylight's splendour,
fange herzlich an zu prangen; denn der Herr voll Heil und Gnaden	there with joy thy praises render unto him whose grace unbounded
will dich jetzt zu Gaste laden;	hath this wondrous banquet founded;
der den Himmel kann verwalten,	high o'er all the heavens he reigneth,
will jetzt Herberg in dir halten.	yet to dwell with thee he deigneth.

Eile, wie Verlobte pflegen,
deinem Bräutigam entgegen,

der mit süssen Gnadenworten
klopft an deines Herzens Pforten;
eile, sie ihm aufzuschliessen,
wirf dich hin zu seinen Füssen;
sprich, mein Heil, lass dich
                    entfassen,
von dir kann ich nimmer lassen.

Ach, wie hungert mein Gemüte,
Menschenfreund, nach deiner
                    Güte!
Ach, wie pfleg ich oft mit Tränen

mich nach dieser Kost zu sehnen!

Ach wie pfleget mich zu dürsten
nach dem Trank den Lebensfürsten,
dass in diesem Brot und Weine
Christus sich mit mir vereine!

Beides, Lachen und auch Zittern,
lasset sich in mir jetzt wittern,
das Geheimnis dieser Speise
und die unerforschte Weise
machet, dass ich früh vermercke,
Herr, die Grösse deiner Werke,

Hasten as a Bride to meet him,
and with loving reverence greet
                    him,
for with words of life immortal
now he knocketh at thy portal;
haste to ope the gates before him,
saying, whilst thou dost adore him,
'Suffer, Lord, that I receive thee,

and I never more will leave thee.'

Ah, how hungers all my spirit
for the love I do not merit!

Oft have I, with sighs fast
                    thronging
thought upon this Food with
                    longing,
in the battle well nigh worsted,
for this cup of life have thirsted,

for the Friend, who here invites us
and to God himself unites us.

Now I sink before thee lowly,
filled with joy most deep and holy,
as with trembling awe and wonder
on thy mighty works I ponder,
how, by mystery surrounded,
depths no man hath ever sounded,

ist auch wohl ein Mensch zu
finden
der dein Allmacht soll ergründen?

none may dare to pierce un-
bidden
secrets that with thee are hidden.

★ ★ ★

Jesu, meine Lebenssonne,
Jesu, meine Freud und Wonne,
Jesu, du mein ganz Beginnen!

Lebensquell und Licht der Sinnen,

hier fall ich zu deinen Füssen,
lass mich würdiglich geniessen
dieser deine Himmelsspeise,
mir zum Heil und dir zum Preise.

Sun, who all my life dost brighten,
light, who dost my soul enlighten,
joy, the sweetest man e'er
knoweth,
fount, whence all my being
floweth,
at thy feet I cry, 'My Maker,
let me be a fit partaker
of this blessed foor from heaven,
for our good, thy glory given.'

★ ★ ★

Jesu, wahres Brot des Lebens,
hilf, dass ich doch nicht vergebens
oder mir viellicht zum Schaden
sei zu deinem Tisch geladen.
Lass mich durch dies Seelenessen
deine Liebe recht ermessen,

dass ich auch, wie jetzt auf Erden,

mög dein Gast im Himmel werden.

Jesus, Bread of life, I pray thee,
let me gladly here obey thee,
never to my hurt invited,
be thy love with love requited;
from this banquet let me measure,
Lord, how vast and deep the
treasure;
through the gifts thou here dost
give me
as thy guest in heaven receive me.

JOHANN FRANCK, 1653
2 st. omitted

CATHERINE WINKWORTH (HG 14), 1863

197
CONSECRATION
HG 548

Liebe, die du mich zum Bilde
deiner Gottheit hast gemacht,
Liebe, die du mich so milde

nach dem Fall hast wieder-
bracht:
Liebe, dir ergeb ich mich,
dein zu bleiben ewiglich.

O Love, who formedst me to wear
the image of thy Godhead here;
who soughtest me with tender
care
through all my wanderings wild
and drear:
O Love, I give myself to thee,
Thine ever, only thine to be.

Liebe, die du mich erkoren,

eh ich noch geschaffen war,

Liebe, die du Mensch geboren

und mir gleich wardst ganz
und gar: . . .

O Love, who ere life's earliest
dawn
on me thy choice hast gently
laid,
O Love, who here as man wast
born
and like to us in all things
made; . . .

Liebe, die für mich gelitten

und gestorben in der Zeit,

Liebe, die mir hat erfritten

ew'ge Lust und Seligkeit, . . .

O Love, who once in time wast
slain,
pierced through and through
with bitter woe;
O Love, who wrestling thus didst
gain
that we eternal joy might know;
. . .

Liebe, die du Kraft und Leben,
Licht und Wahrheit, Geist und
Wort,
Liebe, die sich ganz ergeben

mir zum Heil und Seelenhort:
. . .

O Love, of whom is truth and light,
the Word and Spirit, life and
power,
whose heart was bared to them
that smite,
to shield us in our trial hour, . . .

Liebe, die mich hat gebunden

an ihr Joch mit Leib und Sinn,

Liebe, die mich überwunden

und mein Herz hat ganz dahin:
. . .

O Love, who thus hast bound me
fast,
beneath that gentle yoke of
thine;
Love, who hast conquered me at
last
and rapt away this heart of
mine. . . .

Liebe, die mich ewig liebet
und für meine Seele bitt',
Liebe, die das Lösgeld gibet
und mich kräftiglich vertritt; . . .

O Love, who lovest me for ay,
who for my soul dost ever plead;
O Love, who didst my ransom pay,
whose power sufficeth in my
stead; . . .

Liebe, die mich wird erwecken
aus dem Grab der Sterblichkeit,
Liebe, die mich wird umstecken
mit dem Laub der Herrlichkeit:

O Love, who once shalt bid me rise
from out this dying life of ours;
O Love, who once above the skies
shalt set me in the fadeless
bowers:

Liebe, dir ergeb ich mich,
dein zu bleiben ewiglich.

O Love, I give myself to thee
Thine ever, only thine to be!

J. SCHEFFLER, 1657

CATHERINE WINKWORTH (HG 14), 1863

198
TO GOD ALL PRAISE AND GLORY
HG 640

Sei Lob und Ehr dem höchsten
Gut,
dem Vater aller Güte,
dem Gott, der alle Wunder thut,
dem Gott, der mein Gemüte
mit seinem reichen Trost erfüllt,
dem Gott, der allen Jammer stillt.
Gebt unserm Gott die Ehre!

Sing praise to God who reigns
above,
the God of all creation,
the God of power, the God of love,
the God of our salvation;
with healing balm my soul he fills,
and every faithless murmur stills.
To God all praise and glory!

Es danken dir die Himmelsheer,
o Herrscher aller Thronen,
und die auf Erden, Luft und Meer
in deinem Schatten wohnen,
die preisen deine Schöpfermacht
die alles also wohl bedacht,

Gebt unserm Gott die Ehre!

The angel-host, O King of kings,
thy praise for ever telling,
in earth and sky all living things
beneath thy shadow dwelling,
adore the wisdom that could span,
and power which formed creation's plan.
To God all praise and glory!

Was unser Gott geschaffen hat,

das will er auch erhalten,
darüber will er früh und spat
mit seiner Güte walten.
In seinem ganzen Königreich
ist alles recht, ist alles gleich.
Gebt unserm Gott die Ehre!

What God's almighty power hath
made
his gracious mercy keepeth;
by morning dew or evening shade
his watchful eye ne'er sleepeth;
within the kingdom of his might
lo! all is just, and all is right.
To God all praise and glory!

★ ★ ★

Der Herr ist noch und nimmer
nicht
von seinem Volk geschieden;
er bleibet ihre Zuversicht,
ihr Segen, Heil und Frieden.
Mit Mutterhanden leitet er
die Seinem statig bin und her.
Gebt unserm Gott die Ehre!

The Lord is never far away,

but, through all grief distressing,
an ever-present help and stay,
our peace and joy and blessing;
as with a mother's tender hand
he leads his own, his chosen band.
To God all praise and glory!

★ ★ ★

Ich will dich all mein Leben lang,
o Gott, von nun an ehren;
man soll, Gott, deinen Lobgesang

an allen Orten hören.

Then all my gladsome way along
I sing aloud thy praises,
that men may hear the grateful
song
my voice unwearied raises;

Mein ganzes Herz ermuntre dich,
mein Geist und Leib erfreue dich!

Gebt unserm Gott die Ehre!

Ihr, die ihr Christi namen nennt,

gebt unserm Gott die Ehre!
Ihr, die ihr Gottes Macht bekennt,

gebt unserm Gott die Ehre!
Die falschen Götter macht zu
Spott;
der Herr ist Gott! der Herr ist Gott!
Gebt unserm Gott die Ehre!

J. J. SCHÜTZ, 1675
sts. 4, 6, 9 omitted

be joyful in the Lord, my heart,
both soul and body, bear your
part:
to God all praise and glory!

O ye who name Christ's holy
name,
give God all praise and glory;
all ye who own his power, proclaim
aloud the wondrous story.
Cast each false idol from his
throne:
the Lord is God and he alone:
to God all praise and glory!

FRANCES E. COX (HG 352), 1864

199
. . . AND ALL THAT IS WITHIN ME,
BLESS HIS HOLY NAME
Ps. 103 HG 605

Lobe den Herren, den mächtigen König der Ehren!
Meine geliebete Seele, das ist mein Begehren.
Kommet zu Hauff,
Psalter und Harfe wach't auff,
Lasset die Musicam hören!

Lobe den Herren, der alles so herrlich regieret,
der dich auff Adelers Fittichen sicher geführet.
Der dich erhält
Wie es dir selber gefällt,
Hastu nicht dieses verspüret?

Lobe den Herren, der deinen Stand sichtbar geregnet!
Der aus dem Himmel mit Strömen der Liebe geregnet!
Dencke daran,
was der Allmächtige kan,
der dir mit Liebe begegnet!

Lobe den Herren, was in mir ist, lobe den Namen,
alles was Odem hat, lobe mit Abrahams Samen!
Er ist dein Licht,
Seele, vergiss es ja nicht,
Lobende, schliesse mit Amen!

st. 3 omitted

JOACHIM NEANDER (HG 19), 1680

Praise to the Lord! the Almighty, the King of Creation!
O my soul, praise him, for he is thy health and salvation!
All ye who hear,
now to his temple draw near,
join me in glad adoration.

Praise to the Lord! who o'er all things so wondrously reigneth,
shelters thee under his wings, ye, so gently sustaineth;
Hast thou not seen
how thy desires have been
granted in what he ordaineth?

Praise to the Lord! who doth prosper thy work and defend thee,
surely his goodness and mercy here daily attend thee;
Ponder anew
what the Almighty can do
if with his love he befriend thee!

Praise to the Lord! Oh let all that is in me adore him!
All that hath life and breath, come now with praises before him!
Let the 'Amen'
sound from his people again,
gladly for ay we adore him!

CATHERINE WINKWORTH (HG 14),
1863

200
HOPE IN GOD HG 19

All my hope on God is founded;
he doth still my trust renew.
Me through change and chance he guideth,
only good and only true.
God unknown,
he alone
calls my heart to be his own.

Pride of man and earthly glory,
sword and crown betray his trust;
what with care and toil he buildeth,
tower and temple, fall to dust.
But God's power,
hour by hour,
is my temple and my tower.

God's great goodness ay endureth,
deep his wisdom, passing thought;
splendour, light and life attend him,
beauty springeth out of nought.
Evermore
from his store
new born worlds rise and adore.

Daily doth the almighty Giver
bounteous gifts on us bestow;
his desire our soul delighteth,
pleasure leads us where we go.
Love doth stand
at his hand;
joy doth wait at his command.

Still from man to God eternal
sacrifice of praise be done,
high above all praises praising
for the gift of Christ his Son.
Christ doth call
one and all:
ye who follow shall not fall.

ROBERT BRIDGES (HG 9), 1899, based
on *Meine Hoffnung*, by J. Neander
(HG 19), 1680

201
THIS MAN RECEIVETH SINNERS
Luke 15:1 HG 645

Jesus nimmt die Sünder an,
saget doch dies Trostwort allen,
welche von der rechten Bahn
auf verkerten Weg verfallen!
Hier ist, was sie retten kann:
Jesus nimmt die Sünder an.

Wenn ein Schaf verloren ist,

suchet es ein treuer Hirte;

Sinners Jesus will receive,
tell this word of grace to all
who the heavenly pathway leave,
all who linger, all who fall;
this can bring them back again,
'Christ receiveth sinful men.'

Shepherds seek their wandering
sheep
o'er the mountains bleak and
cold;

Jesus, der uns nie vergisst,
suchet treulich das Verirrte,
das es nicht verderben kann:
Jesus nimmt die Sünder an.

Ich Betrübter komme hier
und bekenne meine Sünden;
lass, mein Heiland, mich bei dir
Gnade zur Vergebung finden,
das dies Wort mich trösten
                        kann:
Jesus nimmt die Sünder an.

Jesus nimmt die Sünder an,
mich hat er auch angenommen
und den Himmel aufgetan,
dass ich selig zu ihn kommen
und auf den Trost sterben kann:
Jesus nimmt die Sünder an.

ERDMANN NEUMEISTER, 1718
sts. 1, 3, 5, 8

Jesus such a watch doth keep
  o'er the lost ones of his fold,
seeking them o'er moor and fen:
Christ receiveth sinful men.

Sick and sorrowful and blind,
  I with all my sins draw nigh;
O my Saviour, thou canst find
  help for sinners such as I;
speak that word of love again,

'Christ receiveth sinful men.'

Christ receiveth sinful men,
  even me, with all my sin;
openeth to me heaven again;
  with him I may enter in.
Death hath no more sting nor
                        pain;
Christ receiveth sinful men.

EMMA FRANCES BEVAN (HG 640),
1858

B

John Wesley's version of these
stanzas

Lo, God is here! let us adore,
  and own how dreadful is this place!   (Gen. 28:22)
Let all within us feel his power
  and silent bow before his face;
who know his power, his grace who prove,
serve him with awe, with reverence love.

Lo, God is here! him day and night
  the united choirs of angels sing;
to him, enthroned above all height
  heav'n's hosts their noblest praises bring:
disdain not, Lord, our meaner song,
who praise thee with a stammering tongue.

Being of beings! may our praise
  thy courts with grateful fragrance fill;
still may we stand before thy face,
  still hear and do thy sovereign will;
to thee may all our thoughts arise,
ceaseless, accepted sacrifice.

1739

202
GOD IS IN THIS PLACE!   HG 850
A

Gott ist gegenwärtig.
Lasset uns anbeten
und in Erfurcht vor ihn treten.
Gott ist in der Mitten.
Alles in uns schweige
und sich innigst vor ihm beuge!

Wer ihn kennt,
wer ihn nennt,
Schlagt die Augen nieder;
kommt, ergebt euch wieder!

Gott ist gegenwärtig,
dem die Cherubinen
Tag und Nacht gebücket dienen;

Heilig, heilig! singen
alle Engelchören
wann sie dieses Wesen ehren.
Herr, vernimm
uns're Stimm',
da auch wir geringen
uns're Opfer bringen!

Majestätisch Wesen!
möcht' ich recht dich preisen
und im Geist dir Dienst erweisen!
Möcht' ich, wie die Engel,
immer vor dir stehen
und dich gegenwärtig sehen!
Lass mich dir
für und für
trachten zu gefallen,
Liebster Gott, in Allen!

G. TERSTEEGEN (HG 741), 1729
sts. 1, 2, 4 of 8

God reveals his presence,
let us now adore him,
and with awe appear before him:
God is in his temple,
all in us keep silence
and before him bow with rever-
                        ence;
  him alone
  God we own;
He's our Lord and Saviour:
praise his name for ever.

God reveals his presence,
whom the angelic legions
serve with awe in heavenly re-
                        gions:
'Holy, Holy, Holy!'
sing the hosts of heaven,
'Praise to God be ever given.'
  Condescend
  to attend
Graciously, O Jesus,
to our songs and praises.

  O majestic Being,
  were but soul and body
thee to serve at all times ready:
  might we like the angels
  who behold thy glory,
with abasement sink before thee,
  and through grace
  be always
in our whole demeanour
to thy praise and honour.

F. W. FOSTER and **J. MILLER** 1789; text
of English, *Moravian Hymn Book*, 1914

203
GRATITUDE FOR CHANGE

We praise and bless thee, gracious Lord,
  our Saviour kind and true,
for all the old things passed away,
  for all thou hast made new.

The old security is gone
  in which so long we lay;
the sleep of death thou hast dispelled,
  the darkness rolled away.

New hopes, new purposes, desires
  and joys, thy grace has given;
old ties are broken from the earth,
  new ties attach to heaven.

But yet how much must be destroyed,
  how much renewed must be,
ere we can fully stand complete
  in likeness, Lord, to thee.

Thou, only thou, must carry on
  the work thou hast begun;
of thine own strength thou must impart
  in thine own ways to run.

So shall we faultless stand at last
  before thy Father's throne,
the blessedness for ever ours,
  the glory all thine own.

Jane Laurie Borthwick (HG 70), 1864,
from the German of **KARL J. P. SPITTA**,
1843.

204
CANTICLE OF THE SUN   HG 13

O most high, almighty, good Lord God,
  to thee belong praise, glory, honour and all blessing.

Praised be my Lord God, with all his creatures;
  and specially our brother the sun, who brings us the day and who
                                                brings us the light.
Fair is he, and shining with a very great splendour:
  O Lord, he signifies to us thee.
Praised be my Lord for our sister the moon:
  and for the stars which he has set clear and lovely in heaven.
Praised be my Lord for our brother the wind:
  and for air and cloud, calms, and all weather by the which thou
      upholdest the life of all creatures.
Praised be my Lord for our sister water:
  who is very serviceable unto us, and humble and precious
                                                and clean.
Praised be my Lord for our brother fire, through whom thou givest us
                                                light in the darkness:
  and he is bright and pleasant and very mighty and strong.
Praised be my Lord for our mother the earth, the which doth sustain us
                                                and keep us:
  and bringeth forth divers fruits, and flowers of many colours and
                                                grass.
Praised be my Lord for all those who pardon one another for his love's
                                                sake:
  and who endure weakness and tribulation.
Blessed are they who peaceably shall endure:
  for thou O most Highest shalt give them a crown.
Praised be my Lord for our sister the death of the body:
  blessed are they who are found walking by thy most holy will.
Praise ye and bless ye the Lord and give thanks unto him:
  and serve him with great humility.

                              ST FRANCIS OF ASSISI (1225),
                              tr. **Matthew Arnold**,* 1865

*This translation, from the first volume of *Essays in Criticism*, reflects the rhythm
and spirit of the original, and has once appeared in a hymnal. The more conventional and better known translation, 'All creatures of our God and King,' will be
found in any hymn book.

205
COME DOWN, O LOVE DIVINE!   HG 123

Discendi, amor santo
visita la mie mente
del tuo amore ardente,
si che di te m'infiammi tutto
                        quanto.

Vienne, consolatore,
nel mio cuor veramente:
del tuo ardente amore
ardel veracemente:
del tuo amor cocente
si forte sie ferito:
vada come smarrito
dentro e di fuore ardendo tutto
                        quanto.

Arda si fortemente
che tutto mi consumi,
si che veracemente
lassi mondan costumi;
li splendenti lumi
lucenti, illuminanti
mi stien sempre davanti
per il quali mi vesta il vero manto.

E'l manto ch'i'mi vesta
sie la carità santa:
sott'una bigia vesta
umilità si canta,
la qual mai nin si vanta
per se nullo ben fare,
non si sa inalzare
ma nel profondo scende con gran
                        pianto.

Si grande è quel disio
ch'allor l'anima sente,
che dir nol sapre ' io,
a ciò non son potente:
nulla umana mente
entender nol potria,
se nol gustasse pria
per la vertù dello Spirito Santo.
                        Deo gracias.

                              BIANCO OF SIENA, d. 1434

  Come down, O love divine,
    seek thou this soul of mine
  and visit it with thine own ardour glowing;

O Comforter, draw near,
  within my heart appear
and kindle it, thy holy flame bestowing.

  O let it freely burn
    till earthly passions turn
  to dust and ashes in thy heat consuming;
    and let thy glorious light
    shine ever on my sight
  and clothe me round, the while my path illuming.

  Let holy charity
    mine outward vesture be
  and lowliness become mine inner clothing:
    true lowliness of heart,
    which takes the humbler part
  and o'er its own shortcomings weeps with loathing.

  And so the yearning strong
    with which the soul will long
  shall far outpass the power of human telling;
    nor none can guess its grace
    till he become the place
  wherein the Holy Spirit makes his dwelling.

                              R. F. LITTLEDALE, 1867

ARTICLE 14:
THE VICTORIAN AGE, 1837-1906 (206-269)

In every respect the English Victorian age was an age of
energy and confidence. Until its very last years, England was
involved in no major war, and during the 64 years 1837-1901,
which are those strictly to be called 'Victorian,' the country
experienced an immense growth in population, economics
and invention. Virtually everything which was 'success' to the
Victorians has come to be questioned in the twentieth century.
But the fashionable use of the word 'Victorian' to describe
what is stolid, philistine, and unimaginative is a dangerous half
truth which, whatever the intellectuals may say, is now being
protested against by the addiction of large numbers of people,
in Britain and America, to documentary entertainments (chiefly on television) which expose with remarkable fidelity, and
not without affection, the true texture of Victorian life.

In hymnody the period conveniently ends at 1906, the year
of the *English Hymnal*; but in this and the next two sections
only a handful of hymns actually fall outside the reign of the
most famous of English queens. And in hymnody the energy
and enterprise of that age is very fully reflected.

In that age of energy there was much controversy. The
hymns in this section respond to three great disputes: (1) that
centred in the Oxford Movement which, after 1833, looked
for and achieved nothing less than a revival of religion in the
Church of England; (2) the passion of the Christian Socialists
against social abuses; and (3), late in the age, what Robert
Schumann would have called the 'march of the armies of David
against the philistines' (the gestures of the literate against the
cheapening of style that was overtaking hymnody itself).

'Cheapening' was the great blessing and the great peril. It
became easy, in the early 19th century, to print and distribute
books and especially to print music. Coincident with this came
a new and clamorous demand for hymnody in the Church of
England. Half-way through the age came several waves of
evangelical revival, mostly aimed from America. A study of the
enormous number of hymnals and song-sheets produced

from about 1860 onwards speedily convinces the reader that in hymnody, as in much else, you could get away with almost anything. A parallel situation developed in the later 20th century where again a new kind of demand produced a massive output, and again standards fell to alarming depths. It was with music as it was with texts; and our third point of controversy was the inevitable response to a feeling, by 1900, that the too liberally sown and too casually tended garden of hymnody needed weeding.

It is a curious and rather mournful fact that literary and theological critics in church circles are still saying what secular criticism and popular taste have now rejected, that the nineteenth century has virtually nothing to offer in the way of good hymnody. Perhaps, in the field of correcting misconceptions, we have no more important chapter in this book than this present one, for it is designed to show what the Victorians were trying to do and what, when they were at their best, they achieved.

This is predominantly the age of Anglican hymnody. The famous case in the church courts which finally legitimized hymnody opened a gate, and the romantics (Article 9) rode through it, liberating hymnody through their special talents (see ## 116-24 for particular examples). (The law against hymnody had long been a dead letter, but members of Thomas Cotterill's congregation in Sheffield chose to make a test case out of the hymnal that their Vicar was inviting them to use, and the Archbishop in the end, after a nice piece of ecclesiastical diplomacy, ruled that hymnody was no longer illegal.)

The first wave of energy was directed at translation work, which we dealt with in articles 11-13. To this Richard Mant made an early, and now mostly forgotten, contribution: his excellent 'Bright the vision' (206) comes from his *Ancient Hymns* of 1837, its place there no doubt being justified by its being based on the *tersanctus* in Isaiah 6. But it is a generation before much original work comes from the Anglicans.

Therefore, after #206 we do not meet an 'Oxford Movement' hymn again until #220. Nonconformity produced many hymnals during the early Victorian time, not least among them being private hymnals for wealthy and populous chapels, the most famous of which was the *Leeds Hymn Book* of 1853, one of whose editors produced the very spirited text of #218. But the creativity of nonconformity was somewhat muted by their 18th-century heritage: the Wesleys for the Methodists, and Watts for the Congregationalists and Baptists. Unitarians, however, produced some choice pieces, like #207, from one of their best minds, which well illustrates the special interest of 19th-century Unitarians in high culture.

But the most productive non-Anglican area turned out to be that of the Roman Catholic Church. This communion, released by emacipation from positive illegality in 1833 and re-establishing its hierarchy in 1850, produced one hymn writer in F. W. Faber (208-12) who had exactly the gift that was needed in that company. Roman Catholics were mostly poor, often immigrants, and in their new-found religious freedom concerned with two great issues: eucharistic devotion, and their mission to convert others to the Catholic faith. Both these notes are sounded by Faber, who had in his make-up a strong influence from evangelicalism. Hymns were, of course, not needed for the Mass, but vernacular hymnody at popular services has never been forbidden to English Catholics, and Faber's purpose, as he said, was to do for his people what the *Olney Hymns*, which he knew and admired, had done for Olney. His talent was equal to neither that of Newton nor that of Cowper,

and he was fatally garrulous, so that his hymns usually need pruning for public use; that is just as well, because he is capable of writing fairly expert doggerel. But on the other hand, there are stanzas in 'My God, how wonderful thou art' and 'O come and mourn with me awhile' which are profoundly beautiful and which sound an ecstatic note that the anti-enthusiastic Anglicans tended to avoid. The argumentative and conversational character of some of the others has an endearing quality, even if it does not always make very polished hymnody. Matthew Bridges' 'Crown him with many crowns' (214) is at a loftier level; it is not too often found now in its original form, many editors preferring the diluted though still serviceable version with stanzas by Godfrey Thring.

With T. T. Lynch (215-7) we stumble on a curious piece of church history. Lynch, a gentle Congregational minister, produced his collection of hymns, *The Rivulet*, in 1855 and enlarged it in 1856. A glance at the texts will indicate a certain nervous originality, a preoccupation with natural imagery, a readiness to deal with religious doubt and hesitation. (216 might have been a text for the 1963 'Honest to God' controversy.) As one of the few nonconformist writers of that time with anything new to say, he commands respect, and one forgives him some bad lines for an equal number of really inspired epigrams, like that at the end of st. 3 of #215, or of st. 3 of #217. One would not put it higher than that, were it not that the book chanced to fall into the hands of one John Campbell, the Scottish Calvinist editor of a denominational paper, whose native heresy-hunting instincts it aroused to such purpose that he reviewed it for seven consecutive weeks, tearing every page to theological shreds. The members of the Congregational Assembly were soon brought to such a tension of dispute between those who thought Campbell a monster and those who thought Lynch an enemy of right-thinking Christians that, in the words of the denomination's best historian of the incident, Albert Peel, the Assembly was 'almost wrecked.' Only Thomas Binney (130) prevailed to secure a peaceful settlement on the second occasion when the matter was debated. Such was the flammable atmosphere in which a nonconformist hymn writer worked; it is hardly surprising that we do not hear much from any but Lynch and Rawson (218) who, in the north country, seems to have kept safely clear of theological storm-centres. The pale examples of Lynch's work that modern hymnals are content with hardly lead anyone to suspect what trouble he got into; we leave those for readers to discover for themselves.

Two 'angry' hymns, ##213 and 219, represent, in this early period, the mind of those who sought to issue calls to social action. Ebenezer Elliott's once famous piece, 'When wilt thou save the people,' is passionate and is also superbly written. Not less so is the only hymn by the author of *Tom Brown's Schooldays* (219), a text which squeamish editors often modify in order to get rid of the rhetorical questions and other acerbities; but they should leave it as it is and sing it to the tune MARTYRS.

And now, with *Hymns Ancient and Modern* (trial edition 1860, first full edition 1861) the Anglicans come into their own. Many hymnals had appeared during the fifties taking the quite new line which *A & M* made famous and standard, that of printing each hymn with a tune appropriate to it, instead of printing a words-edition for the congregation and a tune-book for the precentor, organist, or choir. But, as we have already often seen, it was not the earliest which made the headlines. *Hymns Ancient and Modern*, with 273 hymns in the 1861 edition, very largely translations from Latin, with a sparing selection from the 18th-century evangelicals, proved so abundantly successful that an enlarged edition (with a supplement bringing the total to 386) had to be brought out in 1868, a complete revision (473) in 1875, a supplement to the second edition (score 638) in 1889. The 1875 edition was perhaps the normative one; it was this edition which all editors–Anglican or not–felt they must measure up to, improve on, or react against. It was this edition that made 'Abide with me' (#27) and 'O God our help in ages past' [sic] (#165) the kind of detail that caused people to protest with almost savage violence when the second revision of 1904 rationalized and updated the book and–to their horror–changed all the numbers. To that extent it was a British Institution. (It still is; plenty of churches still use the edition which leaves 27 and 165 where you expect them, and the 1950 revision, while changing much, didn't dare to change those.)

The hymnody there required was a decorous adornment to the Prayer Book. Reacting against the 'enthusiasm' of the evangelicals, these editors said that if we must have hymnody we must avoid the excesses into which it had led those Methodists whom, as agents for the reconversion of England, they most feared. So the book is arranged just as the Prayer Book is arranged, with hymns for Matins coming first, then those for Evensong, then those for the Little Hours (should anyone wish to observe them), then–corresponding to the 'Collect, Epistle and Gospel' section of the Prayer Book–hymns for the Church's Year. Then, for Sundays after Trinity, 'General hymns,' roughly arranged according to subject; then hymns for the Sacraments, for special rites and occasions (corresponding to the 'Occasional Prayers'), a long section of hymns for saints' days, and a handful of litanies.

Although the next series of hymns in this section comes from all manner of sources, the great majority of them appeared at some time in *Hymns A & M*, and nearly all the authors have a place there up to 1904. Every one of the authors is in one or the other of the editions up to 1950.

Hymns A & M was directed by a small committee whose leader was the Reverend Sir Henry Baker, a country parson in one of England's remotest counties–Herefordshire. And the ethos of the book is strictly that of the cosy, conservative, country parish church, the gathering place of those communities which were led by people who had a stake in the land rather than in industry. Not that they sang *about* the countryside any more than they sang about the city. They sang about what was in the Prayer Book, and therefore about what was in the Bible so interpreted.

Perhaps #220 is a good place to begin: a tolerable hymn, for a society that depended so much on the sea but that didn't go to sea much itself, to a rousing pictorial tune that sent shivers down decorous church-going spines. Nos. 221 and 222, by one of the very few laymen (an insurance manager) whom we meet in this section, show the 'domestic' style at its best: neatly written, doctrinal, singable. Nos. 223 and 224 bring in one of the many high dignitaries who contributed to Victorian hymnody; Bp Wordsworth could be dry and could indeed be trivial (there can hardly be a more lamentable travesty of 1 Cor. 13 than 'Gracious Spirit, Holy Ghost'); but he could also be magnificent, as in the massive and scriptural Ascension hymn, or that perfect miniature written for a Confirmation, #224. Monsell, Vicar of Guildford, wrote pleasant lyrics without attempting profundity (226-7). Dean Plumptre again produced good serviceable material; the hymn about knowledge handles

a subject unusual for the time and style (and it did not get into *Hymns A & M*); #229 is like a very well-dressed and well-starched version of #215. But schools and hospitals were multiplying at that time, and most Victorian attempts to meet their needs were far more pedestrian than these. Not so #245, however, which is by an author who knew how to write well and economically. (This was written for the opening of a hospital, though which one it is now difficult to determine–see the *Hymnal Guide*.)

Bishop How is another typical gap-filler, always competent and honest, probably never inspired. Perhaps there is something impressive about the full version of #230 which is to some extent lost when the procession of Apostles, Evangelists and Martyrs is, as always now, dropped out (those stanzas do sit ill on Vaughan Williams' popular tune). No 231 is a good example of the pictorial hymn so much loved by Victorians (indeed, it is, like #262, based on an actual picture, and a very dubious one at that); one can hardly feel that it adequately transmits the message of Revelation 3:20, but at one time it was immensely popular.

Then comes the good Baring-Gould, a man of so many aesthetic interests, leading the children and congregation of his church round the village of Horbury Bridge on Sunday School Procession Day, with the great Tractarian Cross at the head, to the rousing, if mostly superificial, words of 'Onward, Christian Soldiers' (232). Processions, indoors or out, were a great matter for the Oxford Movement. Hardly less strenuous –beginning tolerably, touching real solid scriptural ground, then wilting at the end–is his translation from the Danish (233), still the only hymn we know from that language and so clearly the work of somebody whose culture was wider-ranging than that of the usual parson. 'For the beauty of the earth' (234), now a popular nature hymn, becomes, if you have its full and original text, an earnest eucharistic hymn of considerable dignity.

More pictorial imagery and sonorous language in #235, perhaps the best piece of literature Dean Alford provided for hymnals. (His universally-known harvest hymn is disqualified for inclusion here by its calamitous third stanza.) 'Amen! Come, Lord Jesus' deserves to have had a longer life than in fact it got. 'The church's one foundation' (236) is one of the most theologically substantial of all Victorian hymns and thoroughly deserves its continued popularity. Written by a still young priest in reaction to the Colenso controversy (a heresy-hunt in the Church of England focussed on a popular, tough-minded, and unfortunate South African bishop who was removed from his see for saying that Moses did not write Deuteronomy because it contains an account of his own funeral) and on the side of that controversy with which few people would now be in sympathy, it has become a universal hymn of celebration for great church occasions. Within the author's lifetime such occasions became greater and the processions longer, and to meet organizers' requests he inflated the text to eleven verses (see *Julian*); but they are hack work, new pieces on an old garment, and they have very properly fallen away.

Bishop Bickersteth (238), best known for 'Peace, perfect peace,' was a hymnal editor and an evangelical, and his style was usually trivial and overemotional. This is probably his best work, forgotten in Britain now, though still to be found in America.

It is late in the day to mention Sir Henry Baker as a writer (239, 240); he did indeed contribute one or two pieces to the 1861 *Hymns A & M* which had a certain vogue. But it seems right, here, to quote his best-known hymn followed by his best hymn, and these came later. What could be more typical of countryside Anglicanism than the domesticizing of the 23rd Psalm in #239? King David is no longer 'in presence of his enemies' but at the Communion rail. No. 240 is surely Baker's soundest piece of teaching, with a very well-turned lyric imagination.

Canon John Ellerton (246-7) was editor and hymnologist—one of the first—as well as a prolific author. Here again, as with How and Monsell, we have decent middle-of-the-road hymnody for parishes. 'The day thou gavest' is still one of the authentic 'Anglican sounds' and so is 'Saviour, again to thy dear name we raise.' We offer here two saints' day hymns to show how sensibly Ellerton tackled a subject which too often produced platitude in hymnals. The opening of the third stanza of #247 has a touch of modest genius. Much of his work is still in hymn books and easily come by.

Dean Stanley (248) always seems to have written weightily; he used this ponderous verse-form more than once. This is cathedral-style writing, needing room to speak and space to ponder: urbane and dignified and decent. William Bright has in ##249 and 250 a touch more warmth; 249 is unequal in a fashion that almost makes one welcome the absence of parsonic gloss; 250 is brilliant in its way, a really distinguished saints' day hymn with a splendid climax to the whole argument in the last stanza.

Archbishop Maclagan is now fast disappearing from hymnals, but #251 is worth attention for its very unusual subject: a really brave attempt to write a lyric on the mysteries of Holy Saturday. (Read also, should you have the chance, his workmanlike and unusual piece on St Luke, at 420 in the standard edition of Hymns A & M.) Romanis' hymn for St James is another beautiful piece for a saint's day. The gifted scholar and historian Hatch is now universally famous for 'Breathe on me' (253) whose unfortunate marriage to a detestable tune has hampered its message in America and in parts of England.

So much for the hymns along the main stream of Oxford Movement thinking. But now we must go back and pick up those we omitted.

F. T. Palgrave, of the Golden Treasury, knew his poetry and could write it. His book of that name is the Golden Treasury of Shorter Poems, but he compiled also a similar Treasury of longer poems, and a Treasury of Sacred Song, and from a standpoint near the Unitarian culture he looked pretty objectively at the fashionable hymnody of his time. Almost nothing of his is now sung, except #237 which surely is beautiful literature and beautiful thinking.

Another swimmer-against-the-stream is Henry Twells, an Anglican priest who did not quite fit into the Tractarian picture. I have not seen a picture of him so I do not know positively whether he had two vertical furrows between his eyebrows, but in his famous hymn, #241, we certainly see a very searching and prayerful imagination, and in #242 it is more prominent still. What other hymns for evensong deal with this aspect of Christ's ministry, or what other penitential hymns ask forgiveness for our religion? As for #243: meat too strong for any hymnal except the 1904 and 1916 editions of A & M, written a few days before he died. Why, this is one of the very few Victorian hymns which a frowning contemporary would surely have been proud to have written. Twells is a Victorian who should be looked at again by editors.

The stream of nonconformist hymnody between 1860 and 1890 becomes a mere trickle, but Congregationalism did produce one hymn writer who really seems to have taken it on himself to become that communion's Bishop How. T. H. Gill wrote middle-of-the-road material; I cannot recall any inspired lines in his fairly generous output, but judiciously pruned (he was a bit garrulous), #244 still makes a sturdy hymn for occasions when history is being celebrated.

At #254 we begin to turn new pages. Before the great protest of Bridges, to which we are just coming, there were signs that Anglicans wanted hymnody in new styles and on new subjects. One of these is in Dugmore's two hymns here given. No. 254 waited a long time before becoming as popular as it now is—and it was the Scots, who put it into their 1927 Church Hymnary with a singable tune, who mostly contributed to that. A patristic theologian has pointed out to me that its first two stanzas reflect very vividly the theology of Gregory of Nyssa, one of the abler and more imaginative of the fourth-century Greek-speaking teachers; and as it goes on it does reach out towards the Monday-to-Saturday world, a thing which, excluding the few 'protesters,' had rarely been done since Charles Wesley (67), and which still is hardly attempted by the current Hymns A & M. So it had been a long wait. In the far less familiar #255, Dugmore is experimenting with that meter which most nearly reflects the ethos of the heroic couplet (on which we commented in article 4), and there are lines there, in this immensely sonorous piece, which really do suggest the idiom of Pope.

Rudyard Kipling may or may not have intended #256 to be sung; it found a tune in the year of its first publication, and has been uneasily wedded to different partners for two generations since. Though its historic relevance has been forgotten and the presuppositions of stanza 4 are quite impossible for modern singers, it can still be read as great literature and as a remarkable penitential utterance for a writer so closely associated with celebrations of Empire. Coming on this after reading some other Victorians is like touching real bone after being accustomed to plastic; look at those alliterations, those concrete and clanging monosyllables! Whatever else it may not be, this is real writing, and for about forty years hymnal editors found it irresistible.

And this brings us to the poet Laureate, Robert Bridges, whose single-handed contribution to the history of hymnody in the Yattendon Hymnal we must not here take too much space to celebrate. Here was the man who wrote in a letter, later published, the famous words: 'All I can urge is that they should have at least one service a week where people like myself can attend without being offended or moved to laughter.' He wrote that in 1911, when he was already famous—or notorious—for what he had said and done about Victorian hymnody. He was a trained physician, a leader in the world of letters, fifty-five years old, living on a hill outside Oxford and one of the two or three educated people attending the small parish church at Yattendon when, in 1899, he produced the Yattendon Hymnal. The full music edition of this hymnal is set out on a page thirteen inches by eleven, in open score, in an antique type-face which he invented, with full scholarly notes—sometimes perverse, always trenchant—on each hymn, and contains only two or three tunes later than 1750 (written by his friend, the Slade Professor of fine art at Oxford). The texts are nearly all by himself, designed to carry the original versions of tunes which were either unknown or known only in deformed versions.

His message was: Recover the treasures, not of the theological middle ages, but of the literary and musical past when these two arts were showing a true combination of maturity and innocence. All his material is slightly 'old fashioned,' written by the rules of eighteenth-century rather than nineteenth-century versifying, written to carry old tunes, written to translate or, more often, paraphrase old hymns in other languages. Two hymns of his are rewritings of Isaac Watts. There is a certain kind of profundity you look for in vain in Bridges. He had no ear for the deep notes of devotion in Watts and Wesley; it was not this that he wished to recover. At his best he is gently imaginative and ruthlessly craftsmanlike. His metricization is beautiful; he can write in strange meters, or in familiar ones with the unusual accents demanded by an old tune, as in #257, with effortless ease. But it is hymnody for 'people like him,' for the urbane and cultivated. Uneducated people can grasp Watts and Wesley; the cultivated enjoy Bridges. And why not? It is quite undeniable that up to the time of Karl Barth the settled habit of the church's teaching and preaching was to tell cultivated people to leave their culture and maturity in the church porch. You needed to be a man of the power, the audacity, the opinionated brusqueness, and, one must add, the worldly substance of Bridges to lift up a voice against that.

What Bridges did for texts, Vaughan Williams did for music, and the whole movement to make liturgy humane as well as correct and to bring good taste to the congregations, fused into a success under the guidance of Percy Dearmer, who began his crusade for culture by producing the *English Hymnal* in 1906. Under this spur of new zeal, perhaps the greatest activity was in retranslating some of the old Latin hymns that had been rather woodenly handled by the earlier translators. Our ##137 and 145 are examples of the new style. The *English Hymnal* contained relatively few new texts and tunes—surprisingly few, considering its place as the second most influential hymnal in our history. But it did match Bridges' impertinent plea with Vaughan Williams' equally famous and equally alarming dictum, that good taste is a moral matter. And it did include a good deal of Bridges; it produced Athelstan Riley's festive doxology (266) that made the tune LASST UNS ERFREUEN so famous; it printed some of Dearmer's own early work, and Scott Holland's sturdy 'Judge eternal' (265); and above all, it discovered Chesterton (269) and printed the only hymn he ever wrote for congregational singing, one of the literary masterpieces of the whole field of hymnody.

Another editor was working quietly away, independent at first of this aristocratic movement, though when he finished his work he won their respect; he also was recovering the ancient melodies and (as Dearmer was later to do) reviving the old carols. G. R. Woodward (263-4), who first came out with *Carols for Eastertide* in 1894 containing the now well known 'This joyful Eastertide,' went on to produce the Cowley Carol Book (1902) and *Songs of Syon* (1904, 1910). The expanded edition of this is a collection of over 400 pieces, all set to tunes of exquisite remoteness from the experience of ordinary congregations, many of the texts being his own. He had a style more eloquently antiquated than that of Bridges, and really the book is a collection of sacred madrigals for domestic devotion rather than a parish hymnal. But his contribution to the opening up of the field which Victorian decorum had so rigidly enclosed was substantial enough to earn him a place in the history of the subject, and if the reader is able to hear the incomparable sound of the First Genevan Psalm behind the affectionate text of #264 he will see what Woodward was about.

These dedicated eccentrics, so different from the Ellertons and Hows and Wordsworths in their view of life and their demands of hymnody, rescued English hymnody from the becalmed condition into which some of its text writers (most of whom are not featured in this book at all) and nearly all its musicians had brought it.

RICHARD MANT, Bishop
1776-1848

206
THE VISION OF ISAIAH
Is. 6:1-3

HG 95

Bright the vision that delighted
　　once the sight of Judah's seer;
sweet the countless tongues united
　　to entrance the prophet's ear.

Round the Lord in glory seated
　　Cherubim and Seraphim
filled his temple, and repeated
　　each to each the alternate hymn:

'Lord, thy glory fills the heaven,
　　earth is with its fulness stored;
unto thee be glory given,
　　Holy, Holy, Holy, Lord!'

Heaven is still with glory ringing,
　　earth takes up the angels' cry,
'Holy, Holy, Holy' singing,
　　'Lord of hosts, the Lord most high.'

With his seraph train before him,
　　with his holy church below
thus conspire we to adore him,
　　bid we thus our anthem flow:

'Lord, thy glory fills the heaven;
　　earth is with its fulness stored;
unto thee be glory given:
　　Holy, Holy, Holy, Lord!'

Ancient Hymns, 1837

JAMES MARTINEAU*
1805-1900

207
GETHSEMANE

A voice upon the midnight air,
　　where Kedron's moonlit waters stray　　(John 18:1)
weeps forth in agony of prayer,
　　'O Father, take this cup away.'

Ah, Thou who sorrowest unto death,
　　we conquer in thy mortal fray;
and earth for all her children saith,
　　'O God, take not this cup away.'

O Lord of sorrow! meekly die:
　　thou'lt heal or hallow all our woe;
thy name refresh the mourner's sigh,
　　thy peace revive the faint and low.

Great Chief of faithful souls, arise!
　　none else can lead the martyr-band,

who teach the brave, how peril flies
when faith unarmed uplifts the hand.

O King of earth! the cross ascend;
o'er climes and ages 'tis thy throne;
where'er thy fading eye may bend
the desert blooms, and is thine own.   (Is. 35:1)

Thy parting blessing, Lord, we pray;
make but one fold below, above: (John 10:16)
and when we go the last lone way
Oh, give the welcome of thy love!

Hymns for the Christian Church and
Home, 1840

FREDERICK WILLIAM FABER,
1814-63, *Jesus and Mary,* 1849
HG 175

208
OUR HEAVENLY FATHER   HG 464

My God! how wonderful thou art,
thy majesty how bright,
how beautiful thý mercy-seat
in depths of burning light!

How dread are thine eternal
years,
O everlasting Lord!
by prostrate spirits day and night
incessantly adored!

How beautiful, how beautiful
the sight of thee must be,
thing endless wisdom, boundless
power
and aweful purity!

Oh how I fear thee, living God!
with deepest, tenderest fears,
and worship thee with trembling
hope
and penitential tears.

Yet I may love thee, Living God!
almighty as thou art,
for thou hast stooped to ask of me
the love of my poor heart.

O then this worse than worthless
heart
in pity deign to take
and make it love thee, for thyself
and for thy glory's sake.

No earthly father loves like thee,
no mother half so mild
bears and forbears, as thou hast
done,
with me, thy sinful child.

Only to sit and think of God,
oh, what a joy it is!
To think the thought, to breathe
the Name,
earth has no higher bliss!

Father of Jesus, love's reward,
what rapture will it be,
prostrate before thy throne to lie,
and gaze, and gaze on thee!

209
FAITH OF OUR FATHERS   HG 175

Faith of our fathers! living still
in spite of dungeon, fire and sword:
oh how our hearts beat high with joy
whene'er we hear that glorious word.
Faith of our fathers! Holy Faith!
We will be true to thee till death.

Our fathers, chained in prisons dark,
were still in heart and conscience free:
how sweet would be their children's fate,
if they, like them, could die for thee!
Faith of our Fathers! . . .

Faith of our fathers! Mary's prayers
shall win our country back to thee;
and through the truth that comes from God

England shall then indeed be free.
Faith of our fathers! . . .

Faith of our Fathers! we will love
both friend and foe in all our strife:
and preach thee too, as love knows how
by kindly words and virtuous life:
Faith of our fathers, holy Faith,
we will be true to thee till death.

210
THE RIGHT MUST WIN   HG 826

Oh it is hard to work for God,
to rise and take his part
upon this battlefield of earth
and not sometimes lose heart!

He hides himself so wondrously
as if there were no God;
he is least seen when all the
powers
of ill are most abroad.

Or he deserts us at the hour
the fight is all but lost;
and seems to leave us to ourselves
just when we need him most.

Yes, there is less to try our faith
in our mysterious creed
than in the godless look of earth,
in these our hours of need.

Ill masters good; good seems to
change
to ill with greatest ease;
and, worst of all, the good with
good
is at cross-purposes.

The Church, the Sacraments, the
Faith
their uphill journey take,
lose here what there they gain,
and if
we lean upon them, break.

It is not so, but so it looks;
and we lose courage then;
and doubts will come if God hath
kept
his promises to men.

Ah! God is other than we think;
his ways are far above,
far beyond reason's height, and
reached
only by childlike love.

★   ★   ★

Workman of God! oh lose not
heart,
but learn what God is like;
and in the darkest battlefield
thou shalt know when to strike

Thrice blest is he to whom is given
the instinct that can tell
that God is on the field, when he
is most invisible.

Blest too is he who can divine
where real right doth lie,
and dares to take the side that
seems
wrong to man's blindfold eye.

Then learn to scorn the praise of
men,
and learn to lose with God;
for Jesus won the world through
shame
and beckons thee his road.

God's glory is a wondrous thing,
most strange in all its ways,
and, of all things on earth, least
like
what men agree to praise.

★   ★   ★

Muse on his justice, downcast
soul!
muse and take better heart:
back with thine angel to the field,
and bravely do thy part!

★   ★   ★

For right is right, since God is
God;
and right the day must win;
to doubt would be disloyalty,
to falter would be sin.

Sts. 9, 10, 16, 18 omitted.

211
COME TO JESUS   HG 654

Souls of men! why will ye scatter
like a crowd of frightened
sheep?

foolish hearts! why will ye wander
from a love so true and deep?

Was there ever kindest shepherd
half so gentle, half so sweet,
as the Saviour who would have us
come and gather round his
feet?

It is God: his love looks mighty
but is mightier than it seems:
'Tis our Father: and his fondness
goes far out beyond our
dreams.

There's a wideness in God's mercy
like the wideness of the sea:
there's a kindness in his justice
which is more than liberty.

There is no place where earth's
sorrows
are more felt than up in Heaven;
there is no place where earth's
failings
have such kindly judgment
given.

There is welcome to the sinner,
and more graces for the good;
there is mercy with the Saviour;
there is healing in his Blood.

There is grace enough for thousands
of new worlds as great as this;
there is room for fresh creations
in that upper home of bliss.

For the love of God is broader
than the measures of man's
mind;
and the heart of the Eternal
is most wonderfully kind.

But we make his love too narrow
by false limits of our own;
and we magnify his strictness
with a zeal he will not own.

There is plentiful redemption
in the Blood that has been shed;
there is joy for all the members
in the sorrows of the Head.

'Tis not all we owe to Jesus;
it is something more than all;
greater good because of evil,
larger mercy through the fall.

Pining souls! come nearer Jesus,
and oh come not doubting
thus,
but with faith that trusts more
bravely
his huge tenderness for us.

If our love were but more simple
we should take him at his word;
and our lives would be all sunshine
in the sweetness of our Lord.

212
JESUS CRUCIFIED   HG 501

Oh come and mourn with me awhile!
See, Mary calls us to her side;
oh come and let us mourn with her;
Jesus, our Love is crucified!

Have we no tears to shed for him?
while soldiers scoff and Jews deride?
Ah! look how patiently he hangs;
Jesus, our Love, is crucified!

★   ★   ★

Seven times he spoke, seven words of love,
and all three hours his silence cried
for mercy on the souls of men;
Jesus, our Love, is crucified!

What was thy crime, my dearest Lord?
By earth, by heaven thou hast been tried,
and guilty found of too much love;
Jesus, our Love, is crucified!

Found guilty of excess of love,
it was thine own sweet will that tied
thee tighter far than helpless nails:
Jesus, our Love, is crucified!

★   ★   ★

Oh break, oh break, hard heart of mine!
Thy weak self-love and guilty pride
his Pilate and his Judas were;
Jesus, our Love, is crucified!

★   ★   ★

A broken heart, a fount of tears,
ask, and they will not be denied;
a broken heart Love's cradle is:
Jesus, our Love, is crucified!

O Love of God! O sin of man!
in this dread act your strength is tried;
and victory remains with Love;
for he, our Love, is crucified!

Sts. 3, 4, 8, 10 omitted

EBENEZER ELLIOTT
1781-1849

213
WHEN WILT THOU SAVE THE PEOPLE? HG 812

When wilt thou save the people?
O God of mercy, when?
not kings and lords, but nations,
not thrones and crowns, but men!
Flowers of thy heart, O God, are they,
let them not pass, like weeds, away,
their heritage a sunless day.
God save the people!

Shall crime bring crime for ever,
strength aiding still the strong?
Is it thy will, O Father,
that men should toil for wrong?
'No!' say thy mountains, 'No!' thy skies,
man's clouded sun shall brightly rise
and songs be heard instead of sighs.
God save the people!

When wilt thou save the people?
O God of mercy, when?
The people, Lord! the people! -
not thrones and crowns, but men!
God save the people; thine they are,
thy children, as thy angels fair;
from vice, oppression and despair,
God save the people!

More Prose and Verse (Posth.), 1850

MATTHEW BRIDGES
1800-94
HG 78

214
CROWN HIM WITH MANY CROWNS
Rev. 19:12   HG 157
(This hymn often appears with some quatrains inserted from a similar hymn
written in 1874 by Godfrey Thring: these can be identified by comparison with
the following, which is the original text.)

Crown him with many crowns,
the Lamb upon his throne;
Hark, how the heavenly anthem drowns
all music but its own:
awake, my soul, and sing
of him who died for thee,
and hail him as thy matchless King
through all eternity.

Crown him the Virgin's Son,
the God incarnate born,
whose arm those crimson trophies won
which now his brow adorn:

fruit of the mystic Rose   (Cant. 2:1)
  as of that Rose the Stem;   (Is. 11:1)
the Root whence mercy ever flows,
  the Babe of Bethlehem.

Crown him the Lord of love!
  Behold his hands and side,
rich wounds yet visible above
  in beauty glorified:
  no angel in the sky
  can fully bear that sight,
but downward bends his burning eye
  at mysteries so bright.

Crown him the Lord of peace,
  whose power a sceptre sways
from pole to pole, that wars may cease   (Ps. 46:9)
  absorbed in prayer and praise:
  his reign shall know no end,
  and round his piercèd feet
fair flowers of Paradise extend
  their fragrance ever sweet.

Crown him the Lord of years,
  the Potentate of time,
Creator of the rolling spheres,
  ineffably sublime.
  Glassed in a sea of light,   (Rev. 4:6)
  where everlasting waves
reflect his throne - the Infinite,
  who lives - and loves - and saves.

Crown him the Lord of heaven,
  one with the Father known,
and the blest Spirit through him given
  from yonder triune throne:
  All hail, Redeemer, hail!
  For thou hast died for me!
Thy praise shall never, never fail
  throughout eternity.

Hymns of the Heart, 1851

THOMAS TOKE LYNCH
1818-71
The Rivulet, 1855-6
HG 163

215
SIGNS AND WONDERS

Oh, where is he that trod the sea,
  oh, where is he that spake? -
and demons from their victims flee,
  the dead their slumbers break;
the palsied rise in freedom strong,
  the dumb men talk and sing,
and from blind eyes, benighted long,
  bright beams of morning spring.

Oh, where is he that trod the sea,
  oh, where is he that spake? -
and piercing words of liberty
  the deaf ears open shake;
and mildest words arrest the haste
  of fever's deadly fire,
and strong ones heal the weak, who waste
  their lives in sad desire.

Oh, where is he that trod the sea,
  oh, where is he that spake? -

and dark waves, rolling heavily,
  a glassy smoothness take;
and lepers, whose own flesh has been
  a living loathsome grave,
see with amaze that they are clean,
  and cry, 'Tis he can save.'

Oh, where is he that trod the sea? -
  'Tis only he can save;
to thousands hungering wearily
  a wondrous meal he gave;
full soon, celestially fed,
  their rustic fare they take;
'Twas springtide when he bless'd the bread,
  and harvest when he brake.

Oh, where is he that trod the sea? -
  my soul, the Lord is here:
let all thy fears be hushed in thee,
  to leap, to look, to hear
be thine: thy needs he'll satisfy:
  art thou diseased or dumb?
or dost thou in thy hunger cry?
  'I come,' saith Christ, 'I come.'

216
WHERE IS THY GOD, MY SOUL?

Where is thy God, my soul?
  is he within thy heart?
or ruler of a distant realm
  in which thou hast no part?

Where is thy God, my soul?
  only in stars and sun?
or have the holy words of truth
  his light in every one?

Where is thy God, my soul?
  confined to Scripture's page?
or does his Spirit check and guide
  the spirit of each age?

O Ruler of the sky,
  rule thou within my heart;
O great Adorner of the world,
  thy light of life impart.

Giver of holy words,
  bestow thy holy power;
and aid me, whether work or thought
  engage the varying hour.

In thee I have my help,
  as all my fathers had;
I'll trust thee when I'm sorrowful,
  and serve thee when I'm glad.

1855

217
LIFT UP YOUR HEADS!
Luke 21:28-30

Lift up your heads, rejoice,
  redemption draweth nigh;
now breathes a softer air,
  now shines a milder sky;

the early trees put forth
   their new and tender leaf;
hushed is the moaning wind
   that told of winter's grief.

Lift up your heads, rejoice,
   redemption draweth nigh;
now mount the laden clouds,
   now flames the darkening sky;
the early scattered drops
   descend with heavy fall,
and to the waiting earth
   the hidden thunders call.

Lift up your heads, rejoice,
   redemption draweth nigh;
O note the varying signs
   of earth, and air, and sky: (Luke 12:54)
the God of glory comes
   in gentleness and might,
to comfort and alarm,
   to succour and to smite.

He comes, the wide world's King;
   he comes, the true heart's Friend;
new gladness to begin
   and ancient wrong to end;
he comes, to fill with light
   the weary, waiting eye:
lift up your heads, rejoice,
   redemption draweth nigh.

                                 1856

GEORGE RAWSON, 1807-89
HG 99

218
THE LORD HATH YET MORE LIGHT AND TRUTH
TO BREAK FORTH OUT OF HIS HOLY WORD

(Pastor Robinson to the Pilgrim Fathers, 1620)

We limit not the truth of God
   to our poor reach of mind,
by notions of our day and sect,
   crude, partial, and confined;
no, let a new and better hope
   within our hearts be stirred;
the Lord hath yet more light and truth
   to break forth from his word.

Who dares to bind to his dull sense
   the oracles of heaven,
for all the nations, tongues, and climes
   and all the ages given?
That universe - how much unknown!
   that ocean unexplored!
The Lord hath yet more light and truth
   to break forth from his word.

Darkling our great forefathers went
   the first steps of the way;
'twas but the dawning, yet to grow
   into the perfect day.
And grow it shall; our glorious Sun
   more fervid rays afford:
the Lord hath yet more light and truth
   to break forth from his word.

The valleys past, ascending still,
   our souls would higher climb,
and look down from supernal heights
   on all the bygone time.
Upward we press; the air is clear,
   and the sphere-music heard;
the Lord hath yet more light and truth
   to break forth from his word.

O Father, Son, and Spirit, send
   us increase from above;
enlarge, expand all Christian souls
   to comprehend thy love;
and make us all go on to know
   with nobler powers conferred -
The Lord hath yet more light and truth
   to break forth from his word.

Leeds Hymn Book, 1853

THOMAS HUGHES
1822-90

219
O GOD OF TRUTH   HG 516

O God of truth, whose living word
   upholds whate'er hath breath,
look down on thy creation, Lord,
   enslaved by sin and death.

Set up thy standard, Lord, that we
   who claim a heavenly birth,
may march with thee to smite the lies
   that vex thy groaning earth.

Ah! would we join that blest array
   and follow in the might
of him, the Faithful and the True   (Rev. 19:11)
   in raiment clean and white?

We fight for truth? We fight for God?
   poor slaves of lies and sin!
He who would fight for thee on earth
   must first be true within.   (Ps. 51:6)

Then, God of truth, for whom we long,
   thou who wilt hear our prayer,
do thine own battle in our hearts
   and slay the falsehood there.

Still smite, still burn, till naught is left
   but God's own truth and love;
then, Lord, as morning dew come down,   (Hos. 6:3)
   rest on us from above.

Yea, come! then tried as in the fire   (1 Cor. 3:13)
   from every lie set free,
thy perfect truth shall dwell in us,
   and we shall live in thee.

Lays of the Sanctuary, 1857

WILLIAM WHITING
1825-78

220
FOR THOSE AT SEA   HG 169

Eternal Father, strong to save,
   whose arm doth bind the restless wave,

who bidd'st the mighty ocean deep
its own appointed limits keep: (Ps. 104:9)
O hear us, when we cry to thee,
for those in peril on the sea.

O Saviour, whose almighty word
the winds and waves submissive heard,
who walkedst on the foaming deep   (Matt. 14:25)
and calm amidst its rage didst sleep;   (Mk. 4:38)
O hear us when we cry to thee
for those in peril on the sea.

O sacred Spirit, who didst brood
upon the chaos dark and rude,   (Gen. 1:3)
who bad'st its angry tumult cease
and gavest light and life and peace:
O hear us when we cry to thee
for those in peril on the sea.

O Trinity of love and power,
our brethren shield in danger's hour,
from rock and tempest, fire and foe,
protect them wheresoe'er they go:
and ever let there rise to thee
glad hymns of praise from land and sea.

*Hymns Ancient and Modern, 1860,
1861*

WILLIAM CHATTERTON DIX
1837-98
HG 28

221
EPIPHANY   HG 55

As with gladness men of old
did the guiding star behold,
as with joy they hailed its light,
leading onward, beaming bright,
so, most gracious Lord, may we
evermore be led to thee.

As with joyful steps they sped
to that lowly manger-bed,
there to bend the knee before
him whom heaven and earth adore;
so may we with willing feet
ever seek the mercy-seat.

As they offered gifts most rare
at that manger rude and bare;
so may we with holy joy,
pure and free fron sin's alloy,
all our costliest treasures bring,
Christ! to thee our heavenly King.

Holy Jesus, every day
keep us in the narrow way;
and, when earthly things are past,
bring our ransomed souls at last
where they need no star to guide,
where no clouds thy glory hide.

In the heavenly country bright
need they no created light;
thou, its light, its joy, its crown,
thou its sun which goes not down;
there for ever may we sing
Alleluias to our King.

*1860; in Hymns Ancient and Modern,
1861*

222
REDEMPTION THROUGH THE PRECIOUS BLOOD
HG 28

Alleluia, sing to Jesus,
  his the sceptre, his the throne;
Alleluia, his the triumph,
  his the victory alone:
hark the songs of peaceful Zion
  thunder like a mighty flood;
Jesus, out of every nation,
  hath redeemed us by his Blood.   (Rev. 7:9)

Alleluia, not as orphans
  are we left in sorrow now;
Alleluia, he is near us:
  faith believes, nor questions how;
though the cloud from sight received him
  when the forty days were o'er,   (Acts 1:9)
shall our hearts forget his promise,
  'I am with you evermore'?   (Matt. 28:20)

Alleluia, Bread of angels,   (Ps. 78:25)
  thou on earth our Food, our Stay,
Alleluia, here the sinful
  flee to thee from day to day;
Intercessor, Friend of sinners,
  earth's Redeemer, plead for me
where the songs of all the sinless
  sweep across the crystal sea.   (Rev. 4:6)

Alleluia, King eternal,
  thee the Lord of lords we own;
Alleluia, born of Mary,
  earth thy footstool, heaven thy throne:
thou within the veil hast entered,
  robed in flesh, our great High Priest. (Heb. 10:20)
Thou on earth both priest and Victim
  in the Eucharistic feast.

Altar Songs, 1867

**CHRISTOPHER WORDS-
WORTH**, Bishop. 1807-85
HG 27

223
ASCENSION   HG 636

See the conqueror mounts in triumph, see the King in royal state
riding on the clouds his chariot to his heavenly palace gate;
hark! the choirs of angel voices joyful Alleluias sing
and the portals high are lifted to receive their heavenly King.
          (Ps. 24:7)

Who is he that comes in glory with the trump of jubilee?
Lord of battles, God of armies, he has gained the victory. (Ps. 98:2)
He who on the cross did suffer, he who from the grave arose,
he has vanquished sin and Satan, he by death has spoiled his foes.

While he lifts his hands in blessing he is parted from his friends;
          (Lk. 24:50-1)
while their eager eyes behold him, he upon the clouds ascends;
he, who walked with God and pleased him, preaching truth and doom
          to come,
he, our Enoch, is translated to his everlasting home. (Gen. 5:24)

Now our heavenly Aaron enters with his blood within the veil
          (Heb. 5:4; 10:20)
Joshua now is come to Canaan, and the kings before him quail
          (Jos. 5:1)

now he plants the tribes of Israel in their promised resting place;
now our great Elijah offers double portion of his grace.
(4 Kgs. 2:9-11)

He has raised our human nature on the clouds to God's right hand;
there we sit in heavenly places; there with him in glory stand:
Jesus reigns, adored by angels: man with God is on the throne;
(Heb. 1:5-8)
Mighty Lord, in thine ascension we by faith behold our own.

Holy Ghost, Illuminator, shed thy beams upon our eyes,
help us to look up with Stephen, and to see, beyond the skies,
(Acts 7:55-6)
where the Son of Man in glory standing is at God's right hand,
beckoning on his martyr army, succouring his faithful band.

See him, who is gone before us, heavenly mansions to prepare.
(Jn. 14:2)
see him, who is ever pleading for us with prevailing prayer.
(Heb. 7:23)
See him, who with sound of trumpet and with his angelic train
summoning the world to judgment, on the clouds will come again.
(Mk. 13:26)

Lift us up from earth to heaven, give us wings of faith and love,
gales of holy aspirations wafting us to heaven above;
that with hearts and minds uplifted, we with Christ our Lord may dwell
where he sits enthroned in glory in his heavenly citadel.*

So at last, when he appeareth, we from our graves may spring,
(Is. 40:29)
with our youth renewed like eagles, flocking round our heavenly King
caught up on the clouds of heaven, and may meet him in the air,
(1 Thess. 4:17)
rise to realms where he is reigning, and may reign for ever there.

The Holy Year, 1862
(*) Here the Collect for Ascension Day is paraphrased.

224
CONSECRATION
HG 410

Lord, be thy Word my rule,
in it may I rejoice;
thy glory be my aim,
thy holy will my choice;
thy promises my hope;
thy providence my guard;
thine arm my strong support;
thyself, my great reward.

The Holy Year, 6th edn., 1872

GODFREY THRING
1823-1903

225
MARK 4:37-40
HG 191

Fierce raged the tempest o'er the deep,
watch did thine anxious servants keep;
but thou wast wrapt in guileless sleep,
calm and still.

'Save, Lord, we perish!' was their cry,
'O save us in our agony!'
Thy word above the storm rose high,
'Peace, Be still.'

The wild winds hushed, the angry deep
sank like a little child to sleep.
The sullen billows ceased to leap
at thy will.

So, when our life is clouded o'er,
and storm-winds drift us from the shore,
say, lest we sink to rise no more,
'Peace, be still.'

Congregational Hymn and Tune Book,
1862

**JOHN SAMUEL BEWLEY
MONSELL**, 1811-75
Hymns of Love and Praise,
1863

226
FIGHT THE GOOD FIGHT
HG 193

Fight the good fight with all thy might,   (1 Tim. 6:12)
Christ is thy strength, and Christ thy right;
lay hold on life, and it shall be
thy joy and crown eternally.

Run the straight race through God's good grace,
lift up thine eyes, and see his face;
life with its way before us lies,
Christ is the path, and Christ the prize.

Cast care aside, and on thy Guide
lean, and his mercy will provide;
lean, and the trusting soul shall prove
Christ is its life, and Christ its love.

Faint not nor fear, his arms are near,
he changeth not, and thou art dear;
only believe, and thou shalt see
that Christ is all in all to thee.   (Col. 3:11)

227
GIFTS
HG 576

O worship the Lord in the beauty of holiness!
bow down before him, his glory proclaim;
with gold of obedience, and incense of lowliness,
kneel and adore him: the Lord is his name!

Low at his feet lay thy burden of carefulness,
high on his heart he will bear it for thee,
comfort thy sorrows and answer thy prayerfulness,
guiding thy steps as may best for thee be.

Fear not to enter his courts in the slenderness
of the poor wealth thou wouldst reckon as thine:
truth in its beauty, and love in its tenderness,
these are the offerings to lay on his shrine.

These, though we bring them in trembling and fearfulness,
he will accept for the name that is dear;
mornings of joy give for evenings of fearfulness, (Ps. 30:6)
trust for our trembling and hope for our fear.

O worship the Lord in the beauty of holiness!
bow down before him, his glory proclaim;
with gold of obedience, and incense of lowliness
kneel and adore him, the Lord is his name!

EDWARD HAYES PLUMPTRE,
Dean, 1821-91
Lazarus and other Poems,
1864-5, HG 534

228
THE TEACHER'S PRAYER

O Lord of hosts, all heaven possessing,
  behold us from thy sapphire throne,
in doubt and darkness dimly guessing,
  we might thy glory half have known;
but thou in Christ hast made us thine,
and on us all thy beauties shine.

Illumine all, disciples, teachers,
  thy law's deep wonders to unfold;
with reverent hand let wisdom's preachers
  bring forth their treasures, new and old;   (Matt. 13:52)
let oldest, youngest, find in thee
of truth and love the boundless sea.

Let faith still light the lamp of science,
  and knowledge pass from truth to truth,
and wisdom, in its full reliance
  renew the primal awe of youth;
so holier, wiser may we grow,
as time's swift currents onward flow.

Bind thou our life in fullest union
  with all thy saints from sin set free;
uphold us in that blest communion
  of all thy saints on earth with thee;
keep thou our souls, or there, or here,
in mightiest love, that casts out fear.   (1 Jn. 4:18)

1864

229
MINISTRY OF HEALING   HG 731

Thine arm, O Lord, in days of old
  was strong to heal and save;
it triumphed o'er disease and death,
  o'er darkness and the grave;
to thee they went, the blind, the dumb,
  the palsied and the lame,
the leper with his tainted life,
  the sick with fevered frame.

And lo! thy touch brought life and health,
  gave speech, and strength, and sight;
and youth renewed and frenzy calmed
  owned thee the Lord of light;
and now, O Lord, be near to bless
  Almighty as of yore,
in crowded streets, by restless couch,
  as by Gennesaret's shore.

Be thou our great deliverer still,
  thou Lord of life and death;
restore and quicken, soothe and bless
  with thine almighty breath;
to hands that work, and eyes that see,
  give wisdom's heavenly lore,
that whole and sick, the weak and strong
  may praise thee evermore.

2nd ed., 1865

WILLIAM WALSHAM HOW,
Bishop, 1823-97
HG 75

230
THE PROCESSION OF FAITH   HG 198

For all thy saints, who from their labours rest,
who thee by faith before the world confessed,
thy name O Jesus be for ever blessed. Alleluia!

Thou wast their Rock, their Fortress and their Might;
thou, Lord, their Captain in the well-fought fight;
thou in the darkness drear their one true Light. Alleluia!

For the Apostles' glorious company,
who bearing forth the Cross o'er land and sea,
shook all the mighty world, we sing to thee: Alleluia!
(Acts 17:6)

For the Evangelists, by whose pure word,
like fourfold stream, the garden of the Lord   (Gen. 2:10)
is fair and fruitful, be thy name adored. Alleluia!

For Martyrs, who with rapture-kindled eye
saw the bright crown descending from the sky   (Acts 7:55)
and, seeing, grasped it, thee we glorify. Alleluia!

Oh, may thy soldiers, faithful, true and bold
fight as the saints who nobly fought of old,
and win with them the victors' crown of gold. Alleluia! (Rev. 2:10)

Oh, blest communion! fellowship divine!
we feebly struggle, they in glory shine!
Yet all are one in thee, for all are thine! Alleluia!   (Jn. 17:22)

And when the strife is fierce, the warfare long,
steals on the ear the distant triumph-song,
and hearts are brave again, and arms are strong! Alleluia!

The golden evening brightens in the west;
soon, soon to faithful warriors cometh rest:
sweet is the calm of Paradise the blest. Alleluia!

But lo! there breaks a yet more glorious day;
the saints triumphant rise in bright array;
the King of glory passes on his way! Alleluia!

From earth's wide bounds, from ocean's farthest coast,
through gates of pearl streams in the countless host,
singing to Father, Son and Holy Ghost: Alleluia!

*Hymn for a Saint's Day, and other
Hymns* (Earl Nelson), 1864

231
BEHOLD, I STAND AT THE DOOR
Rev. 3:20   HG 530

O Jesus, thou art standing
  outside the fast-closed door,
in lowly patience waiting
  to pass the threshold o'er;
shame on us, Christian brothers,
  his name and sign who bear,
O shame, thrice shame upon us
  to keep him standing there!

O Jesus, thou art knocking:
  and lo! thy hand is scarred,
and thorns thy brow encircle,
  and tears thy face have marred:

O love that passeth knowledge,
    so patiently to wait!
O sin that hath no equal
    so fast to bar the gate!

O Jesus, thou art pleading
    in accents meek and low,
'I died for you, my children,
    and will ye treat me so?'
O Lord, with shame and sorrow
    we open now the door:
dear Saviour, enter, enter,
    and leave us never more.

Psalms and Hymns (Morrell and How),
Supplement, 1867

SABINE BARING-GOULD
1834-1924
HG 493

232
ONWARD, CHRISTIAN SOLDIERS!   HG 587

Onward, Christian soldiers!
    marching as to war,
with the cross of Jesus
    going on before.
Christ the royal Master
    leads against the foe;
onward into battle
    see, his banners go!
Onward . . .

Like a mighty army
    moves the Church of God;
brothers, we are treading
    where the saints have trod;
we are not divided,
    all one body we,
one in hope and doctrine
                        (Eph. 4:4)
one in charity. . . .

At the sign of triumph
    Satan's legions flee;
on, then, Christian soldiers,
    on to victory.
Hell's foundations quiver
    at the shout of praise;
brothers, lift your voices,
    loud your anthems raise. . . .

Crowns and thrones may perish,
    kingdoms rise and wane,
but the Church of Jesus
    constant will remain;
gates of hell can never
    'gainst that Church prevail;
we have Christ's own promise
    and that cannot fail. . . .

Onward then, ye people,
    join our happy throng,
blend with ours your voices
    in the triumph song;
Glory, laud and honour
    unto Christ the King;
this through countless ages
    men and angels sing:
Onward, Christian soldiers,
    marching as to war
with the cross of Jesus
    going on before.

The Church Times, 15 October, 1864

233
ONE HOPE OF OUR CALLING
Ephesians 4:4   HG 748

Igjennem Nat og Traengsel

  gaar Sjaelens Valfartsgang
med stille Haab og Laengsel,
  med dyb Forventningssang.
Det gjennem Natten luer,

  det lysner gjennem Sky,

Through the night of doubt and
                        sorrow
  onward goes the pilgrim band
singing songs of expectation,
  marching to the Promised Land.
Clear before us through the
                        darkness
  gleams and burns the guiding
                        Light;

til Broder Broder skuer

  og kjender paa ny.

Vor Nat det Lys oplive,

  som aldrig slukkes ud!
Eet sind os alle give
  I Traengsel Trøstens Gud!

Eet Hjerte khaerligt lue
  I hver Korsdragers Bryst!
Een Gud, til hvem vi skue!
  een Tro, eet Haab, een Trøst!

Een Røst fra tusind Munde!

  een Aand i Tusinds Røst!
Een Fred, hvortil vi stunde!
  Een Frelsens, Naadens Kyst!
Een Sorg, eet Savn, een Laengsel!
  Een Fader her og hist!
Een Udgang af al Traengsel!
  Eet Liv i Jesu Christ!

Saa gaa vi med hverandre

  den store Pilgrimsang!
Til Golgatha vi vandre
  I Aand, med Bøn og Sang!
Fra Kors fra Grav vi stige

  med salig Lov og Pris,
til den Opstandnes Rige,
  til Frelsens Paradis!

B. S. INGEMANN, 1859

brother clasps the hand of
                        brother,
  stepping fearless through the
                        night.

One the light of God's own
                        presence
  o'er his ransomed people shed,
chasing far the gloom and terror,
  brightening all the path we
                        tread:
one the object of our journey,
  one the faith which never tires,
one the earnest looking forward,
  one the hope our God inspires.

One the strain that lips of
                        thousands
  lift as from the heart of one:
one the conflict, one the peril,
  one the march in God begun:
one the gladness of rejoicing
  on the far eternal shore,
where the one almighty Father
  reigns in love for evermore.

Onward therefore, pilgrim
                        brothers,
  onward with the cross our aid,
bear its shame and fight its battle
  till we rest beneath its shade.
Soon shall come the great
                        awaking,
  soon the rending of the tomb,
then the scattering of all shadows
  and the end of toil and gloom.

Tr. **Sabine Baring-Gould**, *The
People's Hymnal*, 1867

**FOLLIOTT SANDFORD PIER-
POINT**, 1835-1917

234
OUR SACRIFICE OF PRAISE   HG 201

For the beauty of the earth,
    for the beauty of the skies,
for the love which from our birth
    over and around us lies,
        Christ our God, to thee we raise
        this, our sacrifice of praise.   *

For the beauty of each hour
    of the day and of the night,
hill and vale, and tree and flower,
    sun and moon and stars of light, . . .

For the joy of ear and eye,
    for the heart and brain's delight,
for the mystic harmony
    linking sense to sound and sight, . . .

For the joy of human love,
    brother, sister, parent, child,
friends on earth, and friends above,
    for all gentle thoughts and mild, . . .

For each perfect gift of thine,
    to our race so freely given,
graces human and divine,
    flowers on earth and buds of heaven, . . .

For thy Bride that evermore
   lifteth holy hands above,
offering up on every shore
   this pure sacrifice of love, . . .

For the Martyrs' crown of light,
   for thy prophets' eagle eye,
for thy bold Confessors' might,
   for the lips of infancy, . . .   (Ps. 8:4)

For thy Virgins' robes of snow,
   for thy Maiden-Mother mild,
for Thyself, with hearts aglow,
   Jesus, Victim undefiled,
     Christ our God, to thee we raise
     this, our sacrifice of praise.

Lyra Eucharistica, 1864

* This phrase in the Refrain is taken from the Eucharistic prayer in the Book of
Common Prayer.

HENRY ALFORD, Dean
1810-71
HG 150

235
AMEN! COME, LORD JESUS   HG 681

Ten thousand times ten thousand,   (Rev. 5:11)
   in sparkling raiment bright,
the armies of the ransomed saints
   throng up the steeps of light;
'Tis finished, all is finished,
   their fight with death and sin;
fling open wide the golden gates
   and let the victors in.

What rush of Alleluias
   fills all the earth and sky!
what ringing of a thousand harps
   bespeaks the triumph nigh!
O day for which creation
   and all its tribes were made!
O joy, for all its former woes
   a thousandfold repaid!

O then, what raptured greetings
   on Canaan's happy shore,
what knitting severed friendships up,
   where partings are no more!
Then eyes with joy shall sparkle
   that brimmed with tears of late;
orphans no longer fatherless
   nor widows desolate.

Bring near thy great salvation,
   thou Lamb for sinners slain,
fill up the roll of thine elect,
   then take thy power and reign!
Appear, Desire of nations,
   thine exiles long for home;
show in the heavens thy promised sign:
   thou Prince and Saviour, come!

The Year of Praise, 1867 (St. 4, 1870)

SAMUEL JOHN STONE
1839-1900

236
THE CHURCH'S ONE FOUNDATION   HG 685

The Church's one foundation
   is Jesus Christ her Lord;   (1 Cor. 3:11)
she is his new creation
   by water and the Word;   (Eph. 5:26)
from heaven he came and sought her
   to be his holy bride,
with his own blood he bought her
   and for her life he died.

Elect from every nation
   yet one o'er all the earth,
her charter of salvation -
   'One Lord, one Faith, one Birth.'   (Eph. 4:4)
One holy name she blesses,
   partakes one holy Food,
and to one hope she presses
   with every grace endued.

Though with a scornful wonder
   men see her sore opprest,
by schisms rent asunder,
   by heresies distrest,
yet saints their watch are keeping,
   their cry goes up, 'How long?'   (Rev. 6:9-10)
and soon the night of weeping
   shall be the morn of song.   (Ps. 30:5)

Mid toil and tribulation
   and tumult of her war
she waits for consummation
   of peace for evermore;
till with the vision glorious
   her longing eyes are blest,
and the great Church victorious
   shall be the Church at rest.

Yet she on earth hath union
   with God the Three in One   (Eph. 5:26)
and mystic sweet communion
   with those whose rest is won:
O happy ones and holy!
   Lord, give us grace, that we,
with them the meek and lowly
   on high may dwell with thee.

Lyra Fidelium, 1866

FRANCIS TURNER PALGRAVE
1824-97

237
THE UNWALLED CITY   HG 567

O thou not made with hands,
   not throned above the skies,
nor walled with shining walls,
   nor framed with stones of price,
more bright than gold or gem,
   God's own Jerusalem! -

where'er the gentle heart
   finds courage from above,
where'er the heart forsook
   warms with the breath of love;
where faith bids fear depart,
   City of God, thou art.

Thou art where'er the proud
    in humbleness melts down;
where self itself yields up,
    where Martyrs win their crown;
where faithful souls possess
    themselves in perfect peace;   (Lk. 21:19)

where in life's common ways
    with cheerful feet we go;
where in his steps we tread
    who trod the way of woe;
where he is in the heart,
City of God, thou art.

Not throned above the skies,
    nor golden walled afar,
but where Christ's two or three   (Matt. 18:20)
    in his name gathered are,
be in the midst of them,
God's own Jerusalem.

Hymns, 1867

**EDWARD HENRY
BICKERSTETH**, Bishop
1825-1906

238
O GOD THE ROCK OF AGES
(For the Last Sunday of the Year)   **HG 517**

O God the rock of ages,   (Ps. 90:1)
    who evermore hast been,
what time the tempest rages,
    our dwelling-place serene:
before thy first creations,
    O Lord, the same as now,
to endless generations
    the everlasting Thou!

Our years are like the shadows   (Ps. 90:5-9)
    on sunny hills that lie,
or grasses in the meadows
    that blossom but to die;
a sleep, a dream, a story
    by strangers quickly told,
an unremaining glory
    of things that soon are old.

O thou who canst not slumber   (Ps. 121:4)
    whose light grows never pale,
teach us aright to number   (Ps. 90:12)
    our years before they fall.
On us thy mercy lighten,
    on us thy goodness rest,
and let thy Spirit brighten
    the hearts thyself hast blest.

Lord, crown our faith's endeavour
    with beauty and with grace.   (Ps. 90:17)
till, clothed in light for ever,
    we see thee face to face:
a joy no language measures,
    a fountain brimming o'er;
an endless flow of pleasures,
    an ocean without shore.

1862; in *Psalms and Hymns*, 1867

SIR HENRY WILLIAMS BAKER
1821-77
Hymns Ancient and Modern,
1868, HG 101

239
THE GOOD SHEPHERD   **HG 698**

The King of love my Shepherd is,   (Ps. 23)
    whose goodness faileth never;
I nothing lack if I am his
    and he is mine for ever.

Where streams of living water flow
    my ransomed soul he feedeth,
and where the verdant pastures grow
    with food celestial feedeth.

Perverse and foolish oft I strayed,
    but yet in love he sought me,
and on his shoulder gently laid,
    and home, rejoicing, brought me.   (Matt. 18:12)

In death's dark vale I fear no ill
    with thee, dear Lord, beside me;
thy rod and staff my comfort still,
    thy cross before to guide me.

Thou spread'st a table in my sight;
    thy unction grace bestoweth:
and O, what transport of delight
    from thy pure chalice floweth!

And so through all the length of days
    thy goodness faileth never;
Good Shepherd, may I sing thy praise
    within thy house for ever!

240
THE HOLY SPIRIT   **HG 526**

O Holy Ghost, thy people bless
    who long to feel thy might,
and fain would grow in holiness
    as children of the light.   (Eph. 5:8)

To thee we bring, who art the Lord,
    our selves to be thy throne;
let every deed and thought and word
    thy pure dominion own.

Life-giving Spirit, o'er us move
    as on the formless deep;
give life and order, light and love   (Gen. 1:3)
    where now is death or sleep.

Great gift of our ascended King   (John 16:7-8)
    his saving truth reveal;
our tongues inspire his praise to sing,
    our hearts his love to feel.

True wind of heaven, from south or north
    for joy or chastening, blow;
the garden-spices shall spring forth   (Cant. 4:16)
    if thou wilt bid them flow.

O Holy Ghost, of sevenfold might,   (Is. 11:2)
    all graces come from thee;
grant us to know and serve aright
    our God in Persons Three.

HENRY TWELLS, 1823-1900

241
HG 57

At even, when the sun was set,
 the sick, O Lord, around thee lay;
oh, in what divers pains they met!
 oh, with what joy they went away!

(Mk. 1:32)

Once more 'tis eventide, and we
 oppressed with various ills draw near;
what if thy form we cannot see?
 we know and feel that thou art here.

O Saviour Christ! our woes dispel:
 for some are sick, and some are sad,
and some have never loved thee well,
 and some have lost the love they had;

and some are pressed with worldly care,
 and some are tried with sinful doubt;
and some such grievous passions tear
 that only thou canst cast them out;

and some have found the world is vain,
 yet from the world they break not free;
and some have friends who give them pain,
 yet have not sought a friend in thee;

and none, O Lord, have perfect rest,
 for none are wholly free from sin;
and they who fain would serve thee best
 are conscious most of wrong within.

O Saviour Christ, thou too art Man;
 thou hast been troubled, tested, tried;
thy kind but searching glance can scan
 the very wounds that shame would hide.

Thy touch has still its ancient power;
 no word from thee can fruitless fall:
hear in this solemn evening hour,
 and in thy mercy save us all.

Hymns Ancient and Modern, 1868;
(st. 4 added later)

242
FORGIVE US OUR RIGHTEOUSNESS
HG 485

Not for our sins alone
 thy mercy, Lord, we sue;
let fall thy pitying glance
 on our devotions too,
what we have done for thee,
 and what we think to do.

The holiest hours we spend
 in prayer upon our knees,
the times when most we deem
 our songs of praise will please,
thou Searcher of all hearts,
 forgiveness pour on these.

And all the gifts we bring,
 and all the vows we make,
and all the acts of love
 we plan for thy dear sake,
into thy pardoning thought,
 O God of mercy, take.

And most, when we, thy flock,
 before thine Altar bend,
and strange, bewildering thoughts
 with those sweet moments blend,
by him whose death we plead,
 Good Lord, thy help extend.

Bow down thine ear and hear!
 Open thine eyes and see!
Our very love is shame,
 and we must come to thee
to make it of thy grace
 what thou wouldst have it be.

Hymns Ancient and Modern, 1889

243
THE VOICE SAYS 'CRY!'
Isaiah 40:6

The voice says 'Cry!' What shall we cry?
 'All flesh is grass, and like the flower
its glories droop, its pleasures die,
 its joys but last one fleeting hour.'

The voice says 'Cry!' O piteous cry!
 And are there none to help and save?
Have all that live below the sky
 no other prospect but a grave?

The voice says 'Cry!' Yet glorious cry!
 The Word of God can never fall,
and tells how Jesus, throned on high,
 holds out eternal life to all.

The voice says 'Cry!' Who heeds the cry?
 O brother man! Who heeds it not?
By countless millions, far and nigh,
 'Tis still unheard, despised, forgot.

The voice says 'Cry!' What stops the cry?
 Our greed of wealth, our love of ease,
our lack of earnest will to try
 mankind to save, and God to please.

The voice says 'Cry!' O let us cry!
 Though standing on death's awful brink,
men feast, they jest, they sell, they buy, (Lk. 17:28)
 and cannot see, and will not think.

The voice says 'Cry!' Lord, we would cry,
 but of thy goodness teach us how;
for fast the hours of mercy fly,
 and, if we cry, it must be now!

1900; in S. P. G. Leaflet, 1901. *Hymns
Ancient and Modern*, 1904

THOMAS HORNBLOWER
GILL, 1819-1906
HG 421

244
THE PEOPLE OF GOD
HG 776

We come unto our fathers' God,
 their Rock is our Salvation:
the eternal arms their dear abode,
 we make our habitation:

we bring thee, Lord, the praise they brought;
we seek thee as thy saints have sought
   in every generation.

    ★   ★   ★

The fire divine, their steps that led   (Ex. 40:38)
   still goeth bright before us;
the heavenly shield, around them spread
   is still high holden o'er us:
the grace those sinners that subdued,
the strength those weaklings that renewed,
   doth vanquish, doth restore us.

The cleaving sins that brought them low
   are still our souls oppressing;
the tears that from their eyes did flow
   fall fast, our shame confessing;
as with thee, Lord, prevailed their cry,
so our strong prayer ascends on high
   and bringeth down thy blessing.

    ★   ★   ★

Their joy unto our Lord we bring;
   their song to us descendeth:
the Spirit who in them did sing
   to us his music lendeth.
His song in them, in us, is one;
we raise it high, we send it on -
   the song that never endeth!

Ye saints to come, take up the strain -
   the same sweet theme endeavour!
Unbroken be the Golden Chain!
   keep on the song for ever!
Save in the same dear dwelling-place   (Ps. 90:1)
rich with the same eternal grace,
   bless the same boundless Giver!

The Golden Chain of Praise, 1869
Sts. 2, 5 omitted

CHARLES KINGSLEY
1819-75

245
SKILL AND SCIENCE   HG 215

From thee all skill and science flow,
   all pity, care and love,
all calm and courage, faith and hope -
   O, pour them from above!

And part them, Lord, to each and all,
   as each and all shall need
to rise, like incense, each to thee,
   in noble thought and deed.

And hasten, Lord, that perfect day,
   when pain and death shall cease,
and thy just rule shall fill the earth
   with health, and light, and peace;

when ever blue the sky shall gleam,
   and ever green the sod,
and man's rude work deface no more
   the Paradise of God.

1870 or 1871 (see *Hymnal Guide*)

JOHN ELLERTON
1826-93
HG 80

246
SAINT BARNABAS   HG 560

O Son of God, our Captain of salvation,   (Heb. 2:10)
   thyself by suffering schooled to human grief,
we bless thee for thy sons of consolation,   (Acts 4:36)
   who follow in the steps of thee, their Chief.

Those whom thy Spirit's dread vocation severs
   to lead the vanguard of thy conquering host;
whose toilsome years are spent in brave endeavours
   to bear thy saving name from coast to coast.

Those whose bright faith makes feeble hearts grow stronger,
   and sends fresh warriors to the great campaign,
bids the lone convert feel estranged no longer,
   and wins the sundered to be one again;

and all true helpers, patient, kind and skilful,
   who shed thy light across our darkened earth,
counsel the doubting, and restrain the wilful,
   soothe the sick bed, and share the children's mirth.

Such was thy Levite, strong in self-oblation,
   to cast his all at thine Apostles' feet;
he whose new name through every Christian nation
   from age to age our thankful strains repeat.

Thus, Lord, thy Barnabas in memory keeping,
   still be thy church's watchword, 'Comfort ye';   (Is. 40:1)
till in our Father's house shall end our weeping,
   and all our wants be satisfied in thee.

Church Hymns, 1871

247
THE CONVERSION OF ST PAUL   HG 786

We sing the glorious conquest
   before Damascus gate,
when Saul, the church's spoiler
   came breathing threats and hate;   (Acts 9:1)
the ravening wolf rushed forward
   full early to the prey;   (John 10:11-12)
but lo! the Shepherd met him
   and bound him fast to-day!

O Glory most excelling
   that smote across his path!   (Acts 9:3-4,8-9)
O Light that pierced and blinded
   the zealot in his wrath!
O Voice that spoke within him
   the calm reproving word!
O Love that sought and held him
   the bondman of the Lord!

O Wisdom, ordering all things
   in order strong and sweet,
what nobler spoil was ever
   cast at the Victor's feet?
What wiser master-builder   (1 Cor. 3:10)
   e'er wrought at thine employ,
than he, t'il now so furious
   thy building to destroy?

Lord, teach thy Church the lesson,
   still in her darkest hour
of weakness and of danger
   to trust thy hidden power.
Thy grace by ways mysterious
   the wrath of man can bind,   (Ps. 76:10)
and in thy boldest foeman
   thy chosen Saint can find!

Church Hymns, 1871

ARTHUR PENRHYN
STANLEY*, Dean
1815-81

248
THE LORD IS COME

The Lord is come! on Syrian soil,
the child of poverty and toil;
the Man of sorrows, born to know
each varying shade of human woe:
his joy, his glory to fulfil,
in earth and heaven, his Father's will;
on lonely mount, by festive board,
on bitter Cross, despised, adored.

The Lord is come! in him we trace
the fulness of God's truth and grace;
throughout those words and acts divine
gleams of the eternal splendour shine;
and from his inmost spirit flow,
as from a height of sunlit snow,
the rivers of perennial life,
to heal and sweeten Nature's strife.

The Lord is come! In every heart
where truth and mercy claim a part;
in every land where right is might,
and deeds of darkness shun the light;
in every church where faith and love
lift heavenward thoughts to things above;
in every holy, happy home
we bless thee, Lord, that thou hast come.

Macmillan's Magazine, 1872

WILLIAM BRIGHT
1824-1901

249
AT THE COMMUNION   HG 43

And now, O Father, mindful of the love
   that bought us, once for all, on Calvary's Tree,
and having with us him that pleads above   (Heb. 7:23)
   we here present, we here set forth to thee
that only Offering perfect in thine eyes,
the one true pure immortal sacrifice.

Look, Father, look on his anointed face,
   and only look on us as found in him;
look not on our misusings of thy grace,
   our prayer so languid, and our faith so dim;
for lo! between our sins and their reward
we set the passion of thy Son our Lord.

And then, for those, our dearest and our best,
   by this prevailing Presence we appeal;
O fold them closer to thy mercy's breast,

O do thine utmost for their souls' true weal:
from tainting mischief keep them white and clear,
and crown thy gifts with strength to persevere.

And so we come: O draw us to thy feet,
   most patient Saviour, who canst love us still;
and by this Food, so awful and so sweet,
   deliver us from every touch of ill:
in thine own service make us glad and free,
and grant us never more to part with thee.

The Monthly Packet, 1873; rev. in
Hymns Ancient and Modern, 1875

250
SAINT MATTHEW   HG 277

He sat to watch o'er customs paid,
a man of scorned and hardening trade;
alike the symbol and the tool
of foreign masters' hated rule.

But grace within his breast had stirred;
there needed but the timely word;
it came, true Lord of souls, from thee,
that royal summons, 'Follow me.'

Enough, when thou wast passing by,
to hear thy voice, to meet thine eye:
he rose, responsive to the call,
and left his task, his gains, his all.

O wise exchange! with these to part,
and lay up treasure in thy heart;   (Matt. 6:21)
with twofold crown of light to shine
amid thy servants' foremost line.

Come, Saviour, as in days of old:
pass where the world has strongest hold,
and faithless fear and selfish greed
are thorns that choke the holy seed.   (Matt. 13:22)

Who keep thy gifts, O bid them claim
the steward's, not the owner's name;
who yield all up for thy dear sake,
let them of Matthew's wealth partake.

Hymns Ancient & Modern, 1889

WILLIAM DALYRYMPLE
MACLAGAN, Archbishop
1826-1910

251
HOLY SATURDAY   HG 342A

It is finished! blessed Jesus,
   thou hast breathed thy latest sigh,
teach us the sons of Adam
   how the Son of God can die.

Lifeless lies the piercèd body,
   resting in its rocky bed;
thou hast left the Cross of anguish
   for the mansions of the dead.

In the hidden realms of darkness
   shines a light unseen before,
when the Lord of dead and living
   enters at the lowly door.

Lo! in spirit, rich in mercy
  comes he from the world above,
preaching to the souls in prison   (1 Pet. 3:19)
  tidings of his dying love.

Lo! the heavenly light around him,
  as he draws his people near;
all amazed they come rejoicing
  at the gracious words they hear.

Patriarch and priest and prophet
  gather round him as he stands,
in adoring faith and gladness
  hearing of the piercèd hands.

There in lowliest joy and wonder
  stands the robber by his side,
reaping now the blessed promise
  spoken by the Crucified.   (Lk. 23:43)

Jesus, Lord of our salvation,
  let thy mercy rest on me;
grant me too, when life is finished,
  rest in Paradise with thee.

Hymns Ancient and Modern, 1875:
text of 1904

WILLIAM ROMANIS
1824-99
HG 624

252
SAINT JAMES

Lord, who shall sit beside thee,   (Mk. 10:37-8)
  enthroned on either hand,
when clouds no longer hide thee,
  'mid all thy faithful band?

Who drinks the cup of sorrow
  thy Father gave to thee
'neath shadows of the morrow,
  in dark Gethsemane;

who on thy Passion thinking
  can find in loss a gain,   (Phil. 3:7)
and dare to meet unshrinking
  thy baptism of pain.

O Jesu, form within us
  thy likeness clear and true,
by thine example win us
  to suffer or to do.

This law itself fulfilleth -
  Christ-like to Christ is nigh,
and where the Father willeth
  shall sit with Christ on high.

Wigston Magna School Hymns, 1878

EDWIN HATCH
1835-89

253
THE BREATH OF THE SPIRIT   HG 94

Breathe on me, Breath of God,
  fill me with life anew,
that I may love what thou dost love
  and do what thou wouldst do.

Breathe on me, Breath of God,
  until my heart is pure,   (Matt. 5:3)
until with thee I will one will
  to do or to endure.

Breathe on me, Breath of God,
  till I am wholly thine,
till all this earthly part of me
  glows with thy fire divine.

Breathe on me, Breath of God,
  so shall I never die,
but live with thee the perfect life
  of thine eternity.

Between Doubt and Prayer, 1878

ERNEST EDWARD DUGMORE
1843-1925

254
AN ACCEPTABLE SACRIFICE   HG 30

Almighty Father of all things that be,
our life, our work, we consecrate to thee,
whose heavens declare thy glory from above,
whose earth below is witness to thy love.

For well we know this weary, soilèd earth
is yet thine own by right of its new birth   (Is. 65:1)
since that great Cross upreared on Calvary   (Rev. 21:2)
redeemed it from its sin and shame to thee.

Thine still the changeful beauty of the hills,
the purple valleys flecked with silver rills,
the ocean glistening 'neath the golden rays,
they all are thine, and, voiceless, speak thy praise.   (Ps. 19:4)

Thou dost the strength to workman's arm impart;
from thee the skilled musician's mystic art,
the grace of poet's pen or painter's hand
to teach the loveliness of sea or land.

Then grant us, Lord, in all things thee to own,
to dwell within the shadow of thy throne,
to speak and work, to think, and live, and move,
reflecting thine own nature, which is love;   (1 Jn. 4:7)

that so, by Christ redeemed from sin and shame,
and hallowed by thy Spirit's cleansing flame,
ourselves, our work, and all our powers may be
a sacrifice acceptable to thee.   (Rom. 12:1)

Hymns and Litanies, 1885; text of 1904

255
THE UNORIGINATE

Almighty Father, unoriginate,
  whom no man hath seen, ever, nor can see;
who reignest bless'd and only Potentate,
  light unapproachable encircling thee;
almighty Father, hallowed be thy name,
who ever art, unchangeably the same.   (James 1:17)

Thou lovest us, else had we never been:
  before we were, in ages long ago,
thy love had us and all our wants foreseen,
  creating us that we thy love might know.

Yea, Father, Thou, in whom we live and move,　(Acts 17:28)
hast loved us with an everlasting love.

Thou madest man immortal at the first,
　an image of thine own eternity,　(Gen. 1:26)
and when he fell from life, through sin accurst,
　and lost his right to the life-giving tree,　(Gen. 3:8)
thy love, unconquered, would to him restore
his life ennobled and for evermore.

Such was thy love, thou didst not even spare
　thy Best-Beloved, but gav'st him for us all;　(Rom. 8:32)
to live that human life beyond compare,
　and dying, by his death retrieve our fall.
In him thy love unbounded we behold,
for, giving him, thou canst not aught withhold.

Thou knowest what we are, how frail and blind,
　thou still rememberest that we are but dust:　(Ps. 103:14)
Like as a father pitieth, thou art kind,
　thy justice kindness, and thy kindness just,
Then hear thy children's prayer from heaven thy throne;
'Father, thy kingdom come; thy will be done!'　(Lk. 11:2)

Hymns of Adoration, 1900

RUDYARD KIPLING
1865-1936

256
RECESSIONAL　　　HG 241

God of our fathers, known of old,
　Lord of our far-flung battle-line,
beneath whose awful hand we hold
　dominion over palm and pine -
Lord God of hosts, be with us yet,
lest we forget - lest we forget!

The tumult and the shouting dies;
　the captains and the kings depart:
still stands thine ancient sacrifice,
　an humble and a contrite heart.　(Ps. 51:17)
Lord God of hosts, be with us yet -
lest we forget - lest we forget!

Far-called, our navies melt away:
　on dune and headland sinks the fire:
lo, all our pomp of yesterday
　is one with Nineveh and Tyre!
Judge of the nations, spare us yet,
lest we forget - lest we forget!

If, drunk with sight of power, we loose
　wild tongues that have not thee in awe,
such boastings as the gentiles use,
　or lesser breeds without the Law -
Lord God of hosts, be with us yet,
lest we forget - lest we forget!

For heathen heart that puts her trust
　in reeking tube and iron shard,
all valiant dust that builds on dust,
　and guarding, calls not thee to guard,
for frantic boast and foolish word,
　thy mercy on thy people, Lord!

The Times, 17 July, 1897

ROBERT BRIDGES
1844-1930
The Yattendon Hymnal, 1899
HG 9

257
AMOR PATRIS ET FILII
suggested by a 12th century Latin text　　　HG 443

Love of the Father, love of God the Son,
from whom all came, in whom was all begun;
who formest heavenly beauty out of strife,
creation's whole desire and breath of life;

thou the all-holy, thou supreme in might,
thou dost give peace, thy presence maketh right;
thou with thy favour all things dost enfold,
with thine all-kindness free from harm wilt hold.

Hope of all comfort, splendour of all aid,
that dost not fail nor leave the heart afraid;
to all that cry thou dost all help afford,
the angels' armour, and the Saints' reward.

Purest and highest, wisest and most just,
there is no truth save only in thy trust;
thou dost the mind from earthly dreams recall,
and bring through Christ to him for whom are all.

Eternal glory, all men thee adore,
who art and shalt be worshipped evermore;
us whom thou madest, comfort with thy might,
and lead us to enjoy the heavenly light.

258
LOVE, UNTO THINE OWN WHO CAMEST

Love, unto thine own who camest
　　condescending,
　whom thine own receivèd not:　(John 1:11)
light, that shinedst in the darkness
　　but the darkness
　thy splendour perceivèd not:　(John 1:5)

O blessed were they who saw thee,
　　who were chosen
　first saints of thy saving word:
blessed they who have not seen thee,
　　yet believing　(John 20:29)
　are callèd by thee, O Lord.

Like stars in the night appearing,
　　some are shining,
　leaders high of man's desire:
saints are some, in silent temples
　　ever burning,
　bright lamps of love's living fire.

Thou hidest them, Love almighty,
　　in thy presence,
　from this world's provoking wrongs:
sheltered in thy quiet haven
　　thou dost keep them
　from strife of ungodly tongues.

Love, unto thine own who camest,
　　may thy servants
　thy great love receive aright:
grant, O grant that out of darkness
　　all creation
　may come to thy marvellous light.　(1 Peter 1:12)

259
FEAR NOT, O LAND
Joel 2:21   HG 610

Rejoice, O land, in God thy might;
his will obey, him serve aright;
for thee the saints lift up their voice:
fear not, O land, in God rejoice.

Glad shalt thou be, with blessing crowned,
with joy and peace thou shalt abound;
yea, love with thee shall make his home
until thou see God's kingdom come.

He shall forgive thy sins untold;
remember thou his love of old;
walk in his way, his word adore,
and keep his truth for evermore.

260
PSALM 138   HG 720

Thee will I love,
　　my God and King,
　　thee will I sing,
　　　　my strength and tower;
for evermore
　　thee will I trust,
　　O God most just
　　　　of truth and power;
who all things hast
in order placed
who for thy pleasure hast created;
　　and on thy throne,
　　unseen, unknown,
　　reignest alone
　　　　in glory seated.

Set in my heart
　　thy love I find,
　　my wandering mind
　　　　to thee thou leadest:
my trembling hope,
　　my strong desire
　　　　with heavenly fire
　　　　　　thou kindly feedest.
Lo, all things fair
thy path prepare,
thy beauty to my spirit calleth
　　thine to remain
　　in joy or pain
　　and count it gain
　　　　whate'er befalleth.

O more and more
　　thy love extend,
　　my life befriend
　　　　with heavenly pleasure;
that I may win
　　thy paradise,
　　thy pearl of price,
　　　　thy countless treasure;
since but in thee
I can go free
from earthly care and vain oppression,
　　this prayer I make
　　for Jesus' sake,
　　that thou me take
　　　　for thy possession.

261
OUR FATHER, WHO ART IN HEAVEN

Eternal Father, who didst all create,
　　in whom we live, and to whose bosom move,
　　to all men be thy name known, which is Love,
till its loud praises sound at heaven's gate.

Perfect thy Kingdom in our passing state,
　　that here on earth thou may'st as well approve
　　our service, as thou ownest theirs above,
whose joy we echo and in pain await.

Grant body and soul each day their daily bread:
　　and should in spite of grace fresh woe begin,
　　even as our anger soon is past and dead,
　　be thy remembrance mortal of our sin:

by thee in paths of peace thy sheep be led,
　　and in the vale of terror comforted.

(1876)

[First used as a hymn, 1931, it having been previously discovered by the editors of the *English Hymnal* (see 411) that a sonnet could be sung as a hymn.]

LIONEL B. C. L. MUIRHEAD
1845-1925

262
THE ADORATION OF THE LAMB   HG 684
(the title of a painting by J. van Eyck, which inspired this hymn)

The Church of God a kingdom is,
　　where Christ in power doth reign,
where spirits yearn till seen in bliss
　　their Lord shall come again.

Glad companies of saints possess
　　this Church below, above;
and God's perpetual calm doth bless
　　their paradise of love.

An Altar stands within the shrine,
　　whereon, once sacrificed,
is set, immaculate, divine,
　　the Lamb of God, the Christ,

There rich and poor, from countless lands,
　　praise Christ on mystic Rood;
there nations reach forth holy hands
　　to take God's holy Food.

There pure life-giving streams o'erflow
　　the sower's garden-ground;
and faith and hope fair blossoms show,
　　and fruits of love abound.

O King, O Christ, this endless grace
　　to us and all men bring,
to see the vision of thy face
　　in joy, O Christ our King.

Yattendon Hymnal, 1899

GEORGE RATCLIFFE WOOD-
WARD, 1848-1934
HG 737

263
GLORIA IN EXCELSIS

Praise ye the Lord, ye servants of the Lord:
　　praise ye his name; his lordly honour sing:
　　thee we adore, to thee glad homage bring;
　　thee we acknowledge: God to be adored
for thy great glory, Sovran, Lord, and King.

Father of Christ - that Lamb with blemish none,
　　that took the sins of all mankind away -
　　to thee belongeth worship, day by day;
　　yea, Holy Father, everlasting Son,
and Holy Ghost, all praise be thine for ay!

Songs of Syon, 1904; based on the
Apostolic Constitutions, 4th century

264
HOW DAZZLING FAIR ART THOU

How dazzling fair art thou, my Life, my Light!
How comely is thy countenance, how bright!
Sun uncreate, how keen is the enjoyment
　　that saints and angels find in thine employment!
　　In view whereof sing I, by day and night,
　　'How dazzling fair art thou, my Life, my Light!'

My soul, O lord, is still athirst for thee:　　　(Ps. 42)
　　my heart doth yearn thy seemly face to see:
dim is my sight; but one ray of thy kindness
　　should quickly skill to cure me of thy blindness:
　　meanwhile my song and my complaint shall be,
　　'My soul, O Lord, is sore athirst for thee.'

How lordly are thy mansions, King of love!　　(Ps. 84:1)
How worshipful thy courts in realms above!
Say, Lord, when shall I come to stand before thee,
　　and in thy gallant gates and walls adore thee?
　　Meantime I mourn, as doth the plaintive dove,
　　'How lordly are thy mansions, King of love!'

When shall I come to hear the Angel-song?
Nay, swell the chorus of the heavenly throng?
When join the noble company of Sages
　　who chaunt thy lauds through everlasting ages?
　　Now every day methinks, and all day long,
　　'When shall I come to hear that Angel-song?'

For songs of Syon, Lord, my soul prepare,
　　part in that never-ending round to bear;
to cry, with men of humble heart and lowly,　　(Ps. 148:13)
　　to thy great glory, 'Holy, Holy, Holy';　　　(Is. 6:3)
　　meanwhile shall be the tenor of mine air,
　　'For songs of Syon, Lord, my soul prepare.'

Songs of Syon, 1910
based on J. Scheffler.

HENRY SCOTT HOLLAND
1847-1918

265
JUDGE ETERNAL　　　　　HG 378

Judge eternal, throned in splendour,
　　Lord of lords and King of kings,
with thy living fire of judgment
　　purge this realm of bitter things,
solace all its wide dominion
　　with the healing of thy wings.

Still the weary folk are pining
　　for the hour that brings release,
and the city's crowded clangour
　　cries aloud for sin to cease;
and the homesteads and the woodlands
　　plead in silence for thy peace.

Crown, O God, thine own endeavour:
　　cleave our darkness with thy sword;
feed the faint and hungry heathen
　　with the richness of thy Word:
cleanse the body of this empire
　　through the glory of the Lord.

English Hymnal, 1906

ATHELSTAN RILEY
1858-1945
HG 112

266
THE CHOIR OF HEAVEN　　　　HG 832

Ye watchers and ye holy ones,　　　(Dan. 4:23)
bright seraphs, cherubim and thrones,
　　raise the glad strain, Alleluia!
Cry out, dominions, princedoms, powers,
virtues, archangels, angels' choirs,
　　Alleluia, Alleluia, Alleluia, Alleluia, Alleluia!

O higher than the Cherubim,
more glorious than the seraphim,
　　lead their praises, Alleluia!
Thou bearer of the eternal Word,
most gracious, magnify the Lord, . . .　　(Lk. 1:46)

Respond, ye souls in endless rest,
ye patriarchs and prophets blest,
　　Alleluia! Alleluia!
Ye holy Twelve, ye martyrs strong,
all saints triumphant, raise the song, . . .

O friends, in gladness let us sing
supernal anthems echoing,
　　Alleluia! Alleluia!
To God the Father, God the Son,
and God the Spirit, Three in One,
　　Alleluia, Alleluia, Alleluia, Alleluia, Alleluia!

English Hymnal, 1906

PERCY DEARMER
1867-1936
HG 88

267
PERSEVERANCE　　　　HG 350

Jesu, good above all other,
　　gentle Child of gentle Mother,
　　in a stable born our Brother,
　　　give us grace to persevere.

Jesus, cradled in a manger,
　　for us facing every danger,
　　living as a homeless stranger,
　　　make we thee our King most dear.

Jesus, for thy people dying,
risen Master, death defying,
Lord in heaven, thy grace supplying,
    keep us by thine altar near.*

Jesu, who our sorrows bearest,
all our thoughts and hopes thou sharest,
thou to man the truth declarest;
    help us all thy truth to hear.

Lord, in all our doings guide us,
pride and hate shall ne'er divide us;
we'll go on with thee beside us,
    and with joy we'll persevere!

English Hymnal, 1906
See also 456-458.
* later the author altered this to 'keep
us to thy presence near.'

GABRIEL GILLETT
1873-1948

268
IT IS FINISHED!   HG 342B

'It is finished!' Christ hath known
all the life of men wayfaring,
human joys and sorrows sharing,
    making human needs his own.
Lord, in us thy life renewing,
    lead us where thy feet have trod,
till, the way of truth pursuing,
    human souls find rest in God.

'It is finished!' Christ is slain
on the altar of creation,
offering for a world's salvation
    sacrifice of love and pain.
Lord, thy love through pain revealing,
    purge our passions, scourge our vice,
till, upon the Tree of Healing
    self is slain in sacrifice.

'It is finished!' Christ our King
wins the victor's crown of glory;
sun and stars recite his story;
    floods and fields his triumph sing.
Lord, whose praise the world is telling,
    Lord, to whom all power is given   (Matt. 28:19)
by thy death, hell's armies quelling,
    bring thy saints to reign in heaven.

English Hymnal, 1906

GILBERT KEITH CHESTERTON
1874-1936

269
O GOD OF EARTH AND ALTAR   HG 513

O God of earth and altar
        (Ex. 20:24)
   bow down and hear our cry,
our earthly rulers falter,
   our people drift and die;
the walls of gold entomb us,
   the swords of scorn divide,
take not thy thunder from us,
   but take away our pride.

From all that terror teaches,
   from lies of tongue and pen,
from all the easy speeches
   that comfort cruel men,
from sale and profanation
   of honour and the sword,
from sleep and from damnation
   deliver us, good Lord!

Tie in a living tether
   the price and priest and thrall,
bind all our lives together,
   smite us and save us all;
in ire and exultation,
   aflame with faith, and free,
lift up a living nation,
   a single sword to thee.

English Hymnal, 1906

ARTICLE 15:
WOMEN WRITERS BEFORE 1906 (270-295)

Half of my readers will bristle at this title, but there is no help for it. The Victorian age talked dogmatically about men, women, and children as three distinct species of the genus human, and history insists that until the opening of the twentieth century, at least in hymnology, the women and (in the succeeding article) the children be so treated.

By way of prologue, we present ##270-272, which come from an earlier period. Hardly any hymnody by women comes from the 18th century or earlier and only two or three such compositions have survived at all in modern use. We are obliged to begin with Madame Guyon, about whom Ronald Knox wrote in *Enthusiasm* (1950) so entertainingly and naughtily. She was the leader of the French 'Quietist' movement and personally something of an eccentric. If she had lived in the English 19th century she would probably have got a good deal out of her system by writing novels; in the twentieth, she would have gone to America and started a Movement. As it was, she paraded a somewhat paranoid religiosity, and of her many literary works, Knox says, 'they give an impression of extraordinary glibness . . . of eccentricity rather than originality, of very mediocre taste. Her poems seem to me frankly dull; nor did Cowper, who admired them, manage to make a great deal of them in translation.' Well, #270 comes out as a harmless devotional piece, perhaps not much more than that.

Anne Steele, our first English woman hymnodist, writing surprisingly early, places us on firmer ground in #271, which is still popular; and Anna Barbauld, #272, gives us a hymn which, though rather long, is more impressive in its original than in the truncated version still to be found in hymnals. It is a hymn for springtime or for the late winter, very realistic, and strikingly unsentimental.

Harriet Auber (273-4) still falls technically outside the Victorian era. The less known of the two hymns we here cite is probably the stronger; there are good thoughts and bad lines in #274, which will probably never be divorced now from a disastrous tune.

The tendency for women writers to use meters ending with a short line is something of a curiosity in the 19th century. Charlotte Elliott constantly did it. 'Just as I am' (275), if one uses the whole text, has a very good shape and a telling climax (it again has suffered from abominable tunes). No. 276 is even stronger; in stanza 4–oh, if only she had written 'all with one great voice' instead of 'sweet voice!' That word 'sweet' was run to death by Victorian writers of both sexes. But here is a still sturdy hymn full of good teaching (and there *is* a good tune for this, though few know it).

Now one must understand that the separation of women in

our context reflects the simple fact that women and men in English bourgeois society–hymns don't come from any other section–lived totally different lives. So you find here no echo at all of the controversies that gave the age its energy. On the contrary, you are reminded of the separateness of women by the very titles of some of the sources: look at the source of 275, and of 289. Or look at the novelists, and consider the predicament of any middle-aged woman in Trollope or Dickens or Thackeray. Except when they deal with the 'lower orders' or with country folk who are really rustics, one doesn't know whether to be more terrified of their triviality, if they are trivial, or their officiousness, if they are of the managing kind. At their best they are pictured as dedicated to home and family, or, if unmarried, to good works, which in the best hands really meant disciplined and sacrificial compassion.

It is hardly surprising that with such a complexity of spiritual and mental hazards to negotiate, the one faculty which a Victorian bourgeois woman should have had time to nourish is in fact so lacking in the hymnody she mostly produced: imagination. However, there is imagination in the best Victorian women's hymns; it is there in Charlotte Elliott, and it is there in the Unitarian Sarah Adams, whose 'Nearer, my God, to thee,' if separated from sentimental music (the musicians really did treat these women badly) and from historical association, turns out to be strong literature.

Sunday schools, of course, gave the ladies plenty to do. No. 278 is a famous hymn from that field written by Miss Maude when she was ill and separated from her class for three months, in each week of which she wrote them a letter. The letters were later collected and published, and this little piece was among them. Miss Waring (279) produced a number of poems, some of which are hymns of a pastoral, meditative, and hopeful kind.

But this brings us to Mrs Alexander, and the more one sees of her work the more one is convinced that for sheer honesty and straightforwardness she is the leading Victorian woman hymn writer. She is, indeed, worth closer study than we can here give her. People are often too easily labelled by the part of their work which captures a fickle public imagination; Mrs Alexander is, to most people, a writer of children's hymns. Well, when she was Miss Humphreys, that was what she was. See ##306-8 for some famous examples from her early collection of 1848. But the great thing about her children's hymns is their directness and candour. It does not always suit us now; perhaps it is because several of her children's hymns, like all three of those we cite in the next section, have been appropriated by adults that we look patronizingly upon them. Certainly 'Once in royal David's city,' which begins and ends so well, has one dreadful line: 'mild, obedient, good'; certainly 'There is a green hill' doesn't say all that can be said about the mystery of the Atonement. Equally certainly she perpetrated 'We are but little children weak,' which has an alarming first line, though much sound stuff further on, and 'Within the churchyard side by side are many long, low graves'; but no, even there one has to appreciate the straightforwardness and the candour. In one respect Mrs Alexander was fortunate: she was rarely let down by the musicians. That could be said of one hideous tune to #280, 'Jesus calls us,' which has to be divorced from its A & M tune before it can be seen for the sound piece it is; but for sheer simplicity, #281 is hard to beat, and so is the soundly scriptural #282. When we come to #320 we shall have more to say–that is her greatest piece, written 41 years later than her children's series (see articles 16, 17).

Frances Ridley Havergal (283-4) was an extraordinary person. A maiden lady all her fairly short life, she devoted herself from her early adult years to private evangelism. Not all of us are sure that she might not have proved a somewhat overwhelming guest (read what is said in the Hymnal Guide about 'Take my life'), but one can only admire–even if one keeps a safe distance–her zeal and sincerity. She was a facile writer and fairly frequently wrote doggerel. Our #283, her first hymn, is a modest and moving piece, and #284, one of her best known, shows that, if she did equate Christian service with religious proselytizing, she did at least mean what she said. Among evangelicals her hymnody is always welcome, and certainly it strikes sounder notes than much that evangelicals are now fed with.

No. 285 has greater artistry than Miss Havergal could compass; it is a series of compact and balanced statements so adroitly arranged as to make an eloquent hymn. The comma between stanzas 5 and 6, after the buttoned-up neatness of the first four stanzas, is most dramatic; conviction at last breaks through decorum. Sung to the tune HEINLEIN this is magnificent.

No. 286 became a hymn after its author's death, and perhaps it would have been equally appropriate in section 21; but it is, in its manner, strictly in line with the feminine hymnody of the period. It has to be delivered from the efforts of musicians to overdo the sentiment, but it is a beautiful meditation.

Miss Clephane, the short-lived evangelical hymnist who wrote ##287 and 313, became after her death one of the most sought-after authors of the evangelical missions of the seventies. This one is a highly personalized, atonement-centred piece characteristic of the piety generated by those revivals. This is evangelicalism, the almost direct opposite of resurrection-centred Calvinism, and at the same time the opposite (if such multidimensional geometry be permitted) of demure Anglicanism. This has much in common with those 'Gospel songs' which are dealt with later in section 19.

Could anything be more different from that than the contemplative and charming manner of #288? This poetess, who began her life in Northumbria, a part of England not rich in hymnic associations, embraces the liberal rather than the evangelical culture and presents a human and living Christ rather than a dying Christ. Hymnals have usually rearranged the stanzas, but in those few places where it is still known it brings a message quite unusual in the female hymnody of the time.

Equally unusual is the monumental #289–the only completely objective theological hymn to come from the hand of a 19th-century woman writer. No hymnal includes all the stanzas, and yet, which can really be spared without damaging the shape of the whole?

Christina Rossetti probably did not think of herself as a hymn writer, but from the English Hymnal onwards, fragments of her poetic output have been sought after by singers. The subtle variety in ##290-4, her special facility for writing short, epigrammatic poems of true lyric quality, and her profound evangelical diction combine to make her the most literate and poetically gifted of all these women. She, like Mrs Alexander, has usually been happy in her partnerships with musicians, but she can especially be read for devotional purposes without thought of music, for there is plenty of depth in her words.

Our section ends (295) with Mrs Alderson's hymn on the first Word from the Cross, a successful handling of a meter which often leads writers into exuberant platitude, and one of the very few new texts introduced in the 1904 *Hymns A & M* which has survived into later collections.

JEANNE MARIE BOUVIÈRES DE LA MOTHE (Madame Guyon)* 1648-1717
trs. by **William Cowper**
HG 235

270

O thou by long experience tried,
near whom no grief can long abide,
my Lord! how full of sweet content
my years of pilgrimage are spent.

All scenes alike engaging prove
to souls impressed with sacred love;
where'er they dwell, they dwell with thee,
in heaven, in earth, or in the sea.

To me remains nor place nor time;
my country is in every clime;
I can be calm and free from care
on any shore, since God is there.

While place we seek or place we shun,
the soul finds happiness in none;
but with my God to guide my way
'tis equal joy to go or stay.

Could I be cast where thou art not,
that were indeed a dreadful lot:
but regions none remote I call,
secure of finding God in all.

Then let me to his throne repair,
and never be a stranger there:
then love divine shall be my guard,
and peace and safety my reward.

*Poems Translated from the French of
Mme. Guyon,* 1801 (Posth.)

ANNE STEELE
1716-78

271
THE HOLY SCRIPTURES   HG 185

Father of mercies, in thy word
what endless glory shines!
for ever be thy name adored
for these celestial lines.

Here springs of consolation rise
to cheer the fainting mind;
and thirsty souls receive supplies
and sweet refreshment find.

Here the Redeemer's welcome voice
spreads heavenly peace around;
and life and everlasting joys
attend the blissful sound.

O may these heavenly pages be
my ever dear delight;
and still new beauties may I see,
and still increasing light.

Divine Instructor, gracious Lord,
be thou for ever near;
teach me to love thy sacred word,
and view my Saviour there.

Poems, Chiefly Devotional, 1760

ANNA LAETITIA BARBAULD
1743-1825

272
PRAISE TO GOD, IMMORTAL PRAISE   HG 602

Praise to God, immortal praise
for the love that crowns our days!
Bounteous source of every joy,
let thy praise our tongues employ.

For the blessings of the field,
for the stores and gardens yield;
for the vine's exalted juice,
for the generous olive's use:

flocks that whiten o'er the plain;
yellow sheaves of ripened grain;
clouds that drop their fattening
                              dews;
suns that temperate warmth
                          diffuse;

all that spring with bounteous
                            hand
scatters o'er the smiling land;
all that liberal autumn pours
from her rich o'erflowing stores:

these to thee, my God, we owe,
source whence all our blessings
                              flow;
and for these my soul shall raise
grateful vow and solemn praise.

Yet, should rising whirlwinds tear
                         (Hab. 3:17)
from its stem the ripening ear;
should the fig-tree's blasted shoot
drop her green untimely fruit,

should the vine put forth no more,
nor the olive yield her store;
though the sickening flocks
                         should fall
and the herds desert the stall;

should thine altered hand restrain
                        (James 5:7)
the early and the latter rain;
blast each opening bud of joy,
and the rising year destroy,

yet to thee my soul should raise
grateful vows and solemn praise;
and, when every blessing's flown,
love thee for thyself alone!

Hymns for Public Worship, 1772

HARRIET AUBER
1773-1862
The Spirit of the Psalms, 1829
HG 589

273
THE 78TH PSALM

O praise our great and gracious Lord,
and call upon his name;
to strains of joy tune every chord,
his mighty acts proclaim;
tell how he led his chosen race
to Canaan's pleasant land;
tell how his covenant of grace
unchanged shall ever stand.

He gave the shadowing cloud by day,
the moving fire by night;
to guide his Israel in their way,
he made their darkness light;
and have we not a sure retreat,
a Saviour ever nigh,
the same clear light to guide our feet,
the Dayspring from on high?   (Lk. 1:78)

We too have manna from above,
the Bread that came from heaven;

to us the same kind hand of love
 hath living waters given.
A Rock we have, from whence the spring
 in rich abundance flows;
that Rock is Christ, our Priest, our King (1 Cor. 10:4)
 who life and health bestows.

O let us prize this blessed food,
 and trust our heavenly Guide;
so shall we find death's fearful flood
 serene as Jordan's tide,
and safely reach that happy shore,
 the land of peace and rest,
where angels worship and adore
 in God's own presence blest.

274
THE HOLY SPIRIT   HG 589

Our blest Redeemer, ere he breathed
 his tender, last farewell,
a Guide, a Comfort bequeathed   (John 16:7)
 with us to dwell.

He came in semblance of a dove,   (Mk. 1:10)
 with sheltering wings outspread,
the holy balm of peace and love
 on earth to shed.

He came in tongues of living flame   (Acts 2:3)
 to teach, convince, subdue:
all-powerful as the wind he came,   (Acts 2:2)
 as viewless too.   (John 3:8)

He came sweet influence to impart,
 a gracious, willing guest,
while he can find one humble heart
 wherein to rest.

And his that gentle voice we hear,
 soft as the breath of even,
that checks each fault, that calms each fear,
 and speaks of heaven.

And every virtue we possess,
 and every victory won,
and every thought of holiness
 are his alone.

Spirit of purity and grace,
 our weakness, pitying, see;
O make our hearts thy dwelling-place
 and worthier thee.

CHARLOTTE ELLIOTT
1789-1871
HG 118

275
JUST AS I AM   HG 380

Just as I am, without one plea,
 but that thy blood was shed for me,
and that thou bid'st me come to thee,
 O Lamb of God, I come.

Just as I am, and waiting not
 to rid my soul of one dark blot,
to thee, whose blood can cleanse each spot,
 O Lamb of God, I come.

Just as I am, though tossed about
with many a conflict, many a doubt,
fightings and fears within, without,
 O Lamb of God, I come.

Just as I am, poor, wretched, blind;
sight, riches, healing of the mind,
ye, all I need, in thee to find,
 O Lamb of God, I come.

Just as I am, thou wilt receive,
wilt welcome, pardon, cleanse, relieve,
because thy promise I believe,
 O Lamb of God, I come.

Just as I am, thy love unknown
has broken every barrier down   (Eph. 2:13)
now to be thine, yea, thine alone,
 O Lamb of God, I come.

Just as I am, of that free love
the breadth, length, depth and height to prove (Eph. 3:18)
here for a season, then above,
 O Lamb of God, I come.

                    The Invalid's Hymn Book, 1836

276
WATCH AND PRAY
Mark 14:38   HG 118

'Christian! seek not yet repose,'
 hear thy guardian angel say,
'thou art in the midst of foes:
 Watch and pray!'

Principalities and powers,   (Eph. 6:12)
 mustering their unseen array,
wait for thine unguarded hours:
 watch and pray!

Gird thy heavenly armour on,
 wear it ever night and day;
ambushed lies the evil one:
 watch and pray!

Hear the victors who o'ercame;
 still they mark each warrior's way: (Heb. 12:1)
all with one sweet voice exclaim,
 'Watch and pray!'

Hear, above all, hear thy Lord,
 him thou lovest to obey;
hide within thy heart his word,
 'Watch and pray!'

Watch, as if on that alone
 hung the issue of the day:
pray that help may be sent down:
 watch and pray!

                    Morning and Evening Hymns for a
                    Week, 1839

SARAH FLOWER ADAMS
1805-48

277
NEARER, MY GOD, TO THEE HG 478

Nearer, my God, to thee,
  nearer to thee!
Ev'n though it be a cross
  that raiseth me;
still all my song shall be,
Nearer, my God, to thee,
  nearer to thee!

Though, like the wanderer,   (Gen. 28:20)
  the sun gone down,
darkness comes over me,
  my rest a stone;
yet in my dreams I'd be
nearer, my God, to thee,
  nearer to thee!

There let my way appear
  steps up to heaven;
all that thou sendest me
  in mercy given;
angels to beckon me
nearer, my God, to thee:
  nearer to thee!

Then with my waking thoughts
  bright with thy praise,
out of my stony griefs
  Bethel I'll raise;
so by my woes to be
nearer, my God, to thee,
  nearer to thee.

And when on joyful wing
  cleaving the sky,
sun, moon and stars forgot,
  upwards I fly,
still all my song shall be,
nearer, my God, to thee,
  nearer to thee.

1840; in *Hymns and Anthems* (W. J.
Fox), 1841

MARY FAWLER MAUDE
1819-1913

278
THINE FOR EVER! HG 733

Thine for ever, God of love,
hear us from thy throne above;
thine for ever may we be
here and in eternity.

Thine for ever! Lord of life,
shield us through our earthly strife;
thou the Life, the Truth, the Way   (John 14:6)
guide us to the realms of day.

Thine for ever! oh how blest
they who find in thee their rest!
Saviour, Guardian, heavenly Friend,
O defend us to the end.

Thine for ever! Saviour, keep
us thy frail and trembling sheep;
safe alone beneath thy care
let us all thy goodness share.

Thine for ever; thou our Guide,
all our wants by thee supplied,
all our sins by thee forgiven,
lead us, Lord, from earth to heaven.

Twelve Letters on Confirmation, 1848;
text of 1871

ANNA LAETITIA WARING
1820-1910

279
SAFETY IN GOD HG 332

In heavenly love abiding
  no change my heart shall fear;
and safe is such confiding,
  for nothing changes here:
the storm may roar without me,
  my heart may low be laid;
but God is round about me,
  and can I be dismayed?

Wherever he may guide me,
  no want shall turn me back;
my Shepherd is beside me,
  and nothing can I lack;
his wisdom ever waketh,
  his sight is never dim;
he knows the way he taketh,
  and I will walk with him.

Green pastures are before me,
  which yet I have not seen;
bright skies will soon be o'er me,
  where the dark clouds have been:
my hope I cannot measure,
  my path to life is free;
my Saviour hath my treasure,
  and he will walk with me.

Hymns and Meditations, 1850

CECIL FRANCES ALEXANDER
1818-95
HG 24

280
FOLLOW ME
For St Andrew's Day HG 346

Jesus calls us; o'er the tumult
  of our life's wild restless sea
day by day his sweet voice soundeth,
  saying 'Christian, follow me';

as of old Saint Andrew heard it   (Mk. 1:16)
  by the Galilean Lake,
turned from home, and toil, and kindred,
  leaving all for his dear sake.

Jesus calls us from the worship
  of this vain world's golden store,
from each idol that would keep us,
  saying 'Christian, love me more.'   (John 21:15)

In our joys and in our sorrows,
  days of toil and hours of ease,
still he calls, in cares and pleasures,
  that we love him more than these.

Jesus calls us: by thy mercies,
　Saviour, make us hear thy call,
give our hearts to thine obedience,
　serve and love thee best of all.

Hymns for Public Worship (SPCK),
1852

281
THE ASCENSION HG 689

The golden gates are lifted up,
　the doors are opened wide,
the King of glory is gone in
　unto his Father's side.

Thou art gone up before us, Lord,
　to make for us a place,
that we may be where now thou art,
　and look upon God's face.

And ever on our earthly path
　a gleam of glory lies;
a light still breaks behind the cloud
　that veils thee from our eyes.

Lift up our hearts, lift up our minds,
　let thy dear grace be given,
that, while we wander here below,
　our treasure be in heaven;　　(Matt. 6:21)

that where thou art at God's right hand,
　our hope, our love may be,
dwell thou in us, that we may dwell
　for evermore in thee.

Hymns Descriptive and Devotional,
1858

282
FOR SS. PHILIP AND JAMES

There is one Way, and only one,　　(John 14:6)
　out of our gloom, and sin, and care,
to that far land where shines no sun　　(Rev. 21:23)
　because the Face of God is there.

There is one Truth, the truth of God,
　that Christ came down from heaven to show,
one Life, that his redeeming blood
　has won for all his saints below.

The lore from Philip once concealed,　　(John 14:8-9)
　we know its fulness now in Christ;
in him the Father is revealed,
　and all our longing is sufficed.

And still unwavering faith holds sure
　the words that James wrote sternly down:　　(James 5:7)
except we labour and endure
　we cannot win the heavenly crown.

O Way divine, through gloom and strife
　bring us thy Father's face to see;
O heavenly Truth, O precious Life,
　at last, at last we rest in thee.

Hymns Ancient and Modern, 1875
See also 306-8, 320A.

FRANCES RIDLEY HAVERGAL
1836-79
HG 252

283
WHAT SHALL I RENDER UNTO THE LORD . . . ?
HG 752

Thy life was given for me,
　thy blood, O Lord, was shed,
that I might ransomed be,
　and quickened from the dead;
thy life was given for me:
what have I given for thee?

Long years were spent for me
　in weariness and woe,
that through eternity
　thy glory I might know;
long years were spent for me;
have I spent one for thee?

Thy Father's home of light,
　thy rainbow-circled throne
were left for earthly night,
　for wanderings sad and lone;
yea, all was left for me;
have I left aught for thee?

Thou, Lord, hast borne for me
　more than my tongue can tell
of bitterest agony,
　to rescue me from hell;
thou sufferedst all for me;
what have I borne for thee?

And thou hast brought to me
　down from thy throne above
salvation full and free,
　thy pardon and thy love;
great gifts thou broughtest me:
what have I brought to thee?

O let my life be given,
　my years for thee be spent;
world-fetters will be riven,
　and joy with suffering blent;
thou gav'st thyself for me;
I give myself to thee.

1858; in *Good Words*, 1860

284
THE LAY EVANGELIST HG 434

Lord, speak to me, that I may speak
　in living echoes of thy tone;
as thou hast sought, so let me seek
　thy erring children, lost and lone.

O lead me, Lord, that I may lead
　the wandering and the wavering feet;
O feed me, Lord, that I may feed
　thy hungering ones with manna sweet.

O strengthen me, that while I stand
　firm on the rock and strong in thee,
I may stretch out a loving hand
　to wrestlers with the troubled sea.

O teach me, Lord, that I may teach
   the precious things thou dost impart;
and wing thy words, that they may reach
   the hidden depths of many a heart.

O give thine own sweet rest to me,
   that I may speak with soothing power
a word in season, as from thee,   (Is. 50:5)
   to weary ones, in needful hour.

O fill me with thy fulness, Lord,
   until my very heart o'erflow
in kindling thought and glowing word,
   thy love to tell, thy praise to show.

O use me, Lord, use even me
   just as thou wilt, and when, and where,
until thy blessed face I see,
   thy rest, thy joy, thy glory share.

1872; in *Under the Surface*, 1874

ELISABETH RUNDLE CHARLES
1828-96

285
NEVER FURTHER THAN THY CROSS   HG 479

Never further than thy cross,
   never higher than thy feet;
here earth's precious things seem dross,   (Gal. 6:14)
   here earth's bitter things grow sweet.

Gazing thus, our sin we see,
   learn thy love while gazing thus -
sin, which laid the cross on thee,
   love, which bore the cross for us.

Here we learn to serve and give,
   and, rejoicing, self deny;
here we gather love to live,
   here we gather faith to die.

Symbols of our liberty
   and our service here unite:
captives, by thy cross set free,
   soldiers of thy cross, we fight.

Pressing onwards as we can,
   still to this our hearts must tend,
where our earliest hopes began,
   there our last aspirings end,

till amid the hosts of light
   we in thee redeemed, complete,
through thy cross made pure and white,
   cast our crowns before thy feet.

The Family Treasury, 1860

JEAN INGELOW
1823-97

286
ON THE LOVE OF CHRIST   HG 41

And didst thou love the race that loved not thee?
   and didst thou take to heaven a human brow?
Dost plead with man's voice by the marvellous sea?
   Art thou his kinsman now?

O God, O Kinsman loved, but not enough!
   O man, with eyes majestic after death,
whose feet have toiled along our pathways rough,
     whose lips drawn human breath,

by that one likeness which is ours and thine,
   by that one nature which doth hold us kin,
by that high heaven where, sinless, thou dost shine
     to draw us sinners in;

by thy last silence in the judgment hall,
   by long foreknowledge of the deadly tree,
by darkness, by the wormwood and the gall,
     I pray thee visit me.

Come, lest this heart should, cold and cast away,
   die ere the guest adored she entertain;
lest eyes which never saw thine earthly day
     should miss thy heavenly reign.

Poems, 1863 (cento, 1916)

**ELIZABETH CECILIA
CLEPHANE**, 1830-69

287
BENEATH THE CROSS   HG 82

Beneath the cross of Jesus
   I fain would take my stand -
the shadow of a mighty Rock   (Is. 32:2)
   within a weary land;
a home within a wilderness,
   a rest upon the way,
from the burning of the noontide heat
   and the burden of the day,

O safe and happy shelter!
   O refuge tired and sweet!
O trysting-place where heaven's love
   and heaven's justice meet!
As to the exiled patriarch   (Gen. 28:20)
   that wondrous dream was given,
so seems my Saviour's cross to me
   a ladder up to heaven.

There lies within its shadow,
   but on the further side,
the darkness of an open grave
   that gapes both deep and wide;
and there, between us and the Cross
   two arms outstretched to save,
like a watchman set to guard the way
   from that eternal grave.

Upon the cross of Jesus
   mine eyes at times can see
the very dying form of One
   who suffered there for me.
And from my stricken heart, with tears,
   two wonders I confess, -
the wonders of redeeming love
   and my own worthlessness.

I take, O Cross, thy shadow,
   for my abiding place;
I ask no sunshine other than
   the sunshine of his face:
Content to let the world go by,
   to know no gain or loss. -
my sinful self my only shame,
   my glory all - the Cross!

(posth.), c. 1870
See also 313.

DORA GREENWELL
1821-82

288
IMMANUEL

And art thou come with us to dwell,
  our prince, our guide, our love, our Lord?
And is thy name Immanuel,
  God present with his world restored?

The world is glad for thee; the heart
  is glad for thee, and all is well
and fixed, and sure, because thou art
  whose name is called Immanuel.

The heart is glad for thee: it knows
  none now shall bid it err or mourn,
and o'er its desert breaks the rose   (Is. 35:1)
  in triumph o'er the grieving thorn.

The world is glad for thee! the rude
  wild moor, the city's crowded pen;
each waste, each peopled solitude
  becomes a home for happy men.

Thou bringest all again; with thee
  is light, is space, is breadth and room
for each thing fair, beloved and free
  to have its hour of life and bloom.

Each heart's deep instinct unconfessed;
  each lowly wish, each daring claim;
all, all that life hath long repressed
  unfolds, undreading blight or blame.

Thy reign eternal will not cease;
  thy years are sure and glad and slow;
within thy mighty world of peace
  the humblest flower hath leave to blow.

Then come to heal thy people's smart,
  and with thee bring thy captive train;
come, Saviour of the world and heart,
  come, mighty Victor over pain.

Carmina Crucis, 1869 (in *Congregational Praise*, 1951, this appears as sts. 1, 3, 5, 6, 7, 2).

CAROLINE M. NOEL
1817-77

289
EVERY KNEE SHALL BOW   HG 58

At the name of Jesus   (Phil. 2:11)
  every knee shall bow,
every tongue confess him
  King of glory now.
'Tis the Father's pleasure
  we should call him Lord
who from the beginning
  was the mighty Word.
                    (John 1:1)

Mighty and mysterious
  in the highest height,
God from everlasting,
  very Light of light:
in the Father's bosom
  with the Spirit blest,
love, in love eternal,
  rest, in perfect rest.

At his voice creation   (John 1:3)
  sprang at once to light,
all the angel faces,
  all the hosts of light.
Thrones and dominations,
  stars upon their way,
all the heavenly orders
  in their great array.

Humbled for a season
  to receive a name
from the lips of sinners
  unto who, he came,
faithfully he bore it
  spotless to the last,
brought it back victorious
  when from death he passed.

Bore it up triumphant
  with its human light,
through all ranks of creatures
  to the central height,
to the throne of Godhead,
  to the Father's breast:
filled it with the glory
  of that perfect rest.

Name him, brothers, name him
  with love as strong as death,
but with awe and wonder,
  and with bated breath;
he is God the Saviour,
  he is Christ the Lord,
ever to be worshipped,
  trusted, and adored.

In your hearts enthrone him;
  there let him subdue
all that is not holy,
  all that is not true:
crown him as your captain
  in temptation's hour;
let his will enfold you
  in its light and power.

Brothers, this Lord Jesus
  shall return again,
with his Father's glory,
  with his angel-train;
for all wreaths of empire
  meet upon his brow
and our hearts confess him
  King of glory now.

The Name of Jesus, and Other Verses for the Sick and Lonely, 1870

CHRISTINA GEORGINA ROSSETTI, 1830-94
Poetical Works, 1894

290
IN THE BLEAK MIDWINTER   HG 335

In the bleak midwinter
  frosty wind made moan;
earth stood hard as iron,
  water like a stone;
snow had fallen, snow on snow,
  snow on snow,
in the bleak midwinter,
  long ago.

Our God, heaven cannot hold him,
  nor earth sustain;
heaven and earth shall flee away
  when he comes to reign:
in the bleak midwinter
  a stable-place sufficed
the Lord God Almighty,
  Jesus Christ.

Enough for him whom cherubim
  worship night and day,
a breastful of milk
  and a mangerful of hay;
enough for him, whom angels
  fall down before
the ox and ass and camel
  which adore.

Angels and archangels
  may have gathered there,
cherubim and seraphim
  thronged the air:
but only his mother
  in her maiden bliss
worshipped the Beloved
  with a kiss.

What can I give him,
  poor as I am?
If I were a shepherd
  I would bring a lamb;
if I were a wise man
  I would do my part;
yet what I can, I bring him:
  give my heart.

c. 1872

291
MICHAELMAS

Service and strength, God's angels and archangels;
  his seraphs fires, and lamps his cherubim:
glory to God from highest and from lowest,
  Glory to God in everlasting hymn
    from all his creatures.

Princes that serve, and powers that work his pleasure,
  heights that soar toward him, depths that sink toward him;
flames for out-flaming, chill beside his essence;
  insight all-probing, save where scant and dim
    towards its Creator.

Sacred and free, exultant in God's pleasure,
  his will their solace, thus they wait on him,
and shout their shout of ecstasy eternal,
  and trim their splendours that they burn not dim
    toward their Creator.

Wherefore with angels, wherefore with archangels,
  with lofty cherubs, loftier seraphim,
we laud and magnify our God almighty,
  and veil our faces rendering love to him
    with all his creatures.

Called to be Saints, 1881

292
LOVE CAME DOWN AT CHRISTMAS HG 441

Love came down at Christmas,
  love all lovely, Love divine;
Love was born at Christmas,
  star and angels gave the sign.

Worship we the Godhead,
  love incarnate, love divine;
worship we our Jesus,
  but wherewith for sacred sign?

Love shall be our token,
  love be yours and love be mine,
love to God and all men,
  love for plea and gift and sign.

Time Flies: A Reading Diary, 1885 (rev.
1893)

293
NONE OTHER LAMB
Rev. 5:2 HG 481

None other Lamb, none other name,
none other hope in heaven or earth or sea,
none other hiding place from guilt and shame,
  none beside thee.

My faith burns low, my hope burns low;
only my heart's desire cries out in me,
by the deep thunder of its want and woe,
  cries out to thee.

Lord, thou art life, though I be dead,
love's fire thou art, however cold I be:
nor heaven have I, nor place to lay my head,
  nor home, but thee.

The Face of the Deep, 1892

294
LOVEST THOU ME?
John 21:15

Love is the key of life and death,
  of hidden, heavenly mystery:
of all Christ is, of all he saith
  Love is the key.

As three times to his saint he saith,   (John 21:15)
  he saith to me, he saith to thee,
breathing his grace-conferring breath:
  'Lovest thou me?'

Ah, Lord, I have such feeble faith,
  such feeble hope to comfort me:
but love it is, is strong as death:
  and I love thee.

Poetical Works, 1894
See also 309.

ADA RUNDALL GREENAWAY
1861-1937

295
FATHER, FORGIVE THEM
Luke 23:34 HG 574

O Word of pity, for our pardon pleading,
  breathed in the hour of loneliness and pain:
O voice, which through the ages interceding,
  calls us to fellowship with God again;

O word of comfort, through the silence stealing,
  as the dread act of sacrifice began;
O infinite compassion, still revealing
  the infinite forgiveness won for man;

O word of hope, to raise us nearer heaven,
  when courage fails us, and when faith is dim;
the souls for whom Christ prays to Christ are given, (John 17:12)
  to find their pardon and their joy in him.

O intercessor, who art ever living
  to plead for dying souls that they may live,
teach us to know our sin which needs forgiving,
  teach us to know the love which can forgive.

Hymns Ancient and Modern, 1904

ARTICLE 16:
HYMNS FOR CHILDREN, 1715-1900 (296-319)

While hymns specially written for children came into their own only after the invention of Sunday schools by late 18th-century evangelicals, the young were not overlooked either by Watts or by Wesley. In the 1790 edition of Charles Wesley's children's hymns, published by his brother John after Charles had died, John wrote–and it must have been among the last things he did write–in the preface: 'There are two ways of writing or speaking to children; the one is, to let ourselves down to them; the other, to lift them up to us. Dr. Watts has wrote in the former way, and has succeeded admirably well, speaking to children as children, and leaving them as he found them. The following hymns are written on the other plan: they contain strong and manly sense, yet expressed in such plain and easy language as even children can understand. But when they do understand them, they will be children no longer, only in years and stature.'

Wise old John! As usual, he sees further than most people of his age. Now, in thus writing of Watts I suspect that he did not have in mind our #296 which, as #2 in his *Divine Songs for Children*, is the only piece from either that or the second part of the same little volume, *Moral Songs*, which survives (with two stanzas omitted) in modern books; and when there, it is always treated as an adult hymn. Rather he will have been thinking of the more popular moralistic pieces which very specifically address the condition of children, like

> Let dogs delight to bark and bite,
>   for God hath made them so;
> let bears and lions growl and fight,
>   for 'tis their nature too.
>
> But, children, you should never let
>   such angry passions rise;
> your little hands were never made
>   to tear each other's eyes.

Looking at most of Watts' children's pieces one sees what John Wesley meant. And one sees the contrast in that part of Charles' famous 'Gentle Jesus' which we quote as #297. Even more, of course, one sees it in #72, which it is difficult to think of as having been written for children, but which was, apparently, so devised.

But the axis discerned by John Wesley has continued to be a pattern of children's hymn writing, and during the 19th century, with so many books being published for Sunday school use, one sees a fairly heavy emphasis on the 'Watts' principle. Nowadays the question is put a little differently, though it is the same question; we now ask whether or not children are part of the whole worshipping congregation, and whether it is wise to invite them to sing what their elders—especially those only just older than children—will be embarrassed to sing with them. It is one thing, and a quite legitimate thing, to talk to children as children when only they are present; it is another to do that when one is also addressing adults. And plenty of educationists will now admit that it is the great adult hymns—it hardly matters how profound provided their language is sufficiently evocative of the imagination—that, if they are presented to children, really build up their faith. This is a variation on the 'Wesley' principle.

In the work of the two sisters, Ann and Jane Taylor (Ann having later become Mrs Gilbert), one sees a real attempt to help the children express large thoughts about central things, stilted though the language sometimes is (298-9). In Mary Duncan's tiny piece we have simply a small child being put to bed at home and being given the simplest words for its prayer. Mrs Luke's very well-known piece on the ministry of Christ (301) has the great merit of making the human Jesus real to children, though its language has a cooing archness that sounds odder now than it would have done then. The diction of Jane Leeson's equally well-known hymn (304) is by contrast chaste and restrained and seems to treat a child with just that much more respect.

J. M. Neale, some may be surprised to learn, wrote his first hymns for children long before he began his translations, and at the age of 24. These contain straight teaching; no searching here for ideas and pictures that will appeal especially to children, just a presentation in simple language of the church's teaching. Such of these as now survive are normally used as adult hymns (302-3).

No. 305 is an odd case which we include for textual reasons.

This again is, in either form, a very small child's hymn making a simple moral point which could easily appeal to the very young.

Mrs Alexander (306-8) is the most famous of all children's hymn writers, and she is undoubtedly a 'Wesley-principle' author. These were her earliest hymns, and they are designed to illustrate the catechism. Once again, this is 'Wesley-style' material, upon which we have already commented in article 15. This, too, is usually classed in modern hymnals as suitable for adults.

It will be easy for the reader to assign the rest to their separate categories. We take no account of the terrible rubbish which was so often written for and fed to Victorian children; about each of our examples there is at least a touch of honest workmanship. Baring-Gould's 'Now the day is over' (312) should be especially studied as a model of unaffected simplicity; and Elizabeth Clephane's evangelical song 'There were ninety and nine' (313) raises the point that there is often something strictly juvenile about the hymnody associated with evangelical missions. This, now thought of as very much a 'mission' hymn, was originally a children's hymn. We shall have to take up this point again when we come to Gospel Songs (article 19). Note the grave and simple language of the two children's hymns by writers best known for their adult work, How (315) and Ellerton (317); the open-air touch of #316, by R. S. Hawker, reputedly, in his Cornwall parish, the inventor of the English 'Harvest Festival'; and, above all, the quite remarkable felicity of #319, one of the very few hymns available on that aspect of our Lord's life which Scripture hides from us but which appeals especially to youthful imaginations: 'What was he like when he was eleven years old?'

The writing of children's hymns, like any other aspect of education, needs gifts which not all writers possess. The fatal habit of Victorians was to do what Wesley says Watts did, and do it much worse. Their hymns are littered with the adjective 'little'—and what child wants to think of itself as little? What child of healthy mind wants to stay little? Hymnals in use still contain a good deal of this unhealthy stuff, and the worst incongruities appear when they are used at school assemblies. I cannot easily forgive the authorities who were content to invite my own boys in the 1960s, teenagers then, to rush into school with their breakfast in their throats and bawl

> Our hands are so small,
>   and our words are so weak:
> we cannot teach others;
>   how then shall we seek
> to work for our Lord in his harvest?

There is something truly solemn about the complex infelicities of that in a school housing about 1,600 young Scotsmen. No wonder creatures so trained grow up to despise hymns!

This story is continued in articles 22 and 25.

ISAAC WATTS
1674-1748
HG 10

296
PRAISE FOR CREATION AND PROVIDENCE

HG 320

> I sing the almighty power of God,
>   that made the mountains rise;
> that spread the flowing seas abroad
>   and built the lofty skies.

I sing the wisdom that ordained
   the sun to rule by day;
the moon shines full at his command,
   and all the seas obey.

I sing the goodness of the Lord,
   that filled the earth with food;
he form'd the creatures with his word,
   and then pronounced them good.

Lord, how thy wonders are display'd
   where'er I turn mine eye;
if I survey the ground I tread,
   or gaze upon the sky!

There's not a plant or flower below,
   but makes thy glories known;
and clouds arise, and tempests blow
   by order from thy throne.

Creatures (as numerous as they be)
   are subject to thy care;
there's not a place where we can flee
   but God is present there.

In heaven he shines with beams of love,
   with wrath in hell beneath;
'tis on his earth I stand or move,
   and 'tis his air I breathe.

His hand is my perpetual guard,
   he keeps me with his eye;
why should I then forget the Lord
   who is for ever nigh?

Divine Songs for Children, 1715

CHARLES WESLEY
1707-88
HG 1

297
GENTLE JESUS   HG 216

Lamb of God, I look to thee
thou shalt my Example be;
thou art gentle, meek and mild,
thou wast once a little child.

Fain I would be, as thou art,
give me thine obedient heart;
thou art pitiful and kind,
let me have thy loving mind.

Meek and lowly may I be,
thou art all humility;
let me to my betters bow,
subject to thy Parents thou.

Let me above all fulfil
God my heavenly Father's will,
never his good spirit grieve,
only to his glory live.

Thou didst live to God alone,
thou didst never seek thine own;
thou thyself didst never please,
God was all thy happiness.

Loving Jesu, gentle Lamb,
in thy gracious hands I am,
make me, Saviour, what thou art,
live thyself within my heart.

I shall then show forth thy praise,
serve thee all my happy days;
then the world shall ever see,
Christ, the holy Child, in me.

Hymns and Sacred Poems, (abr.) 1742
(Divided into two parts in *Hymns for
Children*, 1763, of which this is the
second.)

JANE TAYLOR
1783-1824

298
PROVIDENCE   HG 420

Lord, I would own thy tender care,
   and all thy love to me;
the food I eat, the clothes I wear,
   are all bestowed by thee.

'Tis thou preservest me from death
   and dangers every hour;
I cannot draw another breath
   unless thou give me power.

Kind angels guard me every night,
   as round my bed they stay;
nor am I absent from thy sight
   in darkness or by day.

My health and friends and parents dear
   to me by God are given;
I have not any blessing here
   but what is sent from heaven.

Such goodness, Lord, and constant care,
   a child can ne'er repay;
but may it be my daily prayer
   to love thee and obey.

Hymns for Infant Minds, 1809

ANN GILBERT (TAYLOR)
1782-1866
HG 420

299
CONDESCENSION

Great God, and wilt thou condescend
to be my Father and my Friend?
I a poor child, and thou so high,
the Lord of earth, and air, and sky.

Art thou my Father? Canst thou bear
to hear my poor, imperfect prayer?
Or wilt thou listen to the praise
that such a little one can raise?

Art thou my Father? Let me be
a meek, obedient child to thee;
and try, in word and deed and thought,
to serve and please thee as I ought.

Art thou my Father? I'll depend
upon the care of such a Friend;
and only wish to do and be
whatever seemeth good to thee.

Art thou my Father? Then at last
when all my days on earth are past,
send down and take me in thy love
to be thy better child above.

Hymns for Infant Minds (2nd edition),
1810

MARY DUNCAN, 1814-40

300
TENDER SHEPHERD　　　　　HG 369

Jesus, tender Shepherd, hear me,
　　bless thy little lamb tonight;
through the darkness be thou near me,
　　watch my sleep till morning light.

All this day thy hand has led me,
　　and I thank thee for thy care;
thou hast clothed me, warmed and fed me,
　　listen to my evening prayer.

Let my sins be all forgiven,
　　bless the friends I love so well;
take me, when I die, to heaven,
　　happy there with thee to dwell.

　　　　　　　1839; in *Memoir* (Posth.), 1841

JEMIMA LUKE, 1813-1906

301
WHEN JESUS WAS HERE　　　HG 322

I think, when I read that sweet story of old,
　　when Jesus was here among men,
how he called little children as lambs to his fold,
　　I should like to have been with him then.
I wish that his hands had been placed on my head,
　　that his arm had been thrown around me,
and that I might have seen his kind look when he said,
　　'Let the little ones come unto me.'

Yet still to his footstool in prayer I may go,
　　and ask for a share in his love;
and if I now earnestly seek him below,
　　I shall see him and hear him above:
in that beautiful place he has gone to prepare
　　for all that are washed and forgiven.
And many dear children are gathering there,
　　'For of such is the kingdom of heaven.'

But thousands and thousands who wander and fall
　　never heard of that heavenly home;
I should like them to know there is room for them all,
　　and that Jesus had bid them to come.
I long for the joy of that glorious time,
　　the sweetest, and brightest, and best,
when the dear little children of every clime
　　shall crowd to his arms and be blest.

　　　　　　Sunday School Teacher's Magazine,
　　　　　　1841

J. M. NEALE, 1818-66
Hymns for Children
1842
HG 2

302
IN PASSION WEEK

O Thou, who through this Holy Week
　　didst suffer for us all;
the sick to cure, the lost to seek,
　　to raise up them that fall:

we cannot understand the woe
　　thy love was pleased to bear:
O Lamb of God! we only know
　　that all our hopes are there!

Thy feet the path of suffering trod,
　　thy hand the victory won;
what shall we render to our God
　　for all that he hath done?

To God the Father, God the Son
　　and God the Holy Ghost,
by men on earth be honour done
　　and by the heavenly host.

303
GOOD FRIDAY

A time to watch, a time to pray,
a day of wonders is to-day;
the saddest, yet the sweetest too,
that ever man or angel knew:

the saddest; for our Saviour bore
his death, that man might die no more:
the Agony, the Scourge, the Fear,
the Crown of Thorns, the Cross, the Spear;

and yet the sweetest; for to-day
our load of sin was borne away;
and hopes of joy that never dies
hang on our Saviour's sacrifice.

Like straying sheep we wandered wide;　　(Is. 53:6)
thy laws we broke, thy name defied;
on thee the guilt of all was laid;
by thee the debt of all was paid.

O Saviour, blessed be thy name!
Thine is the glory, ours the shame;
by all the pains thy love endured,
let all our many sins be cured.

　　　　　　(The hymn ended with Ken's doxol-
　　　　　　ogy: the last st. of no. 29.)

JANE E. LEESON
1807-82

304
LOVING SHEPHERD　　　　HG 444

Loving Shepherd of thy sheep,
keep thy lamb, in safety keep;
nothing can thy power withstand,
none can pluck me from thy hand.

Loving Saviour, thou didst give
thine own life that we might live;
and the hands outstretched to bless
bear the cruel nails' impress.

I would bless thee every day,
gladly all thy will obey,
like thy blessed ones above,
happy in thy precious love.

Loving Shepherd, ever near,
teach thy lamb thy voice to hear;
suffer not my steps to stray
from the straight and narrow way.

Where thou leadest I will go,
walking in thy steps below,
till before my Father's throne
I shall know as I am known.

Hymns & Songs of Childhood, 1842;
text of 1875

305
LITTLE DROPS OF WATER

[This is a curiosity. The form which was very much used in England a generation or two ago is by an American writer, Mrs Julia A. Carney, b. 1823; it was published in Boston in 1845. A quite different version, but using the same first stanza, was written by Dr E. C. Brewer in a magazine, *Reading and Spelling*, published in England in 1848. The whole story has to be chased through four separate entries in *Julian*, who more than once insists on the superiority of the American version, even when in his earlier edition (1892) he believes the American version to be later than the English, and an adaptation of it. Mrs Carney gets the credit only in the last edition, 1907.]

MRS. CARNEY (U.S.A.)

Little drops of water
 little grains of sand,
make the mighty ocean,
 make the beauteous land.

And the little moments,
 humble though they be,
make the mighty ages
 of eternity.

Little deeds of kindness,
 little words of love,
make our earth an Eden
 like the heaven above.

So our little errors
 lead the soul away
from the paths of virtue
 into sin to stray

Little seeds of mercy,
 sown by youthful hands
grow to bless the nations
 far in heathen lands.

1845

E. C. BREWER (England)

Little drops of water,
 little grains of sand
make the mighty ocean
 and the beauteous land.

Straw by straw the sparrow
 builds its cosy nest;
leaf by leaf the forest
 stands in verdure drest.

Letter after letter
 words and books are made;
little and by little
 mountains level laid.

Drop by drop is iron
 worn in time away;
perseverance, patience
 ever win their way.

Every finished labour
 once did but begin;
try and go on trying:
 that's the way to win.

1848

CECIL FRANCES ALEXANDER
Hymns for Little Children, 1848
HG 24

306
THERE IS A GREEN HILL   HG 725

There is a green hill far away,
 without a city wall,
where the dear Lord was crucified,
 who died to save us all.

We may not know, we cannot tell
 what pains he had to bear,
but we believe it was for us
 he hung and suffered there.

He died that we might be forgiven,
 he died to make us good,
that we might go at last to heaven
 saved by his precious blood.

There was no other good enough
 to pay the price of sin;
he only could unlock the gate
 of heaven, and let us in.

Oh, dearly, dearly has he loved,
 and we must love him too;
and trust in his redeeming blood
 and try his works to do.

(no. 1)

307
CHRISTMAS   HG 583

Once in royal David's city
 stood a lowly cattle-shed,
where a Mother laid her Baby
 in a manger for his bed;
Mary was that Mother mild,
Jesus Christ her little child.

He came down to earth from heaven,
 who is God and Lord of all,
and his shelter was a stable,
 and his cradle was a stall;
with the poor, and mean, and lowly
lived on earth our Saviour holy.

And through all his wondrous childhood
 he would honour and obey,
love and watch the lowly Maiden
 in whose gentle arms he lay;
Christian children all must be
mild, obedient, good as he.

For he is our childhood's pattern,
 day by day like us he grew,
he was little, weak and helpless,
 tears and smiles like us he knew;
and he feeleth for our sadness;
and he shareth in our gladness.

And our eyes at last shall see him,
 through his own redeeming love,
for that Child, so dear and gentle
 is our Lord in heaven above;
and he leads his children on
to the place where he is gone.

Not in that poor lowly stable,
 with the oxen standing by,
we shall see him; but in heaven
 set at God's right hand on high;
when like stars his children crowned,
robed in white shall wait around.

(no. 8)

308
GOD THE FATHER, MAKER OF HEAVEN AND EARTH
HG 24

All things bright and beautiful,
 all creatures great and small,
all things wise and wonderful,
 the Lord God made them all.

Each little flower that opens,
    each little bird that sings,
he made their glowing colours,
    he made their tiny wings.

The rich man in his castle,
    the poor man at his gate,
God made them, high or lowly,
    and ordered their estate.

The purple headed mountain,
    the river running by,
the sunset and the morning
    that brightens up the sky;

the cold wind in the winter,
    the pleasant summer sun,
the ripe fruits in the garden, -
    he made them every one;

the tall trees in the greenwood,
    the meadows where we play,
the rushes by the water
    we gather every day;

he gave us eyes to see them,
    and lips that we might tell
how great is God Almighty
    who has made all things well.

(no. 12)

CHRISTINA GEORGINA
ROSSETTI, 1830-94
HG 335

309
THE SHEPHERDS HAD AN ANGEL

The Shepherds had an angel,
    the wise man had a star;
but what have I, a little child
    to guide me home from far,
where glad stars sing together
    and singing angels are?

Lord Jesus is my guardian,
    so I can nothing lack;   (Ps. 23:1)
the lambs lie in his bosom,   (Is. 40:11)
    along life's dangerous track;
the wilful lambs that go astray
    he bleeding fetches back.   (Matt. 18:12)

Lord Jesus is my guiding star,
    by beacon-light in heaven;
he leads me step by step along
    the path of life uneven;
he, true light, leads me to that land
    whose day shall be as seven.

Those Shepherds through the lonely night
    sat watching by their sheep,   (Luke 8:15)
until they saw the heavenly host
    who neither tire nor sleep
all singing 'Glory, glory'
    in festival they keep.

Christ watches me, his little lamb,
    cares for me day and night,
that I may be his own in heaven:
    so angels clad in white
shall sing their 'Glory, glory'
    for my sake in the height.

1856; in *Poetical Works*, 1894

ALBERT MIDLANE
1825-1909
HG 618

310
THERE'S A FRIEND FOR LITTLE CHILDREN

HG 728

There's a Friend for little children
    above the bright blue sky,
a Friend who never changes,
    whose love will never die;
our earthly friends may fail us,
    and change with changing
                  years,
this Friend is always worthy
    of that dear name he bears.

There's a rest for little children
    above the bright blue sky,
who love the blessèd Saviour
    and to the Father cry;
a rest from every trouble,
    from sin and danger free,
where every little pilgrim
    shall rest eternally.

There's a home for little children
    above the bright blue sky,
where Jesus reigns in glory,
    a home of peace and joy;
no home on earth is like it,
    nor can with it compare;
and every one is happy
    nor could be happier there.

There's a crown for little children
    above the bright blue sky,
and all who look to Jesus
    shall wear it by and by;
a crown of brightest glory,
    which he will then bestow
on those who found his favour
    and loved his name below.

There's a song for little children
    above the bright blue sky,
a song that will not weary,
    though sung continually;
a song which even angels
    can never, never sing;
they know not Christ as Saviour,
    but worship him as King.

There's a robe for little children
    above the bright blue sky,
and a harp of sweetest music,
    and palms of victory.
All, all above is treasured
    and found in Christ alone;
O come, dear little children,
    that all may be your own.

Good News for the Little Ones, 1859

(NOTE: the original order of stanzas, which is never preserved in hymnals was 2, 3, 1, 4, 5, 6. Observe the way in which a thought expressed more profoundly by Isaac Watts in #40 above is reflected in the second half of st. 5)

EMILY MILLER
1833-1913

311
I LOVE TO HEAR THE STORY

HG 317

I love to hear the story
    which angel voices tell,
how once the King of glory
    came down on earth to dwell.
I am both weak and sinful,
    but this I surely know,
the Lord came down to save me
    because he loved me so.

I'm glad my blessed Saviour
    was once a child like me,
to show how pure and holy
    his little ones might be;
and if I try to follow
    his footsteps here below,

he never will forsake me,
because he loves me so.

To tell his love and mercy
my sweetest songs I'll raise;
and though I cannot see him,
I know he hears my praise;
for he himself has promised
that even I may go
to sing among his angels,
because he loves me so.

The Little Corporal, 1867

SABINE BARING-GOULD
1834-1924
HG 493

312
NOW THE DAY IS OVER   HG 493

Now the day is over,
night is drawing nigh,
shadows of the evening
steal across the sky.

Now the darkness gathers,
stars begin to peep,
birds and beasts and flowers
soon will be asleep.

Jesu, give the weary
calm and sweet repose;
with thy tenderest blessing
may our eyelids close.

Grant to little children
visions bright of thee;
guard the sailors tossing
on the deep blue sea.

Comfort every sufferer
watching late in pain;
those who plan some evil
from their sin restrain.

Through the long night watches
may thine angels spread
their white wings above me
watching round my bed.

When the morning wakens,
then may I arise
pure, and fresh, and sinless
in thy holy eyes.

Glory to the Father,
glory to the Son,
and to thee, blest Spirit
whilst all ages run.

Church Times, 16 February, 1867
cf. ##232-3

ELIZABETH CECILIA
CLEPHANE, 1830-69
HG 82

313
THE LOST SHEEP
Matt. 18:12   HG 729

There were ninety and nine that safely lay
in the shelter of the fold,
and one was out on the hills away,
far off from the gates of gold;
away on the mountains wild and bare,
away from the tender Shepherd's care.

'Lord, thou hast here thy ninety and nine;
are they not enough for thee?'
But the Shepherd made answer: 'This of mine
has wandered away from me;
and although the road be rough and steep
I go to the desert to find my sheep.'

But none of the ransomed ever knew
how deep were the waters crossed;
nor how dark the night that the Lord passed through
ere he found his sheep that was lost.
Out in the desert he heard its cry -
sick and hopeless, and ready to die.

'Lord, whence are those blood-drops all the way,
that mark out the mountain's track?'
'They were shed for one that had gone astray
ere the Shepherd could bring him back.'
'Lord, whence are thy hands so rent and torn?'
'They are pierced tonight by many a thorn.'

And all through the mountains, thunder-riven,
and up from the rocky steep,
there arose a cry to the gates of heaven,
'Rejoice! I have found my sheep!'
And the angels echoed around the throne,
'Rejoice, for the Lord brings back his own.'   (Luke 15:10)

The Children's Hour, 1868

SARAH BETTS RHODES
(dates uncertain)

314
GOD, WHO MADE THE EARTH

God, who made the earth,
the air, the sky, the sea,
who gave the light its birth,
careth for me.

God, who made the grass,
the flower, the fruit, the tree,
the day and night to pass,
careth for me.

God, who made the sun,
the moon, the stars, is he
who, when life's clouds come on,
careth for me.

God, who made all things,
on earth, in air, in sea,
who changing seasons brings,
careth for me.

God, who sent his Son
to die on Calvary,
he if I lean on him
will care for me.

When in heaven's bright land
I all his loved ones see,
I'll sing with that blest band,
'God cared for me.'

1870; in *Methodist Sunday School
Hymn Book*, 1879

WILLIAM WALSHAM HOW,
Bishop
1823-97
HG 75

315
A THING MOST WONDERFUL   HG 341

It is a thing most wonderful,
almost too wonderful to be,
that God's own Son should come from heaven
to die to save a child like me.

And yet I know that it is true;
he chose a poor and humble lot,
and wept, and toiled, and mourned, and died
for love of those who loved him not.

I cannot tell how he could love
a child so weak and full of sin;
his love must be most wonderful
if he could die my love to win.

I sometimes think about the Cross,
and shut my eyes, and try to see
the cruel nails and crown of thorns,
and Jesus crucified for me.

But even could I see him die,
I could but see a little part
of that great love, which, like a fire
is always burning in his heart.

It is most wonderful to know
his love for me so free and pure;
but 'tis more wonderful to see
my love for him so faint and poor.

And yet I want to love thee, Lord;
O light the flame within my heart,
and I will love thee more and more
until I see thee as thou art.

Children's Hymns (SPCK), 1872

ROBERT STEPHEN HAWKER
of Morwenstow*
1804-73

316
THE CHILDREN'S HYMN

Sing to the Lord the children's hymn,
his gentle love declare,
who bends amid the seraphim
to hear the children's prayer.

He at a Mother's breast was fed,
though God's own Son was he;
he learnt the first small words he said
at a meek Mother's knee.

He held us to his mighty breast,
the children of the earth;
he lifted up his hands and blessed
the babes of human birth.

Lo! from the stars his face will turn
on us with glances mild;
the angels of his presence yearn
to bless the little child.

Keep us, O Jesus, Lord, for thee,
that so, by thy dear grace,
we, children of the font, may see
our heavenly Father's face.

Poetical Works (posth.), 1879

JOHN ELLERTON
1826-93
HG 80

317
HAIL TO THE LORD WHO COMES   HG 262

Hail to the Lord who comes,
comes to his temple gate!
Not with his angel host
not in his kingly state;
no shouts proclaim him nigh,
no crowds his coming wait;

but borne upon the throne
of Mary's gentle breast,
watched by her duteous love,
in her fond arms at rest;
thus to his Father's house,
he comes, the heavenly Guest.

There Joseph at her side
in reverent wonder stands;
and, filled with holy joy,
old Simeon in his hands   (Lk. 2:28)
takes up the promised child,
the glory of all lands.

Hail to the great First-born
whose ransom price they pay!
The Son before all worlds   (Jn. 8:58)
the Child of man to-day,
that he might ransom us
who still in bondage lay!

O Light of all the earth,
thy children wait for thee!
Come to thy temples here   (Mal. 3:1)
that we, from sin set free,
before thy Father's face
may all presented be!

The Children's Hymn Book, 1881

WALTER J. MATHAMS
1853-1931

318
THE CHILDREN'S FRIEND   HG 348

Jesus, Friend of little children,
be a friend to me;
take my soul, and ever keep me
close to thee.

Show me what my love should cherish,
    what, too, it should shun;
lest my feet for poison flowers
    swift should run.

Teach me how to grow in goodness,
    daily as I grow;
thou hast been a Child, and surely
    thou shouldst know.

Fill me with thy gentle meekness,
    make my heart like thine;
like an altar lamp, then let me
    burn and shine.

Step by step, oh, lead me onward,
    upward into youth;
wiser, stronger, still becoming
    in thy truth.

Never leave me, nor forsake me,
    ever be my Friend;
for I need thee from life's dawning
    to its end.

Psalms and Hymns for School and Home, 1882

EUSTACE ROGERS CONDER*
1820-92

319
THE CHILDHOOD OF CHRIST

Ye fair green hills of Galilee,
    that girdle quiet Nazareth,
what glorious vision did ye see
    when he who conquered sin and death
your flowery slopes and summits trod,
and grew in grace with man and God?

We saw no glory crown his head,
    as childhood ripened into youth;
no angels on his errands sped;
    he wrought no sign. But meekness, truth
and duty marked each step he trod,
and love to man, and love to God.

Jesus! my Saviour, Master, King,
    who didst for me the burden bear,
while saints in heaven thy glory sing,
    let me on earth thy likeness wear.
Mine be the path thy feet have trod, -
duty and love to man and God.

Congregational Church Hymnal, 1887

More children's hymns
at 480-6, 529-35.

ARTICLE 17:
IRISH AND SCOTTISH HYMNODY (320-348)

Scotland and Ireland share a basic Celtic tradition which in Ireland is kept culturally separate from the Protestant tradition of Ulster while in Scotland it is mixed much more freely with the Nordic. Tradition has it that St Patrick (#320) took Christianity to Ireland from Gaul (France) in the late 4th century and founded the Catholic-Celtic pattern of Christianity which is still so peculiarly and natively Irish. Tradition also says (history cannot be asked to document it) that St Patrick wrote the old

Irish original of the 'Breastplate' under circumstances recounted in the *Hymnal Guide* at no. 626.

Whatever historians may eventually find to confirm or refute this, the two versions of the *Breastplate* now in currency make two fine and spacious hymns. Mrs Alexander's translation, easily her finest piece of hymnic literature and written forty years after she began writing hymns, makes of it a credal recitation, entirely appropriate to the ancient rites of baptism (and supremely appropriate to the celebrations of Holy Saturday, or Easter Eve, which are so closely associated in the early church with baptism and confirmation). The Scottish translation of MacAlister is closer to the original and has a slightly greater emphasis on the form of incantation, a primitive song by which the singer warded off the evil spirits and demons whose design was to frustrate his faith. But in both there is a very primitive blending of supernatural faith and natural experience; whether it is a matter of 'binding to myself' or 'arising in the strength of' the subjects of the verses, the sea and rocks and sun and moon are treated on equal terms with the articles of the faith. Since Christian faith is not least a matter of coming to proper terms with the created world, there is nothing theologically improper in this; on the contrary, both hymns in a way not found elsewhere bring heaven and earth together.

St Columba marked the next step in the evangelization of the Celts in taking the faith from Ireland to the west of Scotland and from his centre at Iona dispersing the faith to the mainland. If he is responsible for the Latin original of #321 and the Irish of #322, he has left us two vividly contrasted poems; the Latin one being dogmatic, the Irish one, a song of experience.

Nos. 323 and 324, the former probably medieval, the latter undated, follow the manner of #322 in their highly personal diction, and it will be seen that the Latin poem of Columba is an exception to the normal manner of Celtic song.

Of course, none of this is, in the modern sense, hymnody until it has been translated into hymn-form by English-speaking scholars. The Celtic church was not a hymn-singing church, but the Celts are an essentially poetic people, full of rhyme and music, and this handful of poems, which in translation now enrich the repertory of hymns, brings to that repertory a touch of homespun earthiness that is very welcome when it is contrasted with the rigid liturgical hymnody of the Latin-speaking church, or indeed with the over-spiritualized songs which tend to be contemporary with the translations.

No. 325 is from a Gaelic original written by a relatively modern Gaelic bard; this and the now well-known carol, #326, are about all we have from Gaelic singers of the 19th century. No. 325 is a most attractive piece, based so clearly in the Psalter; and #326 has made its way through being wedded to a haunting tune, as has #324.

If a first appearance in a manuscript from an Irish monastery is evidence of Irish origin, then the original of the Communion hymn, 'Draw nigh and take the body of the Lord' (*EH* 307), and the carol, *Angelus ad Virginem* (*Oxford Book of Carols*, 52), should be added to this list.

But in Scotland the Celtic culture has long had its competitors. There has always been a Catholic stream outside the Gaelic-speaking tradition. There is no direct evidence that William Drummond of Hawthornden was himself a Catholic; but his translation of #327 (which could have been in section 11 but is included here for its Scottish origin) appeared in an English *Primer of the Blessed Virgin* with 18 other hymns and translations ascribed to him, and the making of English versions of medieval Office hymns was not an activity characteristic of Scottish Protestants of the time. This tiny but exquisite piece contains more poetry than most such translations. Apart from this we have no poetry from English-speaking Catholic Scotland.

Far more characteristic, of course, is metrical psalmody (see article 2), and we offer one example of King James VI's complete psalter to show how this exalted writer went to work. The reader will find no difficulty in deducing why the Assembly, hard pressed by one party to adopt this as the authorized psalter, could not see its way to doing so. Musicians would have been hard pressed finding workable tunes for meters like this. The Protestant, Edinburgh-based Scotland of John Knox had no need for hymns; private versions of the psalter were the only variations on psalmody we find until the *Paraphrases* were authorized in 1781 (see article 10). Our #329, which jerks us abruptly into the conventional hymn-singing culture, is the work of an early Scottish Congregationalist and appeared in one of the first hymnals used by that denomination, which, quite unlike the English form of this church-order, was an evangelical reaction *against* Calvinism that began shortly before 1800.

No. 330 was a private venture by a leading Scottish man of letters who was learned in the lore of Europe at a time when few people were, and it remains for Britishers the accepted translation of 'Ein' feste Burg,' more rugged and eloquent than the American version but at one or two points less easy to sing as hymnody–lines 5-8 of the last stanza are a very awkward corner. The zealous and short-lived McCheyne, one of Scotland's most strenuous and celebrated preachers and evangelists, wrote #331 as a devotional poem; its intense spiritual power has attracted the notice of a few hymnal editors, who occasionally adjust the meter of st. 1 to accommodate the singers. This has a touch of the Wesleys in it and, though hardly intended as a hymn, remains one of the greatest devotional pieces Scotland produced in that age.

Nor was #332 aimed at a hymn book–hymns were still not wanted in Scotland–but it was not long after the authorization of hymnody in Scotland that editors grabbed it. Its author was a professor of classics at Edinburgh, and he allows himself a grand freedom of language in his versification of the *Benedicite*. George Macdonald, more a novelist and philosopher than a poet, wrote a few hymns at an early stage (he was for a year or two a Congregational minister in England) of which perhaps it is #333 that is the most useful. And Scotland certainly did produce some good translators: Jane Borthwick (334) and her sister Sarah Findlater in *Hymns from the Land of Luther* (1858) very ably supported the work of Catherine Winkworth (see article 15).

But it is really Horatius Bonar (335-8) who must be called Protestant Scotland's first hymn writer. He was a minister of the Free Church, this communion being the product of the 'Disruption' of 1843 when the Scottish Church split almost down the middle on theological grounds, leaving on one side the Church of Scotland, espousing the conservative cause, and on the other the Free Kirk, which gathered in people of more liberal view. It is natural that the first substantial contribution to hymnody from Scotland should come from that side. Bonar was facile and suffered much from too little self-criticism; too often the contents of *Hymns of Faith and Hope*, three plump little volumes, are garrulous and unevenly written. And not seldom they drink over-deeply of sentimentality. But as an evangelical romantic, Bonar produced work which, with careful pruning, appealed very widely. No. 335 is a good

romantic ballad; #336 I should judge his finest piece, and #337, with half its stanzas taken out, remains deservedly popular. No. 338 comes from a much later date and competes with #336 for the first place; perhaps its unusual modesty and contemplative gentleness gives it the right to be thought of as his best. It is not easy to forgive a writer who could describe the Eucharist, as he did in one of his very well-known hymns, as 'this brief, bright hour of fellowship with thee'; but one can imagine that if hymnody for Scotland was in any sense liberated by him, the very pressure generated by three centuries of prohibition might produce occasional light-headedness in the writing.

If Bonar is the Free Kirk's first hymnist, James Burns (339-40) is usually regarded as the Church of Scotland's first. Compared with Bonar he was less prolific, though hardly more inspired. He shows the same tendency to slip into over-amiable language; #339 was at one time very popular, and history explains why. No. 340 is more vivid and pictorial, a very good children's hymn still, once the lines in st. 2 have been altered from their original form, which caused too many sniggers amongst the young to be allowed to survive:

> The old man meek and mild,
> the priest of Israel slept,
> his watch the temple child,
> the little Levite kept.

(Less casual study of the Scripture forbids us to insist that Samuel at the time was anything younger than a teenager–but never mind.)

With #341 we meet something very different. It can always be shown that when Scotland imitates England it corrupts itself, and that is certainly the case with hymn writers. But in these stanzas from a much longer poem made by Mrs Cousin out of sayings of the venerable 17th-century sage, Samuel Rutherford, we have a warmth and vision that are from beginning to end strictly Scottish. Anyone who can read sts. 2 and 4 unmoved has no soul for prayer.

No. 342 should give the reader a moment's pause. Most readers will think they know this hymn, the work of another Free Kirk minister. But it never now appears as its author wrote it, and a closer look at it in its fuller form shows that it was by no means designed to be one of those general hymns of praise that the parson slams into the praise-list when he is in too much of a hurry to think of anything else but a hymn about the reading of Scripture. Just occasionally editorial tinkering changes the whole personality of a hymn; it has certainly done so here.

We are back to personal devotion with ##343-4. Principal Shairp, Scottish man of letters, one of the very few Scottish laymen who ever wrote a hymn, takes in #343 much the same line as Burns did in #339, but he does it with greater poise. The end of st. 2 has quite unusual distinction. With the more famous George Matheson, we are back in the Kirk of Scotland, and indeed in the parish manse. No. 344 is the one everybody knows. It won a famous tune immediately after being written, and perhaps so delicate a piece should not have ever been exposed to the draughts of congregational singing; but it is real writing, without a word out of place, the work of a natural lyricist. Perhaps one needs to know the delectable folk song 'The Queen's Maries' (all about Mary Queen of Scots and three other friends called Mary) to appreciate the artistry of #345, a poem which only one editor, English, but possibly the greatest of them all, spotted for a hymnal (it is in *Worship Song*). The better known #346 expresses a theology which, at the turn of this century, was very popular, went later into complete eclipse, and has now almost entirely returned to favour. But this hymn got lost in the Barthian period.

No. 347 is known only in America as a hymn; it owes something to the great 'Breastplate,' and has a lyric, almost runic rhythm which is rather captivating. No. 348 is the best known of MacNicol's translations from the works of Tilak, an Indian Christian whom we shall meet again in article 28.

Scottish hymnody, then, is never a very broad stream, though the evangelical revivals generated a good deal of it, and the offerings of Scottish liberals were gratefully received by English editors who wanted relief from episcopal and decanal pedagogy. It might have continued in the same placid way had it not been for the development which we shall celebrate in article 23.

Celtic tradition

320
SAINT PATRICK'S BREASTPLATE   HG 626

(A)

I bind unto myself to-day
  the strong name of the Trinity,
by invocation of the same
  the Three in One and One in Three.

I bind this day to me for ever
  by power of faith, Christ's
              incarnation;
his baptism in Jordan river,
  his death on Cross for my
              salvation;
his bursting from the spicèd tomb,
  his riding up the heavenly way,
his coming at the day of doom
  I bind unto myself to-day.

I bind unto myself the power
  of the great love of Cherubim;
the sweet 'Well done' in judg-
              ment hour,
  the service of the Seraphim,
Confessors' faith, Apostles' word,
  the Patriarchs' prayers, the
              prophets' scrolls,
all good deeds done unto the
              Lord
  and purity of virgin souls.

I bind unto myself to-day
  the virtues of the star-lit heaven,
the glorious sun's life-giving ray,
  the whiteness of the moon at
              even,
the flashing of the lightning free,
  the whirling wind's tempes-
              tuous shocks,
the stable earth, the deep salt sea
  around the old eternal rocks.

I bind unto myself to-day
  the power of God to hold and
              lead,
his eye to watch, his might to stay,
  his ear to hearken to my need.

The wisdom of my God to teach,
  his hand to guide, his shield to
              ward;
the word of God to give me
              speech,
  his heavenly host to be my
              guard.

Against the demon snares of sin,
  the vice that gives temptation
              force,
the natural lusts that war within,
  the hostile men that mar my
              course;
or few or many, far or nigh,
  in every place and in all hours,
against their fierce hostility
  I bind to me those holy powers.

Against all Satan's spells and wiles,
  against false words of heresy,
against the knowledge that defiles,
  against the heart's idolatry,
against the wizard's evil craft,
  against the death-wound and
              the burning,
the choking wave, the poisoned
              shaft,
  protect me, Christ, till thy
              returning.

Christ be with me, Christ within
              me,
  Christ behind me, Christ before
              me,
Christ beside me, Christ to win me,
  Christ to comfort and restore
              me.
Christ beneath me, Christ above
              me,

Christ in quiet, Christ in danger,
Christ in hearts of all that love me,
  Christ in mouth of friend and
              stranger.

I bind unto myself the name,
  the strong name of the Trinity,

by invocation of the same,
  the Three in One and One in
              Three.
Of whom all nature hath creation,
  eternal Father, Spirit, Word:
praise to the Lord of my salvation,
  salvation is of Christ the Lord.

ST PATRICK, 372-466: tr. **Cecil Frances Alexander** (HG 29), 1889

(B)

To-day I arise
invoking the Blessed Trinity,
confessing the Blessed Unity,
Creator of all the things that be.

To-day I arise
by strength of Christ and his mystic birth,
by his Passion and Triumph's saving worth,
by his coming again to judge the earth.

To-day I arise
by seraphs serving the Lord above,
by truths his ancient heralds prove,
by saints in purity, labour, love.

To-day I arise
by splendour of sun and flaming brand,
by rushing wind, by lightning grand,
by depth of sea, by strength of land.

To-day I arise
with God my steersman, stay and guide,
to guard, to counsel, to hear, to bide,
his way before, his hosts beside.

Protecting me now
from crafty wiles of demon crew,
from foemen, be they many or few,
from lusts that I can scarce subdue.

Lord Jesus the Christ,
to-day surround me with thy might;
before, behind, on left and right,
be thou in breadth, in length, in height.

Direct and control
the minds of all who think on me,
the lips of all who speak to me,
the eyes of all who look on me.

To-day I arise,
invoking the Blessed Trinity,
confessing the Blessed Unity,
Saviour, on us salvation be!

tr. **R. A. S. MacAlister** (HG 626), 1927

321
THE HYMNS OF ST COLUMBA   HG 855

(i)

Have mercy, Christ, have mercy
   on all that trust in thee,
for thou art God in glory,
   to all eternity.

O God, make speed to save us
   in life's abounding throes;
O God, make haste to help us
   in all our weary woes.

O God, thou art the Father
   of all that have believed;
from whom all hosts of angels
   have life and power received.

O God, thou art the Former
   of all created things:
the righteous Judge of judges,
   the Almighty King of kings.

The God whose power and glory
   thy countless creatures show -
the love of all above us,
   the dread of all below.

High in the heavenly Sion
   thou reignest God adored;
and in the coming glory
   thou shalt be sovereign Lord.

Beyond our ken thou shinest,
   the everlasting light;
ineffable in loving,
   unthinkable in might.

Thou to the meek and lowly
   thy secrets dost unfold;
O God, thou knowest all things,
   all things both new and old.

I walk secure and blessed,
   in every clime and coast,
in Name of God the Father
   and Son, and Holy Ghost.

(ii)

Christ is the world's Redeemer,
   the lover of the pure,
the font of heavenly wisdom,
   our trust and hope secure;

the armour of his soldiers,
   the Lord of earth and sky;
our health while we are living,
   our life when we shall die.

Christ hath our host surrounded
   with clouds of martyrs bright,
who wave their palms in triumph
   and fire us for the fight.

Christ the red cross ascended
   to save a world undone,
and suffering for the sinful
   our full redemption won.

Down in the realm of darkness
   he lay, a captive bound,
but at the hour appointed
   he rose a victor crowned.

And now to heaven ascended,
   he sits upon the throne,
whence he had ne'er departed,
   his Father's and his own.

All glory to the Father,
   the unbegotten One,
all honour be to Jesus,
   his sole-begotten Son;

and to the Holy Spirit -
   the perfect Trinity.
Let all the worlds give answer -
   'Amen. So let it be!'

In te, Christe, credentium, attr. to **ST
COLUMBA**, 521-597; tr. by **Duncan
MacGregor**, 1898

322
'THOUGH HE SLAY ME . . .'

Alone with none but thee, my God,
   I journey on my way:
what need I fear, when thou art near,
   O King of night and day?
More safe I am within thy hand
than if a host did round me stand.

My destined time is fixed by thee,
   and Death doth know his hour.
Did warriors strong around me throng,
   they could not stay his power;
no walls of stone can man defend
when thou thy messenger dost send.

My life I yield to thy decree,
   and bow to thy control,
in peaceful calm, for from thine arm
   no power can wrest my soul.
Could earthly omens e'er appall
a man that heeds the heavenly call?

The child of God can fear no ill,
   his chosen dread no foe;
we leave our fate with thee, and wait
   thy bidding when to go.
'Tis not from chance our comfort springs:
thou art our Trust, O King of kings.

Poem in the Irish language, attributed
to **ST COLUMBA**, anonymously translated in the Irish *Church Hymnal,*1919

323

How great the tale, that there should be
in God's Son's heart a place for me!
That on a sinner's lips like mine
the cross of Jesus Christ should shine!

Christ Jesus, bend me to thy will,
my feet to urge, my griefs to still;
that e'en my flesh and blood may be
a temple sanctified to thee.

No rest, no calm, my soul may win,
because my body craves to sin;
till thou, dear Lord, thyself impart
peace on my head, light in my heart.

May consecration come from far,
soft shining like the evening star!
My toilsome path make plain to me,
until I come to rest in thee.

MURDOCH O'DALY of Connacht,*
d. 1244, tr. **Eleanor Hull** (HG 72), 1912

324
BE THOU MY VISION   HG 72

Be thou my Vision, O Lord of my heart,
naught be all else to me, save that thou art;
thou my best thought in the day and the night,
waking or sleeping, thy presence my light.

Be thou my Wisdom, be thou my true Word,
I ever with thee, and thou with me, Lord;
thou my great Father, and I thy dear son,
thou in me dwelling, and I with thee one.

Be thou my breastplate, my sword for the fight,
be thou my armour, and be thou my might;
thou my soul's shelter, and thou my high tower,
raise thou me heavenward, O Power of my power.

Riches I heed not, not man's empty praise,
thou mine inheritance through all my days;
thou, and thou only, the first in my heart,
high King of heaven, my treasure thou art!

High king of heav'n, when the battle is done,
grant heaven's joys to me, O bright heav'n's sun!
Heart of my own heart, whatever befall,
still be my Vision, O Ruler of all.

Old Irish poem, tr. **Mary Byrne** and
versified by Eleanor Hull, 1912. Text as
in Irish *Church Hymnal*, 1919

325
A SHLANUIGHEAR RO GLORMHOR

O Lord, I sing thy praises,
  who art my strength and stay,
my leader through life's mazes,
  to bring me to thy way:
thou didst not leave me straying
  when I afar would go   (Matt. 18:12)
with heedless footsteps playing
  upon the brink of woe.

For thou, thy glory showing,
  mad'st me thy beauty see:
thy love has been bestowing
  new life and joy on me.
Thou grace and glory givest,   (Ps. 84:11)
  thou art a Sun and Shield,
thou only ever livest,
  thy words salvation yield.

O lord, do not forsake me,
  but guide me as a friend;
and strong in heart still make me
  for what thy love may send.
Through death's dark vale victorious   (Ps. 23:4)
  O let me lean on thee,
and let me see thee glorious
  through all eternity.

PETER GRANT of Strathspey,* 1783-
1867, tr. from the Gaelic by **Lachlan
Macbean** (HG 102), 1900

326
LEANABH AN AIGH   HG 102

Child in the manger,
  infant of Mary;
outcast and stranger,
  Lord of all!
Child who inherits
  all our transgressions,
all our demerits
  on his fall.

Monarchs have tender
  delicate children,
nourished in splendour,
  proud and gay;
death soon shall banish
  honour and beauty,
pleasure shall vanish,
  forms decay.

But the most holy
  Child of salvation
gently and lowly
  lived below;

now as our glorious
  mighty Redeemer,
see him victorious
  o'er each foe.

Prophets foretold him
  infant of wonder;
angels behold him
  on his throne;
worthy our Saviour
  of all their praises;
happy for ever
  are his own.

MARY MACDONALD, 1817- ?90; tr.
from the Gaelic by **Lachlan Macbean**,
1900

327   HG 865

O lux beata Trinitas,
et principalis unitas,
iam sol recedit igneus,
infunde lumen cordibus.

O Trinity, O blessèd Light,
  O Unity, most principal,
the fiery sun now leaves our sight:
  cause in our hearts thy beams to
                   fall.

Te mane laudum carmine,
te deprecemur vesperi,

Let us with songs of praise divine
  at morn and evening thee
                implore;

te nostra supplex gloria
per cuncta laudet saecula.

and let our glory, bowed to thine
  thee glorify for evermore.

Deo patri sit gloria,
eiusque soli Filio,
cum Spiritu Paraclito,
et nunc et in perpetuum.

To God the Father glory great,
  and glory to his only Son,
and to the Holy Paraclete
  both now and still while ages
                run.

Middle period

WILLIAM DRUMMOND of Hawthorn-
den, 1585-1649
*Primer or Office of the Blessed Virgin
Mary*, 1619

KING JAMES VI of Scotland*
1566-1625

328
THE FIRST PSALM

(Scottish spelling)

That mortal man most happy is and blest
  who in the wickeds counsals doth not walk,
nor zit in sunners wayis doth stay and rest   (that)
  Nor sittis in seats of skornfull men in talk
    but contrair fixis his delicht
      into Jehouas law
    and on his law both day and nicht
      to think is never slaw.   (slow)

He salbe lyk a plesant plantit tree   (shall be)
  vpon a reuer syde increasing tal,   (river)
that yieldis his frute in saison dew, we see;
  whose plesant leif doth neuer fade nor fal.
    Now this is surely for to say
      that quhat he takis in hand,
    it sal withoutin doute alway
      most prosperously stand.

Bot wicked men ar nowayis of that band;
    but as the caffe quhich be the wind is tost (chaff...by)
thairfor they sall not in that iugement stand
nor yett among the iust be sinneris lost.
    For gret Jehoua cleirly knowis
        the iust mans way upricht
    but sure the wickeds way that throwis
        sall perish be his micht.

Psalms (posth.), 1631

RALPH WARDLAW
1779-1853

329
LET GOD ARISE!   HG 541

O Lord our God, arise!
    the cause of truth maintain,
and wide o'er all the peopled world
    extend her blessed reign.

Thou Prince of life, arise!
    nor let thy glory cease;
far spread the conquests of thy grace,
    and bless the earth with peace.

Thou Holy Ghost, arise!
    Expand thy quickening wing,
and o'er a dark and ruined world
    let light and order spring.

All on the earth, arise!
    To God the Saviour sing:
from shore to shore, from earth to heaven,
    let echoing anthems ring.

*A Collection of Hymns for the Use of
the Tabernacles in Scotland,* 1800

THOMAS CARLYLE
1795-1881
translating
Martin Luther

330
EIN' FESTE BURG
[cf. 4]   HG 847

A safe stronghold our God is still,
    a trusty shield and weapon;
he'll help us clear from all the ill
    that hath us now o'ertaken.
        The ancient prince of hell
        hath ris'n with purpose fell;
    strong mail of craft and power
    he weareth in this hour;
    on earth is not his fellow.

With force of arms we nothing can,
    full soon were we down-ridden;
but for us fights the proper Man,
    whom God himself hath bidden.
        Ask ye, who is this same?
        Christ Jesus is his name,
    the Lord Sabaoth's Son,
    he and no other one
    shall conquer in the battle.

And were this world all devils o'er,
    and watching to devour us;
we lay it not to heart so sore;

not they can overpower us.
    and let the prince of ill
    look grim as e'er he will,
    he harms us not a whit;
    for why, his doom is writ;
    a word shall quickly slay him.

God's word, for all their craft and force
    one moment shall not linger,
but, spite of hell, shall have its course:
    'tis written by his finger.
        And though they take our life,
        good, honour, children, wife,
    yet is their profit small;
    these things shall vanish all:
    the city of God remaineth.

Fraser's Magazine, 1831

ROBERT MURRAY
McCHEYNE, 1813-43

331
THE BEATIFIC VISION   HG 811

When this passing world is done,
when has sunk yon glaring sun,
when we stand with Christ in glory,
looking o'er life's finished story,
then, Lord, shall I fully know,
not till then, how much I owe.   (Lk. 7:43)

When I stand before the throne,
dressed in beauty not my own,
when I see thee as thou art,
love thee with unsinning heart,
then, Lord, shall I fully know,
not till then, how much I owe.

When the praise of heaven I hear,
loud as thunders to the ear,
loud as many waters' noise,
sweet as harp's melodious voice,
then, Lord, shall I fully know,
not till then, how much I owe.

Even on earth, as through a glass   (1 Cor. 13:8)
darkly, let thy glory pass;   (Ex. 33:18)
make forgiveness feel so sweet;
make thy Spirit's help so meet;
even on earth, Lord, make me know
something of how much I owe.

Scottish Christian Herald, 1837

JOHN STUART BLACKIE
1809-95

332
BENEDICITE OMNIA OPERA   HG 47

Angels holy,
    high and lowly,
sing the praises of the Lord!
earth and sky, all living nature,
man, the stamp of thy Creator,
    praise ye, praise ye God the Lord!

Sun and moon bright,
    night and noonlight,
starry temples, azure-floored,

cloud and rain, and wild wind's madness,
breeze that floats with genial gladness,
    praise ye, praise ye God the Lord!

    Ocean hoary,
    tell his glory;
cliffs, where tumbling seas have roared,
pulse of waters, blithely beating,
wave advancing, wave retreating,
    praise ye, praise ye God the Lord!

    Rock and high land,
    wood and island,
crag, where eagle's pride hath soared,
mighty mountains, purple-breasted,
peaks cloud-cleaving, snowy-crested,
    praise ye, praise ye God the Lord!

    Rolling river,
    praise him ever,
from the mountain's deep vein poured;
silver fountain, clearly gushing,
troubled torrent madly rushing,
    praise ye, praise ye God the Lord!

    Bond and free man,
    land and sea man,
earth with peoples widely stored,
wanderer lone o'er prairies ample,
full-voiced choir in costly temple,
    praise ye, praise ye God the Lord!

    Praise him ever,
    bounteous giver:
praise him, Father, Friend and Lord;
each glad soul its free course winging,
each blithe voice its free song singing,
    praise the great and mighty Lord!

The Inquirer, 1840

GEORGE MACDONALD
1824-1905
HG 539

333
BLESSED ARE THE POOR IN SPIRIT

Our Father, hear our longing prayer,
    and help this prayer to flow,
that humble thoughts, which are thy care
    may live in us and grow.

For lowly hearts shall understand
    the peace, the calm delight
of dwelling in thy heavenly land,
    a pleasure in thy sight.

Give us humility, that so
    thy reign may come within,
and when thy children homeward go
    we too may enter in.

Hear us, our Saviour; ours thou art,
    though we are not like thee;
give us thy Spirit in our heart,
    large, lowly, trusting, free.

*Hymns and Songs for Sunday Schools
and Social Worship*, 1855

JANE LAURIE BORTHWICK
1813-97
translating
Katharina von Schlegel (1752)

334
BE STILL, MY SOUL
(Stille, mein Wille)   HG 70

Be still, my soul: the Lord is on thy side;
    bear patiently the cross of grief or pain;
leave to thy God to order and provide;
    in every change he faithful will remain.
Be still, my soul: thy best, thy heavenly Friend
through thorny ways leads to a joyful end.

Be still, my soul: thy God doth undertake
    to guide the future as he has the past.
Thy hope, thy confidence let nothing shake;
    all now mysterious shall be bright at last.
Be still, my soul: the waves and winds still know
his voice who ruled them while he dwelt below. (Mk. 4:41)

Be still, my soul: when dearest friends depart,
    and all is darkened in the vale of tears,
then shalt thou better know his love, his heart,
    who comes to soothe thy sorrow and thy fears.
Be still, my soul: thy Jesus can repay,
from his own fulness, all he takes away.

Be still, my soul: the hour is hastening on
    when we shall be for ever with the Lord,
when disappointment, grief and fear are gone,
    sorrow forgot, love's purest joys restored.
Be still, my soul: when change and tears are past,
all safe and blessèd we shall meet at last.

Hymns from the Land of Luther, 1855

HORATIUS BONAR
1807-89
HG 81

335
COME UNTO ME
Matt. 11:28   HG 311

I heard the voice of Jesus say,
    'Come unto me and rest,
lay down, thou weary one, lay down
    thy head upon my breast.'
I came to Jesus, as I was,
    weary, and worn, and sad;
I found in him a resting place,
    and he has made me glad.

I heard the voice of Jesus say,
    'Behold, I freely give   (Rev. 22:17)
the living water: thirsty one
    stoop down, and drink, and live.'
I came to Jesus, and I drank
    of what life-giving stream;
my thirst was quenched, my soul revived,
    and now I live in him.   (Gal. 2:20)

I heard the voice of Jesus say,
    'I am this dark world's light;   (John 8:12)
look unto me, thy morn shall rise,
    and all the day be bright.'
I looked to Jesus, and I found
    in him my Star, my Sun;
and in that Light of life I'll walk
    till travelling days are done.

Hymns Original and Selected, 1846

336
THE LOVE OF GOD   HG 546

O Love of God, how strong and true!
Eternal and yet ever new,
uncomprehended and unbought,
beyond all knowledge and all thought! -

O love of God, how deep and great!
far deeper than man's deepest hate;
self-fed, self-kindled like the light,
changeless, eternal, infinite! -

O heavenly love, how precious still
in days of weariness and ill,
in nights of pain and helplessness,
to heal, to comfort and to bless! -

O wide-embracing, wondrous love,
we read thee in the sky above,
we read thee in the earth below,
in seas that swell and streams that flow!

We read thee best in him who came
to bear for us the cross of shame,
sent by the Father from on high,
our life to live, our death to die.

We read thee in the manger-bed
on which his infancy was laid;
and Nazareth that love reveals,
nestling amid its lonely hills.

We read thee in the tears once shed   (Luke 19:41)
over doomed Salem's guilty head,
in the cold tomb of Bethany,
and blood-drops of Gethsemane.

We read thy power to bless and save
ev'n in the darkness of the grave;
still more in resurrection-light
we read the fulness of thy might.

O love of God, our shield and stay,
through all the perils of our way;
eternal love, in thee we rest,
for ever safe, for ever blest!

Hymns of Faith & Hope II, 1861

337
LIFE'S PRAISE   HG 194

Fill thou my life, O Lord my God,
    in every part with praise,
that my whole being may proclaim
    thy being and thy ways.
Not for the lip of praise alone,
    nor ev'n the praising heart
I ask, but for a life made up
    of praise in every part.

Praise in the common things of life,
    its goings out and in,
praise in each duty and each deed,
    however small and mean.
Praise in the common words I speak,
    life's common looks and tones,
in intercourse at hearth or board
    with my belovèd ones.

★   ★   ★

Fill every part of me with praise;
    let all my being speak
of thee and of thy love, O Lord,
    poor though I be and weak.
So shalt thou, Lord, from me, ev'n me,
    receive the glory due,
and so shall I begin on earth
    the song for ever new.

So shall each fear, each fret, each care,
    be turnèd into song,
and every winding of the way
    the echo shall prolong.
So shall no part of day or night
    from sacredness be free,
but all my life, in every step
    be fellowship with thee.

Hymns of Faith & Hope III, 1863

338
BELOVED, LET US LOVE
1 John 4:7   HG 81

Beloved, let us love;
    love is of God;
in God alone hath love
    its true abode.

Beloved, let us love:
    for they who love,
they only, are his sons,
    born from above.   (John 3:7)

Beloved, let us love;
    for love is rest,
and he who loveth not
    abides unblest.   (1 John 4:8)

Beloved, let us love;
    in love is light,
and he who loveth not
    dwelleth in night.   (1 John 2:11)

Beloved, let us love;
    for only thus
shall we be with that God
    who loveth us.

Psalms and Hymns (Supplement), 1880

JAMES DRUMMOND BURNS
1823-64
The Evening Hymn, 1857
HG 60

339
TRUSTFULNESS

As helpless as a child who clings
    fast to his father's arm,
and casts his weakness on the strength
    that keeps him safe from harm,
so I, my Father, cling to thee,
    and thus I every hour
would link my earthly feebleness
    to thine almighty power.

As trustful as a child who looks
  up to his mother's face,
and all his little griefs and fears
  forgets in her embrace,
so I to thee, my Saviour, look,
  and in thy face divine
can read the love that will sustain
  as weak a faith as mine.

As loving as a child who sits
  close by his parent's knee,
and knows no want while he can have
  that sweet society,
so, sitting at thy feet, my heart
  would all its love outpour,
and pray that thou wouldst teach me, Lord,
  to love thee more and more.

340
SAMUEL
I Sam. 3   HG 302

Hushed was the evening hymn,
  the temple-courts were dark,
the lamp was burning dim
  before the sacred Ark;
when suddenly a voice divine
rang through the silence of the shrine.

* The priest of Israel slept,
  the old man meek and mild,
watch in the temple kept
  the little Levite child;
and what from Eli's sense was sealed
to Hannah's son the Lord revealed.

O give me Samuel's ear,
  the open ear, O Lord,
alive and quick to hear
  each whisper of thy word;
Like him to answer to the call,
and to obey thee first of all.

O give me Samuel's heart,
  a lowly heart that waits
when in thy house thou art,
  or watches at thy gates;
by day and night a heart that still
moves at the breathing of thy will.

O give me Samuel's mind,
  a sweet unmurmuring faith
obedient and resigned
  to thee in life and death;
that I may read with childlike eyes
truths that are hidden from the wise.   (Lk. 10:21)

    * st. 2 follows a later text (1916)

ANNE ROSS COUSIN
1824-1906

341
IMMANUEL'S LAND   HG 712

The sands of time are sinking;
  the dawn of heaven breaks;
the summer morn I've longed for,
  the fair, sweet morn, awakes.

Dark, dark hath been the midnight;
  but dayspring is at hand,
and glory, glory dwelleth
  in Immanuel's land.

The King there in his beauty   (Is. 33:17)
  without a veil is seen;
it were a well-spent journey
  though seven deaths lay between:
the Lamb, with his fair army,
  doth on Mount Zion stand,
and glory, glory dwelleth
  in Immanuel's land.

O Christ! he is the fountain,
  the deep, sweet well of love;
the streams on earth I've tasted,
  more deep I'll drink above;
there to an ocean fulness
  his mercy doth expand,
and glory, glory dwelleth
  in Immanuel's land.

With mercy and with judgment
  my web of time he wove,
and ay the dews of sorrow
  were lustred by his love;
I'll bless the hand that guided,
  I'll bless the heart that planned,
when throned where glory dwelleth
  in Immanuel's land.

I've wrestled on towards heaven,
  'gainst storm and wind and tide;
now, like a weary traveller
  that leaneth on his guide,
amid the shades of evening
  while sinks life's lingering sand,
I hail the glory dwelling
  in Immanuel's land.

The Christian Treasury, 1857
fashioned out of thoughts and phrases
in the works of Samuel Rutherford,
1600-61

WALTER CHALMERS SMITH
1824-1908

342
IMMORTAL, INVISIBLE
1 Tim. 1:17   HG 329

Immortal, invisible, God only wise,
in light inaccessible hid from our eyes,
most blessed, most glorious, the Ancient of Days,   (Dan. 7:9)
Almighty, victorious, thy great name we praise.

Unresting, unhasting, and silent as light,
nor wanting, nor wasting, thou rulest in might;
thy justice like mountains high soaring above,   (Ps. 36:6)
thy clouds which are fountains of goodness and love.

To all life thou givest - to both great and small;
in all life thou livest, the true life of all;
we blossom and flourish as leaves in the tree,
and wither and perish - but nought changeth thee.

Great Father of glory, pure Father of light,
thine angels adore thee, all veiling their sight;

but of all thy rich graces this grace, Lord, impart -
take the veil from our faces, the vile from our heart. (2 Cor. 3:15)

All laud we would render; O help us to see,
'tis only the splendour of light hideth thee;
and so let thy glory, almighty, impart,
through Christ in the story, thy Christ to the heart.

(one stanza omitted)   *Hymns of Christ and the Christian Life,*
                                         1867

JOHN CAMPBELL SHAIRP*
1819-85

343
CHANGELESS LOVE

'Twixt gleams of joy and clouds of doubt
    our feelings come and go;
our best estate is tossed about
    in ceaseless ebb and flow.
No mood of feeling, form of thought,
    is constant for a day:
but thou, O Lord, thou changest not:
    the same thou art alway.

I grasp thy strength, make it mine own,
    my heart with peace is blest;
I lose my hold, and then comes down
    darkness, and cold unrest.
Let me no more my comfort draw
    from my frail hold of thee;
in this alone rejoice with awe,
    thy mighty grasp of me.

Out of that weak, unquiet drift
    that comes but to depart,
to that pure heaven my spirit lift
    where thou unchanging art.
Lay hold of me with thy strong grasp,
    let thy almighty arm
in its embrace my weakness clasp,
    and I shall fear no harm.

Thy purpose of eternal good
    let me but surely know;
on this I'll lean - let changing mood
    and feeling come and go -
glad when thy sunshine fills my soul,
    not lorn when clouds o'ercast,
since thou within thy sure control
    of love dost hold me fast.

                    1871; in *Glen Dessaray and other
                    Poems,* 1888 (posth.)

GEORGE MATHESON
1842-1906
HG 446

344
O LOVE THAT WILT NOT LET ME GO   HG 547

O Love, that wilt not let me go,
    I rest my weary soul on thee;
I give thee back the life I owe,
    that in thine ocean depths its flow
        may richer, fuller be.

O Light that followest all my way,
    I yield my flickering torch to thee;

my heart restores its borrowed ray,
that in thy sunshine's blaze its day
    may brighter, fairer be.

O Joy that seekest me through pain,
    I cannot close my heart to thee;
I trace the rainbow through the rain,
and feel the promise is not vain,
    that morn that tearless be.   (Ps. 30:11)

O Cross that liftest up my head,
    I dare not ask to fly from thee;
I lay in dust life's glory dead,
and from the ground there blossoms red
    life that shall endless be.

                    6 June, 1881; in *Life and Work,* Janu-
                    ary, 1882

345
THREE DOORS

Three doors there are in the temple,
    where men go up to pray,
and they that wait at the outer gate
    may enter by either way.

O Father, give each his answer,
    each in his kindred way;
adapt thy light to his form of night,
    and grant him his needed day.

O give to the yearning spirits
    that only thy rest desire,
the power to bask in the peace they ask,
    and feel the warmth of thy fire.

Give to the soul that seeketh   (Lk. 11:9)
    'mid cloud, and doubt, and storm,
the glad surprise of the straining eyes,
    to see on the waves thy form.   (John 21:7)

Give to the heart that knocketh
    at the doors of earthly care
the strength to tread in the pathway spread
    by the flowers thou hast planted there.

For the middle wall shall be broken,   (Eph. 2:13)
    and the light expand its ray,
when the burdened of brain and the soother of pain
    shall be ranked with them that pray.

                    Sacred Songs, 1890 (written for the
                    Scottish tune, 'The Queen's Maries')

346
GATHER US IN

Gather us in, thou Love that fillest all,
    gather our rival faiths within thy fold,
rend each man's temple's veil and bid it fall,
    that we may know that thou hast been of old:
                    Gather us in.

Gather us in: we worship only thee;
    in varied names we stretch a common hand;
in diverse forms a common soul we see;
    in many ships we seek our spirit-land; . . .

Each sees one colour of thy rainbow-light,
　　each looks upon one tint and calls it heaven;
thou art the fulness of our partial sight;
　　we are not perfect till we find the seven; . . .

Thine is the mystic life great India craves,
　　thine is the Parsee's sin-destroying beam,
thine is the Buddhist's rest from tossing waves,
　　thine is the empire of vast China's dream; . . .

Thine is the Roman's strength without his pride,
　　thine is the Greek's glad world without its graves,
thine is Judaea's law with love beside,
　　the truth that censures and the grace that saves; . . .

Some seek a Father in the heavens above,
　　some ask a human image to adore,
some crave a spirit vast as life and love;
　　within thy mansions we have all and more;
　　　　　　　　　　　　　　　Gather us in.

　　　　　　　　　　　Sacred Songs, 1890

LAUCHLAN McLEAN WATT
1853-1931

347
THRALDOM　　　　　　　　　HG 306

I bind myself this tide
to the Galilean's side,
to the wounds of Calvary,
to the Christ who died for me.

I bind my soul this day
to the brother far away,
to the brother near at hand,
in this town and in this land.

I bind my heart in thrall
to the God, the Lord of all,
to the God, the poor man's friend,
and the Christ whom he did send.

I bind myself to peace,
to make strife and envy cease;
God, knit thou sure the cord
of my thraldom to the Lord!

　　　　　　　　　　　The Tryst, 1907

NICOL MacNICOL
1870-1952
translating
N. V. Tilak
(Indian)

348
INDIAN HYMN OF PENITENCE　　HG 586

One who is all unfit to count
　　as scholar in thy school,
thou of thy love hast named a friend -
　　O kindness wonderful!

So weak am I, O gracious Lord,
　　so all unworthy thee,
that even the dust upon thy feet
　　outweighs me utterly.

Thou dwellest in unshadowed light,
　　all sin and shame above -

that thou shouldst bear our sin and shame,
　　how can I tell such love?

Ah, did not he the heavenly throne　　　(Phil. 2:5ff)
　　a little thing esteem,
and not unworthy for my sake
　　a mortal body deem?

When in his flesh they drove the nails
　　did he not all endure?
What name is there to fit a life
　　so patient and so pure?

So, Love itself in human form,
　　for love of me he came;
I cannot look upon his face
　　for shame, for bitter shame.

If there is aught of worth in me
　　it comes from thee alone;
then keep me safe, for so, O Lord,
　　thou keepest but thine own.

　　　　　　　　　A Missionary Hymn Book, 1922
　　　　　　　　　For Tilak, see also ##577-578.

ARTICLE 18:
AMERICAN HYMNODY TO 1900 (349-389)

No adjective is so difficult to define as 'American.' At different periods in history it means several different things. America (we are bound here to mean by that the United States) is now a complex society in which no civilized race on earth is unrepresented; and if it be said that it was never a racially homogeneous society, the truth is that that complexity has been admitted and has been reflected in an 'American culture' only in the twentieth century.

Nobody thinks that the Pilgrim Fathers discovered America. But they did introduce Protestantism to America, and therefore the first nearly three centuries of American hymnody are entirely a story of what came from, and what reacted against, their influence. Huge tracts of America were unaffected by any such influence at the time of the foundation of the United States in 1776; but those who lived in these tracts were either Catholics or unevangelized Indians or subject Blacks serving white masters who were solidly Protestant.

It is only in the years after about 1950 that American hymnody provides anything but a very one-sided view of American culture. The whole of this present section is concerned with a society which has now virtually passed away: the all-dominating culture of New England and the eastern seaboard down to Baltimore.

New England was colonized by Calvinistic Protestants, and therefore the public praise of the majority of Christians was psalmody. The first book to be printed in this part of America was the *Bay Psalm Book* (1638), a psalter based on the *Old Version* of Sternhold and Hopkins and designed as a simpler and more tractable replacement for Ainsworth's Psalter of 1612, which the Pilgrim Fathers had brought with them. In the 18th century the Episcopals were almost confined to Tate and Brady's *New Version*, which, on the whole, got a more hospitable reception in America than in its own country. And if there was any hymnody here or there it was Watts or Wesley. John Wesley, as we saw earlier (article 6), edited his own hymnal for his Georgia mission and had it printed at Charlestown,

South Carolina in 1737. This predated all Charles Wesley's work and was mostly Watts and members of the Wesley family with incursions into George Herbert. Indeed, we look in vain for native American hymnody in the colonial days, except for the quite remarkable and finely-wrought hymn of Samuel Davies (#349), which stands out as a landmark. It has some of the authentic power of Watts himself. Whether it was ever sung in its author's brief lifetime we cannot tell; it was not printed until some years after his death. But there it stands, monumental and severe, quite unique among American hymns for its theological weight and grandeur.

While psalmody was suffocating hymnody in the cultivated northeast, hymnody began to flourish in the 'southern states' (this is the term applied in America to what is geographically the southeast); but since hardly anybody apart from scholars knew anything about the folk-hymnody of North Carolina, Tennessee, and Kentucky before the second half of our own century, we are leaving that, and the parallel development of the Black Spiritual, to article 23.

Our #350, some fifty years younger than 349, was born of psalmody in that when the American Congregationalists wanted a revision of the Watts psalter they entrusted the work to President Timothy Dwight, part of whose task was to make versions of those psalms which Watts had never versified. 'I love thy Kingdom,' still one of America's favourites, is, surprisingly enough, his version of Psalm 137. Clearly he was almost as hopelessly defeated by that psalm as Watts had been, for his product is strictly a hymn, further away from the psalm than Watts would ever have allowed himself to go. But it alone of his work has survived, and so it is there as another lonely milestone.

One of the earliest hymn writers of the newly-formed United States must have been John Quincy Adams, son of the second president and himself president from 1824 to 1829. He wrote a complete metrical psalter and a small number of original hymns which were published after his death; none of this is interesting enough literature to merit a place here.

We may say that the main stream begins to flow with the two Unitarian ministers whose work is exemplified in ##351 and 352. If #351 looks a rather eccentric production (what tune the author can have ever heard it sung to remains a mystery), #352 gives a very clear indication of how things are going to go. For we are going to find, and our quoted texts will prove it, that the style of hymnody affected by the Unitarian, Congregational, and Presbyterian divines of the American 19th century was, until the century was well advanced, far better literature than the English Anglicans were providing in the same period. Theologically it had its dubious moments, but these New England Calvinists knew how to handle words. It is indeed interesting that so many of these hymns have now been forgotten in America, #351 perhaps understandably, good writing though it is, but #352 incomprehensibly. We shall come to the reasons for this later on.

American hymnody did not make a real impact on English congregations until the century was well advanced, but ##353 and 360 have the distinction of being the two American hymns admitted to the first edition (1861) of Hymns Ancient and Modern. That hymnal was always slow in admitting American influence, and it was not until its 1950 edition that American work was taken seriously by its editors. One curious point is that these two hymns, the first of which certainly has great distinction, were written by authors who were 25 and 19 years old respectively at the time of their publication; the careful

reader will note that eleven of the hymns in this section were written by authors who were less than thirty years old.

No. 354 is another very youthful piece, very mature and poised writing, typical again of the New England style.

Ray Palmer, Congregationalist, is certainly one of America's leading hymn writers. He made a very good beginning with his youthful 'My faith looks up to thee' (355), and his work in the other examples (356-7, with which should be taken 163B and 169B) shows very well his unusually contemplative manner. If American hymnody was subject to any special temptation, it was to the production of surface gloss concealing intellectual commonplaceness. One never finds this in Palmer.

More Unitarian work will be found at ##358, 372, 373 (one of the first Christmas hymns with a social message), #374 (unusual and charming), 378-80, in all of which there is some very good literature. 'City of God' (379) is perhaps the most typical example of a fine lyric whose theological judgments are entirely questionable; the humanistic optimism in this material has found less acceptance in the late twentieth century than it naturally found in the mid-nineteenth. Perhaps #381 qualifies to be called one of the six best American hymns ever written, for here undoubtedly we have a firm base in Scripture and dogma on which a sonorous and beautiful lyric is built; despite the long lines there is not a word wasted here.

The American men of letters contributed plenty to the hymn treasury. Compare that with our Victorian age in which, even if we do steal the occasional piece from Tennyson, no major poet ever wrote a hymn. Emerson, the famous essayist, did not perhaps distinguish himself in hymnody, but #359, an early work written for a local church celebration, has honest candour.

The unwillingness of American editors, both in the 19th century and in this, to fashion hymnody out of the work of recognized poets in the manner we shall investigate in article 20 was no doubt partly the consequence of Puritan prejudice; but the high lyric talent of the American 19th-century writers must have had something to do with it. But there are two large exceptions among the well-known hymns from America: 'Once to every man and nation' (which we shall examine shortly) and Whittier's 'Dear Lord and Father of mankind.'

Whittier was a Quaker poet who was, in the earlier years of a long life, very active in the Abolitionist movement and who spent his later years as a full-time man of letters. His work in current hymnals is the great American exception to the generalization we have just made. In later life he did write one or two hymns, of which 'All things are thine' is the best known; but he wrote those at the wish of people who had already discovered what good hymns could be made out of poetry he did not design for singing. His Quaker background was, of course, not a hymn-singing culture, and it was for quite other purposes that he wrote the poems from which his best 'hymns' actually come. For if nowadays 'Dear Lord and Father' and 'O brother man' are probably his best-known hymns in his own country, it is in the selections given at ##362-6 that we see the best of his contribution to hymnody. These five pieces are, as the notes show and as the Hymnal Guide shows in more detail, stanzas selected from three long poems which run in total to 77 C.M. stanzas and which declare his mature faith. Only 'Immortal love,' the best and most widely used of these selections (363), uses the first stanza of any of these poems.

Two things will at once occur to a thoughtful reader. The first is that if one can make serviceable hymns out of 7-stanza selections so wild and apparently arbitrary as these are, the style of the originals must be fairly loose. The second is that by making such centos the editors have probably altered the thought of the originals to some extent. The first of these notions is only partly true, and the truth about it gives the answer to the second. The original poems are all to some extent argumentative, consisting of the juxtaposition of two opposed ideas of faith. The editors have boiled off the argument, leaving only the positive faith, which, of course, is better for singing than the argument. The controversial elements have not wholly disappeared from the selections we have offered (which will be found at some points different from those in many hymnals); stanza 4 of #365, for example, lifts the curtain for a moment. But it does remain true that Whittier is the only reputable author whose work has been so extensively and at the same time so successfully rearranged in this fashion by hymnal editors.

The 'argument' is, in Whittier, always that of the liberal and cultivated man against doctrinaire rigorism. In true Quaker fashion, what Whittier has to say he says very gently. But 'The Eternal goodness,' from which we take our #366, opens, in our selection, with stanza 4. Here are the first three:

> O friends! with whom my feet have trod
>   the quiet aisles of prayer,
> glad witness to your zeal for God
>   and love of man I bear.
>
> I trace your lines of argument;
>   your logic linked and strong
> I weigh as one who dreads dissent,
>   and fears a doubt as wrong.
>
> But still my human hands are weak
>   to hold your iron creeds;
> against the words ye bid me speak
>   my heart within me pleads.
>
> Who fathoms the eternal thought? . . .

Our selection ends at st. 20. There follow these:

> O brothers! if my faith is vain,
>   if hopes like these betray,
> pray for me that my feet may gain
>   the sure and safer way.
>
> And thou, O Lord, by whom are seen
>   thy creatures as they be,
> forgive me if too close I lean
>   my human heart on thee!

Whittier cannot be called 'orthodox' in his approach to creeds and liturgies, and this is not the place to argue whether it is legitimate to extract stanzas from longer works and, by omitting one strain of thought, modify their author's message. Your present writer's personal opinion is that when this is done with Whittier it is less unsuccessful than we shall find it when we come to Russell Lowell, because the manner of Whittier is gentle, where Lowell's, in the poem from which 'Once to every man and nation' came, is polemical. If one wants a complete Whittier poem, one has one in the very late devotional lyric, #367, which certainly now is a piece for private reading rather than devotional song. If one wants him in a more muscular mood, then the early poem #361 give us that—almost unknown now, recovered only by Garrett Horder in England,

never now sung in the U.S.A. And if there is a case against 'Dear Lord and Father,' which in all conscience is an excellent piece of word-spinning, perhaps it is that there Whittier was writing a polemical piece, a poetic tract contrasting the serenity and sanity of the Christian Faith with the vapourings of a kind of drug-addictive transcendental meditation associated with the drinking of 'Soma,' a potation designed to induce visions. The quietism of the hymn as we know it (it is in fact the last six stanzas, or selections from them, of the poem) takes on a very different tone when its context is made explicit.

American Episcopals did not make a large contribution to 19th-century hymnody; their great days were about 1940. We have already touched on ##353 and 360 which no doubt made the grade in *Hymns A & M* because of their Episcopal origin; for its first century that book was always inhospitable to non-Episcopal writing. Bishop Coxe has a style much less even, much more rugged, than that of the liberals. 'Saviour, sprinkle many nations' is well known to many singers; it is a tolerable hymn somewhat disfigured by an opening line which means nothing much, being based on a venerable mistranslation in the Bible. No. 369 is much more fierce, written by him when he was 26, and passionately interpreting the dark prophecies in Isaiah 63. Nobody knew this in Britain until Vaughan Williams married it to the Welsh tune EBENEZER in the *English Hymnal*, and it proved to be too strong meat for any other hymnal to take it up.

Oliver Wendell Holmes, one of the country's greatest men of letters, is justly famous for 'Lord of all being,' #375; here and in several other hymns he shows the characteristic 'Unitarian' polish and also the length of vision which in less sure hands became sentimental and anti-dogmatic. It is not so here. The 'Battle Hymn of the Republic' (376) is almost too well known to stand comment, and yet, even here, in a piece that has become so popular, what admirable writing in the expansive 19th-century style! Just occasionally, perhaps, it is overexuberant (the 'jubilant feet' and the 'glorious bosom' are not quite up to standard), but few national songs come near this in literary quality. The final stanza, whose authenticity has sometimes been doubted, is perfectly genuine, though the author was unsure whether in the end to include it or not.

Yet another non-cleric, the essayist and journalist Bryant, produced several good pieces. We choose 368 for its social emphasis, which redresses some of the balance against the tendency to over-spiritual writing we have been conscious of up to now. (Great poets do not often make good hymn writers, but the Americans show, and the English showed in Montgomery and Chesterton, how very well the best journalist can rise to the occasion.) Miss Scudder was chiefly a hymn writer. Her vogue has now disappeared, but #380 has plenty of solid merit in the now familiar style.

This brings us to 'Once to every man and nation,' which must be, apart from the two Christmas hymns, the most popular 19th-century hymn in late 20th century America; and possibly American readers will be surprised to learn that the hymn they know so well was really fashioned in England. Russell Lowell's eloquent poem on the Mexican War which we reprint in full at #370 is full of that colorful language and moral hyperbole in which the Boston school of writers excelled; but as it stands it is hardly a hymn.

It was the English editor, William Garrett Horder (1845-1919), who, except for the two hymns so mysteriously annexed earlier by English Episcopals, really introduced American hymnody to England. In *The Hymn Lover*, his book on hymnody, he gave many pages to American hymn writers, and in *Worship Song* (1905) and the collections which preceded it he transcribed scores of these hymns. *Worship Song*, the only hymnal with music that he edited, was a fairly obscure book, but Percy Dearmer, who edited the *English Hymnal*, knew it and admired it, and in 1906 the book that was destined to become England's most enduring hymnal carried many of these hymns which he had learned from Horder's pages. It was Horder who recast Lowell's poem in the form now well known, and it was Dearmer (in a later hymnal, *Songs of Praise*, 1925) who set it to the Welsh tune EBENEZER from which in the USA it is now never separated. Further bibliographical information about this extraordinary piece, which combines at a high pressure theological perverseness and trenchant language, will be found in the *Hymnal Guide* at #585.

In 371 we are able to provide a Lowell hymn rather less well known but at least designed to be sung and of considerable lyric warmth.

The same rich feeling for words is to be found in Burleigh's poem at 382 and in Sears' and Brooks' famous Christmas hymns (373, 383), both of which, when sung in full, have a social emphasis uncommon up to that time in Christmas songs.

With the Congregationalist Wolcott's 'Christ for the world' (384) perhaps we detect a slight falling off into platitudinousness; and the evangelical note appears in Miss Lathbury's 386, which, with 'Day is dying in the west,' she wrote for the Chautauqua Convention, the pioneer of that endless network of conference centers for revival and study which now covers the U.S.A. Possibly it was evangelical influences after 1870 that caused hymn-writers to turn away from the high-toned style of Boston. Hosmer (387-8) is the last of the Unitarians to rise to it. His writing is impeccable, his cast of mind optimistic and, like that of most of the others, wholly unfashionable nowadays. But apart from him we begin now to descend rather steeply into a more conventional hymn style. The euphoria of the Centennial in 1876 may perhaps be blamed for the rather inflated language of 385, and a similar, more local celebration for that of 389; but this, compared with the speculative and imaginative style of the earlier New England work, is poor stuff, associated, unfortunately, with lamentably bombastic music. Both are the work of Episcopals.

I have drawn attention here to the special virtues of the New England style partly because so much of this hymnody has actually passed out of the American repertory now, and much of it got a pretty poor showing in English books. The reason for this extinction of the style in 20th-century hymnals is the changing of a theological fashion. It is entirely understandable that the successive traumas of the 20th century, coming so rudely upon the euphoria of the 19th, should cause people to turn their backs on this sort of material. Whittier's hymn, with its opening verse,

> O sometimes gleams upon our sight,
>   through present wrong, the eternal right,
> and step by step, since time began,
>   we see the steady gain of man . . .

expresses a sentiment which the 20th century caused a whole generation to consider almost blasphemous. Where the English writers were disciplined by their prayer books and bibles and so largely guided by the ideals of the Oxford Movement, the Americans knew no such 'movement' and mostly no such liturgies. So their thoughts turned naturally to speculation, and

they were always vulnerable to the taunt 'It's all very well for you New Englanders; you can afford to talk that way.'

Reflecting the theological stance of the new orthodoxy of 1925-45, critics like Bernard Manning depreciated this kind of material and exalted Watts, Wesley, and the other English Calvinists and early Evangelicals. Nobody (for me) can speak or write too affectionately about those people, but as the 20th century enters its last quarter it is easier than it was forty years before to see certain qualities in the American hymnody which have lately been undervalued. Present-day casualness of language, theological unimaginativeness, seminarial pedagogy, and hatred of poetry and history, not to mention our total aesthetic anarchy, throw a shadow in which the professional literary standards and the religious assurance of the old American writers begin, after being painted grey by our early 20th-century theologians, to glow again with a light we were formerly too complacent to notice.

In a moment we shall see what else happened to American hymnody in the 19th century which will redress to some extent any disbalance a fastidious reader may complain of so far.

And as a postscript: in case anyone accuses the present editor of undue admiration for American work, he will state (following the lead of that great hymnologist, the late Millar Patrick) that that wretched travesty of the 23rd Psalm, 'Father, hear the prayer we offer,' being among the American pieces introduced to England by Garrett Horder and Percy Dearmer, appeals to him as being by far the worst hymn of the century written in either country. For this, the reader will set the dogs on him from a quite different quarter, but at least he will enjoy the change of ground.

SAMUEL DAVIES*
1723-61

349
GREAT GOD OF WONDERS

Great God of wonders! all thy ways
    are matchless, godlike, and divine:
but the fair glories of thy grace
    more godlike and unrivalled shine.
        Who is a pardoning God like thee?
        or who has grace so rich and free?

Crimes of such horror to forgive,
    such guilty, daring souls to spare,
this is thy grand prerogative,
    and none shall in the honor share. . . .

Angels and men, resign your claim
    to pity, mercy, love and grace:
these glories crown Jehovah's name
    with an incomparable blaze. . . .

In wonder lost, with trembling joy,
    we take the pardon of our God -
pardon for crimes of deepest dye,
    a pardon bought with Jesus' blood. . . .

O may this strange, this matchless grace,
    this godlike miracle of love,
fill the wide world with grateful praise,
    and all the angelic hosts above.
        Who is a pardoning God like thee?
        Or who has grace so rich and free?

Hymns (ed. Gibbons: posth.) 1769
text slightly altered

TIMOTHY DWIGHT
1752-1817

350
IF I FORGET THEE, O JERUSALEM
Ps. 137

HG 316

I love thy kingdom, Lord,
the house of thine abode,
the Church our blest Redeemer saved
with his own precious blood.

I love thy Church, O God;
her walls before thee stand,
dear as the apple of thine eye,   (Deut. 32:10)
and graven on thy hand.   (Is. 49:16)

For her my tears shall fall,
for her my prayers ascend,
to her my cares and toils be given,
till toils and cares shall end.

Beyond my highest joy
I prize her heavenly ways;
her sweet communion, solemn vows,
her hymns of love and praise.

Jesus, thou Friend divine,
our Savior and our King,
thy hand from every snare and foe
shall great deliverance bring.

Sure as thy truth shall last
to Zion shall be given
the highest glories earth can yield,
and brighter bliss of heaven.

The Psalms of David, 1801

HENRY WARE JR*
1794-1843

351
EASTER

Lift your glad voices in triumph on high,
for Jesus has risen, and man cannot die;
Vain were the terrors that gathered around him,
and short the dominion of death and the grave;
he burst from the fetters of darkness that bound him,
resplendent in glory to live and to save;
Loud was the chorus of angels on high,
'The Saviour hath risen, and man shall not die!'

Glory to God, in full anthems of joy;
the being he gave us death cannot destroy;
sad were the life we must part with tomorrow,
if tears were our birthright and death were our end. (1 Cor. 15:10)
but Jesus hath cheered the dark valley of sorrow (Ps. 23:4)
and made us, immortal, to heaven ascend.
Lift then your voices in triumph on high,
for Jesus hath risen, and man shall not die!

The Christian Disciple, 1817

JOHN PIERPONT*
1725-1866

352
WORSHIP

O thou, to whom in ancient time
the lyre of Hebrew bards was strung,
whom kings adored in songs sublime
and prophets praised with glowing tongue;

not now on Zion's height alone
thy favoured worshippers may dwell,   (John 4:21)
nor where at sultry noon thy Son   (John 4:5)
sat weary by the patriarch's well;

from every place below the skies
the grateful song, the fervent prayer,
the incense of the heart may rise
to heaven, and find acceptance there.

To thee shall age with snowy hair
and strength and beauty bow the knee,
and childhood lisp with reverent air
its praises and its prayers to thee.

O thou, to whom in ancient time
the lyre of prophet bards was strung,
to thee at last, in every clime
shall temples rise, and praise be sung.

1824; *Psalms and Hymns,* 1840

GEORGE WASHINGTON
DOANE, Bishop
1799-1859
HG 197

353
THE WAY, THE TRUTH AND THE LIFE
John 14:6

HG 738

Thou art the Way; to thee alone
from sin and death we flee;
and he who would the Father seek
must seek him, Lord, by thee.

Thou art the Truth; thy word alone
true wisdom can impart;
thou only canst inform the mind
and purify the heart.

Thou art the Life; the rending tomb
proclaims thy conquering arm,
and those who put their trust in thee
nor death nor hell can harm.

Thou art the Way, the Truth, the Life;
grant us that way to know,
that truth to keep, that life to win
whose joys eternal flow.

Songs by the Way, 1824

SARAH ELIZABETH MILES*
1807-77

354
THE DIVINE COMPASSION

Thou who didst stoop below
to drain the cup of woe,
wearing the form of frail mortality;
thy blessed labours done,
thy crown of victory won,
hast passed from earth, passed to thy throne on high.

Our eyes behold thee not,
yet hast thou not forgot
those who have placed their hope, their trust in thee.
Before thy Father's face
thou hast prepared a place
that where thou art, there they may also be.   (John 14:1-2)

It was no path of flowers
which, through this world of ours,
belovèd of the Father, thou didst tread;
and shall we, in dismay,
shrink from the narrow way
when clouds and darkness are around it spread?

O thou who art our life,
be with us through the strife;
the holy head by earth's fierce storms was bowed:
raise thou our eyes above,
to see a Father's love,
beam, like a bow of promise, through the cloud.   (Gen. 8:22)

And O, if thoughts of gloom
should hover o'er the tomb,
the light of love our guiding star shall be;
our spirit shall not dread
the shadowy path to tread,
Friend, Guardian, Saviour, which doth lead to thee.

The Christian Examiner, 1827

RAY PALMER, 1808-87
HG 370

355
MY FAITH LOOKS UP TO THEE   HG 459

My faith looks up to thee,
thou Lamb of Calvary,
    Saviour divine!
Now hear me when I pray,
take all my guilt away,
O let me from this day
    be wholly thine.

May thy rich grace impart
strength to my fainting heart,
    my zeal inspire;
as thou hast died for me,
O may thy love to me
pure, warm and changeless be,
    a living fire.

While life's dark maze I tread,
and griefs around me spread,
    be thou my guide;
bid darkness turn to day,
wipe sorrow's tears away,
nor let me ever stray
    from thee aside.

When ends life's transient dream,
when death's cold sullen stream
    shall o'er me roll,
blest Savior, then in love
fear and distrust remove;
O bear me safe above,
    a ransomed soul.

Spiritual Songs for Social Worship (L. Mason), 1831

356
WHOM HAVING NOT SEEN, YE LOVE
1 Peter 1:8   HG 370

Jesus, these eyes have never seen
    that radiant form of thine;
the veil of sense hangs dark between
    thy blessed face and mine.

I see thee not, I hear thee not,
    yet art thou oft with me;
and earth hath ne'er so dear a spot
    as where I met with thee.

Like some bright dream that comes unsought,
    when slumbers o'er me roll,
thine image ever fills my thought,
    and charms my ravished soul.

Yet, thou I have not seen, and still
    must rest in faith alone,
I love thee, dearest Lord, and will,
    unseen, but not unknown.

When death these mortal eyes shall seal,
    and still this throbbing heart,
the rending veil shall thee reveal
    all glorious as thou art.

The Sabbath Hymn Book, 1858

357
HOW UNSEARCHABLE ARE HIS JUDGMENTS!
Rom. 11:31

Lord, my weak thought in vain would climb
    to search the starry vault profound;
in vain would wing her flight sublime
    to find creation's utmost bound.

But weaker yet that thought must prove
    to search thy grand eternal plan,
thy sovereign counsels, born of love,
    long ages ere the world began.

When my dim reason would demand
    why that, or this, thou dost ordain,
by some vast deep I seem to stand,
    whose secrets I must ask in vain.

When doubts disturb my troubled breast,
    and all is dark as night to me,
here, as on solid rock, I rest -
    that thus it seemeth good to thee.

Be this my joy, that evermore
    thou rulest all things at thy will;
thy sovereign wisdom I adore,
    and calmly, sweetly, trust thee still.

The Sabbath Hymn Book, 1858
See also 163B, 169B.

STEPHEN G. BULFINCH*
1809-70

358
CHRIST ON THE ROAD

Hath not thy heart within thee burned   (Lk. 24:32)
    at evening's calm and holy hour,
as if its inmost depths discerned
    the presence of a loftier Power?

Hast thou not heard 'mid forest glades,
    while ancient rivers murmured by,
a voice from the eternal shades
    that spake a present Deity?

And as upon the sacred page
    thine eye in rapt attention turned
o'er records of a holier age,
    hath not thy heart within thee burned?

It was the voice of God, that spake
    in silence to thy silent heart;
and bade each holier thought awake,
    and every dream of earth depart.

Voice of our God, O yet be near!
    In low sweet accents whisper peace;
direct us on our pathway here;
    then bid in heaven our wanderings cease.

Contemplations of the Savior, 1832

RALPH WALDO EMERSON*
1803-82

359
THE HOUSE OF GOD

We love the venerable house
    our fathers built to God:
in heaven are kept their grateful vows,
    their dust endears the sod.

Here holy thoughts a light have shed
    from many a radiant face,
and prayers of tender hope have spread
    a perfume through the place.

And anxious hearts have pondered here
    the mystery of life,
and prayed the eternal Light to clear
    their doubts and aid their strife.

From humble tenements around
    came up the pensive train,
and in the church a blessing found
    that filled their homes again;

for faith, and peace, and mighty love,
    that from the Godhead flow,
showed them the life of heaven above
    springs from the life below.

They live with God, their homes are dust;
    yet here their children pray,
and in this fleeting life-time trust
    to find the narrow way.

On him who by the altar stands,
    on him thy blessing fall!
Speak through his lips thy pure commands,
    thou Heart, that lovest all.

1833; *Hymns of the Spirit,* 1864

CHARLES WILLIAM EVEREST
1814-77

360
TAKE UP THY CROSS
Mark 8:34   HG 676

'Take up thy cross,' the Savior said,
    'if thou wouldst my disciple be;
take up thy cross with willing heart
    and humbly follow after me.'

Take up thy cross; let not its weight
    fill thy weak spirit with alarm;
his strength shall bear thy spirit up,
    and brace thy heart, and nerve thine arm.

Take up thy cross, nor heed the shame   (Heb. 12:2)
    and let thy foolish pride be still;
the Lord refused not ev'n to die
    upon a cross, on Calvary's hill.

Take up thy cross, then, in his strength
    and calmly sin's wild deluge brave;
'twill guide thee to a better home,
    and point to glory o'er the grave.

Take up thy cross, and follow on,
    nor think till death to lay it down;
for only he who bears the cross
    may hope to wear the glorious crown.

Visions of Death, and other Poems,
1833

JOHN GREENLEAF WHITTIER
1807-92
HG 11

361
TOWARDS A NEW WORLD

Lord, for the things we see
we trust the things to be;
and present gratitude
insures the future's good.
So in the paths untrod
and the long days of God
our feet shall still be led,
our hearts be comforted.

Others shall sing the song,
others shall right the wrong -
finish what we begin,
and all we fail of, win.
What matter, we or they?
ours or another's day,
so the right word be said
and life the sweeter made?

Hail to the coming singers!
Hail to the brave light-bringers!
forward we reach and share
all that they sing or dare.
The airs of heaven blow o'er us,
a glory shines before us
of what mankind shall be -
pure, generous, brave and free.

The love of God and neighbour,
an equal band at labour,
the richer life where beauty
walks hand in hand with duty.
We feel the earth move sunward,
we join the great march onward,
and take by faith, while living
our freehold of thanksgiving!

Poledom, 1837

362
from MY PSALM
HG 11

All as God wills, who wisely heeds
   to give or to withhold,
and knoweth more of all my needs
   than all my prayers have told!

Enough that blessings undeserved
   have marked my erring track;
that wheresoever my feet have swerved,
   his chastening turned me back;

that more and more a providence
   of love is understood,
making the springs of time and sense
   sweet with eternal good;

that death seems but a covered way
   which opens into light,
wherein no blinded child can stray
   beyond the Father's sight;

that care and trial seem at last
   through memory's sunset air,
like mountain ranges overpast
   in purple distance fair;

that all the jarring notes of life
   seem blending in a psalm,
and all the angles of its strife
   slow rounding into calm;

And so the shadows fall apart,
   and so the west winds play;
and all the windows of my heart
   I open to the day.

1867; sts. 11-17.

363
from OUR MASTER
HG 330

Immortal love, for ever full,
   for ever flowing free,
for ever shared, for ever whole,
   a never-ebbing sea!

Our outward lips confess the name
   all other names above;
love only knoweth whence it came
   and comprehendeth love.

We may not climb the heavenly steeps (Rom. 10:6-7)
   to bring the Lord Christ down;
in vain we search the lowest deeps,
   for him no depths can drown;

but warm, sweet, tender, even yet
   a present help is he,
and faith has still its Olivet,
   and love its Galilee.

The healing of his seamless dress   (Mk. 5:27)
   is by our beds of pain;
we touch him in life's throng and press
   and we are whole again.

Through him the first fond prayers are said
   our lips of childhood frame;
the last low whispers of our dead
   are burdened with his name.

Alone, O love ineffable,
   thy saving name is given: (Acts 4:12)
to turn aside from thee is hell,
   to walk with thee is heaven.

1867; Sts. 1, 2, 5, 13, 14, 15, 31.

364
from OUR MASTER
HG 330

Our Lord and Master of us all,
   whate'er our name or sign,
we own thy way, we hear thy call,
   we test our lives by thine.

Thou judgest us; thy purity
   doth all our lusts condemn;
the love that draws us nearer thee
   is hot with wrath to them;

our thoughts lie open to thy sight;
   and, naked to thy glance,
our secret sins are in the light
   of thy pure countenance.

Yet weak and blinded though we be,
   thou dost our service own;
we bring our varying gifts to thee
   and thou rejectest none.

To thee our full humanity,
   its joys and pains belong;
the wrong of man to man on thee
   inflicts a deeper wrong.

Who hates, hates thee: who loves, becomes (1 John 4:20)
   therein to thee allied:
all sweet accords of hearts and homes
   in thee are multiplied.

Apart from thee all gain is loss,
    all labour vainly done;
the solemn shadow of the Cross
    is better than the sun.

1867; sts. 16-18, 20-22, 30.

365
from OUR MASTER

O Love! O Life! our faith and sight
    thy presence maketh one,
as through transfigured clouds of white
    we trace the noonday sun.

So to our mortal eyes subdued,
    flesh-veiled, but not concealed,
we know in thee the fatherhood
    and heart of God revealed.

Our Friend, our Brother, and our Lord,
    what may thy service be?
Not name, nor form, nor ritual word,
    but simply following thee.

Thy litanies, sweet offices
    of love and gratitude;
thy sacramental liturgies,
    the joy of doing good.

The heart must ring thy Christmas bells,
    thy inward altars raise;
its faith and hope thy canticles,
    and its obedience, praise.

Blow, winds of God, awake, and blow
    the mists of earth away;
shine out, O Light divine, and show
    how wide and far we stray.

We faintly hear, we dimly see,
    in differing phrase we pray;
but, dim or clear, we own in thee
    the Light, the Truth, the Way!   (John 14:6)

1867; Sts. 24, 25, 34, 36, 38, 3, 26.

366
from THE ETERNAL GOODNESS   HG 818

Who fathoms the eternal thought?
    who talks of scheme and plan?
The Lord is God! He needeth not
    the poor device of man.

Here in the maddening maze of things,
    when tossed by storm and flood,
to one fixed ground my spirit clings:
    I know that God is good.

I long for household voices gone,
    for vanished smiles I long;
but God hath led my dear ones on,
    and he can do no wrong.

I know not what the future hath
    of marvel or surprise,
assured alone that life and death
    his mercy underlies.

And if my heart and flesh are weak
    to bear an untried pain,
the bruised reed he will not break,   (Is. 42:3)
    but strengthen and sustain.

And so beside the silent sea
    I wait the muffled oar;
no harm from him can come to me
    on ocean or on shore.

I know not where his islands lift
    their fronded palms in air;
I only know I cannot drift
    beyond his love and care.

1867; sts. 4, 11, 15, 16, 17, 19, 20.

367
AT LAST   HG 808

When on my day of life the night is falling,
    and in the winds, from unsunned spaces blown,
I hear far voices out of darkness calling
    my feet to paths unknown;

thou who hast made my home of life so pleasant,
    leave not its tenant when its walls decay;
O love divine, O helper ever present,
    be thou my strength and stay.

Be near me when all else is from me drifting, -
    earth, sky, home's pictures, days of shade and shine,
and kindly faces, to my own uplifting
    the love which answers mine.

I have but thee, my Father; let thy Spirit
    be with me then to comfort and uphold;
no gate of pearl, no branch of palm I merit,
    nor street of shining gold.

Suffice it if - my good and ill unreckoned,
    and both forgiven through thy abounding grace -
I find myself by hands familiar beckoned
    unto my fitting place,

some humble door among thy many mansions,   (John 14:2)
    some sheltering shade where sin and striving cease,
and flows for ever, through heaven's green expansions,   (Rev. 22:1)
    the river of thy peace.

There, from the music round about me stealing,
    I fain would learn the new and holy song,
and find at last, beneath thy trees of healing,
    the life for which I long.

1882; *The Bay of the Seven Islands*,
1883

WILLIAM CULLEN BRYANT*
1794-1878

368
HOME MISSION

Look from thy sphere of endless day,
    O God of pity and of might;
in pity look on those who stray
    benighted, in this land of light.

In peopled vale, in lonely glen,
    in crowded mart, by stream or sea,

how many of the sons of men
   hear not the message sent from thee.

Send forth thy heralds, Lord, to call
   the thoughtless young, the hardened old,
a scattered homeless flock, till all
   be gathered to thy peaceful fold.

Send them thy mighty word to speak,
   till faith shall dawn, and doubt depart,
to awe the bold, to stay the weak,
   and bind and heal the broken heart.

Then all these wastes, a dreary scene,
   that make us sadden as we gaze,
shall grow, with living waters green
   and lift to heaven the voice of praise.

1840; Songs for the Sanctuary, 1865

ARTHUR CLEVELAND COXE,
Bishop
1818-96
HG 572

369
WHO IS THIS?

Who is this, with garments gory,   (Is. 63:1-6)
   triumphing from Bozrah's way;
this that weareth robes of glory
   bright with more than victory's ray?
Who is this unwearied comer
   from his journey's sultry length,
travelling through Idumè's summer
   in the greatness of his strength?

Wherefore red in thine apparel
   like the conquerors of earth,
and arrayed like those who carol
   o'er the reeking vineyard's mirth?
Who art thou, the valleys seeking   (Is. 63:14)
   where our peaceful harvests wave?
'I, in righteous anger speaking,
   I the mighty One to save;

'I, that of the raging heathen
   trod the winepress all alone   (Is. 63:3)
now in victor-garlands wreathen
   coming to redeem my own:
I am he with sprinkled raiment,
   glorious for the vengeance-hour,
ransoming, with priceless payment,
   and delivering with power.'

Hail, all hail! thou Lord of Glory!
   thee our Father, thee we own;   (Is. 63:16)
Abram heard not of our story,
   Israel ne'er our name hath known,
but, Redeemer, thou hast sought us,
   thou hast heard thy children's wail,
thou with thy dear blood hast bought us:
   Hail, thou mighty Victor, Hail!

Hallowe'en and Other Poems, 1844

JAMES RUSSELL LOWELL
1819-91

370
ONCE TO EVERY MAN AND NATION
(The poem from which the hymn was formed)

When a deed is done for freedom, through the broad earth's aching
           breast
runs a thrill of joy prophetic, trembling on from east to west,
and the slave, where'er he cowers, feels the soul within him climb
to the awful verge of manhood, as the energy sublime
of a century bursts full-blossomed on the thorny stem of time.

Through the walls of hut and palace shoots the instantaneous throe,
when the travail of the Ages wrings earth's systems to and fro;
at the birth of each new Era, with a recognizing start,
nation wildly looks at nation, standing with mute lips apart,
and glad Truth's yet mightier man-child leaps beneath the Future's
           heart.

So the Evil's triumph sendeth, with a terror and a chill,
under continent to continent the sense of coming ill,
and the slave, where'er he cowers, feels his sympathies with God
in hot tear-drops ebbing earthward, to be drunk up by the sod,
till a corpse crawls round unburied, delving in the nobler clod.

For mankind are one in spirit, and an instinct bears along,
round the earth's electric circle, the swift flash of right or wrong;
whether conscious or unconscious, yet Humanity's vast frame
through its ocean-sundered fibres feels the gush of joy or shame; -
in the gain or loss of one race all the rest have equal claim.

Once to every man and nation comes the moment to decide,   *
in the strife of Truth with Falsehood, for the good or evil side;   *
some great cause, God's new Messiah, offering each the bloom or
           blight,   *
parts the goats upon the left hand, and the sheep upon the right,
and the choice goes by for ever 'twixt that darkness and that light.

Hast thou chosen, O my people, on whose party thou shalt stand,
ere the Doom from its warn sandals shakes the dust against our land:
Though the cause of Evil prosper, yet 'tis Truth alone is strong,   *
and, albeit she wander outcast now, I see around her throng
troops of beautiful tall angels, to enshield her from all wrong.

Backward look across the ages and the beacon-moments see,
that, like peaks of some sunk continent, jut through Oblivion's sea;
not an ear in court or market for the low foreboding cry
of those Crises, God's stern winnowers, from whose feet earth's chaff
           must fly;
never shows the choice momentous till the judgment hath passed by.

Careless seems the great Avenger; history's pages but record
one death-grapple in the darkness 'twixt old systems and the Word;
Truth forever on the scaffold, Wrong for ever on the Throne, -   *
yet that scaffold sways the future, and behind the dim unknown   *
standeth God within the shadow, keeping watch above his own.   *

We see dimly in the Present what is small and what is great,'
slow of faith how weak an arm may turn the iron helms of fate,
but the soul is still oracular; amid the market's din,
list the ominous stern whisper from the Delphic cave within, -
'They enslave their children's children who make compromise with
           sin.'

Slavery, the earth-born Cyclops, fellest of the giant brood,
sons of brutish Force and Darkness, who have drenched the earth with
           blood,
famished in his self-made desert, blinded by our purer day,

gropes in yet unblasted regions for his miserable prey; -
shall we guide his gory fingers where our helpless children play?

Then to side with Truth is noble when we share her wretched crust,   *
ere her cause bring fame and profit and 'tis prosperous to be just;   *
then it is the brave man chooses, while the coward stands aside,   *
doubting in his abject spirit, till his Lord is crucified,
and the multitude make virtue of the faith they had denied.   *

Count me o'er earth's chosen heroes, - they were souls that stood
                                              alone,
while the men they agonized for hurled the contumelious stone,
stood serene, and down the future saw the golden beam incline
to the side of perfect justice, mastered by their faith divine,
by one man's plain truth to manhood and to God's supreme design.

By the light of burning heretics Christ's bleeding feet I track,   *
toiling up new Calvaries ever with the cross that turns not back,   *
and these mounts of anguish number how each generation learned
one new word of that grand *Credo* which in prophet-hearts hath
                                            burned
since the first man stood God-conquered with his face to heaven
                                            upturned.

For Humanity sweeps onward: where to-day the martyr stands,
on the morrow crouches Judas with the silver in his hands;
far in front the cross stands ready and the crackling fagots burn,
while the hooting mob of yesterday in silent awe return
to glean up the scattered ashes into History's golden urn.

'Tis as easy to be heroes as to sit the idle slaves
of a legendary virtue carved upon our fathers' graves,
worshippers of light ancestral make the present light a crime; -
was the Mayflower launched by cowards, steered by men behind their
                                            time?
Turn those tracks toward Past or Future, that make Plymouth Rock
                                            sublime?

They were men of present valor, stalwart old iconoclasts,
unconvinced by axe or gibbet that all virtue was the Past's;
but we make their truth our falsehood, thinking that hath made us free,
hoarding it in mouldy parchments, while our tender spirits flee
the rude grasp of that great Impulse which drove them across the sea.

They have rights who dare maintain them; we are traitors to our sires,
smothering in their holy ashes Freedom's new-lit altar-fires;
shall we make their creed our jailer? Shall we, in our haste to slay,
from the tombs of the old prophets steal the funeral lamps away
to light up the martyr-fagots round the prophets of to-day?

New occasions teach new duties; time makes ancient good uncouth; *
they must upward still, and onward, who would keep abreast of
                                      Truth;   *
Lo, before us gleam her camp-fires! we ourselves must Pilgrims be,
launch our Mayflower, and steer boldly through the desperate winter
                                          sea,
nor attempt the Future's portal with the Past's blood-rusted key.

The Present Crisis, December, 1844

Using the lines marked with an asterisk in the above text, W. Garrett Horder
made the following version in England, which was first published in 1896:

      Once to every man and nation
        comes the moment to decide,
    in the strife of Truth with Falsehood,
        for the good or evil side;
      some great cause, God's new Messiah,
        off'ring each the bloom or blight, -

and the choice goes by for ever
    'twixt that darkness and that light.

Then to side with Truth is noble,
    when we share her wretched crust,
ere her cause bring fame and profit
    and 'tis prosperous to be just;
then it is the brave man chooses,
    while the coward stands aside,
till the multitude make virtue
    of the faith they had denied.

By the light of burning martyrs,
    Jesus' bleeding feet I track,
toiling up new Calvaries ever
    with the Cross that turns not back;
new occasions teach new duties;
    time makes ancient good uncouth;
they must upward still and onward
    who would keep abreast of Truth.

Though the cause of evil prosper
    Yet 'tis Truth alone is strong;
though her portion be the scaffold
    and upon the Throne be Wrong,
yet that scaffold sways the future,
    and behind the dim unknown,
standeth God within the shadow,
    Keeping watch above his own.

JAMES RUSSELL LOWELL
1819-91

371
EPIPHANY

'What means this glory round our feet?'
    the Magi mused, 'more bright than morn?'
And voices chanted clear and sweet,
    'To-day the Prince of Peace is born.'

'What means that star?' the shepherds said,
    'that brightens through the rocky glen?'
And angels answering overhead
    sang, 'Peace on earth, good will to men.'

'Tis eighteen hundred years and more
    since those sweet oracles were dumb;
we wait for him, like them of yore;
    alas! he seems so slow to come.

But it was said in words of gold,
    no time or sorrow e'er shall dim,
that little children might be bold,
    in perfect trust to come to him.   (Mk. 10:14)

All round about our feet shall shine
    a light like that the wise man saw,
if we our willing hearts incline
    to that sweet life which is the Law.

So shall we learn to understand
    the simple faith of shepherds then,
and, kindly clasping hand in hand,
    sing 'Peace on earth, good will to men.'

For they who to their childhood cling,
    and keep their natures fresh as morn
once more shall hear the angels sing,
    'To-day the Prince of Peace is born.'

Songs of the Sanctuary, 1865

**THOMAS WENTWORTH
HIGGINSON*, 1823 - ?**

372
WHO HEAREST PRAYER

No human eyes thy face may see;   (Ex. 33:20)
    no human thought thy form may know;
but all creation dwells in thee,
    and thy great life through all doth flow!

And yet, O strange and wondrous thought! -
    thou art a God who hearest prayer   (Ps. 65:2)
and every heart with sorrow fraught
    to seek thy present aid may dare.

And though most weak our efforts seem
    into one creed these thoughts to bind,
and vain the intellectual dream
    to see and know th'Eternal Mind;

yet thou wilt not turn them aside
    who cannot solve thy life divine,
but would give up all reason's pride
    to know their hearts approved by thine.

So though we faint on life's dark hill,
    and thought grow weak and knowledge flee,
yet faith shall teach us courage still,
    and love shall guide us on to thee.

Book of Hymns (Longfellow and
Johnson), 1846

EDMUND HAMILTON SEARS
1810-76

373
PEACE UPON EARTH   HG 339

It came upon the midnight clear,
    that glorious song of old,
from angels bending near the earth
    to touch their harps of gold -
'Peace on the earth, good will to men   (Lk. 2:15)
    from heaven's all gracious King;'
The world in solemn stillness lay
    to hear the angels sing.

Still through the cloven skies they come,
    with peaceful wings unfurled,
and still their heavenly music floats
    o'er all the weary world;
above its sad and lonely plains
    they bend on hovering wing,
and ever o'er its Babel-sounds   (Gen. 11:1ff)
    the blessed angels sing.

Yet, with the woes of sin and strife
    the world has suffered long;
beneath the angel-strain have rolled
    two thousand years of wrong;

and man, at war with man, hears not
    the love-song which they bring:
O hush the noise, ye men of strife,
    and hear the angels sing!

And ye, beneath life's crushing load,
    whose forms are bending low,
who toil along the climbing way
    with painful steps and slow, -
look now, for glad and golden hours
    come swiftly on the wing:
O rest beside the weary road,
    and hear the angels sing!

For lo! the days are hastening on
    by prophet bards foretold   (Virgil, Eclogue IV)
when with the ever-circling years
    comes round the age of gold:
when peace shall over all the earth
    her ancient splendours fling,
and the whole world give back the song
    which now the angels sing.

The Christian Register, 1849

JAMES FREEMAN CLARKE*
1810-88

374
CANA
John 2:1ff

Dear Friend, whose presence in the house,
    whose gracious word benign,
could once, at Cana's wedding feast
    turn water into wine,

come, visit us, and when dull work
    grows weary, line on line,   (Is. 28:10)
revive our souls, and make us see
    life's water turn to wine.

Gay mirth shall deepen into joy,
    earth's hope shall grow divine
when Jesus visits us, to turn
    life's water into wine.

The social talk, the evening fire,
    the homely household shrine,
shall glow with angel-visits when
    the Lord pours out the wine.

For when self-seeking turns to love,
    which knows not mine and thine,
the miracle again is wrought,
    and water changed to wine.

Lyra Sacra Americana, 1855

OLIVER WENDELL HOLMES
1809-94

375
LORD OF ALL BEING   HG 427

Lord of all being, throned afar,
    thy glory flames from sun and star
centre and soul of every sphere,
    yet to each loving heart how near;

Sun of our life, thy quickening ray
sheds on our path the glow of day;
star of our hope, thy softened light
cheers the long watches of the night.

Our midnight is thy smile withdrawn,
our noontide is thy gracious dawn,
our rainbow-arch, thy mercy's sign;   (Gen. 8:22)
all, save the clouds of sin, are thine.

Lord of all life, below, above,
whose light is truth, whose warmth is love,
before thy ever-blazing throne
we ask no lustre of our own.

Grant us thy truth to make us free   (John 8:32)
and kindling hearts that burn for thee,
till all thy living altars claim
one holy light, one heavenly flame.

1848; *The Atlantic Monthly*, 1859

JULIA WARD HOWE
1819-1910

376
THE BATTLE HYMN OF THE REPUBLIC HG 454

Mine eyes have seen the glory of the coming of the Lord;
he is trampling out the vintage where the grapes of wrath are stored
                                                                                    (Is. 63:3)
he hath loosed the fateful lightning of his terrible swift sword:
            his truth is marching on.

I have seen him in the watchfires of a hundred circling camps;
they have builded him an altar in the evening dews and damps;
I have read his righteous sentence in the dim and flaring lamps;
            his day is marching on.

I have read a fiery gospel, writ in burnished rows of steel;
As ye deal with my contemners, so with you my grace shall deal:
let the hero born of woman crush the serpent with his heel;
                                                                (Gen. 3:15)
            our God is marching on.

He has sounded forth the trumpet that shall never call retreat;
he is sifting out the hearts of men before his judgment seat;
O be swift, my soul, to answer him, be jubilant, my feet:
            our God is marching on.

In the beauty of the lilies Christ was born across the sea
with a glory in his bosom that transfigures you and me;
as he died to make men holy, let us die to make men free:
            our God is marching on.

He is coming like the glory of the morning on the wave, (Hos. 6:3)
he is wisdom to the mighty, he is succour to the brave;
so the world shall be his footstool, and the soul of time his slave:
            our God is marching on.

The Atlantic Monthly, February 1862

SAMUEL LONGFELLOW
1819-92
HG 7

377
LOOKING TO GOD   HG 315

I look to thee in every need,
   and never look in vain;

I feel thy strong and tender love
   and all is well again:
the thought of thee is mightier far
than sin and pain and sorrow are.

Discouraged in the work of life,
   disheartened by its load,
shamed by its failures and its fears,
   I sink beside the road;
but let me only think of thee,
and then new heart springs up in me.

Thy calmness bends serene above,
   my restlessness to still;
around me flows thy quickening life,
   to nerve my faltering will;
thy presence fills my solitude;
thy providence turns all to good.

Embosomed deep in thy dear love,
   held in thy law, I stand;
thy hand in all things I behold,
   and all things in thy hand;
thou leadest me by unsought ways,
and turnst my mourning into praise.   (Ps. 30:11)

Hymns of the Spirit, 1864

SAMUEL JOHNSON
1822-82
HG 120

378
LIFE OF AGES   HG 395

Life of ages, richly poured,
   love of God unspent and free,
flowing in the prophets' word
   and the people's liberty; -

never was to chosen race
   that unstinted tide confined;
thine is every time and place,
   fountain sweet of heart and mind.

Breathing in the thinker's creed,
   pulsing in the hero's blood,
shaping noblest thought and deed,
   still inspiring truth and good,

consecrating art and song,
   holy book and pilgrim way,
quelling strife and tyrant-wrong
   widening freedom's sacred sway, -

Life of ages, richly poured,
   love of God unspent and free,
flow still in the prophet's word,
   and the people's liberty!

Hymns of the Spirit, 1864

379
CITY OF GOD   HG 120

City of God, how broad and far
   outspread thy walls sublime!
The true thy chartered freemen are
   of every age and clime.

One holy church, one army strong,
    one stedfast high intent,
one working band, one harvest-song,
    one King omnipotent!

How purely hath thy speech come down
    from man's primeval youth!
How grandly hath thine empire grown
    of freedom, love and truth!

How gleam thy watch-fires through the night
    with never-fainting ray!
How rise thy towers, serene and bright
    to greet the dawning day!

In vain the surges' angry shock,
    in vain the drifting sands;
unharmed upon the eternal Rock,
    the eternal City stands.

Hymns of the Spirit, 1864

ELIZA SCUDDER*
1821-96

380
TRUTH

Thou long disowned, reviled, oppressed,
    strange Friend of human kind,
seeking through weary years a rest
    within our hearts to find; -

how late thy bright and awful brow
    breaks through these clouds of sin;
hail, Truth divine! we know thee now;
    Angel of God, come in!

Come, though with purifying fire
    and swift-dividing sword,
thou of all nations the desire   (Hag. 2:4)
    earth waits thy cleansing word.

Struck by the lightning of thy glance,
    let old oppressions die:
before thy cloudless countenance
    let fear and falsehood fly.

Anoint our eyes with healing grace   (Rev. 3:18)
    to see, as not before,
our Father in our brother's face,
    our Maker in his poor.

Flood our dark life with golden day:
    convince, subdue, enthral;
they to a mightier yield thy sway,
    and Love be all in all.

Hymns of the Spirit, 1864

JOHN WHITE CHADWICK
1840-1904

381
WE WOULD BE ONE   HG 172

Eternal Ruler of the ceaseless round
    of circling planets singing on their way,
Guide of the nations from the night profound
    into the glory of the perfect day;
rule in our hearts, that we may ever be
    guided, and strengthened, and upheld by thee.

We are of thee, the children of thy love,
    the brothers of thy well-belovèd Son;
descend, O Holy Spirit, like a dove,
    into our hearts, that we may be as one, -
as one with thee, to whom we ever tend;
as one with him, our Brother and our Friend.

We would be one in hatred of all wrong,
    one in the love of all things sweet and fair,
one with the joy that breaketh into song,
    one with the grief that trembles into prayer,
one in the power that makes thy children free
to follow truth, and thus to follow thee.

O clothe us with thy heavenly armour, Lord, - (Eph. 6:10)
    thy trusty shield, thy sword of love divine;
our inspirations be thy constant word,
    we ask no victories that are not thine.
Give or withhold, let pain or pleasure be:
enough to know that we are serving thee.

1864; *A Book of Poems*, 1876

WILLIAM HENRY BURLEIGH
1812-71

382   HG 387

Lead us, O Father, in the paths of peace;   (Lk. 1:79)
    without thy guiding hand we go astray,
and doubts appal, and sorrows still increase;
    lead us through Christ, the true and living Way.

Lead us, O Father, in the paths of truth;
    unhelped by thee, in error's maze we grope,
while passion stains and folly dims our youth,
    and age comes on uncheered by faith and hope.

Lead us, O Father, in the paths of right;
    blindly we stumble when we walk alone,
involved in shadows of a darksome night,
    only with thee we journey safely on.

Lead us, O Father, to thy heavenly rest,
    however rough and steep the path may be,
through joy or sorrow, as thou deemest best,
    until our lives are perfected in thee.

Lyra Sacre Americana, 1868

PHILLIPS BROOKS,
Bishop
1835-93

383
O LITTLE TOWN OF BETHLEHEM   HG 535

O little town of Bethlehem,
    how still we see thee lie!
above thy deep and dreamless sleep
    the silent stars go by.
Yet in thy dark streets shineth
    the everlasting light;
the hopes and fears of all the years
    are met in thee tonight.

O morning stars, together
    proclaim the holy birth,
and praises sing to Christ the King,
    and peace to men on earth;
for Christ is born of Mary;
    and, gathered all above,

while mortals sleep, the angels keep
their watch of wondering love.

How silently, how silently
the wondrous gift is given!
So God imparts to human hearts
the blessings of his heaven.
No ear may hear his coming;
but in this world of sin,
where meek hearts will receive him, still
the dear Christ enters in.

Where children pure and happy
pray to the blessèd Child,
where misery cries out to thee,
son of the Mother mild;
where charity stands watching
and faith holds wide the door,
the dark night wakes, the glory breaks,
and Christmas comes once more.

O holy Child of Bethlehem,
descend on us, we pray;
cast out our sin, and enter in,
be born in us to-day.
We hear the Christmas angels
the great glad tidings tell;
O come to us, abide with us,
our Lord, Immanuel.

The Church Porch, 1874

SAMUEL WOLCOTT
1813-86

384
CHRIST FOR THE WORLD! HG 106

Christ for the world, we sing!
the world to Christ we bring
with loving zeal;
the poor and them that mourn,
the faint and overborne,
sin-sick and sorrow-worn,
whom Christ doth heal.

Christ for the world, we sing!
The world to Christ we bring
with fervent prayer;
the wayward and the lost,
by restless passions tossed,
redeemed at countless cost
from dark despair.

Christ for the world we sing!
the word to Christ we bring
with one accord;
with us the work to share,
with us reproach to dare,
with us the cross to bear
for Christ our Lord.

Christ for the world we sing!
the world to Christ we bring
with joyful song;
the new-born souls, whose days
reclaimed from error's ways,
inspired with hope and praise,
to Christ belong.

1869; *Laudes Domini*, 1884

DANIEL CRANE ROBERTS
1841-1907

385
CENTENNIAL HYMN HG 242

God of our Fathers, whose almighty hand
leads forth in beauty all the starry band
of shining worlds in splendor through the skies,
our grateful songs before thy throne arise.

Thy love divine hath led us in the past:
in this free land by thee our lot is cast;
be thou our Ruler, Guardian, Guide and Stay;
thy word our law, thy paths our chosen way.

From war's alarms, from deadly pestilence,
be thy strong arm our ever sure defense;
thy true religion in our hearts increase,
thy bounteous goodness nourish us in peace.

Refresh thy people on their toilsome way,
lead us from night to never ending day;
fill all our lives with love and grace divine,
and glory, laud and praise be ever thine.

1876; *Hymnal* (Episcopal), 1892

**MARY ARTEMISIA
LATHBURY**, 1841-1913

386
BREAK THOU THE BREAD OF LIFE HG 93

Break thou the bread of life,
dear Lord, to me,
as thou didst break the loaves
beside the sea;
beyond the sacred page
I seek thee, Lord;
My spirit longs for thee,
O living Word.

Bless thou the truth, dear Lord,
to me, to me,
as thou didst bless the bread
by Galilee;
then shall all bondage cease,
all fetters fall;
and I shall find my peace,
my All in All.

1877; *Worship Song*, 1896

**FREDERICK LUCIAN
HOSMER**, 1840-1929
HG 483

387
CHRIST ALWAYS PRESENT

We pray no more, made lowly wise,
for miracle and sign;
anoint our eyes to see within
the common, the divine.

'Lo, here, lo there,' no more we cry   (Matt. 24:23)
dividing with our call
the mantle of thy presence, Lord,
that seamless covers all.

We turn from seeking thee afar
and in unwonted ways,

to build from out our daily lives
the temples of thy praise.

And if thy casual comings, Lord,
to hearts of old were dear,
what joy shall dwell within the faith
that feels thee ever near!

And nobler yet shall duty grow,
and more shall worship be,
when thou art found in all our life,
and all our life in thee.

1879; The Thought of God, 1885

388
THY KINGDOM COME!
Luke 11:3   HG 751

'Thy kingdom come,' on bended knee
the passing ages pray;
and faithful souls have yearned to see
on earth that kingdom's day.

But the slow watches of the night
not less to God belong,
and for the everlasting right
the silent stars are strong.

And lo! already on the hills
the flags of dawn appear;
gird up your loins, ye prophet souls,
proclaim the day is near;

the day in whose clear-shining light
all wrong shall stand revealed,
when justice shall be clothed with might,
and every hurt be healed:

when knowledge, hand in hand with peace   (Ps. 85:12)
shall walk the earth abroad -
the day of perfect righteousness,
the promised day of God.

The Thought of God (2nd ed), 1894

WILLIAM CROSWELL DOANE
1832-1913

389
ANCIENT OF DAYS   HG 38

Ancient of Days, who sittest throned in glory,
to thee all knees are bent, all voices pray;
thy love has blest the wide world's wondrous story
with light and life since Eden's dawning day.

O holy Father, who hast led thy children
in all the ages, with the fire and cloud,   (Ex. 40:38)
through seas dry-shod and weary wastes bewild'ring;
to thee, in reverent love our hearts are bowed.

O holy Jesus, Prince of Peace and Savior,
to thee we owe the peace that still prevails,
stilling the rude wills of men's wild behavior,
and calming passion's fierce and stormy gales.

O holy Ghost, the Lord and the Life-giver,
thine is the quickening power that still prevails,

from thee have flowed, as from a pleasant river,
our plenty, wealth, prosperity and peace.

O Triune God, with heart and voice adoring,
praise we the goodness that doth crown our days;
pray we that thou wilt hear us, still imploring
thy love and favor, kept to us always.

1886; Hymnal (Episcopal), 1892

ARTICLE 19:
BLACK AND WHITE SPIRITUALS AND GOSPEL
SONGS (390-408)   HG 223

Very little commentary is needed on these three groups of regional or sectional hymnody peculiar to America. They all have this in common: They depend far more on their music than on their texts for their effect. Less than any other of the material in this collection can they be read without musical association.

For the elements of the history of Black Spirituals, see the *Hymnal Guide* at no. 223, and for ampler and more authoritative information, *120 Negro Spirituals*, by A. Sandilands. Essentially they are the songs of the black people who were brought to America originally from Africa as slaves; the Kentucky Revivals at the end of the 18th century did much to begin to form them into a religious community and to appeal to the instincts which their condition had sought to suppress. We here give only a few texts which seem to be representative of the character of these haunting songs. They are, broadly speaking, (a) scriptural, with a strong emphasis on the liberation of the Exodus (390-1); (b) strongly heaven-centered, as the songs of people in such dismal earthly circumstances well might be (392); (c) full of appeal to the Saviour as comforter of sufferings (393); (d) evangelically Crucifixion-centered (394); (e) very simply didactic (395-6); or (f) hopeful and nursery-rhyme-like (397-8). Almost always they had refrains, as was appropriate to songs for people who were largely illiterate, and they were always vivid, often conversational and even humorous, in their language. Usually they were songs of desperate courage, and often they had an educational slant to give a hopeful pattern to life and to make simple the stories of the Scriptures for the comfort of the slaves.

The use of such songs as these as hymns in the worship of congregations not racially or socially subject to the conditions that generated them is a fairly recent development and is, as much as anything, a gesture of solidarity. Sometimes—though not in the examples here given—the texts are written in a dialect which is really a 'white' transcription of the pronunciation customary among blacks from the southern states. And of course more modern songs, like 'Oh, Freedom' have been written in the style of the 'black classics.' But they remain a regional and sub-cultural form of hymnody whose simple words and music make it perhaps the most powerful section of pure folk-song—material sung before being written down—in the whole literature.

Tunes and texts remain together, and there are hardly any instances at all of a 'black' tune being set to a 'white' text. The most famous exception is the 'black' tune MCKEE, now often sung to 'In Christ there is no East nor West.'

The *White Spiritual* is so called by analogy with the more primitive Black Spiritual, but it is something quite different. This is a generic name sometimes given to the hymnody of the white settlers in the so-called 'southern' states (that expression really means the old slave states), lying either side of the southern Appalachians. This hymnody mostly used texts from evangelical English sources: Isaac Watts most frequently, Charles Wesley sometimes, Toplady and Newton occasionally. Through social and historical accidents, it was known, until recently, only to those communities that lay in that part of the United States, and its special quality is not in its texts but in its music. Certain tunes have now escaped from·that closed environment and found their way all over America, one or two, like the tune of 'Amazing Grace' (whose words are from the Olney Hymns, 1779), all over the world. These tunes are actually in the idiom of the Scottish, Welsh and Irish folk music of the 18th century, when they are not modelled on the evangelical fuguing tunes used by the Methodists—and disapproved by Wesley—from about 1770 onwards.

The communities that use this music are still exceedingly remote, in-bred, mentally conservative, rather anti-educational, and primitive in their religious customs. They devote themselves to agriculture, being the descendants of those British settlers who entered North Carolina and slowly thrust their way through the forests and over the highest range of the Appalachians, which reaches 6,000 feet in several places and is thickly forested to the summit, into Tennessee and Kentucky. There were not slave-owners—they had not the affluence nor stability for that. They were rude pioneers whose behaviour to the Indians in the early stages has been matched in later years, their successors claim without much accuracy, by the brutality of the strip-mining industrialists to them. In Tennessee they still gather for immense hymn-singing marathons, using hymnals that are reprinted without alteration from original editions a hundred and more years old. They sing in a strange nasal style from music books set out in 'shape note' characters, a device that in the United States corresponds to the British sol-fa system as an assistance to easy music reading—and in fact is a great deal better. Their solid conservatism and resistance to change very naturally extinguishes any need for new hymnody, and one rarely finds a native text. When one does, it is distinguished from the Black Spiritual and the Gospel Song by hardly ever having a chorus, for these people could read, and could read music. But when the tune is of the 'English,' rather than of the other British kinds, you often find endless repetitions of words in a Common Meter stanza to accommodate it, and everything in these fascinating old books, which remain monolithically unchangeable in type and temperament, suggests that these songs, for these people, are the whole of their aesthetic culture; they are their drama, their poetry, their symphonies, their pop music. The music itself, having come into their culture from the main stream of British hymnody and folk-song, ran back naturally into the wider culture as soon as it was rediscovered, to the enrichment of everybody concerned. But when sung by people elsewhere in the world it sounds entirely different from what one hears in one of these tiny, primitive, southern churches or at one of their marathon united hymn-singing festivals on a summer night in the countryside.

The *Gospel Song* (402-8) is the third native contribution of Americans to the treasury of hymnody, and it has something in common with both the Black Spiritual and the White Spiritual. It has the simplicity, the repetitiveness, and the addiction to refrains of the Black Song, since it is largely aimed at those who cannot read, or do not propose to. It has the obsessive, ingrown, and entirely petrified character of the White Spiritual in that it never changes its style, as we can easily demonstrate

by presenting songs of this kind ranging over a period of almost a century.

Like the Black Songs, it is Atonement-centered and often didactic, but the only human suffering it knows about is the supposed suffering of the sinner. It is the music of an uncomplicated activist religion that has little time for subtleties, doubts, or speculations and is the reverse of contemplative. A hint was thrown out when we passed #313 of an affinity between this style and that of children's hymns—and indeed there is a ministry to immaturity for which these songs were originally designed. They became known on both sides of the Atlantic through the missions of Moody and Sankey from 1870 onwards and also through the famous travelling choir, the Jubilee Singers from the (Black) Fiske University in Nashville, Tennessee. Their repetitiveness and their very limited vocabulary, nicely combining a very narrow range of words and expressions with just enough theological technicality ('Blood,' 'the Lamb') to attract the uninitiated, made them an ideal vehicle for mass-mission in the industrial parts of both our countries. The music matched, in its unchanging, repetitive, and uncomplicated style, the set of the words.

It was, one need hardly say, very easy to write such lyrics as these. Fanny Crosby (Mrs van Alstyne) is said to have composed more lyrics than Charles Wesley, but it is hardly unfair to say that when you have seen one you have seen them all (403). Ira D. Sankey, the preacher and singer, composed relatively few, and his style had a certain homespun innocence that often avoided sheer platitude; his associate, P. P. Bliss (404), was more prolific and less inventive. The early international success of these songs distinguishes them totally from the Spirituals. In all the decades that followed their first appearance, they have appealed to many and have had such success that nobody has seriously considered any adaptation of their message to changing situations. They therefore have their special place among those religious groups which see the Gospel as a static, unchanging body of truth to which everybody is, in their special language, invited to come. The one variation on the strictly 'Gospel' aspect of these songs turns out to be a naturalistic sentimentality which can plumb alarming depths (406), and it is depressingly true that the integrity of both the Black Spiritual and the Gospel Song has been dangerously compromised by a textual—and far more a musical—concession to the worst of commercialized bad taste. It is no bad exercise to look over the handful of such songs that was admitted to the *English Hymnal* and consider on what grounds the highly sensitive editors of that book thought these the best examples; the ground will be found to be, on the whole, sound. *Hymns Ancient and Modern*, England's monument of hymnic propriety, only ever admitted one such song, our #402, and it disappeared in 1950.

390
GO DOWN, MOSES

When Israel was in Egypt's land (Let my people go!)
oppress'd so hard they could not stand (Let my people go!)
   Go down, Moses,
   way down in Egypt land;
   tell old Pharaoh:
   'Let my people go!'

No more shall they in bondage toil . . .
let them come out with Egypt's spoil . . .

O 'twas a dark and dismal night . . .
when Moses led the Israelites . . .

The Lord told Moses what to do . . .
to lead the children of Israel through . . .

'O come along, Moses, you'll not get lost' . . .
'Stretch out your rod and come across' . . .

When they reached the other shore . . .
they sang a song of triumph o'er . . .

Pharaoh said he would go across . . .
but Pharaoh and his host were lost . . .

O let us all from bondage flee . . .
and let us all in Christ be free . . .

(Exodus 7:1-15, 19)

391
DEEP RIVER

Deep river!
    my home is over Jordan,
Deep river!
    Lord, I want to pass over into camp ground.
O don't you want to go to that Gospel feast,
that promised land where all is peace?
    Lord, I want to pass over into camp ground.
Deep river!
    my home is over Jordan:
Deep river!
    Lord, I want to pass over into camp ground.

(Deut. 11:31)

392
SWING LOW, SWEET CHARIOT

Swing low, sweet chariot,
    coming for to carry me home!
Swing low, sweet chariot,
    coming for to carry me home!

I looked over Jordan, and what did I see,
    coming for to carry me home?
A band of angels coming after me
    coming for to carry me home.

If you get there before I do . . .
tell all my friends I'm coming too . . .

The brightest day that ever I saw . . .
when Jesus washed my sins away . . .

I'm sometimes up and sometimes down . . .
but still my soul feels heavenward bound . . .

(4 Kings 2:11)

393
NOBODY KNOWS

Nobody knows the trouble I see, Lord,
    nobody knows the trouble I see,
    nobody knows the trouble I see, Lord,
    nobody knows like Jesus.

Brothers, will you pray for me,
brothers, will you pray for me,
brothers, will you pray for me
    and help me to drive old Satan away?

Sisters, will you pray for me . . . ? (3)

Mothers, will you pray for me . . . ? (3)

Preachers, will you pray for me . . . ? (3)

(Rev. 2:2, 9; 1 Thess. 5:25)

394
WERE YOU THERE

Were you there when they crucified my Lord?
Were you there when they crucified my Lord?
    Oh, sometimes it causes me to tremble, tremble, tremble,
    Were you there when they crucified my Lord?

Were you there when they nailed him to the tree? . . .

Were you there when they pierced him in the side? . . .

Were you there when the sun refused to shine? . . .

Were you there when they laid him in the tomb? . . .

(Matt. 27:32-61)

395
GOING TO WRITE TO MASTER JESUS

Going to write to Master Jesus,
    to send some valiant soldiers,
    to turn back Pharaoh's army, Hallelu!
    to turn back Pharaoh's army, Hallelujah!
    to turn back Pharaoh's army, Hallelu!

If you want your souls converted,
    you'd better be a praying . . .

When the children were in bondage,
    they cried unto the Lord . . .

You say you are a soldier,
    fighting for your Saviour . . .

(Ex. 14:10; Deut. 26:7)

396
WALK YOU IN THE LIGHT

Walk you in the light, walk you in the light,
Walk you in the light, walking in the light of God.

O children, do you think it's true?
    walking in the light of God,
that Jesus Christ did die for you?
    walking in the light of God?

I think I heard some children say
that they never heard their parents pray:
O parents, that is not the way,
but teach your children to watch and pray. . . .

I love to shout and I love to sing,
I love to praise my heavenly King:
O sisters, can't you help me sing,
for Moses' sister did help him. . . .

(John 12:35; Ex. 15:20ff)

397
JACOB'S LADDER

We are climbing Jacob's ladder,
we are climbing Jacob's ladder,
we are climbing Jacob's ladder,
  soldier of the cross.

Every round goes higher and higher . . . (3)

Sinner, do you love my Jesus . . . (3)

If you love him, why not serve him? . . . (3)

Do you think I'd make a soldier? . . . (3)

We are climbing higher and higher . . . (3)

(Gen. 28:12)

398
BREAKING BREAD

Let us break bread together *on our knees,*
let us break bread together *on our knees,*
  When I fall on my knees
  with my face to the rising sun,
  O Lord, have mercy on me.

Let us drink wine together . . .

Let us praise God together . . .

(Acts 20:7; 1 Cor. 11:23f)

399
WONDROUS LOVE   HG 799

What wondrous love is this, oh my soul, oh my soul!
what wondrous love is this, oh my soul!
  what wondrous love is this,
  that caused the Lord of bliss
to bear the dreadful curse for my soul, for my soul -
to bear the dreadful curse for my soul?

When I was sinking down, sinking down, sinking down,
when I was sinking down, sinking down
  when I was sinking down
  beneath God's righteous frown
Christ laid aside his crown for my soul, for my soul,
Christ laid aside his crown for my soul.

To God and to the Lamb I will sing, I will sing;
to God and to the Lamb I will sing;
  to God and to the Lamb,
  who is the great I AM,
while millions join the theme, I will sing, I will sing,
while millions join the theme I will sing.

And when from death I'm free I'll sing on, I'll sing on,
and when from death I'm free, I'll sing on,
  and when from death I'm free,
  I'll sing and joyful be,
and through eternity I'll sing on, I'll sing on,
and through eternity I'll sing on.

Original Sacred Harp

400
THE WICKED KINGDOM

See how the wicked kingdom is falling every day!
and still our blessed Jesus is winning souls away:
but oh, how I am tempted, no mortal tongue can tell!
So often I'm surrounded with enemies from hell.

With weeping and with praying, my Jesus I have found
to crucify old nature, and make his grace abound.
Dear children, don't be weary, but march on in the way,
for Jesus will stand by you, and be your guard and stay.

If sinners will serve Satan, and join with one accord,
dear brethren, as for my part, I'm bound to serve the Lord;
and if you will go with me, pray give to me your hand,
and we'll march on together unto the promised land.

Southern Harmony, 1835

401
SAFE IN THE PROMISED LAND

Where are the Hebrew children?   (Dan. 3)
  where are the Hebrew children?
Where are the Hebrew children?
  safe in the promised land.
Though the furnace flamed around them
God, while in their troubles, found them,
he with love and mercy bound them,
  safe in the promised land.

Where are the twelve apostles?
Where are the twelve apostles?
Where are the twelve apostles?
  safe in the promised land.
They went up through pain and sighing,
scoffing, scourging, crucifying,
nobly for their Master dying,
  safe in the promised land.

Where are the holy Christians?
Where are the holy Christians?
Where are the holy Christians?
  safe in the promised land.
Those who've washed their robes and made them   (Rev. 7)
white, and spotless pure, and laid them
where no earthly stain can fade them,
  safe in the promised land.

probably by **PETER CARTWRIGHT**,
1785-1872, *Sacred Harp*, 1844

FANNY CROSBY
(Mrs F. J. van Alstyne)
1820-1915
HG 84

402
RESCUE THE PERISHING   HG 617

Rescue the perishing, care for the dying,
snatch them in pity from sin and the grave;

weep o'er the erring one, lift up the fallen,
tell them of Jesus the mighty to save.
Rescue the perishing, care for the dying;
Jesus is merciful, Jesus will save.

Though they are slighting him, still he is waiting,
waiting the penitent child to receive;
plead with them earnestly, plead with them gently,
he will forgive if they only believe. . . .

Down in the human heart, crushed by the tempter,
feelings lie buried that grace can restore;
touched by a loving heart, wakened by kindness,
chords that are broken will vibrate once more. . . .

Rescue the perishing, duty demands it;
strength for thy labor the Lord will provide;
back to the narrow way, patiently win them;
tell the poor wand'rer a Savior has died.
Rescue the perishing, care for the dying;
Jesus is merciful, Jesus will save.

Songs of Devotion, 1870

403
BLESSED ASSURANCE HG 84

Blessed assurance, Jesus is mine!
Oh what a foretaste of glory divine!
Heir of salvation, purchase of God,
born of the Spirit, washed in his blood.
This is my story, this is my song,
praising my Savior, all the day long;
this is my story, this is my song,
praising my Savior all the day long.

Perfect submission, perfect delight,
visions of rapture now burst on my sight:
angels descending bring from above   (John 1:51)
echoes of mercy, whispers of love. . . .

Perfect submission, all is at rest,
I in my Savior now am happy and blest;
watching and waiting, looking above,
filled with his goodness, lost in his love.
This is my story, this is my song,
praising my Savior all the day long.
This is my story, this is my song,
praising my Savior all the day long.

Gems of Praise, 1873

P. P. BLISS
1838-76
HG 447

404
WHOSOEVER WILL

'Whosoever heareth,' shout, shout the sound!
spread the blessed tidings all the world around;
tell the joyful news wherever man is found,
'Whosoever will may come.'   (Rev. 22:17)
'Whosoever will, whosoever will,'
send the proclamation over vale and hill;
'Tis a loving Father calls the wand'rer home:
'Whosoever will may come.'

Whosoever cometh need not delay,
now the door is open, enter while you may;

Jesus is the true, the only living Way;
'Whosoever will may come.' . . .

'Whosoever will,' the promise is secure;
'whosoever will,' for ever must endure;
'Whosoever will!' 'tis life for evermore:
'Whosoever will may come.' . . .

The Prize, 1870

LEWIS EDGAR JONES*
1865-1936

405
THERE IS POWER IN THE BLOOD

Would you be free from the burden of sin?
There's power in the Blood, power in the Blood;
would you o'er evil a victory win?
There's wonderful power in the Blood.
There is power, power, wonder-working power
in the blood, in the blood of the Lamb;
There is power, power, wonder-working power
in the precious blood of the Lamb.

Would you be free from your passion and pride? . . .
come for a cleansing to Calvary's side. . . .

Would you be whiter, much whiter than snow? . . . (Is. 1:18)
sin stains are lost in its life-giving flow. . . .

Would you do service for Jesus your King? . . .
Would you live daily his praises to sing? . . .

Songs of Praise and Victory, 1899

C. AUSTIN MILES*

406
IN THE GARDEN

I come to the garden alone,
while the dew is still on the roses;
and the voice I hear, falling on my ear
the Son of God discloses.
And he walks with me, and he talks with me,
and he tells me I am his own,
and the joy we share as we tarry there
none other has ever known.

He speaks and the sound of his voice,
is so sweet the birds hush their singing;
and the melody that he gave to me
within my heart is ringing. . . .

I'd stay in the garden with him,
though the night around me be falling;
but he bids me go; through the voice of woe
his voice to me is calling. . . .

1912

BAYLUS BENJAMIN
McKINNEY*, 1886-1952 and
MACK WEAVER

407
LORD, LAY SOME SOUL UPON MY HEART

Lord, lay some soul upon my heart
and love that soul through me;
and may I bravely do my part
to win that soul for thee.

Some soul for thee, some soul for thee,
this is my earnest plea,
help me each day on life's highway
to win some soul for thee.

Lord, lead me to some soul in sin,
and grant that I may be
endued with power and love to win
that soul, dear Lord, for thee. . . .

To win that soul for thee alone
will be my constant prayer;
that when I reach the great white throne
I'll meet that dear one there. . . .

Broadman Hymnal, 1940 (St. 1 anonymous)

LEROY McCLARD*

408
JESUS IS LORD OF ALL

Jesus is Savior and Lord of my life,
my hope, my glory, my all;
wonderful Master, in joy and in strife,
on him you too may call.
Jesus is Lord of all,
Jesus is Lord of all,
Lord of my thoughts and my service each day.
Jesus is Lord of all.

Blessed Redeemer, all glorious King,
worthy of reverence I pay;
tribute and praises I joyfully bring
to him, the Life, the Way. . . .

Will you surrender your all to him now?
Follow his will and obey,
crown him as Sovereign, before his throne bow;
give him your heart to-day. . . .

1966

ARTICLE 20:
HYMNS FROM THE POETS (409-448)

If any reader has been reading this book continuously, at this point he will encounter a complete change of pace, something almost like a new start. We are shifted back to England and back to 1600. No poetry anthology would need to put up with any such anomaly; in the history of hymnody it is absolutely inevitable.

More than once we have remarked that great poets, even great lyric poets, are not normally successful hymn writers. That proposition has a positive and a negative sense. Hymn writing, and abundant examples have surely proved it, is a branch of versifying which requires special gifts, special experience, special knowledge. It requires a subordination of many of the poet's natural instincts to the demands of sacred ballad. He cannot do just what he would normally have a right to do with meter, rhyme, and stanza-shape. When one adds to these restrictions the undoubted fact that so much hymn writing has come from people who have a religious experience which their friends would call intense and their enemies narrow or even bigoted, you have adequate explanation of the reason why what we can now call good hymnody is only the tip of an iceberg whose nether parts are nothing but a

congealed mass of bad poetry and worse thinking. If one were attempting to compile an anthology of bad and risible hymnody, the temptation to make it ten times the size of this one would be almost overwhelming. There is indeed terrible Watts and terrible Wesley, and ten times more terrible material from people whose names we do not even refer to here. And yet in its upper reaches, as we have tried to show, the restricted art of the hymn writer produces as excellent material for its purpose as the restricted art of the sonnet writer. It was strictly the hymn-writing tradition, and nothing else, that led to 'Ride on, ride on in majesty,' a hymn by a writer almost all the rest of whose work is not worth mentioning.

If the reader turns back for a moment to article 14, right at the end of that article we mentioned Robert Bridges, and the last few hymns in section 14 were mentioned as examples of the reaction against mediocre hymnody on the part of men of letters. The contents of this present section are as much the contribution to hymnody of those counter-revolutionaries as of their own writers; for we have collected here a group of forty hymns not one of which was intended by its author to be sung, or–with, I think, less than half a dozen exceptions–ever so sung in its author's lifetime.

Once again our historical principle applies: The use of the work of older lyric poets as hymnody was not invented by Bridges, Percy Dearmer, and Garrett Horder, although they were the most successful promoters of this particular kind of hymnology; the practice in fact goes right back to John Wesley, who included a good deal of George Herbert in his Charlestown hymn book of 1737. But he hardly ever did so without alteration, sometimes so drastic as to make the text unrecognizable. (If anybody ever asked John Wesley how he reconciled this treatment with his very famous passage in the 1780 Preface where he remonstrates with people who alter his own and his brother's hymns, did he ever say 'Ah, but *that* was before my conversion'?) None the less, the way he went beyond the hymnody of his own family and of Watts to enrich his hymnal shows how different his approach to the business was from that of most Evangelicals who followed him.

And here and there one will find poems made into hymns well before 1900. Indeed, to make the picture as clear as possible, we provide the date of the book in which, so far as can be ascertained, the poem did first appear as a hymn (excluding, in the case of George Herbert, the Wesley book because of its drastic alterations). These dates form a code which can be unravelled as follows:

1855: *The New Congregational Hymn Book*
1861: *Hymns Ancient and Modern*, 1st edition
1868: (no. 429) *Hymns Ancient & Modern*, 1st edition with Supplement
1868: (no. 431) *The Anglican Hymn Book*
1887: *The Congregational Church Hymnal*
1889: *Hymns Ancient and Modern*, 2nd edition with Supplement
1905: *Worship Song*
1906: *English Hymnal*
1909: *Fellowship Hymn Book*, 1st edition
1916: *Congregational Hymnary*
1925: *Songs of Praise*, 1st edition
1931: *Songs of Praise*, 2nd edition
1951: *The BBC Hymn Book*.

It will at once be seen that the *English Hymnal* and *Songs of*

Praise are by far the richest quarries. Indeed, there is far more material from the poets in *Songs of Praise* (1931 edition) than we have given here, since that book, like its remarkable successor, the *Cambridge Hymnal*, 1967 (from a quite different editorial stable), was designed for educational purposes. In both of these one finds a wealth of exquisite material which any hymn-lover should study even if there are not many chances of actually hearing it sung. What we have here is a selection of those hymns taken from the poets that seem to have found most congregational favour, or to deserve it. They will be more familiar to the English than to the Americans. This is probably understandable. If it was true to say, in the last article but one, that Americans became accustomed to a very polished style of writing and perhaps were less exposed to doggerel than the English in the 19th century, they may have felt less of an urge to nourish hymnody by exploring the poets. But in later years, when this is what they might have done, interest in the texts of hymns was almost extinguished by the custom of making them unreadable by always including them within the music staves of a hymnal. Yet ##447-8 indicate grounds for hope.

It is unnecessary to comment on each item in the present section; it will be better to let the reader read them and allow them to speak for themselves. But one point of guidance may well be useful. It is always necessary to notice that a true poet uses words as precision instruments and often condenses complex ideas into short and memorable phrases. It is always unwise to read–or to sing–the poets too quickly. To take the most obvious example: George Herbert's 'Come, my way' (415) is a tiny poem in which only one word is not a monosyllable. It needs to be read or sung very slowly in order that the words may expand and give off their aroma. Give the whole poem a chance to breathe! And where there is an obscurity, the reader may trust the poet to be delivering good sense instead of–as he might do with a more conventional hymn writer–dismissing him in haste.'

It is proper, however, to give some account of the way in which some of these pieces came into the treasury of hymnody.

We begin with 'God be in my head,' which is, in musical use, less a hymn than an anthem, for it is always sung to a through-composed setting. This was first used in a hymnal in the *Oxford Hymn Book*, 1908, and since then has had several settings. The bracketed word 'at' in the last line appears first in the *Sarum Primer* of 1558.

'Jerusalem, my happy home' (410) has constantly attracted the attention of editors. See the *Hymnal Guide* (344) for a brief account of the way in which it has been used, altered, adapted, and built on. But the first hymnal to include the whole text unaltered was the *English Hymnal*, and while its homely quaintness is sometimes too much for congregations to adjust to, it is something beautiful to read; the imagery of heaven in terms of an English garden, peopled by cheerful saints, has a touch of pathos if it can be believed–it is certainly plausible–that it was composed by a priest in prison under sentence of death.

The Spenser sonnet (411) has found its way into many books since the *English Hymnal* editors hit on the happy solution of the problem of setting fourteen lines to a four-line tune, namely, by repeating the tune's second half for the final couplet (which in a sonnet always sums up the thought of the whole). It was this that prompted the same editors, in *Songs of Praise*, to use a Bridges sonnet (our #261), and indeed, more daringly, a Shakespeare one (*SP* 622).

The Campian songs, part of a delicious little group, were domestic songs to be sung with a lute; *Songs of Praise* took them over as hymns.

Of the George Herbert poems, #414, 'Antiphon' is here printed as the author wrote it. *Hymns Ancient and Modern* seems to have been the first collection (1889) to use it as a hymn, and they did this by repeating the 'antiphon' at the beginning of verse 2. All hymnals have done this since except *Hymns for Church and School* (1964), which sets the hymn twice, once in the corrupt way and once in the original way, offering a new tune which so sets it. (An earlier one did appear privately about 1920 but has not survived). 'King of glory' (416) drops one stanza to make a 24-line hymn which since 1906 has been very popular in England, and appears in every British hymnal now, but hardly ever in the U.S.A.

For nos. 417 and 418 we have to thank the Congregationalists who, in the second edition of their hymn book in 1855, plundered Milton, their own great poet, to excellent purpose. The youthful 'Let us with a gladsome mind,' written when the poet was 15, needed to have some metrical irregularities ironed out in order to become singable; the 1855 editors perhaps went further than they need, and the most faithful hymn-text available is that of the *English Hymnal*. But a comparison of the hymn with its original shows how irresistible the old editors must have found Milton's juvenile venture.

No. 418, almost equally well known now, comes from the same source. Some nameless genius extracted these six stanzas from Milton's version of Psalms 80-88, made in 1648 in strict conformity with the requirements of metrical psalters. Hardly any words are here altered except in the first stanza. The hymn begins with the last lines of Psalm 85, which originally ran:

> Before him righteousness shall go,
>   his royal harbinger,
> then will he come, and not be slow,
>   his footsteps cannot err.

Thereafter the editors took vv. 10-11 of Ps. 85, v. 8 of Ps. 82 and vv. 9-10 of Ps. 86, and, except for the omission sometimes of their st. 2, it has stayed like that ever since.

The next one needing comment is #424, 'Pray that Jerusalem . . . ,' which of course could have appeared among the Scottish Psalms in section 2. But although the Scottish Psalter was virtually unknown in England in the 19th century, this three-stanza fragment was given as a hymn in C. H. Spurgeon's *Our Own Hymn Book* (1866); it was picked up by the *English Hymnal* and is the only fragment of a Scottish Psalm in that book. It has a curiously haunting quality, as if for this one moment in spite of themselves the metricizers broke into poetry. Here and there in later hymnals it is expanded by the use of verses from other psalms, rather in the manner of #418.

No. 425 is one of our few examples of a poem successfully rewritten; we did not care for John Wesley's way of doing it, but the author of this (Earl Nelson, whose version was later amended in details) has produced a magnificent hymn out of the irregular but beautiful original. This first appeared in ten-syllable lines in 1868 as 'Descend to thy Jerusalem, O Lord'; the first appearance of the version which has now found most favour (the one we give) seems to have been in the *Congregational Hymnary*, 1916. It has been picked up by one or two American hymnals, but is never there found in its full five-stanza form.

Vaughan's 'My soul, there is a country' caught the eye of Garrett Horder, who put it into *Worship Song* in 1896; he thought it wise to alter st. 3, to keep the meter and to write 'afar' in st. 1. *Songs of Praise* in 1925 restored the true text but kept Horder's tune.

The Baxter poems at ##428, 429 are parts of much longer pieces. Baxter was splendid but incredibly prolix in prose and verse. In an age before typewriters, he must have been one of the most industrious authors who ever lived, but he is hardly ever damaged by abridgment. It is interesting to note that 'Lord, it belongs not ...' was picked up as early as the 1868 *Hymns A & M.* Probably both these hymns have missed some measure of popularity through beginning with somewhat austere opening lines. One has to pause to recall that 'it belongs not to my care' means not 'I don't care' but 'it is not my business,' and that 'He wants not friends' doesn't mean that 'he is too high minded to bother with friends' but 'he is never without friends.' Once over those initial hurdles, what priceless beauties one enjoys in the rest! As for the superb #430–hardly any of it is actually Baxter. John Hampden Gurney based his hymn on some Baxter verses of which he kept hardly a line intact, and yet he breathes the Puritan spirit of indomitable cheerfulness as if he had been Baxter's close friend. By the way, 'sight' in st. 2 line 6 is certainly the true reading, despite the faithfulness of many hymnals to the oldest existing text (surely misprinted) in writing the foolish rhyme, 'light.'

It is not quite certain that 'My song is love unknown' (431) was never sung in its author's lifetime. It just might have been sung privately, to Lawes' tune for Psalm 47, as some believe. But it did not become a regular hymn until 1868 and perhaps began to be really popular after the Congregationalists took it in 1887. It is always sad when any stanza of this is left out by modern editors.

The two Bunyan hymns (433, 434) speak for themselves, and a comment on #434 will be found in the *Hymnal Guide.* Undoubtedly it was the Dearmer version which made the thing popular, with Vaughan Williams' tune. Americans now always use Dearmer; English editors almost always Bunyan, hobgoblins and all.

The reader may be glad to be reminded that Kit Smart (435-6), who ended his days insane, was the poet who wrote the poems that form the libretto for Benjamin Britten's *Rejoice in the Lamb.* No. 435 is the selection made in *Songs of Praise* except that we restore (for reading) 'He sang' for their 'We sing,' a decent emendation for congregational use.

Blake (437) would have been surprised to find himself in a hymnal; he would have been staggered–probably into apoplexy–to find himself the author of the text for a second English National Anthem, first so used at a rally in support of Women's Guilds in 1916; this is what the song known as 'Jerusalem' amounts to. Whether this is a great poem and a great piece of music which should never have met is an arguable point and one which will not interest American readers. But the *Hymnal Guide* has a word or two about this, and we are here content with the mystical song from 'Songs of Innocence' which the *English Hymnal* so felicitously made into a hymn.

No. 439 is a late addition to this company, having first appeared as a hymn in the *BBC Hymn Book* of 1951. This is another poet who went out of his mind; but this beautiful pastoral, with its dying fall, has proved very popular lately, beginning 'A stranger once did bless ...' and with some of the preceding verses written in, it recovers its original pathos.

John Henry Newman is one of the few poets who, writing verse he did not design as hymnody, heard it sung as hymnody within his own lifetime. 'Lead, kindly light' was a personal poem written under circumstances that are well enough known (*Hymnal Guide,* 384); he was often in later years heard to say that it was because of Dykes' tune that everybody loved it, and when asked what the angel faces in the last verse were he admitted that by that time he had forgotten. *Hymns Ancient and Modern* picked this up in its first edition, and in its second effort of 1868 netted a much more substantial treasure in 'Praise to the Holiest' (442). This is the last part of the 35-stanza 'hymn of the Angelicals' in *The Dream of Gerontius* (1865), and is made into a hymn by repeating its first stanza–which is the first stanza of each of the five parts of the hymn in the original drama–at the end. Those early *A & M* editors were not concerned to quarry among the older poets, but these two, from the intellectual leader of that Oxford Movement which the book served, were something which, despite their author's allegiance to the Church of Rome, the editors could not miss. It is truly astonishing that #442 is not known at all in America outside the Episcopal Church. The third poem of Newman, also from *Gerontius* (441), had to wait till 1906 for its release as a hymn. It is worth observing that both #441 and #442 come from a dramatic poem about an old man who is facing his own death; there are important references to death in both. (The stanza that refers to it in 441 is never used in the hymn version.)

Tennyson could have heard his *In Memoriam* Prologue (443) sung as a hymn if (as was most unlikely) at the end of his life he went into a Congregational Church that had laid in its new hymnal, for the 1887 *Congregational Church Hymnal* seems to have been the first such book to set it to music. It made an instant appeal to the people who were enjoying the speculative, liberal hymnody in which the Americans excelled. And, of course, it is beautiful writing. Theologians are worried by 'seemest' in stanza 3, but the rest of it has perhaps not wholly deserved the relegation which it has suffered in Britain. There is less to argue about in #444 and more in which to take the purest pleasure. But Tennyson would not have heard this sung; it waited for 1909 to get into a hymnal.

No. 445, which has some fine lofty lines, was first used as a hymn in the *Congregational Hymnary* of 1916, and #446, whose author's untimely death in the First World War alone prevented his living to hear sung, was taken by *Songs of Praise* in 1925. It is, as far as we can find, the earliest-dated hymn to address the Deity in the 'you' form, though not quite the only one in the 1925 book to do so.

A few pages back we said that the use of poetry as hymns has appealed less to Americans, but we end our section with two pieces which owe their place in this anthology mostly to American enterprise. Auden's fragment (447) was actually first included as a hymn in the 1967 *Cambridge Hymnal,* but Auden became an American citizen in 1938; Elizabeth Poston, joint editor of the *Cambridge Hymnal,* was probably the English musician who knew most about American literature at that time. Moreover, it was its inclusion, with a wholly manageable tune, in the American *Worshipbook* (1972), rather than the Cambridge association, or its appearance in the Episcopal Supplement of 1971, that really launched it on its hymnic career. A younger author, and a less recondite text, appears at #448; Richard Wilbur is a wholly American poet, and since the poem was first set to music for use as a hymn in the Lutheran *Contemporary Worship* I in 1969, it has been much sought after. It uses the meter of the German carol 'Es ist ein' Ros' entsprungen,' and, if the Auden is regarded as not wholly American, it may be the first instance (apart from the Whittier poems which were made into hymns by English editors) of

American non-hymnic poetry entering the field of hymnody.

There is much more to find in English books, and the plundering of the poets was rarely ill-judged. (It is something quite different from de-contexting attractive tunes from symphonic classics.) Its purpose was to cleanse the stream of hymnic literature through a new appreciation of poetic precision. You cannot be a poet and write cliches, or write carelessly, or write–at least before 1900–in in-group language. Poets make the faith public. They minister to the educated and the educable. This enrichment was greatly needed in the early 20th century.

409
GOD BE IN MY HEAD
HG 225

Jésus soit en ma teste
　et mon entendement.
Jésus soit en mes yeux
　et mon regardement.
Jésus soit en ma bouche
　et en mon parlement.
Jésus soit en mon coeur
　et en mon pensement.
Jésus soit en ma vie
　et mon trespassement.

God be in my head
　and in my understanding;
God be in my eyes
　and in my looking;
God be in my mouth
　and in my speaking;
God be in my heart
　and in my thinking.
God be at my end
　and [at] my departing.

Book of Hours, printed for Antoine Verard (British Museum) c. 1497

Book of Hours, Salisbury, 1514

410
JERUSALEM, MY HAPPY HOME
HG 344

Jerusalem, my happy home,
　when shall I come to thee?
when shall my sorrows have an
　　　　　　　　　　end?
　thy joys when shall I see?

O happy harbour of the saints!
　O sweet and blessed soil!
in thee no sorrow may be found,
　no grief, no care, no toil.

In thee no sickness may be seen,
　no hurt, no ache, no sore;
in thee there is no dread of death,
　but life for evermore.

No dampish mist is seen in thee,
　no cold nor darksome night;
there every soul shines as the sun;
　there God himself gives light.

There lust and lucre cannot dwell;
　there envy bears no sway,
there is no hunger, heat nor cold,
　but pleasure every way.

Jerusalem, Jerusalem,
　God grant I once may see
thy endless joys, and of the same
　partaker ay may be.

Thy walls are made of precious
　　　　　　　　　stones,
　thy bulwarks diamonds square;

thy gates are of right orient pearl,
　exceeding rich and rare;

thy turrets and thy pinnacles
　with carbuncles do shine;
thy very streets are paved with
　　　　　　　　　　gold
　surpassing clear and fine;

Thy houses are of ivory,
　thy windows crystal clear;
thy tiles are made of beaten gold -
　O God that I were there!

Within thy gates no thing doth
　　　　　　　　　　come
　that is not passing clean,
no spider's web, no dirt, no dust,
　no filth may there be seen.

Ah, my sweet home, Jerusalem,
　would God I were in thee!
would God my woes were at an
　　　　　　　　　　end,
　thy joys that I might see!

Thy saints are crowned with glory
　　　　　　　　　great:
　they see God face to face;
they triumph still, they still
　　　　　　　　　rejoice;
　most happy is their case.

We that are here in banishment
　continually do mourn;

we sigh and sob, we weep and
　　　　　　　　　wail,
　perpetually we groan.

Our sweet is mixed with bitter
　　　　　　　　　gall,
　our pleasure is but pain,
our joys scarce worth the looking
　　　　　　　　　on,
　our sorrows still remain.

But there they live in such delight,
　such pleasure and such play,
as that to them a thousand years
　doth seem as yesterday.
　　　　　　　　　(Ps. 90:4)

Thy vineyards and thy orchards
　　　　　　　　　are
　most beautiful and fair,
full furnished with trees and fruits,
　most wonderful and rare;

thy gardens and thy gallant walks
　continually are green;
there grow such sweet and
　　　　　　　　pleasant flowers
　as nowhere else are seen.

There's nectar and ambrosia
　　　　　　　　　made,
　there's musk and civet sweet;
there many a fair and dainty drug
　is trodden under feet.

There cinnamon, there sugar
　　　　　　　　　grows,
　there nard and balm abound;
what tongue can tell, or heart
　　　　　　　　conceive
　the joys that there are found!

Quite through the streets with
　　　　　　　　silver sound
　the flood of life doth flow
　　　　　　　　　(Rev. 22:1)
upon whose banks on every side
　the wood of life doth grow

There trees for evermore bear
　　　　　　　　　fruit,
　and evermore do spring;
there evermore the angels sit,
　and evermore do sing;

there David stands with harp in
　　　　　　　　　hand
　as master of the choir:
ten thousand times that man were
　　　　　　　　　blest
　that might this music hear.

Our Lady sings Magnificat
　　　　　　　　　(Lk. 1:46)
　with tune surpassing sweet;
and all the Virgins bear their parts
　sitting about her feet.

Te Deum doth Saint Ambrose
　　　　　　　　　sing,
　Saint Austin doth the like †
Old Simeon and Zachary
　　　　　　　　　(Lk. 1:68, 2:29)
　have not their songs to seek.

There Magdalene hath left her
　　　　　　　　　moan
　and cheerfully doth sing
with blessed Saints, whose
　　　　　　　　harmony
　in every street doth ring.

Jerusalem, my happy home,
　would God I were in thee!
Would God my woes were at an
　　　　　　　　　end,
　thy joys that I might see!

'F.B.P.,' who may have been a Catholic priest under sentence of death in London, c. 1593: based on a passage in the Meditations of St. Augustine.

† This refers to a tradition that the Te Deum was composed by SS Ambrose and Augustine singing antiphonally. This is no more than a pious and affectionate legend.

EDMUND SPENSER
1552-99

411
AMORETTI: Sonnett 68
HG 457

Most glorious Lord of life, that on this day
　didst make thy triumph over death and sin:
and, having harrowed hell, didst bring away
　captivity thence captive, us to win:
　this joyous day, dear Lord, with joy begin,
and grant that we, for whom thou diddest die
　being with thy dear blood clean washed from sin,
may live for ever in felicity.

And that thy love we weighing worthily,
  may likewise love thee for the same again:
and for thy sake that all like dear didst buy
  with love may one another entertain.
So let us love, dear Love, like as we ought:
love is the lesson that our Lord us taught.

Amoretti and Epithalamion, 1595
(1906)

THOMAS CAMPIAN*
1567-1620

412
TWO LUTE SONGS

Never weatherbeaten sail more willing bent to shore,
never tired pilgrim's limbs affected slumber more,
than my wearied sprite now longs to fly out of my troubled breast.
O come quickly, sweetest Lord, and take my soul to rest.

Ever blooming are the joys of heaven's high paradise,
cold age deafs not there our ears, nor vapour dims our eyes;
glory there the sun outshines, whose beams the blessed only see;
O come quickly, glorious Lord, and raise my sprite to thee.

413

Sing a song of joy, praise our God with mirth.
His flock who can destroy? is he not Lord of heaven and earth?

Sing we then secure, tuning well our strings,
with voice as echo pure, let us renown the King of kings.

First who taught the day from the east to rise?
whom doth the sun obey when in the seas his glory dies?

He the stars directs that in order stand:
who heaven and earth protects but he that formed them with his hand?

All that dread his name, and his hests observe,
his arm will shield from shame, their steps from truth shall never
swerve.

Let us then rejoice, sounding loud his praise,
so will he hear our voice, and bless on earth our peaceful days.

Books of Ayres, c. 1613 (1931)

GEORGE HERBERT
1593-1632
from
The Temple
1633
HG 137

414
ANTIPHON   HG 389

Let all the world in every corner sing,
  my God and King!

The heavens are not too nigh,
  his praises there may fly;
the earth is not too low,
  his praises there may grow.

Let all the world in every corner sing,
  my God and King!

The Church with psalms must shout,
  no door can keep them out;
but, above all, the heart
  must bear the longest part.

Let all the world in every corner sing
  my God and King!

(1889)

415
THE CALL   HG 137

Come, my Way, my Truth, my Life: (John 14:6)
  such a way as gives us breath,
  such a truth as ends all strife,
  such a life as killeth death.

Come, my light, my feast, my strength:
  such a light as shows a feast,
  such a feast as mends in length,
  such a strength as makes his guest.

Come, my joy, my love, my heart:
  such a joy as none can move,
  such a love as none can part,
  such a heart as joys in love.

(1925)

416
PRAISE   HG 381

King of glory, King of peace,
  I will love thee;
and that love may never cease,
  I will move thee.
Thou hast granted my request,
  thou hast heard me;
thou didst note my working breast,
  thou hast spared me.

Wherefore with my utmost art
  I will sing thee,
and the cream of all my heart
  I will bring thee.
Though my sins against me cried,
  thou didst clear me;
and alone, when they replied,
  thou didst hear me.

Seven whose days, not one in seven,
  I will praise thee;
in my heart, though not in heaven
  I can raise thee.
Small it is, in this poor sort
  to enrol thee:
ev'n eternity's too short
  to extol thee.

(1906)

JOHN MILTON
1608-74

417
PSALM 136

HG 394

1

Let us with a gladsom mind
praise the Lord, for he is kind,
for his mercies ay endure,
ever faithfull, ever sure.

1

Let us with a gladsome mind
praise the Lord, for he is kind:
for his mercies shall endure,
ever faithful, ever sure.

2

Let us blaze his name abroad,
for of gods he is the God. . . .

2

Let us sound his name abroad,
for of gods he is the God. . . .

3

O let us his praises tell
that doth the wrathful tyrants
quell. . . .

4

That with his miracles doth make
amazed Heaven and Earth to
shake. . . .

★   ★   ★

7

That by his all-commanding might
did fill the new-made world with
light, . . .

3

He with all-commanding might
filled the new-made world with
light. . . .

8

and caus'd the golden-tressèd
Sun
all the day long his course to
run, . . .

4

He the golden-tressèd sun

caused all day his course to
run. . . .

9

the hornèd moon to shine by
night
amongst her spangled sisters
bright. . . .

10

He with his thunder-clasping
hand
smote the first-born of Egypt
land. . . .

★   ★   ★

13

The floods stood still like Walls of
Glass
while the Hebrew bands did
pass. . . .

14

But full soon they did devour
the Tawny King with all his
power. . . .

15

His chosen people he did bless
in the wastefull wilderness. . . .

6

He his chosen race did bless
in the wasteful wilderness. . . .

★   ★   ★

20

He hath with a piteous eye
beheld us in our misery. . . .

7

He hath, with a piteous eye
looked upon our misery. . . .

★   ★   ★

22

All living creatures he doth feed
and with full hand supplies their
need. . . .

5

All things living he doth feed;
his full hand supplies their
need. . . .

23

Let us therefore warble forth
his mighty Majesty and worth. . . .

8

Let us then with gladsome mind
praise the Lord, for he is kind. . . .

written before 1624

(1855)

418
From THE PSALMS

HG 706

The Lord will come, and not be slow,
his footsteps cannot err;
before him righteousness shall go,
his royal harbinger.

Mercy and Truth, that long were missed,
now joyfully are met
sweet peace and righteousness have kissed,
and hand in hand are set.

Truth from the earth like to a flower
shall bud and blossom then,
and justice from her heavenly bower
look down on mortal men.

Rise, God, judge thou the earth in night,
this wicked earth redress,
for thou art he who shalt by right
the nations all possess.

The nations all whom thou hast made
shall come, and all shall frame
to bow them low before thee, Lord
and glorify thy name.

For great thou art, and wonders great
by thy strong hand are done;
thou in thy everlasting seat
remainest God alone.

Nine of the Psalms done into Metre,
1648 (1855)

JOHN DONNE*
1573-1631

419
A HYMNE TO GOD THE FATHER

Wilt thou forgive that sin, where I begun,
which was my sin, though it were done before?
Wilt thou forgive those sins, through which I run,
and do run still; though still I do deplore?
When thou hast done, thou hast not done,
for I have more.

Wilt thou forgive that sin by which I've won
others to sin? and made my sin their door?
Wilt thou forgive that sin which I did shun
a year or two: but wallowed in, a score?
When thou hast done, thou hast not done,
for I have more.

I have a sin of fear, that when I've spun
   my last thread, I shall perish on that shore;
swear by thyself, that at my death thy Son
   shall shine as he shines now, and heretofore;
and having done that, thou hast done:
      I fear no more.

Poems (posth.) 1633 (1906)

PHINEAS FLETCHER*
1582-1650

420
A LITANY

Drop, drop, slow tears,
   and bathe those beauteous feet
which brought from heaven
   the news and Prince of Peace:
cease not, wet eyes,
   his mercy to entreat;
to cry for vengeance
   sin doth never cease.
In your deep floods
   drown all my faults and fears;
nor let his eye
   see sin, but through my tears.

*Piscatorial Eclogs and other Poetical
Miscellanies,* 1633 (1906)

FRANCIS QUARLES*
1592-1644

421
WHY DOST THOU SHADE THY LOVELY FACE?

Why dost thou shade thy lovely face? O why
does that eclipsing hand so long deny
the sunshine of thy soul-enlivening eye?

Without that light, what light remains in me?
Thou art my life, my way, my light; in thee
I live, I move, and by thy beams I see.

* Thou art my life; if thou but turn away
my life's a thousand deaths: thou art my way;
without thee, Lord, I travel not, but stray.

* My light thou art; without thy glorious sight,
my eyes are darkened with perpetual night.
My God, thou art my way, my life, my light.

* Thou art my way; I wander, if thou fly:
thou art my light; if hid, how blind am I!
Thou art my life; if thou withdraw, I die.

Mine eyes are blind and dark, I cannot see;
to whom, or whither should my darkness flee,
but to the light? and who's that light but thee?

My oath is lost, my wandering steps do stray;
I cannot safely go, nor safely stay;
whom should I seek but thee, my path, my way?

    ★   ★   ★

Thou art the pilgrim's path, the blind man's eye;
the dead man's life: on thee my hopes rely;
if thou remove, I err, I grope, I die.

* Disclose thy sun-beams, close thy wings and stay;
   see, see how I am blind and dead, and stray,
   O thou that art my light, my life, my way.

Emblemes, 1635. Sts. 8-14 omitted.
Starred stanzas form hymn version
(1931).

SIDNEY GODOLPHIN*
1610-43

422
WISE MEN AND SHEPHERDS

original

Lord, when the wise men came
             from far,
led to thy cradle by a star,
then did the shepherds too
             rejoice,
instructed by thy angel's voice.
Blest were the wisemen in their
             skill,
and shepherds in their harmless
             will.

Wisemen in tracing nature's laws
ascend unto the highest cause,
shepherds with humble
             fearfulness
walk safely, though their light be
             less:
though wisemen better know the
             way,
it seems no honest heart can stray.

There is no merit in the wise
but love (the shepherds' sacrifice).
Wisemen, all ways of knowledge
             past,
to the shepherds' wonder come at
             last;
to know, can only wonder breed,
and not to know, is wonder's seed.

A wiseman at the altar bows
and offers up his studied vows
and is received; may not the tears
which spring too from a
             shepherd's fears,
and sighs upon his frailty spent,
though not distinct, be eloquent?

'Tis true, the object sanctifies
all passions which within us rise,
but since no creature
             comprehends
the Cause of causes, End of ends,
he who himself vouchsafes to
             know
best pleases his Creator so.

1925 cento

Lord, when the wise man came
             from far,
led to thy cradle by a star,
shepherds with humble
             fearfulness
walked safely, though their
             light was less.

Wise men in tracing nature's laws
ascend unto the highest cause;
though wise men better know the
             way,
it seems no honest heart can stray.

And since no creature
             comprehends
the Cause of causes, End of ends,
he who himself vouchsafes to
             know
best pleases his Creator so.

There is no merit in the wise
but love, the shepherds' sacrifice;
wise men, all ways of knowledge
             past
to the shepherds' wonder came
             at last.

Percy Dearmer, in *Songs of Praise,*
1925

(the whole poem appears in *School
Worship,* 1926)

When then our sorrows we apply
to our own wants and poverty,
when we look up in all distress
and our own misery confess,
sending both thanks and prayers
above,
then, though we do not know, we
love.

manuscript. Published in G. Saints-
bury, *Caroline Poets*, 1906

ROBERT HERRICK*
1591-1674

423
THE WHITE ISLAND: or PLACE OF THE BLEST

In this world (the *Isle of Dreams*)
while we sit by sorrow's streams,
tears and terrors are our themes
reciting:

but when once from hence we fly,
more and more approaching nigh
unto young eternity
uniting:

in that whiter Island, where
things are evermore sincere;
candour here, and lustre there
delighting:

there no monstrous fancies shall
out of hell a horror call,
to create (or cause at all)
affrighting.

There in calm and cooling sleep
we our eyes shall never steep;
but eternal watch shall keep
attending

pleasures, such as shall pursue
me immortaliz'd, and you:
and fresh joys, as never to
have ending.

Noble Numbers, 1647 (1925)

The Scottish Psalter,
1650: a fragment in Spurgeon's
Hymn Book, 1866

424
PRAY FOR THE PEACE OF JERUSALEM
From Psalm 122   HG 607

Pray that Jerusalem may have
peace and felicity:
let them that love thee and thy peace
have still prosperity.

Therefore I wish that peace may still
within thy walls remain,
and ever may thy palaces
prosperity retain.

Now for my friends' and brethren's sake,
'Peace be in thee,' I'll say;
and for the house of God our Lord
I'll seek thy good alway.

JEREMY TAYLOR,
Bishop
1613-67

425
'THY KINGDOM COME'   HG 167

Lord! come away!
Why dost thou stay?
Thy road is ready; and thy paths made straight
with longing expectation wait
the consecration of thy beauteous feet!
Ride on triumphantly! Behold, we lay
our lusts and proud wills in thy way!

Hosanna! Welcome to our hearts! Lord, here
thou hast a temple too; and full as dear
as that of Sion, and as full of sin;
nothing but thieves and robbers dwell therein:
enter, and chase them forth, and cleanse the floor!
Crucify them, that they may never more
profane that holy place
where thou hast chose to set thy face!
And then, if our stiff tongues shall be
mute in the praises of thy Deity,
the stones out of the temple wall
shall cry aloud, and call
'Hosanna!' and thy glorious footsteps greet! Amen!

The Golden Grove, 1655

Revised
1868, 1916

'Draw nigh to thy Jerusalem, O Lord,'
thy faithful people cry with one accord:
'Ride on in triumph; Lord, behold, we lay
our passions, lusts and proud wills in thy way.'

Thy road is ready; and thy paths, made straight,
with longing expectation seem to wait
the consecration of thy beauteous feet,
and silently thy promised advent greet.

Hosanna! Welcome to our hearts; for here
thou hast a temple too, as Sion dear;
yes, dear as Sion, and as full of sin:
how long shall thieves and robbers dwell therein?

Enter and chase them forth, and cleanse the floor;
o'erthrow them all, that they may never more
profane with traffic vile that holy place
where thou hast chosen, Lord, to set thy face.

And then, if our stiff tongues shall faithlessly
be mute in praises of thy Deity,
the very temple stones shall loud repeat
'Hosanna!' and thy glorious footsteps greet.

HENRY VAUGHAN
1622-95

426
MY SOUL, THERE IS A COUNTRY   HG 475

My soul, there is a country
far beyond the stars,
where stands a wingèd sentry
all skilful in the wars.

There, above noise and danger,
sweet Peace sits crowned with smiles,

and One born in a manger
   commands the beauteous files.

He is thy gracious Friend,
   and - O my soul, awake -
did in pure love descend
   to die here for thy sake.

If thou canst get but thither,
   there grows the flower of peace,
the Rose that cannot wither,
   thy fortress and thy ease.

Leave then thy foolish ranges,
   or none can thee secure,
but One, who never changes,
   thy God, thy Life, thy Cure.

Silex Scintillans, 1655 (1905)

THOMAS PESTEL
?1584-?1659

427
PSALM FOR CHRISTMAS DAY   HG 77

Fairest of morning lights, appear,
   thou blest and holy day,
on which was born our Saviour dear;
   arise and come away!

This day prevents his day of doom;
   his mercy now is nigh;
the mighty God of Love is come,
   the Dayspring from on high!

Behold, the great Creator makes
   himself a house of clay;
a robe or virgin flesh he takes
   which he will wear for ay.

Hark, hark, the wise eternal Word
   like a weak infant cries;
in form of servant is the Lord,
   and God in cradle lies.

This wonder struck the world amazed,
   it shook the starry frame;
squadrons of spirits stood and gazed,
   then down in troops they came.

Glad shepherds ran to view this sight;
   a quire of angels sings;
and eastern sages with delight
   adore this King of kings.

Join then, all hearts that are not stone,
   and all our voices prove
to celebrate this Holy One,
   the God of peace and love.

Sermons and Devotions Old and New,
1659 (1906)

RICHARD BAXTER, 1615-91
from *Poetical Fragments*, 1681

428
From THE RESOLUTION   HG 278

He wants not friends that hath thy love,
   and may converse and walk with thee
and with thy saints, here and above,
   with whom for ever I must be.

In the communion of saints
   is wisdom, safety and delight;
and when my heart declines and faints,
   it's raisèd by their heat and light.

As for my friends, they are not lost;
   the several vessels of thy fleet,
though parted now, by tempests tost,
   shall safely in the haven meet.

Still we are centred all in thee,
   members, though distant, of one Head;
in the same family we be,
   by the same faith and Spirit led.

Before thy throne we daily meet
   as joint-petitioners to thee;
in spirit we each other greet
   and shall again each other see.

The heavenly hosts, world without end,
   shall be my company above;
and thou, my best and surest friend,
   who shall divide me from thy love?   (Rev. 8:37)

1663 (1906)

429
From THE CONCORDANT DISCORD OF A
BROKEN-HEARTED HEART: *London. At the*
Door of Eternity, 1681   HG 424

Lord, it belongs not to my care
   whether I die or live;
to love and serve thee is my share
   and this thy grace must give.

If life be long, I will be glad
   that I may long obey;
if short, yet why should I be sad
   to soar to endless day? *

Christ leads me through no darker rooms
   than he went through before;
he that into God's kingdom comes
   must enter by that door.

Come, Lord, when grace hath made me meet
   thy blessed face to see;
for if thy work in earth be sweet,
   what will thy glory be?

Then shall I end my sad complaints,
   and weary, sinful days,
and join with the triumphant saints
   that sing Jehovah's praise.

My knowledge of that life is small;
  the eye of faith is dim;
but 'tis enough that Christ knows all,
  and I shall be with him.

(1868)

* as altered for *Hymns A & M*, 1868

430
YE HOLY ANGELS BRIGHT   HG 829

Ye holy angels bright,
  who wait at God's right hand,
or through the realms of light
  fly at your Lord's command,
    assist our song,
      for else the theme
      too high doth seem
    for mortal tongue.

Ye blessed souls at rest,
  who ran this earthly race,
and now, from sin released
  behold your Father's face,
    his praises sound,
      as in his sight
      with sweet delight
    ye do abound.

Ye saints, who toil below,
  adore your heavenly King,
and onward as ye go
  some joyful anthem sing;
    take what he gives,
      and praise him still
      through good or ill,
    whoever lives.

My soul, bear thou thy part,
  triumph in God above,
and with a well-tuned heart
  sing thou the songs of love.
    Let all thy days
      till life shall end,
      whate'er he send,
    be filled with praise.

J. H. Gurney (1802-62), based
on BAXTER [1862]

SAMUEL CROSSMAN
?1624-1684

431
MY SONG IS LOVE UNKNOWN   HG 473

My song is love unknown,
  my Saviour's love to me,
love to the loveless shown
  that they might lovely be.
    O, who am I,
      that for my sake
      my Lord should take
    frail flesh, and die?

He came from his blest throne
  salvation to bestow;
but men made strange, and none
  the longed-for Christ would
    know.

But, O my Friend,
  my Friend indeed,
who at my need
  his life did spend!

Sometimes they strew his way
  and his sweet praises sing;
resounding all the day
  hosannas to their King.
    Then 'Crucify!'
      is all their breath,
      and for his death
    they thirst and cry.

Why, what hath my Lord done?
  what makes this rage and spite?
He made the lame to run,
  he gave the blind their sight.
    Sweet injuries!
      Yet they at these
      themselves displease
    and 'gainst him rise.

They rise, and needs will have
  my dear Lord made away;
a murderer they save,
  the Prince of life they slay.
    Yet cheerful he
      to suffering goes

(Heb. 12:2)

    that he his foes
    from thence might free.

In life no house, no home
  my Lord on earth might have;
in death, no friendly tomb
  but what a stranger gave.
    What may I say?
      heaven was his home;
      but mine the tomb
    wherein he lay.

Here might I stay and sing
  no story so divine;
never was love, dear King,
  never was grief like thine.
    This is my Friend,
      in whose sweet praise
      I all my days
    could gladly spend.

The Young Man's Meditation, 1664

HENRY MORE
1614-87
HG 229

432
INCARNATION

The holy Son of God most high,
  for love of Adam's lapsed race
quit the sweet pleasures of the sky
  to bring us to that happy place.

His robes of light he laid aside,
  which did his majesty adorn,
and the frail state of mortals tried
  in human flesh and figure born.   (Phil. 2:5-11)

Whole choirs of angels loudly sing
  the mystery of his sacred birth,
and the blest news to shepherds bring,
  filling their watchful souls with mirth.

The Son of God thus man became,
  that men the sons of God might be,
and by their second birth regain
  a likeness to his deity.

cento from *Divine Hymns*, 1668 (1925)

JOHN BUNYAN
1628-88
HG 821

433
THE SHEPHERD BOY'S SONG IN THE VALLEY OF
HUMILIATION

He that is down needs fear no fall,
  he that is low, no pride;
he that is humble ever shall
  have God to be his guide.

I am content with what I have,
  little be it or much;
and, Lord, contentment still I crave
  because thou savest such.

Fullness to such a burden is
    that go on pilgrimage;
here little, and hereafter bliss
    is best from age to age.

The Pilgrim's Progress, II, 1684

434
VALIANT FOR TRUTH
HG 821

Who would true valour see,
    let him come hither;
one here will constant be,
    come wind, come weather;
there's no discouragement
shall make him once relent
his first-avowed intent
    to be a pilgrim.

Who so beset him round
    with dismal stories,
do but themselves confound;
    his strength the more is.
No lion can him fright,
he'll with a giant fight,
but he will have a right
    to be a pilgrim.

Hobgoblin nor foul fiend
    can daunt his spirit;
he knows he at the end
    shall life inherit.
Then fancies fly away!
He'll fear not what men say,
he'll labour night and day
    to be a pilgrim.

JOHN BUNYAN, 1684 (1916)

He who would valiant be
    'gainst all disaster,
let him in constancy
    follow the Master.
There's no discouragement
shall make him once relent
his first-avowed intent
    to be a pilgrim.

Who so beset him round
    with dismal stories,
do but themselves confound;
    his strength the more is.
No fees shall stay his might,
though he with giants fight:
he will make good his right
    to be a pilgrim.

Since, Lord, thou dost defend
    us with thy Spirit,
we know we at the end
    shall life inherit.
Then fancies flee away!
I'll fear not what men say;
I'll labour night and day
    to be a pilgrim.

PERCY DEARMER, 1906

CHRISTOPHER SMART*
1722-71

435
SONG OF DAVID

He sung of God, the mighty Source
of all things, the stupendous force
    on which all strength depends,
from whose right arm, beneath whose eyes,
all period, power and enterprise
    commences, reigns, and ends.

Glorious the sun in mid career,
glorious the assembled stars appear,
    glorious the comet's train,
glorious the trumpet and alarm,
glorious the almighty out-stretched arm,
    glorious the enraptured main.

The world, the clustering spheres he made,
the glorious light, the soothing shade,
    dale, champaigne, grove and hill,
the multitudinous abyss,
where secrecy remains in bliss,
    and wisdom hides her skill.

Strong is the lion, like a coal
his eyeball, like a bastion's mole
    his chest against the foes:

strong the gier-eagle on his sail;
strong against tide the enormous whale
    emerges as he goes;

but stronger still - in earth and air
and in the sea - the man of prayer;
    and far beneath the tide,
and in the seat to faith assigned,
where ask is have, where seek is find,
    where knock is open wide.

Song to David, 1763
Sts. 18, 84, 21, 76, 78 of original 86
(1925)
Hymn version begins 'We sing . . .'.

436
EASTER DAY

Awake, arise! lift up thy voice,
    which as a trumpet swell!
Rejoice in Christ! again rejoice,
    and on his praises dwell!

Let us not doubt, as doubted some,
    when first the Lord appeared;
but full of faith and reverence come,
    what time his voice is heard.

And even as John, who ran so well,
    confess upon our knees
the Prince who locks up death and hell,
    and has himself the keys.

And thus through gladness and surprise
    the saints their Saviour treat;
nor will they trust their ears and eyes
    but by his hands and feet:

those hands of liberal love indeed
    in infinite degree,
those feet still frank to move and bleed
    for millions and for me.

O Dead, arise! O Friendless, stand
    by seraphim adored!
O Solitude, again command
    thy host from heaven restored!

A Translation of the Psalms of David,
1765 (1925)

WILLIAM BLAKE
1757-1827

437
INNOCENCE
HG 759

To Mercy, Pity, Peace and Love,
    all pray in their distress,
and to these virtues of delight
    return their thankfulness.

For Mercy, Pity, Peace, and Love
    is God our Father dear;
and Mercy, Pity, Peace and Love
    is Man, his child and care.

For Mercy has a human heart,
    Pity, a human face;

and Love, the human form divine,
and Peace, the human dress.

Then every man, of every clime,
that prays in his distress,
prays to the human form divine:
Love, Mercy, Pity, Peace.

And all must love the human form,
in heathen, Turk, or Jew;
where Mercy, Love and Pity dwell,
there God is dwelling too.

Songs of Innocence, 1789 (1906)

THOMAS MOORE
1779-1852
HG 148

438

Thy heaven, on which 'tis bliss to look
shall be my pure and shining book,
where I shall read, in words of flame
the glories of thy wondrous name.

There's nothing brought, above, below,
from flowers that bloom to stars that glow,
but in its light my soul can see
some feature of thy deity:

There's nothing dark, below, above,
but in its gloom I trace thy love,
and meekly wait that moment, when
thy touch shall turn all bright again.

Sacred Songs, 1816 (1925)

(A different cento in *The Sacred Min-strel* [USA], 1846).

JOHN CLARE
1793-1864

439
THE STRANGER   HG 4

When trouble haunts me,
need I sigh?
no, rather smile away
despair;
for those have been more sad
than I,
with burthens more than I
could bear;
aye, gone rejoicing under
care
where I had sunk in black
despair.

When pain disturbs my peace
and rest,
am I a hopeless grief to
keep,
when some have slept on
torture's breast
and smiled as in the
sweetest sleep,
aye, peace on thorns, in faith
forgiven,
and pillowed on the hope of
heaven?

Though low and poor and
broken down,
am I to think myself distrest?
No, rather laugh where others
frown
and think my being truly
blest;
for others I can daily see
more worthy riches worse
than me.

Aye, once a Stranger blest the
earth
who never caused a heart to
mourn,
whose very voice gave sorrow
mirth -
and how did earth his love
return?
It spurned him from its lowliest
lot,
the meanest station owned him
not;
an outcast thrown in sorrow's
way,

a fugitive that knew no sin,
yet in lonely places forced to stay -
men would not take the
Stranger in.

Yet peace, though much himself
he mourned
was all to others he returned.

His presence was a peace to all,
he bade the sorrowful rejoice.
Pain turned to pleasure at his call,
health lived and issued from his
voice.
He healed the sick, and sent
abroad
the dumb rejoicing in the Lord.

The blind met daylight in his eye
the joys of everlasting day;
the sick found health in his reply
the cripple threw his crutch
away
Yet he with troubles did remain
and suffered poverty and pain.

Yet none could say of wrong he
did
and scorn was ever standing by
accusers by their conscience chid
when proof was sought, made
no reply
Yet without sin, he suffered more
than ever sinners did before.

The Village Minstrel, 182

(as a hymn, from st. 3, beginning 'A
stranger once . . .', 1951)

JOHN HENRY NEWMAN
1801-90

440
LEAD, KINDLY LIGHT   HG 38

Lead, kindly Light, amid the encircling gloom,
lead thou me on;
the night is dark, and I am far from home,
lead thou me on.
Keep thou my feet; I do not ask to see
the distant scene; one step enough for me.

I was not ever thus, nor prayed that thou
shouldst lead me on;
I loved to choose and see my path; but now
lead thou me on.
I loved the garish day, and, spite of fears,
pride ruled my will: remember not past years.

So long thy power hath blest me, sure it still
will lead me on
o'er moor and fen, o'er crag and torrent, till
the night is gone,
and with the more those angel-faces smile
which I have loved long since, and lost awhile.

The British Magazine, March, 1834
[1861]

441
SANCTUS FORTIS   HG 19

Sanctus fortis, sanctus Deus,
de profundis oro te,
miserere, Judex meus,
parce mihi, Domine.

Firmly I believe and truly,
God is Three and God is One;
and I next acknowledge duly
manhood taken by the Son.

And I trust and hope most fully
in that manhood crucified;
and each thought and deed unruly
do to death, as he has died.

Simply to his grace and wholly
light and life and strength belong,

and I love, supremely, solely,
  him the holy, him the strong.

    Sanctus, fortis, sanctus Deus,
      de profundis oro te,
      miserere, Judex meus,
      parce mihi, Domine.

And I hold in veneration
  for the love of him alone,
holy Church as his creation,
  and her teachings as his own.

And I take with joy whatever   †
  now besets me, pain or fear,
and with a strong will I sever
  all the ties which bind me here.

Adoration ay be given
  with and through the angelic host
to the God of earth and heaven,
  Father, Son and Holy Ghost.

    Sanctus fortis, sanctus Deus,
      de profundis oro te,
      miserere, Judex meus,
      mortis in discrimine.

The Dream of Gerontius, 1865, lines
72-107; English stanzas (except that
marked †) as a hymn (1906).

442
PRAISE TO THE HOLIEST   HG 603

Praise to the Holiest in the height
  and in the depth be praise,
in all his words most wonderful,
  most sure in all his ways.

O loving wisdom of our God,
  when all was sin and shame
a second Adam to the fight
  and to the rescue came.

O wisest love, that flesh and blood,
  which did in Adam fail,
should strive afresh against the foe,
  should strive, and should prevail;

and that a higher gift than grace
  should flesh and blood refine,
God's presence and his very self,
  and essence all-divine.

O generous love! that he who smote
  in man for man the foe,
the double agony in man
  for man should undergo;

and in the garden secretly,
  and on the cross on high,
should teach his brethren, and inspire
  to suffer and to die.

(Praise to the Holiest in the height,
  and in the depth be praise,
in all his words most wonderful,
  most sure in all his ways.)

The Dream of Gerontius, 1865
St. 1 repeated at end in hymn version

ALFRED, LORD TENNYSON
1809-92

443
STRONG SON OF GOD   HG 666

Strong Son of God, immortal love,
  whom we, that have not seen thy face,
  by faith, and faith alone, embrace,
believing where we cannot prove;

thou wilt not leave us in the dust:
  thou madest man, he knows not why;
  he thinks he was not made to die;
and thou hast made him: thou art just.

Thou seemest human and divine,
  the highest, holiest manhood, thou;
  our wills are ours, we know not how;
our wills are ours, to make them thine.

Our little systems have their day;
  they have their day and cease to be:
  they are but broken lights of thee,
and thou, O Lord, art more than they.

We have but faith: we cannot know;
  for knowledge is of things we see;
  and yet we trust it comes from thee,
a beam in darkness: let it grow.

Let knowledge grow from more to more,
  but more of reverence in us dwell;
  that mind and soul, according well,
may make one music as before,

but vaster. We are fools and slight;
  we mock thee when we do not fear;
  but help thy foolish ones to bear -
help thy vain worlds to bear thy light.

In Memoriam, 1850 (1887)

444
RING OUT, WILD BELLS   HG 620

Ring out, wild bells, to the wild sky,
  the flying cloud, the frosty light:
  the year is dying in the night;
ring out, wild bells, and let him die.

Ring out the grief that saps the mind,
  for those that here we see no more;
  ring out the feud of rich and poor,
ring in redress to all mankind.

Ring out a slowly dying cause,
  and ancient forms of party strife;
  ring in the nobler modes of life,
with sweeter manners, purer laws.

Ring out false pride in place and blood,
   the civic slander and the spite;
  ring in the love of truth and right,
  ring in the common love of good.

Ring out old shapes of foul disease;
   ring out the narrowing lust of gold;
   ring out the thousand wars of old,
  ring in the thousand years of peace.

Ring in the valiant man and free,
   the larger heart, the kindlier hand;
  ring out the darkness of the land,
  ring in the Christ that is to be.

In Memoriam, 1850 (1909)

**FREDERICK WILLIAM HENRY
MYERS**, 1843-1901

445
HARK, WHAT A SOUND   HG 271

Hark, what a sound, and too divine for hearing,
  stirs on the earth and trembles in the air!
Is it the thunder of the Lord's appearing?
  is it the music of his people's prayer?

Surely he cometh, and a thousand voices
  shout to the saints, and to the deaf are dumb;
surely he cometh, and the earth rejoices,
  glad in his coming who hath sworn, 'I come.'

This hath he done, and shall we not adore him?
  This shall he do, and can we still despair?
Come, let us quickly fling ourselves before him,
  cast at his feet the burden of our care.

Yea, through life, death, through sorrow and through sinning
  he shall suffice me, for he hath sufficed:
Christ is the end, for Christ was the beginning,
  Christ the beginning, for the end is Christ.

from *St Paul*, 1867 (1916)

DONALD HANKEY*
1884-1916

446
LORD OF THE STRONG

Lord of the strong, when earth you trod
  you calmly faced the angry sea,
  the fierce unmasked hypocrisy,
   the traitors kiss, the rabble hiss,
  the awful death upon the tree:
   all glory to be God.

Lord of the weak, when earth you trod,
  oppressors writhed beneath your scorn;
  the weak, despised, depraved, forlorn
   you taught to hope and know the scope
  of love divine for all who mourn:
   all glory be to God.

Lord of the rich, when earth you trod,
  to Mammon's power you never bowed,
  but taught how men with wealth endowed
   in meekness' school might learn to rule
  the demon that enslaves the proud:
   all glory be to God.

Lord of the poor, when earth you trod,
  the lot you chose was hard and poor;
  you taught us hardness to endure,
   and so to gain through hurt and pain
  the wealth that lasts for evermore:
   all glory be to God.

Lord of us all, when earth you trod,
  the life you led was perfect, free,
  defiant of all tyranny;
   now give us grace that we may face
  our foes with like temerity,
   and glory give to God.

The Spectator, c. 1915 (1925)

W. H. AUDEN
1907-75

447
HE IS THE WAY

He is the Way.
Follow him through the Land of Unlikeness;
you will see rare beasts and have unique adventures.

He is the Truth.
Seek him in the Kingdom of Anxiety:
you will come to a great city that has expected your return for years.

He is the Life
Love him in the World of the Flesh:
and at your marriage all its occasions shall dance for joy.

For the Time Being, 1945 (1967)

RICHARD WILBUR
b. 1921

448
A STABLE LAMP

A stable lamp is lighted,
  whose glow shall wake the sky;
the stars shall bend their voices,
  and every stone shall cry
   and straw like gold shall shine;
a barn shall harbor heaven,
  a stall become a shrine.

This child through David's city
  shall ride in triumph by;
the palm shall strew its branches,
  and every stone shall cry,
   though heavy, cold and dumb,
and lie within the roadway
  to pave his kingdom come.

Yet he shall be forsaken,
  and yielded up to die,
the sky shall groan and darken,
  and every stone shall cry
   for stony hearts of men:
God's blood upon the spearhead,
  God's blood refused again.

But now, as at the ending,
  the low is lifted high,
the stars shall bend their voices
  and every stone shall cry
in praises of the Child
  by whose descent among us
    the worlds are reconciled.

from *Advice to a Prophet, and other Poems*, 1961 (1967)

ARTICLE 21:
ENGLISH HYMNODY, 1906-51 (449-479)

This period defines itself very naturally. It begins with the *English Hymnal*, where Article 14 left off, and ends with the first wave of new hymnals after the Second World War. It is dominated by *Songs of Praise*, which appeared first in 1925 and in its enlarged and extremely successful edition in 1931; if one compares that book with the *English Hymnal*, to which it owed so much and with which it shares its general editor and musical editor (Dearmer and Vaughan Williams), one sees at once the direction of the main thrust of hymnody during the first quarter of the century: from liturgical richness towards aesthetic and intellectual liberalism.

That indeed is the shape of Dearmer's own development. It is as if, having written the *Parson's Handbook* and got the *English Hymnal* rolling, he felt free to develop that crusade against the enthronement of religious cant which was his other passion. His is one of the most interesting spiritual stories of that time. Some have judged that he abandoned his earlier liturgical interests for the social gospel, but that is putting it far too naively. Throughout his very busy and creative life, a life during which admittedly he became more and more of a misfit so far as orthodox Anglicanism was concerned, he was saying, 'If you are going to do it at all, do it, for heaven's sake, *right*.' His liturgical work had a social gospel at its very heart; he used to storm at all those who wanted the Catholic liturgies for sentimental reasons and who put up cheap buildings and devised cheap vestments, whose cheapness, he was never tired of saying, was achieved by sweated labour. Similarly, he detested cheap music and cheap piety, and the musicians he gathered round him, Vaughan Williams and, even more, Martin Shaw, abetted the crusade by campaigning vigorously in favour of the proposition that what was popular need not be trivial, which meant in practice a re-evaluation of the folk-song heritage of a much earlier Britain.

The hymnody of these very important years is divided simply into that which was and that which was not directly influenced by Dearmer and his group. Broadly speaking this means a division between the Anglican and the non-Anglican, though when one realizes how much Dearmer did to bring the work of American Unitarians into English currency, one has to judge him an ecumenical Christian. His eyes were turned towards literature and away from the in-group language of the evangelicals. He had little use for Watts, not very much more for Wesley; Doddridge was mostly a closed book to him. The one way in which he noticeably changed in his theology is that in his later books he would never have dreamed of including Cowper's 'There is a fountain,' and would no longer countenance in 'O for a thousand tongues' the stanza, 'his blood availed for me.'

Take first the group composed of #452, 454 and 456-8, all of which were in the earlier edition of *Songs of Praise*, except

458. Nos. 452 and 454 come from the First World War and are petitions for peace, Clifford Bax's poem being very largely humanistic, Housman's being decisively Christian, both exquisitely written, both lyrical—and, one has to add, both now more sung in America than in England. The First World War lent impetus to the movement for the revival of English art which was focussed, just after its end, in the League of Arts. Both these pieces were much promoted in their literature (which itself had much influence on the contents of the early *Songs of Praise*). In Dearmer's own work, of which in the later *Songs of Praise* there is, perhaps, too much, we see a strenuous forward thrust and a tendency to pull congregations away from that which is bigoted and philistine. No. 456 really does bring John the Baptist into the twentieth century (he is ill served elsewhere by hymn writers); #457, based on a famous passage in the 2nd-century *Didache* (compare #552), removes mystery from the Eucharist and substitutes the atmosphere of the primitive love-feast in a manner one would have expected more of a neo-sacramental nonconformist. And as for #458, which thanks God for prophets and philosophers but not for Jesus Christ, this takes the Dearmer style as far in the direction of 'mission to pagans' as it ever went. Incidentally it also illustrates a habit which he formed of writing new hymns based on the opening words, and singable to the tunes, of hymns already well known (cf. 198), a practice which brought down on him much puristic wrath at the time.

Puristic wrath and pedantic contempt are quite the wrong response to Dearmer, exasperating though his orthodox colleagues must have found him in some ways. The real essence of Dearmer's contribution to religious culture is to be found in the *Oxford Book of Carols* (1928), whose preface is one of the classics of carol literature. We must add to that what we demonstrated in section 20: the way he threw great lyric poetry at his singers, especially at the schools for which *Songs of Praise* was partly devised. Thirdly we must celebrate the work of other authors whom he urged to write for him. Having discovered Chesterton's 'O God of earth and altar' in 1906, he commissioned or promoted such excellent things as Charter Piggott's memorial hymn (459), by far the best and healthiest of such hymns available; Bishop Bell's magnificent ecumenical celebration, #465 (now becoming very popular through the rearrangement of its lines to carry a simpler tune than any to be found in its original meter) and the often delicious pieces of Jan Struther, of which I take #466 to be the best and sanest of all marriage hymns. Piggott was a well-known Congregationalist preacher, Bell the most dedicated and outspoken of all his Episcopal contemporaries, and Jan Struther a virtually humanist novelist. Dearmer spread his net wide, and in respect of Jan Struther, whom we shall meet once more, we may perhaps offer a word in defence of a writer who was especially singled out for vilification by the many enemies which Dearmer's work made. If there is any place for hymns (like #458) which can be sung communally by gatherings including a proportion of uncertain and not yet fully-committed Christians, hymns which perhaps at a more mature stage such people may, if they ever reach it, leave behind, the delicacy and metrical skill of Jan Struther was a talent which such songs could especially use.

G. W. Briggs became at a later stage a colleague of the *Songs of Praise* team. A much more evangelical Anglican than Dearmer, he was even more of an educationist. A navy chaplain during the war, Briggs developed his hymn-writing in the twenties, and was the kind of Christian minister who is often heard using the word 'manly.' He had a much higher respect for Wesley than Dearmer had (this increased as he got older), and his work is much less experimental and trendy than most of Dearmer's. At its best it has a very successful combination of virility and tenderness. No. 460, one of his earlier and one of his best, has a Wesleyan touch in its use of massive words in the last stanza (and in its meter) and the teacher's touch in the narrative style of its earlier stanzas. No. 461, very popular now, is in the old-fashioned biblical style, very simple and direct. No. 462 is a good example of his later work, a meditation on the new terrors of the nuclear bomb; #463, which may be his last hymn, first printed when he was 82, may also be his very finest. One can see how with advancing years he went back towards the style of Cowper, Wesley and the other great evangelicals. Yet it is not imitative stuff. It is strictly twentieth-century hymnody, succeeding through the simplicity of its expression. He is now easily the most sought-after of the writers of his time, and with full justice.

Studdert-Kennedy, the author of #455, was one of the major lyricists of the First World War and one of the two best-known military chaplains. (The other was P. B. Clayton, founder of 'Toc H.') He had a vivid, slashing style in which he often expressed his—and everybody's—indignation at the folly of war. This piece, which Dearmer collected from an Industrial Christian Fellowship leaflet, is one of three he included in *Songs of Praise*; theologians may hesitate at stanza 5, but this is one of the first English hymns to use the modern urban imagery which the Americans had already begun to attempt, and of which we shall shortly hear more.

Bishop Rees (453), of whose work Dearmer does not seem to have known, was a monk of the Community of the Resurrection at Mirfield, Yorkshire, an Anglo-Catholic body dedicated to missions at home and abroad. The preaching of these talented men often took them to places where Gospel Songs and highly seasoned evangelical or eucharistic hymnody were the normal fare, and their first hymn book (1922), which included this piece, is generously endowed with material of that kind. Rees' 'God of love' could be called the greatest of all 'Gospel songs'; it has their rhythmic and repetitive simplicity, but it adds a severity and concreteness which they never attempt, and now (1951) that it has received a worthy musical setting it has begun to travel far.

No. 467 is something quite unique, in being a collaboration between two able hymn-writers. Ronald Knox was in his day equal to G. K. Chesterton in his fame as a Catholic apologist; witty, urbane, with a crossword-puzzle mind, he wrote satire, detective stories, theological works and many hymn-translations. C. A. Alington, Head Master of Eton, later Dean of Durham, was also an able hymn-writer, several of whose pieces have appeared in many books. Knox, when he collaborated in this, was probably still an Anglican. (He joined the Catholic Church in 1918, being himself the son of the Bishop of Manchester.) The remarkable thing about this composition is its use of Scripture, which is more strictly exegetical and interpretative than anything since Charles Wesley (223 would be its only competitor). It was first included in a hymnal for schools and is less well known than it deserves to be. Alington's 'solo' at #468 is again closely and devoutly scriptural, though elsewhere his work is more lyrical and less didactic.

The *BBC Hymn Book* of 1951, a very brave attempt to provide an ecumenical book with some of the characteristics of *Songs of Praise* and designed primarily for use at the daily broadcast service, was again musically adventurous but at its best in

selecting from older hymns rather than in devising new texts. It suddenly comes to life in its harvest section, however, producing Andrew Young's exquisite poem (474) for the first time as a hymn, and three tiny gems by the journalist and sports-commentator, John Arlott, or which we have two at 475-6. All our three examples show a special sense of the beauty of words and have nourished with sanity the harvest observances in church which were until so recently disfigured by the use of hymns of an oppressively moralistic kind.

Something of the same gift—less impressive, perhaps, and a little more ecclesiastical in tone, but often producing some excellent hymns—is found in the under-used author T. C. Hunter-Clare who, in a series of privately printed booklets for his parish, included several pieces which are only now coming into their own. 'God of the pastures' (472) is an excellent hymn about the blessing of labour, and #473 is a welcome respite from the trivial piece by Wordsworth on the same passage.

Apart from the prodigious and sometimes eccentric labours of Dearmer and the substantial contribution of Briggs, the Anglicans were not writing a great deal in these years. The one other tradition that produced anything like a steady stream was that of the Congregationalists. With a single exception, all the rest of the hymns in this section come from them.

The *Congregational Hymnary* of 1916 showed no sign of being influenced by the Dearmer group. It appeared in the depths of World War I, its musical taste was already rather dated, and it produced very little in the way of enduring new texts. But it did have its moments. The now-accepted version of #425 was one of them. Its most distinguished contribution, however, was in making known some of the hymns of Howell Elvet (Hywel Elfed) Lewis, the leading Welsh poet and preacher of his time. Elfed, to give him his bardic name, wrote in Welsh and in English, but normally he did not translate his own work from one language to the other; his English hymns do not have any special Welsh accent. He has his place in this section because it is strictly the twentieth century that has appreciated him, but actually #450 was written in 1883. It was a memorable experience to hear him broadcasting a sermon seventy years later, only a month or two before he died at 93, in which he quoted this hymn and told how he wrote it for the first church in which he ministered. It is still an admirable piece and too little known. No. 451 is much more widely used, and the *Hymnary* was the first to print it.

No. 449 was also first printed in the *Hymnary* and is the work of a minister whose most famous charge was in Bristol; the only known hymn of this author, it has real distinction. In some books it begins 'Lord Christ, who . . . ,' but the alteration is entirely unnecessary, and this is still one of the most satisfying hymns of Christian service. Doddridge showed the right path (51), but ever since his day Christian writers on this subject, following Wesley, tended to equate the life of service with the specific purpose of making conversions. This one shows the liberal mind at its graceful best.

No. 459, also by a Congregationalist, we have already mentioned. The three authors represented in ##469-471 and 477-479, virtually representing three generations, are an interesting trio. Henry Carter (477), minister for 37 years of his denomination's most eminent campus church (Cambridge), wrote only two published hymns; but this, a new interpretation of a passage in Scripture which Charles Wesley had handled in a famous hymn 'Soldiers of Christ, arise,' is great writing; 'The whole armour of God' is here expounded by a lifelong pacifist, and to tell the truth it communicates the sense of that passage to the twentieth century better than the older and better-known text.

Albert Bayly (469-71) has proved to be the most sought-after writer of his generation. He is a Congregational minister who has spent a long working life in a succession of small charges, mostly in the country. In *Rejoice, O People*, a privately-published collection he put out in 1949, he showed himself to be a writer who could successfully handle what were then modern ideas and modern language. No. 469, with its astronomical context, makes a good Christian layman's prayer in a scientific milieu; #470 is one of a whole series he wrote on the minor prophets and expounds Scripture with admirable directness and candour; #471 is a lyric in an unusual meter written much later in the third of his published collections.

The third one of the trio, George Caird, revives for the twentieth century the tradition of the scholar-poet, and in this, in this century, he is unique. He is, at the time of writing, Dean Ireland Professor of New Testament in the University of Oxford, having spent all but three years of his working life in matters academic and having established himself as one of the international leaders in Biblical studies. The merest glance at the texts of ##478 and 479 shows him to be capable of handling Scripture as subtly and tellingly as Charles Wesley himself; he may indeed be the last of the great line of hymn writers whose language and thought are wholly inspired by the King James Version. Both these weighty, condensed, shapely pieces were written before his thirtieth year—#478 when he was a student, #479 during his first years as a minister—and both were answers to challenges, the earlier having been written for a college hymn-writing competition (in a meter suggested by a friend who wanted to get a great tune into currency), the latter on a friend's suggestion that the great epigram of Pastor Robinson famously expounded in #218 could bear a new interpretation in the twentieth century. (Nos. 479 and 218 should be compared.)

This leaves only that strange and lonely figure, Thomas Tiplady, whom we certainly must not overlook (464). Tiplady was unusual in most ways. He was just about the only early twentieth-century Methodist to dare to write hymns at all; the shadow of the great Charles still shut out most of the sun. And, very unusually for a Methodist, he spent 23 years in one place, a mission on the south bank of the Thames within sight of the Archbishop's palace. Here he held evening services directly aimed at the unchurched heathen and the poor; he used to say that it was not unusual for men to come in smoking cigarettes and keeping their caps on. He found nothing in the traditional services of his church that would serve, so he held services featuring films (he was one of the very first to do this though later many did), and he found no hymns to speak to their condition, so he wrote his own for them. These he published in small booklets, and they are found to be hymns dealing quite directly with the kind of life and world known to the underprivileged of Lambeth. Normally their style is less interesting than their subject-matter, and they suffer from a certain casualness and, often, shallowness. During his lifetime his own countrymen never took to his work, though he was able to say that eleven American hymnals used it. (None of the more recent American books does.) In 1944 his mission was completely destroyed in an air-raid, but he battled on for several years after this, picking up the pieces. And in #464 we surely have a charming miniature which would grace anybody's hymnal. It is our tribute, anyhow, to one of the most courageous and off-beat ministers in that very orthodox age and among that then very orthodox Protestant communion.

The emphasis, then, in these early twentieth-century hymns is either towards culture (in the Anglicans) or towards the restatement of theology in orthodox but up-to-date language (in the nonconformists). On all sides there is a quietening down after the explosion of the 19th century, not least due to the quite new standards which seemed now to be applicable to hymn writing after Dearmer had made his gestures. Fewer people perhaps wanted to do it, but fewer people thought they had the capacity to do it, and this application of the brake was probably a healthy sign.

HENRY ARNOLD THOMAS
1848-1924

449
SERVICE
HG 98

Brother, who on thy heart didst bear
  the burden of our shame and sin,
and stoopest ever still to share
  the fight without, the fear within;

whose patience cannot know defeat,
  whose pity will not be denied,
whose loving kindness is so sweet,
  whose tender mercies are so wide:

O Brother man, for this we pray,
  thou brother Man and sovereign Lord,
that we thy brethren, day by day
  may follow thee and keep thy word;

that we may care, as thou hast cared,
  for sick and lame and maimed and blind,
and freely share, as thou hast shared
  in all the woe of all mankind;

that ours may be the holy task
  to help and bless, to heal and save;
this is the privilege we ask,
  and this the happiness we crave.

So in thy mercy make us wise,
  and lead us in the ways of love,
until, at last, our wondering eyes
  look on thy glorious face above.

Congregational Hymnary, 1916

HOWELL ELVET LEWIS
1860-1953
HG 430

450
A PSALM OF CHEERFUL TRUST

The days that were, the days that are,
  they all are days of God;
with psalms of cheerful trust we tread
  where Christ's own freemen trod.

We bless the love of larger noon
  that moved the loyal heart
in evil times to trust the true
  and choose the better part.

God of the fathers! God of Christ!
  keep us in simple ways;

and in the calm of silent hours
  train us for clamorous days.

For those who find the tempest strong,
  make us a hiding place,
a shadow in a weary land
  for healing and for grace.

When love for man is growing cold,
  and many faithless prove,
then may the Man of Sorrows come
  and teach us how to love.

We tarry, Lord, thy leisure still,
  the best is yet to be;
naught ever comes too late for man
  that is in time for thee.

God of our fathers, God of Christ!
  keep us in simple ways;
and may the sharpness of the strife
  be to thy greater praise.

1883; Cheltenham Ladies' College,
Hymnal, 1892
Congregational Hymnary, 1916

451
THY WILL BE DONE   HG 430

Lord of light, whose name outshineth
  all the suns and stars of space,
deign to make us thy co-workers
  in the kingdom of thy grace;
use us to fulfil thy purpose
  in the gift of Christ thy Son;
  Father, as in highest heaven
    so on earth thy will be done.

By the toil of lowly workers
  in some far outlying field;
by the courage where the radiance
  of the cross is still revealed;
by the victories of meekness,
  through reproach and suffering won: . . .

Grant that knowledge, still increasing,
  at thy feet may lowly kneel;
with thy grace our triumphs hallow,
  with thy charity our zeal;
lift the nations from the shadows
  to the glory of the sun: . . .

By the prayers of faithful watchmen,
  never silent day or night;
by the cross of Jesus bringing
  peace to men, and healing light;
by the love that passeth knowledge,
  making all thy children one:
Father, as in highest heaven,
  so on earth thy will be done.

Congregational Hymnary, 1916

CLIFFORD BAX
1886-1962

452
TURN BACK, O MAN   HG 764

Turn back, O man, forswear thy foolish ways.
Old now is earth, and none may count her days,
  yet thou, her child, whose head is crowned with flame,
  still wilt not hear thine inner God proclaim -
'Turn back, O man, forswear thy foolish ways.'

Earth might be fair, and all men glad and wise.
Age after age her tragic empires rise,
  built while they dream, and in that dreaming weep:
  would man but wake from out his haunted sleep,
earth might be fair, and all men glad and wise.

Earth shall be fair, and all her people one:
nor till that hour shall God's whole will be done.
  Now, even now, once more from earth to sky
  peals forth in joy man's old undaunted cry -
'Earth shall be fair, and all her people one!'

1916; Motherland Song Book, 1919

TIMOTHY REES, Bishop
1874-1939

453
HALLOWED BE THY NAME

God of love and truth and beauty,
  hallowed be thy name,
fount of order, law and duty,
  hallowed be thy name.
As in heaven thy hosts adore thee,
and their faces veil before thee,
so on earth, Lord, we implore thee,
  hallowed be thy name.

Lord, remove our guilty blindness,
  hallowed be thy name.
Show thy heart of lovingkindness,
  hallowed be thy name.
By our heart's deep-felt contrition,
by our mind's enlightened vision,
by our will's complete submission,
  hallowed be thy name.

In our worship. Lord most holy,
  hallowed be thy name.
In our work, however lowly,
  hallowed be thy name.
In each heart's imagination,
in the Church's adoration,
in the conscience of the nation,
  hallowed be thy name.

1916; Mirfield Mission Hymn Book,
1922

LAURENCE HOUSMAN
1865-1959

454
PEACE   HG 177

Father eternal, Ruler of creation,
  Spirit of life, which moved ere form was made,
through the thick darkness covering every nation,
  light to man's blindness, O be thou our aid:
    Thy kingdom come, O Lord, thy will be done.

Races and peoples, lo, we stand divided,
  and, sharing not our griefs, no joy can share;
by wars and tumults love is mocked, derided;
  his conquering cross no kingdom wills to bear. . . .

Envious of heart, blind-eyed, with tongues confounded,
  nation by nation still goes unforgiven,
in wrath and fear, by jealousies surrounded,
  building proud towers which shall not reach to heaven. . . .

Lust of possession worketh desolations;
  there is no meekness in the sons of earth;
led by no star, the rulers of the nations
  still fail to bring us to the peaceful birth: . . .

How shall we love thee, holy, hidden Being,
  if we love not the world which thou hast made?
O give us brother-love for better seeing
  thy Word made flesh, and in a manger laid:
    Thy kingdom come, O Lord, thy will be done.

1918; Songs of Praise, 1925

**GEOFFREY ANKETELL
STUDDERT-KENNEDY**
1883-1929
HG 62

455
HIS COMING

When through the whirl of wheels, and engines humming,
  patiently powerful for the sons of men,
peals like a trumpet promise of his coming
  who in the clouds is pledged to come again;

when through the night the furnace fires a-flaring,
  shooting out tongues of flame like leaping blood,
speak to the heart of Love, alive and daring,
  sing of the boundless energy of God;

when in the depths the patient miner striving
  feels in his arms the vigour of the Lord,
strikes for a kingdom and his King's arriving,
  holding his pick more splendid than the sword;

when in the sweat of labour and its sorrow,
  toiling in twilight flickering and dim,
flames out the sunshine of the great to-morrow
  when all the world looks up because of him -

then will he come with meekness for his glory,
  God in a workman's jacket as before,
living again the eternal gospel-story,
  sweeping the shavings from his workshop floor.

*Industrial Christian Fellowship hymn
leaflet, 1921; Songs of Praise, 1925*

PERCY DEARMER
1867-1936
Songs of Praise
HG 88

456
MAKE STRAIGHT THE WAY

Lo, in the wilderness a voice
  'Make straight the way,' is crying:
when men are turning from the light
  and hope and love seem dying,

the prophet comes to make us clean,
'There standeth one you have not seen,
  whose voice you are denying.'

God give us grace to hearken now
  to those who come to warn us,
give sight and strength, that we may kill
  the vices that have torn us,
lest love professed should disappear
in creeds of hate, contempt and fear
  that crash and overturn us.

When from the vineyard cruel men
  cast out the heavenly powers
and Christendom denies its Lord,
  the world in ruin cowers.
Now come, O God, in thy great might!
Unchanged, unchanging is thy right,
  unswayed thy justice towers.

1925; rev. 1931

457
THE LOVE FEAST

As the disciples, when thy Son had left them,
  met in a love-feast, joyfully conversing,
all the stored memory of the Lord's last supper
      fondly rehearsing;
so may we here, who gather now in friendship,
  seek for the spirit of those earlier churches,
welcoming him who stands and for an entrance
      patiently searches. (Rev. 3:20)

As, when their converse closed and supper ended,
  taking the bread and wine they made thanksgiving,
breaking and blessing, thus to have communion
      with Christ the living;
so may we here, a company of brothers,
  make this our love-feast and commemoration,
that in his Spirit we may have more worthy
      participation.

And as they prayed and sang to thee rejoicing,
  ere in the night-fall they embraced and parted,
in their hearts singing as they journeyed homeward,
      brave and true-hearted;
so may we here, like corn that once was scattered
  over the hill-side, now one bread united,
led by the Spirit, do thy work rejoicing,
      lamps filled and lighted.

1931

458
SING PRAISE TO GOD

Sing praise to God, who spoke through man
  in differing times and manners (Heb. 1:1)
for those great seers who've led the van,
  truth writ upon their banners;
for those who once blazed out the way,
for those who still lead on to-day,
  to God be thanks and glory.

For Amos, of the prophets first
  the vast confusion rending
of many gods that bless'd or curs'd,
  to find one, Good, Transcending;

for all who taught mankind to rise
out of the old familiar lies,
    to God be thanks and glory.

For Socrates who, phrase by phrase,
    talked men to truth, unshrinking,
and left for Plato's mighty grace
    to mould our ways of thinking;
for all who wrestled, sane and free,
to win the unseen reality,
    to God be thanks and glory.

For all the poets, who have wrought
    through music, words and vision
to tell the beauty of God's thought
    by art's sublime precision,
who bring our highest dreams to shape
and help the soul in her escape,
    to God be thanks and glory.

1931

**WILLIAM CHARTER
PIGGOTT, 1872-1943**

459
FOR THOSE WE LOVE   HG 204

For those we love within the veil,
    who once were comrades of our way,
we thank thee, Lord; for they have won
        to cloudless day;

and life for them is life indeed,
    the splendid goal of earth's strait race;
and where no shadows intervene,
        they see thy face.

Not as we knew them any more,
    toilworn, and sad with burdened care:
erect, clear-eyed, upon their brows
        thy name they bear.

Free from the fret of mortal years,
    and knowing now thy perfect will,
with quickened sense and heightened joy
        they serve thee still.

O fuller, sweeter is that life,
    and larger, ampler is the air;
eye cannot see nor heart conceive
        the glory there,

nor know to what high purpose thou
    dost yet employ their ripened powers,
nor how at thy behest they touch
        this life of ours.

There are no tears within their eyes;
    with love they keep perpetual tryst;
and praise and work and rest are one
        with thee, O Christ.

Songs of Praise, 1925
See also 481.

**GEORGE WALLACE BRIGGS
1875-1959
HG 110**

460
CHRIST'S MINISTRY

Son of the Lord most high,
    who gave the worlds their birth,
he came to live and die,
    the Son of man on earth.
In Bethlehem's stable born was he
and humbly bred in Galilee.

Born in so low estate,
    schooled in a workman's trade,
not with the high and great
    his home the Highest made:
but labouring by his brethren's side
life's common lot he glorified.

Then, when his hour was come
    he heard his Father's call;
and leaving friends and home,
    he gave himself for all;
good news to bring, the lost to find,
to heal the sick, the lame, the blind.

Toiling by night and day,
    himself oft burdened sore,
where hearts in bondage lay,
    himself their burden bore:
till, scorned by them he died to save
himself in death, as life, he gave.

O lowly majesty,
    lofty in lowliness!
Blest Saviour, who am I
    to share thy blessedness?
Yet thou hast called me, even me,
Servant divine, to follow thee.

Prayers and Hymns for use in Schools,
1927

461
THE LIGHT OF THE WORLD   HG 110

Christ is the world's true light,
    its Captain of salvation,
the daystar clear and bright
    of every man and nation;
new life, new hope awakes
    where'er men own his sway;
freedom her bondage breaks
    and night is turned to day.

In Christ all races meet,
    their ancient feuds forgetting,
the whole round world complete
    from sunrise to its setting:
when Christ is throned as Lord,
    men shall forsake their fear,
to ploughshare beat the sword,
    to pruning-hook the spear.

One Lord, in one great name
  unite us all who own thee;
cast out our pride and shame
  that hinder to enthrone thee;
the world has waited long,
  has travailed long in pain;
to heal its ancient wrong
  come, Prince of Peace, and reign.

Songs of Praise, 1931

462
SCIENCE

God, who hast given us power to sound
  depths hitherto unknown:
to probe earth's hidden mysteries,
  and make their might our own:

great are thy gifts: yet greater far
  this gift, O God, bestow,
that as to knowledge we attain
  we may in wisdom grow.

Let wisdom's godly fear dispel
  all fears that hate impart;
give understanding to the mind,
  and with new mind, new heart.

So for thy glory and man's good
  may we thy gifts employ,
lest, maddened by the lust of power
  man shall himself destroy.

The Times, 10 January, 1954;
rev. in *Hymns of Faith*, 1957

463
THE FRIEND OF SINNERS

Jesus, whose all-redeeming love
  no pentitent did scorn,
who didst the stain of guilt remove
  till hope anew was born:

to thee, Physician of the soul,
  the lost, the outcast came:
thou didst restore and make them whole,
  disburdened of their shame.

'Twas love, thy love, their bondage brake,
  whose fetters sin had bound:
for faith to love did answer make,
  and free forgiveness found.

Thou didst rebuke the scornful pride
  that called thee 'sinners' friend,'
thy mercy as the Father's wide,
  God's mercy without end.

Along life's desecrated way
  where man despairing trod,
thy love all-pitying did display
  the pitying love of God.

Jesus, that pardoning grace to find,
  I too would come to thee:
O merciful to all mankind,
  be merciful to me.

Hymns of Faith, 1957

THOMAS TIPLADY*
1882-1964

464
CHRIST WALKS IN BEAUTY

From Nazareth the Lord has come
  and walks in Galilee
along the narrow crowded streets,
  and by the tideless sea.
The people throng to hear his words
  of sweet celestial grace;
and, by the way he leaves behind
  his pathway all may trace.
    Christ walks in beauty, grace and power
      along life's common ways,
    and, like the dawn in summer time
    awakes the voice of praise.

From Galilee, the Risen Lord
  now comes to every land,
to share his love with every race
  and lead it by the hand;
no more in darkness shall men grope,
  for he their light shall be;
and from the bonds of sin and fear
  the truth shall make them free.   (John 8:36)
    Christ walks in beauty, grace and power
      along life's common ways,
    and, like the dawn in summer time
    awakes the voice of praise.

100 New Hymns of Praise, c. 1930

**GEORGE KENNEDY
ALLEN BELL**, Bishop
1883-1959

465
THE COMMUNION OF SAINTS   HG 108

Christ is the King! O friends, rejoice;
brothers and sisters, with one voice,
let all men know he is your choice.
Ring out, ye bells, give tongue, give tongue!
Let your most merry peal be rung,
while our exultant song is sung.

O magnify the Lord, and raise
anthems of joy and holy praise
for Christ's brave saints of ancient days,
who with a faith for ever new
followed the King, and round him drew
thousands of faithful men and true.

O Christian women, Christian men,
all the world over, seek again
the way disciples followed then.
Christ through all ages is the same;
place the same hope in his great name,
with the same faith his word proclaim.

Let Love's unconquerable might
your scattered companies unite
in service to the Lord of light;
so shall God's will on earth be done,
new lamps be lit, new tasks begun,
and the whole Church at last be one.

Songs of Praise, 1931

JAN STRUTHER
1901-53
HG 428

466
MARRIAGE

God, whose eternal mind
rules the round world over,
whose wisdom underlies
all that men discover:
grant that we, by thought and speech,
may grow nearer each to each;
Lord, let sweet converse bind
lover unto lover.
Bless us, God of loving.

Godhead in human guise
once to earth returning,
daily through human eyes
joys of earth discerning:
grant that we may treasure less
passion than true tenderness,
yet never, Lord, despise
heart to sweetheart turning.
Bless us, God of loving.

God, whose unbounded grace
heaven and earth pervadeth,
whose mercy doth embrace
all thy wisdom madeth:
grant that we may, hand in hand,
all forgive, all understand;
keeping, through time and space,
trust that never fadeth.
Bless us, God of loving.

God, who art Three in One,
all things comprehending,
wise Father, valiant Son
in the Spirit blending:
grant us love's eternal three -
friendship, rapture, constancy;
Lord, till our lives be done,
grant us love unending.
Bless us, God of loving.

Songs of Praise, 1931

RONALD A. KNOX, 1888-1957
and
CYRIL A. ALINGTON
1872-1955

467
PROPHECY

Awake, awake, put on thy strength, O Zion   (Is. 52:1)
God's purpose tarries, but his will stands fast;   (Hab. 2:3)
of Judah's tribe is born the mighty Lion,   (Gen. 49:9; Rev. 5:5)
and Man shall bruise the serpent's head at last.   (Gen. 3:15)
Promise and covenant God surely keeps;   (Ps. 111:9)
He watching o'er us slumbers not nor sleeps.   (Ps. 121:4)

Ho, ye that thirst, the pleasant fountains wait you;   (Is. 55:1)
Ye that are poor, ye shall be freely fed;
why give ye gold for wine that cannot sate you?   (Is. 55:2)
Why strive your hands for that which is not bread?   (Jn. 6:27)

For now the low estate of his handmaiden
God hath regarded and she shall be blest;   (Lk. 1:48)
Hear him that saith, 'Come, all ye heavy-laden,
come unto me and I will give you rest.'   (Mt. 11:28)

Scornful we looked, and lo! his face was stained,   (Is. 53:4)
His visage marred beyond the sons of men;   (Is. 53:2-3)
Yet those his stripes our life and peace regained,   (Is. 53:6)
Those hands shall heal us that were pierced then.

Arise and shine, thy battlements are shining,   (Is. 60:1)
upon thee breaks the glory of the Lord;
and from the east, thy royalty diving,   (Is. 60:2-7)
the Gentiles come to see thy peace restored.
Promise and covenant God surely keeps;
he watching o'er us slumbers not nor sleeps.

The Public School Hymn Book, 1919

**CYRIL ARGENTINE
ALINGTON**, Dean
1872-1955
HG 253

468
KINGS AND PRIESTS

Ye that know the Lord is gracious,   (1 Pet. 2:4-10)
ye for whom a corner-stone
stands, of God elect and precious,
laid that ye may build thereon,
see that on that sure foundation
ye a living temple raise,
towers that may tell forth salvation,   (Is. 60:18)
walls that may re-echo praise.

Living stones, by God appointed
each to his appointed place,
kings and priests, by God anointed,
shall ye not declare his grace?
Ye, a royal generation,
tell the tidings of your birth,
tidings of a new creation   (2 Cor. 5:17)
to an old and weary earth.

Tell the praise of him who called you
out of darkness into light,
broke the fetters that enthralled you,
gave you freedom, peace and sight:
tell the tale of sins forgiven,
strength renewed and hope restored,   (Is. 40:28)
till the earth, in tune with heaven,
praise and magnify the Lord!

Hymns Ancient and Modern, 1950

ALBERT FREDERICK BAYLY
1901-

469
LORD OF THE UNIVERSE   HG 537

O Lord of every shining constellation
that wheels in splendour through the midnight sky;
grant us thy Spirit's true illumination
to read the secrets of thy work on high.

And thou who had'st the atom's hidden forces,
    whose laws its mighty energies fulfil;
teach us, to whom thou giv'st such rich resources
    in all we use, to serve thy holy will.

O Life, awaking life in cell and tissue,
    from flower to bird, from beast to brain of man;
O help us trace, from birth to final issue
    the sure unfolding of thine ageless plan.

Thou, who hast stamped thine image on thy creatures,   (Gen. 1:26)
    and though they marred that image, lov'st them still;
uplift our eyes to Christ, that in his features
    we may discern the beauty of thy will.

Great Lord of nature, shaping and renewing,
    who mad'st us more than nature's sons to be;
help us to tread, with grace our souls enduing,
    the road to life and immortality.

Rejoice, O People, 1950

470
DO JUSTLY, LOVE MERCY
Micah 6:6-8

HG 796

What doth the Lord require
    for praise and offering?
What sacrifice desire
    or tribute bid thee bring?
        Do justly;
        love mercy;
    walk humbly with thy God.

Rulers of men, give ear!
    Should you not justice know?
Will God your pleading hear
    while crime and cruelty grow?
        Do justly;
        love mercy;
    walk humbly with your God.

Masters of wealth and trade;
    all you for whom men toil:
think not to win God's aid
    if lies your commerce soil.
        Do justly;
        love mercy;
    walk humbly with your God.

Still down the ages ring
    the prophet's stern commands.
To merchant, worker, king
    he brings God's high demands.
        Do justly;
        love mercy;
    walk humbly with your God.

How shall my soul fulfil
    God's law so hard and high?
Let Christ endue thy will
    with grace to fortify.
        Then justly;
        in mercy;
    thou'lt humbly walk with God.

Rejoice, O People, 1950

471
JOY

Joy wings to God our song,
    for all life holds
        to stir the heart,
        to light the mind
    and make our spirit strong.

Joy wings our grateful hymn,
    for home and friends,
        and all the love
        that fills our cup
    of gladness to the brim.

Joy wings to God our praise,
    for wisdom's wealth,
        our heritage
        from every age,
    to guide us in his ways

Joy wings to God our prayer.
    All gifts we need
        of courage, faith,
        forgiveness, peace,
    are offered by his care.

Joy wings our heart and voice
    to give ourselves
        to Christ who died
        and, risen, lives
    that we may all rejoice.

Again I say, Rejoice, 1971

T. C. HUNTER-CLARE*
1910-

472
LABOUR

God of the pastures, hear our prayer,
    Lord of the growing seed,
bless thou the fields, for to thy care
    we look in all our need.

God of the rivers in their course,
    Lord of the swelling sea,
where man must strive with nature's force,
    do thou his guardian be.

God of the dark and sombre mine,
    Lord of its hard-won store,
in toil and peril all be thine;
    thy help and strength are sure.

God of the city's throbbing heart,
    Lord of its industry,
bid greed and base deceit depart,
    give true prosperity.

God of authority and right,
    Lord of all earthly power,
to those who rule us grant thy light,
    thy wisdom be their dower.

God of the nations, King of men,
Lord of each humble soul,
we seek thy gracious aid again:
come down and make us whole.

The Voice of Melody, 1949

473
I CORINTHIANS 13

Lord, thy word hath taught
that our deeds are naught
if no flame of love doth fire us,
nor with godly grace inspire us;
from thy holy hill
love in us instil.

Send thy Spirit down,
and thy children crown
with this jewel best and rarest,
in thy diadem and fairest,
rich, all gold above,
gracious, holy love.

Faith and hope beyond,
of true peace the bond,
all man's virtues love uniteth
and thine image in him writeth,
who hath not its light
lives not in thy sight.

Hear us for his sake,
who our flesh did take,
send us love that never faileth,
love that o'er all foes prevaileth;
through thy Son our Lord
this great gift afford.

The Voice of Praise, 1950

ANDREW YOUNG*
1885-

474
LAMMAS

Lord, by whose breath all souls and seeds are living
with life that is and life that is to be,
first-fruits of earth we offer with thanksgiving
for fields in flood with summer's golden sea.

Lord of the earth, accept these gifts in token
thou in thy works art to be all-adored,
from whom the light as daily bread is broken,
sunset and dawn as wine and milk are poured.

Poor is our praise, but these shall be our psalter;
lo, like thyself they rose up from the dead;
Lord, give them back when at thy holy altar
we feed on thee, who art our living Bread.

BBC Hymn Book, 1951

JOHN ARLOTT
1914-
BBC Hymn Book
1951
HG 251

TWO COUNTRY HYMNS
475

We watched the winter turn its back,
its grip is loosened now,
and shoot and leaf have signed their green
on brown of field and bough.

From ambushed frost that kills by night,
and storm with bludgeoned hand,
from soft and secret-moving blight,
dear God, protect our land.

and send soft rain to feed the crops,
sun-warm them gold and red;
so grant the prayer we learned from Christ,
give us our daily bread.

476

God, whose farm is all creation,
take the gratitude we give;
take the finest of our harvest,
crops we grow that men may live.

Take our ploughing, seeding, reaping,
hopes and fears of sun and rain,
all our thinking, planning, waiting,
ripened in this fruit and grain.

All our labour, all our watching,
all our calendar of care,
in these crops of your creation,
take, O God; they are our prayer.

HENRY CHILD CARTER*
1875-1954

477
THE WHOLE ARMOUR OF GOD
Eph. 6:10-15

Give me, O Christ, the strength that is in thee,
that I may stand in every evil hour;
faints my poor heart except to thee I flee,
resting my weakness in thy perfect power.

Give me to see the foes that I must fight,
powers of the darkness, throned where thou shouldst reign,
read the directings of thy wrath aright,
lest, striking flesh and blood, I strike in vain.

Give me to wear the armour that can guard,
over my breast thy blood-bought righteousness,
faith for my shield, when fiery darts rain hard,
girded with truth, and shod with zeal to bless.

Give me to wield the weapon that is sure,
taking, through prayer, thy sword into my hand,
word of thy wisdom, peaceable and pure,
so, Christ my Conqueror, I shall conqueror stand.

Congregational Praise, 1951

GEORGE BRADFORD CAIRD
1917-

478
STEWARDSHIP

HG 32

Almighty Father, who for us thy Son didst give
that men and nations in his precious death might live,
in mercy guard us, lest by sloth and selfish pride
we cause to stumble him for whom the Saviour died.   (1 Cor. 8:9)

We are thy stewards; thine our talents, wisdom, skill;   (Matt. 18:24)
our only glory that we may thy trust fulfil;
that we thy pleasure in our neighbours' good pursue,   (Matt. 19:19)
if thou but workest in us both to will and do.   (Phil. 2:13)

On just and unjust thou thy care dost freely shower;   (Matt. 5:45)
make us thy children, free from greed and lust for power,
lest human justice, yoked with man's unequal laws,
oppress the needy, and neglect the humble cause.

Let not thy worship blind us to the claims of love;
but let thy manna lead us to the feast above,   (Heb. 9:4, 11)
to seek the country which by faith we now possess,   (Heb. 11:14)
where Christ our treasure reigns in peace and righteousness.

1942; *Congregational Praise*, 1951

479
MORE LIGHT AND TRUTH

Not far beyond the sea, nor high
above the heavens, but very nigh   (Deut. 30:11-14)
    thy voice, O God, is heard.
For each new step of faith we take
thou hast more light and truth to break
    forth from thy holy Word.

The babe in Christ thy Scriptures feed   (Heb. 5:13-14)
with milk sufficient for his need,
    the nurture of the Lord.
Beneath life's burden and its heat   (Matt. 20:12)
the full-grown man finds stronger meat
    in thy unfailing Word.

Rooted and grounded in thy love,   (Eph. 3:17-18)
with saints on earth and saints above
    we join in full accord
to grasp the breadth, length, depth and height,
the crucified and risen might
    of Christ, the Incarnate Word.

Help us to press toward that mark,   (Phil. 3:14)
and, though our vision now is dark,   (1 Cor. 13:12)
    to live by what we see.
So, when we see thee face to face,
thy truth and light our dwelling-place
    for ever more shall be.

1945; *New Songs*, 1962

ARTICLE 22:
HYMNS FOR CHILDREN, 1906-51 (480-486)

This very brief selection does scanty justice to the development of thinking about children's hymns during this period, which in hymnody was one of its most important aspects.

The *English Hymnal* had a strictly Victorian selection of children's hymns. It is a poor selection, but it is good compared with what was offered by the book universally popular in nonconformist Sunday schools, the *Sunday School Hymnary*,

1905, which packed its section for older children with 'junior Gospel-Songs' and moralistic doggerel. The temptation to include in section 20 H. W. Longfellow's 'Tell me not in mournful numbers,' which this book picked up, was easy to resist.

It may well have been because parents after 1914 had a good deal more contact with their own children than, in the hymn-writing section of society, they had earlier, that children's hymnody took on so decisive a new look. Dearmer, in his educational phase, had a good deal to do with it too. In *Songs of Praise* his children's section, especially in the 1931 edition, is strictly for young children and shows the results of good searching for good children's poetry.

We had had enough, anyhow, of 'writing down' to children. The offensive aspect of it was not so much when adults spoke their language in front of children (which children don't mind) but when they seemed, in the stilted and pompous language they affected, not to be taking children seriously. Many new books of children's hymns appeared between about 1920 and 1950, all of which were doing their best to find the right balance in this delicate form of communication. Undoubtedly the two most interesting were the *Church and School Hymnal* and *School Worship*, the one Anglican, the other Congregationalist, both of which came out in 1926.

No. 480 is a good example of the kind of material that appeared in the *Church and School Hymnal* and #481 of that which appeared in *School Worship*. No. 480 is very good, sturdy and swinging, with a very pictorial and at the same time faithful handling of Scripture. Perhaps #481 is, here and there, a little overdone; the 'chivalry' motif was, in this and many other hymns of the period, a concession to romanticism by people who had been brought up on Tennyson. But at least it takes trouble and takes the youngsters seriously.

No. 482, from *School Worship* again, is really remarkable; its author was the Public Orator in the University of Cambridge, a classical scholar, and a Baptist. He builds up, for small children, a vivid picture of the youth of Jesus in a manner which shows the influence of the Schweitzerian *Quest for the Historical Jesus* and of the preaching which was influenced by that line of thought. This book, though getting old now, is still worth careful study by people looking for children's hymns.

With ##483 and 484 we return to the Anglican book and introduce that remarkable children's poet, Canon Crum. We shall probably never be able to decide whether #483 goes well over the edge of risibility, or whether it just gets by. Its genial, frankly humorous approach to the sort of thing that Isaac Watts wrote about in his *Divine Songs* certainly sounds a new note and a refreshing one. Its author would have been the last person to expect us to take it very seriously. He always had a very delicate and serene style, and a feeling for the right word, and in #484, which surely is entirely beautiful, he shows us what heights he could reach. Fairly often elsewhere he is a bit arch and sometimes sentimental, but hardly in the ponderous way which the older books insisted was the right way.

Lesbia Scott's hymn of the saints, #485, was written in England but first published in America and much later taken back to England. She here has a slightly Crum-like twinkle. (One supposes an American would now have to read 'planes' for 'trains' in st. 3 line 6; and what he does about 'tea' is his own problem.) Perhaps 'just like me' in the last line but one is a shade questionable; but at the time it was certainly a very good effort at clearing cant out of children's hymnody.

No. 486 is our one example from *Songs of Praise*, but we

would gladly suggest that the reader look carefully at the 1931 edition of that book. Here is chivalry again, which nowadays will hardly do as a Christian image; but here also is rhythmical, friendly writing which children have in fact always fallen for. We should add that G. W. Briggs (460-3) wrote some of the best children's hymns that are available, and that they are in *Songs of Praise*.

But this should be enough to alert the reader to the fact, which he will find confirmed in the hymnals of this period, that if the Victorians were in danger always of being stuffy and repressive, the later writers were in equal danger of being sweet and over-mellifluous. One healthy sign in the hymnals of this period is the way in which they tend to shorten their children's sections and to close the gap between what is appropriate to children above the age of about ten and what is appropriate for everybody. The adults have for a long time been appropriating the best children's hymns ('Once in royal David's city' is still a children's hymn in *Hymns A & M*, but not so elsewhere), and increasingly those who look after children know that children will always welcome the most direct and commanding of the adult hymns. Now that a family is a family and not so much a household, this is as it should be.

C. ERSKINE CLARKE

480
DAVID AND HIS SON

O David was a shepherd lad,
and guarded well the sheep;
by night and day, good times or bad,
his watch he used to keep.
But David's less than David's Son,
though a shepherd too is he;
through all the world his pastures run
and of his flock are we.

O David was a shepherd lad,
and more he dared to do;
Goliath all in armour clad
with sling and stone he slew.
But David's Son, more daring yet,
put weapons all away;
all evil things with goodness met,
and stronger was than they.

O David was a shepherd lad,
and a kingdom he attained;
and gold and glory great he had,
and forty years he reigned.
But David's Son is rich in love,
and reigns eternally;
for King he is in heaven above,
and on the earth shall be.

1926

**WILLIAM CHARTER
PIGGOTT**, 1872-1943
HG 204

481
THE HOLY WAR

Christ rides to the holy war again,
leading his own to a new campaign;
for love of God and for love of man,
who will be with him and lead the van?

The Master leads as of old he led
the hero band of our hallowed dead;
to help the poor and the overborne,
who rides with him in the breaking dawn?

To free the body as once the soul,
making like happy and sweet and whole,
to give to labour its heritage,
who will with him in the work engage?

To give to the children smiles for tears,
glad rest for care to the hoary years,
to woman peace, and to manhood power,
who follows him in the present hour?

For Christ is out, and he turns not back,
though fierce the war and though long the track,
till he makes an end of want and woe -
who, then, is ready with him to go?

Yes, Christ is out, and when he comes in
he comes victorious over sin,
as Lord and Brother of love-bound men, -
who will go with him and stay till then?

1926

T. REAVELY GLOVER

482
JESUS AND JOSEPH

Jesus and Joseph day after day	(Matt. 13:55)

chiselled and planed and hammered away
in the shop at Nazareth.

Mary the Mother ground at the mill; (? Matt. 13:55)
eight little hungry mouths she must fill
in the home at Nazareth.

Four little boys for kindling were sent; (ibid.)
pulling and grasses and flowers they went
o'er the hills at Nazareth.

Grasses and flowers so pretty and gay,
packed in the oven they smoulder away (Matt. 6:30)
in the yard at Nazareth.

Soon it grows hot, her loaves she can bake;
bread, and not stones, for dinner they take (Matt. 7:9)
in the home at Nazareth.

'Where is the coin that fell?' with her broom (Lk. 15:8)
Mary goes sweeping over the room
in the home at Nazareth.

'Look! There it is!' She ran in her joy
telling the news to the man and the boy
in the shop at Nazareth.

Patching their clothes by the candle's light (Matt. 9:16)
Mary would sew far into the night
in the home at Nazareth.

Games in the market - what did they play? (Matt. 11:16)
Weddings and funerals, that was their way,
boys and girls at Nazareth.

So he grew up, our Saviour dear (Lk. 2:52)
sharing the life of all of us here
in his home at Nazareth.

All that he did, he did for our sake,
seeking a home for us all to make
in heaven like that at Nazareth.

1926

J. M. C. CRUM, Canon
HG 494

483
NATURE'S GOOD HUMOUR

O once in a while
we obey with a smile
and are ever so modest and prudent,
but it's not very long
before something is wrong,
and somebody's done what he shouldn't.

In meadow and wood
the cattle are good
and the rabbits are thinking no evil;
the anemones white
are refined and polite,
and all the primroses are civil.

O Saviour, look down
when we sulk or we frown
and smooth into kindness our quarrels;
till our heart is as light
as a little bird's flight
and our life is as free as a squirrel's!

1926

484
LOVE IS OUR SHEPHERD

Love is our shepherd. All is well.
By meadow green and quiet pool
on summer noons he'll make us lie
among the elmtree shadows cool.

And when the surly winter comes
and all the shade is bleak with snows,
Love is our Shepherd, we'll not fear
to go where Love our Shepherd goes.

For he'll not suffer one lost lamb
to wander bleating on the fell;
he'll lift it up and bear it home.
Love is our Shepherd. All is well.

1926

LESBIA SCOTT

485
SAINTS NOW   HG 319

I sing a song of the saints of God,
patient and brave and true,
who toiled and fought and lived and died
for the Lord they loved and knew.
And one was a doctor and one was a queen,
and one was a shepherdess on the green:

they were all of them saints of God; and I mean,
God helping, to be one too.

They loved their Lord so good and dear,
and his love made them strong;
and they followed the right, for Jesus' sake,
the whole of their good lives long.
And one was a soldier, and one was a priest,
and one was slain by a fierce wild beast:
and there's not any reason, not the least
why I shouldn't be one too.

They lived not only in ages past,
there are hundreds of thousands still;
the world is bright with the joyous saints
who love to do Jesus' will.
You can meet them in school, or in lanes, or at sea,
in church, or in trains, or in shops, or at tea,
for the saints of God are just like me,
and I mean to be one too.

1929

JAN STRUTHER
1901-53
HG 428

486
CHIVALRY

When a knight won his spurs, in the stories of old,
he was gentle and brave, he was gallant and bold;
with a shield on his arm and a lance in his hand
for God and for valour he rode through the land.

No charger have I, and no sword by my side,
yet still to adventure and battle I ride,
though back into storyland giants have fled,
and the knights are no more and the dragons are dead.

Let faith be my shield and let joy be my steed
'gainst the dragons of anger, the ogres of greed;
and let me set free, with the sword of my youth,
from the castle of darkness the power of the truth.

1931

ARTICLE 23:
BRITISH HYMNODY, 1952-75 (487-520)

Following the year 1951, in which the first wave of post-war hymnals spent its force, the period of consolidation continued for a while. Then came the beginnings of a revolution. This was, in the first place, musical, and the first shots were fired with the publication in 1957 of the *Folk Mass* by Geoffrey Beaumont (1906-71), which at once raised the question whether styles up to then regarded as quite alien to English church music could be used in worship and which also gave at once a new connotation to the word 'Folk.'

Since the first phases of this were all musical–devising new tunes for hymns already well-known–they do not here concern us. And when the quest for new texts began, its early phases produced texts that went with new kinds of (in the new sense) folk music. These we shall consider in the next article.

What concerns us here is that in the years 1956-65 English hymnody took what one can only describe as a pasting. Many people were saying that the new styles must irretrievably replace the old. Many hasty judgments were made, both by those who espoused them and those who rejected them. It looked as if the main stream of hymnody might dry up.

As it turned out this was certainly not the case, and we must here, in introducing a set of hymns from the period 1964-1975, recount one or two of the events which released again the stream of 'straight' hymnody. As will be seen, it began to flow perhaps more clearly and unpollutedly than it had done for many years.

The first thing to say about the years 1964-75 is that they are the beginning of the age of 'Supplements.' The earlier years had seen a considerable production and marketing of informal books of religious songs; but the red light of inflation had already begun to glow. The consequence was that, what with the considerable store of new material that was coming, the difficulty of judging its durability in a hurry, the danger that too much hospitality to it might empty the hymnals of too much that was classic and still valuable, and the cost of making full hymnals, the major denominations all decided that the right thing to do was to produce an updating supplement to be used alongside the existing book. This had immense advantages: The editors of a new supplement could concentrate on what was new, without feeling that one new piece meant the extinction of one old one; and the relatively inexpensive supplement might be renewable in a shorter time than economics would dictate in the case of a full-sized book.

But, while the fashion of Supplements was introduced by two major collections which appeared almost simultaneously in 1969, *Hymns and Songs* (Methodist) and *100 Hymns for To-day* (Anglican, primarily for *Hymns A & M*), the story really begins in 1962 in a remote and pleasant Scottish village called Dunblane. So important is this story in the recent history of hymnody that it must here be recounted by one who was privileged to be a participant in the enterprise.

Around 1960, a row of cottages in Dunblane, about forty miles from both Edinburgh and Glasgow, was bought by the Scottish Churches' Council, a new ecumenical body representing the seven major denominations in Scotland, as a small retreat house and conference center. Pleasantly furnished and equipped with a small chapel in a cave which was reputedly the cell of the medieval Saint Blane, this house was placed in the charge of Dr Ian Fraser (see 488-9), a minister of the Church of Scotland who had served in a dockside parish at Rosyth. His brief was to organize a program of conferences –what in America are called workshops–to discuss and report on any issue of importance that might be appropriate, either from study of ancient matters or from examination of new political, economic, or ecclesiastical problems that came from time to time. In his wisdom Dr Fraser, himself not a musician, decided that one of these workshops should be devoted to church music. As will have already been seen, no time in history since the 16th century was a better one for the close and zealous examination of the place of music in the church.

It should be understood that the background of this was a feeling that the church must change its shape, its manner, and its attitudes. They were saying the same thing at the time at the Second Vatican Council in Rome, and everybody was saying it. So what was the musician's response? Dr Fraser himself was and remains–though he is not now in charge at Dunblane–an able disciple of the Iona Community, which from its foundation by Dr George (later Lord) McLeod was the most active and successful instrument of renewal in the Church of Scotland and collected members from all denominations

and from all over the world.

So the spirit in which some twenty-four people, half musicians and half clergy (not excluding several clerical musicians), met was a spirit of excitement and expectation. Now what must here be said, and must be said by a partisan with all possible objectivity, is that the 'report' which this workshop was to produce was from the first designed to be a collection of experimental hymns, or whatever other church music occurred to it, for the consideration of the authorities of the Church of Scotland, who were known to be already working on a revision of their official hymn book, the *Church Hymnary*. The question remained open whether whatever Dunblane produced should be issued as a supplemental book by that Church or incorporated into its thinking for the new book. The issue, which was known publicly only in 1973 when the *Church Hymnary, Third Edition* was published, was that, with the single exception of the Rimaud/Langlais hymn (no. 568 in our collection), this is the only major hymnal in recent years which totally ignored the products of the Dunblane group.

However, that is jumping ahead in the story. The conference set up a small working party, after some close thinking about principles, who were to search for or, if necessary, write new material. The products of the first working party appeared in a very informal booklet–hastily written out in the secretary's abominable manuscript and on an electric typewriter–called *Dunblane Praises*. Issued in an edition of 200 copies in 1964, it was retailed at (what used to be) two shillings, about twenty cents. It was distributed to churches and individuals who wanted it, and the edition had to be reprinted until a halt was called at 1,400 copies. There were 16 pieces, of which eight were new tunes to old hymns; but our #497 was in it, and this, with #568, has travelled a long distance since then.

The whole enterprise was repeated in 1966, and the product of that was *Dunblane Praises* II (1967); and a third meeting produced some more material, mostly in the form of canticles and responsive music, which was taken by Galliard Ltd. (now Stainer & Bell/Galaxy) and published as *New Songs for the Church* I and II, together with gleanings from the two *Dunblane Praises* books.

Now, considering that this material was produced by a fairly small bunch of writers and musicians from several denominations under pressure–they were in any case busy people who could only spare about 48 hours at a time for meetings–the modest success of their materials is, I think, fit to celebrate. As it happens, the only texts we have by members of that working party are ##488-9 and 504; but the ascriptions of several others will indicate that they were collected and first published by this group.

At this point it is worth looking at the two pieces by Dr Fraser, ##488-9; if Scotland had been tardy in producing literature in hymnody, in the person of Ian Fraser it certainly woke up. He has written much more than this. He has a zestful style, a poetic imagination, and an impatience of cliché which produces sometimes a most endearing roughness of texture. As for #504, all that needs to be said is that we include it here because it qualifies for inclusion in the *Hymnal Guide*, which see for a note on the odd circumstances of its composition.

But, going on from there, the Congregationalist minister John Geyer, a very able theologian, was laid under contribution in #491; and his other hymn, #492, first in *Hymns and Songs* (1969), has travelled some distance since. These are both weighty theological utterances saying quite new things about their subjects.

Brian Wren (497) was in the 1964 booklet, and we hardly knew then that we were coming in on the early work of a writer who was to achieve major importance. But since then he has done so. Wren, Kaan, and Pratt Green (to whom we shall come almost at once) are the leading triumvirate of English hymn writers at the moment (1975), and each has his special gifts. Wren's is for the felicitous expression of profound theological ideas. His communion hymn (498) brings together as no other does the equally important individual and communal factors in the grace that the sacrament confers: 'I' becomes, before the end, 'we,' a beautiful piece of timing and reconciliation. We present #499 for the same kind of reason; who else has written a hymn on the subject, 'How dare you presume to serve?' Place this alongside, say, #284, and see what has happened. And in #500 we have one of many hymns, and the best so far, on the now fashionable subject of ecology; note again the disciplined choice of words, and the lyric passion that compensates entirely for the absence of rhyme.

No. 503, one of many hymns written by Ian Ferguson, an ex-classics professor who is now Dean of Arts in the Open University in England, is probably the best known of all the Dunblane products. Informality masks a ferocious seriousness in this characteristically social-oriented poem.

That disposes of Dunblane. Before turning to the Supplements of the more official sort, we must mention #487, which comes from a book prepared for public (residential) schools in 1964, a book which remains the model for all future editors in matters of style, presentation, and precision of textual reading. The new texts in this book are not many, or specially distinguished, but their finest discovery was Donald Hughes, who just before his untimely death had begun to develop a very promising gift for hymnody. Hughes was a Methodist Head Master, a devoted admirer of Charles Wesley and of Bernard Manning, and in #487 (which he wrote in 'thou,' but his executor has authorized the perfectly natural changes to 'you') he produced a perfect lyric, serious but hopeful, not a word out of place, with a Wesley-like balance between the massive words and the small ones.

One other important hymnal of the same period is the *Anglican Hymnal* (1965), a book for Anglican evangelical congregations containing a good deal more of the classic Calvinist and Methodist hymnody than one finds in the other two hymnals used in that church. Among the new texts to be found there is #501, by an author, Timothy Dudley-Smith, who here and later elsewhere proves himself to have a polished and direct style. 'Tell out, my soul' is no doubt the first hymn to be directly inspired by the text of the New English Bible (compare #517) and has become very popular. Less well known, but often equally admirable, is his work in *Psalm Praise* (1974), a book of hymns, often in popular style, based on the Psalter. No. 502 is an example of this, and his work is easily the most valuable in that collection.

The first of the official Supplements to appear, *Hymns and Songs*, virtually introduced the work of Frederick Pratt Green. It is true that one of his pieces was in the *Methodist School Hymn Book* of 1950, but it is only since 1969 that, having been before a poet and dramatist as well as a minister, he emerged as one of the leaders among hymn writers. That he undoubtedly now is. It is safe to say that no hymnal that ignores him can claim to be fully literate. He has one very unusual gift: he especially enjoys writing 'to order' and does his best work when so stimulated. In such circumstances he always writes at once and sends a revision a few days later. No. 505 was

written to carry a certain tune, and how majestically simple and trenchant it is. It has a timeless quality and yet could only have been written in the mid-twentieth century because of the especially modern juxtaposition of ancient ideas that it achieves. No. 506 is one of his finest pieces, and again note how, by the use of none but simple words, he tells the singer so much about the doctrine of the Trinity—even, in St. 2, its history—that nobody else tells him. From the now considerable bulk of his work I chose #507, published previously only on a leaflet printed for the occasion it celebrates, for its beautiful combination of sheer ingenuity and hymnic eloquence. It is unlikely that the original version will be much sung, for you have to know a little of the Lady Julian to catch its allusions, especially in st. 4. But even if one doesn't know Julian, one can appreciate the climax of that stanza. The more general version once again says quite new things about saints. (What an unsmiling and fraught company they are in the more pedestrian of the Victorian hymns!)

Both the Methodist supplement and *100 Hymns for To-day* carry ## 508 and 509, featuring two of our most gifted women writers. Rosamund Herklots mostly writes hymns for children, but this admirable piece (508) has gone far enough to get into the *Hymnal Guide*. Miss Chisholm's very dramatic piece on Peter (509), written originally with a special dramatic ceremony in mind, is full of telling and alarming messages and is also proving a good traveller.

Nos. 510-514 are our first encounters with the new Catholic hymnody. It will later be necessary to say that Vatican II, with its liberation of vernacular hymnody, has yet to liberate any good texts in the U.S.A., but England and Scotland have been more fortunate. James Quinn, of the Lauriston Jesuit Fathers in Edinburgh, produced single-handed a book in 1969 which contained a hundred pieces, some translations, some original, in a very finished and professional style, thus giving his co-religionists a good start. In England, although an understandable eagerness to cash in on the new hymnic permissiveness produced a certain amount of hastily written material and hastily edited literature, the *New Catholic Hymnal* of 1971, a learned and demanding collection mostly showing fairly lofty taste, discovered a brilliant new writer in Brian Foley; and *Praise the Lord*, a more parish-oriented collection put together by three youthful scholars, gives us some fine material in a different key. The two Foley pieces (512-3) are very polished, modest, and moving; the energy and rhythm of the two from *Praise the Lord* (514-5) have already evoked some fascinating music, and deservedly so. Ever since 1964, Protestants have hoped that Catholics would avoid the errors into which Protestants fell in their hymn-singing customs. That was, it turned out, too much to hope for, but the excellent example of these two books and of *Worship-II* in America and the *Catholic Book of Worship* (1972) in Canada is one that we all hope will be widely followed.

The Third Edition of the *Church Hymnary* in Scotland admitted relatively few new texts and, as we said, missed many chances, but here and there it provides a new text worth anybody's respect. Dr Hunter, very well known as a scholar in New Testament studies, paraphrases what all his pupils know to be his favorite Biblical passage in #516, in a most unusual and entirely appropriate meter. Ian Pitt-Watson, perhaps Scotland's most accomplished minister-musician, has metricized three psalms (see #517) using the language of the New English Bible and surprising many by finding so much poetry there. His versions are beautifully done and are a good augury for any revision of the Scottish Psalter that may, within the next thousand years or so, be in view.

Some of the 'Supplement' material already mentioned appears in *New Church Praise* (1975), such as our #500. Of the many authors appearing there for the first time, it is, we hope, not invidious to select the two who seem to be the best metrists. John Gregory (#518, written long before publication) takes a Genevan meter otherwise handled only by Bridges (260) for his spacious Communion hymn, and Caryl Micklem, English scholar and musician, (519) shows considerable versatility in his substantial contribution to that book, not least in writing for children (535). He is one of the very few authors outside the 'folk' circle who successfully write their own music for their lyrics.

This leaves us only with the fascinating and unclassifiable Fred Kaan. Kaan, as many already know, is a Dutch-born minister of the United Reformed Church (formerly Congregationalist) who began in the 1960's writing hymns for his own congregation in Plymouth, England. He has never written hymns in his own language, but he has made English so much his own as to have developed a quite inimitable and distinctive style. His hymns up to 1971 were collected in the last edition of *Pilgrim Praise* (Galliard Ltd), but he issued some of them privately at an earlier stage in an informal typescript booklet and then in a printed booklet neither of which needed music because he always wrote in the meter of a well-known hymn tune.

What Kaan has done primarily is to focus the contemporary desire for hymns about modern ideas and situations, especially hymns about the city, and respond to it. Two of his best-known hymns are 'Sing we of the modern city,' and 'Sing we a song of high revolt'; I happen to think that both contain blemishes which make them less appropriate for inclusion here than the four I have ventured to choose from the collection of 68. These, surely, repay careful attention.

The one to look at first is #495, and the line to note is 'and for the love we owe the modern city,' which in its context is pure, vintage Kaan. Then look at #496, the very simple Communion hymn, and notice how naturally and yet how dramatically the 'machine' is accommodated in it; also the wonderful phrase, 'Pass from hand to hand the living love of Christ.' After this consider #493. Here one sees the other special gift of Kaan, which is a feeling for words so intense as to produce strange and often exhilarating word-associations. His title, 'Come to your senses,' is a good example of the ambiguity he loves to play with. And the spirit of joyful surprise is nowhere better communicated than in the first and last stanzas of this. Even more elusive, perhaps, is #494, in which the word 'tree' takes on a dreamlike, shifting quality, prepared for by the image of the 'gardener.' Among his many remarkable compositions I believe this to be the most searching and distinguished. In Kaan we have indeed the archetypal 'new-European' hymn writer. He will appear again in our last section.

The reader is, of course, encouraged to look about in contemporary books for new material, and if he does so he will encounter plenty more not only from the authors mentioned but from others. The third quarter of the twentieth century, after a quiet start followed by an alarming episode, has brought out of English hymn-writers a form of song which is at the same time traditional in form and new and fresh in content. Especially it expresses contemporary doubts (and, at its best, their resolutions), contemporary hesitations (and, at its best, penitence), and contemporary observation (and, at its best, concreteness).

The signature-hymn for some people for the whole of this modern movement is #490, perhaps the most famous of all 'contemporary' hymns in traditional form. The reader must decide whether the author has succeeded in making poetry out of motorways and pylons and railways; every new hymnal has it and almost always to a different tune. The best comment on it is what one young scientist of semi-agnostic cast of mind is known to have said when it first appeared: 'This is the first time the church has said anything that indicates that it, or God, is interested in what I do with my life.' 'God of concrete' is the central and archetypal hymn of mission to technology, and as such it deserves honour. Its author is a Methodist; Charles Wesley might possibly knit his brows over it, but John, whose special genius was in being observant and in despising cant, would certainly have responded with a surprised and delighted chuckle.

DONALD W. HUGHES
1911-67

487
PENITENCE

HG 156

Creator of the earth and skies,
   to whom the words of life belong,   (John 6:67)
grant us your truth to make us wise;
   grant us your power to make us strong.

Like theirs of old, our life is death,
   our light is darkness, till we see   (John 9:41)
th' eternal Word made flesh and breath,
   the God who walked by Galilee.

We have not known you; to the skies
   our monuments of folly soar,
and all our self-wrought miseries
   have made us trust ourselves the more.

We have not loved you: far and wide
   the wreckage of our hatred spreads,
and evils wrought by human pride
   recoil on unrepentant heads.

For this, our foolish confidence
   our pride of knowledge and our sin,
we come to you in penitence;
   in us the work of grace begin.   (Phil. 1:6)

Teach us to know and love you, Lord,
   and humbly follow in your way.
Speak to our souls the quickening word,
   and turn our darkness into day.

Hymns for Church and School, 1964,
text of 1969.

IAN FRASER,*
1917-

488
CHRIST BURNING

Christ, burning
   past all suns,
stars beneath thy feet
   like leaves on forest floor:
man, turning
   spaceward, shuns

knowledge incomplete,
fevered, to e..plore.

Christ, holding
atoms in one
loom of light and power
to weave creation's life:
man, moulding
rocket, gun,
turns creation sour,
plots dissolving strife.

Christ, festive
in gay bird,
rush of river flood,
joy on lovers' part:
youth, restive
seeks new word,
beat of life in blood,
chill of death in heart.

Christ, humble
on our side,
snatching death's grim keys,
ending Satan's scope:
we gamble
on our Guide,
inch our gains of peace,
work a work of hope.

Dunblane Praises, I, 1964

489
LORD, BRING THE DAY TO PASS

Lord, bring the day to pass
when forest, rock and hill,
the beasts, the birds, the grass
will know your finished will:
when man attains his destiny
and nature its lost unity.

Forgive our careless use
of water, ore and soil -
the plenty we abuse
supplied by others' toil:
save us from making self our creed,
turn us towards our brother's need.

Give us, when we release
creation's secret powers,
to harness them for peace,
our children's peace, and ours:
teach us the art of mastering
which makes life rich, and draws death's sting.

Creation groans, travails,   (Rom. 8:22)
futile its present plight,
bound - till the hour it hails
the new-born sons of light
who enter on their true estate.
Come, Lord: new heavens and earth create! (Rev. 21:1)

New Songs for the Church, I, 1969

RICHARD G. JONES
1926-

490
THE EARTH IS THE LORD'S   HG 237

God of concrete, God of steel,
God of piston, and of wheel
God of pylon, God of steam,
God of girder and of beam,
God of atom, God of mine,
all the world of power is thine.

Lord of cable, Lord of rail,
Lord of motorway and mail,
Lord of rocket, Lord of flight,
Lord of soaring satellite,
Lord of lightning's livid line,
all the world of speed is thine.

Lord of science, Lord of art,
God of map and graph and chart,
Lord of physics and research,
word of Bible, faith of church,
Lord of sequence and design,
all the world of truth is thine.

God, whose glory fills the earth,
gave the universe its birth,
loosed the Christ with Easter's might,
saves the world from evil's blight,
claims mankind by grace divine,
all the world of love is thine.

Methodist Recorder, 1964

JOHN BROWNLOW GEYER*
1932-

491
OUR RISEN LORD

Our risen Lord we will adore
who broke the gates of hell;
the Tyrant's power shall hold no more,
and earth with praise shall swell.

So great the Lord is and our King
in majesty doth reign;   (Ps. 99:1)
all men his greatness ever sing
and shout aloud his name.

The elemental powers are dead,   (Gal. 4:9)
the rule of sin and fear,
all by our God are captive led,   (Ps. 68:18)
his kingdom now draws near.

The powers of war and peace are caught,
all other fame is loss;   (Phil. 3:8)
the stonied soul, her freedom bought,   (Job 17:8)
rejoices in his cross.

With all your being show his praise,
who feeds us with his leaven;   (1 Cor. 5:8)
in song his mighty deeds upraise
and rise with him to heaven.

Dunblane Praises, I, 1964

492
BAPTISM AND RESURRECTION
Romans 6:9

We know that Christ is raised and dies no more:
embraced by futile death he broke its hold:
and man's despair he turned to blazing joy:
    Alleluia!

We share by water in his saving death:
this union brings to being one new cell,
a living and organic part of Christ:
    Alleluia!

The Father's splendour clothes the Son with life:
the Spirit's fission shakes the Church of God:
Baptized we live with God the Three in One:
    Alleluia!

A new Creation comes to life and grows
as Christ's new Body takes on flesh and blood:
the universe restored and whole will sing
    Alleluia!

Hymns and Songs, 1969

FREDERIK HERMANN KAAN
1929-
Pilgrim Praise, 1967, 1971
HG 202

493
COME TO YOUR SENSES

If you have ears, then listen
    to what the Spirit says
and give an open hearing
    to wonder and surprise.

If you have ears for hearing
    the word in human form,
then let your love be telling
    and your compassion warm.

If you have buds for tasting
    the apple of God's eye,
then go, enjoy creation
    and people on the way.

If you have hands for caring,
    then pray that you may know
the tender art of loving
    our world of touch and go.

If you can smell the perfume
    of life, the feast of earth,
then sow the seeds of laughter
    and tend the shoots of mirth.

Come, people, to your senses,
    and celebrate the day!
For God gives wine for water,   (John 2:1-12)
    the gift of light for grey.

494
THE TREE SPRINGS TO LIFE   HG 781

We meet you, O Christ,
    in many a guise,
your image we see
    in simple and wise.

You live in a palace,
    exist in a shack.
We see you, the gardener,   (John 20:15)
    a tree on your back.

In millions alive,
    away and abroad;
involved in our life
    you live down the road.
Imprisoned in systems
    you long to be free,
We see you, Lord Jesus,
    still bearing your tree.   (Lk. 23:26)

We hear you, O man,
    in agony cry.
For freedom you march,
    in riots you die.
Your face in the papers
    we read and we see.
The tree must be planted
    by human decree.

You choose to be made
    at one with the earth;
the dark of the grave
    prepares for your birth.
Your death is your rising,
    creative your word;
the tree springs to life
    and our hope is restored.

495
FROM WORSHIP TO SERVICE   HG 409

Lord, as we rise to leave this shell of worship,
called to the risk of unprotected living,
willing to be at one with all your people,
    we ask for courage.

For all the strain with living interwoven,
for the demands each day will make upon us,
and for the love we owe the modern city,
    Lord, make us cheerful.

Give us an eye for openings to serve you;
make us alert when calm is interrupted,
ready and wise to use the unexpected:
    sharpen our insight.

Lift from our life the blanket of convention;
give us the nerve to lose our life to others.
Be with your church in death and resurrection,
    Lord of all ages!

496
COMMUNION

As we break the bread
    and taste the life of wine
we bring to mind our Lord,
    Man of all time.

Grain is sown to die;   (John 11:24)
    it rises from the dead,
becomes through human toil
    our common bread.

Pass from hand to hand
the living love of Christ!
Machine and man provide
bread for this feast.

Jesus binds in one
our daily life and work;
he is of all mankind
symbol and mark.

Having shared the bread
that died to rise again,
we rise to serve the world,
scattered as grain.

BRIAN ARTHUR WREN
1936-

497
CHRISTIAN UNITY   HG 413

Lord Christ, the Father's mighty Son,
whose work upon the cross was done
all men to receive,
make all our scattered churches one,
that the world may believe.

To make us one your prayers were said.
To make us one you broke the bread
for all to receive.
Its pieces scatter us instead:
how can others believe?

Lord Christ, forgive us, make us new!
What our designs could never do
your love can achieve.
Our prayers, our work, we bring to you
that the world may believe.

We will not question or refuse
the way you work, the means you choose,
the pattern you weave,
but reconcile our warring views
that the world may believe.   (John 17:21)

Dunblane Praises, I, 1964

498
CHRIST MAKING FRIENDS

I come with joy to meet my Lord,
forgiven, loved and free,
in awe and wonder to recall
his life laid down for me.

I come with Christians far and near,
to find, as all are fed,
man's true community of love
in Christ's communion bread.

As Christ breaks bread for men to share
each proud division ends,
the love that made us, makes us one,
and strangers now are friends.

And thus with joy we meet our Lord,
his presence, always near,
is in such friendship better known:
we see, and praise him here.

Together met, together bound,
we'll go our different ways,
and as his people in the world
we'll live and speak his praise.

The Hymn Book (Canada), 1971

499
PRIDE AND SERVICE

Lord Jesus, if I love and serve my neighbour
out of my knowledge, leisure, power or wealth,
open my eyes to understand his anger
if from his helplessness he hates my help.

When I have met my brother's need with kindness
and prayed that he could waken from despair,
open my ears if, crying now for justice
he struggles for the changes that I fear.

Lord, though I cling to safety or possessions,
yet from the cross love's poverty prevails:
open my heart to life and liberation,
open my hands to bear the mark of nails.

New Church Praise, 1975

500
CARING FOR PLANET EARTH

Thank you, Lord, for water, soil and air -
large gifts supporting everything that lives.
Forgive our spoiling and abuse of them.
Help us renew the face of the earth.

Thank you, Lord, for minerals and ores -
the basis of all building, wealth and speed.
Forgive our reckless plundering and waste.
Help us renew the face of the earth.

Thank you, Lord, for priceless energy -
stored in each atom, gathered from the sun.
Forgive our greed and carelessness of power.
Help us renew the face of the earth.

Thank you, Lord, for weaving nature's life
into a seamless robe, a fragile whole.
Forgive our haste, that tampers unawares.
Help us renew the face of the earth.

Thank you, Lord, for making planet earth
a home for us and ages yet unborn.
Help us to share, consider, save and store.
Come and renew the face of the earth.

New Church Praise, 1975

TIMOTHY DUDLEY-SMITH,
Archdeacon
1928-

501
MAGNIFICAT

(based on the New English Bible version of Luke 1:46-54)

Tell out, my soul, the greatness of the Lord!
Unnumbered blessings, give my spirit voice;
tender to me the promise of his word;
in God my Saviour shall my heart rejoice.

Tell out, my soul, the greatness of his name!
  Make known his might, the deeds his arm has done;
his mercy sure, from age to age the same;
  his holy name - the Lord, the Mighty One.

Tell out, my soul, the greatness of his might!
  Powers and dominions lay their glory by,
proud hearts and stubborn wills are put to flight,
  the hungry fed, the humble lifted high.

Tell out, my soul, the glories of his word!
  Firm is his promise, and his mercy sure.
Tell out, my soul, the greatness of the Lord
  to children's children and for evermore!

1961; *Anglican Hymn Book*, 1965

502
NON NOBIS, DOMINE
(Psalm 115)

Not to us be glory given
  but to him who reigns above,
Glory to the God of heaven
  for his thankfulness and love!
What though unbelieving voices
  hear no word and see no sign,
still in God my heart rejoices,
  working out his will divine.

Not what human fingers fashion,
  gold and silver, deaf and blind,
dead to knowledge and compassion,
  having neither heart nor mind -
lifeless gods, yet men adore them,
  nerveless hands and feet of clay;
all become, who bow before them,
  lost indeed, and dead as they.

Not in them is hope of blessing -
  hope is in the living Lord!
High and low, his name confessing,
  find in him their shield and sword.
Hope of all whose hearts revere him,
  God of Israel, still the same!
God of Aaron! Those who fear him
  he remembers them by name.

Not the dead, but we the living
  praise the Lord with all our powers;
of his goodness freely giving -
  his is heaven: earth is ours.
Not to us be glory given
  but to him who reigns above;
Glory to the God of heaven
  for his faithfulness and love!

Psalm Praise, 1974

IAN FERGUSON
1920-

503
AM I MY BROTHER'S KEEPER?   HG 36

'Am I my brother's keeper?'   (Gen. 4:9)
  the muttered cry was drowned
by Abel's life-blood shouting
  in silence from the ground.

For no man is an island,
  divided from the main;
the bell which tolled for Abel
  tolled equally for Cain.

The ruler called for water,
  and thought his hands were clean,   (Matt. 27:24)
Christ counted less than order,
  the man than the machine.
The crowd cried 'Crucify him!'
  their malice wouldn't budge,
so Pilate called for water,
  and history's his judge.

As long as people hunger,
  as long as people thirst,
and ignorance and illness
  and warfare do their worst,
as long as there's injustice
  in any of God's lands,
I am my brother's keeper;
  I dare not wash my hands.

Dunblane Praises II, 1967

ERIK ROUTLEY
1917-

504
THE LORD IS THERE   HG 25

All who love and serve your city,
  all who bear its daily stress,
all who cry for peace and justice,
  all who curse, and all who bless,

in your day of loss and sorrow,
  in your day of helpless strife,
honour, peace and love retreating,
  seek the Lord, who is your life.

In your day of wealth and plenty,
  wasted work and wasted play,
call to mind the word of Jesus,
  'Work ye yet while it is day.'   (John 9:4)

For all days are days of judgment,
  and the Lord is waiting still,
drawing near to men who spurn him,   (Lk. 19:41)
  offering peace on Calvary's hill.

Risen Lord, shall yet the city
  be the city of despair?
Come to-day, our Judge, our Glory,
  be its name, 'The Lord is there.'   (Ezek. 48:35)

Dunblane Praises II, 1967

FREDERICK PRATT GREEN
1903-

505
THE UNIQUENESS OF CHRIST   HG 109

Christ is the world's Light, he and none other;
born in the darkness, he became our Brother.
If we have seen him, we have seen the Father: (John 14:9)
  Glory to God on high.

Christ is the world's Peace, he and none other;
no man can serve him and despise his brother.   (1 John 4:20)

Who else unites us, one in God the Father?   (John 17:21)
   Glory to God on high.

Christ is the world's Life, he and none other;
sold once for silver, murdered here, our Brother -
he, who redeems us, reigns with God the Father:
   Glory to God on high.

Give God the glory, God and none other;
give God the glory, Spirit, Son and Father;
give God the glory, God in man my brother:
   Glory to God on high.

Hymns and Songs, 1969

506
HYMN IN HONOUR OF THE HOLY AND UNDIVIDED TRINITY

Rejoice with us in God the Trinity,
the Three for ever One, for ever Three,
Fountain of Love, Giver of Unity.

We would rejoice again, and yet again
that God reveals his truth to mortal men,
      unveils for all to see
in what he is, what man himself may be.

How long and earnestly the Fathers strove
to frame in words a faith we cannot prove;
      but O, how dead our creeds
unless they live in Christ-like words and deeds.

So let us all, rejecting none, remove
whatever thwarts a reconciling love,
      all ills that still divide
the fold of Christ, and all the world beside.

Rejoice with us that man may yet achieve
what God himself has dared us to believe:
      that many live as one,
each loving each, as Father, Spirit, Son.

26 Hymns, 1971

507
THE REVELATIONS OF DIVINE LOVE

(Note: Originally this was written for a celebration at Norwich, England, of the 600th anniversary of the 'Revelations of Divine Love,' which The Lady Julian of Norwich wrote in 1373. Green wrote also a version for use on any saint's day, which is here version (b); in version (a) he incorporates many expressions and one direct quotation from the *Revelations*.)

(A)

Rejoice in God's saints
   this day of all days!
A world without saints
   forgets how to praise!
Rejoice in their courage,
   their spiritual skill:
in Julian of Norwich
   rejoice, all who will!

The candle she lit
   six centuries gone,
by darkness beset
   shines quietly on.
Her cell is no prison,
   though narrow and dim,

(B)

Rejoice in God's saints,
   this day of all days!
A world without saints
   forgets how to praise!
Their joy in exploring
   far reaches of prayer,
their depth of adoring,
   Lord, help us to share.

Rejoice in God's saints,
   the grave and the gay!
Some march with events,
   some live but to pray.
The world in its folly
   they wake from its dream:

(A)

for Jesus is risen
   and she lives in him.

How bright in her cell
   the showings of God!
No writings could tell
   what love understood.
She suffers His Passion,
   she grieves over sin,
and shares that compassion
   which makes us all kin.

How courteous is God!
   All love and all light!
In God's Motherhood
   she finds her delight.
She pleads for the sinner,
   she wrestles with Hell;
God answers: *All manner*
   of thing shall be well!

Dear Lord, we would learn
   to walk in this way;
with patience discern
   how best to obey.
The disciplined spirit,
   the saintly, how rare!
Lord, help us to wear it -
   the habit of prayer!

ROSAMUND E. HERKLOTS
1905-

(B)

in love that is holy
   there's power to redeem.

Rejoice in God's saints!
   what patience is theirs!
They shame our complaints.
   our comforts, our cares.
The disciplined spirit,
   the saintly, how rare!
Lord, help us to wear it,
   this habit of prayer!

Rejoice in God's saints
   this day of all days!
A world without saints
   forgets how to praise.
In loving, in living,
   they prove it is true:
the way of self-giving,
   Lord, leads us to you!

ms. 1973

508
FORGIVENESS   HG 207

'Forgive our sins as we forgive,'
   you taught us, Lord, to pray,
but you alone can grant us grace
   to live the words we say.

How can your pardon reach and bless
   the unforgiving heart
that broods on wrongs, and will not let
   old bitterness depart?

In blazing light your Cross reveals
   the truth we dimly knew,
how small the debts men owe to us,
   how great our debt to you.   (Lk. 7:41-2)

Lord, cleanse the depths within our souls
   and bid resentment cease;
then, reconciled with God and man,
   our lives will spread your peace.

Hymns and Songs, 1969

EMILY CHISHOLM*
1910-

509
PETER FEARED THE CROSS

Peter feared the cross for himself and his Master;
Peter tempted Jesus to turn and go back.
      O Lord, have mercy,
      lighten our darkness.
      We've all been tempters,
      our light is black.

Judas loved his pride and rejected his Master;
Judas turned a traitor, and lost his way back.
> O Lord, have mercy,
> lighten our darkness,
> we've all been traitors,
> our light is black.

Peter, James and John fell asleep when their Master
asked them to be praying a few paces back.
> O Lord, have mercy,
> lighten our darkness.
> We've all been sleeping,
> our light is black.

Peter, vexed and tired, thrice denied his own Master;
said he never knew him, to stop a girl's clack.
> O Lord, have mercy,
> lighten our darkness.
> We've all denied you,
> our light is black.

Twelve all ran away, and forsook their dear Master;
left him, lovely prisoner, a lamb in wolves' pack.
> O Lord, have mercy,
> lighten our darkness.
> We've all been failures,
> our light is black.

Pilate asked the crowd to set free their good Master.
'Crucify!' they shouted, 'we don't want him back!'
> O Lord, have mercy,
> lighten our darkness.
> We crucified you,
> our light is black.

We have watched the Cross and we've scoffed at our Master;
thought the safe way better, and tried our own tack.
> O Lord, have mercy,
> lighten our darkness.
> We've all reviled you,
> our light is black.

Hymns and Songs, 1969

JAMES QUINN, S.J.
1919-
Hymns for All Seasons, 1969
HG 867

510
UBI CARITAS

God is love, and where true love is, God himself is there
Here in Christ we gather, love of Christ our calling.
Christ, our love, is with us, gladness be his greeting.
Let us fear him, yes, and love him, God eternal.
Loving him, let each love Christ in all his brethren.

> God is love, and where true love is, God himself is there.

When we Christians gather, members of one Body,
let there be in us no discord, but one Spirit.
Banished now be anger, strife and every quarrel.
Christ, our God, be always present here among us.

> God is love, and where true love is, God himself is there.

Grant us love's fulfilment, joy with all the blessed.
when we see your face, O Saviour, in its glory.
Shine on us, O purest Light of all creation,
be our bliss while endless ages sing your praises.

> God is love, and where true love is, God himself is there.

From the Liturgy of Maundy Thursday.

511
FORTH IN THE PEACE OF CHRIST

Forth in the peace of Christ we go:
> Christ to the world with joy we bring;
Christ in our minds, Christ on our lips,
> Christ in our hearts, the world's true King.

King of our hearts, Christ makes us kings;   (1 Pet. 2:9)
> kingship with him his servants gain;
with Christ the Servant-Lord of all,
> Christ's world we serve to share Christ's reign.

Priests fo the world, Christ sends us forth
> the world of time to consecrate,
the world of sin by grace to heal,
> Christ's world in Christ to re-create.   (2 Cor. 5:17)

Christ's are our lips, his word we speak;
> prophets are we whose deeds proclaim
Christ's truth in love that we may be
> Christ in the world, to spread Christ's name.

We are the Church; Christ bids us show
> that in his Church all nations find
their hearth and home where Christ restores
> true peace, true love, to all mankind.

BRIAN FOLEY*
New Catholic Hymnal, 1971

512
THE SUFFERING SERVANT
Isaiah 53:1-6

See, Christ was wounded for our sake
> and bruised and beaten for our sin,
so, by his sufferings we are healed,
> for God has laid our guilt on him.

Look on his face, come close to him -
> see, you will find no beauty there:
despised, rejected, who can tell
> the grief and sorrow he must bear?

Like sheep that stray, we leave God's path
> to choose our own and not his will;
like sheep to slaughter he has gone,
> obedient to his Father's will.

Cast out to die by those he loved,
> reviled by those he died to save,
see, how sin's pride has sought his death,
> see how sin's hate has made his grave.

For on his shoulders God has laid
> the weight of sin that we should bear;
so by his Passion we have peace,
> through his obedience and his prayer.

513
LORD, AS I WAKE
(Psalm 5)

Lord, as I wake I turn to you,
> yourself the first thought of my day:
my King, my God, whose help is sure,
> yourself the help for which I pray.

There is no blessing, Lord, from you
    for those who make their will their way,
no praise for those who will not praise,
    no peace for those who will not pray.

Your loving gifts of grace to me,
    those favours I could never earn,
call for my thanks in praise and prayer,
    call me to love you in return.

Lord, make my life a life of love,
    keep me from sin in all I do;
Lord, make your law my only law,
    your will my will, for love of you.

'PETER ICARUS'*

514
OFFERTORY

Reap me the earth as a harvest to God,
    gather and bring it again,
all that is his, to the Maker of all,
    lift it and offer it high.
        Bring bread, bring wine, give glory to the Lord.
        Whose is the earth but God's? Whose is the praise but his?

Go with your song and your music, with joy,
    go to the altar of God.
Carry your offerings, fruits of the earth,
    work of your labouring hands. . . .

Gladness and pity and passion and pain,
    all that is mortal in man,
lay all before him, return him his gift,
    God, to whom all shall go home. . . .

Praise the Lord, 1972

LUKE CONNAUGHTON*

515
BREAD AND WINE

Bread from the earth, wine from the soil, Adam made of clay:
bring to the Lord - sing to the Lord! - gifts of red and gold.
Red is the wine, royal and rich, golden gleams the wheat.

Fashioned from dust, what can you give, man, so weak, so poor?
Bring to the Lord - sing to the Lord! - what he gave to you:
Spirit of flame, mastering mind, body fine and proud.

Cry on his name, worship your God, all who dwell on earth.
Bring to the Lord - sing to the Lord! - heart and voice and will.
Father and Son, Spirit most high, worship three in One.

Praise the Lord, 1972

ARCHIBALD MacBRIDE
HUNTER*, 1906-

516
KENOSIS
Phil. 2:5-11

Though in God's form he was,
    Christ Jesus would not snatch
    at parity with God.

Himself he sacrificed,
    taking a servant's form,
    being born like every man;

revealed in human shape,
    obediently he stooped
    to die upon a cross.

Him therefore God raised high,
    gave him the name of Lord,
    all other names above;

that at the Saviour's name
    no knee might be unbowed
    in heaven or earth or hell;

and every tongue confess,
    to God the Father's praise,
    that 'Jesus Christ is Lord.'

Church Hymnary III, 1973

IAN PITT-WATSON*

517
FROM PSALM 139

Thou art before me, Lord, thou art behind,
    and thou above me hast spread out thy hand;
such knowledge is too wonderful for me,
    too high to grasp, too great to understand.

Then whither from thy Spirit shall I go,
    and whither from thy presence shall I flee?
If I ascend to heaven thou art there,
    and in the lowest depths I meet with thee.

If I should take my flight into the dawn,
    if I should dwell on ocean's farthest shore,
thy mighty hand would rest upon me still,
    and thy right hand would guard me evermore.

If I should say, 'Darkness will cover me,
    and I shall hide within the veil of night,'
surely the darkness is not dark to thee,
    the night is as the day, the darkness light.

Search me, O God, search me and know my heart,
    try me, O God, my mind and spirit try;
keep me from any path that gives thee pain,
    and lead me in the everlasting way.

Church Hymnary III, 1973
(Based on the New English Bible
translation.)

JOHN K. GREGORY
b. 1929

518
OFFERTORY

Good is our God who made this place
whereon our race is plenty liveth.
    Great is the praise to him we owe,
that we may show 'tis he that giveth.
    Then let who would for daily food
give thanks to God who life preserveth;
    offer this board to our good Lord,
and him applaud who praise deserveth.

Praise him again whose sovereign will
grants us the skill of daily labour;
   whose blessed Son to our great good
fashioned his wood to serve his neighbour.
   Shall we who sing not also bring
of this world's wages to the Table? -
   giving again of what we gain,
to make it plain God doth enable.

So let us our Creator praise
who all our days our life sustaineth;
   offer our work, renew our vow,
adore him now who rightly reigneth;
   that we who break this bread, and take
this cup of Christ to our enjoyment,
   may so believe, so well receive,
never to leave our Lord's employment.

New Church Praise, 1975
(The meter and rhyme-scheme in this
hymn follow exactly those of #260)

CARYL MICKLEM*
1925-
New Church Praise, 1975

519
THINK ON THESE THINGS
Phil. 4:6-8

We praise you, Lord, for all that's true and pure -
clean lines, clear water, and an honest mind.
Grant us your truth, keep guard over our hearts,
   fill all our thoughts with these things.

We praise you, Lord, for all that's excellent -
high mountain peaks, achievement dearly won.
Lift up our eyes, keep guard over our hearts,
   fill all our thoughts with these things.

We praise you, Lord, for all of good report -
the spur to us of others' noble lives.
Show us your will, keep guard over our hearts,
   fill all our thoughts with these things.

We praise you, Lord, the man of Nazareth -
you lived for others, now you live for all.
Jesus, draw near, keep guard over our hearts,
   fill all our thoughts with these things.

520

Give to me, Lord, a thankful heart
   and a discerning mind:
give, as I play the Christian's part,
the strength to finish what I start
   and act on what I find.

When, in the rush of days, my will
   is habit-bound and slow
help me to keep in vision still
what love and power and peace can fill
   a life that trusts in you.

By your divine and urgent claim
   and by your human face
kindle our seeking hearts to flame
and as you teach the world your name
   let it become your place.

Jesus, with all your church I long
   to see your kingdom come:
show me your way of righting wrong
and turning sorrow into song
   until you bring me home.

ARTICLE 24:
ENGLISH 'FOLK' HYMNODY (521-528)

There are special reasons why the representation of the English 'folk' style in this collection is altogether disproportionate to the output of its promoters. One of the chief reasons is that almost always it means very little without its music. In all but one of the eight pieces we present here the music is composed by the author of the words, and this is the normal fashion, which at once distinguishes the style from that of 'main line' hymnody.

It is too early yet to judge how much of this material will prove to be enduring; our selection turns out to include three pieces from the founding father of the cult in England and five from three other authors who are far less celebrated than some of those we might have chosen. The point we hope to make will become clear after a little discussion of that extraordinary figure who during the 1960's leapt to fame and prominence in England, Sydney Carter.

Carter is a journalist and folk-singer of whom in the year 1960 probably only his close friends had ever heard. By 1970 two or three of his pieces had been translated into many languages and were sought after by the editors of many hymnals. By then he had had several long-run programs on English television, and his songs had become well known through records mostly made either by himself or by his intimate friend, Donald Swann. His work, after first appearing in 1962 in a very modest booklet called *9 Ballads or Carols*, was taken up by an enterprising English publisher and by 1970 was available in many books featuring songs of this kind written by what had by then become a fairly wide-ranging group of his disciples and imitators. The best collection of his songs, which includes a comment by himself on each piece, is *Green Print for Song* (Stainer and Bell, 1973); the sources of his songs apart from this are so numerous and followed each other so quickly that it is best now to give that as the definitive source.

The ingredients in what we call, for want of a better way of putting it, the 'Folk' style are informality and protest. Upon those two, one might say, hang all its subsidiary properties. Consider first some of Sydney Carter's very well-known songs –too well-known to need including here–such as 'Lord of the Dance,' 'When I needed a neighbour,' and 'No use knocking on the window.' In these, as certainly also in #521, the informality breaks down into a sense of the physical, a sense of movement, and a free-ranging imaginative and–in Carter's case–poetic perception. The protest breaks down into a series of gestures against the over-abstraction (anti-physical) and the conventionality (anti-movement) of institutional religion. Consider that bird in #521: the image of the bird is free and outdoor; it is cruel to cage it. Consider two of Carter's favourite words, the noun 'dance' and the verb 'travel': negatively, English religion doesn't–in some cases mustn't–*dance*; positively, and here he is certainly on sound theological ground, it must always *travel*. One does, of course, notice in Carter a habit of impressionism in theology allied with a ruthless and severe concreteness in image and precept. The (assumed, not always fairly) callousness of Christians to the poor, the contrast between institutional opulence and practical meagreness, the shut-in quality of the kind of religion he seems to know most about are always under attack in his songs.

Now, these songs are an incursion into Christianity of a demotic art-form which has always had a vigorous underground existence. It derives from traditional folk-song in being the product of a culture which depends on oral tradition rather than on writing. Carter always says it doesn't matter if you alter his words or how you harmonize his tunes; it is incongruous and inept ever to say 'This, and this only, is the definitive text.' It is not that world. It is the world of the young –specifically the young of the 1950's–who were learning to reject the conventional world, finding ways of lampooning its absurdities and demonstrating against its injustices, and, when met together in cellars in London and Newcastle, the two metropolitan centres of this culture, making up songs that expressed their aspirations. The essence of folk-song is always that it is unprinted; it is hardly too much to say that at its most genuine it is unprintable! This is the world in which Carter had already found a sort of senior membership before he became famous as a Christian gadfly. The musical instrument of these singers was always the extremely portable and informal guitar –you can't carry a church organ down to the cellar. The language is conversational, and there is no reason why it should not be crude. It is as 'in-group' as that of the lower grade of eighteenth-century evangelical hymn, or as that of some of the Gospel Songs. It has no public manner because a public manner is just what the folk-people dislike and distrust.

Carter has professionalized all this to some extent. He has a public manner: a deadpan stance, a rasping voice, and a fairly settled frown. He is as near as we have ever seen in our time to the sort of Old Testament prophet who could produce the ironic and penetrating song in the beginning of Isaiah 5. He never tries to make a beautiful sound; he prints his songs in keys comfortable for him but hideous for any trained voice except a full bass; and although there is humour and a twinkle in many of his secular songs, in his religious pieces he never sings in any mood but that of exasperated censoriousness. (I am about to say that #522 is as near an exception to this as he ever gets.) Even 'Lord of the Dance' is a protest; he sings as if dancing is the last thing his hearers will ever do.

Now this is no affectation. Every word of it is meant, and every word of it is, in a wry sense, inspired. In 'The Bird of Heaven' you have the contrast he is always painting: a Blake-like picture of the imprisoned formal culture over against the blessed and joyful freedom he wants to communicate. A touch of this sanctified dissent is part of the equipment of any religious song-writer. There is something in the background he wants to change. Isaac Watts had it, gentle spirit that he was, when he wrote of ineffable visions and impossible demands. Charles Wesley had it when he wrote of the inconceivable grace of Christ. Perhaps the almost-absence of it is what gives the great American Unitarians their vulnerability, for there indeed Carter would recognize 'style and nothing more,' at least in some cases such as 'Dear Lord and Father of mankind.'

But it is this quality that produces the imagination that conceived 'Every star' (522). 'Why *shouldn't* there be an incarnation on Saturn?' asks Carter in his usual tone. He produces as a result of this question what some believe–I among them–to be his most innocent and lovable piece.

But not his greatest. Without question, that is #523, one of his earlier and most startling compositions. Here is a drama, here is irony, here is a theological exploration which opens up a terrifying vision of the real source of human grievance. 'It's

God they ought to crucify.' Well, I know of two short theological books that are written with that song as their text. I know also of many people whom the song has offended because they mistook it for a piece in the same universe of discourse as 'Praise, my soul.' But this is Carter; he is a folk poet in that he expresses the unexpressed thoughts of ordinary human beings about Jesus, about grief, about the church, and even about the Cross. He exposes them as alarmingly as this. In this he is in line with the greatest of hymn writers. But he has to be publicly sung with circumspection.

Carter is a layman. The next two authors might be described as laicized clergy in that both were ordained, and both are now serving the community in secular employment–Goodall in education, Stewart in the media–without in any sense having deserted the faith into which they were ordained. David Goodall, of whom more ought to have been heard, exercises still the professional ministry of the United Reformed Church in recognizable ways. Whether Goodall can be called a disciple of Carter is doubtful, for he was writing songs like ##524 and 525 before Carter had become famous. But here again is civilized protest and baptized poetry. Goodall is a far more cultivated musician than Carter (as a matter of history he succeeded the British political leader Edward Heath as organ scholar at Balliol College, Oxford, in 1938), and a far subtler writer; in addition, he refuses to abandon his theological insights. The result in #524 is a very tight-knit piece expressing the deep Christian unease at the conventionalities of outward religion; and in #525 it is a beautifully witty and well-turned song of the Carter kind expressing the contradictions within the mind and intentions of what he calls 'a not-quite-Christian.'

Malcolm Stewart, at one time a Roman Catholic priest and always a cultivated musician, in his *Gospel Songs for To-day* (in America, called *Now Songs*), spends little time protesting and most of the time either gently musing or positively teaching. His best-known song is 'When he comes back,' which is a strictly scriptural homily in verse; one could say the same of #527. His #526 is more contemplative and narrative, but it has the same slightly wistful manner which makes him one of the most engaging of these singers.

There are, as we have said, dozens, scores, maybe by now hundreds of people writing in this style. One of the most reliable sources of modern carol and folk-song material is the three volumes called *Faith Folk and Clarity / Nativity / Festivity*, published in 1967-9 by Stainer and Bell/Galaxy. From one of these we take #528, the only one of these pieces whose tune is not by its author. The tune here, which one has to have in mind when reading it, is 'The Keel Row,' the rollicking Northumbrian song whose accents and cadences Michael Hewlett, the one full-time clergyman in our group, has very carefully followed in his entertaining lyric.

In our last two articles we shall glance at some products of this style outside England. Here it will be enough to say that without any doubt Sydney Carter and his circle made the style fit to mention as a genuine part of Christian hymnody, as sectional, perhaps, as the Spirituals or the Gospel Songs, but no less authentic. Indeed, you might say that these are today's real Gospel Songs with their choruses, their informality, and their closeness to simple human emotions. It need not be stressed here, only gently admitted, that the style simply invites writers less disciplined than those we have quoted to indulge in every possible form of public sloth, bad manners, and unfair-mindedness. Most writers of this kind of material have

failed to see that any artistic discipline is implied in the pro-
ductions of the real creative artists. That, one must suppose,
indicates the extent to which Carter and his circle are masters
of the 'art that conceals art.'

SYDNEY CARTER
1915-
HG 173

521
BIRD OF HEAVEN

Catch the bird of heaven,
  lock him in a cage of gold;
look again to-morrow,
  and he will be gone.
    Ah! the bird of heaven!
      Follow where the bird has gone;
    Ah! the bird of heaven!
      keep on travelling on.

Lock him in religion,
  gold and frankincense and myrrh,
carry to his prison,
  but he will be gone. . . .

Temple made of marble,
  beak and feather made of gold,
all the bells are ringing,
  but the bird has gone. . . .

Bell and book and candle
  cannot hold him any more,
for the bird is flying
  as he did before.
    Ah! the bird of heaven!
      follow where the bird has gone;
    if you want to find him,
      keep on travelling on.

522
EVERY STAR SHALL SING A CAROL   HG 173

Every star shall sing a carol.
  Every creature, high or low
come and praise the King of heaven
  by whatever name you know.
    God above, man below.
    Holy is the name I know.

When the King of all creation
  had a cradle on the earth,
holy was the human body,
  holy was the human birth. . . .

Who can tell what other cradle
  high above the Milky Way
still may rock the King of heaven
  on another Christmas day? . . .

Who can count how many crosses,
  still to come or long ago
crucify the King of heaven?
  Holy is the name I know. . . .

Who can tell what other body
  he will hallow for his own?
I will praise the Son of Mary,
  Brother of my blood and bone. . . .

Every star and every planet,
  every creature high or low
come and praise the King of heaven
  by whatever name you know.
    God above, man below,
    Holy is the name I know.

523
FRIDAY MORNING

It was on a Friday morning that they took me from the cell,
and I saw they had a carpenter to crucify as well.
You can blame it on to Pilate, you can blame it on the Jews,
you can blame it on the Devil: it's God I accuse.
  'It's God they ought to crucify instead of you and me,'
  I said to the carpenter a-hanging on the tree.

You can blame it on to Adam, you can blame it on to Eve,
you can blame it on the Apple (but that I can't believe).
It was God who made the Devil, and the Woman and the Man,
and there wouldn't be an Apple if it wasn't in the plan. . . .

Now Barabbas was a killer, and they let Barabbas go,
but you are being crucified for nothing here below.
Your God is up in heaven, and he doesn't do a thing:
with a million angels watching, who never turn a wing. . . .

To hell with Jehovah, to the carpenter I said,
I wish that a carpenter had made the world instead.
Goodbye, and good luck to you: our ways will soon divide;
remember me in heaven, the man you hung beside.   Lk. 23:43
  'It's God they ought to crucify instead of you and me.'
  I said to the carpenter a-hanging on the tree.

DAVID STANTON
GOODALL*
b. 1922

524
PIOUS PRAYERS

When the pious prayers we make
  are a wall of pride,
lest the faithful few awake
  to the world outside;
when a man won't mix with a race
  which he disapproves,
only God descends to make clean the face
  of the world he loves.

Through the bright persuading voice
  of the lies we read,
in the self-deceiving choice
  of our lust and greed,
though the word of man is a mesh
  that our blindness proves
we have seen the Word of the Lord made flesh
  in the world he loves.

Beat the dust and noisy pain
  of our town and street;
watch him flinching at the stain
  of our hands and feet;
hand the heart of God upon high
  though he reigns above -
and then see him conquering come to die
  for the world he loves.

Dunblane Praises I, 1964

525
I WANT TO GO OUT

I want to go out,
I want to go home.
I want to be single,
I want to belong.
I want to grow up.
I want to stay young.
I want to do both and all at once and anything else that
takes my fancy, whether it hurts or helps to pass the time of day:
show me the way!

Now tell me a tale,
or say me a prayer,
bring on the preacher
and let him declare,
'We're going to heaven,
for heaven's up there.'
But what of the folks who stay below and live and die and never
recollect the tales they heard in their forgotten youth?
Tell them the truth!

One Saturday night
I sat all alone,
and when it was Sunday
went out on my own.
I came to the church,
they opened the door.
But when I got in the congregation looked the same as me and every
one as lonely as a man without a wife,
looking for life.

I want to get out,
I want to stay here,
I want to be welcomed,
I want to keep clear:
I want to believe,
I want to be sure.
Show me the Man who knows the way, the truth, the life, and who
is yesterday to day and everlastingly the same.
Tell me his name!

[Jn. 14:6; Heb. 13:8]

Dunblane Praises II, 1967

MALCOLM STEWART*
b. 1936
Gospel Songs for To-day, 1969

526
THE SUN AND THE HILL

In a garden one night on a bed of bracken and grief
two men slept while another man cried in grief.
Let them sleep and take their rest
let him face his lonely test -
for how could they understand
that the hour of dark was close at hand
till they saw their friend carried off in the chains of a thief?

In an upstairs room where once was light and bread
two men sat and thought of one now dead.
Two days and two nights till on the third,
they heard tell of the woman's word
but what else could it seem
but that she's sown a wish to reap a dream?
For never in the world had such a thing been said.

Before that dawn, when the night hung over the hill,
those two men came running while the rest of the world lay still.
They ran till they came to an open cave;
all they found was an empty grave,
then Peter and John both knew,
Peter and John knew the word was true,
and Peter and John saw the sun come over the hill -
yes - Peter and John saw the sun come over the hill.

527
BEATITUDES

You are blessed who are poor in desires
never seeking the riches of earth, which the fires
can consume, turn to dust,
or the waters can rust;
the kingdom is yours, you are just.

You are blessed who are sad but whose crying
is not for yourself, for your self must be dying.
Your tears shall have worth
when they share in the cares of the earth,
for a cross brings the kingdom to birth.

You are blessed who are gentle and meek,
for the war-cries of rage are the tunes of the weak.
Your silence is long
and the trumpets of anger blow strong;
but the Kingdom will dance to your song.

You are blessed, you who hunger and thirst
for the waters of love to abound. They are cursed
who still foster and keep
only deserts, and selfishness reap -
in the Kingdom love's waters run deep.

★ ★ ★

You are blessed when they seek you to kill
and to wound like the Master himself on a hill.
amid laughter and scorn;
so his wounds as a mark must be worn
to recall where the kingdom was born.

(Sts. 5-7 omitted)

MICHAEL HEWLETT*

528
SONG AND DANCE
(to the tune of 'Well may the Keel row')

When God almighty came to be one of us,
masking the glory of his golden train,
dozens of plain things kindled by accident,
and they will never be the same again.
Sing, all you midwives, dance, all the carpenters,
sing, all the publicans and shepherds too,
God in his mercy uses the commonplace,
God on his birthday had a need of you.

Splendour of Rome and Local Authority,
working on policy with furrowed head,
joined to locate Messiah's nativity,
just where the prophets had already said.
Sing, all you tax-men, dance, the commissioners,
sing, civil servants and policemen too,
God for his purpose uses the governments,
God on his birthday had a need of you.

Wise men they called them, earnest astrologers,
watching for meaning in the moving stars,
science or fancy, learned or laughable,
theirs was a vision that was brought to pass.
Sing, all you wise men, dance all the scientists,
whether your theories are false or true,
God uses knowledge, God uses ignorance,
God on his birthday had a need of you.

Sing, all creation, made for his purposes,
called by his providence to live and move:
none is unwanted, none insignificant,
Love needs a universe of folk to love.
Old men and maidens, young men and children (Ps. 148:12)
black ones and coloured ones and white ones too,
God on his birthday, and to eternity,
God took upon himself the need of you.

Faith, Folk and Festivity, 1969

ARTICLE 25:
HYMNS FOR CHILDREN, 1952-75 (529-535)

Continuing from where we left off in article 22, we find that hymnody for children, after a period of considerable activity, did not make any noticeable progress until the later sixties. The period 1906-51 was, we said, a pedagogic period, and while there was a great deal of progress then in writing hymns for children that at least achieved a tolerable style and got rid of the peculiar awkwardness of Victorian stiffness, a pedagogic period was not likely to be the period of real breakthrough in children's hymn-writing.

What our small selection here seems to indicate is that during the later sixties a few writers, at least, managed to do the one thing that was required: lose their adult self-consciousness and really celebrate in a Christian way the thoughts that children might be thinking themselves. This is, for the first time, a third choice alongside the two that John Wesley offered: You can stoop down to the children, or you can lift them up to you, said he. In other words, you, an adult, can talk to children as children, or you can help them to talk as adults. But either way you are still talking *to* them. Is it possible to get them to say, as the ordinary hymn-writer wants to get his singers to say, '*That's* what I meant; thank you for helping me to articulate it'?

Paul Townsend (529) produces a song which is partly carol, partly (but very little) hymn, to which one reacts by saying, 'Yes, that's what a child might well say when learning for the first time about time zones.' It is in a ballad style, varied by the extra-metrical stanza 4, and it has been very delightfully set to music by Donald Swann. Ian Fraser of Dunblane succeeded in several children's hymns in getting inside the minds of children in the same way. One part of the Dunblane project (see article 23) was to try to invent new kinds of children's hymns; and all submissions were put before a Christian child psychologist before being published.

No. 531 also first appeared in the Dunblane book, but it originated in a class of children at Emmanual Church, Cambridge, where their leader, who is a professional musician, invited them as a group to invent a hymn by saying, 'How should we thank God? How about thinking what the world would be without—now what?' The full text was designed to be sung at intervals during a young people's service. The children also to some extent invented the music.

The short-lived Eric Reid left a little church music which

indicated that had he been spared he would have been a major contributor in the field. Himself an educationist and teacher, he wrote a few of the Dunblane children's hymns, of which ##532 and 533 are examples. Both of these are in *New Songs for the Church* Book I. 'Trotting,' in itself a delightful conception, depends for its success partly on a remarkably graceful tune. The other one is a quite remarkable essay in interpreting the mystery of the Trinity to young minds.

A very creative and useful book for children ages eight to eleven is *New Orbit*, published in 1972 by Stainer & Bell; our #534, a kind of very simple junior *Benedicite*, is one sample from it; but several of the pieces in this and the preceding section are in it as well.

And from a more recent publication we offer Caryl Micklem's meditation on 'Light' from *New Church Praise*. There is no room for more, but in the best contemporary books this is the kind of material one may look for. It is partly the consequence of the liberation of vocabulary which the 'folk' writers achieved (and 'folk' at its best, of whatever period, is always a good nourishment for children), and partly it comes from the new attitude to children in education and in church which has become normal since intelligent people who have families now have uninterrupted and direct contact with their children, a situation which, so evidently, did not apply in the 19th century.

PAUL TOWNSEND*

529
THE CLOCK CAROL

When the bells chime noon in London,
New York begins its day,
good morning in Toronto spells
good-night for Mandalay.

When the sun shines on the pyramids,
Alaska's in the dark;
at one tick of the clock God hears
both nightingale and lark.

For he is there through nights and days,
through rain and cold and heat;
behind the chatter of the clocks
we sense his timeless beat.

Midday, midnight, the bells are always ringing,
the world keeps turning into day and night:
sunshine, moonshine, the light and shadow bringing,
patterns they make from God's one light.

While some work at their benches,
their brothers work in fields,
yet one Creator is the source
of what their labour yields.

Men of all kinds and colours,
in factory or field,
have on their faces, black or white,
God's image there revealed.

For East and West in him are one,
and colour, race and clime;
his love will reach beyond the bounds
of night and day and time.

1965; *Faith, Folk and Clarity*, 1962

IAN FRASER
b. 1917

530

Lord, I love to stamp and shout
testing lungs and muscles out;
other times I curl up still
dreaming till I've had my fill
- still as mouse, or ranting free:
what strange mixture makes me me?

Lord, I love to watch things fly,
whizzing, zooming, flashing by;
engines, aircraft, speedboats, cars,
spacecraft shooting to the stars;
- as I learn and think and grow
let my life say, 'Go, man, go!'

Lord, I love to probe and pry,
seeking out the reason why;
looking inside things and out,
finding what they're all about;
- make me curious to find
what will really bless mankind.

Lord, I'm many things and one,
though my life's not long begun;
you alone my secret see
what I am cut out to be:
take this life - it's almost new -
make your dreams for it come true.

Dunblane Praises II, 1967

DOREEN NEWPORT*
b. 1922

531
THINK OF A WORLD

Think of a world without any flowers,
    think of a world without any trees,
think of a sky without any sunshine,
    think of the air without any breeze.
We thank you, Lord, for flowers and trees and sunshine,
we thank you, Lord, and praise your holy Name.

Think of a world without any animals,
    think of a field without any herd,
think of a stream without any fishes,
    think of a dawn without any bird:
We thank you, Lord, for all your living creatures,
we thank you, Lord, and praise your holy Name.

Think of a world without any paintings,
    think of a room where all the walls are bare,
think of a rainbow without any colours,
    think of the earth with darkness everywhere.
We thank you, Lord, for paintings and for colours,
we thank you, Lord, and praise your holy Name.

Think of a world without any poetry,
    think of a book without any words,
think of a song without any music,
    think of a hymn without any verse.
We thank you, Lord, for poetry and music,
we thank you, Lord, and praise your holy Name.

Think of a world without any science,
    think of a journey with nothing to explore,
think of a quest without any mystery,
    nothing to seek, and nothing left in store.
We thank you, Lord, for miracles of science,
we thank you, Lord, and praise your holy Name.

Think of a world without any people
    think of a street with no-one living there,
think of a town without any houses,
    no one to love, and nobody to care.
We thank you, Lord, for families and friendships,
we thank you, Lord, and praise your holy Name.

Think of a world without any worship,
    think of a God without his only Son,
think of a cross without a resurrection,
    only a grave, and not a victory won.
We thank you, Lord, for showing us our Saviour,
we thank you, Lord, and praise your holy Name.

Thanks to our Lord for being here among us,
    thanks be to you for sharing all we do;
thanks for our Church and all the love we find here,
    thanks for this place, and all its promise true.
We thank you, Lord, for life in all its richness,
we thank you, Lord, and praise your holy Name.

Dunblane Praises II, 1967

ERIC REID*
1936-70
Dunblane Praises II, 1967

532
TROTTING, TROTTING

Trotting, trotting through Jerusalem,
Jesus, sitting on a donkey's back,
children waving branches singing,
'Happy is he that comes in the name of the Lord!'

Many people in Jerusalem
thought he should have come on a mighty horse
leading all the Jews to battle -
'Happy is he that comes in the name of the Lord!'

Many people in Jerusalem
were amazed to see such a quiet man
trotting, trotting on a donkey,
'Happy is he that comes in the name of the Lord!'

Trotting, trotting through Jerusalem,
Jesus, sitting on a donkey's back,
let us join the children singing,
'Happy is he that comes in the name of the Lord!'

533
TRINITY

God is our Friend,
Jesus is our Friend,
and the Holy Spirit is our Friend,
all made into one.

God keeps us safe,
God makes us strong;
he's very sad when he sees us go wrong,
God will help us all.

Jesus like us
played in the street,
grew up to heal, and made life complete
helping everyone.

Nobody hears,
nobody knows;
quiet as sunshine the Holy Spirit grows
into everyone.

God is our Friend,
Jesus is our Friend,
and the Holy Spirit is our Friend,
all made into one.

GRACIE KING*

534
BLESS THE LORD!

When I see the salmon leap the fall,
or the airplane's silver trail -
or a drop of water magnified,
    then my eyes and soul bless the Lord.

When I hear the frosty crunch of snow,
or the sun-drenched hum of the bee,
or a well-tuned engine whine with power,
    then my ears and soul bless the Lord.

After rain a smell of clean fresh air
blows soft and cool and free;
when the strawberries are turned to jam,
    then my nose and soul bless the Lord.

At the taste of berries gathered free,
or the tang of seafood, mint or treacle,
touch of velvet, feel of cold smooth stones,
    hands and tongue and soul bless the Lord.

New Orbit, 1972

THOMAS CARYL MICKLEM
b. 1925

535
ALL KINDS OF LIGHT

Father, we thank you, -
for the light that shines all the day;
    for the bright sky you have given,
    most like your heaven;
Father, we thank you.

Father, we thank you, -
for the lamps that lighten the way;
    for human skill's exploration
    of your creation;
Father, we thank you.

Father, we thank you, -
for the friends who brighten our play;
    for your command to call others
    sisters and brothers;
Father, we thank you.

Father, we thank you, -
for your love in Jesus to-day,
    giving us hope for tomorrow
    through joy or sorrow;
Father, we thank you.

New Church Praise, 1975

ARTICLE 26:
AMERICAN HYMNODY, 1901-75 (536-559)

A subtle change comes over the story of American hymnody after the turn of the century, the center of gravity moving from the Unitarians towards the Episcopals. Until about 1940 the best American writers were doing as well as, sometimes better than, their English cousins, though the stream begins to run rather less broadly.

True, the first six in our selection come from non-Anglicans, and indeed form a direct continuation of the tradition we celebrated in Article 18. Louis Benson, a Presbyterian minister, is known as the founding father of serious American hymnology and the library he bequeathed to Princeton Theological Seminary is one of the finest hymnological collections in the world. As #536 shows, he was also an excellent hymn writer; this one on the life of Christ is his best known, and is one of the best of its kind.

Frank Mason North (537) was a Methodist, and in his famous 'city' hymn antedated the English city pioneers (Scott Holland and Chesterton) by a year or two. Perhaps it is now somewhat dated, especially in its assignation of work to men and tears to women in st. 3, but it set the fashion which others followed more successfully. Shepherd Knapp (538) is another Presbyterian, and, using a meter which American writers were always partial to, he writes a typically fervent and forthright hymn for ministers. (This meter invites garrulousness, but he avoids it well.)

W. P. Merrill, Presbyterian, is best known for his muscular, almost Pelagian, 'Rise up, O men of God'; in his hymn for a national occasion, #539, he gives us what amounts to America's answer to Kipling's *Recessional* (256): less stirring literature, but better hymn-writing. Yet another Presbyterian, Henry van Dyke, wrote a poem on the dignity of work from which different hymnals take different centos, of which #540 is one. Americans, one sees, are developing in the first decade of the century a reaction to the over-spiritualized manner of the great Unitarians. The same reaction is seen in the very warmly-felt lines of the great Presbyterian missionary to Japan, W. M. Vories (541), who wrote these lines while contemplating the power-struggle in Europe which was, even in 1908, developing into a world-wide threat.

The Episcopal line begins with W. R. Bowie (542-3), a pastor of great distinction, who contributed in these two pieces not only two hymns of great power but two on strictly twentieth-century subjects. The 'city' hymn is surely a long step forward from F. M. North: both more visionary and more concrete. And #543, written at the request of F. W. Dwelly, first Dean of Liverpool Cathedral in England, to try to say to this age what the *Dies Irae* said to former generations, is a masterpiece which is as well known in England as in the U.S.A.

H. H. Tweedy (544), a Presbyterian professor, was the editor of a successful hymnal and the writer of a text which has also become as well known in England as in America; only one word mars it, 'ban' in st. 4, which one fervently wishes had been 'shun' (banning ugliness just isn't possible); but the hymn was written when the Hymn Society of America advertised its search for modern missionary hymns, and as such it certainly says some quite new and very trenchant things. Even more famous, the best known of all twentieth-century American hymns, is Harry Fosdick's 'God of grace' (545). This was written for the dedication of the enormous Riverside Church in New York, in 1930. It cannot be too often stated that the association of this text with the tune CWM RHONDDA was an association he deplored. During its fairly short life this admirably downright text has suffered more abuse by sentimental and careless choosers than it deserved.

Nos. 546-552 bring the Episcopal contribution to its peak. Though a small Christian community in the U.S.A. and not generating a large number of hymn writers, it is probably fair to say that in the first half of this century it produced the half-dozen finest hymns. For this, apart from Bowie already mentioned, we have chiefly to thank Robbins and Tucker. The contributions of Robbins to the 1940 Episcopal *Hymnal* all repay close study–especially his translation of St Francis' 'Canticle of the Sun,' which is not better than Draper's, but certainly is a fascinating variation. We here include #546, his most daring and unusual composition; #547, a straightforward hymn of spiritual resolution; and #548, an unusually poetic miniature, to show what variety of styles he could handle.

Tucker is even finer. He often goes to ancient sources for his material. No. 549, from Abélard, is exquisite not only in its handling of the subject but in the unusually subtle way it disposes its important syllables; almost any good tune seems to give the 'lift' required by the third line of each stanza. This admirable craftsmanship, this complete rejection of the cliché, is found all through his work. No. 550 (compare #516) paraphrases Philippians 2 most felicitously, though of course less closely than #516.

No. 551, from *Diognetus* (the most beautiful of all the sub-Apostolic writings) I find the most moving of all his texts, a tender and penetrating exposition of the idea in 'They will reverence my Son' in the parable of the rebellious Husbandmen. The famous #552, taken from another very early Christian source, is now, very properly, in all reputable hymnals. Again the author has seized upon the central idea in a fine passage of ancient literature. There is no better twentieth-century writing in either of our countries than is to be found in Tucker.

Georgia Harkness, the distinguished American scholar, wrote #553 for a promotion by the Hymn Society similar to that mentioned above under #544, and her hymn, perhaps not quite free from cliché but containing some fine lines, has found very wide acceptance in America. Women writers in the U.S.A. do not seem to flourish yet in great numbers.

The one later writer, however, who, in a very different way, can be thought of as standing alongside Tucker is the Lutheran Martin Franzmann (554-5). Lutherans, especially of the Germanic Missouri Synod, have not until very recently been energetic hymn writers; the pietist chorales did for them what Wesley did for later Methodists. But Franzmann, whose style has a rough-cast ruggedness about it, certainly avoids cliché; indeed, it is so dense that it needs a good deal of careful thinking before it delivers its full message. His hymns seem always to frown before they smile, and this in itself is a refreshment after the fixed and euphoric beam that we get from some of the earlier American poets. (Incidentally, Franzmann has been served in both these pieces with special distinction by musicians whose settings exactly reflect the dark colours and bright endings of these fine poems.)

Of a very different kind, but from the same cultural background, is the impressionistic Communion hymn, #556; one of the few hymns without a single finite verb and without any punctuation. It is something of a *tour de force* and another example of the new talent for poetry that Lutherans are fostering in America.

Finally, among orthodox American hymns, we offer two new pieces from the newest (at this date) American hymnal. This is the book that serves the church that contains the ex-Congregationalists of America as well as the Evangelical and Reformed Church; these two contrasted pieces, chosen with some difficulty from a very fair offering of good new material in this modest and fascinating hymnal, seem to pick up the best in those traditions. No. 558 is one of several by a distinguished academic who, following Tucker's lead, goes to ancient sources for his subjects and versifies them with considerable skill. In this case the difference between the use of analogies in the three stanzas is no fault of his; it faithfully reflects Cyprian, who wrote the tract *De Unitate Ecclesiae* in a mood of white-hot anger and probably did not give himself leisure to polish it. For sheer originality, expressed, we have to say, in poetry which aspires more often than it succeeds, the United Church *Hymnal* is a book to be respected.

In the matter of American Folk Hymnody we regret that technical difficulties prevent our offering any examples. This is material which in any case is difficult to present without music. Very often the text and the tune come from the same hand. Very often, too, they are skillful and trenchant. The best known of these pieces probably are James Theim's 'Sons of God,' Ray Repp's 'All your peoples clap your hands,' and Peter Scholtes' 'They'll know we are Christians by our love.' It is, like its English counterpart, informal hymnody, and not infrequently the doctrinal and scriptural content of these modern 'Gospel Songs'–for that is what they are–is impressive. In others there is a tendency to stray into romantic ecumenism and a somewhat unfocussed zeal to serve those deemed to be underprivileged. At their worst they are crude, and it is probably fair to say that the Roman Catholic communities in America, with their sudden new need for hymns, have been the most vulnerable to the assaults of commercialized hymnody of this kind. That fact should not too much prejudice a reader against the whole *genre*, which at its best has brought much vitality to American worship. Our lack of representation of this kind of song must be taken in terms of the line we took about Spirituals and Gospel Songs: they are available everywhere; they need their music to make their effect; and sometimes they are hideously expensive to reprint.

The section ends with a tiny piece which is unique and unclassifiable and therefore anachronistically placed. Apart from the work of Whittier, American hymnbook editors have not plundered their poets as freely as have the English. But Sidney Lanier, short-lived and in his time obscure, left some haunting lines, including those here given (559), which were picked up by American Methodists in 1905 but otherwise have appeared oftener in British than in American books. They fittingly conclude a section which illustrates the great variety of styles that has developed in America since 1900.

LOUIS F. BENSON, 1855-1930

536
THE LIFE OF CHRIST

HG 559

O sing a song of Bethlehem,
   of shepherds watching there,
and of the news that came to them
   from angels in the air;
the light that shone on Bethlehem
   fills all the world to-day;
of Jesus' birth and peace on earth
   the angels sing alway.

O sing a song of Nazareth,
   of sunny days of joy,
O sing of fragrant flowers beneath
   and of the sinless Boy:
for now the flowers of Nazareth
   in every heart may grow;
now spreads the fame of his dear name,
   on all the winds that blow.

O sing a song of Galilee,
   of lake and woods and hill,
of him who walked upon the sea
   and bade its waves be still:
for though, like waves on Galilee,
   dark seas of trouble roll,
when faith has heard the Master's word
   falls peace upon the soul.

O sing a song of Calvary,
   its glory and dismay,
of him who hung upon the tree
   and took our sins away;
for he who died on Calvary
   is risen from the grave,
and Christ our Lord, by heaven adored,
   is mighty now to save.

School Hymnal, 1899

FRANK MASON NORTH
1850-1935

537
THE CROWDED WAYS OF LIFE

HG 813

Where cross the crowded ways of life,
   where sound the cries of race and clan,
above the noise of selfish strife,
   we hear thy voice, O Son of Man.

In haunts of wretchedness and need,
   on shadowed thresholds dark with fears,
from paths where hide the lures of greed,
   we catch the vision of thy tears. (Lk. 19:41)

From tender childhood's helplessness,
   from woman's grief, man's burdened toil,
from famished souls, from sorrow's stress,
   thy heart has never known recoil.

The cup of water given for thee (Matt. 10:42)
   still holds the freshness of thy grace:
yet long these multitudes to see
   the sweet compassion of thy face.

O Master, from the mountain-side (Mk. 9:10ff)
   make haste to heal these hearts of pain;
among these restless throngs abide,
   O tread the city's streets again:

till sons of men shall learn thy love,
   and follow where thy feet have trod;
till glorious from thy heaven above,
   shall come the city of our God. (Rev. 21:1ff)

The Christian City, 1903

SHEPHERD KNAPP, 1873-1946

538
CHRISTIAN VOCATION

HG 416

Lord God of hosts, whose purpose, never swerving,
   leads toward the day of Jesus Christ thy Son,
grant us to march among thy faithful legions,
   armed with thy courage, till the world is won.

Strong Son of God, whose work was his that sent thee,
   one with the Father, thought and deed and word,
one make us all, true comrades in thy service,
   and make us one in thee, with God the Lord.

O Prince of peace, thou bringer of good tidings,
   teach us to speak thy word of hope and cheer -
rest for the soul, and strength for all men's striving,
   light for the path of life, and God brought near.

Lord God, whose grace has called us to thy service,
   how good thy thoughts towards us, how great their sum! (Ps. 139:17)
We work with thee, we go where thou wilt lead us,
   until in all the earth thy kingdom come.

WILLIAM PIERSON MERRILL
1867-1954

539
THANKSGIVING

HG 482

Not alone for mighty empire,
   stretching far o'er land and sea,
not alone for bounteous harvests,
   lift we up our hearts to thee.
Standing in the living present,
   memory and hope between,
Lord, we would with deep thanksgiving
   praise thee most for things unseen.

Not for battleship and fortress,
   not for conquests of the sword,
but for conquests of the spirit
   give we thanks to thee, O Lord,
For the heritage of freedom,
   for the home, the church, the school,
for the open door to manhood
   in a land the people rule.

For the armies of the faithful,
   souls that passed and left no name;
for the glory that illumines
   patriot lives of deathless fame;
for our prophets and apostles,
   loyal to the living word,
for all heroes of the spirit,
   give we thanks to thee, O Lord.

God of justice, save the people
from the clash of race and creed,
from the strife of class and faction,
make our nation free indeed;
keep her faith in simple manhood
strong as when her life began,
till it find its full fruition
in the brotherhood of man!

1909; *The Continent*, 1911

HENRY VAN DYKE, 1852-1933
HG 377

540
THE DIGNITY OF WORK

Jesus, thou divine companion,
by thy lowly human birth
thou hast come to join the workers,
burden-bearers of the earth.
Thou the carpenter of Nazareth,
toiling for thy daily food,
by thy patience and thy courage
thou hast taught us toil is good.

They who tread the path of labour
follow where thy feet have trod;
they who work without complaining
do the holy will of God.
Thou, the peace that passeth knowledge,
dwellest in the daily strife;
thou, the Bread of heaven, art broken
in the sacrament of life.

Every task, however simple,
sets the soul that does it free;
every deed of love and kindness
done to man is done to thee.   (Matt. 25:35)
Jesus, thou divine companion,
help us all to work our best;
bless us in our daily labor,
lead us to our sabbath-rest.

The Toiling of Felix, 1898;
Hymns of the Kingdom of God, 1909

WILLIAM MERRELL VORIES
1880-1964

541
LET THERE BE LIGHT   HG 392

Let there be light, Lord God of hosts,
let there be wisdom on the earth;
let broad humanity have birth,
let there be deeds, instead of boasts.

Within our passioned hearts instill
the calm that endeth strain and strife;
make us thy ministers of life;
purge us from lusts that curse and kill.

Give us the peace of vision clear
to see our brothers' good our own,
to joy and suffer not alone -
the love that casteth out all fear.

Let woe and waste of warfare cease,
that useful labor yet may build
its homes with love and laughter filled;
God, give thy wayward children peace.

The Advocatè of Peace, 1909

WALTER RUSSELL BOWIE
1882-1969
HG 414

542
THE HOLY CITY   HG 525

O holy city, seen of John,
where Christ the Lamb doth reign,   (Rev. 21)
within whose four-square walls shall come
no night, nor need, nor pain,
and where the tears are wiped from eyes
that shall not weep again! -

★   ★   ★

O shame to us who rest content
while lust and greed for gain
in street and shop and tenement
wring gold from human pain,
and bitter lips in blind despair
cry 'Christ hath died in vain!'

Give us, O God, the strength to build
the City that hath stood
too long a dream, whose laws are love,
whose ways are brotherhood,
and where the sun that shineth is
God's brace for human good.

Already in the mind of God
that city riseth fair:
lo, how its splendour challenges
the souls that greatly dare -
yea, bids us seize the whole of life
and build its glory there.

Hymns of the Kingdom of God, 1910
St. 2 omitted

543
DIES IRAE   HG 414

Lord Christ, when first thou cam'st to men,
upon a cross they bound thee,
and mocked thy saving kingship then
by thorns with which they crowned thee;
and still our wrongs may weave thee now
new thorns to pierce that steady brow
and robe of sorrow round thee.

O awful love, which found no room
in life where sin denied thee,
and, doomed to death, must bring to doom
the power which crucified thee,
till not a stone was left on stone,
and all a nation's pride, o'erthrown,
went down to dust beside thee!

New advent of the love of Christ,
shall we again refuse thee,
till in the night of hate and war
we perish as we lose thee?

From old unfaith our souls release
to seek the kingdom of thy peace
by which alone we choose thee.

O wounded hands of Jesus, build
in us thy new creation;
our pride is dust, our vaunt is stilled,
we wait thy revelation:
O Love that triumphs over loss,
we bring our hearts before thy cross
to finish thy salvation.

1928; *Songs of Praise*, 1931

HENRY HALLAM TWEEDY
1868-1953

544
LOVE, TRUTH AND BEAUTY   HG 170

Eternal God, whose power upholds
both flower and flaming star,
to whom there is no here or there,
no time, no near or far,
no alien race, no foreign shore,
no child unsought, unknown,
O send us forth, thy prophets true,
to make all lands thine own!

O God of love, whose spirit wakes
in every human breast,
whom love, and love alone, can know,
in whom all hearts find rest,
help us to spread thy gracious reign,
till greed and hate shall cease,
and kindness dwell in human hearts,
and all the earth be peace!

O God of truth, whom science seeks
and reverent souls adore,
who lightest every earnest mind
of every clime and shore,
dispel the gloom of error's night,
of ignorance and fear,
until true wisdom from above
shall make life's pathway clear!

O God of beauty, oft revealed
in dreams of human art,
in speech that flows to melody,
in holiness of heart;
teach us to ban all ugliness
that blinds our eyes to thee,
till all shall know the loveliness
of lives made fair and free.

O God of righteousness and grace,
seen in the Christ, thy Son,   (John 14:9)
whose life and death reveal thy face,
by whom thy will was done,   (John 4:34)
inspire thy heralds of good news
to live thy life divine,
till Christ is formed in all mankind,
and every land is thine!

The Hymn Society, 1929

HARRY EMERSON FOSDICK
1878-1969

545
GOD OF GRACE AND GOD OF GLORY HG 239

God of grace and God of glory,
on thy people pour thy power;
crown thine ancient church's story,
bring her bud to glorious flower.
Grant us wisdom,
grant us courage
for the living of this hour.

Lo! the hosts of evil round us
scorn thy Christ, assail his ways!
From the fears that long have bound us
free our hearts to work and praise.
Grant us wisdom,
grant us courage
for the living of these days.

Cure thy children's warring madness;
bend our pride to thy control;
shame our wanton, selfish gladness,
rich in things and poor in soul.
Grant us wisdom,
grant us courage,
lest we miss thy kingdom's goal.

Set our feet on lofty places;
gird our lives that we may be
armored with all Christlike graces
in the fight to set men free.
Grant us wisdom,
grant us courage
that we fail not man or thee.

Save us from weak resignation
to the evils we deplore;
let the search for thy salvation
be our glory evermore.
Grant us wisdom,
grant us courage
serving thee whom we adore.

1930; *Methodist Hymnal*, 1932

**HOWARD CHANDLER
ROBBINS**, 1876-1952
HG 609

546
ASCENSION

And have the bright immensities
received our risen Lord,
where light-years frame the Pleiades
and point Orion's sword?
Do flaming suns his footsteps trace
through corridors sublime,
the Lord of interstellar space
and Conqueror of time?

The heaven that hides him from our sight
knows neither near nor far:
an altar candle sheds its light
as surely as a star;
and where his loving people meet
to share the gift divine,
there stands he with unhurrying feet;
there heavenly splendors shine.

Living Church, 1931

547
THE SPIRIT'S MIGHT   HG 609

Put forth, O Lord, thy Spirit's might
  and bid thy church increase
in breadth and length, in depth and height,
  her unity and peace.

Let works of darkness disappear
  before thy conquering light;
let hatred and tormenting fear
  pass with the passing night.

Let what apostles learned of thee
  be ours from age to age;
their stedfast faith our unity,
  their peace our heritage.

O Judge divine of human strife!
  O Vanquisher of pain!
To know thee is eternal life,
  to serve thee is to reign.

New Church Hymnal, 1937

548
SUNSET TO SUNRISE

Sunset to sunrise changes now,
  for God doth make his world anew;
on the Redeemer's thorn-crowned brow
  the wonders of that dawn we view.

Ev'n though the sun withholds its light,
  lo! a more heavenly lamp shines here,
and from the cross, on Calvary's height
  gleams of eternity appear.

Here, in o'erwhelming final strife
  the Lord of life hath victory;
and sin is slain, and death brings life,
  and sons of earth hold heaven in fee.

Preaching the Gospel, 1939

FRANCIS BLAND TUCKER
b. 1895
HG 22

549
SOLUS AD VICTIMAM   HG 34

Alone thou goest forth, O Lord,
  in sacrifice to die;
is this thy sorrow naught to us
  who pass unheeding by?

Our sins, not thine, thou bearest, Lord,
  make us thy sorrow feel,
till through our pity and our shame
  love answers love's appeal.

This is earth's darkest hour, but thou
  dost light and life restore;
then let all praise be given thee,
  who livest evermore.

Give us compassion for thee, Lord,
  that, as we share this hour,
thy cross may bring us to thy joy
  and resurrection power.

The Hymnal, 1940
from Peter Abélard, 1079-1142

550
KENOSIS   HG 22

All praise to thee, for thou, O King divine
didst yield the glory that of right was thine,
that in our darkened hearts thy grace might shine,
    Alleluia!

Thou cam'st to us in lowliness of thought;
by thee the outcast and the poor were sought,
and by thy death was God's salvation wrought.
    Alleluia!

Let this mind be in us which was in thee,
who wast a servant that we might be free,
humbling thyself to death on Calvary,
    Alleluia!

Wherefore, by God's eternal purpose, thou
art high exalted o'er all creatures now,
and given the name to which all knees shall bow,
    Alleluia!

Let every tongue confess with one accord
in heaven and earth that Jesus Christ is Lord;
and God the Father be by all adored,
    Alleluia!

The Hymnal, 1940
Philippians 2:5-12

551
HE SENT HIS SON

The great Creator of the worlds,
  the sovereign Lord of heaven,
his holy and immortal truth
  to men on earth hath given.

He sent no angel of his host
  to bear this mighty word,
but him through whom the worlds were made,
  the everlasting Lord.

He sent him not in wrath and power,
  but grace and peace to bring;
in kindness, as a king might send
  his son, himself a king.

He sent him down as sending God;
  as man he came to men;
as one with us he dwelt with us,
  and died and lives again.

The Hymnal, 1940
from the *Epistle to Diognetus*, 2nd
century (sts. 5-6 omitted)

552
EUCHARISTIC THANKSGIVING   HG 188

Father, we thank thee, who hast planted
  thy holy name within our hearts.
Knowledge and faith and life immortal
  Jesus thy Son to us imparts.
Thou, Lord, didst make all for thy pleasure,
  didst give man food for all his days,
giving in Christ the Bread eternal;
  thine is the power, be thine the praise.

Watch o'er thy church, O Lord, in mercy,
  save it from evil, guard it still,
perfect it in thy love, unite it,
  cleansed and conformed unto thy will.
As grain, once scattered on the hillsides,
  was in this broken bread made one,
so, from all lands thy church be gathered
  into thy kingdom by thy Son.

The Hymnal, 1940
from the *Didache*, 2nd century

GEORGIA HARKNESS
1891-1975

553
HOPE OF THE WORLD   HG 292

Hope of the world, thou Christ of great compassion,
  speak to our fearful hearts by conflict rent.
Save us, thy people, from consuming passion
  who by our own false hopes and aims are spent.

Hope of the world, God's gift from highest heaven,
  bringing to hungry souls the bread of life,
still let thy Spirit unto us be given
  to heal earth's wounds and end her bitter strife.

Hope of the world, afoot on dusty highways,
  showing to wandering souls the path of light,
walk thou beside us lest the tempting byways
  lure us away from thee to endless night.

Hope of the world, who by thy cross didst save us
  from death and dark despair, from sin and guilt,
we render back the love thy mercy gave us;
  take thou our lives and use them as thou wilt.

Hope of the world, O Christ, o'er death victorious,
  who by this sign didst conquer grief and pain,
we would be faithful to thy gospel glorious;
  thou art our Lord! Thou dost for ever reign!

The Hymn Society, 1954

MARTIN FRANZMANN*
1907-76

554
GOOD NEWS FOR A SAD WORLD

O God, O Lord of heaven and earth,
  thy living finger never wrote
  that life should be an aimless note,
a deathward drift from futile birth.
Thy Word meant life triumphant hurled
through every cranny of thy world.
  Since light awoke and life began
  thou hast desired thy life for man.

Our fatal will to equal thee,
  our rebel will, wrought death and night.
  We seized and used in thy despite
thy wondrous gift of liberty.
We housed us in this house of doom,
where death had royal scope and room,
  until thy servant, Prince of Peace,
  breached all its walls for our release.

Thou camest to our hall of death,
  O Christ, to breathe our poisoned air,
  to drink for us the dark despair
that strangled man's reluctant breath.
How beautiful the feet that trod
the road that leads us back to God.
  How beautiful the feet that ran
  to bring the great good news to man.

O Spirit, who didst once restore
  thy Church that it might be again
  the bringer of good news to men,
breathe on thy cloven church once more,
that in these gray and latter days
there may be men whose life is praise,
  each life a high doxology
  to Father, Son and unto thee.

Worship Supplement, 1969

555
WEARY OF ALL TRUMPETING

Weary of all trumpeting,
  weary of all killing,
weary of all songs that sing
  promise, non-fulfilling.
We would raise, O Christ, one song,
  we would join in singing
that great music, pure and strong
  wherewith heaven is ringing.

Captain Christ, O lowly Lord,
  Servant-King, your dying
bade us sheathe the foolish sword,
  bade us cease denying.
Trumpet with your Spirit's breath
  through each height and hollow:
into your self-giving death
  call us all to follow.

To the triumph of your cross
  summon all men living;
summon us to live by loss,
  gaining all by giving.
Suffering all, that men may see
  triumph in surrender;
leaving all, that we may be
  partners in your splendour.

1971

JAROSLAV J. VAJDA,* b. 1919

556
NOW

Now the silence Now the peace
Now the empty hands uplifted

Now the kneeling Now the plea
   Now the Father's arms in welcome

Now the hearing Now the power
   Now the vessel brimmed for pouring

Now the body Now the blood
   Now the joyful celebration

Now the wedding Now the songs
   Now the heart forgiven leaping

Now the Spirit's visitation
   Now the Son's epiphany
      Now the Father's blessing
         Now

Worship Supplement, 1969

WILLIAM NELSON, 1967

557
NOT MY WILL BUT YOURS

The mountains rise in ranges far and high
above the walls men throw against the sky;
I cannot bid them stay on border lines,
embossing earth the way my will defines.

The mighty rivers cannot choose to flow
through this land, and through that, refuse to go;
they take the water from one neighbor's rain,
and make another's desert green with grain.

I cannot cause a partial sun to shine
on those whose color is the same as mine,
and keep in darkness those who should be free
to build a better world along with me.

If neither mountain, flowing stream, nor sun
can choose one people and another shun,
then I, O Lord, must let no barrier stand
between me and my brother's outstretched hand.

*Hymnal of the United Church of
Christ*, 1975

FORD L. BATTLES*
1915-

558
THE CHURCH OF CHRIST IS ONE

The Church of Christ is one:
many are the rays of the sun,
but only the one parent light.
   Take a ray from the sun,
uncleft the sun remains;
   the church of Christ is bathed
suffused in the Lord's undying light;
although on all the earth diffused,
   ever its light is one.

The church of Christ is one:
many are the branches of a tree,
but rooted in the earth one trunk.
   Break a branch from the tree,
the branch will cease to grow;
   the branches of the church
are spread through all the earth, and still
the body of the church remains,
   whole, unbroken, one.

The church of Christ is one:
many are the streams of a spring:
the source undivided stands.
   Choke a stream at the source,
the stream will fail - go dry;
   the well-spring of the church
outflows in many streams, and still
the head thereof is always one,
   one alone the source.

From Cyprian of Carthage,
De Unitate, 252 A.D.
*Hymnal of the United Church of
Christ*, 1975

SIDNEY LANIER
1842-81

559

Into the woods my Master went,
clean forspent, forspent;
into the woods my Master came,
forspent with love and shame;
but the olives they were not blind to him,
the little grey leaves were kind to him,
the thorn tree had a mind to him,
   when into the woods he came.

Out of the woods my Master went,
and he was well content;
out of the woods my Master came
content with death and shame.
When death and shame would woo him last,
from under the trees they drew him last:
'twas on a tree they slew him, last,
   when out of the woods he came.

Methodist Hymnal, 1905

ARTICLE 27:
CANADA AND AUSTRALIA (560-569)

T. S. Eliot wrote rather austerely that a 'classic' can emerge only from a society with a long historical tradition. This may explain why Canada, Australia and other English-speaking communities in the British Commonwealth have not yet produced a Charles Wesley. Young cultures do produce hymnody, and the article after this one will indicate how picturesque and refreshing such hymnody can be. One must remember that in 1776, America south of the Canadian border was by no means a young culture; the vigour of U.S.A. hymnody in the 19th century can be ascribed largely to the high culture of that very unusual community which is New England and perhaps also to the simple fact that already a great many people were living there.

Canada has only recently emerged as a significant source of hymnody, and we have the very forward-looking enterprise of the 1971 *Hymn Book* jointly used by the United Church and the Episcopal Church in Canada to thank for that. And it has to be said that the first two well-known Canadian hymns turn out to be by Britishers. One is Scriven's 'What a friend we have in Jesus' (which combines very wide popularity with a fairly low level of literature and which therefore we did not feel it necessary to transcribe), and the other is the Duke of Argyll's version of Psalm 121 (560). The Duke was Governor-General of Canada when he wrote it, and the hymn is among those most dearly loved by Canadians; he was, of course, a

Scottish aristocrat, and the Scottish influence in Canada extended to a widespread Presbyterian suspicion of hymnody, which contributed to that country's slow start in hymnody but which this piece effectively challenged.

It is difficult to find anything distinguished from Canada until we come to authors who are, at the time of writing, still alive. R. B. Y. Scott's 'O day of God' (561) has been on the road since 1938 and found its way to England for the first time in 1951 (*BBC Hymn Book*). All the rest (562-6) are taken from the 1971 *Hymn Book* and represent only a small fraction of the new material to be found there. Not the least of the distinctions of that book is the set of translations of medieval hymns by John Willis Grant which it includes. And #565 features the youngest authors in our collection, a further indication of the versatility of the New Canadian hymnody.

Australia has been rather slower in getting off the ground, though there are indications that in a few years' time we may be able to say more than we can now. The one Australian hymn to achieve the status of a 'classic' is that of Principal Merrington (566) in which there are four stanzas of universal value. The *Australian Hymn Book* (1977), however, has abundant signs of hope. Our nos. 567-9 come from that book, no. 567 being by its general Editor. This book, though in its contents very unlike the Canadian one of 1971, is like it in being an ecumenical publication designed for use in most of the major denominations in Australia, and in this it is a portent of hope.

JOHN DOUGLAS
SUTHERLAND CAMPBELL, 9th
Duke of Argyll, 1845-1914

560
PSALM 121

HG 766

Unto the hills around do I lift up
    my longing eyes;
O whence for me shall my salvation come,
    from whence arise?
From God the Lord doth come my certain aid,
from God the Lord, who heaven and earth hath made.

He will not suffer that thy foot be moved:
    safe shalt thou be.
No careless slumber shall his eyelids close,
    who keepeth thee.
Behold our God, the Lord, he slumbereth ne'er,
who keepeth Israel in his holy care.

Jehovah is himself thy keeper true,
    thy changeless shade;
Jehovah thy defence on thy right hand
    himself hath made.
And thee no sun by day shall ever smite,
nor moon shall harm thee in the silent night.

From every evil shall he keep thy soul,
    from every sin;
Jehovah shall preserve thy going out,
    thy coming in.
Above thee watching, he whom we adore
shall keep thee henceforth, yea, for evermore.

The Book of Psalms, 1877

ROBERT B. Y. SCOTT, b. 1899

561
THE DAY OF THE LORD

HG 503

O Day of God, draw nigh
    in beauty and in power,
come with thy timeless judgment now
    to match our present hour.

Bring to our troubled minds,
    uncertain and afraid,
the quiet of a stedfast faith,
    calm of a call obeyed.

Bring justice to our land,
    that all may dwell secure,
and finely build for days to come
    foundations that endure.

Bring to our world of strife
    thy sovereign word of peace,
that war may haunt the world no more,
    and desolation cease.

O Day of God, draw nigh
    as at creation's birth,
let there be light again, and set
    thy judgments in the earth.   (Ps. 105:7)

Hymns for Worship, 1939

T. HERBERT O'DRISCOLL*
1928-

562
SCRIPTURE

God, who hast caused to be written thy word for our learning,
grant us that, hearing, our hearts may be inwardly burning.
    (Luke 24:32)

    give to us grace
    that in thy Son we embrace
    life, all its glory discerning.

Now may our God give us joy, and his peace in believing
    (Rom. 15:13)
all things were written in truth for our thankful receiving.
    (2 Tim. 3:16)
    As Christ did preach
    from man to man love must reach:
    grant us each day love's receiving.

Lord, should the powers of the earth and the heavens be shaken
    (Heb. 12:26)
grant us to see thee in all things, our vision awaken.
    Help us to see
    though all the earth cease to be,   (Matt. 5:18)
    thy truth shall never be shaken.   (Ps: 117:2)

From an ancient Collect
The Hymn Book (Canada), 1971

JOHN EDWARD SPEERS*
b. 1916

563
PENTECOST
Psalm 68

In thy pentecostal splendour
    rise, O living God, arise,
smoke of battle blurs and blinds us,
    blow thy wind and clear our eyes:
        Alleluia!
    thou art God of victories.

Thou of old didst lead thy people
    through the desert as they went;
thou upon the mount to Moses
    didst thy tenfold rule present:
        Alleluia!
    Thou art law and covenant.

Him who stooped to die for sinners
    thou hast glorified again;
he captivity led captive,
    now obtaineth gifts for men.
        Alleluia!
    Thou art giver, now as then.

Thou at Pentecost didst shower
    gracious rain from heaven above,
on all flesh didst pour thy Spirit,
    silver-winged, descending dove;
        Alleluia!
    Thou art liberty and love!

Let the fire of thy near presence
    melt our fears, like wax, away;
touch our lips with songs of courage,
    teach us with thy saints to say,
        Alleluia!
    Thou, God, lead'st us all the way.

The Hymn Book (Canada), 1971

GEORGE BRANDON*
b. 1924

564
SPIRIT OF WISDOM

O God, whose mighty wisdom moves
    the minds of men to seek thy way,
by thee our fathers sought the law;
    Lord, keep us in that quest to-day,
that in thy light we yet may see
the path that leads through truth to thee.

O God, whose perfect holiness
    inspires our search to find thy will,
by thee the prophets spoke of old;
    Lord, let us hear them speaking still,
that in thy light we yet may see
the path that leads through truth to thee.

O God, whose tender, yearning heart
    gave us thy Son, the living Word;
by thee men sent the good news forth;
    Lord, let this gospel now be heard
that in thy light we yet may see
the path that leads through truth to thee.

O God, whose surging Spirit stirs
    within the minds of all on earth,
by thee the Scriptures bring new life,
    and hopes forgotten find rebirth;
Lord, grant us in thy light to see
the path that leads through truth to thee.

1951; The Hymn Society of America,
1952.
The Hymn Book (Canada), 1971

DAVID KENNETH BENTLEY
b. 1948; **DOREEN MARGARET
JEAL**, b. 1940; **MARSHA
COBURN KAHALE**, b. 1947;
ROBERT KYBA,* b. 1949

565
SHARING

On this day of sharing
    gladly do we come
to the Lord's own table,
    gathering at one.

See the Table laden
    with the bread and wine,
sign of Christ's own presence,
    pledge of love divine!

Food and drink, symbolic
    on his life on earth:
peace, goodwill to all men,
    promised from his birth.

In the bread that's broken,
    in the wine that's poured,
be the name of Jesus
    evermore adored!

Many urgent problems
    face the human race -
war and vice and hunger:
    God seems out of place.

Yet our Saviour sends us
    to this world of sin,
calling men to Jesus:
    'Let Christ enter in!'

Then, depart to serve him;
    worship him as God;
follow as he leads us
    in the way he trod.

First sung at Easter Communion, 1966,
Rosedale United Church, Montreal.
The Hymn Book (Canada), 1971

**ERNEST NORTHCROFT
MERRINGTON**, 1876-1953

566
GOD OF ETERNITY   HG 238

God of eternity, Lord of the ages,
    Father and Spirit and Saviour of men!
Thine is the glory of time's numbered pages;
    thine is the power to revive us again.

Thankful we come to thee, Lord of the nations,
  praising thy faithfulness, mercy and grace,
shown to our fathers in past generations,
  pledge of thy love to our people and race.

Far from our ancient home, sundered by oceans,
  Zion is builded and God is adored:
lift we our hearts in united devotions!
  Ends of the earth, join in praise to the Lord!   (Ps. 48:10)

Beauteous this lands of ours, bountiful Giver!
  brightly the heavens thy glory declare;
streameth the sunlight on hill, plain and river,
  shineth thy cross over fields rich and fair.

Pardon our sinfulness, God of all pity,
  call to remembrance thy mercies of old;   (Ps. 25:6)
strengthen thy church to abide as a city
  set on a hill for a light to thy fold.   (Matt. 5:14-15)

Head of the church on earth, risen, ascended!
  thine is the honour that dwells in this place;
as thou hast blessed us through years that have ended,
  still lift upon us the light of thy face.

Brisbane, 1912; Church Hymnary, 1927

WESLEY MILGATE
b. 1916

567
FOR ABSENT FRIENDS

Our God, we know your providence
  and love are everywhere,
the wheeling stars, a sparrow's fall
  are equally your care.

Much more to us of little faith
  your power and love extend:
the church is given your Spirit's power,
  our loneliness, a friend.

No power on earth can separate
  us from the love of God;
and in that love, though parted, we
  in union tread his road.

Those absent from our family
  we bring to you in prayer,
that where they are they'll seek and find
  a present helper there.

Through Christ we pray for all we love -
  his love is all our might;
increase our faith, confirm our trust,
  surround us with your light.

Australian Hymn Book, 1977

JAMES PHILIP McAULEY
1917-76

568
SING A NEW SONG

Sing a new song, sing a new song
and wait upon the promise of the Lord.

Creation sings a new song to the Lord,
the universal energies rejoice,

through all the magnitudes of space and time
  creatures proclaim the grandeur of Christ.

The mountains and the valleys and the plains,
the cattle and the wild beasts and the birds,
the shadows and the clouds, the rain and snow,
  praise and reflect the bounty of Christ.

The ocean deeps, the currents and the tides,
the diatoms, the fishes and the whale,
the storm, the reef, the waterspout, the calm
  praise and reflect the wonder of Christ.

The fruit trees in their seasons and the vine,
the eucalypt, the cedar and the palm,
the lotus and the orchid and the rose
  praise and reflect the beauty of Christ.

The human eye, the shaping hand, the mind,
with number and with symbol and design,
in work and play and artistry and prayer
  praise and reflect the wisdom of Christ.

The love of man and woman clear as dawn,
the will for truth and justice broad as day,
the wisdom of the heart profound as night
  praise and reflect the glory of Christ.

Australian Hymn Book, 1977

GRANTON DOUGLAS HAY
b. 1943

569
A LAMP FOR OUR FEET

A lamp for our feet has been given,
  a light has been set on a hill;
God's word in its truth may be trusted
  by all who surrender their will:
to order the chaos of darkness,
  give hope in the midst of despair,
to make of our lives new creations
  and lighten the burdens we bear.

Lord, worship and praise we would offer
  in thanks for the grace we've received;
your word is our rock and our tower,
  in trusting we are not deceived.
The prophets of old had their visions,
  your word often came in their dreams,
but we see the word now incarnate
  in Christ, and in those he redeems.

Lord, grant to us eyes ever watchful,
  and ears ever open to hear
the word that in love you are speaking,
  the word that defeats all our fear.
In suffering love you have claimed us,
  forgive us for flesh that is weak;
you know that our spirits are willing:
  give strength with the word that you speak.

Australian Hymn Book, 1977

ARTICLE 28:
CANTATE DOMINO: HYMNS FROM MODERN FOREIGN SOURCES (570-592)

Our final section is headed by the quotation from Psalm 96 which is also the title of the best-known international hymn book, and it contains a small handful of hymns all of which come from what are in some sense new hymn-cultures of non-English-speaking background.

Looking back over the whole story, we find that it is, naturally enough, centered in the English language. The only other language in which such a book as this could have been compiled is the German; there is a vast treasury of hymnody originating in that tongue. But even so it would have been a very different kind of book, for only in the English-speaking tradition has so much hymn-writing been combined with so much translation. The German tradition is Lutheran or Reformed, and German hymnaries have never taken much notice of hymnody (other than medieval) from other languages. Until recently the same has been true of the Scandinavian language groups. As for the Catholic countries, until 1964 they had no tradition of hymnody apart from that which was founded and concluded in the Middle Ages.

The distinguishing quality of twentieth-century church life has been, as everyone knows, ecumenism. This means not only the meeting of Christians of hitherto hostile denominations, but also, in our field, the meeting of languages. The Ecumenical Movement found its focus in the conferences which led to the establishment in 1948 of the World Council of Churches, and it was its associated junior instrument (junior in standing but senior in foundation), the World Student Christian Federation, which produced the first editions (1924, 1930, 1950) of the multilingual and international hymnal, *Cantate Domino*. They appear to have invented the idea of collecting hymns that could be sung in several languages by groups representing many cultures, and their books in the successive editions have had a modest and significant success. This suggested to other groups the provision of similar books, like the hymnal *Laudamus* and the worship book *Venite Adoremus*, of the World Lutheran Federation.

It was only, however, in 1974 that *Cantate Domino* could show how the specially valuable fruits of Roman Catholic participation. This edition was published by the World Council of Churches, and a glance at it will show that it is ampler, and much further-ranging in styles and in places of origin, than its predecessors. Indeed, in the preparation of this book the Eastern Orthodox Churches also participated for the first time, although, since they have no tradition of congregational hymnody, their contribution was confined to liturgical pieces.

Developments of this kind show that a new horizontal dimension has been introduced into hymnody in the twentieth century. It is no longer a single historical stream of the kind we have been following right up to this point. The Catholic churches have since 1964 been developing vernacular hymnody of a quite new kind. The churches in countries which were regarded not much more than a hundred years ago as mission-receiving countries are now developing indigenous qualities and indigenous hymnody. Even a generation ago it was difficult, with the best will in the world, to find true indigenous hymnody from Africa, India, and the Far East; it is not so now.

Profound difficulties remain and will become more intractable as communication increases. They are not only theological and ecclesiastical, although the more 'indigenous' a church becomes, the stranger its ways of thinking may well appear to traditional 'western' minds. People from the southern hemisphere are now arguing forcibly with those who stand in the Latin tradition of Christianity on the most fundamental principles. But the aesthetic of these countries also creates difficulties of understanding, as when their traditional ideas of poetic expression, or of the musical scale, are wholly foreign to those of Europe. Naturally all this has to be faced and will, one hopes, be creatively resolved in the many centuries that are left to our descendants. At the moment we are in a kind of 'honeymoon' stage in which the excitement and newness of the hymnody that comes through from lands whose praise we never before shared overrides the difficulties.

Translation, of course, presents new hazards. Sometimes the originals are, so far as our present talents go, almost untranslateable into English. Or they look unusual and peculiar when so translated. Some of the best English pieces taken from foreign originals may be, like #585, paraphrases made by a poet, who does not kow the original language, out of a prose translation furnished by a linguist.

The contents of this last section are arranged roughly geographically, and they begin with two offerings from Catholic France. These show only a hint of the strenuous activity in psalmody and hymnody that has come from the Centre Nationale de Pastorale Liturgique in Paris, whose chief poet is Didier Rimaud and whose leading musician, the celebrated Joseph Gelineau.

No. 570 is historic, in being a biblical canticle written before 1964. Its occasion was the Conference on 'Bible and Liturgy' held in Strasbourgh in July 1957, when at the service of Vigils before the High Mass the psalmody was entirely in the vernacular and included this specially-composed hymn with music by Jean Langlais. The original French processional is in nine stanzas; the English translation, made for *Dunblane Praises I*, 1964, (see article 23) uses that part of it which appears on a record made at the time.

No. 571 is another canticle, the most spacious and majestic of all the many such responsive songs written by the C.N.P.L. team. These canticles are always profoundly biblical, and therefore in the highest tradition of hymnody. Other work of the kind by Lucien Deiss has become very well known in Europe and America.

Nos. 572-4 are from Germany. In a quite understandable sense, the new German hymnody is a new culture. Right down to 1933, German hymnody was dominated by the chorale, where it was not corrupted by romantic perversions. It was isolated and remote; it used virtually no translations from contemporary sources. The first great break came with the Hitler persecutions, which forced the Confessional Church, the resisting part of the Lutheran communion, into reassessments of its customs and its role. Out of this came a small quantity of new hymnody, much of it by the heroic Bishop Dibelius. It was almost all a throw-back to the hymnody of the Thirty Years' War, and in their praise the new-style congregations revived the ancient chorales and rejected the romantic accretions. No. 572 is probably the only hymn from this period that has gone into English; it is translated by a writer who has written no other hymns, and it has appeared only in his translation of the original author's book, *The Iron Ration of a Christian*.

No. 573, by a martyr of the Resistance and the most influential theologian of his generation, Bonhoeffer, was not designed as a hymn. It is part of a poem that was printed at the end of the book known in English as *Letters and Papers from Prison*. It has been used as a hymn in Germany, but the English translation was made for *Cantate Domino*. Another Bonhoeffer text, 'Men go to God when they are sorely pressed,' by the Canadian translator Walter Farquharson, is now deservedly finding acceptance.

But the most remarkable development in hymnody in Germany during the postwar years has been what we may for convenience call the *Kirchentag* style. The *Kirchentag* was originally a large convention of religious people from all over Europe, mostly young, who met for a quite unusual kind of religious revival. Immediately after World War II this enterprise, which organized several of these gatherings, was mostly organized by that great Christian von Thadden. Outwardly, the sight of a hundred thousand people in a large German stadium met for religious purposes might suggest the kind of activity widely associated with the name of Billy Graham. But the tone was radical, not conservative; the politics were left, not right; the preaching was intellectual rather than emotional. And the hymnody was in a quite unusual way professional; it could not be less like the Lutheran or Pietist chorales. It was rhythmical and syncopated; it presupposed guitars rather than organs, sometimes indeed jazz-groups; it was antiphonal, and, in abounding in refrains, it shared just one quality with 'Gospel Songs.' Some of the most creative minds in German music contributed to these songs. The lyrics are almost always biblical and radical at the same time.

Long after the *Kirchentag* phase passed, this German version of 'folk' or 'pop' hymnody persisted, and indeed, it is still, in 1976, in full cry. There is much that we might have quoted, though like other 'folk' material it loses much of its force when separated from its music and is usually, especially in translation, unsatisfactory for reading. But special honour should be done to Provost Dieter Trautwein of Frankfurt, who in earlier years was a distinguished leader in German religious youth work, who has composed a number of these new lyrics; we choose his Communion hymn (574) because it seems to embody most of the characteristics of this style: new thinking, intimacy, informality, ruggedness, and sincerity.

The Netherlands, traditionally even more conservative than Germany in its public praise, since the Reformed Church had the same addiction to metrical psalms that we found in the Church of Scotland, has been producing some excellent new material. Its best-known religious poet is Huub Oosterhuis (575), whose most famous hymn is here given; this one has travelled a long way.

Sweden, whose hymnody anybody in 1950 would have thought irretrievably petrified, has experienced a similar explosion of creativity. The recent *Psalmer och Visor* (1975) shows how violent the explosion has been. Olov Hartman, their best religious dramatist and poet, has written a number of hymns, and #576 exhibits their biblical background and imaginative quality. Anders Frostenson (#577) is their most energetic hymn writer; a good deal of the lyric in *Psalmer och Visor* is his own, and here again we find a special celebration of the Bible, especially of the Old Testament, which makes his work unlike anything that the English-speaking writers are producing at the moment.

From here on we go farther from the English scene. No. 578 is, it has to be admitted, a paraphrase based on a prose translation, the text as you have it being the work of an author who does not know a word of Hungarian. It probably is as near the original as some of Bridges' work was to his sources; that may

well be the only context in which it would be decent to invoke the name of Bridges in this connection. But it is just about all that is yet available from Hungarian Protestantism.

Africa is producing a good deal of religious lyric. As yet in translation it is immature, though it is always zestful. No. 579 is from a French original by a minister who comes from and works in Cameroun, and it was written to be sung to the tune of a traditional funeral dance. (It will be readily recalled that funeral customs in those regions are a good deal less oppressive and decorous than ours.) It is a simple Easter narrative, with a double refrain; the absence of the refrain at the climactic point is especially dramatic.

We met the Indian poet Tilak at #348. In #580 he has another characteristic lyric, beautifully rendered by a different translator, and at 581 a third, in MacNicol's translation. Later Indian material is, as is fitting, dance-like and ecstatic and, more than most, needs its music to make its effect. We should mention the work of the Portuguese-Indian priest Christopher Coelho of Goa, who has written many antiphonal canticles with music that combine western tonality with Indian turns of phrase, and some of which may be found in *Cantate Domino*. We may hazard a guess that hymnody as understood by western Protestants will not come easily to either of the two leading temperaments in the Indian sub-continent, the contemplative Hindu or the activist Moslem. But the Bible, especially the Book of Psalms, provides a good ground for some very vital new hymnody among the beleaguered Christians of that region.

No. 582 introduces that extraordinary ecumenical figure, D. T. Niles, who, in editing the *East Asia Christian Council Hymn Book* (1963), circulated so many valuable translations of contemporary lyrics from India and the Far East. 'Slaves of Christ' comes from that source and from the Tamil language. There is a touch of resemblance between some of this hymnody and the negro spiritual. In the next few years we are going to hear from these quarters a great deal about 'liberation,' a para-theological concept which is much exercising ecumenical Christians at present and which has the same origin as the liberation-yearning we hear from the first-generation black slaves.

China before 1948 was beginning to develop a hymnody of its own after being brought up, like all the farther regions, on translations of Watts, Wesley, and American Unitarians. Nos. 583-586 represent different strains in the very varied scene of Chinese Christianity. Probably it will be some time before Chinese Christians, who have now for so long been in exile or silence, develop what one could call an indigenous Christian style. They are, as here evidenced, very good pupils of western preachers. Nos. 584-5 are translations by missionaries who knew the language; ## 583 and 586 are paraphrases, but both admirably done. (The *East Asia Hymn Book*, the only source of 583, misses a point by providing a tune in the wrong meter.) The Korean hymn, #587, which many western books have found useful, is even more obviously a western evangelical product. It might be noted that it was written well before the 1950 Korean war.

Japan, perhaps religiously the most mysterious of all nations, not least because of the extraordinary Japanese capacity for assimilating the surface qualities of alien cultures, has produced a small quantity of Christian lyric, and it is certainly right for us to include the very forward-looking song about Christ's working life (588) and the haunting, though undogmatic, lines of that great Christian Kagawa (589).

In this almost indecent scamper through the part of the

world where the great majority of human beings actually live, we finally touch down in Latin America and in the Caribbean. Latin America–principally Brazil but including the central states–has a vigorous Protestant tradition, Presbyterian and Methodist, which until recently used western evangelical hymnody for its praise. But #590 is a quite remarkable departure from that style. The original is in Portuguese, and although it is pessimistic, it is certainly passionate.

Caribbean Christianity, where it is not of the Black culture, is very largely the product of missions from Europe and the U.S.A. Ethnically those delicious islands are in the late twentieth century experiencing profound racial and political problems, and there is a certain tender pathos in the poem (591) by the exiled John Hoad, formerly a College Principal in Jamaica. Here, though it is the work of a white Christian, is something which really evokes the life of Jamaica in the way in which Kagawa evoked that of traditional Japan a few pages back.

Finally, in #592, we give the text of what seems to be one of the very best hymns written lately by an English missionary for a foreign country. Its author was the editor of that quite remarkable collection, *Africa Praise* (1968), and he contributed this to that book, most of which is strictly Africa and not material exported from Britain. He wrote it for an African tune; a rather beautiful British one appears with it in the *Church Hymnary*, 3rd Edition. The sharing of western talent in this fashion is something quite different from the exporting of western-style hymnody, in the past, necessary, but now inappropriate.

This section is, in any case, only the prologue to a development in hymnody which is already energetic and will become decisive. Perhaps the very swiftness of the journey round the world, which has had a touch of Pan Am Flight One about it, will cause the reader to feel a due sense of the vastness of the field and the speed of progress. From the severe biblicism of Sweden to John Hoad's glow-worms in the tropics–fifty years ago no English knew a word of this or conceived of its happening; even ten years ago we did not know much of it.

None the less, the circle must for the moment be closed, not with a wall but with an easily-opened gate. Isaac Watts shall have the last word. Nobody who writes or sings hymns in any language or climate will be able to afford to ignore what Watts says in his last couplet.

570
WE BEHELD HIS GLORY

God, your glory we have seen in your Son, (John 1:14)
    full of truth, full of heavenly grace;
      in Christ make us live, his love shine on our face
    and the nations shall see in us the triumph you have won.

In the fields of this world his good news he has sown,
    and sends us out to reap till the harvest is done. (John 4:35-6)

In his love like a fire that consumes he passed by;
    the flame has touched our lips: let us shout, 'Here am I.' (Is. 6:8)

He was broken for us, God-forsaken his cry; (Matt. 27:46)
    and still the bread he breaks: to ourselves we must die.

He has trampled the grapes of new life on his Cross; (Is. 63:3)
    now drink the cup and live: he has filled it for us.

He has founded a kingdom that none shall destroy;
    the corner-stone is laid. Go to work, build with joy.

God, your glory we have seen in your Son,
    full of truth, full of heavenly grace;
      in Christ make us live, his love shine on our face,
    and the nations shall see in us the triumph you have won.

DIDIER RIMAUD, 1957.
Tr. (Refrain) **Ronald Johnson** and
(verses) **Brian Wren**, 1964.

571
CANTICLE OF THE CROSS

By the Cross which did to death our only Saviour,
this blessed vine from which grapes are gathered in,
    Jesus Christ, we thank and bless you.
By the Cross which casts down fire upon our planet,
this burning bush in which love is plainly shown,   (Ex. 3:4)
    Jesus Christ, we glorify you.
By the Cross on Calvary's hill securely planted,
this living branch which can heal our every sin,
    Conquering God, we your people proclaim you!

By the Blood with which we marked the wooden lintels, (Ex. 12:21-2)
for our protection the night when God passed by, . . .
by the blood which in our Exodus once saved us,
when hell was sealed up by God's engulfing sea...   (Ex. 14:16)
By the Blood which kills the pioson in bad fruitage,
and gives new life to the dead sap in the tree, . . .

By the Death on Calvary's hill of him the First-born
who bears the wood and the flame for his own pyre . . .
By the Death, amid the thorns, of God's own Shepherd,
the Paschal Lamb who was pierced by our despair, . . .
By the death of God's Beloved outside his vineyard   (Mk. 12:8)
that he might change us from murderer into heir: . . .

By the Wood which sings a song of nuptial gladness,
of God who takes for bride our human race: . . .
By the Wood which raises up in his full vigour
the Son of Man who draws all men by his grace...   (John 12:32)
By the Wood where he perfects his royal Priesthood
in one High Priest who for sin is sacrifice...   (Heb. 9:11-14)

Holy Tree which reaches up from earth to heaven,
that all the world may exult in Jacob's God: . . .   (Gen. 28:10)
Mighty Ship which snatches us from God's deep anger,
saves us, with Noah, from drowning in the flood, . . .   (1 Pet. 3:20)
Tender Wood which gives to brackish water sweetness   (Ex. 15:25)
and from the Rock shall strike fountains for our good, (1 Cor. 10:4)
    Conquering God, we your people proclaim you!

DIDIER RIMAUD, c. 1963;
tr. **F. Pratt Green**, 1972

572

Der Herr wird für dich streiten,	O faithless, fearful army,
du angstverstörtes Heer,	for you the Lord doth fight.
und Seinen Weg bereiten	For you, through oceans stormy
dir mitten durch das Meer;	he cleaves his path of light.
das Eine und das Grösste	Determined is the issue,
liess er an dir gescheh'n,	the crucial victory past;
der Gott, der dich erlöste,	and God who has redeemed you
lässt dich nicht untergeh'n!	upholds you to the last.
Warum willst du verzagen	Why downcast, why despairing,
vor Feindes Übermacht,	in face of hostile power;
Als müsstest du nun schlagen	as though alone you're bearing

mit deiner Kraft die Schlacht.
Und ob gleich Tod und Hölle
die unausweichlich droh'n.
er trat an deine Stelle,
des Vaters ein'ger Sohn.

Mit Seinem Leib und Leben
deckt Er Sein Eigentum,
du darfst dich Ihm nur geben,
Er ist dein Heil und Ruhm!
Er ist der rechte Krieger
in Gottes grosser Schlacht, -
Herr Christ, Du bist der Sieger,
Dein Werk ist schon vollbracht!

HEINRICH VOGEL*
Eiserne Ration eines Christen, 1937

the stresses of this hour?
To death and hell appointed -
see, conquering in your place,
the Son of God, the Anointed,
Elect by soveriegn grace!

His death and resurrection
he clothes upon his folk,
bound to him in subjection
by faith and love and hope.
O Warrior true and glorious,
thou hast God's battle won!
Lord Christ, for us victorious,
thy perfect work is done.

tr. **W. A. Whitehouse***
The Iron Ration of a Christian, 1945

573
NEW YEAR'S EVE
(from a poem composed by Bonhoeffer on what was to prove the last New Year's Eve of his life)

By gracious powers so wonderfully sheltered,
and confidently waiting come what may,
we know that God is with us night and morning
and never fails to greet us each new day.

Yet is this heart by its old foe tormented,
still evil days bring burdens hard to bear;
O give our frightened souls the sure salvation
for which, O Lord, you taught us to prepare.

And when this cup you give is filled to brimming
with bitter sorrow, hard to understand,
we take it thankfully, and without trembling
out of so good, and so beloved a hand.

Yet when again, in this same world, you give us
the joy we had, the brightness of your sun,
we shall remember all the days we lived through,
and all our life shall then be yours alone.

Now when your silence deeply spreads around us,
O let us hear all your creation says:
that world of sound which soundlessly invades us,
and all your children's highest hymns of praise.

DIETRICH BONHOEFFER,* 1944;
tr. **Frederick Pratt Green**, 1972, HG 109

574
AT MANY TABLES

Lord, you are at many tables
an invited, honoured guest.
Even of those, Lord, who are self-sufficient
you let none bear you down;
Come, share the meal with us!
Come, share the meal with us!
unite those who part without loving.

Lord, you are at many tables
an invited, honoured guest.
You also speak, Lord, to those who see nothing
except tomorrow's cares.
Come, share the meal with us!
Come, share the meal with us!
give light to the eyes of the weary.

Lord, you are at many tables
an invited, honoured guest,
You come to people who do without you.
False piety you hate.
Come, share the meal with us!
Come, share the meal with us!
then, Lord, we shall trust what you offer.

Lord, you are at many tables
an invited, honoured guest.
But as our host, Lord, you make sure we carry
each other's load of care.   (Gal. 6:8)
Come, share the meal with us!
Come, share the meal with us!
here, now, and at each of our tables.

DIETER TRAUTWEIN,* 1967;
tr. **Frederick Pratt Green** (HG 109),
1972.

575
FULL OF PEOPLE

While still the earth is full of people,
and earth to man her increase gives,
we give our thanks to you, the keeper
and Father God of all that lives.

As long as human words are spoken,
and for each other we exist,
you give your love as faithful token:
we thank you in the name of Christ.

You feed the birds in tree and rafter,
you clothe the flowers of the field.   (Matt. 6:25ff)
You shelter us, now and hereafter,
and to your care our days we yield.

You are our light and our salvation,
you raise your people from the dead,
you gave your Son for every nation,
his body is the living bread.

The world is bound to bow before you,
you brought it by your love to birth;
you live among us, we adore you,
we are your children down to earth.

HUUB OOSTERHUIS* (Netherlands),
1965
tr. **Fred Kaan** (HG 202), 1972

576
BABEL

See them building Babel's towel   (Gen. 11:3)
slaves the stones are carrying:
here no man cares for brother man:
Kyrieleison.

Far astray that upward road,
man, become a stranger
goes hungry at his brother's board:
Kyrieleison.

'Brotherhood,' forgotten word
down the grassy hillside
rejected from that building lies: (Mk. 12:10)
Kyrieleison.

Men one day will find it there
and will recognize it
as keystone of God's hill and house:
Hallelujah!

Then their cry will rise, and we,
each in his own language   (Acts 2:11)
shall hear of brotherhood once more:
Hallelujah!

Mighty wind of heaven's rule,
storming every barrier,
will blow for ever where it wills: (John 3:8)
Hallelujah!

So shall Babel come to naught,
where it stood shall flourish
the harvest of God's brotherhood.
Hallelujah!

OLOV HARTMAN,* 1970; tr. **T. Caryl**
and **Ruth Micklem,** * 1972

577
FAITH

Faith, while trees are still in blossom,
plans the picking of the fruit:
faith can feel the thrill of harvest
when the buds begin to sprout.

Long before the dawn is breaking
faith anticipates the sun.
Faith is eager for the daylight,
for the work that must be done.

Long before the rains were coming,
Noah went and built an ark;   (Gen. 6:13)
Abraham, the lonely migrant,
saw the light beyond the dark.   (Gen. 12:1)

Faith, uplifted, tamed the water
of the undivided sea   (Ex. 14:15-16)
and the people of the Hebrews
found the path that made them free.

Faith believes that God is faithful -   (Rom. 4:3)
'He will be that he will be' -   (Ex. 3:14)
Faith accepts his call, responding,
'I am willing: Lord, send me.'   (Is. 6:3)

ANDERS FROSTENSON,* 1960
tr. **Fred Kaan** (HG 202), 1972

578
THE TREE OF LIFE

There in God's garden stands the Tree of wisdom   (Gen. 2:16)
whose leaves hold forth the healing of the nations,   (Rev. 22:2)
Tree of all knowledge, Tree of all compassion,
Tree of all beauty.

Its name is Jesus, name that says 'Our Saviour'   (Matt. 1:21)
There on its branches are the scars of suffering;
see where the tendrils of our human selfhood
feed on its life-blood.

Thorns not its own are tangled in its foliage;
our greed has starved it; our despite has choked it.
Yet, look, it lives! Its grief has not destroyed it
nor fire consumed it.   (Ex. 3:2)

See how its branches reach to us in welcome;
hear what the voice says, 'Come to me, ye weary!' (Matt. 11:28)
Give me your sickness, give me all your sorrow:
I will give blessing.'

This is my ending; this my resurrection;
into your hands, Lord, I commit my spirit;   (Ps. 31:5)
this have I searched for; now I can possess it.
This ground is holy!   (Ex. 3:5)

All heaven is singing, 'Thanks to Christ, whose Passion
offers in mercy healing, strength and pardon.
All men and nations, take it, take it freely!'   (Rev. 22:17)
Amen! My Master!

Based on a hymn by **IMRE PÉCSELY
KIRÀLY** (Hungary); tr. in *Cantate
Domino,* 1974.

579
EASTER

Our Jesus is Saviour, Lord and friend;
he searched all our life from end to end.
and he came down to earth to shed his blood on Calvary
all to give life to men.

The city rejoices, the children sing:
'A day of joy: behold, our King!'
and he came down to earth to shed his blood on Calvary,
all to give life to men.

The Table is set in an upper Room;
the bread and the wine foretell his doom.
And he came down to earth to shed his blood on Calvary
all to give life to men.

In form of a servant he washes their feet,
and says, 'thus humbly each other greet.'
and he came down to earth to shed his blood on Calvary,
all to give life to men.

They all go with him to Gethsemane,
but in Pilate's courts there is none but he
and he came down to earth to shed his blood on Calvary,
all to give life to men.

'Not guilty!' says Pilate, and washes his hands.
'Away with him now!' the crowd demands,
and he came down to earth to shed his blood on Calvary
all to give life to men.

Before evening falls it is all done;
the tomb receives our Holy One.
And he came down to earth to shed his blood on Calvary
all to give life to men.

Where are the disciples? where now are his friends?
The Lord is dead; and here all hope ends.
Pause

Two nights and a day, and the news is abroad:
not end but beginning! Alive is the Lord
Sing Alleluia, for Christ the Lord is risen
all to give life to men.   (sing twice)

So praise we God's love for what Jesus has done.
Now death is defeated and victory won
  sing Alleluia for Christ the Lord is risen
    all to give life to men.

ABEL NJUINJI (Cameroun), 1965;
tr. in *Cantate Domino*, 1974

580
THE LOWEST PLACE

Grant me to give to men what they desire,
  and for my portion take what they do slight,
grant me, my Lord, a mind that doth aspire
  to less than it may claim of proper right.

Rather, the lowest place, at all men's feet,
  that do thou graciously reserve for me.
This only bounty I would fain entreat,
  that thy will, O My God, my will may be.

NARAYAN VAMAN TILAK, 1862-1919
(Marathi); tr. **Jack Winslow,*** 1920

581
AS THE LYRE TO THE SINGER

As the lyre to the singer,
  as one's thought to spoken word,
as the rose to fragrant odour,
  so to me is Christ the Lord.

As the mother to the baby,
  as the traveller to his guide,
as the lake to streaming rainfall
  stands the Saviour by my side.

As the sun to gladdening dayspring,
  as the oil is to the flame,
as the fish is to the water,
  so to me is his sweet name.

Bound to him and by him holden
  as the flute and breath accord,
his for now and his for ever
  is my soul to Christ the Lord.

NARAYAN VAMAN TILAK, 1862-1919
(Marathi); tr. **Nicol MacNicol,** 1922

582
SLAVES OF CHRIST

Slaves of Christ, his mercy we remember,
and his will that our lands for him we win,
that he reign - our witness we shall bear
        for all his brethren care,
        and his communion share
        in all our work and prayer.
Slaves of Christ, his mercy we remember
and his will that our lands for him we win.

Calling men, the labouring and the laden,
to his feet that their burdens he may lift   (Matt. 11:28)
At his word - their sorrows fully past
        their troubles on him cast,
        their sickness healed at last,
        will men to him hold fast.
Slaves of Christ, his mercy we remember
and his will that our lands for him we win.

Bringing him, our Master and our Saviour,
where his sword must all false pretences slay,
that his peace may shatter human pride,
        the right from wrong divide,
        the widow's cause decide,
        injustice set aside,
Slaves of Christ, his mercy we remember,
and his will that our lands for him we win.

D. T. NILES* (Sri Lanka), paraphrasing
from the Tamil of V. Santiago, 1962.

583
SAVING LOVE

God, the love that saved mankind,
  raised the Cross upon life's road,
    guiding us through winding ways.
Praise we him who brought the blind
  grace, which to them sight restored
    by the truth he set ablaze.

Babel voices round us rise;
  grief and torment, blood and dust
    hide all meaning and all light.
Burdened hearts and aching eyes
  seek their Lord in love and trust,
    praying that he end their night.

Quiet from the earth is fled;
  vain is hope, and striving vain,
    like dead water and dead wood
severed from the fountain-head.
  Send thou down like healing rain
    grace that brings forth truth and good.

Where a cross-road comes we stand
  rent by inner questioning,
    aims that differ and delude.
Stretch thou forth thy guiding hand,
  and thy wandering people bring
    into peace and plenitude.

Free the vanquished and enslaved,
  and those sunk in pain and haste,
    by thy glorious sacrifice.
Lead thou them whom thou hast saved
  upward through the narrow gate
    to the joy of paradise.

Anonymous Chinese hymn
tr. **Margaret Barclay,*** 1950

584
MY HEART LOOKS IN FAITH

My heart looks in faith
  to the Lamb divine;
his precious blood he shed
  for this life of mine.

My heart waits in hope
  the great God to see;   (Ps. 42:2)
sure are his promises,
  they encompass me.

My heart dwells in love
  by the Spirit blest;
he heals my sicknesses,
  sets my soul at rest.

All faith, hope and love
are by Jesus given,
on earth to give us strength
and his peace in heaven.

T. C. CHAO* (China)
tr. **Frank W. Price,*** 1962

585
THE BREAD OF LIFE

O Bread of life, for all men broken,
of God's own love his dear token,
we hear the words so gently spoken,
  'When you do this, do in remembrance.' (1 Cor. 11:24)

Humbly we seek the help of thy grace
for our own souls, for all our race.
We feel the love in thy blood-stained face,
  'Come unto me, all heavy-laden.'   (Matt. 11:28)

Now may thy life to us descending
enter our lives, all veils rending;
Immanuel, our joy unending;
  'I am with you, this day and always.'   (Matt. 28:20)

TIMOTHY T'ING FANG LEW* (China)
tr. **W. R. O. Taylor,*** 1936

586
THE HEAVENLY CITY

Salem, from heaven descending,   (Rev. 21:1ff)
  Home, Light, Felicity,
beneath man's sore oppressions
  our hearts cry out for thee.
The hope of thy pledged coming
  assuages grief and pain,
kindles to high emprises,
  the weak makes strong again.

Salem from heaven descending,
  here milk and honey flow,
here rules the Son of Mary
  whose head was cradled low;
here sorrows shall be ended,
  nor gold nor power divide,
nor brethren here be sundered
  by huckster's guile or pride.

Salem from heaven descending -
  here reigns in joy and peace
the Lamb who bore our sorrows,
  that we might find release.
No more the list of empire,
  nor rift of race-disdain!
Sword shall be turned to ploughshare   (Is. 2:4)
  and slaughter shall be slain.

Salem from heaven descending,
  where heart and mind are free,
behold, the Word eternal
  is Light and Lord to thee.
Here violence is vanquished,
  nor bars nor bonds prevail;
and who now travel darkling
  shall see without a veil.

Salem from heaven descending,
  Home, Light, Beatitude,
the hopes of thy pledged coming
  our grief and pain extrude.
On earth, as now in heaven,
  God's holy will be done;
may we, from doubt delivered,
  in toil and hope be one.   (1 Cor. 15:58)

TIMOTHY T'ING FANG LEW* (China)
Paraphrased by Nathaniel Micklem
(HG 724), 1937

587
REDEMPTION

The Saviour's precious blood
hath made all nations one,
united let us praise this deed
the Father's love hath done.

In this vast world of men,
a world so full of sin,
no other theme can be our prayer
than this - 'Thy kingdom come!'

In this sad world of war
can peace be ever found?
Unless the love of Christ prevail,
true peace will not abound.

The Master's new command
was - love each other well,   (John 13:34)
O brothers, let us all unite
to do his holy will.

TAI JUN PARK (Korea); tr. **William
Scott** and **Yung Oon Kim,** 1950

588
NAZARETH

Long ago in little Nazareth lived the Son of Man,
planing wood, the carpenter, working to the plan
which his father gave him daily, whatever it was,
from his brow the sweat drops falling until evening's pause.
  God made a workman, occupied with human toil,
  God here accepting as his own our blood and soil.

God's salvation is no theory based on empty thought,
with his calloused working hands was salvation wrought,
not in human wisdom nor found in learned book,
but by Holy Spirit's fire within the flesh he took.
  Man made a brother sharing life with God's own son,
  the labourer finding life anew in Christ begun.

Toiler, trader, peasant, farmer: each enriched by grace
given freely, irrespective of man's name or place.
Let us then the hammer lift, or turn the heavy wheels,
draw the water for the field, or hoe till evening steals.
  Work, for the Father worketh even until now.   (John 5:17)
  He will the work complete. He only knoweth how.   (Phil. 1:6)

GUMPEI YAMAMURO (Japan)
tr. **D. T. Niles,*** 1962

589
BLACK SOIL

Oh black fruitful soil, presenting a gladsome scene,
          dressed in garments green,
bedecking earth with beauty - tree and flower and vine -
youth lead their cows to pasture in the bright sunshine.
    Revive the land where poverty lies,
     for God, a Mother true, their every need supplies,
     and his grace is their perpetual surprise.

Come, brothers, unite to guard all our homes and land,
          joined in heart and hand,
that we may lift the burdens of the poor, the weak;
and, to the sick and lonely, words of comfort speak.

God's love, oh, how deep! Unceasing the mercy which
          flows from Jesus rich;
when we through sin inflict on him most grievous pain,
ev'n then his love, unchanging, claims us once again.

              TOYOHIKO KAGAWA (Japan)
              tr. **Vern Rossman**, 1962

590
THE MODERN CITY

Modern man has the city for his home,
    where his life is walled in by want and dread,
pained by nights without sleep and days of grinding work
    in the struggle to earn his daily bread.
In our cities, immense and growing out
    there are millions from faith and love estranged,
who need to recapture hope of better things,
    and whose hearts, by the grace of Christ, can change.

In the dark of our noisy city life,
    men and women are groping for the light.
human beings who hunger to see right prevail,
    unaware of the liberating Christ.

In the great, giant cities of our globe,
    hollowed out by the ways of greed and crime,
we are set to reflect the likeness of our God
    and to act out renewal's great design.

Grow, then, cities, to house the world of man,
    with your skyscrapers blotting out the sun.
Let Christ be the light to shine from human homes
    in the high-rising blocks of steel and stone.

            JOAO DIAS DE ARAUJO, 1967;
            tr. **Fred Kaan** (HG 202), 1972

591

Take the dark strength of our nights,
soft with peeny-wallies' lights   [glow-worms]
Take the star-signs wheeling round
while the steel-drum melts to sound.
Take and weave a womb of night
    that we may live.

Take the protest of our need,
what the garden? what the weed?
Take the orb and break the chain,
break the shackles of the brain.
Take and weave a womb of right
    that we may live.

Take the islands' human skills,
dancing seas and wise old hills.
Take our Jesus and his power,
match his people to this hour.
Take and weave a womb of right
    that we may live.

            JOHN HOAD* (Jamaica), 1971

ARTHUR MORRIS JONES
b. 1899

592
SPIRIT OF LIGHT

Spirit of Light - Holy,
shine in this world of thine;
lighten thou our darkness, clear
blindness from out our minds.
Guide thou our ways, so may we
walk in the light of thy truth,
come, Spirit, come.

Spirit of Love - Holy,
fire thou this world of thine;
chasten thou the pride of race
marring our common life.
Kindle our love, that loving
all may true brotherhood find,
come, Spirit, come.
Spirit of Life - Holy,
breathe o'er this world of thine;
teach us all to know and do
all that will make men free.
Thy kingdom come, on earth as
in thy blest heaven above,
come, Spirit, come.

Spirit of Power - Holy,
mighty and infinite;
work within this world of thine
breaking the powers of sin.
Take thou thy throne, and reigning,
claim the whole world for thine own.
Great Spirit, come.

           Church Hymnary III, 1973;
           Africa Praise, 1968

EPILOGUE

593

A SONG OF PRAISE TO THE BLESSED TRINITY

We give immortal praise
  to God the Father's love
for all our comforts here
  and better hopes above;
he sent his own eternal Son
to die for sins that man had done.

To God the Son belongs
  immortal glory too,
who bought us with his blood
  from everlasting woe:
and now he lives, and now he reigns,
and sees the fruit of all his pains.

To God the Spirit's name
  immortal worship give,
whose new-creating power
  makes the dead sinner live:
his work completes the grand design,
and fills the soul with joy divine.

Almighty God, to thee
  be endless honours done;
the undivided Three
  and the mysterious One:
where reason fails with all her powers,
there faith prevails and love adores.

ISAAC WATTS (HG 10), *Hymns*, 1707,
III 38

TABLE OF CURRENT SOURCES

Should any reader wish to compare a hymn in our collection with what is now to be found in current hymnals, to find a tune for it, or for any other reason to turn it up in an accessible source, we provide the following table to help in such a search. It lists the hymns in the 26 hymnals used in the *Hymnal Guide* as control sources, adding three and removing one. The three added are *Songs of Praise, Worship Song* and *Cantate Domino*; the *New Catholic Hymnal*, which so often provides revised texts, and which in any case is easy to refer to because it is arranged in alphabetical order of first lines, we have omitted.

Certain signs carry the following meanings:

* * in first column - non-English original
* * elsewhere - Supplemental Hymnal (see list below)
* + alternative translation, version, or first line

The initials at the head of the columns refer to the following books:

AMS	- *Hymns Ancient and Modern*, Standard Edition, 1922
AMR	- *Hymns Ancient and Modern*, Revised Edition, 1950
AMR*	- *100 Hymns for To-day*, 1969
An	- *Anglican Hymn Book*, 1965
B	- *Baptist Hymn Book*, 1962
B*	- *Praise for To-day*, 1974
BB	- *BBC Hymn Book*, 1951
CH2	- *Church Hymnary*, Revised Edition, 1927
CH3	- *Church Hymnary*, Third Edition, 1973
CP	- *Congregational Praise*, 1951
CP*	- *New Church Praise*, 1975
E	- *English Hymnal*, 1906, 1933
E*	- (below 125) *English Praise*, 1975 (300-335) *English Hymnal Service Book*, 1962 (above 744) *Hymnal for Scotland*, 1951 (Scottish Supplement)

M	- *Methodist Hymn Book*, 1933
M*	- *Hymns and Songs*, 1969
PL	- *Praise the Lord*, 1972
WS	- *Worship Song*, 1905 (chiefly for American texts in England)

American Hymnals

B	- *Baptist Hymnal*, 1975
BP	- *The Book of Praise* (Canada), 1972
Can	- *The Hymn Book* (Canada), 1971
CLB	- *Catholic Liturgy Book*, 1975
CW1	- *Christian Worship* (Baptists and Disciples), 1941
CW2	- *Hymnal for Christian Worship*, (as above), 1970
Hy	- *The Hymnal, 1940* (Episcopal), 1943
Hy*	- *More Hymns and Spiritual Songs*, 1971
L	- *Lutheran Book of Worship*, 1978 (numbers in parenthesis refer to the *Service Book and Hymnal*, 1958)
M	- *Methodist Hymnal*, 1966
P1	- *The Hymnal* (Presbyterian), 1933
P2	- *The Hymnbook* (Presbyterian), 1955
P3	- *The Worshipbook* (Presbyterian), 1972
Pm	- *Pilgrim Hymnal*, 1958
Pm*	- *Westminster Praise*, 1976
W2	- *Worship-II* (Catholic), 1975

International

CD	- *Cantate Domino*, 1974
EAC	- (in final section) *East Asia Christian Council Hymnal*, 1962

British Hymnals: columns AMS–WS. American Hymnals: columns BP–W2. Int.: column CD.

Hymn #	AMS	AMR	An	B	BB	CH2	CH3	CP	E	M	PL	SP	WS	BP	Can	B	CW1	CW2	Hy	L	M	P1	P2	P3	Pm	W2	CD
1				153			268	761	210					191				171	60	134				327		45	92
2				457+		407	381+	359+										89+		295	526+						
3			98+		48+	56+	188+	78+	126+						411+			132+	22-3+	51+					121+	89*	
4	678+	[See 330]												86	135+	137	155	31	551	228+	20	266	19	274	363	2	146
5‡																											
6				362											Mennonite Hymnal (1969) 344.												
7	166	166	231	2	450	229	1	1	365	2	11	443	172	42	12	17		71	278	245	21	1	24	288	4	14	1
8B						Sc_{124} Ps	392																				
9E	93*	93*	511	73	480	Sc_{23} Ps	387	729	313*	50	115			9	131	341	40			451	68	97	104	592	84		
9F			178		474			43	93	51		653													(10) / 14*		
9-10	9A-D and 10 not in modern sources. 16th century psalm tunes appropriate.																										
12-14	See Scottish Psalter, 1929, for recommended tunes for these.																										
15	238	314	516	571	451			390	367	455		449		18			185	80	450	452	255	317	322		390		
16	290	290	512	589	481			46	502	427		677	234	15	137			25		(420)	56	83			81		
17	93	93				401			84													503			580		
18	Not in modern sources. Psalm tunes up to 1677 appropriate.																										
19	[See 140.]																										
20								29	296																		
21	Not in modern sources. Psalm tunes up to 1677 appropriate, or proper tune in Playford, 1671.																										
22	62	62	123	113	61	42+	174+	80	30	129	157	82		127	405	97		126	13	(22)	394	120	169	643	146	309	
23								151				176															
24						Sc_{148} Ps		744				657															
25								4+		20+			163+														
26												605	208														
27								382																			
28	Not in modern sources; tune composed for it is WHITEHALL (Lawes Psalm 8), EH 234 ii, CP 470 &c.																										

Hymn #	British Hymnals										American Hymnals																Int.
	AMS	AMR	An	B	BB	CH2	CH3	CP	E	M	PL	SP	WS	BP	Can	B	CW1	CW2	Hy	L	M	P1	P2	P3	Pm	W2	CD
29	3/23	3/23	34/64	672/694	403/414	256/291	42/641	590/617	257/267	931/943	302/317	25/45	531/563	547/560	357/363		148	68	151/165	269/278	180/493	278/42	50/63	292	32/56	16	83
30								6	404	78		526	191+		20												
31								605																			
32	Not in modern sources. CM tunes up to 1800 suitable.																										
33								7	635	6																	
34			266	175		165	304	176		96				248						(412)					229		
35	536	285	436	614	254	592	536	359	498	649		201	505	538		504			586	(583)							
36	682		570	572	300			489		418		451															
37	623	571	462	404	229			358	197	831		204	503	317	503	498			337	(594)	533						
38	108	108	164	151	97	106	254	131	107	182	177	133	120	178	109	111	228	171		482	435	152	198	635	177		
39				156				129	28*	48*															46*		
40	Not in modern sources. SM tunes up to 1800 suitable.																										
41								294																			
42								50										10	29*					477	14*	182	
43	220	220	320	184	460	388	413	158	420	272		545	472	385	164	282	527	288	542	530	472	377	496	443	202	147	99
44	165	165	244	71	467	601	611	52	450	878	286	598	2	87	133	223	585	23	289	320	28	77	111	549	1	203	2
45 (b)																	477		389			346					
46		179			477			48	491																		
47	517	117	568	77	22	26	150	49	511	413		694	346	99	207	468			297	264	70	81	119		84		
48	662	170	232	74	21	10	143	30	297	44		659	623	96	85		164	3	309	(442)	43	69	97	595	72		
49	61	61	97	93	46	54	190	83	21	120		73	91	126					16	(19)					127		
50	Not in modern sources. LM tunes up to 1800 suitable.																										
51		45*			379	345+	459+	669		36*				494						(565+)				410			
52	53	53	82	81	490	40	160	74	6	82		62	84	110	385				7	35							
53										193											428						
54	510																										

Hymn #	British Hymnals																		American Hymnals								Int.
	AMS	AMR	An	B	BB	CH2	CH3	CP	E	M	PL	SP	WS	BP	Can	B	CW1	CW2	Hy	L	M	P1	P2	P3	Pm	W2	CD
55	600		494	460		459	96	469		433		670	331	377					464	(391)	531						
56			504	208				470		370				405	118					(376)	127						
57								395		496																	
58			496	426		110		472		371				173				241			527						
59	60	60	112	98	50	46	169	84	24	117		74	92	132	407	83	189	123	27	60	388	117	163	411	120	111	
60+	522	196	270	212	278	166	371	180	446	1		595	63	247	48	69	262	72	325	559	1	199	141	493	223		
61	7	7	36	673	137	261	114	594	258	924		26		149	362			285	153	265	401	26	47	332	43		
62	774	343		767	4	416		495	378	339	150	476								(471)	529						
63										142																	
64	556								333	771				356						202							
65	195	195	531	772		428		428		434											285						
66	520	205	625	595	328	479	437	179	437	431	113	573	61	233	241	58	379	297	479	315	283	308	399	471	228	172	
67	8	336	604	629	406	651	463	593	259	590		29	439	456	306				150	505	152				406		129
68				712						956				576													
69								496		608																	
70										594																	
71	702	328	602	461		518				578						407	373				150		301				
72			69		397			606	302*	661	19			334													
73	601	631	249	30	283	571	358	12	646	21		398	5	531	22+	25+	124+	81+	285	544	30+	8+	89+	587+	14+	230+	
74	Not in modern sources except Oxford Hymnal (1908). WAREHAM (EH 475) is suitable.																										
75			45	682				595																			
76	196	296	555	541	140	564	89	500	397	615		508	366	504	269	202	393	251	434+	343	271	104	339	409	93		
77				304				244																			
78	134	134	194	157	105	119	264		133	205	195	145		190	465	115		174	85	151	443	163	204	440	187	145	
79						561+		401													147+						
80	184	210	492	458	296	413	83	477	477	498		636	209	397		163	294		471	327	120	237	271		259		

Hymn #	British Hymnals																		American Hymnals								Int. CD
	AMS	AMR	An	B	BB	CH2	CH3	CP	E	M	PL	SP	WS	BP	Can	B	CW1	CW2	Hy	L	M	P1	P2	P3	Pm	W2	
81	155	153	222		163				631			184		255	485		110		111	(118)							
82	292	368	29	24	16	35	37	13	535	13		624	12	67	10	11		79		540	42	10	3	554	13	229	
83								68					32														
84	300	217	265	180	118	139	382	163	364	91		440	73	237	42	42	253	284	355	328	73	192	132	285	196	10	
85	176	192	260	203	142	419	376	182	405	99		527	64	249	116	464	264		455	345	81	310	130		221	125	
86	545	257	424	257	176	206	421	243	393	706		500		297	144		431	354	385	358	293	339	434	379	267	92	
87			[See CAMBRIDGE HYMNAL (1967) 113.]																						44*		
88			519	573				396	511																		
89								397																			
90	630	326	147	599	333	457	663	476	445	461		112	290	415			310		416	(466)	268	259	319		349		
91	633		509	148		692		765	332	201				180		107				(373)	421	241	276				
92	260	344	523	414		417	676	374	400	432		510	292	372					459			224	263				
93	246		616	658			312	322		904																	
94	373	181	403	53	8	31	147	56	394	503		503	233	101	159	439	162	29	310	483	215	103	112	391	87		
95		176	530	585	485	439	69	398		527		643	352			221	581		443	(495)	231	296	418				
96	512	299	561	550	495	562	72	55	447	607		596	361	510	263		174		497	477		98	342	496	389		
97			416			365									162												
98	80+	80+	133	110	496	57	168	75	43	139		96		154	430						361+		153				
99			143			400		386		342			276	402	72								125				
100	201	204	213	178	498	140	295	184	316*				129	213		125							389				
101			619	593	488	481	395	394						419	111								328				
102			521		484	483	396	393		5*				224	151								120				
103	283+	117+						766	85+			117+															
104	200	215	162	150	95	109	258	132	510	196		132	116	170	110				340	344							
105	301	218	207	192	132	131	286	164	147	244	213	175	175	204	108				106	173	458	195	211	589	200	266	
106	360	266	333	46	185	364	494	328	553	803	272	303	468	95	235	303	536		272	400	480	392				279	

Hymn #	British Hymnals																		American Hymnals							Int.	
	AMS	AMR	An	B	BB	CH2	CH3	CP	E	M	PL	SP	WS	BP	Can	B	CW1	CW2	Hy	L	M	P1	P2	P3	Pm	W2	CD
107			317			389		325	306*	829			478															
108	219	219	129	80	457	154	347	326	45	245	164	87	469	113	154		257	113	545	87		111	146		105	110	
109	585		328	387	159	386	496	323					477	387	233				256	388		207	242	528	279		
110	247	317	609		344			444	78	539										438							
111		611		340	347			445+	474	533		630		432+		400	335			(458)	252		391		336+		
112					468	473	665	403																			
113				326+				302		766							465+	311	213+	(269)	313	356	446		280	242+	
114			556	141		113	259	134	409	183			119	174	113	70	237	208	336	104	416	154	195	437	157		
115						367							332														
116	160	160	227	42	169	1	352	223	162	36	222	187	10	277	50	1	107	70	266	165	26	57	11	421	251	118	
117	642	75	125	91	63	64	201	94	41	122		85	93	150	432		202		46	84	400	136	175	318	126		
118	714	409	371	310	503	318	574	303	305	756		265	713	358	326		453	303	196	(279)	323	353	445		282		
119		174	174									533															
120	99	99	167	128	89	92	234	122	620	192	185	137	107	176	449		223	156	64	121	425	150	188	563	176	255	
121	4	4	43	678	408	259	47	596	260	927		31	531	548	360				155	(201)	499	31	45		36		
122	24	24	62	703	424	292	647	621	274	942		55	562	553					166	(226)	502	37	56		50		
123	Not in this form in modern sources except (abridged) Oxford Hymn Book. TALLIS FIFTH (SP 483) suitable.																										
124	168	168	134	76	8	8		35	497	43		664	621	91+			435+										
125	167	167	248	22	471	9	35	17	466	8	226	618	26	76	127	30	94	67	288	548	473	2	26	533	6		
126	298	365	247	23	15	21	360	18	470	12	95	623	8	250	30	8	259	73	282	549	66	14	31	551	16	228	
127						544		767	432	458		104	255														
128	27	27	500	686	298	286	695	622	363	948		437	557	533	180	217	138	47	467	272	289	33	64	278	209		
129		57							13																		
130			4	51		36	357	21		544			275	529					478								
131		239	297	239		183	107	210		289			139	253	60		275	196	370		461	212	243	574	241	256	
132			302	248		201		229					449	283			436		400		368		254		256	256	

Hymn #	AMS	AMR	An	B	BB	CH2	CH3	CP	E	M	PL	SP	WS	BP	Can	B	CW1	CW2	Hy	L	M	P1	P2	P3	Pm	W2	CD
									British Hymnals									American Hymnals									Int.
133	659	175	239	194	26	25		58	312*				6	88	32							83					
134	318	411	370	309	200			304	304	769		264			340				212					313	281		
135								247																			
136								187																			
137									49			44															
138	95						652		81											273							
139	1	1	44			258	45		254		307			543	361				159	268							
140	9+	11+							255		305+								160								
141	10	12							261		311+								161								
142	11	14			413				262		309+								162								
143	15	16			405				264		312+				371				164	277							
144		10+	40+	675		263	43	588	165		306	28		546	359		102	62	157	267	504	24	43	365	41	78	
145									68	123-4									61								
146	128	129			113+				125						472												
147	126	158	226		167				160+		220+				489					169							
148 Pt. 3		602		159	107 108								13		474				98	94							
149	430	503			234		540		175						497+				132+					581	188+	260	
150		564							242						506				123								
151	295					14		789	494																		
152	156+	156+	225+	228+		186	105	203	155	287+	216+	180			248+				109+							56+	
153	398	466							351	646									468								
154	76+	76+			64		199	76	40	83	158	84		146+	431+			140+	48+	81	405+	A85				70+	
155	56	58	109	85	57	60	198	125	613	63*	140	387		137	429	62		139	20	42	357		7	534	111	216	58
156	97	97	161	146	90	108	256		95		181	129			446				66	118						225	
157					130		305	150	146					206						157+				273+			

British Hymnals: AMS, AMR, An, B, BB, CH2, CH3, CP, E, M, PL, SP, WS, BP, Can, B, CW1, CW2
American Hymnals: Hy, L, M, P1, P2, P3, Pm, W2, CD

Hymn #	AMS	AMR	An	B	BB	CH2	CH3	CP	E	M	PL	SP	WS	BP	Can	B	CW1	CW2	Hy	L	M	P1	P2	P3	Pm	W2	CD
158	396	620	660		445	207	10	237	169	7*		190		304	145				383	367	298	336	433	325	263	43	
159	98	98	166	144	77	91	233	120	622	84	261	135	105	240	447	39	221	155	62	108	424	146	187	284	155	9	
160A		152							154		9							197									100
160B	157	157	216	226	151	182	342	199	153	779		178	161	256					217	472	467		237	335	575		
160C				230		184	118	200	156	293		181	150						371	164					310	62	
161+	235	281			252	224	535	349	465			200			186				589	337		430	424		310		

NB 162 (1) The world is very evil (2) Brief life is here our portion (3) For thee, O dear dear country (4) Jerusalem the golden.

Hymn #	AMS	AMR	An	B	BB	CH2	CH3	CP	E	M	PL	SP	WS	BP	Can	B	CW1	CW2	Hy	L	M	P1	P2	P3	Pm	W2	CD
162 (1)	226	276							495																		
162 (2)	225	275			241	597		350	371	652		459	514						596	(527)			430				
162 (3)	227	277				598		351	392										598	(534)			429				
162 (4)	228	278	432	406	248	599	537	352	412	652		198	515	528	184		569		597	347	303	435	428		309		
163A	178	189	536 542	205 188	322	422 423	377 378	173	419	108 107		547	69 68	243 245	120 121	73	392	282	462	316 537	82	309	401		226	149	
163B	190	387	380	207	323	420	571	291		109		549	721	231	343	72	419	320	485	356	329	354	215	510	290		
164	309	383	383	326+	208		578	314+	326*	63+	334	286+							199+	120						225	

References for familiar translations of 165 - Thee we adore and (+) Humbly we adore thee given on next line. Tunes there given appropriate for 165B.

Hymn #	AMS	AMR	An	B	BB	CH2	CH3	CP	E	M	PL	SP	WS	BP	Can	B	CW1	CW2	Hy	L	M	P1	P2	P3	Pm	W2	CD
165	312	385		330	217	319	584		331		65+	279			329			319+	204+	199				599			
165A	Westminster Hymnal (1940) 73																										
165B																										5	
166	117	118			80	99	246		115	689	229				455			164+	76	110							
167	173	187		126	73	223	223	63	459	62					100			146	344	88	451	167		518	150		
168	130	130			110	124	277	724	626			143		194	467			179	99	139			206	527	191	312	
169A	314+	389+			209				321		74+								192	222+							
169B								292		768			723														
170	431	506	459		226			654	178	788																	
171	78	78			68				46																		
172	49	49	83	83	36	149	165	72	8+	257	131	66		116	390	78	182	108	2	34	354	109	147	489	110	195	53

Hymn #	British Hymnals																American Hymnals										Int.
	AMS	AMR	An	B	BB	CH2	CH3	CP	E	M	PL	SP	WS	BP	Can	B	CW1	CW2	Hy	L	M	P1	P2	P3	Pm	W2	CD
173	58+	63+			349			82	27	140																	
174	273+																										
175	59	59	106	104	55	55	191	85	28	118	139	78	90	120	415	81	205	121	12	45	386	116	170	486	132	193	65
176	180	198			94						182																
177A	18	18	54	695	416	281	54	612		931																	
178	133	133		155			269	140	131		198	144		199	464		242	173	94	132	448	168	205	344	186	58	
179	132	132	190	162	112	123	267	141	137	208		146	125	193	374		247	183	96	141	437	166	208	584	192		
180		390		102	204		577		318	38*	171	273+		354	332			114	197	198	324	112	148	449	376	157	152
181		88*	386	328	215		588	313	329	30	278				348				201	218						88	164
182		417			244		325	315	310						307				492								
183	185	200	138	565		403	80	380	77	239	104	106						255	417	309	284	239	270		314	167	
184						458	95	431																	407		
185														227					11	33	353	187	232		201	269	
186	224	68	90	87	41		192		19	618									18	18							
187		289	582	551		577		517	452																		
188		55+	77+		40+	162+	315+	760	12	255+		687+		152	394+			112+	3+	31+				614+	108+	291+	163
189‡	214		130	261	141	216	202	508	435	33*	283	349	458	295	117	145	430	287	329	76	399	321	415	521			
190B		253	405		179		491			729					272				395	366	412				378		
191B	379		151	137	500		251	775	70	177	175	99		175	443			162	71	123	49	158	191	280	163	6	110
192	379	379	22	18	277	29	368	42	533	10	93	350	19	103	197	234	598	99	276	533		459	9	481	29	189	
193A			57							946				557						276		505+	66+				
193B		34		707	427		57	629	278			57							181	(228)							
194A	111+	111+			86				102		179+	128							75							211+	
194B			158	145		107	253	127		202				181	452		231	163		116+	418	151	194	524	170		82
195A																			446								
195B	692+	310+	482	574	313+	546/547	669+	487		507§		479	239	503+		224+				(579+)							

Hymn #	British Hymnals																American Hymnals										Int.
	AMS	AMR	An	B	BB	CH2	CH3	CP	E	M	PL	SP	WS	BP	Can	B	CW1	CW2	Hy	L	M	P1	P2	P3	Pm	W2	CD
196		393		314	510	324	567	293	306			267		353	333			310		224+	318			351			
197	192	203			361	496		436	460	447		608	219														
198	293	366	565	28	18		142		478	415	228			75		22		26		542+	4		15	568	20	249	
199	657	382	246	25	17	22	9	45	536	64	14	626		83	29	10	98	57	279	543	55	6	1	557	15	231	108
200		3*	492	299	448	405	417	417		70	278	442		104	134		354	20							339		
201			478			394				322+					167+				377		227						
202A			5	41+		234	355	224+		31+			179+	322	16	16	123	61	477	249+		51	3	384	3		
202B	526	249		16	264			261	637	683				89	21					(162)					499		
203								404					337														
204												434															
205	670	235	214	224	149	191	115	204	152	273	7	177		257	67				376	508	466			334	239	49	102
206	161	161	15	26+	269	2+	353+	16	372	25+		460		69+	43		156+		269+	(177+)		15+					
207								123				124	109									375					
208	169	169	10	64	12	23	356	24	441	73		581	25						284	524	151	267	348	361	365	75	
209				466						402			454		187	143	348	253	393	500					369		
210	739			535		520	670	544		489																	
211	634	364	480	419	20	395	218	369	499	318		666	485	409	76	171	172	13	304	290	69	93	110	601	101		
212	114	113	173	144		96	243	135	111	187		140	108	187			233	168	74	(86)		159	193		114		
213				654				567	566	909		314	796				563		496								
214	304	224	209+	182+	124+	136+	298+	166+	381	271+	223		132	218+	480+	52+	250+	184+	352+	170+		190	213	349+	199+	63+	
215													103														
216													135														
217													341														
218				254				230	449				447						547								
219	513+	309		517	359	531		522				597	201		209		365										
220	370	487	408	665	384	626	527	680	540	917		336	753	435	221		610	370	512	467	538	492	521	356+	429	71	

British Hymnals / American Hymnals concordance

Hymn #	AMS	AMR	An	B	BB	CH2	CH3	CP	E	M	PL	SP	WS	BP	Can	B	CW1	CW2	Hy	L	M	P1	P2	P3	Pm	W2	Int. CD
						British Hymnals										American Hymnals											
221	79	79	126	90	62	63	200	95	39	132	159	83	98	153	435		196	141	52	82	397	135	174	302	119	27	
222	316	399	383	168	197	138			301		66	260			49			294	347	158						19	
223	148	148	208	171	129				145	223	212	173							103	(112)		173					
224	701	327	299						751*		279				98	394									37*		
225	285	313	553	117		83		108	541	167		489	101										359		367		
226	540	304	577	289	302	517	442	512	389	490		491	226	487	175		376	256	560	461	240	270					
227		77	11	35	267	232	40	275	42	9	162	93	182	148	33		106					7			31		
228									458																		
229	369	478				86		672	526			287	757							431						80	
230	437	527	460	403	227	220	534	363	641	832	242	202	513	310	501	144	577	279	126	174	536	429	425	369	306		
231	198	355	416	418		397			578	330			484				279			(386)	108	228	266		329		
232	391	629	562	520		535	480	527	643	822		397	799	301	178	393	482		557	509	305	365	350	542	382		
233	274	292	566	559	186	214	423	504	503	616		678	349	514			481		394	355		345	475		387	81	
234	663	171	18	8	272	17	367	37	309§	35	263	494	336	98	199	54	167	7	296	561	35	71	2	372	66		
235	222	284	437	407	253	221			486	828			502				568		590	(595)		427	427		311		
236	215	255	425	263	184	205	420	254	489	701	271	249	453	307	146	236	423	290	396	369	297	333	437	582	260	261	
237		259			180			550	464	707		615	195				478		491+								
238				67						958			35				154			(176)		62	92				
239	197	197	546	72	475	438	388	61	490	76	114	654	46	80	132	215	169	49	345	456	67	99	106	590	79	268	
240	211	234	221		156			215																			
241	20	20	49	688	442	277	52	632	266	689		42	592	555					168	(232)	501	43	55		55		
242	528	324	490	449	345					743																	
243	686																										
244				265	255	211	14	250		71			771	314					303		58	342	16				
245		479	398	635		351	535	671	525			285	756	497	230			270	515	(216)	485		315	623	271		
246	413	550				360																386					

234

Hymn #	British Hymnals																American Hymnals										Int.
	AMS	AMR	An	B	BB	CH2	CH3	CP	E	M	PL	SP	WS	BP	Can	B	CW1	CW2	Hy	L	M	P1	P2	P3	Pm	W2	CD
247	406	541	453						207										114								
248									48			95	85														
249	322	397		307	198	320			302			261							189	(278)		355			292		
250	615	563	450				580		240	759		237		344	331												
251	122	124							120																		
252									232			234															
253	671	236	287	592	148	194	103	216	300*	300	6	458	154	259	240	317		200	375	(470)	133	213	235		233		
254				626		503	451	461						475													
255	660																										
256						637		573	558	889		317	763				560		147	(347)					341		
257		238			522		335	217	438											(125)							
258					502																						
259		582	663	651	433			571	475	882		631							520						430		
260				75	314		403	430		65*		661															5
261												484															
262	675	254			183				488			248							387								
263					280																						
264	Songs of Syon, 330																										
265			662	643	393	636	519	572	423	883		552		592	213		515		518	418	546	417	517	447	435	155	
266			263		288		111		519						7				599	175	19		34		30	313	
267		45*			72			464	598					164					322								
268									118			139							78						22*		
269					394	638	520	578	562		105	308		594	214		546	373	521	428	484	419	511	497	436		41
270													242														
271	531	251	300	245	189			227		302				292			440			240	367	218	249				
272		485													386		595	95	140					556	464		

Hymn #	British Hymnals															American Hymnals											Int.
	AMS	AMR	An	B	BB	CH2	CH3	CP	E	M	PL	SP	WS	BP	Can	B	CW1	CW2	Hy	L	M	P1	P2	P3	Pm	W2	CD
273	293								461																		
274	207	230	233	236	160	180	336	209	157	283		182	145	260					368			205					
275	255	349	472	443	292	411	79	385	316	353		254	211	394	284	187	295	216	409	296	119	230	272		320		
276	269	308	573	507	340	523		505	374	491		467	377	434													
277	277	352		598	332	475	689	480	444	468		586	287	519	254		329		465	(577)	263	261	326		351		
278	280		364	586		504		252	344	569		258	228						427	(511)		248					
279			524	581		442	681	412		528				505	204		384		431	(574)	230	284	417		343	138	
280	403	533	442	416	354	500	211	451	205	157		217	489	374	166	367	281	204	566	494	107	223	269	439	322		
281		439	204		131	130	298	155		224		174	128														
282	411																										
283	259		643							391							289			(513)		229	262		397		
284	356		597	514		338	485	552		781			428	477	302	276	470	344	574	403	195	399	298				
285			560					453		198			113								430						
286				140		144		109		149		447										330					
287	667		152	427	301	691	684		567	197				185	440	360	235	159	341	107	417	162	190	308+	160		
288								169		259			56									134					
289	306	225	254	199	120	178	300	167	368	249		382	77	234	39	363		291	356	179	76		143	303	197	30	
290		67	100	99	51	50	178	90	25	137		75		121	418			135	44	(36)	376				128		
291												240															
292			105	103	53	52	194	717		138		92		138	422			134		(37)	375	133					
293			617	169				308		94				410													
294									119	435																	
295	121	123				103	250																				
296			241	58				33		46					81	154		4			37	65					
297	568	451		739		662		700	591	842		356		452					251				84	628	68	133	
298	572	443	538			655	419		601																		

Hymn #	British Hymnals																American Hymnals										Int.
	AMS	AMR	An	B	BB	CH2	CH3	CP	E	M	PL	SP	WS	BP	Can	B	CW1	CW2	Hy	L	M	P1	P2	P3	Pm	W2	CD
299						550							677														
300			348	750		654	656	703	599	844		364		562					241	(235)		449					
301			346	120		82		104	595	865			675				213		246	(497)		442	460		483		
302									109+											(73)					154		
303			171		76																						
304	334	444	337	287	146	668	93		602																		
305									600					490													
306	332	214	163	149	92	105	241	136	106	180		131	670	186	101		230		65	114	414	157	202		172		
307	329	432	107	106	58	69	193	89	605	859		368	658	129	112			125	236	(41)		454	462	559		220	
308	573	442	233	733	3	18	154	684	587	851		444	700	105	86			2	311		34		456		478	17	
309								91				372															
310	337		358	615		593			607	839										(592)							
311	330	445	347	119		71	227		594	856			662	167		461	428					447					
312	346	431	59	698	420	288	653	627	603	944		49	701				149		172	280	495	35	51		51		
313				425		685			584	334			490														
314			237			20	151	690				358		393					248								
315		435	350	142	81	436	385	137	597	854		669															
316	571	446	441						606	30*	165									(335)							
317	611	544							209						266				115								
318			357	747		667	100	701		841		363	688	507													
319						75		106					663														
320A	655	162	229	433	170	506	402	753	212	392	221	528		276	68				268	188				428+	53*	127	
320B						505	401																				
321A						454	397		756*														93	504			
321B						179	301		758*													123	136				
322							398		74*																		

237

British Hymnals columns: AMS, AMR, An, B, BB, CH2, CH3, CP, E, M, PL, SP, WS, BP.
American Hymnals columns: Can, B, CW1, CW2, Hy, L, M, P1, P2, P3, Pm, W2. Int.: CD.

Hymn #	AMS	AMR	An	B	BB	CH2	CH3	CP	E	M	PL	SP	WS	BP	Can	B	CW1	CW2	Hy	L	M	P1	P2	P3	Pm	W2	CD
323	Irish Church Hymnal (1960) #324.																										
324	10*		571	462	316	477	87	432	755*	632	289			458	253	212	321	90			256	325	303	304	391		123
325						570																					
326			96	92	45	53	180		757*					136		84											
327	14+	15+				4	56		164+			51+							271+	133+		59+	245+				
328	No modern source and no contemporary tune known.																										
329	678+		331	385	25	376	495	327						380													
330		183	402	562	297	526	406	485	362	494		436	238		135		see	4									146
331				616		582		772		643		419		541													
332				5				39		27		448+	9									76			73		
333								452																			
334			520			556	673							417						(267)	209	281	374		77	36	
335	257	351	513	346	143	410	212	376	574	154		529	59	369	115	288		223	424	497	117	236	280			130	
336				69	10			69		52	274	607	52					16							99		
337	705	373	621	628	271		457	22	304*	604		492	345	462		460						500			396		
338	703			591	373	488		539		444			384														
339													241														
340	574			474		251	123	455		848			683									434					
341				776	175	581	694	773		637														433			
342		372	242	61		12	32	28	407	34		535	1	70	26	32	159	75	301	526	27	66	85		7	135	
343						559	675						205														
344	699	359		20		424	677	774		448			500	447	192	368	388	17	458	324		234	307	519	399		
345													416														
346												497	496														
347																	302	219				243	286				
348				456		406	82	388		159										(384)		234			330		

238

British Hymnals: AMS–WS · American Hymnals: BP–W2 · Int.: CD

Hymn #	AMS	AMR	An	B	BB	CH2	CH3	CP	E	M	PL	SP	WS	BP	Can	B	CW1	CW2	Hy	L	M	P1	P2	P3	Pm	W2	CD
349								67		356																	
350						210		246		708+			456	305		240		348	388	368	294	537	455		626+	269	
351	Hymns Ancient and Modern (1904) #153.																										
352								273					168		259												278
353		199	455	220	338	173	121	102		160									361	464	75	254	221				
354						147							118												348		
355			507	549		415	81	479	439	238		580	250	398	285	382	355	244	449	479	143	285	378				
356		347	534	206		418	674	188	421	111		550	71							(469)		319					
357												563	20														
358													140														
359													177														
360	263	333	589	510	369	501	430	515	484			119	492	454	176	370	285	151			160		293				
361													803														
362					1			407+		629		438	328														
363		208	537	121		141	306	186	408	102		536	53	160		329	254	12	360	(476)	157	178	229	434	230		
364			272	125		513	439	186	456	103		603	54	481	287				501						224		
365	Congregational Hymnary (1916) 167: some stanzas of this appear in WS 54.																										
366						558				513		530+	520+	518		492+			441+	(593+)	290+						
367				777		589		770		642		697	529	535													
368						340							482														
369									108																		
370	689+								563			309	783		167	385	558	247	519	(547)	242		361	540	441		
371													94														
372													230														
373		66	104	101	52	47	170	88	26	130	138	76	86	144	427	86	191	119	19	54	390	127	160	438	129	242	
374													100														

Hymn #	British Hymnals																American Hymnals										Int.
	AMS	AMR	An	B	BB	CH2	CH3	CP	E	M	PL	SP	WS	BP	Can	B	CW1	CW2	Hy	L	M	P1	P2	P3	Pm	W2	CD
375			245	63	11	24	34	23	434	32		564	17	93			151		291	170	64	87	87	463	89		
376						155	318	170		255		578	800	225	156				28*	332	545			474	443	178	
377									406			532	39					239		(490)	219	79	114		92		
378				630				580		908		559	40				177		373			95			236		
379		258		255	173	209	422	253	375	703		468	795	303	147		426			(330)		338	436		261		
380												673	75														
381		20*	419	358	321	489	514	554	384	892		485	388	473	252	506				373		406		358	275	73	134
382				546	308	566		514		613		357					566		433	(462)	269		341		376		
383	642	65	122	105	56	48	172	718	15	125	142	79	661	130	421	85	184	120	21	41	381	121	171	521	134	207	
384		11*		364	172		500	333		805			461	382			538		537	(311)	292	378	489		295		
385																149	551	22	143	567	552	414	515	394	433	101	
386			303+	243+		202		233+		309+			711	285		138+	461	327+		235	369	216	250	317			
387								459				577	267														
388		263		398	28	153	323	585	504	742		680	480		278		539		591	(331)		363	484				
389																	99		274	137	459	58	246	297	249		
390-398: The tunes to these texts are indivorcibly associated with them. See Hymnal Guide at #223.																											
399										94*						106		157	69*	385	432				25*		79
400																Sacred Harp, 157											
401																Sacred Harp, 133											
402	764			522		681				338						283					175						
403				493						422						334	412				224		139				
404																184											
405																159											
406																428											
407																298											
408																353											

Table: Hymn concordance (British Hymnals / American Hymnals / Int.)

Hymn #	AMS	AMR	An	B	BB	CH2	CH3	CP	E	M	PL	SP	WS	Can	B	CW1	CW2	Hy	L	M	P1	P2	P3	Pm	W2	CD
				British Hymnals														American Hymnals								Int.
409	695	332	623	471	512		433	745	305*	405	111	501			69			432	(466)				395		393	
410		623			247	595		354	638	655		395							331	587						
411			73		398		44	602	283			22														
412												587														
413												639														
414+	548	375	243	13	275	15	361	3	427	5		556	29	71	2	24		83	(290)	418	10	9	22	5*		159
415								15*	12*		110	474			258				513					36*		53
416	665	367	539	12	325		364	426	424	23	295	553		476	195	27		3	521	415	61	64	28	453	71	3
417		377	20	15	461	11	33	44	532	18	259	12	34	60	28						468					
418		52	89	195	479	151	321	156	492	813		658	467	118		128			318	327		185	230		95	
419									515			123														
420									99			125														
421												670														
422A					172																					
422B								434				571														
423												348														
424					472	Ps 122	489	742	472	61*		628		55												
425		599+	168					121					106+				154+				148+			156+		
426		286				463	693	356	86*	466		585	519	181										21*		
427		69			44		197	79	20			72														
428		274	430	360	245	225		355	401	714		514														
429	535	342		612	355	549		435	433	647		105	323		190			445+	(308)	218						
430	546	371	24	36	286	39	363	5	517	26		701		6+				600+	(409)					23		
431		102	155	143	84		224	128	308*	144	178	127		442	486			27*	94					169	183	80
432												80														
433		301			304	557		38*				513														

School Worship (1926) (note appears at row 422A, An/B columns)

241

Hymn #	British Hymnals													American Hymnals													Int.
	AMS	AMR	An	B	BB	CH2	CH3	CP	E	M	PL	SP	WS	BP	Can	B	CW1	CW2	Hy	L	M	P1	P2	P3	Pm	W2	CD
434A	676	293		561	371	576	443	486		620	285				293												
434B									402			515		520		284	364	252	563	498	155	276	345	414	371		
435												690															
436												151															
437								537	506						138											283	
438												679															
439		2*		633	70														56*								
440	266	298		545	306	568	682	509	425	612		554	364	516	270		578	46	430	(523)	272	289	331		215		
441		186			168		400	71	390	17*	219	625	51		40			386	343								
442	172	185	160	216	88	32	238		471	74	180	648	82	252			349	15	365	(411)	146	175	228		597		
443						142		192	483	86														578			
444												633											526+		453		
445					32		314			254		511										110	150				
446												568								74				466			
447																			12*					413	20*		
448								556																			
449		55*+		636	380+																						
450								664																			
451				380		337	510	560						489	280		504			405							147
452				89*			84	586		912	329				73		567	339	536	(348)	475	424	490		451	286	42
453		35*			273				102*																		116
454						645	507					326			279			265	532	413	469		486	362	445	76	
455												698													422		
456		51*							50*			561															
457		8*										262							49*								155
458												640							299								

Hymn #	AMS	AMR	An	B	BB	CH2	CH3	CP	E	M	PL	SP	WS	BP	Can	B	CW1	CW2	Hy	L	M	P1	P2	P3	Pm	W2	CD
459				610	243	218	538	364	657			289							222	(598)							
460		87*						117																			
461		13*	418	659			505	171	101*	9*		60		111		274			258		408		492	326	198		
462										25*																	
463		50*																									
464	100 New Hymns of Praise (1944) 29. Possible tune AMR 445.																									
465		12*		356			474	365				242		316				353	543	386						44	143
466												282															
467	Public School Hymn Book (1949) #346																									
468		260																							51*		
469		78*		64*			141			56*	266				83									512			
470		99*		94*															37*								
471								48*																			
472		37*						34*		26*																	
473			136																								
474					437																			457			
475					435																						
476		37*		726	440			34*		26*	300				381						514						
477								532																			
478		5*	591	639				564							291			234			141				26*		
479		68*						67*		49*															361		
480		449																									
481	School Worship (1926) #313																									
482	School Worship #44																									
483	Church and School Hymnal (1926) #277																									
484	Church and School Hymnal #245																									

						British Hymnals													American Hymnals								
Hymn #	AMS	AMR	An	B	BB	CH2	CH3	CP	E	M	PL	SP	WS	BP	Can	B	CW1	CW2	Hy	L	M	P1	P2	P3	Pm	W2	Int. CD
485				259	353														243						48		
486								535				377															
487		18*		12*				17*		15*	99								5*						57*	61	
488				8*				8*																			
489				50*				54*																			
490		33*		28*				32*		23*					90												
491	*New Songs for the Church* (1969) I - 23																										
492										72*										189							95
493	*Ecumenical Praise* (1977) #83																										
494				91*											104				36*								
495		52*		49*				53*						320	305				18*								
496								5*							339												
497		53*		51*				55*	96*									347	19*							165	139
498				40*				39*							328												
499								58*																	55*		
500								93*																			
501		89*	439	77*			164	92*	49*					244	495										18*		
502	*Psalm Praise* (1974) # 122																										
503								2*	99*		293													295	58*	21	34
504				3*				1*		3*					168				1*	436				293	56*		40
505								10*		8*					119									7*			97
506	*26 Hymns* (1971) # 1																							11*			
507	Leaflet 1973, Norwich Cathedral (A) Ms (B)																										
508		29*		22*				25*	24*	18*					74				9*	307						84	
509		81*		67*						90*																	
510				35*				29*			62																

Hymn #	AMS	AMR	An	B	BB	CH2	CH3	CP	E	M	PL	SP	WS	BP	Can	B	CW1	CW2	Hy	L	M	P1	P2	P3	Pm	W2	CD
				British Hymnals												American Hymnals											Int.
511				Hymns for Celebration (1974) # 25							53																
512				New Catholic Hymnal (1971) # 209																							
513									86*																		
514				69*				82*			62																
515											53																
516							399																				
517							68																				
518								37*																			
519								104*																			
520								27*																			
521				Green Print for Song (1973) p. 24																							
522	21*			13*				20*		77*	154				428				53*					359		74	
523				Green Print for Song (1973) p. 28																							
524								42*																			
525				New Songs for the Church (1969) I - 18																							
526				Gospel Song Book (1967) p. 56																							
527				Gospel Song Book (1967) p. 54																							
528				Faith, Folk and Festivity (1969) p. 2																							
529				New Orbit (1972)																							
530				New Songs for the Church (1969) I - 11+																							
531				New Songs for the Church I - 10																							
532				88*				100*		92*												138	177	526			
533								31*																			
534								105*																			
535								22*																			
536	80*					74	220									99											

Hymn #	AMS	AMR	An	B	BB	CH2	CH3	CP	E	M	PL	SP	WS	BP	Can	B	CW1	CW2	Hy	L	M	P1	P2	P3	Pm	W2	Int. CD
				British Hymnals										American Hymnals													
537				533			512			895				496	303	311	519	268	498	429	204	410	507	642	423		
538																						368	288	460	411		
539																	597		145	437	548	416	512	479	338		
540																									409		
541																	513	331				402	480	451	449	161	
542		76*					509								160				494	(332)	481	409	508	505	420	204	
543		54*					235	172		906		562						222	522	421	355				325		
544					23		499								236	535				(322)	476		485	357	294	72	
545		34*			391		88	563		24*				465	223	265	378	245	524	415	470		358	393	366		29
546																			354	391							
547																			380	(243)			477	559			
548																			81						165		
549			169	139	79		242								454			169	68		427			294	159		
550		4*	253	198	119		297	197		2*					107	43		59	366		74			290	147	15	
551																			298					588			
552		24*		315	201		586		62*	16*	69				225	315			195		307			366	289	79	
553																364		236		493	161		291	423	398		
554																	225			396					28*	199	
555																									59*	301	
556																				205							
557	*United Church of Christ Hymnal (1974) #44*																										
558	*United Church of Christ Hymnal (1974) #153*																								32*		
559												126				90	225					96					
560			567											54	129		166	21		445							
561		72*		187	24		511			52*				598	275			266	525		477			492	444		
562				31*											99												

Hymn #	AMS	AMR	An	B	BB	CH2	CH3	CP	E	M	PL	SP	WS	BP	Can	B	CW1	CW2	Hy	L	M	P1	P2	P3	Pm	CD	EAC
							British Hymnals											American Hymnals								Int.	
563															484												
564															264												
565															335												
566					390	642	517	577							57												
567	Australian Hymn Book (1977) 118																										
568	Australian Hymn Book (1977) 102																										
569	Australian Hymn Book (1977) 341																										
570						469		36*												11*						96	
571																										78	
572																											
573																									47*	48	
574																										159	
575																										74	
576								85*																		135	
577																										44	
578																									30*	131	
579																										86	
580																											159
581																											115
582																											179
583																											182
584																										124	165
585					538																		447			157	171
586																											
587										68*																	183
588																											177

| Hymn # | British Hymnals | | | | | | | | | | | | | | | | American Hymnals | | | | | | | | | | Int. |
	AMS	AMR	An	B	BB	CH2	CH3	CP	E	M	PL	SP	WS	BP	Can	B	CW1	CW2	Hy	L	M	P1	P2	P3	Pm	CD	EAC
589																											180
590																										35	
591																										31	
592							340																				
593								220		40																	

248

BIOGRAPHICAL APPENDIX

If the author appears in the *Hymnal Guide* refer to the HG number given either against the hymn in this book or, if the hymn here quoted is not in the *Hymnal Guide* or if the first of several here quoted is not there, against the author's name. Where an author's name is followed by an asterisk, no biographical notice will be found for him in the *Hymnal Guide*; it is these authors for whom notice is given in this present appendix.

Ord. = ordained.   † = died.

ARNOLD, Matthew, b. Laleham, Middx., 24 xii 1822; ed. Rugby, Winchester, Balliol, Oxf.; Newdigate Prize for Poetry. Fellow of Oriel, Oxf., '45; Priv. Sec. to Lord Lansdowne, '48; inspector of schools, '51; prof. Poetry, Oxf., '57-67; thereafter devoted himself to writing. Leading poet and critic, publishing substantial books of poetry '53, '55, and '67, and much religious literature with a critical slant. Finally retired from inspectorate, '86. Visited USA, '83. † 15 iv 1888 (65).

AUDEN, Wystan Hugh, b. York (England), 21 ii 1907; ed. Gresham's and Christ Ch., Oxf.; was for a short time a schoolmaster but soon became full time man of letters; became US citizen, '38; Prof. Poetry, Oxf., '56-59; † 1975 (68).

AUSTIN, John, b. Walpole, Norfolk, 1613; ed. St John's, Camb.; became Roman Catholic & studied for the bar; later private tutor, but mainly a man of letters, writing a modest amount of poetry and prose incl. 39 hymns (some adapted from the greater R.C. poet Crashaw, whom see below). † London, 1669.

BEDDOME, Benjamin, b. Henley in Arden, 1717, son of Bapt. minister; apprenticed to a surgeon in Bristol, joined Bapt ch. and Ord. Bapt.; pastor, Bourton on the Water (Glos) 1740 - † 1795. Wrote hymns each Sunday for his congn., wh. were collected posth. and pub. 1817; these numbered 830.

BEZA, Theodore, b. 1519 Vezelay, Burgundy; studied under M. Wolmar who became a Protestant & made his house a Protestant center in Bourges which Calvin often visited; studied law at Orleane from '35 to '39; officially became Protestant '48; prof. Greek at Lausanne, '49; published Latin trsln. of Greek Testament, '56. Completed Marot's edn. of Genevan Psalms, 1561, and after Calvin's death became leader of Swiss Protestants. Discovered *Codex Bezae* 1562 & edited & published it, 1582. † 1605 (86).

BONHOEFFER, Dietrich, b. Breslau, 4 ii 1906, son of a psychiatrist; ed. Tübingen and Berlin; Vicar in Barcelona, 1928; member of faculty of theol. in Berlin, '29; studied at Union Theo. Sem., New York, '30-1; declared public opposition to Hitler in a radio broadcast when he came to power, '33; pastor of 2 German congregations in London; then directed a secret seminary in Germany for ministerial training, at Zingst, later at Finkelwande. Promoted Resistance movement in Germany until arrested '43 and imprisoned. Executed 9 iv 1945 in Flossenburg prison. Author of many works, mostly posth. publ., including (in trnsln) *The Cost of Discipleship, Ethics,* and *Letters & Papers from Prison.* His posth. influence on late 20th-century theology is probably greater than that of any single person of his generation.

BRANDON, George, b. 4 ii 1924; ed. Univ. Pacific in history but took up musical career; MSM Union Seminary, New York, '52. Instructor in music, Eureka Coll., Illinois, and since 1959 Assoc. Prof. mus. and chairman of Fine Arts, William Penn Coll., Oskaloosa, Iowa. Has pub. more than 200 choral and organ works.

BRYANT, William Cullen, b. 3 xi 1794 Cummington, Mass.; ed. William Coll. & admitted to the bar; after 10 years in law, entered journalism & became well-known poet and essayist. Founded *New York Review* and for nearly 50 years edited *New York Evening Post.* † 12 vi 1878 (84).

BULFINCH, Stephen Greenleaf, b. Boston, Mass., 18 vi 1809, his father being the architect of the Capitol in Washington, to which they moved, 1818; ed. Columbian Coll. and Cambridge Theol. School; Ord. Unit., '31; later pastor in Pittsburgh, Pa., Washington ('38),

Nashua, N.H. ('45), Dorchester, Mass. ('52), East Cambridge, Mass., ('65) † there, 12 x 1870 (61).

CAMPIAN, Thomas, b. Witham, Essex, c. 1575; ed. Cambridge; trained in law and then medicine, which he practised in London for the rest of his life. Notable musician and writer, celebrated for his two *Books of Ayres* and for musicological writings. † London, 1619 (about 44).

CARTER, Henry Child, b. Clapton (London), 1875, ed. Mill Hill, Oriel and Mansfield Colls., Oxf.; Ord. Cong. (never officially ordained because of personal scruples about the rite); minister Queen Street, Wolverhampton 1901-10 and Emmanuel, Cambridge '10-44. Celebrated pastor and preacher. † Bishops Stortford, Herts, 1 viii 1954 (79).

CARTER, Sydney, b. Camden (London) 6 v 1915; ed. Christ's Hospital & Balliol, Oxf. Became a schoolmaster but during World War II joined Friends' Ambulance Unit in Middle East. Developed journalistic skills, became a broadcast script writer and lecturer; attributes his development as folk-song artist to the 2 war years he spent in Greece. During the years after c. 1962 became a leader of the folksong renaissance in Engl. ch. mus. through many TV appearances and through his publications.

CLARKE, C. Erskine, all that is traceable is that he was born in 1871 and died in 1926, at which time he was Vicar of Battersea (London).

CLARKE, James Freeman, b. Hanover, N.H., 4 iv 1810; ed. Harvard; Ord. Unit., 1833; pastor at Louisville, Ky., '33-40; Boston, Mass., '41-50 and from '53 till † 8 vi 1888 (77).

CONDER, Eustace Rogers, b. St Albans, Herts, 1820 (son of Josiah Conder, hymn-writer & editor); ed. Spring Hill Coll. Birmingham; Ord. Cong. and ministered at Poole, Dorset, then Leeds, '61-91. Chairman of Congl Union, 1873. † Bournemouth, 1892 (72).

CRASHAW, Richard, b. about 1613, London, ed. Charterhouse & Cambridge; Fellow of Peterhouse; refused to accept Solemn League & Covenant and dismissed from Camb., 1643; went to France, became R.C., suffered much poverty before being made Secretary to Cardinal Palotta; Canon of Ch. of Loreto, Italy, '49; died there 21 viii 1649 (about 35). Mystical poet who has been compared with George Herbert.

DAVIES, Samuel, b. New Castle, Del., 1726; ed. priv., Ord. Presb., 1748 & ministered in Virginia; eventually, after a visit to Britain, succeeded Jonathan Edwards as President of New Jersey Presb. Coll., Princeton (now Princeton Univ.); † Princeton, 1761 (35).

DONNE, John, b. 1572, London; ed. as R.C. for Law, but later joined C/E, and spent much time in travel and literary activities; Ord. C/E, 1610 (at suggestion of King James I who recognized his literary talent); Dean of St Paul's, London, 1621; acknowledged as the greatest of the English metaphysical poets, † London, 31 iii 1631.

EMERSON, Ralph Waldo, b. Boston, Mass., 25 iii 1803; ed. Harvard; schoolmaster then Ord. Unit.; resigned ministry 1832, visited Europe, returned to Boston and entered on career of literature & lecturing which he followed for the rest of his life. Lived at Concord 1853-† there 1882 (79).

FLETCHER, Phineas, b. Cranbrook, Kent, 8 iv 1582; ed. Eton & King's, Camb.; Fellow 1600-16; Ord. C/E; rector of Hillgay, Norfolk 1621-† 1650 (68).

GEYER, John Brownlow, b. Wakefield 1932; ed. Silcoates Sch., St John's Camb., Mansfield Coll., Oxf.; Ord. Cong. '59; minister, St Andrews (Scotland), Drumchapel, Glasgow; Tutor in O.T. studies, Cheshunt Coll., Camb., '64-7; Minister, Little Baddow, Chelmsford, '67. O.T. Scholar.

GODOLPHIN, Sidney, b. Godolphin, Cornwall, 1610; ed. Exeter Coll., Oxf., practised law. M.P. for Helston (Cornwall) 1628. Raised a troop for royalist cause in English Civil War; killed in battle 1643.

GOODALL, David Stanton, b. Barnet, 1922; ed. Mill Hill, Balliol & Mansfield, Oxf.; Organ scholar at Balliol, 1938-41; Ord. Congl., '50;

minister at Brill, Bucks, '50-3; Bursar, Mansfield Coll., Oxf.; served later with Educ. Depts of Sunderland (Technical College) and Manchester (City). Organist, composer, preacher. Minister, 1970— of churches (URC) in Cheshire.

GRANT, Peter, b. Ballentua, Strathspey (Scotland) 1783; self-educated; crofter, Gaelic-speaking. Baptist lay preacher from age 19. Composed spiritual songs at first to supplant lewd and secular songs sung at weddings and even at wakes (funerals), which had great success and became known throughout the Scottish highlands. Minister at Grantown (Scotland) 1826-67, and † there 1867 (84).

GUYON, Madame (Jeanne Marie Bouvières de la Mothe), b. Montargis, 1648; m. Jacques Guyon, 1664; widowed '76; cultivated mystical beliefs of an eccentric kind, toured France 5 years in company with Barnabite friar, F. Lacombe, propagating their beliefs; arrested 1687 & Lacombe imprisoned 12 years; Mme. Guyon freed from prison early & became prominent at court of Louis XIV. Her most eminent disciple was Fénélon. After renewed theol. controversy, she demanded a hearing, and on its findings was arrested again (1695) & imprisoned 7 years. Meanwhile her cause was constantly defended by Fénélon against J. B. Bossuet, most eminent theologian of the time. Leader of quietist movement, highly influential. She † 1717 (69).

HANKEY, Donald William Alers, b. Brighton, 1884; ed. Rugby, entered military academy at Woolwich, 1901; commissioned 1903, joined Royal Garrison Artillery, Sheerness. Resigned commission '07, went to Leeds Clergy School to prepare for ordination; travelled steerage to Australia '12, returned '14, to live in poorest part of London; rejoined army '15, and was killed 1916 at Battle of the Somme. Wrote a considerable amount of poetry and prose with religious reference.

HAWKER, Robert Stephen, b. Plymouth (Eng), 1804; ed. Pembroke Coll., Oxf.; Newdigate prize for poetry, '27. Ord. C/E, Vicar of Morwenstow, Cornwall from '34. Transformed semi-barbarous customs among fishermen there (who unscrupulously raided each other's catches) into thanksgiving service in parish ch., which is reputed to have been the origin of the Harvest Festival. A great eccentric, he wrote several books of poetry. † Plymouth, 1875 (71).

HERRICK, Robert, b. London 1591, apprenticed to goldsmith's trade, then ed. Cambridge and Ord. C/E, Vicar of Dean Prior, Devon '29-'47 when he was ejected by Puritan faction; returned '62. Leading lyric poet of his age; described, despite clerical status, as 'the most pagan of English poets.' † Dean Prior, Devon, 1674 (83).

HIGGINSON, Thomas Wentworth, b. Cambridge, Mass., 22 xii 1823; ed. Harvard; Ord. Unit., pastor Newburyport, Mass., '27, Worcester '52-8; retired '58 & devoted himself to literature. Colonel of the first negro regiment raised in S. Carolina during Civil War; leading contrib. to Atlantic Monthly and author of several books of essays.

HUNTER, Archibald McBride, b. 16 i 1906; ed. Hutcheson's Sch., Glasgow, Univ. Glasgow, Marburg, Oxf. Ord. C/Scot; Minister Comrie, Perthshire, '34-7; Prof. N.T., Mansfield College, Oxf., '37-'42. Minister Kinnoull, Perth, '42-'45; Prof. N.T. Univ. Aberdeen '45-71; Master, Christ's Coll., Aberdeen, '57-'71. Leading N.T. author, lecturer, popularizer.

JAMES, King; b. Edinburgh 1566, s. of Mary Queen of Scots; crowned King James VI of Scotland on his mother's abdication, 1567; crowned King James I of England and VI of Scotland in London, 1603; instituted Hampton Court Conference from which emerged, 1611, the Authorized Version of the Bible, often called the King James Version. Author of several polemical books. † London, 1625 (59).

JOHNSON, Sir Ronald (Ronald Ernest Charles), b. 3 v 1913 Portsmouth; ed. Portsmouth Grammar Sch., St John's, Camb. Entered civil service in Scottish office, '35; Secretary, Scottish Home & Health Dept, '63-'72; Secretary of Commissions for Scotland '72- . Kt, 1970. Organist of St Columba's (Episc.) Ch., Edinburgh.

JONES, Lewis Edgar, b. Yates City, Ill., 8 ii 1865; ed. Moody Bible Inst., went into YMCA work; gen. sec. YMCA's in Fort Worth, Tx., then Santa Barbara, Cal. † Santa Barbara, 1 ix 1936 (71).

McCLARD, Leroy, b. Cape Girardeau, Mo., 18 iii 1926; ed. Southeast Missouri State Univ., Oklahoma Bapt Univ., Southwestern Bapt

Seminary; minister of music at Bapt chs in Cleburne, Tx., Shawnee, Okla., Little Rock, Ark., before becoming state mus. dir for Bapt chs in Arkansas ('55-63), Illinois ('64-6). Research and Program Design Consultant, Bapt Sunday School Board, Nashville, Tenn., '66-'71, then supervisor of Youth-Adult-General Materials Sectn of that Board.

McKINNEY, Baylus Benjamin, b. Heflin, La, 22 vii 1886; ed. Mt Lebanon Academy, La, Southwestern Bapt Seminary, & Buch Conservatory, Chicago. Mus.D. Oklahoma Bapt Univ., '42. Faculty of Sch. of Sac. Mus., Southwestern Bapt Sem., Fort Worth, Tx., 1919-32. Mus. Ed. for Robt H. Coleman, publisher, '18-'35. Asst pastor Travis Av. Bapt Ch., Fort Worth, '31-5; mus. ed. Bapt Sunday Sch. Board, '35-'41; Sec. Mus. Dept from its inception '41; compiler of Broadman Hymnal and other songbooks. † as result of car accident, Bryson City, N.C., 7 ix 1952 (66).

MAROT, Clément, b. Cahors, France, c. 1496; court poet for Francis I of France; his metrical psalms, written for the court, attracted the attention of Calvin who appointed him to edit the first Strasbourg metrical psalter, 1539, then Genev. Psalters from 1542. When he † 1544, Beza (q.v.) completed his work.

MICKLEM, Thomas Caryl, b. Oxford, 1 viii 1925; ed. Mill Hill, New Coll. & Mansfield, Oxf.; Ord. Cong 1949, minister at Oundle, Northants, '49-53, Banstead, Surrey, '53-8 and Kensington Chapel, London, '58-'78, St Columba's, Oxford, '78- English scholar and musician. Contrib. to New Church Praise both texts & music.

MILES, C. Austin, b. Lakehurst, N.J., 7 i 1868; ed. Philadelphia Coll. of Pharmacy and Univ. Pennsylvania; after some years in pharmacy went to work for gospel-song publisher Hall-Mack of Philadelphia; remained there 1898-1935 & continued with Rodeheaver-Hall-Mack thereafter. † Pitman, N.J., 5 vi 1955 (87).

MILES, Sarah Elizabeth, nee Appleton, b. Boston, Mass., 28 iii 1807; m. 1833 Solomon P. Miles, HM of Boston High Sch. (who † 1842). After this lived with son at Brattleborough, Vt. † there 23 i 1877 (69).

O'DALY, Donnchadh, d. 1244, member of dynasty of medieval Irish poets (his poem prob. erroneously attrib. to his brother Muiredhach) to whom more than 30 major devotional poems are attributed.

O'DRISCOLL, Thomas Herbert, b. near Cork, Ireland, 17 x 1928; ed. locally (Gaelic speaking) then Trinity Coll., Dublin. Ord. Episc.; curate Monkstown '52-4; emigr. to Canada; asst in Christ Ch. Cathedral, Ottawa; chaplain, Shearwater Base, Dartmouth, '57-60; Rector of Carp, Ont., '60-62; Rector, St John's, Ottawa '62-8; Dean of Christ Ch. Cathedral, Vancouver since '68.

PAYNE, Ernest Alexander, b. 19 ii 1902; London; ed. Regents Pk Coll., St Catherines and Mansfield, Oxf.; Ord. Bapt; minister at Bugbrooke, Northants, '28-32; Bapt Miss. Soc. staff, '32-40; Senior Tutor, Regents Pk Coll., Oxf., '40-'51; Gen. Sec. Bapt Union of Gt Brit., '51-67; Vice-Chm., Central Cttee of World Council of Churches, '54-'68; President, World Council of Churches since '68. Leading Bapt administrator & historian.

PEMBROKE, Countess of: see SIDNEY, Mary, along with S., Sir Philip.

PIERPONT, John, b. Litchfield Conn., 6 iv 1785; ed. Yale; taught in New Haven, Conn. and Charleston. S.C., then admitted to the bar 1812; shortly left that for business, and in 1816 went to Harvard Div. Sch. to train for ministry; Ord. Unit., pastor Hollis St, Boston, Mass., 1819; resigned 1840 after controversy provoked by his liberal views on slavery; pastor, Troy, N.Y., '45-9, Medford, Mass., '49-59. Chaplain to US army '62, and, in retirement, govt clerk in US Treasury at Washington. Many of his poems & hymns were on the anti-slavery theme. † Medford 27 viii 1866 (81).

QUARLES, Francis, b. Romford, Cambs, 8 v 1592; studied law at Lincoln's Inn; Travelled on continent & was cup-bearer to Elizabeth of Bohemia (d. of King James I of Eng.) Secretary to Archbp Ussher in Ireland, and (1639) Chronologer to the City of London. Espoused royalist cause in Civil War; his home was raided by Cromwell's forces who destroyed all his books & mss. In consequence he † 8 ix 1644 (52). Pub. several books of poems of which Divine Emblems was v. popular.

SANDYS, George, b. 1578, ed. St Mary Hall, Oxf.; travelled widely 1610-15; treasurer of Virginia Company, '21; member of privy Council, '24-40. Published much verse; remained agent of Virginia Company & petitioned successfully ('42) for re-establishment of its privileges under govt of Cromwell, † 1644 (66).

SCUDDER, Eliza, b. Boston, Mass., 14 xi 1821 (niece of E. H. Sears who wrote 'It came upon the midnight clear'); left Unit. ch. for Episcopal in later life. † Salem, Mass., 1896 (75).

SHAIRP, John Campbell, b. Houstoun, Linlithgowshire, 1819; ed. Edinburgh Academy, Univ. Glasgow, Balliol, Oxf.; Schoolmaster at Rugby '45-56; dep. Prof. of Greek, Univ. Glasgow, '56; asst Prof. Humanity, St Andrews, '57; Prof., '61; Principal, United College at St Andrews, '68-† and concurrently Prof. of Poetry at Oxford, '77-†. Wrote much poetry and was highly revered as a teacher, † Ormsary, Argyllshire, 1885 (66).

SIDNEY, Sir Philip, b. 30 xi 1554, Penshurst, Kent; ed. Shrewsbury and Oxf.; diplomatic career took him to France, Germany, Italy and Ireland; engaged in the war with the Netherlands 1585 and died in battle of Zutphen, 17 x 1586 (31). His sister Mary, who became Mary Herbert & later Countess of Pembroke (1561-1621) caused his work to be edited & pubd after his death, and collaborated with him in version of the Psalms which she completed after his death.

SMART, Christopher, b. Shipbourne, Kent, 11 iv 1722; ed. Cambridge; Fellow of Pembroke Coll., '45. Thereafter lived in London as a poet and satirist, but became mentally ill and wrote his most impressive work, *Song to David*, in a mental institution. After leaving it, fell into debt and died in the King's Bench prison, where he was incarcerated for debt, 21 v 1771 (49).

SPEERS, John Edward, b. Saskatchewan 29 xii 1916; ed. Moose Jaw, Sask., and Victoria College, then lecturer in English at Univ. Winnipeg from '45. Entered Trinity Coll., Toronto, '50, to train for ministry; Ord. Episc., '63; Rector of Trinity Ch., Barrie, since '72.

STANLEY, Arthur Penrhyn, b. Alderley, Ches., 13 xii 1815; ed. Rugby & Oxf.; Ord. C/E '39; Canon of Canterbury '51; Dean of Westminster '64; Prof. Eccl Hist. at Oxf. '56-'62. Well-known author on subjects associated with ch. hist. † Westminster, London, 18 vii 1881 (65).

STEWART, Malcolm, b. 1936, was trained for and ord. into the R.C. priesthood, later laicized and became ('68) a producer for Thames Television, London.

STERNHOLD, Thomas, b. 1500, prob. at Southampton; ed. Oxf.; Groom of the Royal Wardrobe to King Henry VIII and his successor Edward VI. † London, 23 viii 1549.

TAYLOR, Walter Reginald Oxenham, b. Portsmouth, 1 viii 1889 of missionary parents; ed. China Inland Mission, Chefoo, China and Univ. Durham; Ord. C/E, served with missionary socty in China, 1924-49. Served with T. T. Lew (q.v.) on committee of *Hymns of Universal Praise*. Retired to Sevenoaks, Kent, where † 1974 (85).

TIPLADY, Thomas, b. 1 i 1882 at Gayle, Wensleydale (Lancs), in which area the name is still found; ed. Methodist Day School and Evening School at Nelson, Lancs, then Richmond (Methodist) Theol Coll., Surrey; during earlier period of education worked, after age 13, in cotton mill part-time. During WW I, chaplain with British Forces; visited USA, 1919; his great work was done 1922-42 at the Lambeth Mission (see text) which was destroyed by enemy action, '42.

During the 1930's and 40's his hymns were much in demand in USA. † in London 1964 (82).

TRAUTWEIN, Dieter, b. 1928, Ord. Luth., was for some years a director of church youth work in Germany, and in 1970 was appointed Probst (Provost) of the Cathedral at Frankfurt. He was a member of the cttee compiling *Cantate Domino* (4th edn, 1974).

WARE, Henry, b. Hingam, Mass., 21 iv 1794; ed. Harvard; Ord. Unit., 1815; pastor, Second Church, Boston, 1 i '17; asst pastor apptd to him '29 as Ralph Waldo Emerson (q.v.); Prof. Pulpit Eloquence & Pastoral Care, Harvard Theol. School, '30-'42; † Framingham, Mass., 25 ix 1843 (49).

WESLEY, Samuel (senior), b. Whitchurch, Dorset, 1662, son of John Wesley, Vicar of that parish; ed. at Dissenting Academy, but decided to enter C/E ministry; attended Exeter Coll., Oxf, and Ord. C/E; Vicar of South Ormsby, Lincs, 1693, and of Epworth, Lincs, 1697, where his 2 most famous sons, John and Charles, were born. Suffered many doctrinal difficulties, also financial straits, in middle life, but the later years were peaceable, and he † at Epworth 1735 (72).

WESLEY, Samuel (junior), eldest child of the above, b. in or near London, 1691; ed. Westminster Sch. Christ Ch. Oxf.; returned to Westmnr Sch. as Usher (schoolmaster); soon after, Ord. C/E, but advancement in the church was precluded by his friendship with Dean (later Bp) Atterbury, of whom publ. opinion disapproved. Head Master of Free School, Tiverton, Devon, 1732 - † there 6 xi 1739 (48).

WILBUR, Richard, b. New York, 1 iii 1921; ed. Amherst Coll., Mass., and Harvard; Member of Soc. of Fellows, Harvard '47; asst Prof. of English '50; asst Prof. of English, Wellesley Coll., Mass., '55; Prof. English at Wesleyan Univ., Middletown, Conn. since 1957. Publ. several volumes of verse and regarded as one of the leading US poets of his generation.

WHITEHOUSE, Walter Alexander, b. Shelley, nr Huddersfield, Yorks, 27 ii 1915; ed. Penistone Gram. Sch., St John's Camb., Mansfield, Oxf.; Ord. Cong; minister Elland, Yorks, '40-44; Chaplain, Mansfield Coll., '44-7; Reader in Divinity, Univ, Durham, '47-'65; Principal, St Cuthbert's Coll., Durham, '55-'60; Prof. of Theology, Univ. Kent from '65; Master, Eliot College, Univ. Kent, '65-'70 and from '73-'77; Minister (URC) Ravenstonedale, Yorks, '77—.

WITHER, George, b. Bentworth, Hants, 11 vi 1588; ed. Magd. Coll., Oxf.; but withdrawn from there by his father before taking degree; abandoned country life fairly soon for the law, but became a well-known writer & pamphleteer; imprisoned 1612 for writing a pamphlet, *Abuses Whipt & Stript*, which later ran into 4 large editions. Succeeded in getting letters patent to have his *Hymns and Songs* (1623) bound up with the Prayer Book; this was contested by Stationers' Company who held the patent rights, and who had the patent quashed; hence the unknown status of Wither's hymns. In the Civil War (from 1640) he first raised a troop for the King's party, but later (1643) became a supporter of Cromwell, by whom he was created Major General (1650). After the Restoration he spent some time in Newgate prison for his defection, but was eventually released and † 2 v 1667 (78). His wife was an Emerson, of the family from whom R. W. Emerson was descended (q.v.).

YOUNG, Andrew John, b. Elgin, Scot., 1885; ed. Edinburgh Royal High Sch. and Univ.; Ord. C/E and in later life was Vicar of Stonegate, Sussex, and Canon of Chichester Cathl. Queen's Medal for Poetry, 1952.

INDEX OF AUTHORS

Translations are indicated by †; originals of translations by * (if in
parentheses, the original is not in this book)

INDEX OF FIRST LINES